D1088333

Rodolphe Töpffer

Rodolphe Töpffer

THE COMPLETE COMIC STRIPS

Compiled, translated, and annotated by DAVID KUNZLE

University Press of Mississippi / Jackson

Publication is made possible in part from a
grant from Pro Helvetia, Zürich, Switzerland
prohelvetia
with special thanks to Pierre Schaer

www.upress.state.ms.us

Designed by Todd Lape

The University Press of Mississippi is a member of the
Association of American University Presses.

Manufactured in the United States of America

First edition 2007
∞
Library of Congress Cataloging-in-Publication Data

Töpffer, Rodolphe, 1799–1846.
[Comic strips. 2007]
Rodolphe Töpffer : the complete comic strips / translated and annotated by David Kunzle. — 1st ed.
p. cm.
Includes bibliographical references.
ISBN-13: 978-1-57806-946-0 (cloth : alk. paper) 1. Comic books, strips, etc. I. Kunzle, David. II. Title.
PN6790.S93T56 2007
741.5'973—dc22 2006030571

British Library Cataloging-in-Publication Data available

To Marjoyrie, comme toujours
To Marianne, comme il faut

Contents

The Comic Strips

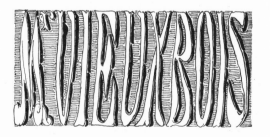

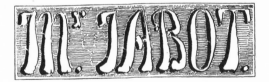

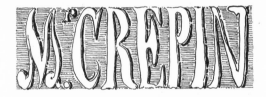

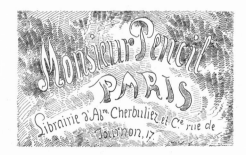

Le Docteur Festus
PARIS
Librairie d'Abm. Cherbuliez et Ce. rue de Tournon. 17.

Histoire d'Albert.
par Simon de Nantua

Histoire de
Monsieur
Cryptogame
1845.

Mr. Trictrac est dévoré de l'amour de la Science.

Appendixes

Preface

Rodolphe Töpffer (1799–1846), Genevan schoolmaster, university professor, writer of short stories, novels, travel accounts, and theatrical farces; art critic, aesthetic philosopher, social moralist, polemical journalist, tireless correspondent; caricaturist, illustrator and author of innumerable sketches of landscape and genre scenes, *and* above all, virtual inventor of the modern comic strip, is, alas, almost unknown to the English-speaking public today. He was, to be sure, very much a Genevan and a Swiss, but in his own time and down to the present, he was well known in France and translated into German. His writing was approved as a school text, pure in style and pure in moral reach, quite unlike his caricature. It is true that the bulk of his writing—curious, witty, and at times surprising as it can be—may be too bound to his time and place to ever enjoy universal appeal, but his authorship of eight picture stories, or comic strips or graphic novels as we would call them today, should earn him immortality and truly international renown, which is the modest purpose of this volume.

Although a few crude plagiaries with English captions for the British and American children's market were published in his own time, this is the first time that Töpffer's comic strips as a whole have been translated into English, and this is the first time they are treated, as a body, with the kind of scholarly apparatus that any great artist deserves. I may add that, although this fulfils a lifelong dream, I was inspired to see what Hans Ries did with the massive oeuvre of Wilhelm Busch, the German who is with Töpffer the other great master of the comic strip in the nineteenth century, three huge volumes of historical-critical scholarship, the complexity and sheer extent of which, happily, I do not have to approach here.

As yet, only a few of the most popular comic strip masters of the twentieth century, mostly American, have been given historical-critical editions or oeuvre catalogs, although some (like Carl Barks) have their collected editions. This has been done with something akin to patriotic fervor, as if the comic strip were quintessentially American. Perhaps it is, but it is an excess of such fervor, a nationalistic chauvinism which insists, as many American experts have, that the comic strip was *invented* in the United States, usually citing the Yellow Kid in 1896 which is not a comic or narrative strip at all.

No invention is entirely new. Töpffer may reasonably be said to have *virtually* invented a genre, the comic strip and comic book, which has become, in the twentieth century, the largest iconographical field ever, consumed by millions around the globe. I have to say "virtually" because Töpffer himself gave explicit credit to his model William Hogarth, and only him for he did not know about the numerous Hogarth imitators in England and Germany. Hogarth in the mid-eighteenth century pioneered the idea of telling long, complete, moral stories in pictures. But Hogarth's amazing series of narrative paintings and engravings, with their densely packed, minutely crafted, intensely topical satire, look much more different from the work of his Swiss heir a century later than the Swiss does from our modern versions of the genre. For the Swiss invented an appropriate, speed-driven comic strip graphic style, as well as a fantasy-driven narrative technique. If Töpffer is the father of the comic strip, Hogarth is the grandfather.

Töpffer combined literary and artistic virtues and skills seldom united in one person: the cryptic wit of the captions and the surreal craziness of the plot lines; the touching nervousness of the graphic line which matches the nervous energy of his heroes with that of the caprices of Fate driving them; the mastery of the physiognomic doodle, which he theorized and systematized (quite a feat for man who professed to hate all systems), catching for this alone the respectful attention of Ernst Gombrich in his *Art and Illusion* (1960). Paradoxically, Töpffer was aware that he was pioneering a hybrid genre, but he could not accept, much less foresee, its importance, vis-à-vis the established genres of novel writing and painting. He always disparaged—later, I think, pretending to disparage—the idea that something of real cultural value could be expressed in this impure literary-pictorial form. The comic strip, indeed, bore a snobbish cultural stigma, akin to that suffered by film, well into the twentieth century. But the comic strip albums, which he sketched, lithographed, and published himself, became quickly popular, and even a significant source of income. Töpffer was amused, delighted, and bit puzzled by all this, but loved his creations as alter egos, as friends and real-life familiars, and looked eagerly forward to a bilingual (German and French) collected edition.

The reasons that Töpffer delayed in publishing his "silly stuff," are rooted in his sense that they were indeed just the throw-away pastime of a schoolmaster tired and bored during supervision time, and also in his (justified) fear that once he became a university professor, the academic and clerical stick-in-the-muds of Calvinist Geneva would regard them as unbefitting a man of his exalted calling. Even the all-important accolade of Goethe, early on, did not change his mind at the time. Some justification of his reserve came with the first full-blown appraisal, in 1840, by the big French critic Sainte-Beuve, who enlarged upon his literary merits but disparaged his efforts in caricature. By this time, however, professional and social security allowed him to bypass critical prejudice, but his albums never bore his full name as author in his lifetime, only his initials. These were semi-acknowledged bastard children, but his children nevertheless, to which he bids anxious farewell in each preface as to a child leaving on his travels into an uncertain world: Va, petit livre . . . Go, little book, and seek your world . . .

Although the stories were initially written and sketched for and under the laughing eyes of the boys of his school, their success with family and friends, as the manuscripts circulated in ever widening ripples, soon convinced him that this was adult fare too. There is perhaps no example of work written for the young that looks so adult. Edward Lear and Lewis Carroll, much as adults enjoy them, leave us in no doubt that young children are the primary audience. The difference of course is that Töpffer's first audience was older, the adolescent offspring of highly educated families who expected first-class, sophisticated teaching. They were teenagers with a keen appreciation of social and political satire such as might speak to the high spirits, irreverence, and rebelliousness natural to their time of life. At the same time, they loved plain silliness, a virtue only the more fortunate adults retain. Although Töpffer invariably dismissed his comic albums as "nonsense" and "little follies," he knew, and we know, that they contain much serious truth, especially regarding certain social and intellectual pretensions.

There is an even more surprising origin, apart from context of schoolroom and schoolboy audience: the frustrated ambitions of a would-be painter. Early on, Töpffer realized that his weak eyesight, which he feared would eventually make him completely blind, would prevent him following in his father's footsteps as a genre and landscape painter. It is easy now to see this as a catalyst in his search for new combinations of his senses: the incompleteness of his ocular vision would be compensated by a literary and narrative vision such as most visual artists manage without. He learned to draw as quickly as he wrote, in monochrome of course, and with a pen which hurried from the feet of his characters to the lettering scribbled below. Speed, leaving all inessentials aside: that was his aesthetic philosophy in a nutshell, all nuts and no shell, all essence, no mere surface description. So the doodle, first fling of his unconscious, was drawn out into faces, figures, and scenarios, careering haphazardly, a little blindly one might say, turning obstacles into launching pads, and logic upside down. Graphic and narrative trajectories remained open. The "open line" was Töpffer's "great" discovery, the saying of less to express more, enlarging and parading the Gombrichian "share of the beholder," which has become the quintessence of modernist aesthetic.

Töpffer did not die blind, like his mother, but his was, by Genevan standards, a short life. The speed with which he thought and drew, the speed with which his protagonists move, on land, by sea, and in the air, was the speed of a man who always feared the onset of a final incapacity of hand and eye to move at all. So we need not pity him for having been denied his true métier, but marvel at the one he found or created almost by accident. He would have appreciated the irony.

Critical Apparatus

Dismissive as he pretended to be of his "little follies," the author took great pains to improve the initial sketches when he came to redraw them on lithographic transfer paper for printing. I note these changes when they go beyond mere systematization of the line and amplification of the background, for they are often curious testimony to second thoughts, occasionally involving self-censorship in light of his expanded audience. Since most of the stories were sketched around 1830, but not published until many years later, there was time for the author to have reached a fresh and more critical perspective. Sometimes however he cut parts that we would have had him retain, that are different and still amusing; I have, accordingly, included these omitted passages in an appendix.

Careful examination of the sketchbooks containing the first drafts revealed notes for changes, the significance of which I have tried to elucidate. There is more work to be done here, for one cannot doubt that psychological insight into a new creative process is always valuable, in the case of the world's first true comic strips doubly so.

A most complicated situation emerges with *Monsieur Cryptogame*, one of the first stories sketched but the last published. This was the only story that first appeared in a mass-distribution French periodical, *L'Illustration*, in 1845 in installments. It was necessarily translated into woodcut, by a competent young admirer of Töpffer in Paris called Cham, who would eventually become as famous as Daumier. Cham's translation onto wood, when cut by the specialists, is, inevitably, rather wooden. Töpffer started a lithographic version but was too ill to complete it. Our edition here follows tradition in preferring a combination of manuscript and lithographic version over Cham's (which satisfied the nineteenth century in innumerable editions) as the more authentic. I have however departed from tradition in reinstating Töpffer's original drawings for scenes 9–26 in preference to the (I believe, inferior) existing lithographs which he started at the end of his life, when his mind and eye were much weakened. The whole operation of fitting a Töpffer picture story into a mass-circulation magazine, overseen in lengthy correspondence with the publisher and Cham, makes for the kind of scholarly challenge that I have puzzled out elsewhere.

This edition includes *M. Trictrac*, a major, unfinished story "stolen" from the author and apparently never recovered, thus unpublished at the time and for long afterwards, and excluded from modern collected editions. I also include fragments of stories started and never pursued, and an exceptional complete unillustrated scenario written for *The Story of M. Berlu*, done at the end of his life when he was too ill to draw. Normally, he made the drawings first, as is confirmed by the sketchbooks where the captions are often fitted awkwardly and haphazardly. I have also included some appealing title pages of early collected editions. All this has never been published before.

The translation of Töpffer's captions has presented few problems. The only one that I am conscious of is his habit of proceeding to a subordinate clause immediately after giving the subject (e.g., "Milord, having donned the Mayor's clothes, goes on his way"), instead of "Having donned the Mayor's clothes, Milord goes on his way" which would be more normal word order in both French and English today. This is a tactic adopted by the author in order to give a formal, slightly archaic feel to actions intended to be read, in part, as mock epic. I have however normalized the original word order in some cases.

I have, generally speaking, followed the author's casually inconsistent capitalization of proper nouns and normalized the punctuation.

Original documents cited are in the Musée d'art et histoire in Geneva (MAH, for the sketchbooks) and Bibliothèque publique et universitaire in Geneva (BPU, for the letters and other manuscripts). Most letters are cited by date only, because they are awaiting publication in the Droin edition.

This volume, the first English edition and the first complete edition of Töpffer's comic strips, is intended to accompany the simultaneous publication of my critical monograph, *Father of the Comic Strip: Rodolphe Töpffer* (University Press of Mississippi; referred to here as Kunzle 2007), which contains a more complete bibliography. In the "critical apparatus" appended here, I have kept to a minimum the historical information required for an understanding of the stories in their context, trying to avoid duplication of information with Kunzle 2007 and lending the present volume a certain independence. The notes are otherwise of a rather technical nature, relating to dating and offering quite detailed comparison of first sketches to published versions and different published versions, with listing of plagiaries and some later editions. The comparison of versions, which has never been done in any language, is more than a matter of technical interest, however: it gives insight into the creative process of the inventor of what is virtually a totally new artistic-literary genre. Ideally, of course, the two books are to be seen as inseparable twin claimants to your bookshelf space.

First of all I thank Marianne Gourary, co-dedicatee of this volume, who has built up over the years what must be the finest Töpffer library in the U.S., which she generously opened to me, and which was the happy link to our lasting friendship. Her affection and encouragement of this project have always been precious to me. Philippe Kaenel, the leading Töpffer specialist of Switzerland, was always forthcoming in advice and comment; Danielle Buyssens and Jean-Daniel Candaux have also encouraged me. Above all I acknowledge the generosity of the indefatigable editor of Töpffer correspondence, Jacques Droin, who put at my disposal printouts of that massive corpus previous to their publication (the world still awaits the printing of three of a projected five volumes). I was thus able to use in its entirety material never before available to scholars. His advice and the gastronomic hospitality in their home presided by his wife Monique were always appreciated.

The University Press of Mississippi, efficiently presided by Seetha Srinivasan, with the careful editing of Anne Stascavage and the elegant design of Todd Lape, has been a pleasure to work with. Töpffer himself would have applauded, as Töpfferians today applaud, the decision to publish in a format oblong like the original albums. I thank the Press for engaging in this extra expense. This volume reproduces the drawings in the same size as the original albums.

Chronology

1799 Born 31 January, in Geneva. His grandfather was a haberdasher immigrant from Franconia in Germany. His father, Wolfgang-Adam Töpffer (1766–1847), is a moderately successful genre and landscape painter, with a sideline in privately circulated caricature. Wolfgang-Adam visits England and brings back engravings by and enthusiasm for William Hogarth, who will be the son's model both for the idea of picture stories and the popular moralizing role of art.

1819–20 Rodolphe studies Greek and other subjects in Paris. While learning and practicing drawing and caricature under his father, he discovers that his ambition to become a painter is being thwarted by poor eyesight.

1822 He becomes assistant master in the Pension Heyer. First Alpine excursions with boys of the school.

1823 He marries Anne-Françoise ("Kity") Moulinié, daughter of a wealthy watchmaker, whose dowry helps him set up his own boarding school for boys in 1824. They will have two sons and two daughters. The school soon flourishes, with a body of thirty to forty pupils drawn locally and from Europe and the U.S.

1825–42 He takes students on annual excursions to the Alps, France, German-speaking Switzerland, Savoy, and Italy as far as Turin and Milan. He writes up and illustrates these trips, at first circulating them privately and later publishing them broadly in an extensive series known as the *Voyages en Zigzag*. These chronicles, which mix romantic descriptions of scenery with amusing and critical anecdotes about inns, innkeepers, guides, and fellow tourists, are edited in later years and for publication, and often inflated with much social moralizing. They become a minor classic of French and travel literature.

1824 Publishes an edition of Demosthenes to establish his credentials as a classicist.

1827 He sketches his first picture story, *Les Amours de Mr. Vieux Bois*, and in immediately succeeding years executes the first drafts of most of his "comic strip" oeuvre, which would be published many years later (1835–45). They would be done at first under the eyes of and to the active applause of the boys, during evening "prep" time, and circulated among his friends as well.

1828 Writes his first theatrical farce, for private production. He will write six more, none published until recently.

1830 Begins a regular series of articles for the *Bibliothèque Universelle*, a Genevan cultural and scientific magazine.

1832 The first important and public approbation is that of Goethe in Weimar, to whom he sent samples of the first drafts of his picture stories. The initial oral imprimatur is quickly printed in *Kunst und Alterthum* after the old poet's death, but RT is reluctant to publish the sketches since he is aware such trivial things, as he always referred to them in half-sincere self-disparagement, would not redound to his growing reputation as head of one of Geneva's best schools. He is, moreover, from 1832 a lecturer in French literature at the Academy of Geneva, and from 1834 a silent member of the lower house advisory body of the city and cantonal government, the Conseil Représentatif de Genève.

1832 He publishes his first short story, *My Uncle's Library*, which is still today the universal favorite of his works in prose. From then until his death, short stories, novels, art criticism, and social commentary pour forth from his indefatigable pen. He also maintains an enormous correspondence, now being at last published in its entirety.

1833 He lithographs and self-publishes *Histoire de Monsieur Jabot*, in a process he later explains in his *Essai d'Autographie* (1842), by "auto-lithography," done by direct drawing with a pen on special paper before transfer onto the stone, resulting in a double reversal back to the original direction when printed. This permitted the combination of drawing and handwriting on one page, which gives a visual and psychological unity to what was essentially a newly invented hybrid of literature and draftsmanship. He called the picture stories (when not "my scribbling") "histoires en estampes," literally "engraved novels," or "graphic novels," a term now used for the longer and more ambitious kind of comic book. He withdraws *Jabot* from circulation, for fear of repercussions, until 1835.

1837 He publishes *Mr. Crépin* and *Les Amours de Mr. Vieux Bois*.

1839 He publishes a second edition of *Vieux Bois*, which had been plagiarized in Paris.

1840 He publishes *Le Docteur Festus* and *Monsieur Pencil*.

1841 A long article by the famous French critic Sainte-Beuve launches him onto the big French literary scene. The critic scants the picture stories and lauds Töpffer the prose artist for his gentle irony, subtle characterization, moral purity, and provincial archaisms—stereotypical criteria which were to endure through the nineteenth century and seem so inadequate to assessment of his comic strip oeuvre.

1842–43 Passionately opposed to the democratic and radical demands fermenting in Geneva, he launches and writes innumerable articles for *Le Courrier de Genève*. This nakedly political partisanship inspires his last new picture story, *L'Histoire d'Albert* (1844), aimed at the radical leader James Fazy, who would take power in Geneva just after RT's death.

1845 Publication in eleven installments of *Histoire de M. Cryptogame* in *L'Illustration*, a new illustrated weekly published by his cousin Jacques-Julien Dubochet in Paris. Its great success in this form (the first comic strip in a magazine) would be affirmed subsequently in autonomous album form. Since the magazine could only use woodcuts, and RT could not draw on wood because of his eyesight and his need for speed, the task was given to his first imitator in Paris, Cham (Amédée de Noé), who had been publishing original imitations of Töpffer picture strips. The captions, alas, had to be set in standard type.

1845 *Essai de Physiognomonie*. Now fatally ailing, he reveals his "secret" for stimulating the narrative imagination and inventing funny characters: the doodle, which he systematizes, and the feeling of which he insists can be preserved in final versions. The various drafts of RT picture stories prove, however, that he put much effort into improving them. There is a whole modernist aesthetic theory embedded in this essay, cannily picked up by Gombrich in 1960, which also runs through much of RT's copious art criticism, itself a kind of meandering intellectual doodle.

1846 After several useless visits to spas to cure a swollen spleen, and having given up his school in 1845, he dies, probably of leukemia.

The Comic Strips

Mr. JABOT.

DE Mr. JABOT.
GENÈVE 1833..

Prèface.

Ci-derrière commence l'histoire vèritable de Monsieur Jabot, et comme quoi, rien que par ses manières comme il faut, et sa bonne tenue, il sut rèussir dans le monde.

Va, petit livre, et choisis ton monde, car aux choses folles, qui ne rit pas, baîlle; qui ne se livre pas, rèsiste; qui raisonne, se mèprend; et qui veut rester grave, en est maître.

(Autographié chez. J. Freydig; Genève, 1833.)

Preface. Here begins the true story of Mr. Jabot, and how, by his polite manners and his good deportment alone, he managed to succeed in the world.

Go, little book and choose your world, for at crazy things, those who do not laugh, yawn; and those who do not yield, resist; and those who reason, are mistaken, and those who would keep a straight face, can please themselves.

1.
Monsieur Jabot se disposant à réussir dans le monde, fréquente les promenades publiques.
Mr Jabot croit devoir prendre une glace au premier café de l'endroit.
Ayant mangé sa glace, Mr. Jabot se remets en position.
R.T.

Mr. Jabot with a mind to succeeding in the world, frequents the public promenades.

Mr. Jabot thinks it proper to take an ice in the smartest café of the area.

Having eaten his ice, Mr. Jabot resumes his attitude.

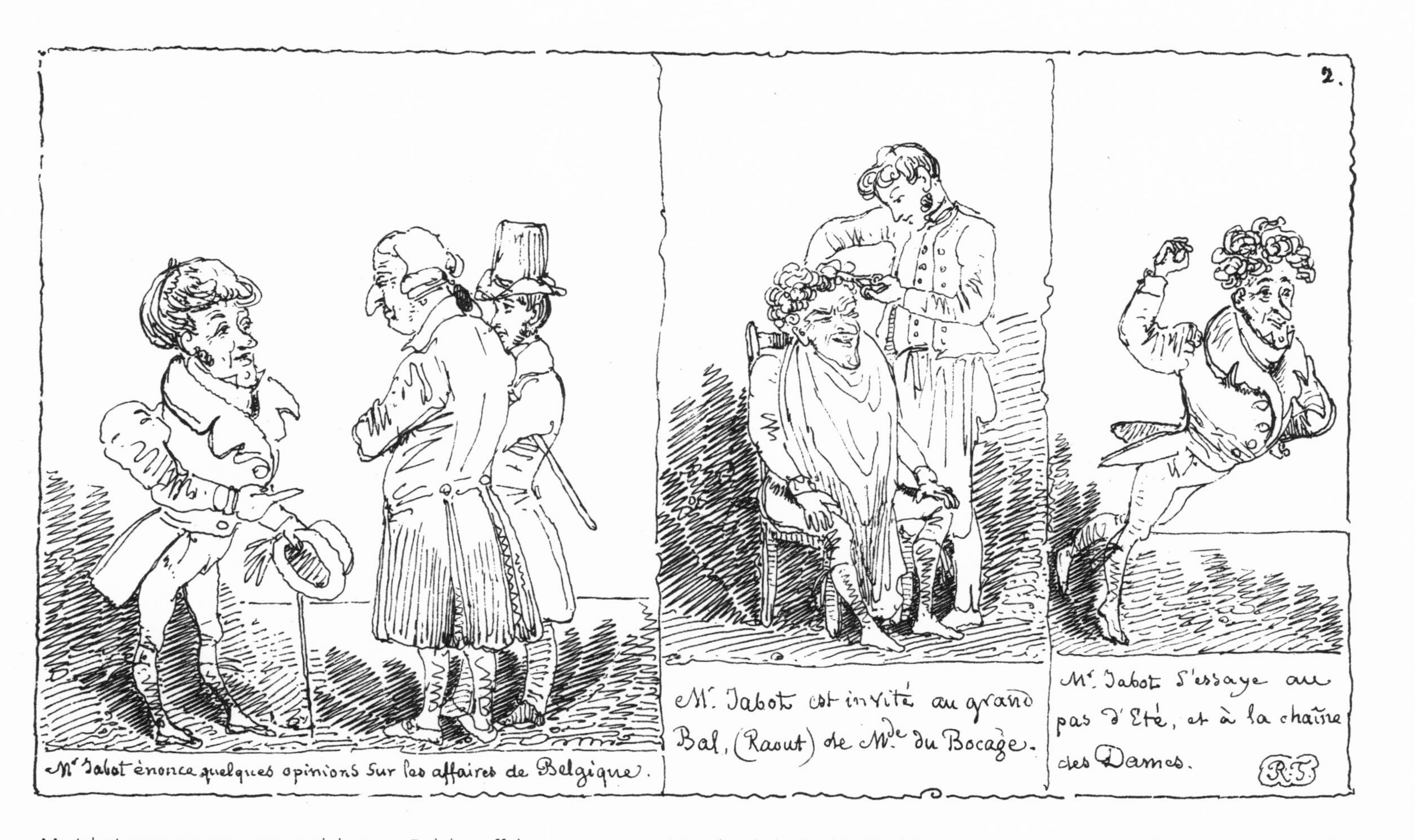
2.
Mr Jabot énonce quelques opinions sur les affaires de Belgique.
Mr. Jabot est invité au grand Bal, (Raout) de Mde du Bocage.
Mr. Jabot s'essaye au pas d'Eté, et à la chaîne des Dames.
R.T.

Mr. Jabot pronounces some opinions on Belgian affairs.

Mr. Jabot is invited to the big Ball (Reception) given by Mrs. du Bocage.

Mr. Jabot tries out his Pas d'Eté, and the Ladies' Chain.

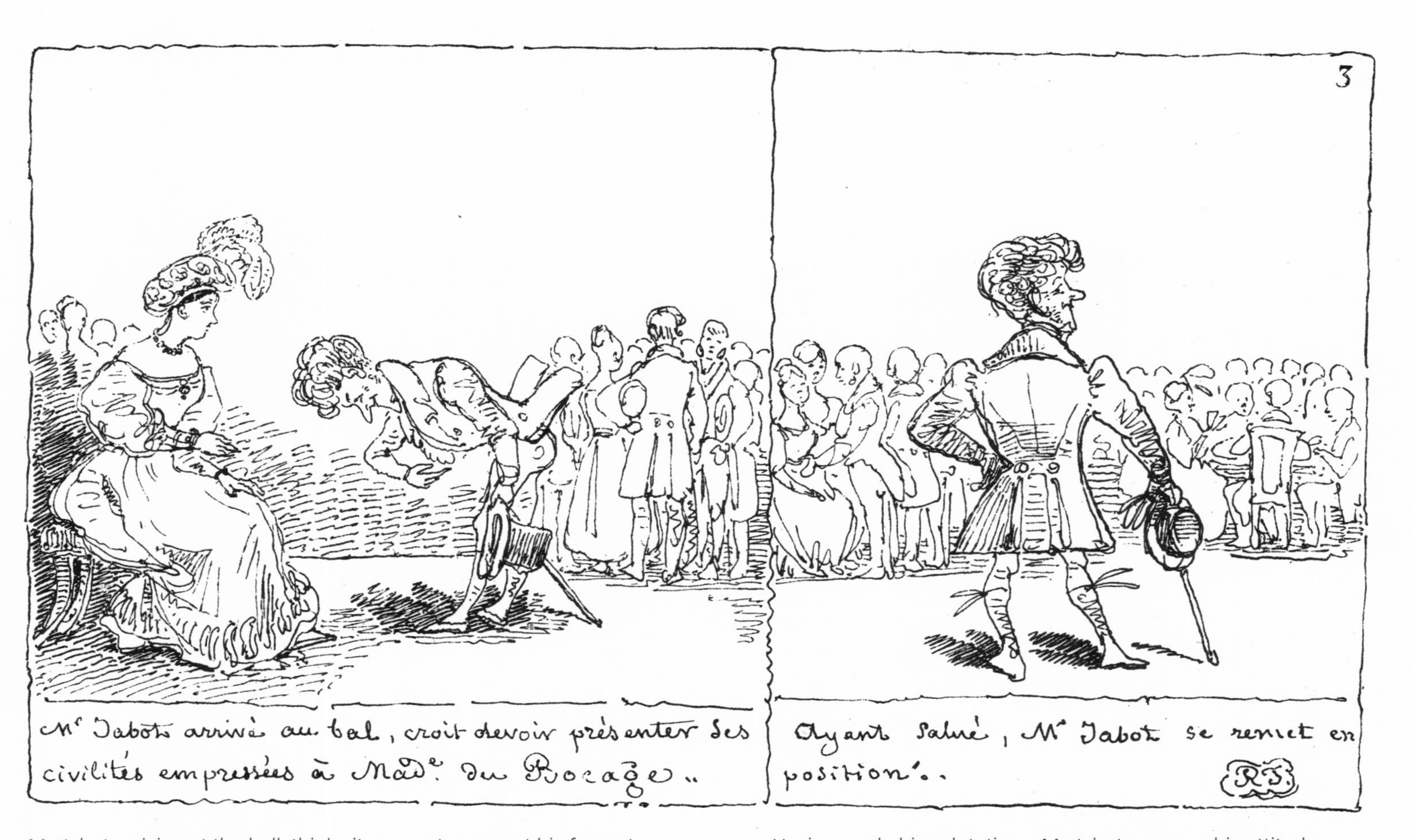
3
Mr Jabot arrivé au bal, croit devoir présenter ses civilités empressées à Madme. du Bocage..
Ayant salué, Mr Jabot se remet en position!..
RT.

Mr. Jabot arriving at the ball, thinks it proper to present his fervent respects to Mrs. du Bocage.

Having made his salutations, Mr. Jabot resumes his attitude.

4.
Mr Jabot croit devoir énoncer quelques mots agréables et galans, à Mad.elle du Bocage.
Mr Jabot croit devoir causer chasse, avec Mr du Bocage le fils aîné.
Mr Jabot croit devoir regarder avec bienveillance, les jeux enfantins du jeune du Bocage, le cadet.
R.T.

Mr. Jabot thinks it proper to offer some agreeable and gallant words to Miss du Bocage.

Mr. Jabot thinks it proper to talk hunting with Mr. du Bocage, the elder son.

Mr. Jabot thinks it proper to watch with a benevolent eye the childish games of the du Bocage boy, the youngest.

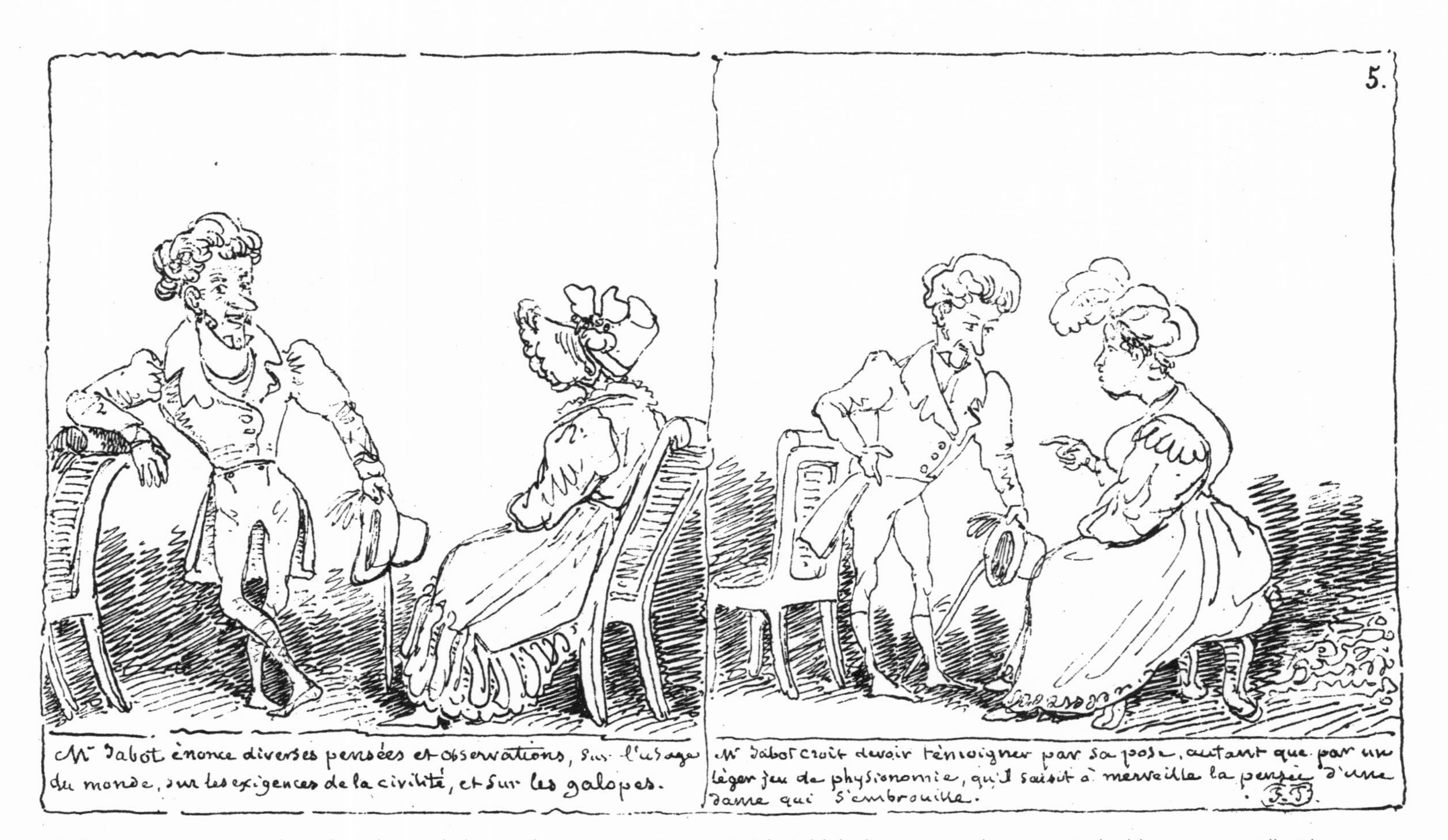
5.
Mr Jabot énonce diverses pensées et observations, sur l'usage du monde, sur les exigences de la civilité, et sur les galopes.
Mr Jabot croit devoir témoigner par sa pose, autant que par un léger jeu de physionomie, qu'il saisit à merveille la pensée d'une dame qui s'embrouille.

Mr. Jabot pronounces various thoughts and observations on fashionable customs, on the demands of civility, and on gallopades.

Mr. Jabot thinks it proper to demonstrate by his pose, as well as by a slight facial expression, that he perfectly grasps the thoughts of a lady who gets confused.

6.
Après quoi Mr Jabot se remet en position.
Mr Jabot énonce d'après les Débats l'inquiétude que lui cause le parti populaire dans un moment où l'Autocrate arme.
Mr Jabot croit devoir s'éloigner d'un groupe qui lui paraît renfermer une Société mêlée.

After which Mr. Jabot resumes his attitude.

Mr. Jabot following the *Débats* expresses the concern caused him by the popular party at a moment when the Autocrat is arming.

Mr. Jabot thinks it proper to withdraw from a group that seems to him to be of a mixed character.

7.
Mr antoine, le marchand de bas, qui est cousin de Mr Jabot, croit le reconnoître, et marche vers lui.
Ayant aperçu son cousin le marchand de bas Mr Jabot croit devoir éluder une entrevue familière au milieu d'un Raout.
Mr Jabot ayant fait une habile évolution autour d'une grosse Dame le cousin antoine le perd de vue.

Mr. Antoine, the haberdasher, who is a cousin of Mr. Jabot, recognizes him and makes towards him.

Perceiving his cousin the haberdasher, Mr. Jabot thinks it proper to avoid any familiarity in the midst of a Reception.

Mr. Jabot having made a deft maneuver around a plump lady, cousin Antoine loses sight of him.

8
après quoi Mr Jabot se remet en position.
Mr Jabot croit devoir s'effacer pour laisser passer la galopa; d'où la basse perd le son.
Le Bassier s'étant fâché, Mr Jabot lui affirme qu'il est un insolent, et que s'il n'était pas d'une classe subalterne il lui demanderait raison.
RT

After which Mr. Jabot resumes his attitude.

Mr. Jabot thinks it proper to efface himself in order to let the gallopade pass: which silences the double bass.

The bassist becoming annoyed, Mr. Jabot calls him an insolent fellow, and if he weren't of an inferior class, he would demand satisfaction of him.

9.
Jugeant que le temps convenable est arrivé, Mr Jabot se dispose à danser.
Mr Jabot engage Melle du Bocage en personne, si, dit-il, sa demande n'est pas trop inefficace.
Mr Jabot prélude à la danse par de gracieux propos.

Judging that the time is now right, Mr. Jabot prepares to dance.

Mr. Jabot engages Miss du Bocage in person, if, he says, his request is not too ineffective.

Mr. Jabot offers some gracious remarks as a prelude to the dance.

10.
Les propos étant peu goûtés Mr Jabot croit devoir approprier des gestes de bon goût à des expressions choisies.
Les expressions ayant peu d'effet, Mr Jabot croit devoir se renfermer dans une attitude décelant l'observation fine et la plaisanterie de bon ton.
Après quoi Mr Jabot conduit la galopade avec le plus heureux succès.

His remarks being little appreciated, Mr. Jabot thinks it proper to adapt some tasteful gestures to well-chosen expressions.

The expressions having little effect, Mr. Jabot thinks it proper to withdraw into an attitude betraying subtle powers of observation and a tasteful sense of fun.

After which Mr. Jabot leads the gallopade with the greatest success.

11.
Malheureusement Mr Jabot glisse au plus beau moment.
Ce qui cause du dérangement dans le reste de la galope.
RT

Unfortunately Mr. Jabot slips at a critical moment.

Which causes some disturbance among the rest of the gallopade.

12.
Mr Jabot croit devoir dissimuler une forte douleur lombaire, et rejette la faute sur la basse qui écorche la mesure.
Après quoi Mr. Jabot se remet en position.
Mr Jabot entre en relation avec Milord Felou, qui lui parle bécassines.

Mr. Jabot thinks it proper to affect an acute back pain, and throws the blame on the bassist who mangled the tempo.

After which, Mr. Jabot resumes his attitude.

Mr. Jabot makes a connection with Lord Felou, who talks snipe with him.

13.
Malheureusement le Cousin Antoine qui n'a pas vu Mr Jabot depuis 3 ans, prend ce moment pour lui Sauter au cou.
Mr Jabot croit devoir affirmer au cousin Antoine qu'il se méprend grossièrement. Le cousin Antoine tombe des nues.
RT

Unfortunately Cousin Antoine, who has not seen Mr. Jabot for 3 years, takes this opportunity to embrace him.

Mr. Jabot thinks it proper to tell his cousin Antoine that he is vastly mistaken. Cousin Antoine is thunderstruck.

14.
après quoi Mr Jabot reprend ses relations avec Milord, et croit devoir plaisanter sur cet étrange individu.
Mr. Jabot est présenté à Milady.
RT

After which Mr. Jabot resumes relations with Milord [Felou], and thinks it proper to make fun of that strange individual.

Mr. Jabot is presented to Milady.

15
Beau moment ! Mr. Jabot fait faire à Milady un tour de salle.
Mr. Jabot croit devoir marquer à Milady une préférence délicate. Un lampion s'éteint et fume.
Aussitôt Mr. Jabot s'empresse de remédier à cette odeur, inopportune. La galope approche.

A fine moment! Mr. Jabot takes Milady on a turn around the room.

Mr. Jabot thinks it proper to show a delicate preference for Milady. A candelabra goes out and smokes.

Mr. Jabot immediately hastens to suppress the unwelcome smell. The gallopade approaches.

16.
La galope arrive, renverse la chaise, et Mr. Jabot a le malheur de rester accroché au clou.
Mr. Jabot est décroché par le retour de la galope.

The gallopade arrives, knocks over the chair, and Jabot suffers the misfortune of being caught on the hook.

Mr. Jabot is unhooked by the return of the gallopade.

17.
à peine relevé Mr Jabot est cogné par la galope à son troisième tour.
L'habit de Mr Jabot s'étant accroché à la galope, il est entraîné.
Le Bassier pressant la mesure, la galope accélère prodigieusement
RT

Hardly has he got up, Mr. Jabot is knocked about by the gallopade on its third round.

With his coattails caught up in the gallopade, he is dragged off.

The Bassist increasing the tempo, the gallopade rushes past at prodigious speed.

18.
M. Jabot est lancé par la galope, dans une partie d'échecs.
R.T.
Mr Jabot a une explication très vive avec le joueur d'échecs. Il s'en suit qu'il lui offre satisfaction pour demain à neuf heures.

Mr. Jabot is thrown by the gallopade into a game of chess.

Mr. Jabot engages in a lively altercation with the chess player. The result is that he offers satisfaction for the morrow at nine o'clock.

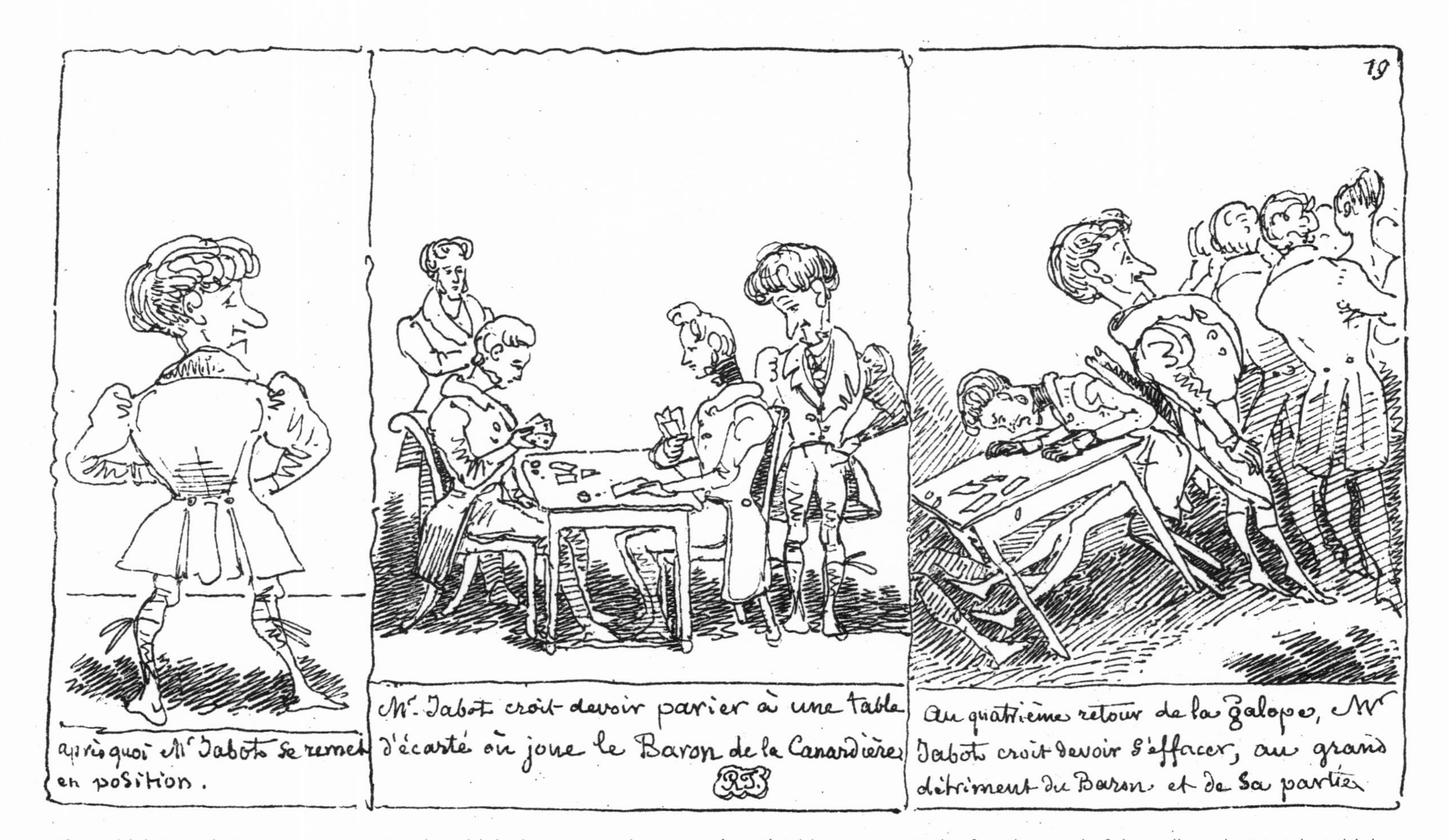
après quoi Mr Jabot se remet en position.
Mr. Jabot croit devoir parier à une table d'écarté où joue le Baron de la Canardière
RT.
19
Au quatrième retour de la galope, Mr Jabot croit devoir s'effacer, au grand détriment du Baron et de sa partie

After which Mr. Jabot resumes his attitude.

Mr. Jabot thinks it proper to bet at an écarté table where the Baron de la Canardière is playing.

At the fourth round of the gallopade, Mr. Jabot thinks it proper to efface himself, to the great detriment of the Baron and his game.

20.
Explication excessivement vive avec le Baron. Mr Jabot croit devoir lui demander satisfaction pour demain à 10 heures.
RTf
Après quoi Mr Jabot se distingue dans un quadrille.

Excessively lively altercation with the Baron. Mr. Jabot thinks it proper to demand satisfaction for the morrow at 10 o'clock.

After which Mr. Jabot distinguishes himself in a quadrille.

21
Malheureusement Mr Jabot termine son dernier entrechat sur le pied droit de Mde Posomby, sa danseuse, qui prend mal.
Mr Posomby prend mal la chose. Il montre la porte à Mr Jabot qui croit devoir lui demander satisfaction pour demain à 11 heures.

Unfortunately Mr. Jabot ends his final entrechat on the right foot of Mrs. Posomby, his partner, who is taken ill.

Mr. Posomby takes the matter ill. He shows the door to Mr. Jabot who thinks it proper to demand satisfaction for the morrow at 11 o'clock.

22.
aprèsquoi Mr Jabot se remet en position.
Mr Jabot a l'avantage de retrouver Milady. Il est prié par Milord, à une partie de chasse avec Mr Dubocage, pour après demain.
Inestimable Situation. — J'irai si je ne suis pas mort! — mort? — Trois affaires d'honneur, milady! — Que vous êtes donc imprudent! — qu'est-ce que ma vie! — Mais c'est bien quelque chose. — Je la donnerais pour ce mot! Milady! . . . .

after which Mr. Jabot resumes his attitude.

Mr. Jabot has the luck to find Milady again. He is invited by Milord to a hunting party with Mr. Dubocage, for the day after next.

Incomparable situation! —I shall go if I am not dead! —Dead? —Three affairs of honor, Milady! —How imprudent you are! —What is my life worth! —But it is worth something. —I would give it for those words, Milady! . . . .

23
Mr Jabot croit devoir prendre une attitude qui exprime l'état de son ame.
Mot très heureux. Mr Jabot est présenté à Melle Plouplou indigène d'infiniment d'esprit. — Et c'est vous, monsieur que la galope a si fort maltraité ? — De la part des galopins, mademoiselle, on peut s'attendre à tout.
Mr Plouplou qui a conduit la galope, trouve le mot très impoli. — Les galopins, c'est vous petit Brimborion ! — Mr Jabot demande Satisfaction pour demain à midi.
RST

Mr. Jabot thinks it proper to adopt an attitude expressive of the state of his soul.

Very fortunate expression. Mr. Jabot is presented to Miss Plouplou, a native of infinite wit. —Was it you, sir, so ill-treated by the gallopade? —May *galloping* consumption, Mademoiselle, overtake them all.

Mr. Plouplou who led the galope, finds this repartee very rude. —The galloping consumption take you, you little Wretch! —Mr. Jabot demands satisfaction for the morrow at midday.

24
Mr Jabot conduit Milady aux rafraîchissemens
Mr Jabot fend la presse.
Mot charmant, d'un sens profond. — Ah quelle horreur que d'être pressée de la sorte! — Pour le coup, Milady, je cesse d'être partisan de la presse. Je me fais Tory.

Mr. Jabot leads Milady to the refreshments.

Mr. Jabot squeezes through the press of people.

Charming phrase, with profound meaning. —Oh, how horrible to be pressed like that! —For my part, Milady, I cease to be a partisan of the press. I will become a Tory.

25.
Lord Bricbroc demande l'explication de ce mot. — Mr Jabot répond qu'il ne doit compte à personne de ses opinions politiques.
Lord Bricbroc qui a bu du Champagne, s'emporte et tire son épée. Mr Jabot se met en garde. Milady s'enfuit. Tout s'arrange moyennant une rencontre, pour demain à 1. heure.

Lord Bribrac demands an explanation of this remark. —Mr. Jabot replies that he owes no one an account of his political opinions.

Lord Bribrac who has drunk champagne, gets angry and draws his sword. Mr. Jabot places himself on guard. Milady flees. All is settled by means of a rendez-vous, for the morrow at one o'clock.

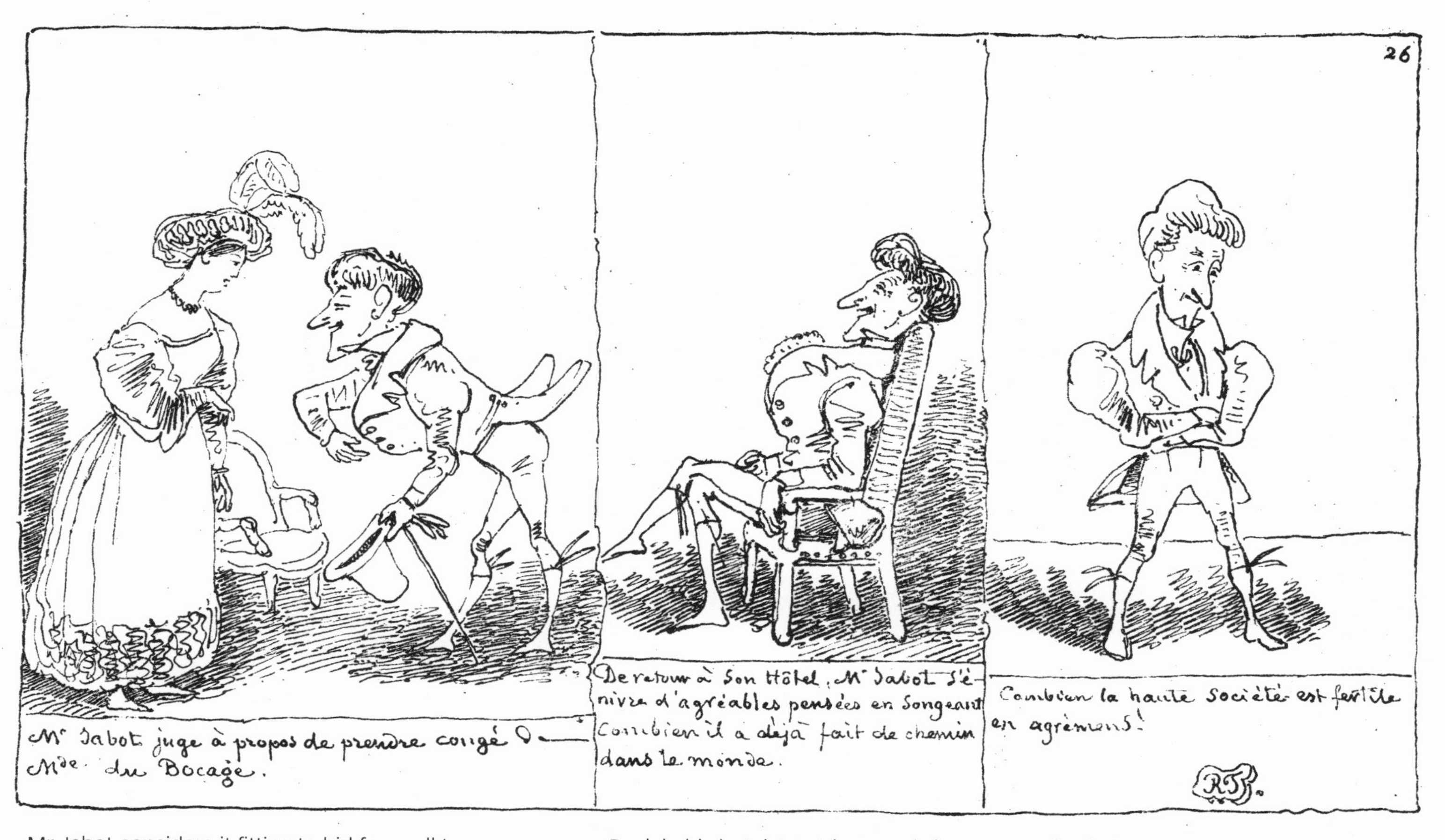
26
Mr Jabot juge à propos de prendre congé de Mde du Bocage.
De retour à son Hôtel, Mr Jabot s'énivre d'agréables pensées en songeant combien il a déjà fait de chemin dans le monde.
Combien la haute Société est fertile en agrémens!
RT.

Mr. Jabot considers it fitting to bid farewell to Mrs. du Bocage.

Back in his hotel, Mr. Jabot revels in agreeable thoughts, reflecting what progress he has already made in the world.

How fertile high society is in pleasures!

27.
Combien il a été heureux en impayables reparties !
Combien Milady fut aimable et son tendre intérêt visible !!
Et cinq affaires d'honneur !!!! Quel début brillant !
RT
Mr Jabot fait ses dispositions testamentaires, écrit à Milord pour qu'il lui serve de second, et au chirurgien pour qu'il se trouve prêt.

How successful he has been in unimaginable repartees!

How agreeable Milady was, and apparent her tender interest!

And five affairs of honor! ! ! ! What a brilliant début!

Mr. Jabot draws up his will, writes to Milord [Felou] to ask him to serve as his second, and to the surgeon to be ready on hand.

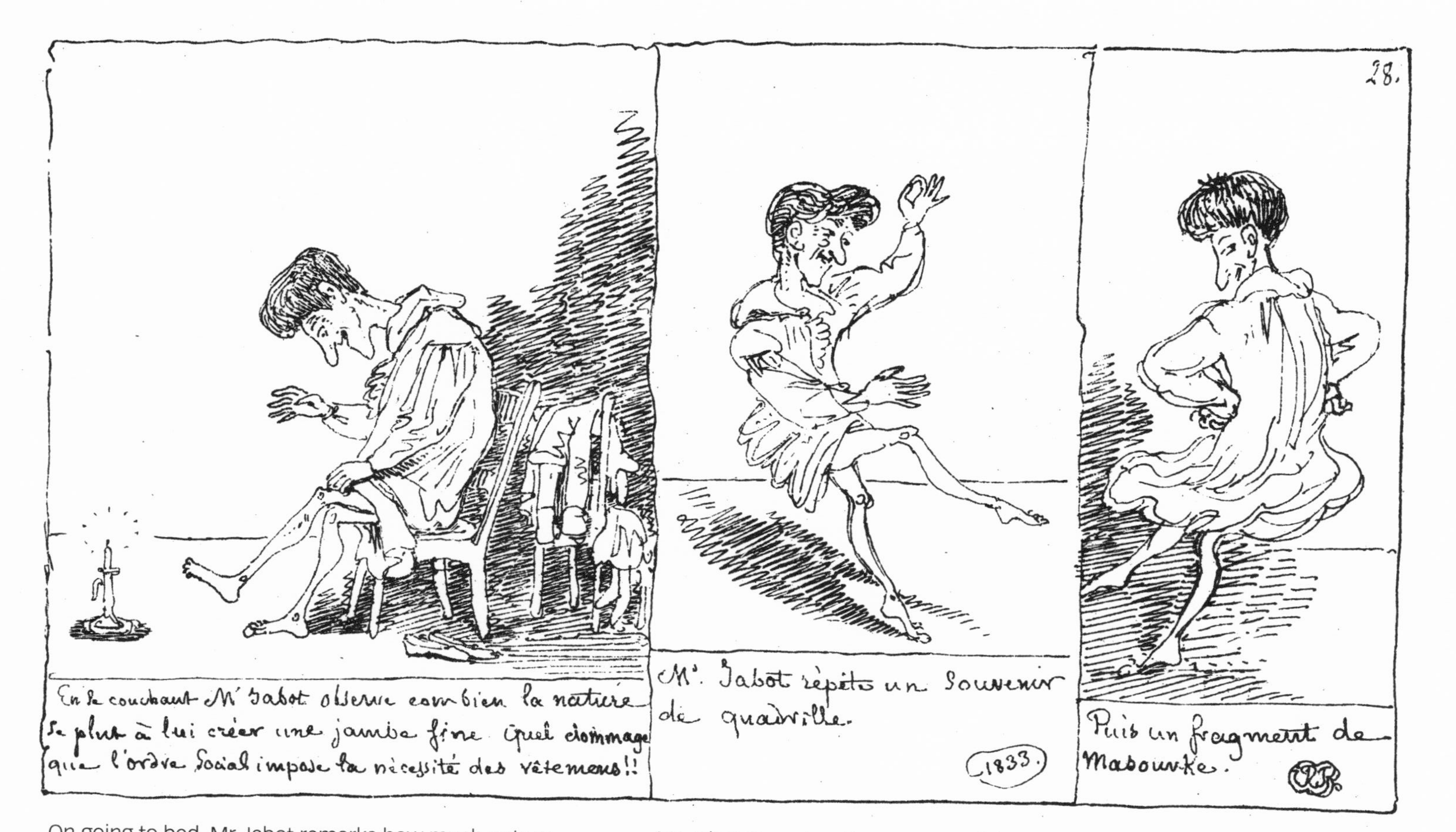
28.
En se couchant Mr Jabot observe combien la nature se plut à lui créer une jambe fine. Quel dommage que l'ordre social impose la nécessité des vêtemens!!
Mr. Jabot répète un souvenir de quadrille.
1833.
Puis un fragment de Mazourke.

On going to bed, Mr. Jabot remarks how much nature favored him by giving him slender legs. What a shame that decency imposes the necessity of clothing! !

Mr. Jabot re-evokes the memory of the quadrille.

—Then a fragment of the Mazurka.

29
Mr Jabot ayant entendu un petit bruit, s'arrête tout court.
Le bruit partant de derrière Mr Jabot se retourne subitement et ne voit rien.
Mr Jabot va se coucher, très décidé à changer totalement son régime dès le lendemain.

Mr. Jabot having heard a slight noise, stops abruptly.

The noise emanating from behind, Mr. Jabot suddenly turns around and sees nothing.

Mr. Jabot goes to bed, very much decided to change his diet totally from the next day.

30
Mr Jabot ne peut dormir que d'un oeil.
Mr. Jabot rêve des airs de mazourke.
Mr. Jabot rêve des choses énivrantes.
Mr Jabot rêve des hauts faits en présence d'une femme adorable.

Mr. Jabot can sleep with one eye only.

Mr. Jabot dreams of Mazurka music.

Mr. Jabot dreams of intoxicating things.

Mr. Jabot dreams of great deeds in the presence of an adorable woman.

31.
M. Jabot change d'oeil vers deux heures, après minuit.
Cependant les Seconds de Mr. Jabot et de ses adversaires s'assemblent de bon matin. Un premier propose le pistolet. — Arrêté. — Un second, que l'on charge les armes avec des boulettes de mie de pain, puisque l'honneur sera également satisfait — arrêté, comme juste et conforme à l'usage. — Un troisième, que l'on en prévienne les parties, afin de leur épargner une inquiétude inutile. — Adopté à l'unanimité.
Mr. Jabot devant tirer le dernier, essuie noblement le premier feu.

Mr. Jabot switches eyes around two after midnight.

Meanwhile Mr. Jabot's and his adversaries' Seconds gather early in the morning. One proposes pistols. —Agreed. —A second, that the arms be loaded with bread-balls, since honor would be equally well satisfied that way. —Agreed, as proper and consistent with custom. —A third, that the parties concerned should be informed in advance, in order to spare them useless worry. —Adopted unanimously.

Mr. Jabot, who fires last, comes nobly under the first fire.

32.
Mr Jabot tire noblement en l'air, après quoi les témoins accourent déclarent que l'honneur est satisfait et qu'il ne reste plus qu'à déjeuner ensemble.
Mr Jabot s'anime au champagne; il est déclaré unanimement galant homme.
RT

Mr. Jabot fires nobly into the air, after which the witnesses run up declaring that honor is satisfied and there remains only to take breakfast together.

Mr. Jabot becomes animated at the champagne; he is unanimously declared a man of honor.

33.
Mr Jabot ayant satisfait cinq fois à l'honneur, est ramené chez lui un peu replet.
Aussitôt Mr Jabot, songeant à sa partie de chasse, s'occupe d'acheter une petite meute

Mr. Jabot having satisfied the demands of honor five times, is brought home rather full.

Mr. Jabot, thinking of his hunting party, immediately busies himself with the purchase of a little pack of dogs.

34.
Les chiens sont si gentils que Mr Jabot les trouve presque trop familiers.
Aussi Mr Jabot rentré à l'Hôtel attache-t-il ses chiens au pied de son lit.
Mr Jabot s'empresse ensuite de porter chez Mr du Bocage 15 cartes, la famille se composant de 15 personnes

The dogs are so nice that Mr. Jabot finds them almost too friendly.

So returning to his hotel, Mr. Jabot ties his dogs to the foot of his bed.

Mr. Jabot then wastes no time in dropping off at Mr. du Bocage's 15 cards, the family being composed of 15 persons.

35.
Au retour Mr Jabot s'achète un fusil à deux coups, tout chargé.
Cependant les chiens font bonne garde.
Ce qui complique la migraine de la Marquise, Veuve de Mirliflor, qui occupe la chambre voisine.

On the way back Mr. Jabot buys himself a double-barreled gun, ready loaded.

Meanwhile the dogs do good guard-duty.

Which worsens the migraine of the Marquise, Widow de Mirliflor, who occupies the neighboring room.

36
Mr Jabot après s'être acheté une gibecière toutes pleines, rentre chez lui où il s'occupe à dresser ses chiens en leur criant : Tayaut ! Tayaut ! et autres termes de chasse. Les chiens lui paraissent pleins d'ardeur.
Les chiens fatigués s'endorment. Mr Jabot va se coucher. Il remarque avec peine que sa tournure a un peu perdu.

Mr. Jabot, after having bought himself a game-bag ready filled, returns home where he busies himself with training his dogs by shouting: Tally-ho! Tally-ho! and other exhortations of the chase. The dogs seem to him to be full of zeal.

Tired out, the dogs go to sleep. Mr. Jabot retires to bed. He notices to his grief that his figure has deteriorated somewhat.

37.
Ce qui le rassure, ce sont ses jambes.
C'est aussi certain moelleux dans les contours
certaine grâce dans les articulations. Cependant
le feu prend à sa chemise
Certaine chaleur!!.... certaine flamme amoureuse!..... et Sympathique!
RT

What reassures him is his legs.

And also something easy in his contours, a certain grace in the articulations. Meanwhile his shirt catches fire.

A certain warmth! ! . . . a certain amorous . . . . . and Sympathetic flame!

38
Entendant parler de flamme amoureuse, la Marquise de Mirliflor juge qu'elle pourrait bien y être pour quelque chose.
Ayant senti de la chaleur au dos, Mr Jabot fait neuf fois le tour de sa chambre en criant: Je brûle!.. Je brûle!!!
La Marquise ne doute plus qu'elle n'ait inspiré une passion d'une violence extraordinaire.

Hearing speak of amorous flame, the Marquise de Mirliflor considers that she might well be in question here.

Having felt the heat in his back, Mr. Jabot runs nine times around his room shouting I am burning! . I am burning! ! !

The Marquise no longer doubts that she has inspired a passion of extraordinary violence.

39
Holà !! Holà !! au feu !! au feu !!
La Marquise qui entend Hélas! Hélas! ô feux !! ô feux !! se confirme dans son idée.
Les chiens sentans une odeur de chair grillée se raniment.
Le chien de la Marquise aussi.
Le feu se communique au fusil qui part.

Hallo! ! Hallo! ! Fire! ! Fire! !

The Marquise who heard Alas! Alas! O fires! ! O fires! ! is confirmed in her idea.

The dogs smelling an odor of burnt flesh, revive.

The Marquise's dog also.

The fire reaches the gun, which goes off.

40
Persuadée que c'est un Suicide en sa faveur, la Marquise s'évanouit.
Son chien aussi.
Mr. Jabot sauve ses jours en changeant de linge
Ce qui fait plaisir à Mr. Jabot c'est que ses jambes n'ont pas souffert le moins du monde

Persuaded that this means a suicide on her account, the Marquise faints.

Her dog also.

Mr. Jabot saves his life by changing his shirt.

What pleases Mr. Jabot is that his legs have not suffered in the least.

41
Cependant la fumée tire des yeux de M. Jabot, d'abondantes larmes.
Revenue à elle, la Marquise se hasarde à jeter un coup d'oeil furtif. Elle voit son amant plein de vie et tout en larmes! Douces larmes!!!
Le chien de la Marquise se hasarde à revenir à lui.
M. Jabot s'étant écrié: Il y a de quoi périr!! La Marquise en est profondément touchée. Le chien aussi
RT

Meanwhile the smoke causes Mr. Jabot to weep copious tears.

Recovering, the Marquise ventures a furtive look. She sees her lover alive and bathed in tears! Sweet tears! ! !

The Marquise's dog ventures to revive.

Mr. Jabot having cried out: "This could be the end of me! !" the Marquise is profoundly touched. The dog too.

42
La Marquise extrêmement agitée, combattue, attendrie, fléchie, se va coucher, et ne peut dormir que d'un oeil.
Il vient une idée à Mr. Jabot, c'est d'ouvrir toutes les portes et fenêtres, pour laisser échapper la fumée.
après quoi Mr. Jabot va se coucher.
Cependant la fumée en pénétrant dans la chambre de la Marquise fait éternuer celle-ci. des chiens qui font bonne garde s'élancent vers le bruit.

The Marquise, extremely agitated, exhausted, melting, affected, goes to bed, and can sleep only with one eye.

Mr. Jabot has an idea, it is to open all the doors and windows to let the smoke out.

After which Mr. Jabot goes to bed.

Meanwhile the smoke penetrating into the Marquise's bedroom, makes her sneeze. Jabot's eager dogs on guard dash towards the noise.

Les chiens, en s'élançant, entraînent le lit de Mr. Jabot dans la chambre de la Marquise. après quoi ils se cou= chent épuisés.
Et le chien de la Marquise aussi.
Vers minuit, la Marquise s'étant mise à ronfler, Mr Jabot croit que c'est lui qui a de l'asthme, et se lève pour aller boire.
Mr Jabot se croyant dans sa chambre, prend sur la table de nuit de la Marquise sa veilleuse qui s'est éteinte

As they dash, the dogs drag Mr. Jabot's bed into the Marquise's chamber. After which they lie down, exhausted.

The Marquise's dog also.

Towards midnight, the Marquise having begun to snore, Mr. Jabot thinks it must be he with his asthma, and rises to find a drink.

Mr. Jabot believing himself to be in his bedroom, takes from the Marquise's bedside table her night-light which has gone out.

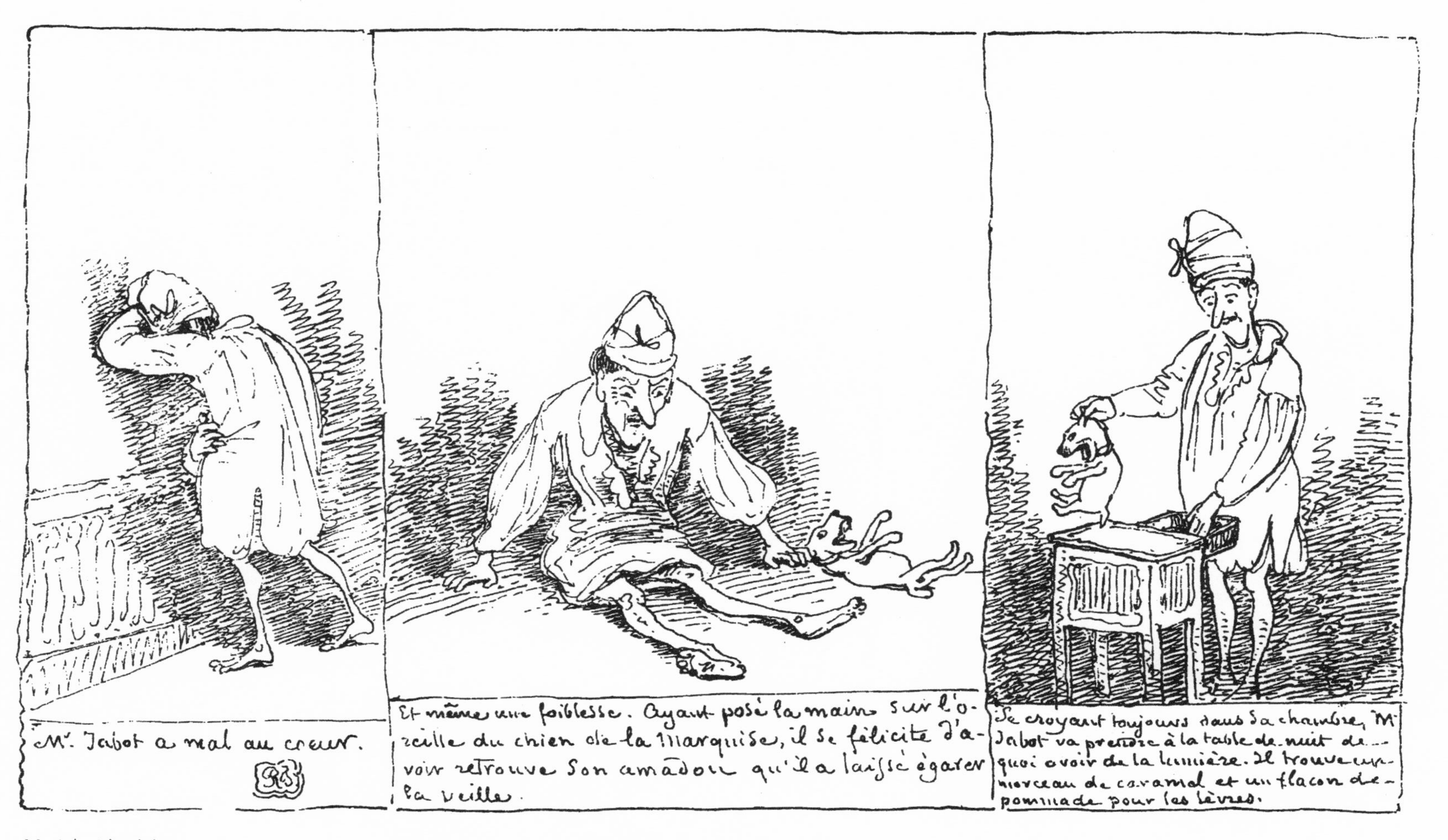
Mr. Jabot a mal au cœur.
Et même une foiblesse. Ayant posé la main sur l'oreille du chien de la Marquise, il se félicite d'avoir retrouvé son amadou qu'il a laissé égarer la veille.
Se croyant toujours dans sa chambre, Mr Jabot va prendre à la table de nuit de quoi avoir de la lumière. Il trouve un morceau de caramel et un flacon de pommade pour les lèvres.

Mr. Jabot is sick.

And feels faint. Having placed his hand on the ear of the Marquise's dog, he congratulates himself on having found the tinder that he lost the night before.

Still thinking he is in his own room, Mr. Jabot goes to take from the bedside table something to make a light with. He finds a piece of caramel and a pot of lip pomade.

45.
après quoi, Mr Jabot bat briquet infructueusement. Le chien crie mais il croit que ce sont les siens.
Ne pouvant avoir de la lumière par cette voie Mr Jabot s'habille pour en aller chercher. Il ne conçoit plus rien à sa culotte.
Mr Jabot tend à s'embrouiller.
Mr Jabot charge sa culotte d'imprécations, et jure qu'il quittera son tailleur dès le lendemain.

After which Mr. Jabot tries in vain to strike a light. The dog howls but he thinks it is his own dogs.

Failing to get a light this way, Mr. Jabot dresses to look for one. He cannot make head or tail of his underpants.

Mr. Jabot tends to get all mixed up.

Mr. Jabot curses his underpants roundly, and swears he will find another tailor the very next day.

46.
Cependant la Marquise se réveille au bruit, et persuadée que c'est un voleur, se lève et va furtivement dans la chambre de Mr. Jabot— où elle crie: Homme généreux! au secours! un voleur!!!
Entendant la voix du sexe, Mr Jabot se dégage et accourt dans sa chambre qu'il prend pour celle de la Marquise: Où est-il? Où est-il? femme adorable!!
Cependant l'aubergiste se lève pour aller voir ce que signifie ce bruit.
Lempoignant à l'entrée, Mr Jabot s'écrie: Je le tiens, je l'étouffe! L'aubergiste n'y comprend rien.

Meanwhile the Marquise awakens at the noise, and convinced that it is a burglar, gets up and steals into Mr. Jabot's room, where she cries "Generous man! Help! A burglar! ! !"

Hearing the voice of the fair sex, Mr. Jabot frees himself and runs into his room which he takes for that of the Marquise: Where is he? Where is he? Adorable woman! !

Meanwhile the innkeeper rises from his bed to see what all the ruckus is about.

Seizing him at the doorway Mr. Jabot shouts: I've got him! The innkeeper understands nothing of all this.

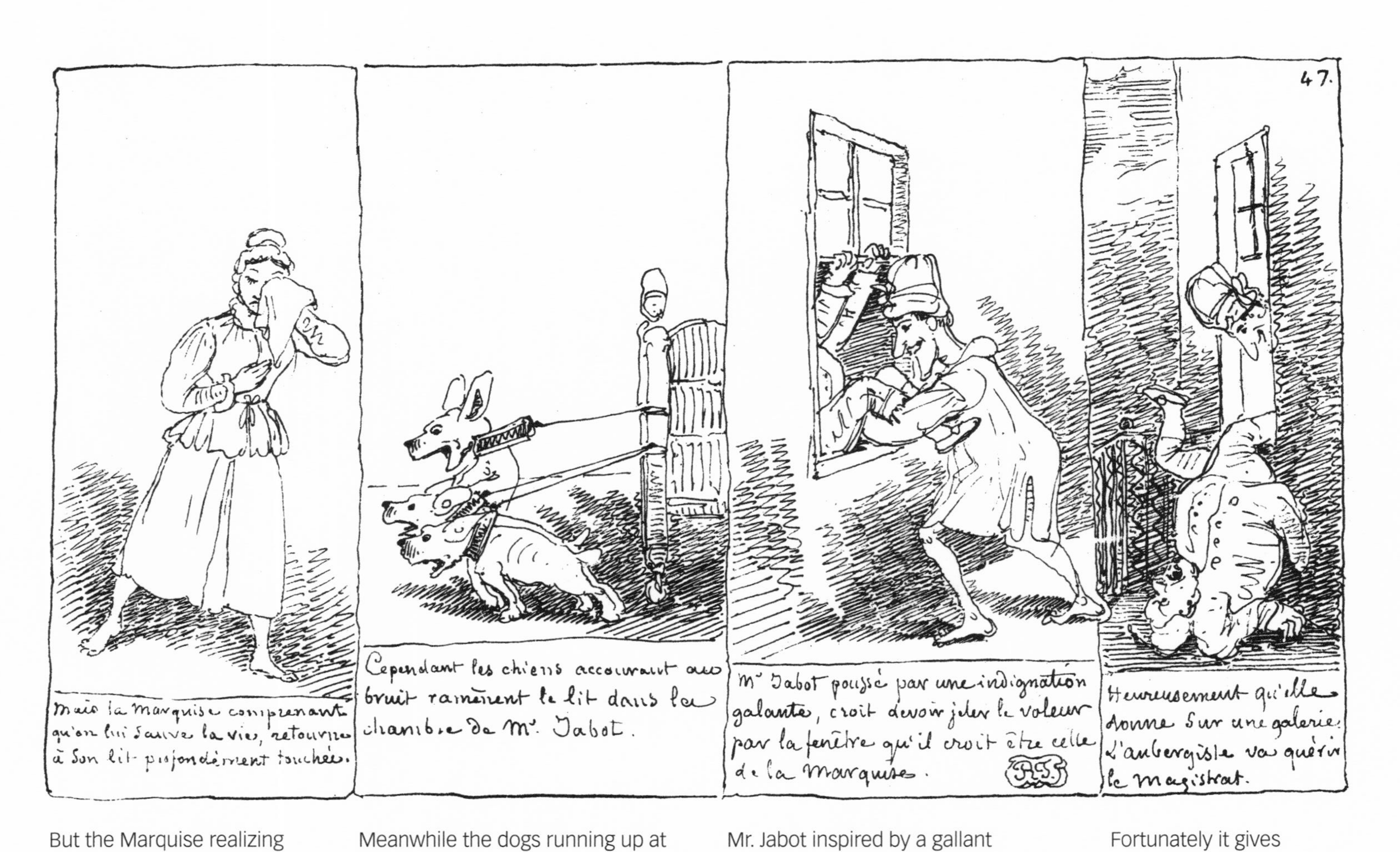
47.
Mais la Marquise comprenant
qu'on lui sauve la vie, retourne
à son lit profondément touchée.
Cependant les chiens accourant au
bruit ramènent le lit dans la
chambre de Mr. Jabot.
Mr Jabot poussé par une indignation
galante, croit devoir jeter le voleur
par la fenêtre qu'il croit être celle
de la Marquise.
Heureusement qu'elle
donne sur une galerie;
L'aubergiste va quérir
le magistrat.

But the Marquise realizing that she is having her life saved, returns to her bed profoundly touched.

Meanwhile the dogs running up at the noise bring the bed back to Mr. Jabot's room.

Mr. Jabot inspired by a gallant indignation, thinks it proper to throw the burglar out of the window, which he thinks is that of the Marquise.

Fortunately it gives onto a corridor. The innkeeper goes to fetch a magistrate.

48.
Guidé par le bruit des chiens, Mr. Jabot retourne à son lit, ravi d'une aventure aussi chevaleresque.
S'étant rendormi Mr Jabot rêve qu'il sauve deux beautés mourantes des injustes persécutions d'un trop coupable oppresseur.
La Marquise s'étant levée de bon matin est profondément attendrie à la vue de son libérateur. Toutefois elle ferme la porte. Son chien aussi.

Guided by the noise made by the dogs, Mr. Jabot returns to his bed, delighted at so chivalrous an adventure.

Asleep again Mr. Jabot dreams that he is rescuing two beauties dying from the unjust persecutions of all-too-guilty an oppressor.

The Marquise having got up early, is profoundly moved at the sight of her liberator. However she closes the door. Her dog also.

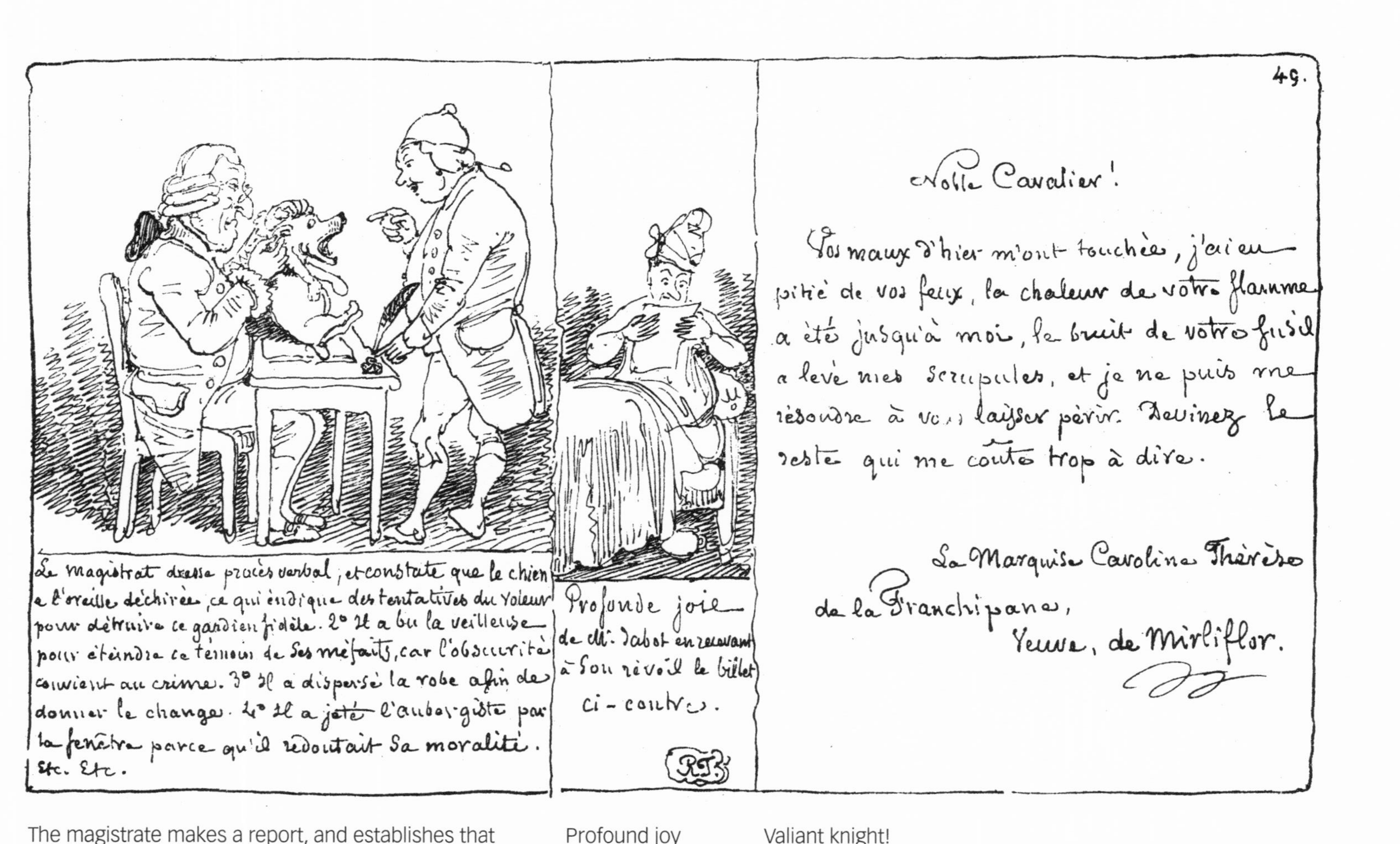
49.
Le magistrat dresse procès verbal, et constate que le chien
a l'oreille déchirée, ce qui indique des tentatives du voleur
pour détruire ce gardien fidèle. 2° Il a bu la veilleuse
pour éteindre ce témoin de ses méfaits, car l'obscurité
convient au crime. 3° Il a dispersé la robe afin de
donner le change. 4° Il a jeté l'aubergiste par
la fenêtre parce qu'il redoutait sa moralité.
Etc. Etc.
Profonde joie
de Mr. Jabot en recevant
à son réveil le billet
ci-contre.
RT
Noble Cavalier!
Vos maux d'hier m'ont touchée, j'ai eu
pitié de vos feux, la chaleur de votre flamme
a été jusqu'à moi, le bruit de votre fusil
a levé mes scrupules, et je ne puis me
résoudre à vous laisser périr. Devinez le
reste qui me coûte trop à dire.
La Marquise Caroline Thérèse
de la Franchipane,
Veuve, de Mirliflor.

The magistrate makes a report, and establishes that the dog has a torn ear, which indicates attempts on the part of the burglar to destroy this faithful guardian. 2nd He has drunk oil from the night-light in order to extinguish this witness of his deeds, for crime thrives in darkness. 3rd He tossed the dress about in order to lay down a false scent. 4th He threw the innkeeper out of the window because he feared his honesty. Etc. Etc.

Profound joy of Mr. Jabot on receiving at his awakening the following note.

Valiant knight!

Your troubles of yesterday touched me, I took pity on the fire of your love, the warmth of your flame reached me, the sound of your gun removed my scruples, and I cannot take it upon myself to let you perish. Divine the rest which costs me too much to say.

Marquise Caroline Thérèse de la Franchipane, Widow, de Mirliflor.

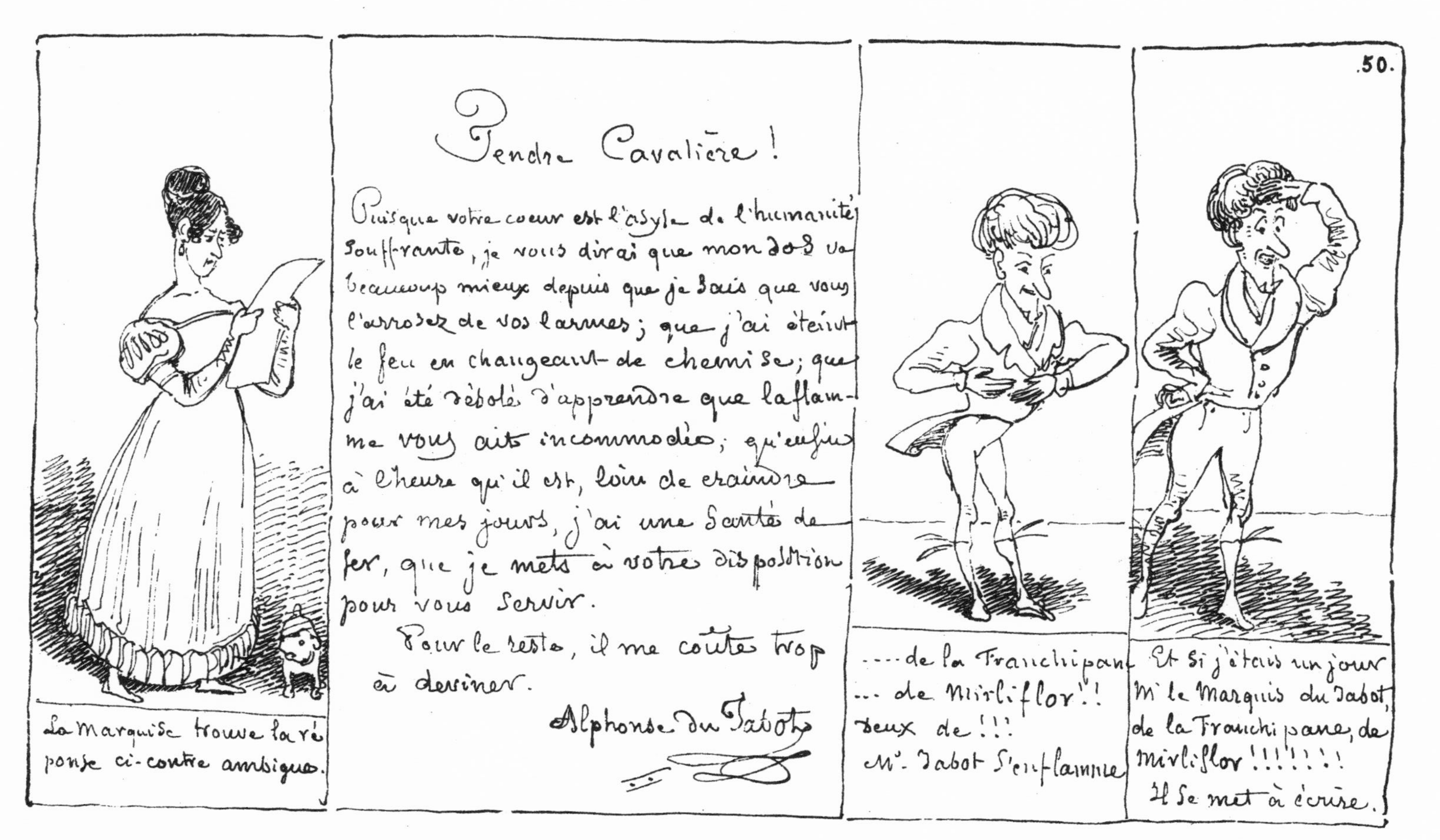
50.
La Marquise trouve la réponse ci-contre ambigue.
Tendre Cavalière!
Puisque votre coeur est l'asyle de l'humanité souffrante, je vous dirai que mon dos va beaucoup mieux depuis que je sais que vous l'arrosez de vos larmes; que j'ai éteint le feu en changeant de chemise; que j'ai été désolé d'apprendre que la flamme vous aits incommodée; qu'enfin à l'heure qu'il est, loin de craindre pour mes jours, j'ai une santé de fer, que je mets à votre disposition pour vous servir.
Pour le reste, il me coûte trop à deviner.
Alphonse du Jabot
....de la Franchipane
... de Mirliflor!!
deux de!!!
Mr. Jabot s'enflamme
Et si j'étais un jour Mr le Marquis du Jabot, de la Franchipane, de Mirliflor!!!!!!!
Il se met à écrire.

The Marquise finds the following response puzzling.

Tender Lady Knight! Since your heart is the asylum of suffering humanity, I will tell you that my back is much better since I know that you water it with your tears; that I put out the fire by changing my shirt; that I was distressed to learn that the flame incommoded you, and finally that at this time far from fearing for my life, my health is as iron, which I put at your disposition in order to serve you. As for the rest, it costs me too much to guess. Alphonse du Jabot.

. . . . de la Franchipane
. . . de Mirliflor! ! Two partitives! ! !

Mr. Jabot is enflamed.

And if I became one day Marquis du Jabot, de la Franchipane, de Mirliflor! ! ! ! ! ! !

He sits down to write.

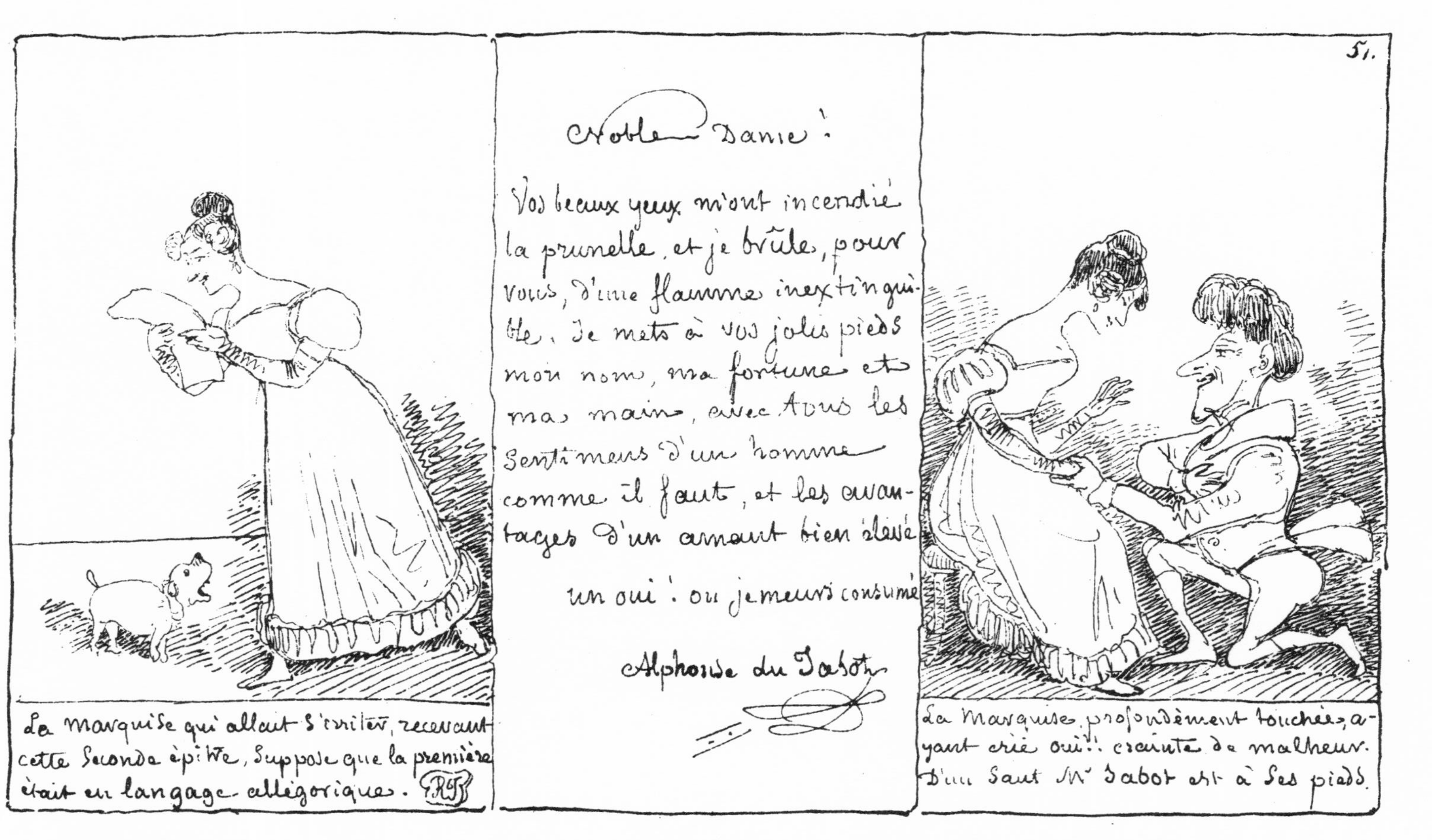
51.
La Marquise qui allait s'irriter, recevant cette Seconde épitre, suppose que la première était en langage allégorique.
Noble Dame!
Vos beaux yeux m'ont incendié la prunelle, et je brûle, pour vous, d'une flamme inextinguible. Je mets à vos jolis pieds mon nom, ma fortune et ma main, avec tous les sentimens d'un homme comme il faut, et les avantages d'un amant bien élevé
un oui! ou je meurs consumé
Alphonse du Jabot
La Marquise, profondément touchée, ayant crié oui!! crainte de malheur. D'un saut Mr Jabot est à ses pieds.

The Marquise who was about to get annoyed, receiving this second epistle supposes that the first was in an allegorical language.

Noble lady! Your beauteous looks have set fire to my eyes, and I burn, for you, with an inextinguishable flame. I put at your pretty feet my name, my fortune, and my hand, with all the sentiments of a man of breeding, and the advantages of a well-brought-up lover. A Yes! or I die, consumed. Alphonse du Jabot.

The Marquise, profoundly moved, having cried yes! ! for fear of some misfortune. In a single bound, Mr. Jabot is at her feet.

52.
Surprise de Mr. Jabot. Les trois chiens s'étant pris de querelle pendant son absence, se sont battus avec une telle voracité qu'il ne reste plus que les trois queues. Mr. Jabot saisit ce prétexte pour contremander sa partie de chasse.
Mr. Jabot part dès la journée même pour s'aller marier en Beaujolais.
Fin.

Surprise of Mr. Jabot. The three dogs having quarreled during his absence, have fought each other with such voracity that the three tails are all that is left of them. Mr. Jabot seizes the pretext to cancel his hunting party.

Mr. Jabot sets off that very day for his marriage in Beaujolais.
End

Mr CREPIN

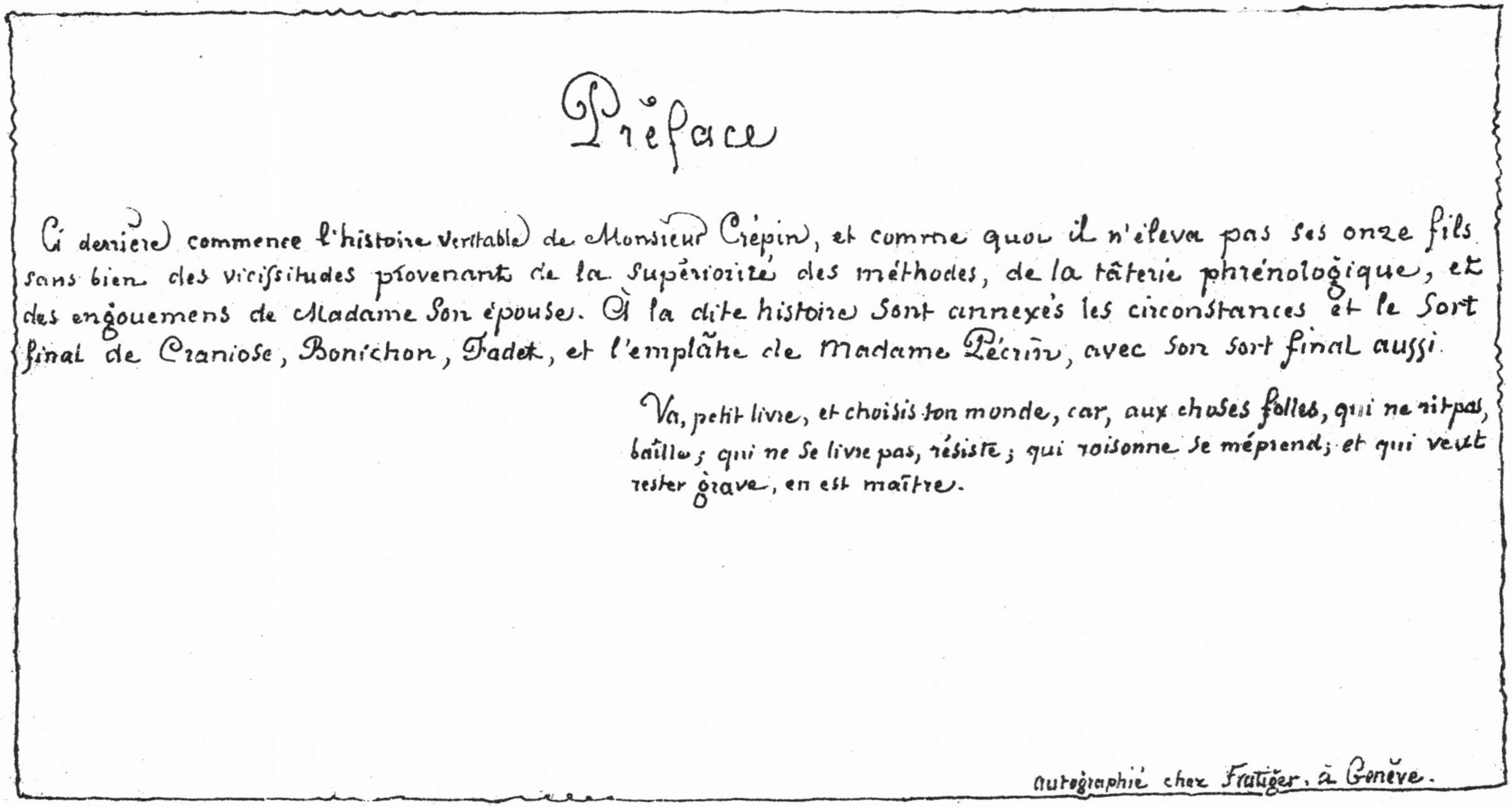
Préface

Ci derrière commence l'histoire véritable de Monsieur Crépin, et comme quoi il n'éleva pas ses onze fils sans bien des vicissitudes provenant de la supériorité des méthodes, de la tâterie phrénologique, et des engouemens de Madame son épouse. A la dite histoire sont annexés les circonstances et le sort final de Craniose, Bonichon, Fadet, et l'emplâtre de Madame Pécrin, avec son sort final aussi.

Va, petit livre, et choisis ton monde, car, aux choses folles, qui ne rit pas, bâille; qui ne se livre pas, résiste; qui raisonne se méprend; et qui veut rester grave, en est maître.

Autographié chez Frutiger, à Genève.

Preface.

Hereafter begins the true story of Monsieur Crépin, and how his attempts to raise his eleven children were attended with many vicissitudes resulting from the superiority of certain methods, from phrenological palpations, and from the infatuations of Madame his wife. To the said story are appended the particulars and what finally happened to Craniose, Bonichon, Fadet, and the plaster of Mrs. Pécrin, and what happened to that too.

Go little book and choose your world, for at crazy things, those who do not laugh, yawn; and those who do not yield, resist; and those who reason, are mistaken, and those who would keep a straight face, can please themselves.

De retour de son voyage, Mr Crépin éprouve le plaisir de serrer sa famille dans ses bras.
(3.)

Returning from his travels, Mr. Crépin experiences the pleasure of embracing his family.

Les enfans de Mr. Crépin témoignent à leur père toute leur filiale allégresse
(4)

Mr. Crépin's children demonstrate to their father all their filial joy.

Monsieur Crépin assiste aux jeux de ses enfans.
Monsieur Crépin assiste au repas de ses enfans.
(5.)

Mr. Crépin attends his children’s games.

Mr. Crépin attends his children’s meals.

L'Instituteur des jeunes Crépin est présenté à Monsieur leur père
(6)

The young Crépins' tutor is presented to their father.

Monsieur Crépin assiste à la promenade du soir, dont l'Instituteur lui explique les propriétés dans son Système. (7)

Mr. Crépin attends the evening walk, the properties of which in his system the Tutor explains.

Monsieur Crépin assiste à la couchée dont l'Instituteur lui explique les propriétés et l'organisation dans son Système
(8)

Mr. Crépin attends bedtime, the properties and organization of which according to his system the Tutor explains.

Mr. Crépin se trouve un peu fatigué de cette première journée
L'Instituteur lui explique comment, dans son Système
il procède du général au particulier.
Madame Crépin ajoute sur le Système
de l'Instituteur quelques particularités que celui-ci avait omises par
modestie.
Mr. Crépin ne ferme pas l'oeil de toute la nuit.
19.
9

Mr. Crépin finds himself a bit tired after this first day. The Tutor explains how, in his system, he proceeds from the general to the particular.

Mrs. Crépin adds to the Tutor's system some particularities that he had omitted out of modesty.

Mr. Crépin cannot close his eyes the whole night long.

De grand matin, Mr Crépin assiste aux Soins de propreté, dont l'Instituteur lui explique la portée hygiénique
et morale, dans son système.
(10)

Early in the morning, Mr. Crépin attends the ablutions, the hygienic and moral purpose of which, in his system, the Tutor explains.

Pendant que les jeunes Crépin font un devoir, Mr Crépin demande où en est l'instruction. L'Instituteur répond que tous commencent à procéder très bien du général au particulier.
Ayant fait venir Joseph, l'Instituteur lui demande où est Besançon. Joseph répond instantanément que Besançon est dans l'ensemble des choses, qui comprend l'Univers, qui comprend le monde, qui comprend les quatre parties du monde, qui comprennent l'Europe, où se trouve Besançon.
Mr Crépin ayant appelé Léopold, lui demande lui-même, combien couteront huit Livres de Saindoux, à cinq florins la livre? Léopold répond instantanément que le Saindoux est dans l'ensemble des choses, qui comprend l'Univers, qui comprend les trois règnes, qui comprennent le règne animal, qui comprend le cochon qui comprend le Saindoux
(11)

While the young Crépins are engaged in homework, Mr. Crépin asks how the teaching is going. The Tutor replies that all are beginning to proceed quite effectively from the general to the particular.

Summoning Joseph, the Tutor asks him where Besançon is. Joseph replies immediately that Besançon is in the totality of things, which includes the Universe, which includes the world, which includes the four parts of the world, which include Europe, where Besançon is.

Calling up Léopold, Mr. Crépin himself asks how much eight pounds of lard would cost at five florins a pound? Léopold replies immediately that lard is in the totality of things, which includes the universe, which includes the three kingdoms, which includes the animal kingdom, which includes the pig, which includes lard.

Mr. Crépin trouve son fils Léopold peu avancé sur l'arithmétique. L'Instituteur lui explique que dans son système; l'arithmétique est la dernière chose que Léopold saura, parce qu'il doit auparavant savoir l'algèbre, qu'il ne commencera qu'après avoir préalablement approfondi la quantité en général.
Mr Crépin expose pourquoi le système lui semble absurde; Madame Crépin rétorque comme quoi il est admirable. L'Instituteur s'en rapporte entièrement à Madame qui seule en a suivi les applications et les succès vraiment étonnans
L'affaire s'échauffant, Madame Crépin prend mal, et Monsieur Crépin argumente vivement. L'Instituteur le traite de stupide, incapable de saisir une méthode, et de comprendre un système.
(12)

Mr. Crépin finds his son Léopold rather backward in arithmetic. The Tutor explains that in his system arithmetic is the last thing that Léopold will learn, because he has first to learn Algebra, which he will not start until he has thoroughly mastered quantity in general.

Mr. Crépin shows why he thinks the system absurd; Mrs. Crépin retorts that it is quite admirable. The Tutor appeals to Madame alone, who alone has followed its applications and truly astonishing achievements.

The discussion growing heated, Mrs. Crépin faints away, and Mr. Crépin argues vigorously. The Tutor calls him stupid, incapable of understanding a method, or understanding a system.

Mr Crépin ayant intimé à l'Instituteur l'ordre de sortir sur le champ de chez lui, l'Instituteur se retranche derrière le mobilier, et y proclame énergiquement la supériorité, l'efficacité et l'antériorité de son système.
Les jeunes Crépin accourent au bruit et croyant que Mme Crépin a reçu un coup de chaise, escaladent l'Instituteur et procèdent contre lui du général au particulier.
(13)

When Mr. Crépin orders the Tutor out of his house forthwith, the Tutor barricades himself behind the furniture, and loudly proclaims the superiority, efficacy, and anteriority of his system.

The young Crépins rush up at the noise, and thinking that Mrs. Crépin has been hit by a chair, climb all over the Tutor and proceed against him from the general to the particular.

Après quoi, les jeunes Crépin étant revenus, et retrouvant madame leur mère saine et sauve, lui sautent au cou pour lui en té = moigner toute leur joie.
L'Instituteur laissé dans un fossé, y soutient envers et contre tous la Supériorité, et l'antériorité de son Système.
(14)

After which, the young Crépins turn back, and finding their mother safe and sound, jump on her as a demonstration of their joy.

Abandoned in a ditch, the Tutor defends against all and sundry the superiority and anteriority of his system.

Pour venger son système méconnu, l'Instituteur casse les vitres de la ferme.
Le Garde champêtre ayant paru, l'Instituteur proclame à la face du Ciel que ni la force brutale, ni la violence stupide, ni une soldatesque effrénée, n'auront la moindre action sur ses convictions intimes
(15)

To avenge his misunderstood system, the Tutor smashes the farm windows.

At the appearance of the Rural Guard the Tutor vows to the heavens above that neither brute force, nor stupid violence, nor unbridled soldiery, shall have the slightest effect on his innermost convictions.

La Commune étant accourue au bruit, l'Instituteur se réfugie sur un poirier, d'où il proclame que les fureurs d'une populace imbécille ne pourront pas davantage sur ses convictions intimes.
La branche ayant cassé, l'Instituteur tombe sur le Marguillier, et l'oblige à confesser la supériorité et l'antériorité de son système, pendant que la commune s'enfuit à toutes jambes.
(16)

The Commune running up at the noise, the Tutor takes refuge in a pear tree, from where he proclaims that the fury of an imbecile mob shall not affect his innermost convictions, either.

When a branch breaks, the Tutor falls on the Churchwarden, and forces him to admit the superiority and anteriority of his system, while the commune takes to its heels.

Après quoi l'Instituteur échappe comme il peut aux chiens de garde.
Cependant Monsieur Crépin, déjà fort embarrassé de l'éducation de ses enfans, reçoit comme il peut les reproches de Madame Crépin, qui regrette un Système qu'elle avait compris.
(17.)

After which the Tutor flees the watchdogs as best he can.

Meanwhile already very worried about the education of his children, Mr. Crépin suffers as best he can the reproaches of Mrs. Crépin, who bewails a system she had understood.

Monsieur Crépin ayant demandé un Instituteur, par les petites affiches, plusieurs viennent se présenter chez lui.
(18)

On Mr. Crépin's advertising for a Tutor, several show up at his house.

Monsieur Crépin ayant choisi un Instituteur qui lui plaît; madame Crépin lui en propose un qui lui plairait da=vantage.
Mr Crépin déjà fort embarrassé de l'éducation de ses enfans; est contrarié par les propos de Mde Crépin qui lui reproche d'avoir chassé un homme d'esprit pour prendre une bête
(19)

Mr. Crépin chooses a Tutor he likes, Mrs. Crépin proposes another whom he would like even more.

Already very worried about the education of his children, Mr. Crépin is vexed by Mrs. Crépin, who upbraids him with having gotten rid of a clever man and taken on a fool.

Monsieur Crépin, par manière de conciliation, engage les deux Instituteurs et leur as=
signe à chacun un local particulier
(20)

Mr. Crépin by way of a compromise engages the two Tutors and assigns each of them their own schoolroom.

Mr Bonichon met aussitôt les Crepin cadets à sa méthode qui consiste à étudier la physique dans les Aventures de Télémaque, à la manière Jacotot.
Mr Fadet met aussitôt les Crepin aînés à sa méthode qui consiste à tout réduire en nombres fractionnaires, selon un système dont il est l'inventeur.
21.

Mr. Bonichon immediately introduces the younger Crépins to his method, which consists of studying physics in the *Adventures of Telemachus*, Jacotot style.

Mr. Fadet immediately introduces the older Crépins to his method, which consists in reducing everything to fractions, according to a system he himself invented.

Le soir étant venu, les deux Instituteurs se promènen
dans la grande allée, et sont d'accord sur ce point
que leur prédécesseur n'y entendait rien.
Les Crépin cadets ayant mis toute la cuisine en physique, Mr. Crépin reçoit les plaintes de sa cuisinière.
22.

In the evening, the two Tutors take a walk in the main drive and agree on this much, that their predecessor understood nothing about anything.

When the younger Crépins turn the whole kitchen into a physics lab, Mr. Crépin is subjected to the complaints of the cook.

Les Crépin ainés mettant tout le Salon en nombres fractionnaires, Madame en augure avec délices qu'ils entreront tous à l'École polytechnique.
Madame Crépin complimente Mr Fadet, Fadet en prend occasion de développer sa théorie, tant sous le rapport interne, que sous le rapport externe ou extérieur.
23.

The elder Crépins reduce the whole drawing room to fractions. A delighted Madame can see in advance that they will all get into the Polytechnic School.

Mrs. Crépin compliments Mr. Fadet. Fadet takes the opportunity to develop his theory, in its internal as in its external or exterior relations.

Cependant la cuisinière verse un pot d'eau grasse sur Bonichon pour lui apprendre à physiquer sa cuisine.
Mr. Bonichon porte plainte. Mr Crépin donnant tort à la cuisi= nière, est contrarié par Madame Crépin qui donne tort à l'Instituteur.
24.

Meanwhile the cook empties a pot of dirty dishwater over Bonichon, to teach him to physic her kitchen.

Mr. Bonichon lodges a complaint. Mr. Crépin blames the cook and is opposed by Mrs. Crépin who blames the Tutor.

Pendant que Mr Bonichon va changer de linge, Mr Fadet donne raison à Madame Crépin, et prouve que tout le mal vient de la méthode vicieuse de son confrère.
Entendant cela Bonichon revient sur ses pas, pour défendre sa méthode, et foudroie d'un sorite et de deux dilemmes la cuisinière qui donne raison à Mr Fadet et à Mde Crépin
(25)

While Mr. Bonichon goes off to change, Mr. Fadet sides with Mrs. Crépin, and proves that the whole problem is caused by the faulty method of his colleague.

Hearing which, Bonichon returns to defend his method, and with one sorites and two dilemmas blasts the cook, who sides with Mr. Fadet and Mrs. Crépin.

L'affaire s'échauffant, Madame Crépin s'évanouit, et Mr Crépin qui donne raison à Bonichon, retient les jeunes Crépin dans leur chambre
La Cuisinière ayant été chercher sa lèchefrite délivre Mr Fadet, et expulse Bonichon de la maison, à perpétuité.
(26)

As the matter gets heated, Mrs. Crépin faints, and Mr. Crépin siding with Bonichon, keeps the younger Crépins in their room.

The cook takes up her grease-pan, rescues Mr. Fadet and drives Bonichon from the house, in perpetuity.

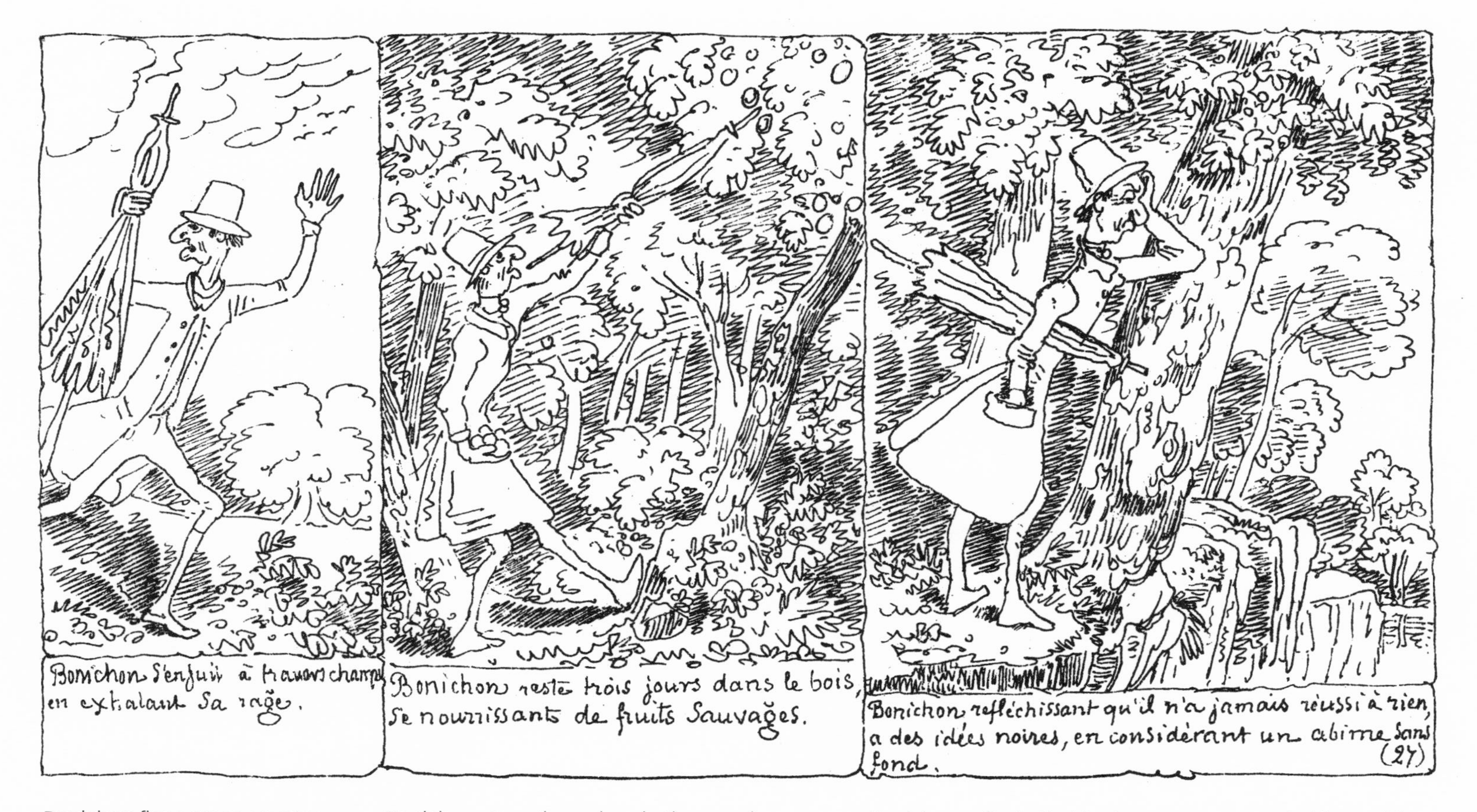
Bonichon s'enfuit à travers champs
en exhalant sa rage.
Bonichon reste trois jours dans le bois,
se nourrissant de fruits sauvages.
Bonichon réfléchissant qu'il n'a jamais réussi à rien,
a des idées noires, en considérant un abîme sans
fond.
(27)

Bonichon flees cross country, venting his rage.

Bonichon stays three days in the wood, living on wild fruit.

Bonichon reflects that he has never succeeded in anything, and becomes sunk in dark thoughts as he contemplates a bottomless abyss.

Se méfiant de lui-même, Bonichon regagne la plaine avant la nuit.
DOUANE ROYALE
Arrivé dans la plaine, Bonichon obtient par la protection secrète de Monsieur Crépin une place de Sous=douanier.
(28)

Mistrusting himself, Bonichon returns to the plain before nightfall.

On his arrival in the plain, the secret patronage of Mr. Crépin gets Bonichon a job as assistant customs officer.

Fadet qui a beaucoup souffert, reçoit les félicitations de ses jeunes élèves, pendant que Mr. Crépin est vivement sollicité par sa femme et par sa cuisinière de lui confier l'éducation de tous ses enfans.
Fadet enchanté attribue son triomphe à la supériorité de sa méthode. Mr. Crépin le prie de laisser là sa méthode et de donner de bonnes manières à ses enfans.
(29)

The long-suffering Fadet is congratulated by his young pupils, while Mr. Crépin is earnestly entreated by his wife and his cook to entrust to him the education of all his children.

The delighted Fadet attributes his triumph to the superiority of his method. Mr. Crépin asks him to drop his method and give his children good manners.

Fadet ayant fait acheter aux jeunes Crépins un lorgnon et un chapeau, leur enseigne les règles de l'urbanité française.
Comment, en écoutant un Supérieur, on fléchit légèrement le dos, et on marque l'empressement avec la jambe gauche.
(30)

Fadet has the young Crépins buy a lorgnette and a hat, and teaches them the rules of French etiquette.

How, on listening to a superior, one gives a slight bow, using a forward left leg to express devoted attention.

Comment, interpellé par un inférieur, on marque la distance sociale, en retournant seulement le buste, pour lorgner ce que demande cet individu.
Comment, à un homme qui vous insulte on se borne à présenter avec calme sa carte d'adresse.
Comment, si un supérieur éternue, on s'incline légèrement, en simulant un souhait du bras gauche.
(31)

How, called upon by an inferior, one marks social distance by turning the upper body alone, to stare through the lorgnette at what this individual might want.

How when insulted, one does no more than calmly present one's card.

How, if a superior sneezes, one bows slightly, gesturing a "bless you" with the left arm.

Comment si une incongruité quelconque se fait apercevoir, on feint d'admirer le paysage, ou l'on suppose avoir entendu un petit bruit dans la rue.
Comment, dans une société légère et spirituelle, on se pose pour causer spectacles, casinos, et en général les superfluités à la mode.
Comment on se lève en partant d'un éclat de rire, à un trait d'esprit échappé à un Supérieur.
(32)

How in the event of some accidental impropriety, one pretends to admire the view, or to have heard some slight noise in the street.

How, in a free and witty society, one sits down to talk of theater, casinos, and fashionable nothings in general.

How one rises with a burst of laughter when a superior cracks a joke.

Comment on se subordonne avec con-
venance à la maîtresse de la maison.
Comment on prend congé.
Les jeunes Crépin en se subordonnant avec
convenance à Madame leur mère lui
causent une admiration mélangée d'un
doux attendrissement.
(33)

How one properly submits to the pleasure of the lady of the house.

How one takes one's leave.

Properly submitting to the pleasure of Madame their mother, the young Crépins arouse in her an admiration mingled with sweet tenderness.

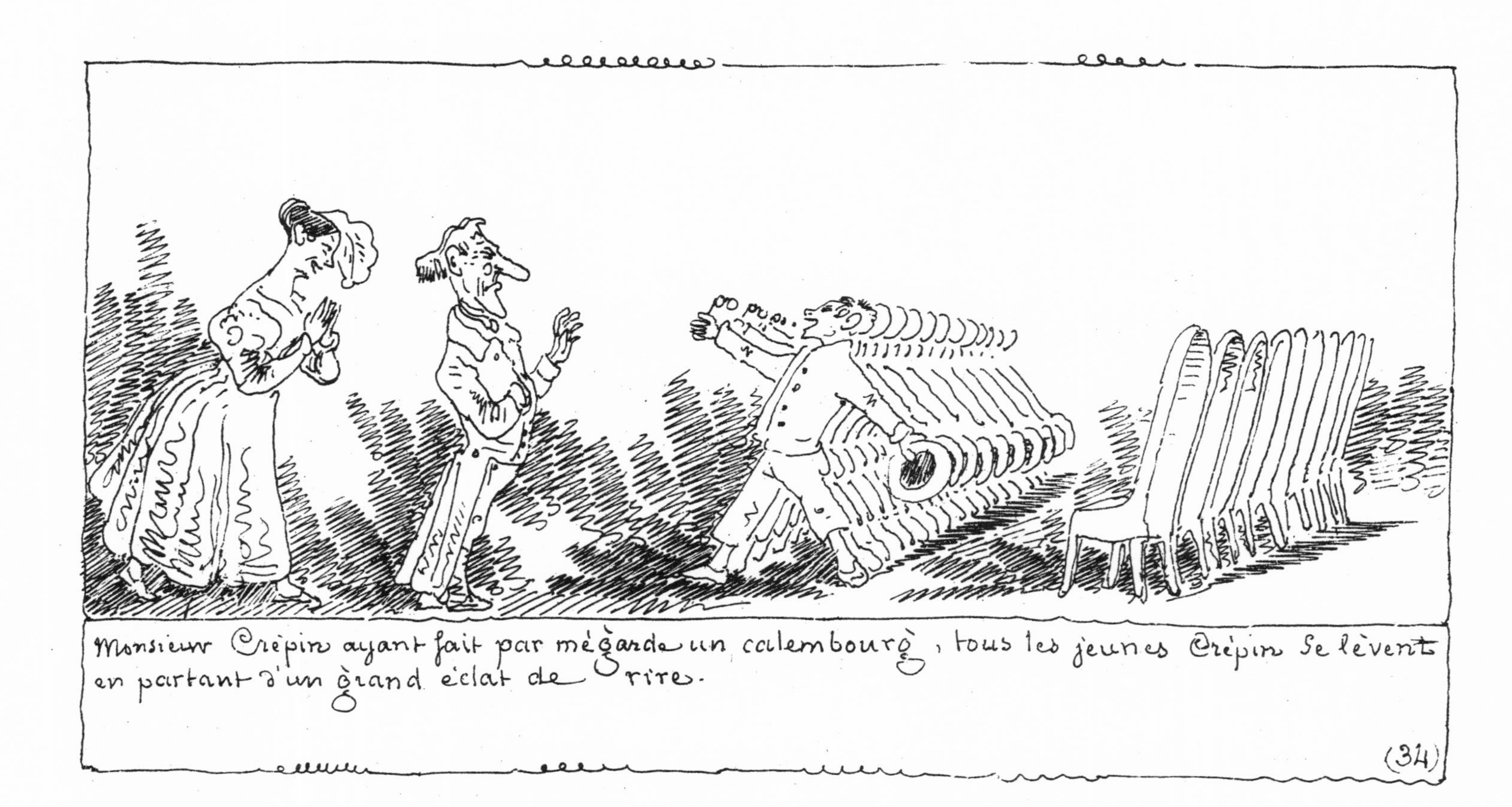
Monsieur Crépin ayant fait par mégarde un calembourg, tous les jeunes Crépin se lèvent en partant d'un grand éclat de rire.
(34)

Mr. Crépin having unwittingly made a pun, all the young Crépins jump up with great bursts of laughter.

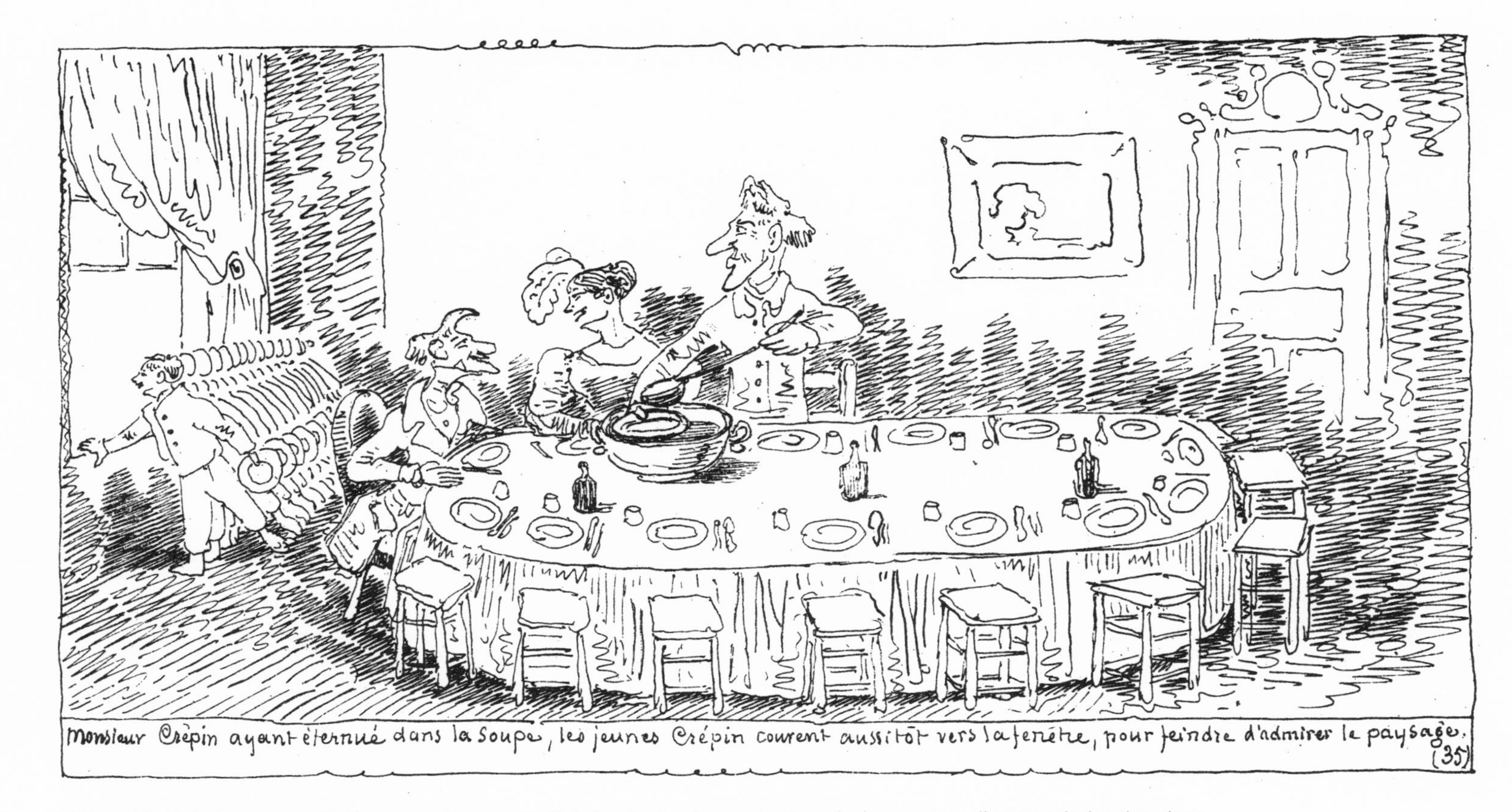
Monsieur Crépin ayant éternué dans la soupe, les jeunes Crépin courent aussitôt vers la fenêtre, pour feindre d'admirer le paysage.
(35)

When Mr. Crépin sneezes in the soup, the young Crépins instantly run to the window, pretending to admire the view.

à la promenade du soir, Fadet fait remarquer à Mr Crépin, combien sa famille a gagné en urbanité française.
Au retour les jeunes Crépin, passant auprès d'une vigne, y entrent deux à deux.
(36)

During the evening walk, Fadet brings to Mr. Crépin's attention how much the family has gained in French urbanity.

On the way back, passing by a vineyard, the young Crépins enter it two by two.

Interpellés par le garde champêtre, les jeunes Crépin retournent seulement le buste, pour lorgner ce que demande cet individu.
(37)

Challenged by the rural guard, the young Crépins merely turn their torsoes, to peer questioningly through their lorgnettes at the individual.

Le garde champêtre s'emportant en insultes, les jeunes Crépin se bornent à lui présenter avec calme leur carte d'adresse.
(38)

When the rural guard explodes in insults, the young Crépins content themselves with quietly presenting their cards.

Pour s'assurer de l'amende, le garde champêtre enfile d'un coup de sabre les onze chapeaux et s'enfuit.
N'ayant plus leur chapeau, les jeunes Crépin jettent leur lorgnon, perdent leur tenue et font de mauvaises manières en re tournant chez eux.
(39)

In order to make sure of his fine, the rural guard spits the eleven hats with a single thrust of his saber, and runs off.

Now being hatless, the young Crépins throw away their lorgnettes, run wild, and misbehave on the way home.

PLAINTE
L'autorité civile arrive avec une plainte et demande de dommages et intérets. Mr Crépin s'emporte contre Fadet à qui il reproche de corrompre le naturel bien né de ses enfans.
PLAINTE
Mr Crépin continuant à s'emporter, Fadet admire et déplore en même temps la stupidité d'un pareil homme.
(40)

The civic authority arrives with a complaint and demand for damages with interest. Mr. Crépin gets furious with Fadet, whom he blames for corrupting his children's naturally good disposition.

When Mr. Crépin does not abate his fury, Fadet simultaneously marvels at and deplores the stupidity of such a man.

plainte
Mr Crépin s'emporte contre sa femme qui intercède en faveur d'un système qu'elle avait compris, et déclare qu'il chasse Fadet à l'instant même.
plainte
A ce mot insultant Fadet présente avec calme sa carte d'adresse et Made Crépin s'évanouit.
(41)

Mr. Crépin gets furious with his wife for interceding in favor of a system she had understood, and declares that he will get rid of Fadet that very instant.

At this insult, Fadet quietly presents his card, and Mrs. Crépin faints.

L'autorité s'impatientant, Fadet déclare qu'il se rend caution et otage de l'urbanité française de ses jeunes élèves, et se rend volontairement en prison.
Fadet en prison jette sur le papier quelques quatrains sur sa captivité.
Fadet refusant une grossière nourriture maigrit assez pour pouvoir, au bout de quelques jours passer à travers les barreaux.
(42)

When the Authority loses patience, Fadet offers himself as bail and hostage for the French urbanity of his young pupils, and goes voluntarily to jail.

In jail Fadet jots down on paper a few quatrains on his captivity.

Rejecting the coarse food given to him, in a few days Fadet becomes thin enough to slip through the bars.

Fadet ayant poussé du pied la guérite, emprisonne la force armée, et s'enfuit.
Fadet va se cacher dans le comble de la maison Crépin, où la cuisinière lui apporte un bouillon.
Ayant levé quelques tuiles, Fadet lorgne la beauté du paysage.
(43)

Kicking over the sentry box, Fadet immobilizes the armed force and flees.

Fadet goes into hiding in the attic of the Crépin house, where the cook brings him a broth.

Lifting some tiles, Fadet gazes at the beauty of the countryside through his lorgnette.

Fadet réfléchissant qu'il n'a jamais réussi à rien, est préservé de toute idée sinistre par des idées avantageuses.
Après un mois passé dans le comble, Fadet obtient par la protection secrète de Mme Crépin une place de teneur de livres dans une maison de cravates en crinoline, imperméables.
Cependant Mr Crépin, fort embarrassé de l'éducation de ses enfans, conjure Madame Crépin de se désévanouir.
(44)

Reflecting that he has not made a success of anything, Fadet is saved from fatal thoughts by ideas to his advantage.

After he has spent a month in the attic, the secret influence of Mrs. Crépin gets Fadet a job as bookkeeper in a waterproof crinoline cravat business.

Mr. Crépin however, very worried about the education of his children, beseeches his wife to recover from her faint.

L'évanouissement se prolongeant Monsieur Crépin envoie en toute hâte Léopold chercher le Docteur.
Le Docteur s'étant trompé de nom va chez Madame Pécrin à qui il ordonne un emplâtre de neuf pouces sur les reins.
Le Docteur ne venant pas, Mr. Crépin se rend chez celui-ci qui lui apprend qu'il en sort, et que l'ordonnance est déjà chez le pharmacien.
(45.)

Since the fainting fit is protracted, Mr. Crépin hurriedly sends Léopold to fetch the Doctor.

The Doctor mistaking the name, goes to Mrs. Pécrin, for whom he prescribes a nine-inch poultice on her back.

Since the Doctor fails to show up, Mr. Crépin goes to find him and is told that he has just come from there, and that the prescription is already at the pharmacist's.

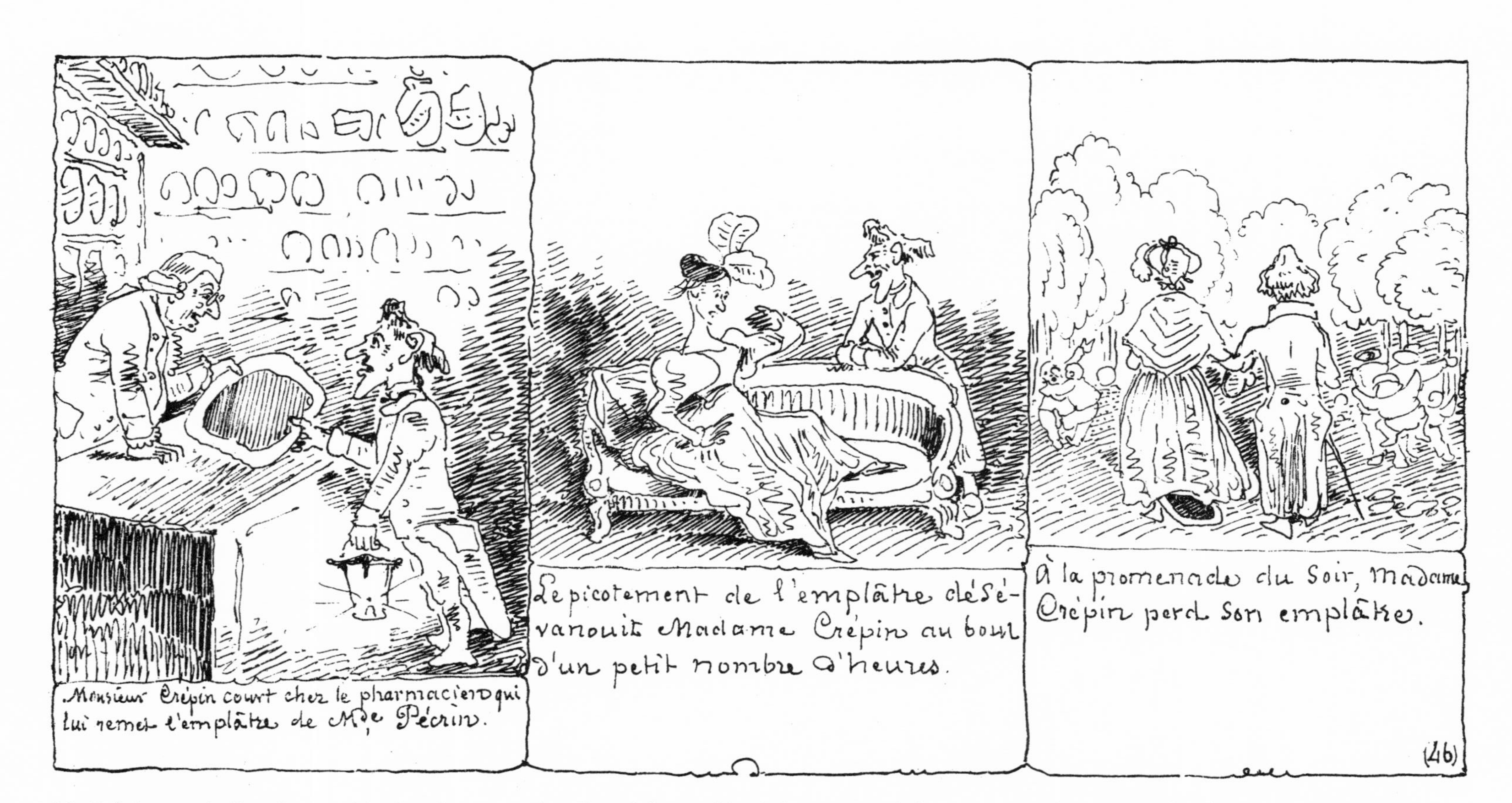
Monsieur Crépin court chez le pharmacien qui lui remet l'emplâtre de Mme Pécrin.
Le picotement de l'emplâtre désévanouit Madame Crépin au bout d'un petit nombre d'heures.
À la promenade du Soir, Madame Crépin perd son emplâtre.
(46)

Mr. Crépin runs to the pharmacist who gives him Mrs. Pécrin's poultice.

The sting of the poultice brings Mrs. Crépin round after a few hours.

In the course of their evening walk, Mrs. Crépin loses her poultice.

L'emplâtre est ramassé par Jean Chiffon
qui le vend pour cinq sous à Grené=taz l'Ecrivain public.
PICIER
qui le vend pour vingt sous à Gagne=prin, l'Epicier frater.
(47)

The poultice is picked up by Jean Chiffon

who sells it for five sous to Grenétaz the public letter-writer

who sells it for twenty sous to Gagneprin, the barber grocer.

qui le vend pour trente sous à Bonichon
qui s'en fait du bien.
Cependant Monsieur Crépin étant déjà très perplexe quant à l'éduca=
tion de ses enfans, est très contrarié de la visite d'un phrénologue
célèbre qui lui est recommandé.
(48)

who sells it for thirty sous to Bonichon, who finds it useful.

Mr. Crépin meanwhile, very worried about the education of his children, is much vexed at the visit of a famous phrenologist recommended to him.

Le Phrénologue ayant été prié à diner, tâte, en passant, la cuisinière, et lui reconnait la bosse des bonnes Sauces et des coulis Succulens, si elle s'applique bien.
Mr Crépin étant Survenu, prend à part Mr. Craniose, et le prie qu'il ait à s'abstenir de toute phrénologie dans sa maison.
(49)

The Phrenologist, invited to dinner, palpates the cook's head in passing, and recognizes in her the bump of good sauces and succulent gravies, if she applies herself enough.

Mr. Crépin appears, and taking Mr. Craniose aside, begs that he abstain from all phrenology in his house.

Le repas est fort gai, mais ce qui contrarie Mr. Crepin, c'est que sa femme raffolle de la phrénologie, et meurt d'envie d'être tâtée. (50)

The meal is cheerful enough, but what vexes Mr. Crépin, is that his wife is crazy about phrenology, and is dying to be palpated.

au dessert, Mr Crépin prend à part Mde Crépin et la prie de ne
pas attirer la conversation sur ce sujet.
madame Crépin n'y pouvant plus tenir engage Mr Craniose
à démontrer sur une bouteille, rien que pour voir. Monsieur Crépin s'y oppose vivement, en déclarant que la
phrénologie est une science immorale et matérialiste
(51)

At dessert, Mr. Crépin takes Mrs. Crépin aside and begs her not to draw the conversation onto that topic.

Mrs. Crépin is unable to hold out any longer, and urges Mr. Craniose to demonstrate on a bottle, just to see. Mr. Crépin is much opposed to this, declaring that phrenology is an immoral and materialist science.

Mr Craniose est charmé d'entendre parler ainsi, afin d'avoir l'occasion de détruire des préventions aussi honorables qu'injustes. « La phrénologie, monsieur, la phrénologie est au contraire une Science éminemment Spiritualiste; en effet réduisant tout à l'organisation et à la matière, elle laisse l'ame absolument en dehors de ses investigations. Donc, ne s'occupant pas de l'ame, elle est loin de l'attaquer. » Madame Crépin donne raison à Mr Craniose.
Passant ensuite aux applications les plus élémentaires de cette Science sublime à la législation, à l'éducation, à la religion, à la morale, à l'hygiène, à l'anthropologie, à la polygamie, à l'ontologie, ... etc, etc, Mr Craniose recule en entrevoyant l'avenir qui attend les Sociétés!!!!
(52)

Mr. Craniose is delighted to hear such language, which gives him the chance to confound objections as honorable as they are unjust. "Phrenology, Sir, phrenology is on the contrary an eminently spiritual science for, reducing all things to organization and matter, it leaves the soul absolutely outside its investigations. So that, having nothing to do with the soul, it is far from impugning it." Mrs. Crépin sides with Mr. Craniose.

Passing from the most elementary applications of this sublime science, to legislation, education, religion, morality, hygiene, anthropology, polygamy, ontology, . . . etc, etc, Mr. Craniose recoils when he foresees the future that awaits society! ! ! !

Passant ensuite à la preuve démonstrative, Mr Craniose déballe sa collection, et démontre que la phrénologie s'appuie sur des faits, que ces faits sont des bosses, que ces bosses indiquent le vol dans les têtes qui ont appartenu à un voleur, le meurtre dans les crânes qui ont appartenu à un meurtrier, et le savoir dans les crânes qui ont appartenu à un savant
53.

Passing on to demonstrative proof, Mr. Craniose unpacks his collection, and demonstrates that phrenology is supported by facts, that these facts are bumps, that these bumps indicate theft in the heads that belonged to a thief, murder in the skulls that belonged to a murderer, and knowledge in skulls that belonged to a man of learning.

Madame Crépin n'y pouvant plus tenir, exige de son mari qu'il lui permette de se laisser tâter.
Mr Craniose, tâtant sans rien dire, Mr Crépin lit dans son expression.
54

Mrs. Crépin, unable to stand it any longer, demands that her husband let her be palpated.

As Mr. Craniose palpates in silence, Mr. Crépin reads his expression.

Mr Craniose ayant poussé un cri de découverte, Mr Crépin pousse un cri involontaire.
L'Opération terminée, Mr Craniose, malgré les instances de Mme Crépin déclare qu'il n'a rien dit, et qu'il ne dira rien.
55

Mr. Craniose utters a cry of discovery, and Mr. Crépin utters an involuntary cry.

Once the Operation is over, despite the instances of Mrs. Crépin, Mr. Craniose declares that he has said nothing and that he will say nothing.

Alors Madame Crépin Supplie son mari de se faire tâter.
Madame Crépin ordonne, exige, et menace de se r'évanouir
56.

Then Mrs. Crépin begs her husband to have himself palpated.

Mrs. Crépin commands, demands, and threatens to faint away all over again.

Mr Crépin se livre en protestant. Mr. Craniose, du premier coup, déclare que c'est-là un des plus curieux crânes qu'il ait rencontrés, une conquête pour la Science.
Passant à l'analyse détaillée, Mr Craniose trouve dans ce crâne là des montagnes de sagesse, mais malheureusement une petite bosse de préventions portée sur une petite bosse de préjugés qui tend à disparaître sous une bosse de Scientivité que l'on sent croître. Il y trouve, en second lieu un rudiment d'hommicidité qui a été étouffé par un mammelon d'humanitivité enté lui-même sur une petite colline de paternitivité. Il y trouve en troisième lieu une légère bosse d'entêtement qui combat une bosse de faiblesse, et, entre deux une bosse de jugement qui combat l'une par l'autre. Il y trouve en quatrième lieu, un monticule de religiosité qui a écrasé deux tertres voltairiens. Il y trouve enfin toutes les bosses d'un époux aimable, dévoué, soumis, digne en un mot de la compagne accomplie à laquelle il a associé son sort.
57.

Mr. Crépin submits unwillingly. Mr. Craniose immediately declares that here there is one of the strangest skulls that he has encountered, a conquest for science.

Passing on to a detailed analysis, Mr. Craniose finds in this skull mountains of wisdom, but also, unfortunately a little bump of bias mounted on a little bump of prejudice tending to disappear under a bump of scientivity that one can feel growing. He discovers, in the second place, a rudiment of homicidity, stifled by a little knoll of humanitivity, itself grafted on a hillock of paternitivity. In the third place he finds a slight bump of obstinacy struggling against a bump of weakness, and between the two, a bump of judgment using the one to balance the other. He finds, in the fourth place, a monticule of religiosity which has crushed two Voltairean mounds. Finally he finds all the bumps of an amiable spouse, devoted, submissive, worthy in a word of the accomplished companion with whom he has associated his destiny.

Monsieur Crépin est moins irrité, et Madame Crépin toujours plus ravie de cette phrénologie.
58.
Craniose donne communication à ses hôtes d'un grand projet de Société modèle qu'il se propose de soumettre à l'approbation du gouvernement. Cette Société sera fondée sur les bosses. A la religion, à la morale et aux lois, Craniose substitue le Grand Tâteur. Le Grand Tâteur tâte tous les ci-

Mr. Crépin calms down, and Mrs. Crépin gets more and more excited by this phrenology.

Craniose announces to his hosts a grand new project for a model Society that he proposes to submit for government approval. This Society will be based on bumps. For religion, morality, and laws, Craniose substitutes the Great Palpator. The Great Palpator palpates all cittoyens qui ont atteint l'âge de quinze ans et les répartit selon leurs bosses. Ceux qui ont la bosse de la limonade, il les fait limonadiers; la bosse du pain de sucre, épiciers; la bosse du dos et coin, relieurs; la bosse de l'hémistiche, poètes; la bosse du bleu de prusse, peintres; la bosse du bois de réguelisse, droguistes; du ventilateur, fumistes; de la roue de rencontre, horlogers; et ainsi de suite. Après cela, mettant à part tous ceux qui ont la bosse du vol, du meurtre, de la strangulation, de la pendaison, du suicide, de l'asphyxie par charbon ou autrement, il les déporte pour coloniser des contrées lointaines et sauvages. De cette façon Craniose obtient une Société admirablement organisée, où tout procédant de la bosse, qui procède du Grand Tâteur, les lois, la morale, et la religion deviennent superflues: les lois, parce qu'il n'y a plus de crimes; la morale, parce que chacun suit sa bosse; la religion, parce qu'il n'en est plus question.

Madame Crépin trouve le système admirable, et se réjouit d'en être; Monsieur Crépin déclare qu'une pareille Société serait aussi méprisable qu'impossible.

59.

izens who have reached the age of fifteen years, and categorizes them according to their bumps. Those who have the bump of lemonade, are made lemonade sellers, those with the bump of sugar-loaf become pastry-cooks, with the bump of back-and-corner, bookbinders, the bump of metre and rhyme, poets, the bump of Prussian blue, painters, the bump of licorice root, pharmacists, the bump of duck-egg, quacks; the bump of the balance-wheel, watchmakers; and so on. After which, setting aside all those with the bump of theft, of murder, of strangulation, of hanging, of suicide, of suffocation by carbon monoxide fumes or otherwise, he deports them to colonize distant and savage countries. Thus does Craniose achieve an admirably organized society, and all proceeding from the bump, which proceeds from the Grand Palpator, laws, morality, religion become superfluous: laws because crime is no more; morality because everyone follows their bump, religion because there is now no need for it.

Mrs. Crépin finds the system admirable and is delighted to be part of it; Mr. Crépin declares that such a society would be contemptible as well as impossible.

Pendant que Mr Crépin est sorti pour qques instans, Madame Crépin supplie Craniose de faire le Grand Tâteur à l'égard de Léopold. Craniose est enchanté des bosses et monticules de l'enfant, qu'il augure digne, en un mot, de la mère accomplie à laquelle il doit le jour. Il lui trouve en outre la bosse des Saillies et de la calembourgivité, entée sur la bosse de l'esprit de répartie: le tout annonçant un homme d'infiniment d'esprit
60.
ayant la bosse des saillies, Léopold commence par faire une cabriole qui renverse la collection. Ce qui simplifie singulièrement les bosses de plusieurs gredins célèbres.

While Mr. Crépin has gone out for a few moments, Mrs. Crépin begs Craniose to play the Great Palpator on Léopold. Craniose is delighted with the child's bumps and monticules, which he foresees to be worthy, in a word, of the accomplished mother to whom he owes his life. He finds moreover the bump of banter and punsterism, grafted on the bump of repartee: the whole promising a man of infinite wit.

Having the bump of banter, Léopold begins by cutting a caper that upsets the whole collection. Which makes for a singular simplification of the bumps of various celebrated rogues.

Monsieur Crépin revient au bruit, demandant quel est ce vacarme.
Léopold, ayant de l'esprit de repartie, lui repart :
Papa, c'est un vacarme ;
Si vous avez de l'alarme
Prenez de l'eau des Carmes
Pendant que Mr Crépin est sorti pour morigéner Léopold, Mde Crépin
fait tâter Gustave. Mr Craniose, qui a de l'humeur, lui trouve
la bosse d'un sot moineau.
61.

The noise brings back Mr. Crépin, who demands to know what all the commotion is about. Léopold, having the bump of banter, banters thus:

> Papa, it's a commotion
> If alarmed at this notion
> Try a tonic lotion.

While Mr. Crépin is out scolding Léopold, Mrs. Crépin has Gustave palpated. Mr. Craniose, out of humor, finds the bump of a sparrow-brain.

Mr Crépin revient. Etant Sot moineau, Gus-
tave s'en prévaut pour sauter sur le dos
de son papa, en fourrant ses pieds dans
ses poches.
Pendant que Mr Crépin est sorti pour morigéner
Gustave, Mde Crépin fait tâter Samuel. Craniose lui
trouve la bosse des langues.
Samuel qui déteste le latin se met à
pleurer. Mad. Crépin demande pour
lui une autre bosse.
62.

Mr. Crépin returns. Having a sparrow-brain, Gustave takes advantage of it by jumping on his father's back, and sticking his feet into his pockets.

While Mr. Crepin is out scolding Gustave, Mrs. Crépin has Samuel palpated. Craniose finds the bump of languages.

Samuel who detests Latin begins to cry. Mrs. Crépin asks Craniose to give him a different bump.

Mr. Crépin étant revenu, et trouvant Samuel rétif et pleurard, ne conçoit rien au dérangement moral de ses enfans, et en impute la cause à Fadet qui a gâté leur naturel bien né.
Madᵉ Crépin fait tâter Nicolas. Craniose lui montre la bosse de la capacité universelle, sur la tête de Nicolas.
Mr Crépin découvrant qu'on tâte ses fils, se fâche tout rouge contre la phrénologie, pendant que Madᵉ Crépin se livre à une joie bien naturelle.
63.

Returning to find Samuel stubborn and whiny, Mr. Crépin cannot understand the moral disorder of his children, and blames Fadet for spoiling their natural good disposition.

Mrs. Crépin has Nicolas palpated. Craniose shows her, on Nicolas's head, the bump of universal capacity.

Discovering that more of his sons are being palpated, Mr. Crépin becomes really furious with phrenology, while Mrs. Crépin gives herself up to a very natural joy.

64.
L'affaire s'échauffant, Monsieur Crépin jette tous les cranes par la fenêtre, et Mde Crépin s'évanouit.

As the affair gets heated, Mr. Crépin throws all the skulls out of the window, and Mrs. Crépin faints.

Les jeunes Crépins qui se trouvaient dans le jardin, font aussitôt une partie de quilles.
65.

The young Crépins, out in the garden, immediately organize a game of skittles.

Craniose étant descendu pour reprendre ses crânes de gredins est re=
poussé avec perte.

Going down into the garden to recover his rogues' skulls, Craniose is repulsed with losses.

Craniose se réfugie dans la loge du
chien et les jeunes Crépin continuent
leur partie.

66.

Craniose takes refuge in the dog kennel and the young Crépins carry on with their game.

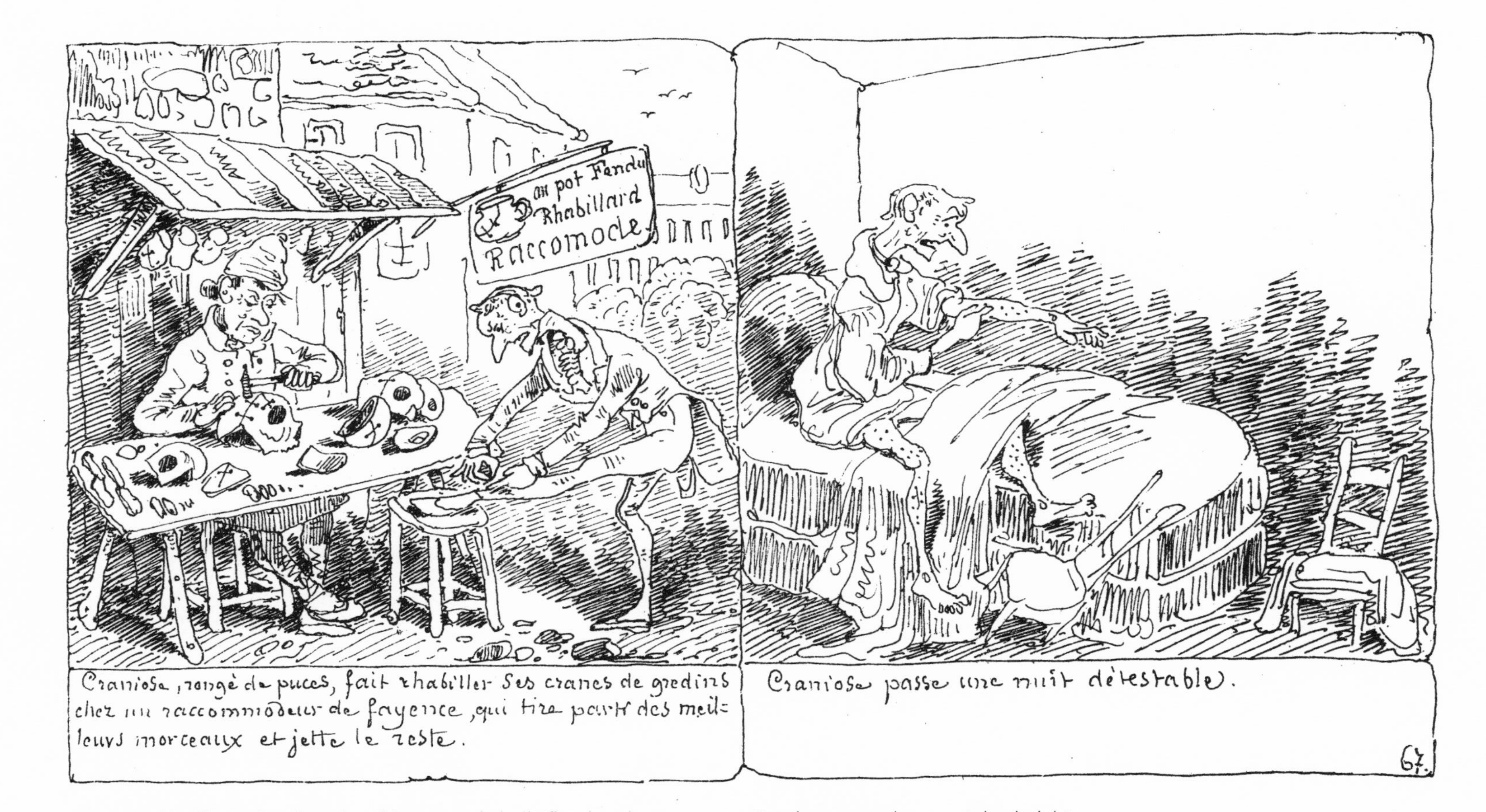
au pot Fendu
Rhabillard
Raccomode
Craniose, rongé de puces, fait rhabiller ses cranes de gredins chez un raccommodeur de fayence, qui tire parti des meilleurs morceaux et jette le reste.
Craniose passe une nuit détestable.
67.

Devoured by fleas, Craniose has his rogues' skulls fixed up by a man who repairs broken crockery. He uses the best parts and discards the rest. [Sign: The Broken pot The Fixer mends]

Craniose spends a wretched night.

Ayant emballé sa collection, Craniose va le lendemain prendre une place dans la diligence de Bruxelles.

La diligence étant arrivée à la frontière Bonichon recule d'horreur à la vue des effets du Phrénologue Craniose.

68

After packing up his collection, on the next day Craniose goes to take his seat in the Brussels coach.

The coach arrives at the frontier and Bonichon recoils in horror at the sight of the Phrenologist Craniose's effects.

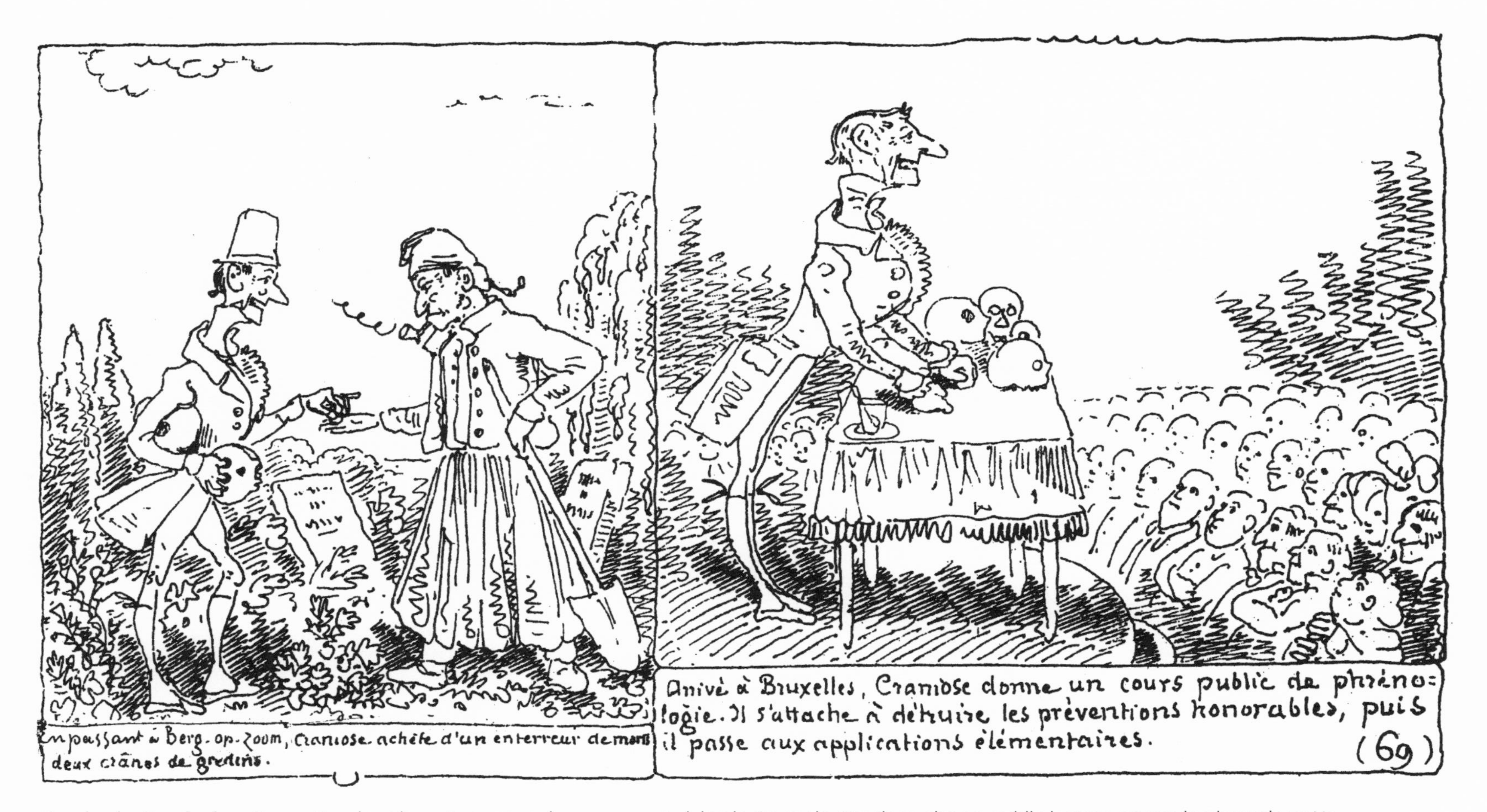
En passant à Berg-op-Zoom, Craniose achète d'un enterreur de morts deux crânes de gredins.
Arrivé à Bruxelles, Craniose donne un cours public de phrénologie. Il s'attache à détruire les préventions honorables, puis il passe aux applications élémentaires.
(69)

Passing by Berg[en]-op-Zoom, Craniose buys two rogues' skulls from a gravedigger.

Arriving in Brussels, Craniose gives a public lecture course in phrenology. He studiously clears away honorable reservations, then passes on to elementary applications.

Puis passant à la preuve démonstrative, Craniose montre que la phrénologie s'appuie sur des faits, et que ces faits sont des bosses de gredins.

Then passing to demonstrative proof, Craniose shows that phrenology is based on facts, and that these facts are the rogues' bumps.

Puis ayant développé sa théorie du Grand Tâteur, Craniose recule en entrevoyant l'avenir qui attend les Sociétés. (70.)

After expounding his theory of the Great Palpator, Craniose recoils on foreseeing the future that awaits society.

Cependant Mr Crepin déjà fort embarrassé de l'éducation de ses enfans est encore contrarie par Mme Crépin qui, ayant repris ses sens, lui reproche vivement de l'avoir privée d'un systéme qu'elle avait compris.
Mr Crépin renonce au systéme des Instituteurs à domicile, et visite des institutions, pour y placer ses enfans. Monsieur Gribouille lui explique sa méthode où tous les éléves remportent des prix, parce qu'elle est fondée sur l'émulation.
(71.)

Meanwhile Mr. Crépin, already very worried about the education of his children, is still thwarted by Mrs. Crépin who, recovering her senses, reproaches him sharply with depriving her of a system that she had understood.

Mr. Crépin gives up on the domestic tutor system, and visits schools to put his children in. Mr. Gribouille explains his method where all the pupils get prizes, because it is based on emulation.

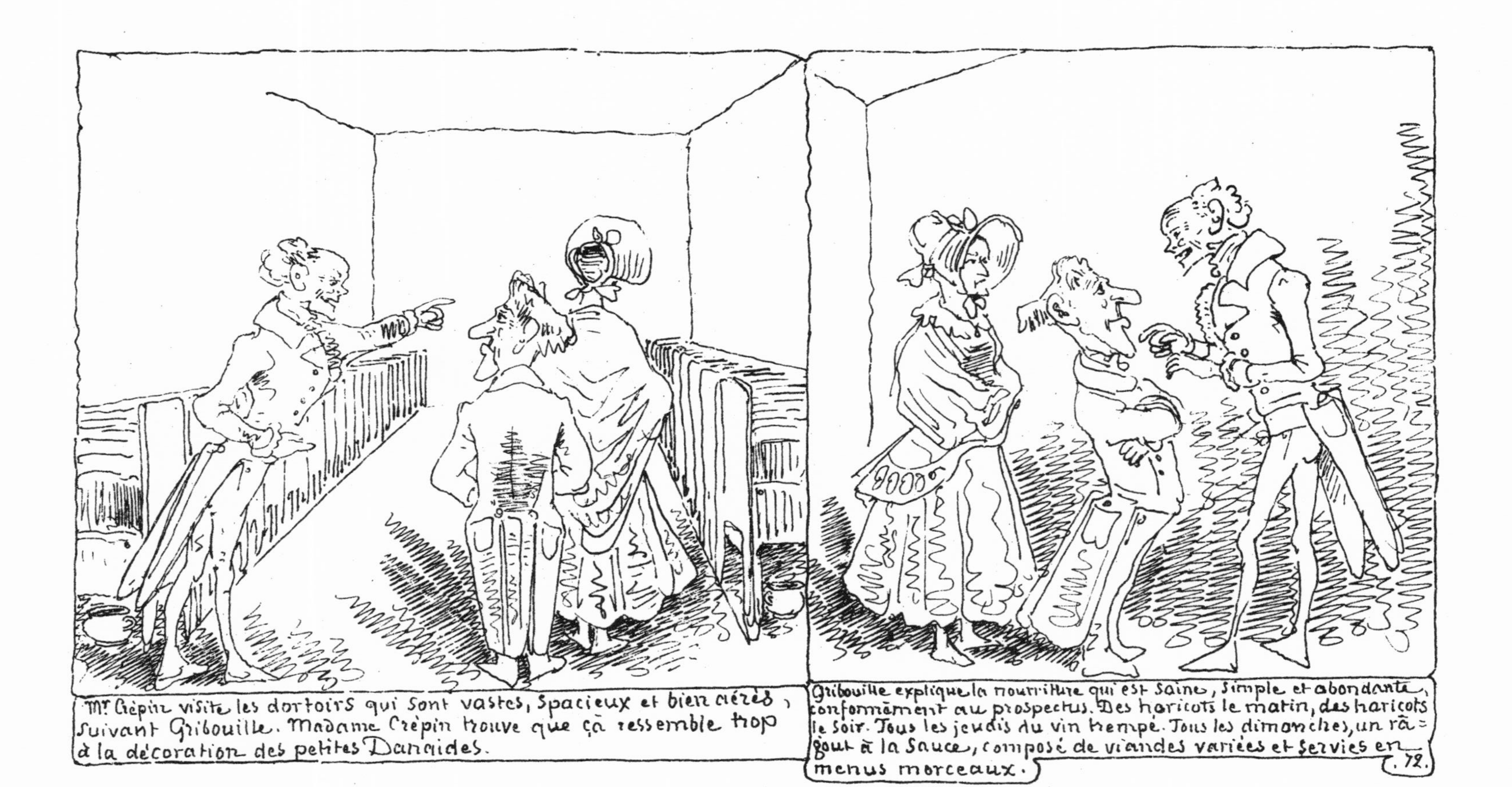
Mr Crépin visite les dortoirs qui sont vastes, spacieux et bien aérés, suivant Gribouille. Madame Crépin trouve que ça ressemble trop à la décoration des petites Danaïdes.
Gribouille explique la nourriture qui est saine, simple et abondante, conformément au prospectus. Des haricots le matin, des haricots le soir. Tous les jeudis du vin trempé. Tous les dimanches, un râgout à la sauce, composé de viandes variées et servies en menus morceaux.
. 72.

Mr. Crépin visits the dormitories which according to Gribouille are vast, spacious, and well ventilated. Mrs. Crépin finds that all this is too much like the decoration of the little Danaides.

Gribouille explains that the food is wholesome, simple, and abundant, in conformity with the prospectus. Beans in the morning, beans at night. Every Thursday, watered wine. Every Sunday, a well-sauced stew, composed of various kinds of meat and served in small pieces.

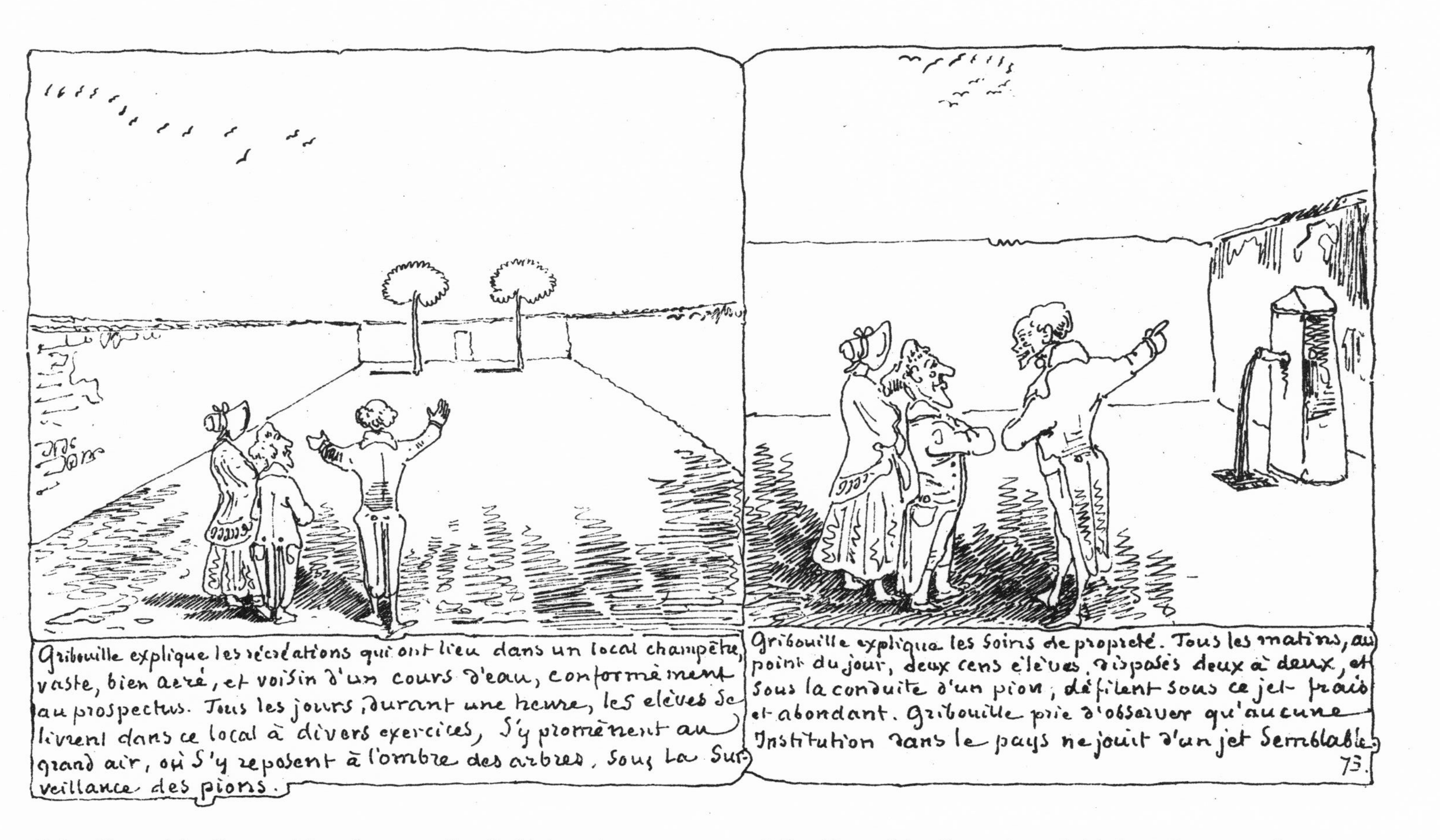
Gribouille explique les récréations qui ont lieu dans un local champêtre, vaste, bien aéré, et voisin d'un cours d'eau, conformément au prospectus. Tous les jours, durant une heure, les élèves se livrent dans ce local à divers exercices, s'y promènent au grand air, où s'y reposent à l'ombre des arbres, sous la surveillance des pions.
Gribouille explique les soins de propreté. Tous les matins, au point du jour, deux cens élèves, disposés deux à deux, et sous la conduite d'un pion, défilent sous ce jet frais et abondant. Gribouille prie d'observer qu'aucune Institution dans le pays ne jouit d'un jet semblable.
73.

Gribouille explains the provisions for recreation that takes place in a vast, airy, rural area, close to a stream, in conformity with the prospectus. Every day, for an hour, the pupils devote themselves here to various exercises, walk about in the open air and rest in the shade of the trees, under the watchful eye of the assistant masters.

Gribouille explains the system of ablutions. Every morning, at daybreak, two hundred pupils file two by two by this cooling and abundant fountain. Gribouille begs to observe that no institution in the country enjoys such a spout of water.

Gribouille explique les soins d'hygiène. Conformément au prospectus, tous les élèves, sous la surveillance des pions, sont purgés mensuellement à l'infirmerie qui est vaste, bien aérée, et voisine aussi d'un cours d'eau.
Mr Crépin visite un Institut-modèle, où il retrouve le premier instituteur de ses enfans qui enseigne en procédant du général au particulier.
74.

Gribouille explains the hygienic arrangements. In conformity with the prospectus, all the pupils, under the watchful eye of the assistant masters, are given a monthly purge at the infirmary which is vast, airy, and also close to a stream.

Mr. Crépin visits a Model Institute, where he finds his children's first tutor teaching by proceeding from the general to the particular.

Mr Crépin visite l'Institution Farcet, où la méthode est d'instruire en amusant.
Dans ce moment, c'est la leçon d'histoire, où le maître fait danser la pyrrhique
à deux petits macédoniens en carton.
Mr Crépin visite l'Institution Parpaillozzi, où la méthode est de
faire autrement qu'ailleurs.
75.

Mr. Crépin visits the Farcet Institute, where the method is to teach by entertaining. At this moment it is a history class, where the master makes two little cardboard Macedonians dance the pyrrhic.

Mr. Crépin visits the Parpaillozzi Institute, where the method is to do otherwise than elsewhere.

Mr Crépin visite l'Institution Bonnefoi, où la méthode est de faire comme on peut et pour le mieux.
Les fils Crépin entrant dans l'Institution Bonnefoi où, classés, d'après leur force, ils occupent le dernier banc.
Madame Crépin communique à Mr Crépin une iniquité révoltante. Son fils Nicolas lui écrit que malgré sa capacité universelle Mr Bonnefoi l'a placé le dernier de la classe.
76.

Mr. Crépin visits the Bonnefoi Institute, where the method is to do as one can and for the best.

The Crépin children enter the Bonnefoi school where, placed according to their abilities, they sit on the last bench.

Mrs. Crépin informs Mr. Crépin of a revolting iniquity. Her son Nicolas writes to tell her that despite his universal capacity, Mr. Bonnefoi has put him at the bottom of the class.

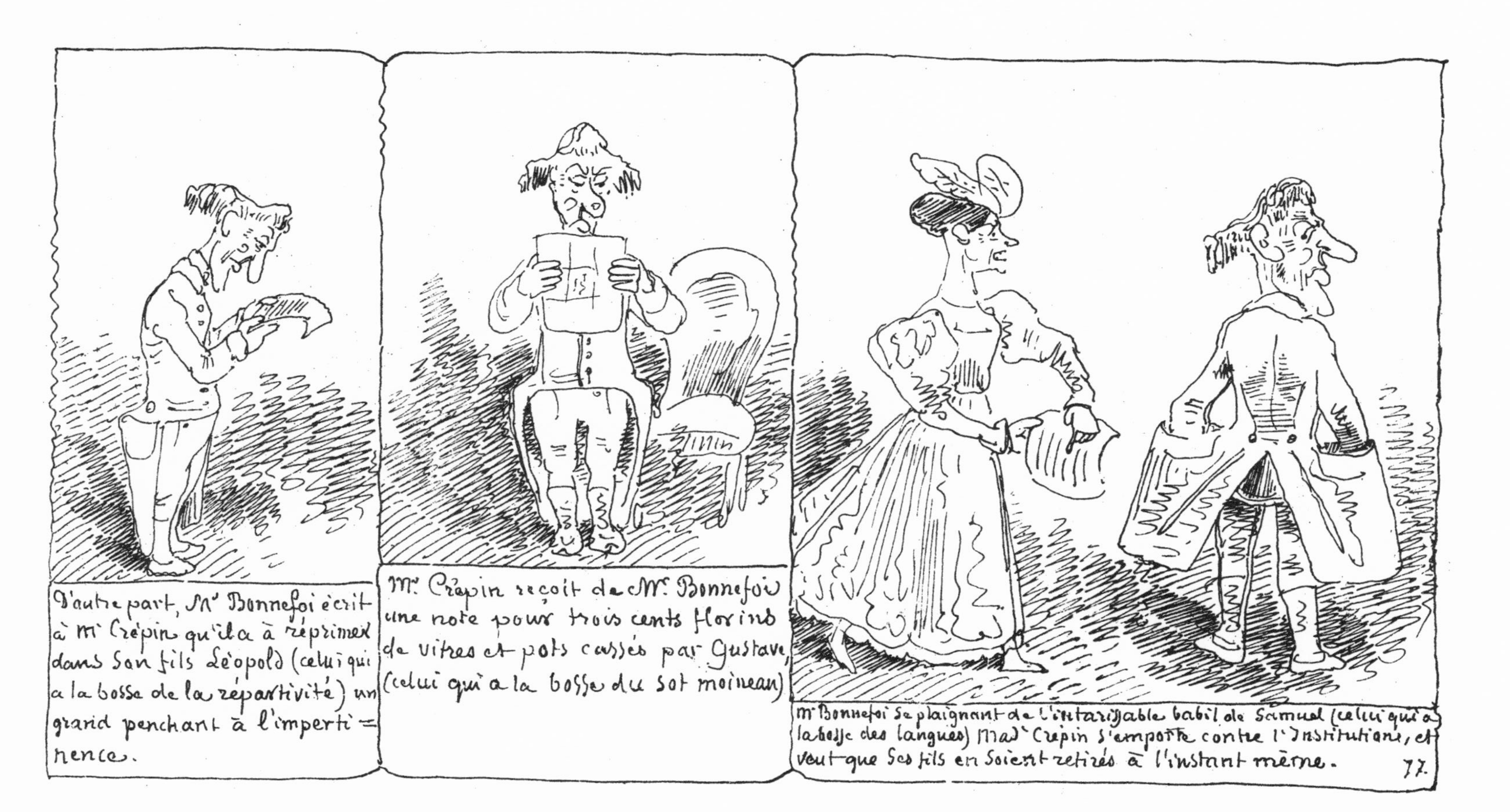
D'autre part, Mr Bonnefoi écrit à Mr Crépin qu'il a à réprimer dans son fils Léopold (celui qui a la bosse de la répartivité) un grand penchant à l'imperti=nence.
Mr. Crépin reçoit de Mr. Bonnefoi une note pour trois cents florins de vitres et pots cassés par Gustave, (celui qui a la bosse du sot moineau)
Mr Bonnefoi se plaignant de l'intarissable babil de Samuel (celui qui a la bosse des langues) Mad. Crépin s'emporte contre l'Institution, et veut que ses fils en soient retirés à l'instant même.
77.

Moreover, Mr. Bonnefoi writes to Mr. Crépin that he has to curb a marked tendency to impertinence in his son Léopold (the one with the bump of banterdom).

Mr. Crépin receives a bill for three hundred florins worth of windows and pots broken by Gustave (the one with the bump of a sparrow's brain).

Mr. Bonnefoi complains of the incessant chatter of Samuel (the one with the bump of languages), and Mrs. Crépin rails against the School, and demands that her children be withdrawn immediately.

Mr. Crépin s'y opposant formellement, Madame Crépin a une crise.
Mr Crépin se promène en long et en large, en attendant que la crise soit passée.
Madame Crépin revient à elle pour déclarer qu'elle mourra si on ne lui rend Fadet, Craniose, Farcet, Gribouille et tous les systèmes qu'elle avait compris.
78.

Mr. Crépin flatly refuses, which gives Mrs. Crépin a fit.

Mr. Crépin paces up and down, waiting for the fit to pass.

Mrs. Crépin recovers to declare that she will die if Fadet, Craniose, Farcet, Gribouille, and all the systems she had understood, are not restored to her.

L'affaire s'échauffant, Mr Crépin se retire précipitamment dans son cabinet, d'où il déclare que Mr Bonnefoi lui semble préférable, et que ses enfans y resteront.
Cependant Bonichon donne la chasse à un chien tout chargé d'horlogerie et de bijouterie.
79.

The affair gets heated, and Mr. Crépin withdraws in a hurry to his study, from where he declares that he really prefers Mr. Bonnefoi, and that his children will stay there.

Meanwhile Bonichon chases after a dog loaded with watches and jewelry.

Mort de Bonichon. Le contrebandier lui tire dessus pour délivrer son chien.

Death of Bonichon. The smuggler shoots him to save his dog.

Cependant Craniose continue à professer publiquement dans la contrée, de façon que ses idées s'y répandent dans le public.
80.

Meanwhile Craniose continues to give his public lectures in the region, so that his ideas take hold among the people.

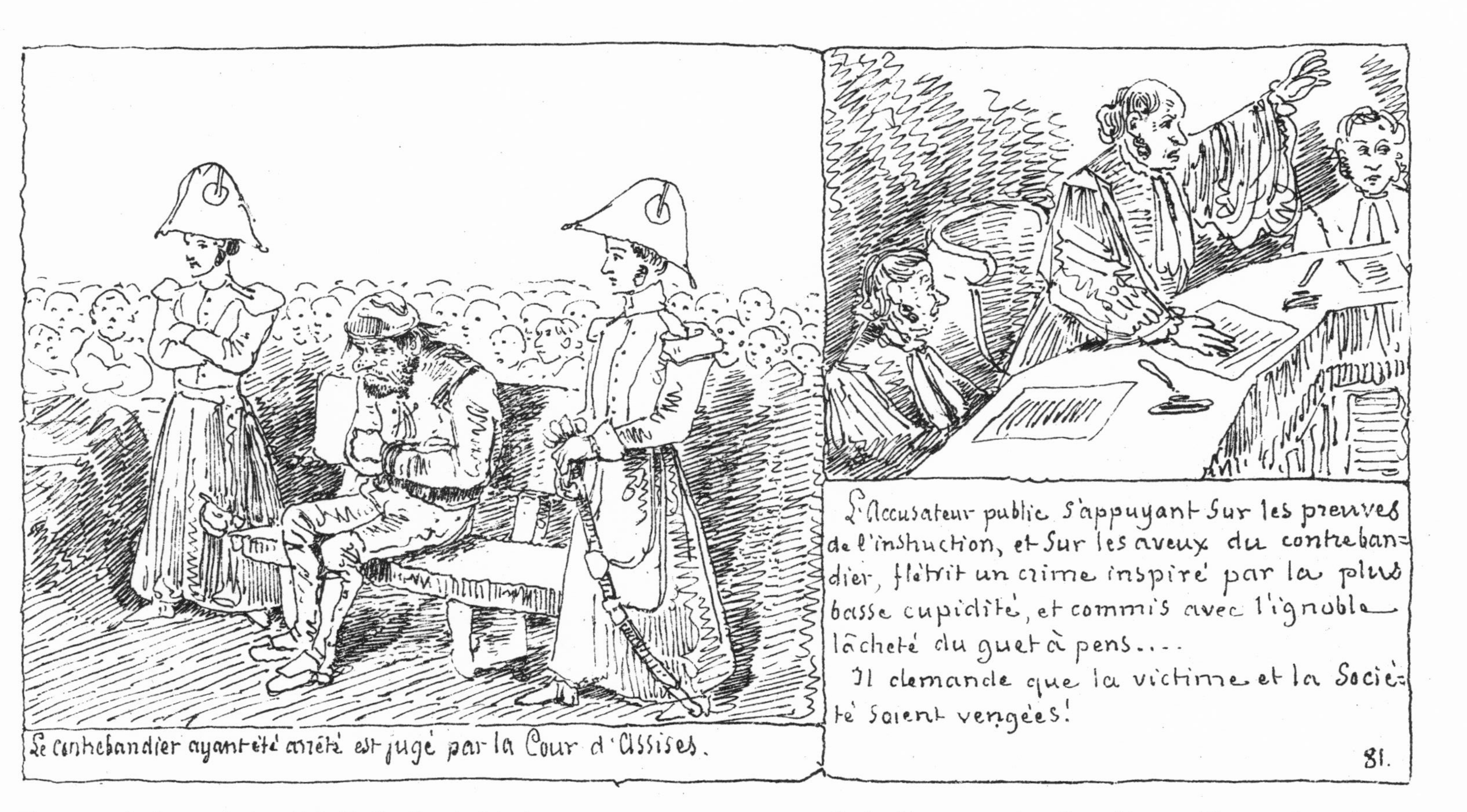
Le contrebandier ayant été arrêté est jugé par la Cour d'Assises.
L'Accusateur public s'appuyant sur les preuves de l'instruction, et sur les aveux du contrebandier, flétrit un crime inspiré par la plus basse cupidité, et commis avec l'ignoble lâcheté du guet à pens....
Il demande que la victime et la Société soient vengées!
81.

The smuggler is arrested and tried in the Court of Assizes.

Basing his argument on the evidence of the enquiry and the confessions of the smuggler, the Public Prosecutor denounces a crime inspired by the foulest greed, and committed by means of a vile and cowardly ambush. . . . He demands the victim and society be avenged!

L'avocat convient que les apparences sont contre son client. Il le suppose même coupable. Mais il se demande s'il n'est pas des hommes que la fatalité de leur organisation pousse au crime par une pente inévitable. Il se demande si, de nos jours, lorsque la Science portant ses investigations jusque dans les replis les plus cachés du cerveau y a découvert et analysé avec toute la Sûreté de son Scalpel la cause fatale et première des passions et des forfaits, il est bien permis à la Société de punir des crimes obligatoires, comme s'ils étaient des forfaits volontaires! Pour lui, il a visité, dans la prison, son infortuné client, et dès le premier aspect, il fut frappé des Signes de férocité native que présentait ce crâne aplati à sa sommité et développé sur ses flancs, comme celui de la hyène ou du Jaguar (Ici, un des Jurés demande à son voisin ce que c'est que le Jaguar; son voisin lui répond que c'est une Sorte de Caïman.)

Immolerez vous, continue l'avocat, dans un chaleureux mouvement, immolerez-vous celui qui, en dehors de toute moralité, a tué par appétit, par instinct par obéissance aux lois d'une nature marâtre envers lui! Non; vous ne l'immolerez pas! Mais il y a plus; la Science, messieurs, la Science prouve aussi que la vie de l'homme est inviolable, que nul n'a le droit de l'ôter à son semblable; irez-vous, méconnaissant cette doctrine de haute civilisation, vous rendre complices en quelque sorte, du crime de l'accusé.... à une vie, ajouter la perte, l'irréparable perte, d'une autre vie; à un cadavre, ajouter un cadavre; à une tombe, une tombe!! Non, Jurés, vous ne le ferez pas... J'en ai pour garants ces lumières par lesquelles vous surpassez vos pères, ces lumières aujourd'hui concentrées tout particulièrement dans cette classe moyenne à laquelle vous faites l'honneur d'appartenir! J'ai dit.

L'avocat se rassied et reçoit les félicitations de ses collègues.

82.

The Counsel for the Defense admits that appearances are against his client. He supposes him even to be guilty. But he wonders whether there is not a kind of man whom the fatal accident of their makeup does not drive down an inevitable path towards crime. In these times when science, carrying its investigations into the most hidden recesses of the brain, has discovered there and analyzed with surgical precision the fatal cause and origin of passions and the blackest of crimes, may one not wonder whether society may be allowed to punish involuntary felonies as if they were voluntary crimes? He himself, on visiting his unfortunate client in prison, from the very first sight of him was struck by the signs of innate ferocity presented by this skull flat at the top and bulging at the sides, like that of a hyena or Jaguar. (Here, one of the jury asks his neighbor what a Jaguar is; the neighbor replies that it is a sort of Alligator).

Would you sacrifice, continues the counsel, warming up, would you sacrifice one who, beyond all considerations of morality, killed out of lust, instinct, in obedience to the harsh laws of nature! No, you would not sacrifice him. But there is more; since, gentlemen, science also proves that human life is inviolable, that no one has the right to deprive a fellow human of it; will you, disregarding this doctrine of advanced civilization, render yourselves in some way accomplices of the crime of the accused. . . . To the loss of one life, add the loss, the irretrievable loss, of another life; to a corpse, add a corpse, to a tomb, a tomb! ! No, gentlemen of the jury, you would not do this. . . . I am guaranteed this by your enlightened views which surpass those of your fathers, those enlightened views concentrated today most particularly in that middle class to which you have the honor to belong! I rest my case.

The lawyer sits down again to the congratulations of his colleagues.

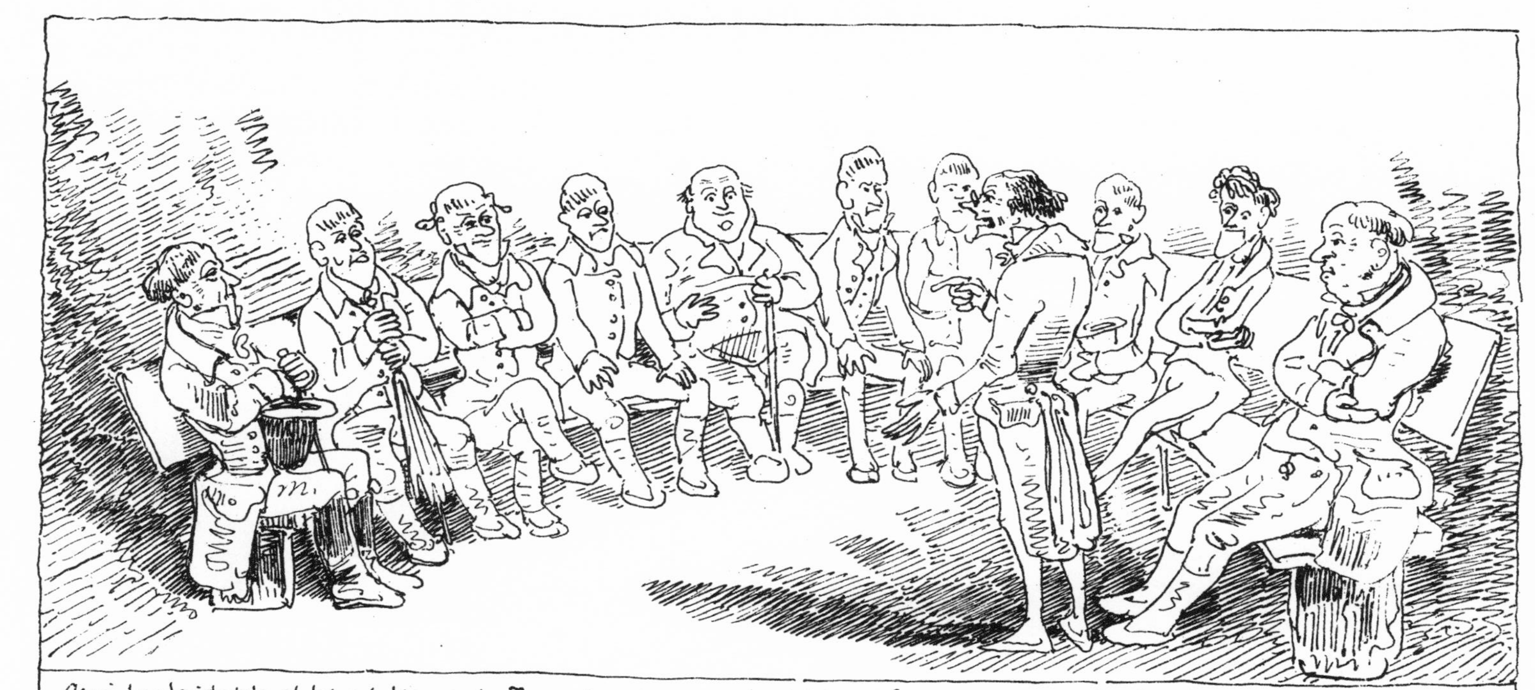
Après la plaidoirie et les répliques, le Jury se retire pour délibérer. Sur les quinze Jurés, huit qui ont suivi les cours
de Craniose et vu des bosses de gredins trouvent la défense bien forte, et les sept autres qui ont ouï parler de l'abolition de
la peine de mort, ne la jugent pas faible. Mr. Péclot affirme avoir reconnu sur la tête de l'accusé la même bosse que le
Professeur Craniose signalait sur le crâne d'un tueur de quatre vingt neuf. Mr Bonhomme affirme avoir fait la
même observation, et de plus... la même observation.
83.

When Prosecution and Defense have done, the Jury retires to deliberate. Of the fifteen Jurymen, eight having taken Craniose's lecture course and seen the bumps on the dead criminals' skulls, find the defense very persuasive, and the seven others who have heard talk of abolition of the death penalty, find it not bad. Mr. Péclot asserts that he recognized on the head of the accused the same bump that Professor Craniose pointed out on the skull of a killer of eighty-nine. Mr. Bonhomme asserts he had noticed the same thing, and moreover . . . the same thing.

Le Jury rentre en Cour, et son chef porte au président qui en donne lecture, la réponse du Jury conçue en ces termes: Non, l'accusé n'est pas coupable. Le contrebandier est aussitôt remis en liberté.
84.

The Jury return to the courtroom, and their head delivers to the president who reads it out, the Jury's verdict conceived in these terms: No, the accused is not guilty. The smuggler is immediately released.

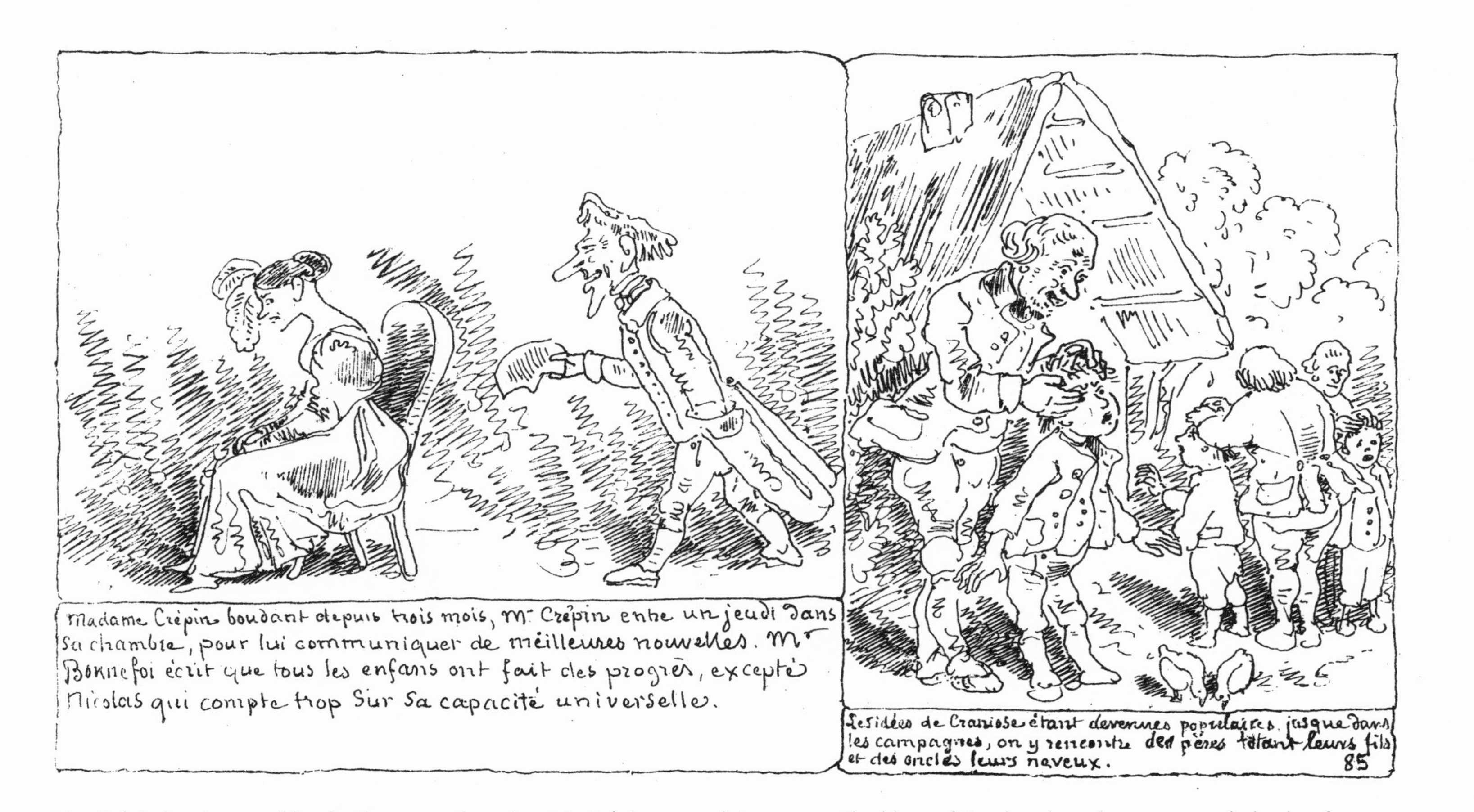
Madame Crépin boudant depuis trois mois, Mr Crépin entre un jeudi dans sa chambre, pour lui communiquer de meilleures nouvelles. Mr Bonnefoi écrit que tous les enfans ont fait des progrès, excepté Nicolas qui compte trop sur sa capacité universelle.
Les idées de Craniose étant devenues populaires, jusque dans les campagnes, on y rencontre des pères tâtant leurs fils et des oncles leurs neveux.
85

Mrs. Crépin has been sulking for three months, when Mr. Crépin comes into her room one Thursday to give her better news. Mr. Bonnefoi writes to say that all the children have made progress, except Nicolas who is still relying too much on his universal capacity.

The ideas of Craniose have become popularized as far as the countryside, where fathers can be found palpating their children, and uncles their nephews.

GRAND COURS
DE
GIE APP UEE
SOCIETE
BONH
RELIGIO
MORALE
LEGISLA
ION
EUR
THEORIE D
TATEUR E
LIMONADE
AVEC AUTO
Mais à mesure que les idées de Craniose deviennent populaires, elles deviennent moins à la mode parmi le beau monde. Craniose n'a plus de souscripteurs à ses cours, bien qu'il se ruine en affiches.
Au bout de deux ans, Mr Bonnefoi écrit à Mr Crépin que dix de ses fils sont maintenant en état d'entrer au collège, et de suivre l'instruction publique, ce qui vaut toujours mieux. Il gardera Nicolas jusqu'à ce qu'il soit revenu de sa capacité.
Déjà dans une grande gêne, Craniose en est réduit à composer un livre pour vivre.
(86)

But in becoming more popular, the ideas of Craniose become less fashionable among the upper crust. No one subscribes to his courses any more, although he ruins himself in posters.

After two years, Mr. Bonnefoi writes to Mr. Crépin that ten of his children are now ready to enter college, and to take courses in the public schools, which is always better. He will keep Nicolas until he has recovered from his universal capacity.

In the direst straits, Craniose is reduced to writing a book to make a living.

Au bout de onze mois Craniose meurt de misère un Jeudi matin, au septiè= me étage. Il laisse un testament olo= graphe, par lequel il lègue sa théorie au monde, et son crâne à la Science.
Nul ne réclamant sa succession Craniose est porté en terre, et, avec lui, ses trente six crânes de gredins.
Au bout de cinq ans Fadet meurt un Samedi matin, pour avoir trop serré sa crinoline im= perméable.
(87)

Eleven months later, Craniose dies of starvation one Thursday morning, on the seventh floor. He leaves a holographic will, in which he bequeaths his theory to the world, and his skull to science.

Since no one claims his succession, Craniose is carried to burial in the company of his thirty-six rogues' skulls.

Five years later Fadet dies one Saturday morning, having over-tightened his waterproof crinoline cravat.

P. 88
Fin de l'Histoire de Monsieur Crépin 1837.
R.T.
Les fils de Mr. Crépin après avoir achevé leurs études, embrassent diverses carrières et s'y comportent tous honorablement. Au bout de quelques années, Mr Crépin profitant d'un moment où tous ses fils sont auprès de lui, donne un dîner à Mr Bonnefoi. Au dessert s'étant levé, Mr Crépin porte ce toast: Rien de si commun que les méthodes, rien de plus rare que la conscience. Buvons, messieurs, à Mr Bonnefoi dont les soins, les lumières et la patience, vous ont mis dans la voie du travail et de l'honnêteté.

After finishing their studies, the sons of Mr. Crépin embrace various careers in which they all conduct themselves honorably. After a few years, Mr. Crépin takes the opportunity when all his sons are at home, to give a dinner in honor of Mr. Bonnefoi. At dessert, Mr. Crépin rises to propose this toast: nothing so commonplace as methods, nothing more rare than good sense. Let us drink, Gentlemen, to Mr. Bonnefoi, whose care, insight, and patience have guided you on the path of hard work and respectability.

End of the Story of Mr. Crépin 1837.

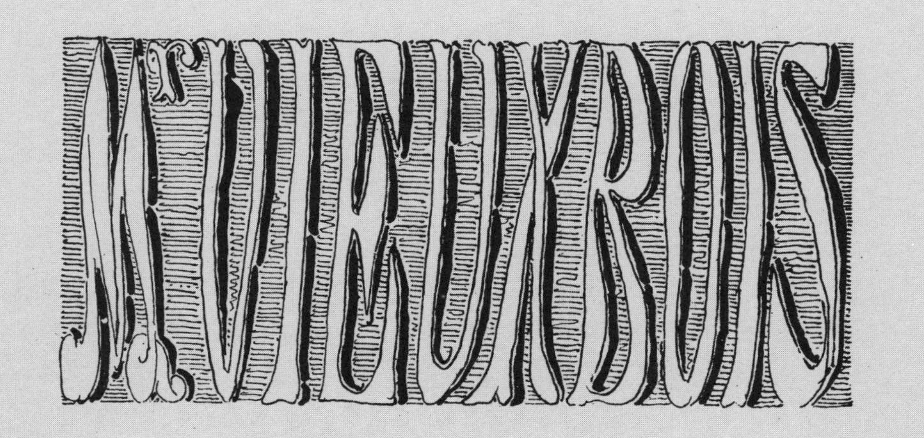
Mr VIEUXBOIS

Les amours de Mr Vieux Bois
PREFACE.
Ci derrière commence l'Histoire véritable des amours de monsieur VieuxBois, et comme quoi après bien des vicissitudes, il épousa l'Objet aimé.
Va, petit livre, et choisis ton monde; car aux choses folles, qui ne rit pas baille; qui ne se livre pas résiste; qui raisonne se méprend, et qui veut rester grave, en est maître.
Seconde, Edition,
Geneve
1839

The Loves of Mr. Vieux Bois. Second edition, Geneva 1839.

Preface. Here begins the True History of the loves of Mr. Vieux Bois, and how after many vicissitudes, he married the Beloved Object.

Go, little book, and choose your world, for at crazy things, those who do not laugh, yawn; those who do not yield, resist; those who reason, are mistaken, and those who keep a straight face, can please themselves.

Rencontre de Mr. Vieux Bois.....!!!!!!!
Mr Vieux Bois voit avec amertume que l'on s'éloigne.
Mr Vieux Bois sent, au feu intérieur que c'est pour la vie....!!!
(2)

Encounter of Mr. Vieux Bois . . . . . ! ! ! ! !

Mr. Vieux Bois takes bitter note of the withdrawal.

The fire burning within his breast tells Mr. Vieux Bois that it is for life . . . . ! ! !

Mr. VieuxBois cherche à se distraire par l'étude.
L'étude ne lui procurant aucun soulagement, Mr. VieuxBois passe à la musique.
Mr VieuxBois sent l'inutilité de ses efforts!
3.

Mr. Vieux Bois tries to distract himself by study.

Study giving him no relief, Mr. Vieux Bois tries music.

Mr. Vieux Bois senses the uselessness of his efforts!

Mais s'étant mis à la fenêtre, Mr Vieux Bois entrevoit l'Objet aimé......
Descendu dans la rue, Mr Vieux Bois n'entrevoit plus l'Objet aimé...
Mr Vieux Bois se décide à écrire.
4.

But from the window, Mr. Vieux Bois catches a glimpse of the Beloved Object.

Passing into the roadway, Mr. Vieux Bois no longer catches a glimpse of the Beloved Object . . .

Mr. Vieux Bois decides to write.

Songe de Monsieur Vieux Bois

Dream of Mr. Vieux Bois.

Mr. Vieux Bois ne reçoit point de réponse.

Mr. Vieux Bois receives no reply.

Monsieur Vieux Bois se tue...... Heureusement l'épée passe sous son bras.

5.

Mr. Vieux Bois kills himself . . . . . . Fortunately the sword passes under his arm.

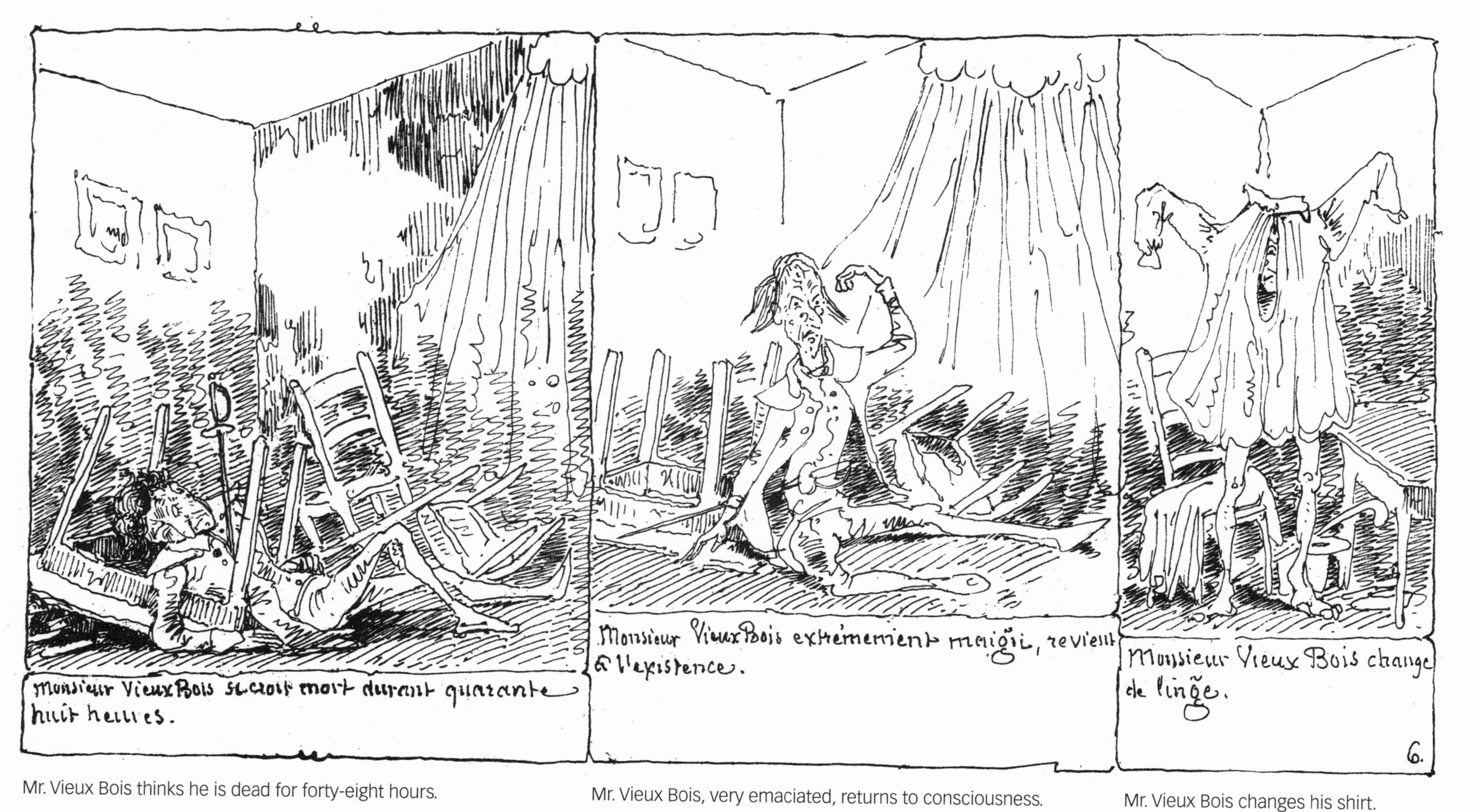
Monsieur Vieux Bois se croit mort durant quarante huit heures.
Monsieur Vieux Bois extrêmement maigri, revient à l'existence.
Monsieur Vieux Bois change de linge.
6.

Mr. Vieux Bois thinks he is dead for forty-eight hours.

Mr. Vieux Bois, very emaciated, returns to consciousness.

Mr. Vieux Bois changes his shirt.

Troisième rencontre. Déclaration, Soupirs, espoir.

L'Objet aimé s'éloigne.....

Soupçons naissans.

7.

Third encounter. Declaration, sighs, hope.

The Beloved Object withdraws. . . . .

Dawning suspicions.

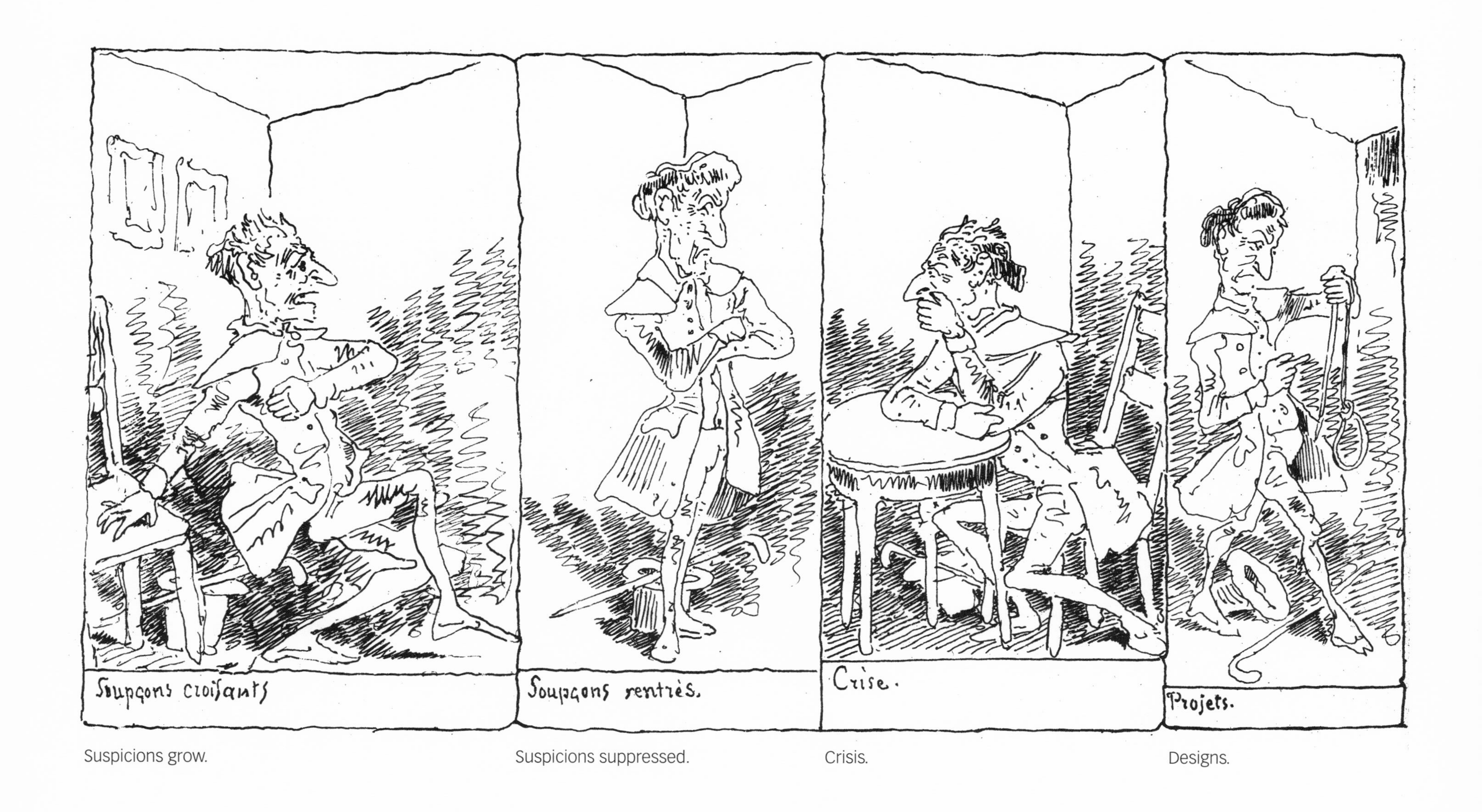
Soupçons croisants
Soupçons rentrés.
Crise.
Projets.

Suspicions grow.

Suspicions suppressed.

Crisis.

Designs.

Mr Vieux Bois se tue..... Heureusement la corde est trop longue.
Au bout de quarante huit heures, entendant la voix de l'Objet aimé dans la rue, Mr Vieux Bois oublie qu'il est pendu, et se précipite de ce côté.
Mr Vieux Bois entraîne la Solive à laquelle il s'est pendu.
9.

Mr. Vieux Bois kills himself . . . . . Fortunately the rope is too long.

After forty-eight hours, hearing the voice of the Beloved Object outside, Mr. Vieux Bois forgets he is hanged, and rushes in that direction.

Mr. Vieux Bois drags with him the beam from which he hanged himself.

Ce qui cause du désagrément au bourgeois.
10.

Which causes unpleasantness to the citizenry.

Et non moins à la garde nationale.

And no less to the national guard.

Mr. Vieux Bois touche presque à l'Objet aimé.

11.

Mr. Vieux Bois almost touches the Beloved Object.

Au moment d'atteindre l'Objet aimé, Mr Vieux Bois est arrêté net par un Sort jaloux.
Mr Vieux Bois voulant rentrer chez lui, ne peut.
12.

At the moment of catching the Beloved Object, Mr. Vieux Bois is stopped short by a jealous fate.

Mr. Vieux Bois trying to return home, fails.

Mr. Vieux Bois invente un procédé pour rentrer chez lui.

Rentré chez lui Mr. Vieux Bois change de linge.

Ayant changé de linge Mr. Vieux Bois éprouve des palpitations. 13.

Mr. Vieux Bois invents a method for returning home.

Back home, Mr. Vieux Bois changes his shirt.

Having changed his shirt, Mr. Vieux Bois experiences palpitations.

Mr. Vieux Bois consulte le médecin.
Mr. Vieux Bois prend le lait d'anesse.
14.

Mr. Vieux Bois consults the doctor.

Mr. Vieux Bois takes asses' milk.

Sur l'ordre du médecin, Mr Vieux Bois achète un cheval arabe, pour sa santé.

On doctor's orders, Mr. Vieux Bois buys an Arab horse for his health.

Mr Vieux Bois prend l'exercice du cheval.

15.

Mr. Vieux Bois takes exercise on horseback.

Chûte de Mr. Vieux Bois. L'Arabe retourne à ses Lares.
Mr. Vieux Bois, au moment où il se relève, aperçoit l'Objet aimé qui n'est pas seul ! ! ! ! !
16.

Fall of Mr. Vieux Bois. The Arab returns home.

Mr. Vieux Bois, as he picks himself up, sees the Beloved Object who is not alone! ! ! ! !

ayant feint de feindre, afin de mieux dissimuler, Mr Vieux Bois sur un arbre perché, découvre un tête à tête ! !

Having feigned pretense, in order the better to deceive, Mr. Vieux Bois perched on a tree, discovers a tête à tête! ! !

Explication très vive. L'Objet aimé s'enfuit.

17.

Very lively explanation. The Beloved Object flees.

Satisfaction. Mr. Vieux Bois tue le Rival.... Heureusement l'épée passe sous le bras.
Le Rival extrêmement rassuré revient à l'existence.
18.

Satisfaction. Mr. Vieux Bois kills the Rival . . . . Fortunately the sword passes under his arm.

The Rival, much heartened, recovers consciousness.

Mr Vieux Bois, heureux vainqueur, fait la demande aux parens, en présence de l'Objet aimé.

Mr Vieux Bois accepté, rentre chez lui, et s'y livre pendant trois heures à des sauts de joie.

19.

Mr. Vieux Bois, the happy victor, makes his request to the parents, in the presence of the Beloved Object.

Accepted, Mr. Vieux Bois returns home and gives himself up for three hours to bounds of joy.

Au bout de la troisième heure, les voisins accourent irrités.
Mr Vieux Bois est mis en prison pour tapage nocturne.
Ses parens étant venus pour rendre à Mr Vieux Bois sa visite, apprennent avec étonnement qu'il est en prison.
20

After the three hours, irritated neighbors confront him.

Mr. Vieux Bois is put in jail for disturbing the peace by night.

The parents having come to return Mr. Vieux Bois's visit, are astonished to learn that he is in prison.

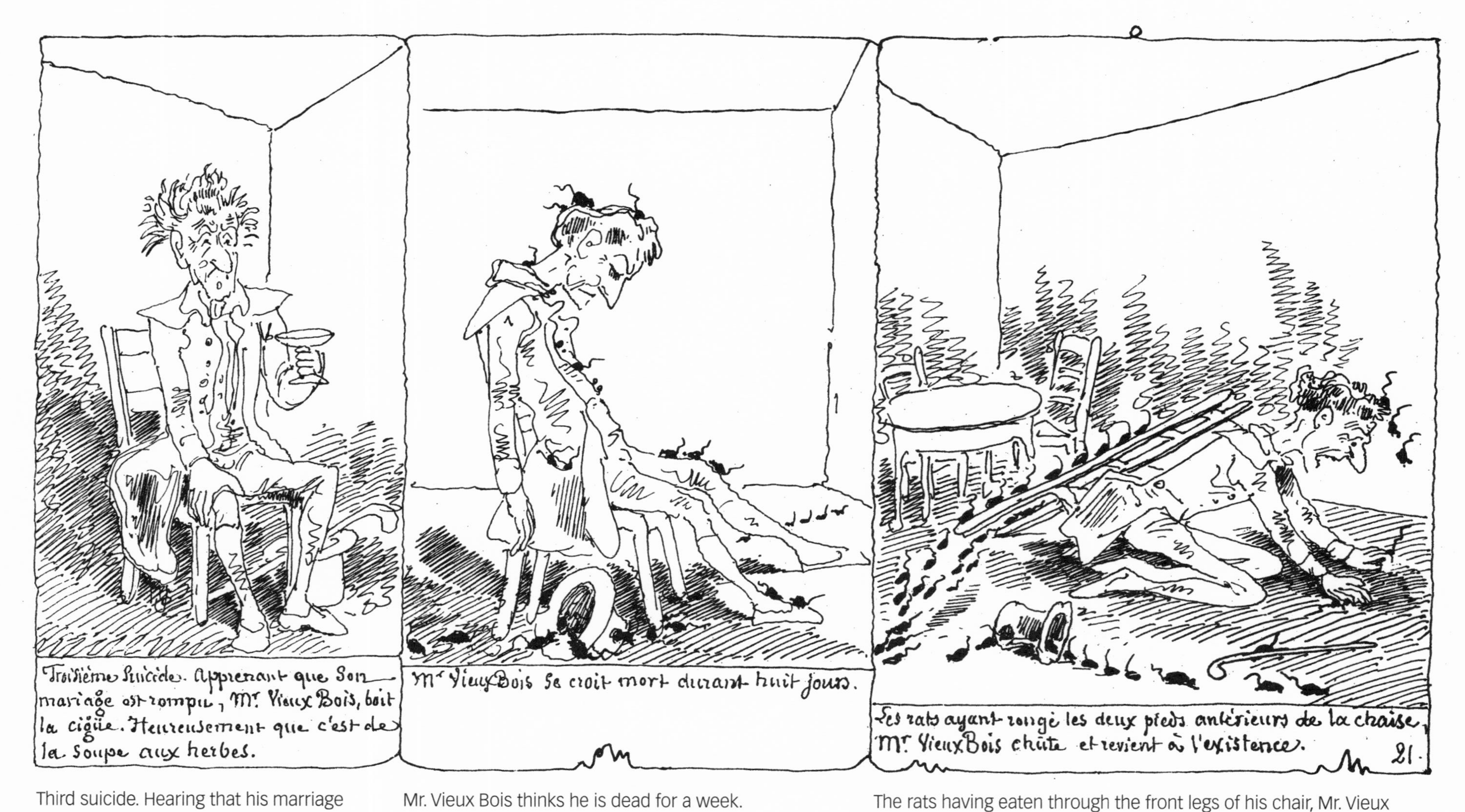
Troisième Suicide. Apprenant que son mariage est rompu, Mr. Vieux Bois, boit la cigüe. Heureusement que c'est de la soupe aux herbes.
Mr Vieux Bois se croit mort durant huit jours.
Les rats ayant rongé les deux pieds antérieurs de la chaise, Mr. Vieux Bois chûte et revient à l'existence.
21.

Third suicide. Hearing that his marriage is broken off, Mr. Vieux Bois drinks the hemlock. Fortunately it is herb soup.

Mr. Vieux Bois thinks he is dead for a week.

The rats having eaten through the front legs of his chair, Mr. Vieux Bois falls and recovers consciousness.

Mr. Vieux Bois change de linge.
ROUTE DE PARIS
S'étant acheté un chien de garde, Mr. Vieux Bois se décide à voyager.
ayant aperçu des brigands, Mr Vieux Bois se cache, lui, et son cheval, derrière un arbre.
22.

Mr. Vieux Bois changes his shirt.

Having bought himself a watchdog, Mr. Vieux Bois decides to take a trip.

Having seen brigands, Mr. Vieux Bois hides, with his horse, behind a tree.

Mr Vieux Bois dévalisé par les brigands, se réfugie dans un antre Sauvage où il déplore sa destinée.

Mr. Vieux Bois, robbed by brigands, takes refuge in a cave in the wilds and deplores his destiny.

Découvert par un hermite, Mr Vieux Bois en reçoit de grandes consolations.

Discovered by a hermit, Mr. Vieux Bois is much consoled by him.

Mr Vieux Bois se fait Hermite.

23.

Mr. Vieux Bois becomes a Hermit.

M. V.Bois éprouve que d'être hermite, ça ne fait pas le bonheur.
Et que ça attise, plus que ça n'éteint.
Et d'affreux soupçons.
Et un déplorable abattement.
24.

Mr. Vieux Bois finds that being a hermit does not bring happiness.

And that it fans the flames, rather than dowsing them.

And frightful suspicions.

And a deplorable dejection.

Mr VBois s'ennuyant, s'échappe du Couvent, déguisé en femme.

Mr. Vieux Bois, getting bored, escapes from the monastery disguised as a woman.

Mr VBois est accosté en route par un voyageur sur la personne duquel il croit reconnaître son habit en personne.

Mr. Vieux Bois is accosted en route by a traveler on whose person he seems to recognize his clothes in person.

Le souper est fort gai mais Mr VBois croit toujours plus reconnaître sa casquette elle-même. 25.

The supper is very cheerful. But Mr. Vieux Bois is more and more convinced that it is his very own cap.

aussi, dès que le Voyageur est endormi, Mr. Vieux Bois se hâte de rentrer dans sa propriété.
Mr. Vieux Bois retire son cheval d'un précipice où il gisait depuis quinze jours.
Mr Vieux Bois déplore l'état affreux de son cheval.
26

So, as soon as the Traveler is asleep, Mr. Vieux Bois hastens to recover his property.

Mr. Vieux Bois drags up his horse from a precipice where it was lying for two weeks.

Mr. Vieux Bois deplores the miserable condition of his horse.

Mr Vieux Bois se décide à tirer parti de son cheval, sans le fatiguer.
Arrivé dans un fertile vallon, Mr Vieux Bois lance son cheval dans de gras pâturages.
27.

Mr. Vieux Bois decides to profit from his horse, without tiring it out.

Reaching a fertile valley, Mr. Vieux Bois releases his horse into rich pastures.

Au bout de quelques jours, le cheval ne peut plus avancer, par trop d'embonpoint.
La Solitude du pâturage rallume la passion de Mr. Vieux Bois.
Heureusement Mr Vieux Bois tourne au tendre. 28

After a few days, the horse is no longer capable of moving, being too fat.

The solitude of the pastures reignites Mr. Vieux Bois's passion.

Mr. Vieux Bois turns happily tender.

Et il se plaît à errer.

And he enjoys wandering around.

Le cheval éclate d'embonpoint. Mr Vieux bois se voit dans le cas de retourner chez lui à pied.

The horse explodes with obesity. Mr. Vieux Bois sees himself obliged to return home on foot.

Rentré chez lui, Mr Vieux Bois y trouve une lettre de l'Objet aimé. 29.

Returning home, Mr. Vieux Bois finds a letter from the Beloved Object.

Mr Vieux Bois répond à l'Objet aimé par un bouquet allégorique.
Mr Vieux Bois donne une Sérénade à l'Objet aimé, et compte 48 mesures.
Mr Vieux Bois enlève l'Objet aimé.
30.

Mr. Vieux Bois replies to the Beloved Object with an allegorical bouquet.

Mr. Vieux Bois serenades the Beloved Object, and counts 48 bars.

Mr. Vieux Bois abducts the Beloved Object.

Mr Vieux Bois repris par les moines est mis en prison d'un côté.. — l'objet aimé, de l'autre.

31

Mr. Vieux Bois is recaptured by the monks and thrown into prison on one side. . —the Beloved Object on the other.

Quatrième Suicide.
Heureusement Mr. Vieux Bois reste accroché à l'aiguille du Cadran Solaire.
Mr. Vieux Bois change de linge.
Mr. Vieux Bois, atteint d'un grand découragement tombe malade.
32.

Fourth suicide.

Fortunately Mr. Vieux Bois is caught on the index of a Sundial.

Mr. Vieux Bois changes his shirt.

Mr. Vieux Bois, falling into great despondency, becomes ill.

Monsieur VieuxBois, profitant de sa maigreur extrême, s'introduit par la cheminée, ce qui effraie fort l'Objet aimé.

Evasion par un Soupirail étroit 33.

Mr. Vieux Bois, taking advantage of his extreme thinness, introduces himself through the chimney, which greatly frightens the Beloved Object.

Escape through a narrow vent hole of the cellar.

Suite de l'évasion.
Succès presque assuré de l'évasion.
Néanmoins au passage du fossé, Mr Vieux Bois boit beaucoup d'eau.
34.

Continuation of the escape.

Almost assured success of the escape.

Nevertheless on crossing the stream, Mr. Vieux Bois drinks a great deal of water.

Pendant que l'Objet Aimé se sèche au soleil, Mr. Vieux Bois noie un petit moine qui les a découverts.

While the Beloved Object dries herself in the sun, Mr. Vieux Bois drowns a little monk who has discovered them.

Mr. Vieux Bois embarque sa chère cargaison et retourne chez lui par eau.

35.

Mr. Vieux Bois embarks his precious cargo and returns home by water.

Cependant les parens de l'Objet aimé, faisant leur promenade du soir au bord du grand Canal, croient reconnaître au loin leur enfant chéri.
Mr Vieux Bois profite des avantages de sa situation pour parlementer, et obtient la main de l'Objet aimé.
Et la nôce a lieu dès le lendemain
36.

Meanwhile the parents of the Beloved Object, taking their evening walk on the bank of the Grand Canal, seem to recognize their dear child in the distance.

Mr. Vieux Bois takes advantage of the situation to negotiate, and obtains the hand of the Beloved Object.

And the wedding takes place the next day.

Au moment d'entrer à l'Eglise, Mr Vieux Bois se souvient qu'il a enfermé son chien chez lui, et il revient sur ses pas pour lui ouvrir.

At the very moment of entering the church, Mr. Vieux Bois remembers that he has locked his dog up in his house, and he retraces his steps to let him out.

Retourné à l'Eglise, Mr Vieux Bois n'y retrouve plus ni les parens, ni l'objet Aimé.

Back at the church, Mr. Vieux Bois finds no one there, neither the parents, nor the Beloved Object.

Dispositions Sinistres. Il disculpe son chien, rend les parens responsables de sa mort, et charge la police de son inhumation.

Sinister dispositions. He exculpates his dog, blames his death on the parents, and charges the police with his burial.

Cinquième Suicide. Mr Vieux Bois se précipite dans le grand Canal. 37.

Fifth suicide. Mr. Vieux Bois throws himself into the Grand Canal.

Heureusement des Voleurs qui en veulent à l'habit de noce, repêchent Mr Vieux Bois. Mr. Vieux-
Bois ne s'en croit pas moins bien et duement noyé.
Mr Vieux Bois est laissé nu sur la plage
38.

Fortunately some Thieves with an eye to his wedding clothes, fish out Mr. Vieux Bois. Mr. Vieux Bois believes himself to be nonetheless well and properly drowned.

Mr. Vieux Bois is left naked on the canal bank.

La police relève Mr. Vieux Bois, et le porte en terre.

Deterré par les oiseaux de proie, Mr. Vieux Bois revient à l'existence.

39.

The police pick Mr. Vieux Bois up and carry him to burial.

Unearthed by birds of prey, Mr. Vieux Bois recovers consciousness.

Mr. Vieux Bois s'étant revêtu du linceul d'un mort, pour retourner chez lui est poursuivi comme fantôme par les populations.
Mr. Vieux Bois, de retour chez lui, cause une vive frayeur à ses héritiers.
40.

Mr. Vieux Bois having donned a shroud of the dead to return home in, is pursued as a ghost by the people.

Mr. Vieux Bois, back home, scares his heirs out of their wits.

Mr Vieux Bois change de linge

Mr. Vieux Bois changes his shirt.

Les héritiers ayant porté plainte, Mr Vieux Bois est arrêté comme prévenu de tapage diurne.

The heirs having registered a complaint, Mr. Vieux Bois is arrested for disturbing the daytime peace.

Mr Vieux Bois plaide lui-même sa cause. Il débute par un exorde rempli de calme et de noblesse.
41.

Mr. Vieux Bois pleads his cause himself. He begins with an exordium filled with calm and nobility.

Mr. Vieux Bois jette quelques Sels dans sa narration.
En approchant de sa péroraison, Mr Vieux Bois s'échauffe par degrés.
S'enflamme en apostrophes.
Et enfin frappe les grands coups.
42.

Mr. Vieux Bois throws some spice into his narrative.

As he approaches his peroration, Mr. Vieux Bois gets progressively warmer.

Becomes inflamed in admonitions.

And finally goes for broke.

Mr. Vieux Bois qui s'est entendu condamner à deux ans de prison est reconduit dans son cachot. Abreuvé d'amertume, il médite un plan d'évasion.

Mr. Vieux Bois after hearing himself condemned to two years in jail, is brought back to his cell. Overwhelmed with bitterness, he contemplates a plan for escape.

Exécution du plan

Execution of the plan.

Mr Vieux Bois passe, du toit de la prison sur le toit d'une maison voisine.

Mr. Vieux Bois passes from the prison roof onto the roof of a neighboring house.

Mr Vieux Bois sonde avec son chien, une cheminée voisine aussi.
43.

Mr. Vieux Bois also sounds a neighboring chimney with his dog.

La cheminée se trouve être celle de l'Objet aimé. Frayeur mortelle des parents.
L'Objet aimé ayant reconnu le chien, s'élance, et l'embrasse étroitement, au moment où, par malheur, Mr. Vieux Bois retire la corde.
44.

The chimney happens to be that of the Beloved Object. Mortal terror of the parents.

The Beloved Object having recognized the dog, darts forward and embraces it firmly, at the moment when, unfortunately, Mr. Vieux Bois pulls up the rope.

Monsieur Vieux Bois sent un grand poids.
Au plus beau moment la corde casse.
Mr Vieux Bois, tombant dans un reverbère, est sauvé.
45

Mr. Vieux Bois feels a great weight.

At the critical moment the rope breaks.

Mr. Vieux Bois falling into a street-lamp, is saved.

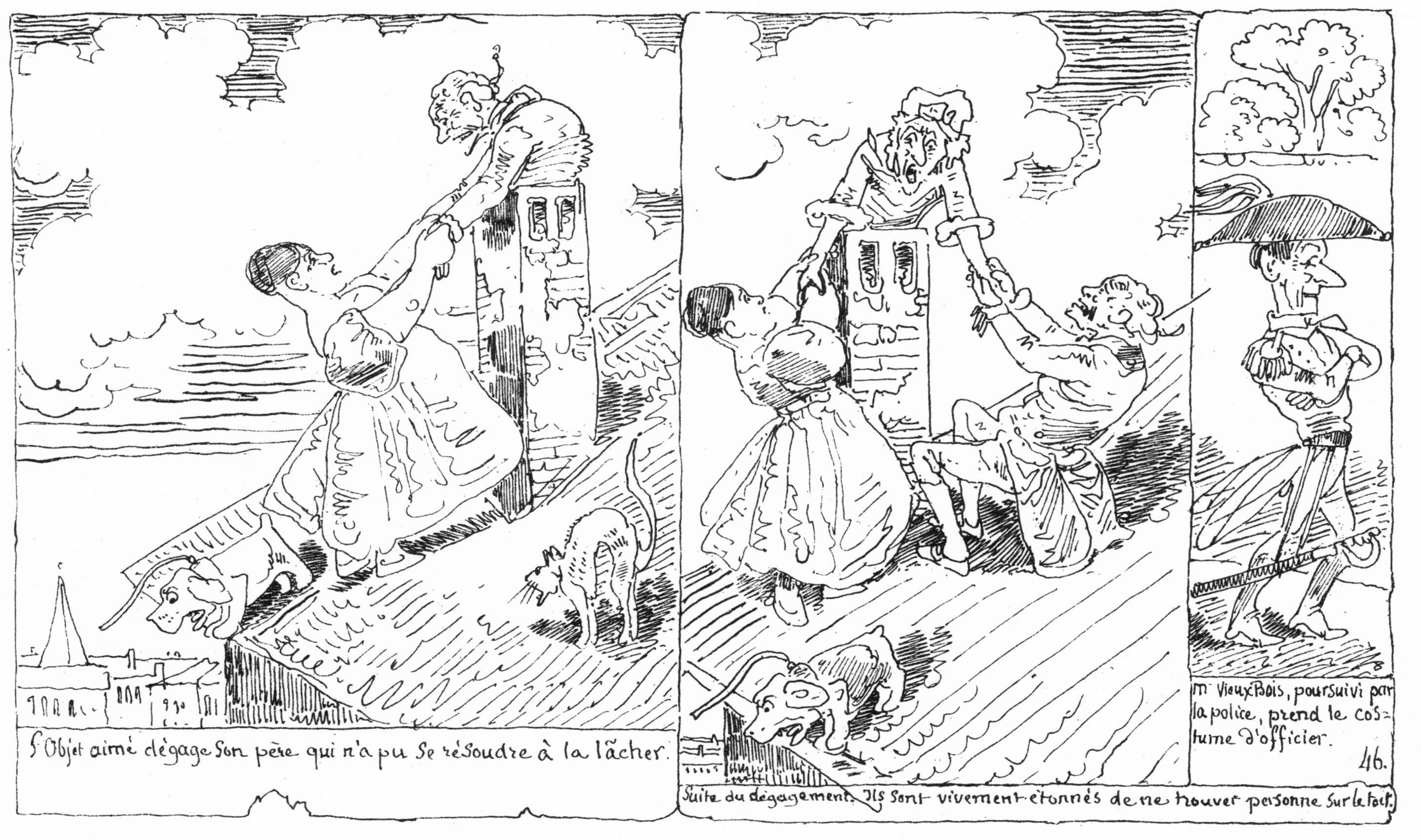
L'Objet aimé dégage son père qui n'a pu se résoudre à la lâcher.
Suite du dégagement. Ils sont vivement étonnés de ne trouver personne sur le toit.
Mr Vieux Bois, poursuivi par la police, prend le costume d'officier.
46.

The Beloved Object frees her father who could not decide to let go of her.

The disengagement continues. They are most surprised not to find anyone left on the roof.

Mr. Vieux Bois, pursued by the police, puts on an officer's uniform.

S'étant rendu chez l'Objet aimé, Mr Vieux Bois apprend avec surprise que toute la famille a disparu depuis trois jours.

Présumant qu'il y a complot, Mr Vieux Bois part pour la recherche de l'Objet Aimé.

47.

Reaching the Beloved Object's home, Mr. Vieux Bois learns to his surprise that the whole family has been gone for three days.

Scenting a plot, Mr. Vieux Bois sets off in search of the Beloved Object.

La famille, ignorant comment elle est venue là se livre à une douleur bien naturelle. Heureusement qu'au bout de quatre jours elle est découverte par un ramoneur.
Mr Vieux Bois, passant auprès d'un paturage, met pied à terre, pour tenir son cheval.
48.

The family, with no idea how they came to be there, surrender to a very natural grief. Fortunately after four days they are discovered by a chimney sweep.

Mr. Vieux Bois, passing by a pasture, alights to hold his horse.

Mr. Vieux Bois ayant rencontré un des moines, dans une solitude, lui coupe la barbe avec un extrême plaisir.

Mr Vieux Bois échappe à une légion de moines vengeurs.

49.

Mr. Vieux Bois having met one of the monks in a deserted place, takes great pleasure in cutting off his beard.

Mr. Vieux Bois escapes a legion of vengeful monks.

Mr Vieux Bois apprend du petit ramoneur que l'Objet Aimé a passé quatre jours sur un toit avec sa famille.
Mr Vieux Bois prend en croupe le petit ramoneur pour se faire montrer le toit en question.
Arrivé sur le toit, Mr Vieux Bois comprend toute l'affaire, et retrouva son chien exténué.
50.

Mr. Vieux Bois learns from the little chimney sweep that the Beloved Object spent four days on a roof with her family.

Mr. Vieux Bois mounts the little chimney sweep behind him on the horse, to show him the roof in question.

Reaching the roof, Mr. Vieux Bois understands everything, and finds his dog much emaciated.

Mr Vieux Bois cherche à établir une correspondance avec l'Objet Aimé.
Les parens de l'Objet aimé ayant abandonné leur apparte=ment depuis leur grande frayeur, Mr Vieux Bois attend en vain une réponse, depuis huit jours.
Au neuvième jour Mr Vieux Bois a l'ivresse de sentir un grand poids. Il se flatte que c'est l'Objet aimé lui-même.
51.

Mr. Vieux Bois tries to establish correspondence with the Beloved Object.

The parents of the Beloved Object having abandoned their apartment since their great scare, Mr. Vieux Bois awaits a reply in vain, for a good week.

On the ninth day Mr. Vieux Bois is enraptured to feel a great weight. He flatters himself that it is the Beloved Object herself.

Les nouveaux locataires qui ont pris la corde de Mr Vieux Bois pour une crémaillère, sont horriblement effrayés en voyant la marmite monter.
Amer désappointement de Mr. Vieux Bois.
52.

The new tenants who took Mr. Vieux Bois's rope for a pot hook, are horribly afraid as they see the pot rise.

Bitter disappointment of Mr. Vieux Bois.

Tout à coup, Mr Vieux Bois a l'ivresse d'apercevoir l'Objet aimé, à une croisée, de l'autre côté de la rue.
S'étant livré à un saut de joie bien naturel, Mr Vieux Bois enfonce la toiture et disparaît.
53

Suddenly Mr. Vieux Bois experiences the rapture of seeing the Beloved Object at a window on the other side of the street.

Delivering himself up to a most natural leap of joy, Mr. Vieux Bois crashes through the roof and disappears.

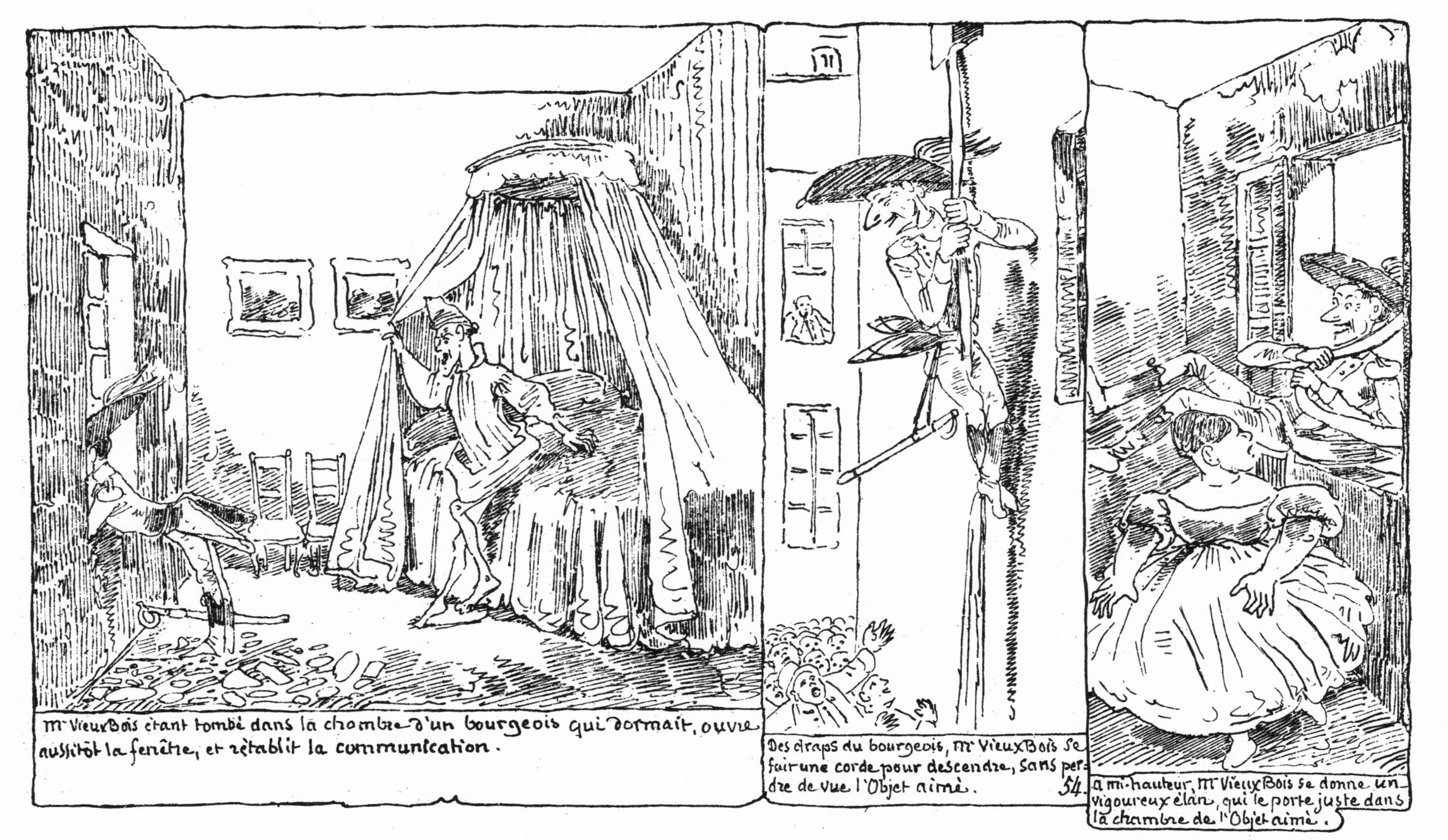
Mr Vieux Bois étant tombé dans la chambre d'un bourgeois qui dormait, ouvre aussitôt la fenêtre, et rétablit la communication.
Des draps du bourgeois, Mr Vieux Bois se fait une corde pour descendre, sans perdre de vue l'Objet aimé.
54.
A mi-hauteur, Mr Vieux Bois se donne un vigoureux élan, qui le porte juste dans la chambre de l'Objet aimé.

Mr. Vieux Bois having fallen into the chamber of a sleeping citizen, immediately opens the window and reestablishes communication.

From the citizen's sheets Mr. Vieux Bois makes a rope for his descent, without losing the Beloved Object from view.

Halfway down Mr. Vieux Bois gives himself a powerful, deft swing into the Beloved Object's bedroom.

Précieux momens qui dédommagent de bien des peines.

Tout en se dédommageant de bien des peines, Mr Vieux Bois observe fortement les localités.

55.

Le bourgeois qui est allé chercher la police n'ayant personne à lui montrer, est provisoirement arrêté comme mauvais drôle, un peu farceur.

Precious moments which amply repay his pains.

Even as he is amply repaid for his pains, Mr. Vieux Bois keeps a wary eye on the surroundings.

The citizen who went to fetch the police, having no one to show for it, is provisionally arrested as a trickster, a bit of a buffoon.

Second enlèvement dans une chaise fermée à clef, pour éviter tout Soupçon, et tout danger.
Mr Vieux Bois ayant aperçu un moine, pique des deux, et ne s'aperçoit pas de l'accident.
56.

Second abduction in a locked chaise, to avoid all suspicion and all danger.

Mr. Vieux Bois having spied a monk, gallops off, not noticing the accident.

Monsieur Vieux Bois, allant toujours plus vite, fait dix huit lieues à l'heure.
57.

Mr. Vieux Bois traveling ever faster, does eighteen leagues per hour.

La chaise est trouvée par la diligence de Paris. On la charge sur l'impériale.
La diligence ayant versé, l'Objet aimé favorisé du Sort, flotte au gré des eaux.
58.

The chaise is found by the Paris stagecoach. It is loaded onto the top.

The coach having tipped over, the Beloved Object, favored by fate, floats at the mercy of the waters.

Un des Voyageurs étant revenu sur l'eau cherche un refuge sur la chaise.
Horrible frayeur du Voyageur, à l'ouïe de la chaise qui l'appelle par son nom.
Le Voyageur qui n'est autre que le rival de Mr Vieux Bois, reconnaît une voix chérie, et presse la chaise avec tendresse, pendant que l'Objet aimé lui raconte ses aventures.
59.

One of the Travelers having risen to the surface, seeks safety on the chaise.

Horrible fear of the Traveler, hearing himself called by name from the chaise.

The Traveler who is none other than Mr. Vieux Bois's Rival, recognizes a beloved voice, and embraces the chaise tenderly, while the Beloved Object recounts her adventures.

S'étant aperçu de l'accident, Mr Vieux Bois se hâte de revenir sur ses pas.
60.

Having noticed the accident, Mr. Vieux Bois hastens to retrace his steps.

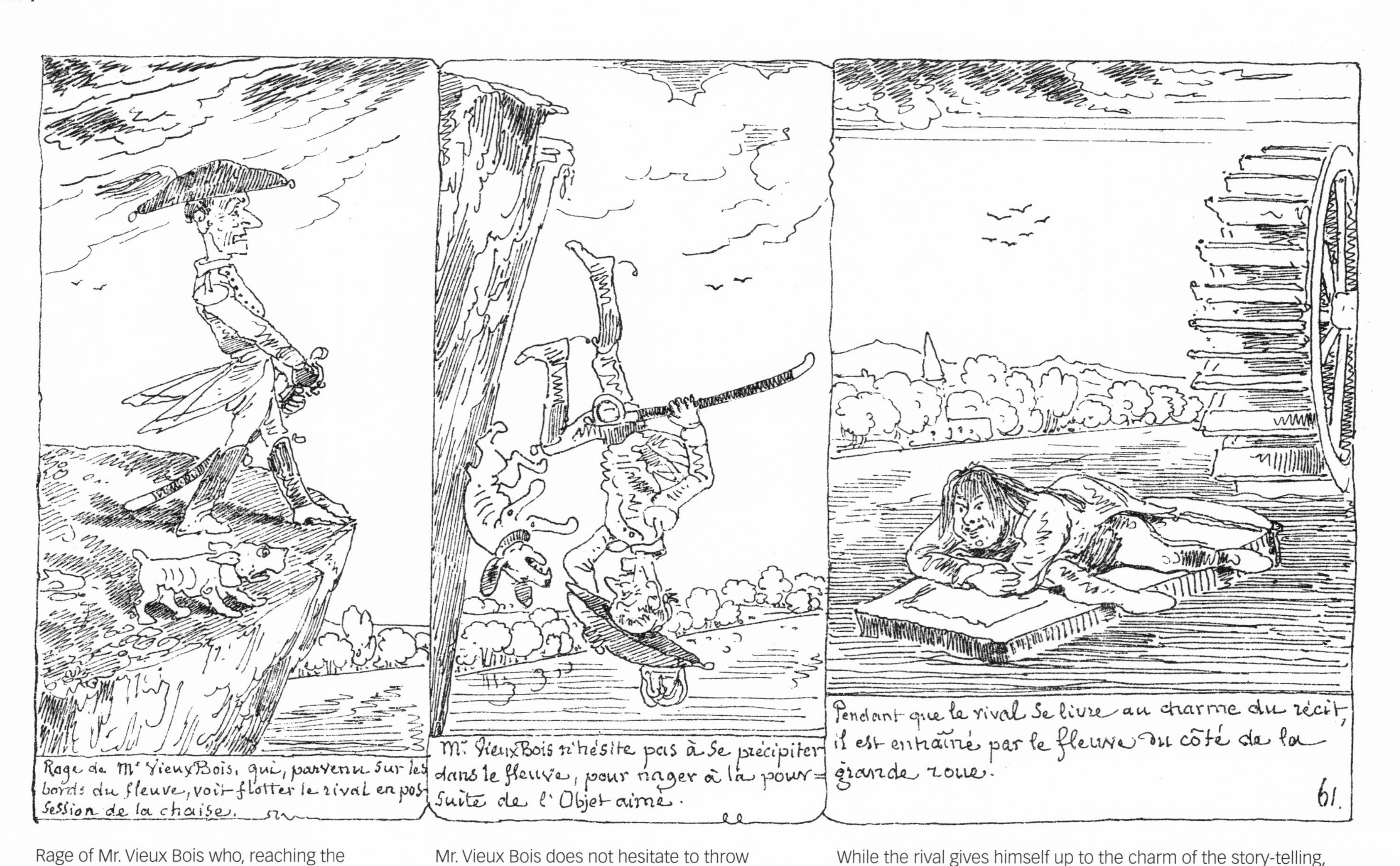
Rage de Mr Vieux Bois, qui, parvenu sur les bords du fleuve, voit flotter le rival en possession de la chaise.
Mr. Vieux Bois n'hésite pas à se précipiter dans le fleuve, pour nager à la poursuite de l'Objet aimé.
Pendant que le rival se livre au charme du récit, il est entraîné par le fleuve du côté de la grande roue.
61.

Rage of Mr. Vieux Bois who, reaching the banks of the river, sees the rival floating in possession of the chaise.

Mr. Vieux Bois does not hesitate to throw himself into the river, to swim in pursuit of the Beloved Object.

While the rival gives himself up to the charm of the story-telling, he is carried off by the river towards the great waterwheel.

Happé au plus beau moment par la grande roue, le Rival est prodigieusement saucé à chaque tour.
Ayant atteint la chaise, Mr. Vieux Bois y prend place, et gouverne avec son chapeau.
Mr Vieux Bois cherche, pour y débarquer, une rive émaillée de fleurs.
62.

Caught up at the height of the story by the big waterwheel, the Rival is thoroughly soused at every turn.

Having reached the chaise, Mr. Vieux Bois takes his place and steers with his hat.

Mr. Vieux Bois seeks a flower-studded shore suited to disembarkation.

Cependant le Rival continue d'être prodigieusement saucé à chaque tour.

Ayant débarqué sur une rive fleurie, Mr. Vieux Bois dégage l'Objet aimé, et, par façon de plaisanterie, repousse la chaise dans le fleuve, en criant au Rival qu'il lui en fait cadeau maintenant.

L'Objet aimé étant extrêmement amoindri, Mr. Vieux Bois le mène boire le lait à la montagne.

63.

Meanwhile the Rival continues to get thoroughly soused at every turn.

Having disembarked on a flowery bank, Mr. Vieux Bois extracts the Beloved Object and, just for fun, pushes the chaise back into the river, shouting to the Rival that he can take it now as a gift.

The Beloved Object being now in an extremely reduced state, Mr. Vieux Bois takes her to drink milk in the mountains.

Le Rival persiste à être prodi=
gieusement saucé à cha=
que tour.
Mr Vieux Bois embrasse la vie pastorale, pour la santé de l'Objet Aimé, et prend le nom provisoire
de Tircis.
64.

The Rival continues to get thoroughly soused at every turn.

Mr. Vieux Bois embraces the pastoral life, for the sake of the Beloved Object's health, and takes the provisional name of Thyrsis.

Le Rival persiste à être prodigieusement saucé à chaque tour.

Mr Vieux Bois, sous le nom provisoire de Tircis, s'adonne à traire en faveur de l'Objet aimé

65.

The Rival continues to get thoroughly soused at every turn.

Mr. Vieux Bois, under the provisional name of Thyrsis, devotes himself to milking on behalf of the Beloved Object.

Le Rival persiste à être prodigieusement saucé à chaque tour.
Mr. Vieux Bois, sous le nom provisoire de Tircis, récrée l'Objet aimé par des danses bucoliques.
Mr. Vieux Bois, sous le nom provisoire de Tircis, déniche en faveur de l'Objet Aimé.
66.

The Rival continues to get thoroughly soused at every turn.

Mr. Vieux Bois, under the provisional name of Thyrsis, entertains the Beloved Object with bucolic dances.

Mr. Vieux Bois, under the provisional name of Thyrsis, goes bird's nesting on behalf of the Beloved Object.

Le Rival persiste à être prodigieusement saucé à chaque tour.

Aux premières froidures, Mr Vieux Bois, sous le nom provisoire de Tircis, quitte les hauteurs, et vient chercher dans les plaines embaumées de plus tièdes zéphirs.

Cependant les eaux ayant considérablement baissé, la chaise laissée à sec, échoue non loin du Couvent.

67.

The Rival continues to get soused at every turn.

At the first signs of cold, Mr. Vieux Bois, under the provisional name of Thyrsis, quits the heights and seeks out warmer zephyrs in the balmy plains.

Meanwhile, the waters having appreciably subsided, the chaise is left high and dry and lands not far from the Monastery.

Par la même cause, la grande Roue cesse de tourner, et le Rival prend te re.
Et puis se sèche au Soleil.
La vie pastorale ayant singulièrement engraissé l'Objet aimé, Mr. Vieux-Bois commence à en concevoir de l'inquiétude.
68.

For the same reason, the big waterwheel ceases turning, and the Rival finds solid ground.

And then dries himself in the sun.

The pastoral life having led singularly to fattening the Beloved Object, Mr. Vieux Bois begins to experience misgivings.

Une fois séché, le Rival trouve un âne, et s'en trouve bien.
Mr Vieux Bois, ayant composé un palanquin bucolique, confie à deux pâtres le Soin de le porter dans sa patrie.
Les pâtres trouvant la besogne rude, profitent du Sommeil des amans pour les déposer Sur le grand chemin, et S'enfuient très allégés.
69.

Once dried out, the Rival finds an ass, and is glad of it.

Mr. Vieux Bois, having constructed a bucolic palanquin, entrusts two shepherds with the task of carrying it back to his homeland.

The shepherds finding the work laborious, profit from the sleep of the lovers by leaving them on the highway, and flee in great relief.

Le Rival étant venu à passer par là, reprend l'Objet aimé, le charge tout-endormi sur son âne, et poursuit sa route au plus vite.
Profonde surprise de Mr. Vieux Bois, à son réveil.
70.

The Rival happening to pass by the place, retrieves the Beloved Object, loads her still asleep on his ass, and pursues his way as fast as possible.

Profound surprise of Mr. Vieux Bois, on awakening.

Persuadé que c'est un tour des porteurs, Mr Vieux Bois se lance à leur poursuites. 15 lieues en trois heures.

Convinced that the porters have tricked him, Mr. Vieux Bois dashes off in pursuit of them. 15 leagues in three hours.

Une fois lancé, Mr Vieux Bois ne pouvant ni se détourner, ni s'arrêter à temps, s'enfonce dans une meule de foin.

71.

Once launched, Mr. Vieux Bois is unable to turn or stop in time, and plunges into a haystack.

Arrivé au même endroit, le Rival décharge l'Objet aimé, et
fait manger son âne qui attrape le pied de Mr. Vieux Bois
Mr. Vieux Bois pousse en vain un cri affreux dans la meule
L'âne mangeant beaucoup de foin
Mr. Vieux Bois commence à se déga=
ger Tourmens de la jalousie. 72

Reaching the same spot, the Rival unloads the Beloved Object and gives fodder to his ass which seizes Mr. Vieux Bois's foot. Mr. Vieux Bois utters in vain a frightful scream from within the haystack.

The ass eats so much hay that Mr. Vieux Bois begins to free himself. Torments of jealousy.

Une fois dégagé, Mr. Vieux Bois prend sa revanche, et s'éloigne au plus vite.

S'étant réveillé, l'Objet aimé demande où sont les porteurs, et pourquoi cet âne.

73

Once free, Mr. Vieux Bois takes his revenge, and makes off double quick.

Waking up, the Beloved Object asks where are the porters and why this ass.

Le Rival persiste à dormir prodigieusement.
Mr Vieux Bois continue sa route. Momens sans pareils. Et son chien aussi.
74

The Rival continues to sleep prodigiously.

Mr. Vieux Bois goes on his way. Incomparable moments. And his dog too.

Devant repasser sur les terres des Moines, Mr. Vieux Bois se déguise en meunier, et déguise l'Objet aimé en sac de farine.

Les moines, ayant droit de péage, sondent le sac qui se crispe, en poussant un cri affreux.

75.

Having to pass through the Monks' territory again, Mr. Vieux Bois disguises himself as a miller, and the Beloved Object as a sack of flour.

The monks, having toll rights, sound the sack, which buckles, uttering a horrible scream.

A la vue du Sac qui se met à marcher, les moines croyant que c'est le Diable en personne, s'enfuient à toutes jambes au grand plaisir de Mr. Vieux Bois.
76.

At the sight of a sack walking off, the monks thinking it is the Devil in person, flee in a panic, to Mr. Vieux Bois's great satisfaction.

Le sac s'étant fortuitement délié, les Moines reviennent à la charge, et en tirent l'Objet aimé en personne

77.

The sack happening to have come undone, the Monks return to the charge, and extract the Beloved Object in person.

Mr Vieux Bois et l'Objet aimé reconnus, jugés et condamnés par le Chapitre sont conduits au bucher.
78

Mr. Vieux Bois and the Beloved Object are recognized, judged, and condemned by the Chapter, and led to the stake.

Le feu ayant d'abord consumé la base des poteaux, Mr. Vieux Bois et l'Objet aimé s'échappent, en profitant de la fumée qui les dérobe à la vue du Chapitre.

Les deux amans tout brûlans d'une ardeur infinie, se jettent dans le fleuve pour éteindre, et nagent vers la rive opposée 79

The fire having first of all consumed the base of the posts, Mr. Vieux Bois and the Beloved Object escape, under the cover of the smoke that hides them from the sight of the Chapter.

The two lovers all burning with infinite ardor, throw themselves into the river in order to quench it, and swim towards the bank opposite.

arrivés à l'endroit où la chaise a échoué, Mr Vieux Bois et l'Objet aimé se sèchent au soleil.
Mr Vieux Bois ayant redressé la chaise, monte dessus pour observer s'il est poursuivi.
80

Reaching the place where the chaise landed, Mr. Vieux Bois and the Beloved Object dry themselves in the sun.

Mr. Vieux Bois having stood the chaise upright, climbs up on it to see if he is being pursued.

Ayant observé deux moines qui le poursuivent, Mon=
sieur VieuxBois combine un malin Stratagême.

Son stratagême combiné, Mr VieuxBois veut ouvrir la chaise; mais il est presque renversé par les grenouilles qui en sortent.

81.

Having spotted two monks pursuing him, Mr. Vieux Bois thinks up a cunning stratagem.

With his stratagem in place, Mr. Vieux Bois tries to open the chaise, but he is almost knocked over by the frogs which spring out of it.

Les Moines approchant, Mr Vieux Bois se hâte de se cacher dans la chaise avec l'Objet aimé, et de fermer en dedans après avoir semé quelques écus autour.
82.

As the Monks approach, Mr. Vieux Bois hurriedly hides himself in the chaise with the Beloved Object, and shuts himself into it after having scattered some coins around it.

Les deux moines jugeant au poids et aux écus que c'est un immense trésor, font une fosse pour enfouir à eux deux.

Quand le trou est assez profond, Mr Vieux Bois sort doucement de la chaise, pousse les deux moines dans la fosse, et y rejette promptement la terre.

83.

The two Monks supposing from the weight and the coins that it contains an immense treasure, dig a pit to bury it for their mutal benefit.

When the hole is deep enough, Mr. Vieux Bois quietly leaves the chaise, pushes the two Monks into the pit, and quickly throws earth into it.

Quand Mr Vieux Bois a proprement enterré les deux Moines, il prend congé, et s'enfuit au plus vite.
84.

When Mr. Vieux Bois has thoroughly buried the two Monks, he takes his leave and escapes as fast as possible.

le Rival s'étant réveillé ne trouve plus l'Objet aimé, et le redemande aux échos.

The Rival having awakened, finds the Beloved Object missing and demands that the echoes give her back to him.

Les échos ne lui apprenant rien, le Rival s'adresse au Ciel et à la nature entière.

The echoes having nothing to tell, the Rival addresses himself to Heaven and nature entire.

Découragé entièrement le Rival se dirige vers le fleuve pour s'y précipiter. 85.

Totally discouraged the Rival sets off for the river, to throw himself into it.

Les deux moines trouvent le temps long.
La fuite qui se prolonge ne laisse pas que de fatiguer l'Objet aimé.
30
86.

The two Monks find the time drags.

The prolonged flight does not fail to fatigue the Beloved Object.

Aussi Mr Vieux Bois saisit-il galamment l'occasion de voiturer l'Objet aimé.

So Mr. Vieux Bois gallantly seizes the occasion to give the Beloved Object a lift.

Grand déploiement de forces de Mr. Vieux Bois.

87

Great exertion on the part of Mr. Vieux Bois.

ayant lâché pied, la brouette lui passe sur le ventre, et redescend vers la plaine
Entendant un grand bruit derrière eux, les deux moines crient au secours de toute leur force
88.
Entendant des cris, le Rival qui allait se précipiter dans le fleuve, s'arrête court

When Mr. Vieux Bois loses his footing, the wheelbarrow passes over his belly and runs down towards the plain.

Hearing a loud noise behind them, the two Monks shout for help with all their might.

Hearing the shouts, the Rival who was going to throw himself into the river, suddenly pauses.

Voyant de quoi il s'agit, le Rival s'empresse d'accourir, et il s'adjuge de nouveau l'Objet Aimé.

Seeing what is up, the Rival hurries up and repossesses himself of the Beloved Object.

Revenu à lui, Mr Vieux Bois reprend sa grande course. Quinze lieues en trois heures.

89.

Coming to, Mr. Vieux Bois resumes his headlong course. Fifteen leagues in three hours.

Arrivé auprès des deux Moines, Mr Vieux Bois apprend d'eux ce qui s'est passé, et en reconnoissance de ces indications, il les déterre. Après quoi, il reprend sa grande course. Vingt lieues en deux heures
La nuit étant venue le Rival goûte q.ques instans de sommeil sans lâcher la brouette, pour plus de sureté.
90.

Reaching the two Monks, Mr. Vieux Bois is told by them what has happened, and in gratitude for this information, he digs them up. After which he resumes his headlong course. Twenty leagues in two hours.

At nightfall the Rival enjoys a few moments of sleep keeping hold of the wheelbarrow for greater safety.

Mr Vieux Bois étant survenu, profite du sommeil du Rival pour lui attacher les deux mains à la brouette, puis l'ayant utilisé de cette façon, il reprend le chemin de sa patrie.

On his arrival there, Mr. Vieux Bois takes advantage of the Rival's sleep to tie his hands to the wheelbarrow, then having fixed him like this, resumes the way to his country.

De retour dans sa patrie, Mr Vieux Bois change de linge.

91.

Back in his country, Mr. Vieux Bois changes his shirt.

HEUREUX DENOUEMENT DE L'HISTOIRE DE MONSIEUR VIEUX BOIS. GENEVE 1839.
92.

HAPPY CONCLUSION TO THE STORY OF MR. VIEUX BOIS, GENEVA 1839.

Monsieur Pencil
PARIS
Librairie d'Abm. Cherbuliez et Cie. rue de
Tournon, 17.

Autographié à Genève par l'Auteur

Monsieur Pencil

1840

Ci derrière commencent les Aventures de Monsieur et de Madame Jolibois, simples particuliers, combinés avec les faits et gestes du Docteur, et les choses merveilleuses relatives au Bourgeois et à Mr. Pencil. Le tout mêlé aux drôleries du temps présent, et comme quoi George Luçon échappa sauf au Vingtième léger qui avait bu un coup de trop chez le Maire.

Va, petit livre, et choisis ton monde, car aux choses folles, qui ne rit pas, baîlle; qui ne se livre pas, résiste; qui raisonne se méprend et qui veut rester grave, en est maître.

Lithographie de Schmid

Mr. Pencil, autographed in Geneva by the author, 1840, Schmid Lithography

Here begin the Adventures of Mr. and Mrs. Jolibois, private individuals, together with the exploits of the Professor, and marvelous matters relating to the Burgher and Mr. Pencil. All mingled with the fun of our times, and showing how George Luçon escaped from the Twentieth Light who had drunk a drop too much at the Mayor's.

Go, little book, and choose your world, for those who do not laugh, yawn at crazy things; those who do not yield, resist; those who reason, are mistaken; and those who would keep a straight face, can please themselves.

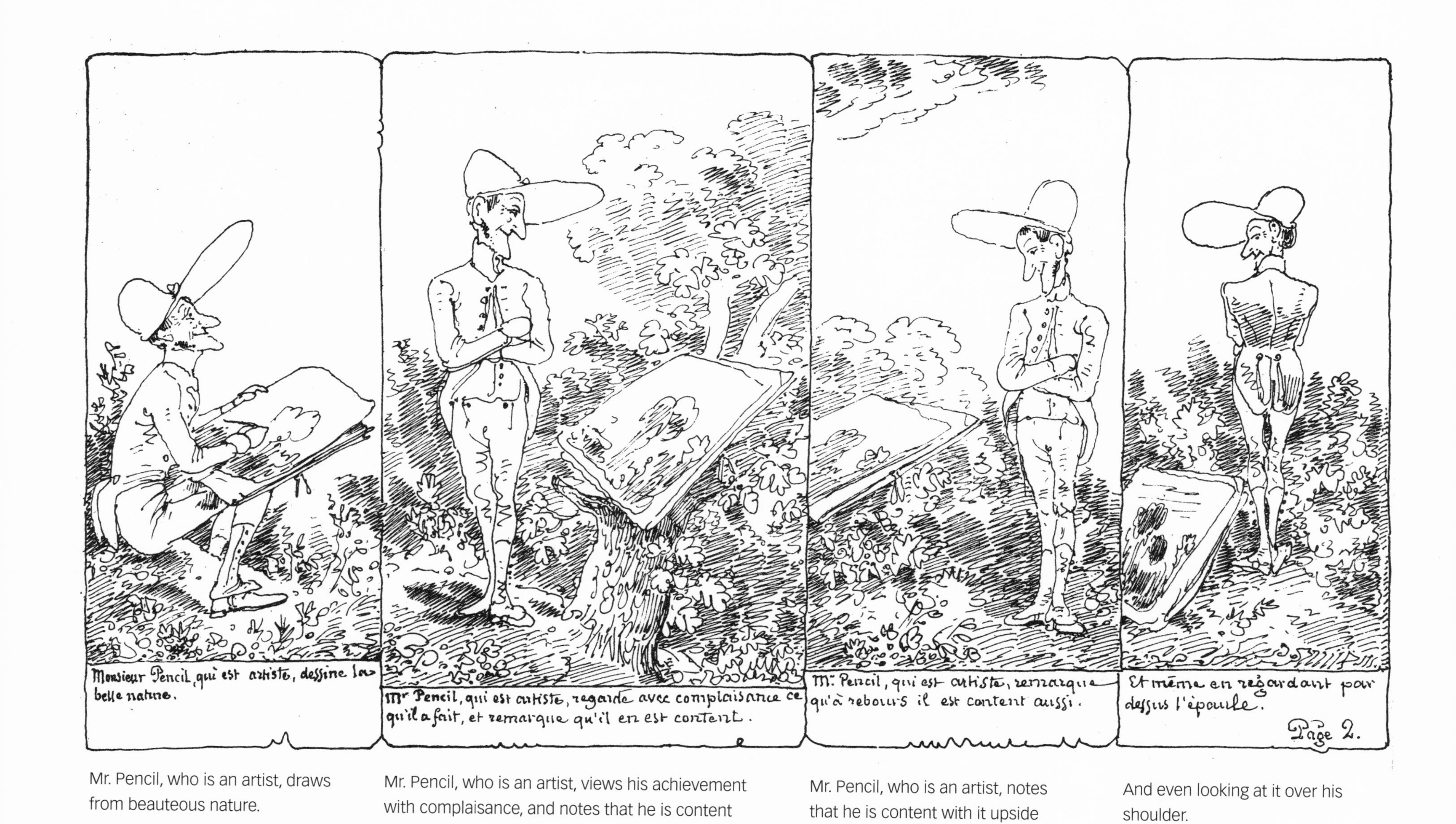
Monsieur Pencil, qui est artiste, dessine la belle nature.
Mr Pencil, qui est artiste, regarde avec complaisance ce qu'il a fait, et remarque qu'il en est content.
Mr. Pencil, qui est artiste, remarque qu'à rebours il est content aussi.
Et même en regardant par dessus l'épaule.
Page 2.

Mr. Pencil, who is an artist, draws from beauteous nature.

Mr. Pencil, who is an artist, views his achievement with complaisance, and notes that he is content with it.

Mr. Pencil, who is an artist, notes that he is content with it upside down as well.

And even looking at it over his shoulder.

Ayant essayé de ne regarder que le revers M. Pencil, qui est artiste, remarque avec plaisir qu'il est encore content.

Pendant que M. Pencil remarque avec plaisir qu'il est content un petit zéphir s'amuse à lui enlever sa casquette.

En ayant assez de la casquette, le petit zéphyr rebrousse pour s'amuser avec le dessin.

3.

Having tried looking at just the reverse side, Mr. Pencil, who is an artist, notes with pleasure that he is still content.

While Mr. Pencil is noting with pleasure that he is content, a little zephyr playfully blows off his cap.

Tiring of the cap, the little zephyr turns back to play with the drawing.

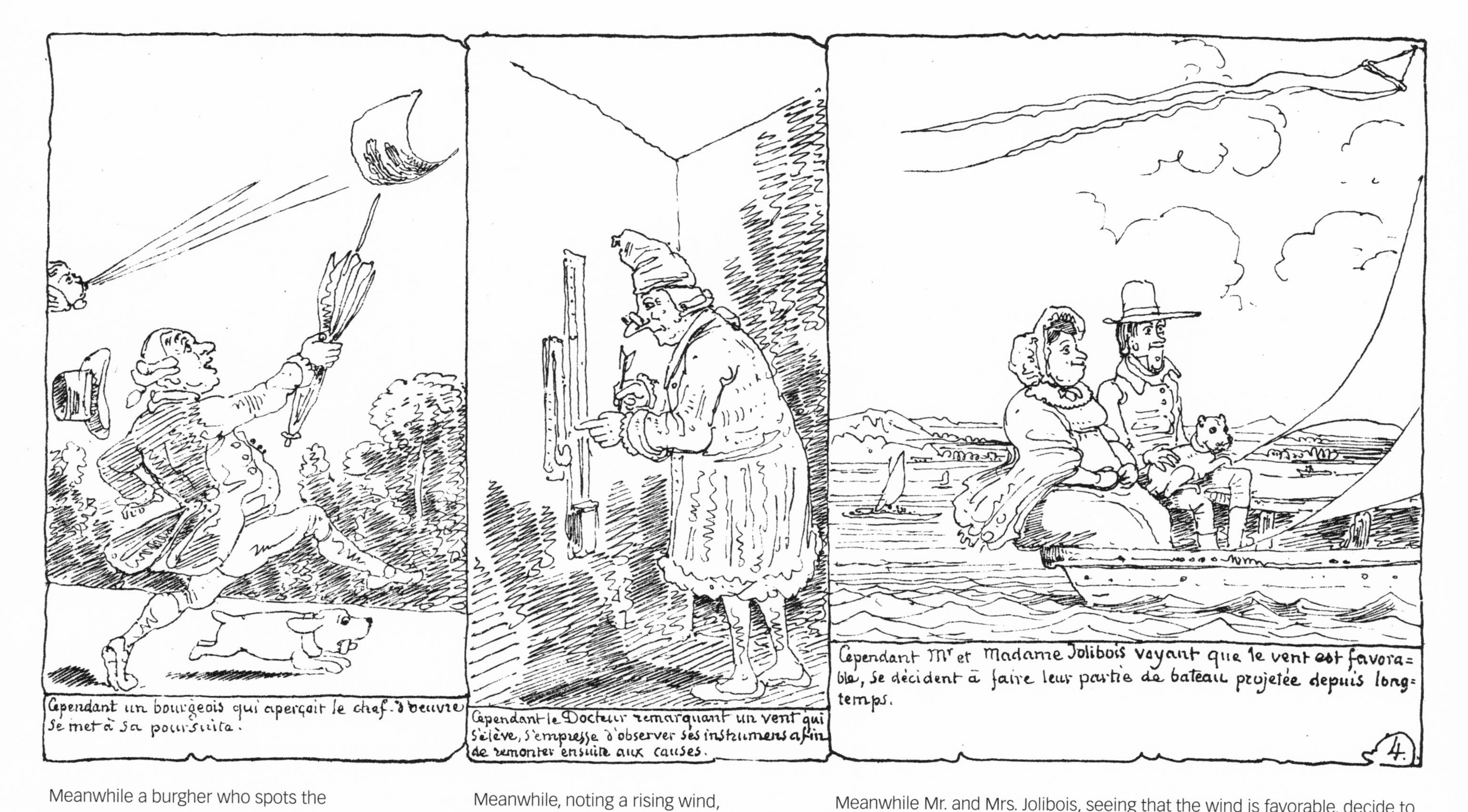
Cependant un bourgeois qui aperçoit le chef-d'oeuvre se met à sa poursuite.
Cependant le Docteur remarquant un vent qui s'élève, s'empresse d'observer ses instrumens afin de remonter ensuite aux causes.
Cependant Mr et Madame Jolibois voyant que le vent est favorable, se décident à faire leur partie de bateau projetée depuis longtemps.
4.

Meanwhile a burgher who spots the masterpiece, sets off after it.

Meanwhile, noting a rising wind, the Professor hastens to check his instruments, so as to determine causation.

Meanwhile Mr. and Mrs. Jolibois, seeing that the wind is favorable, decide to embark on the boat trip they had been planning for a while.

En ayant assez du dessin, le petit zéphir passe au Bourgeois, et s'amuse à ouvrir son parapluie.
Puis il souffle d'en bas, ferme.
Ayant senti du froid, le Docteur se rhabille, et s'en va rédiger sa découverte d'un vent souterrain tout nouveau.
Par suite du vent souterrain, Mr. et Madame Jolibois commencent à être dans un sérieux embarras.
5.

Tiring of the drawing, the little zephyr passes on to the Burgher, and playfully opens his umbrella.

Then he blows upward, hard.

Feeling the cold, the Professor dresses again, and goes off to write up his discovery of an entirely new subterranean wind.

As a consequence of the subterranean wind, Mr. and Mrs. Jolibois find themselves in serious trouble.

qui va croissant.
Le petit zéphir s'amuse à pousser le bourgeois dans les bras de Mme Jolibois. Mr Jolibois, (car hélas la passion aveugle) ressent les tourmens d'une atroce jalousie.
Et il se noierait s'il n'y avait pas trop de fond dans cet endroit
Cependant le Docteur ayant cru remarquer que son vent souterrain est chargé de particules odorantes, s'occupe d'en remplir des phioles à l'appui du grand mémoire qu'il prépare.
6.

Which only increases.

The little zephyr playfully pushes the burgher into the arms of Mrs. Jolibois. Mr. Jolibois (for passion blinds, alas) experiences the torments of an atrocious jealousy.

And he would have drowned himself, were not the water too deep at that point.

Meanwhile the Professor, thinking he has observed that his subterranean wind is filled with odorous particles, busies himself filling some phials with it, in support of the great scientific report that he is preparing.

Finding only his portfolio, Mr. Pencil is delighted that his drawing should have been taken off by some lover of the truly beautiful.

Having made another drawing, Mr. Pencil takes cover, so as to find out who the art lover may be.

Meanwhile the Professor, having bottled his data, busies himself with writing up his great report on an entirely new subterranean wind.

Le bourgeois ayant imprudemment lâché le parapluie, a le bonheur de tomber sur les épaules de Mme Jolibois
Ce que voyant, (car hélas la passion aveugle) Mr Jolibois se persuade que c'est sa femme qui enlève son amant. Aussitôt il se dépouille de ses vêtemens pour chercher la mort dans les flots mais il trouve que la chose est malaisée.
Porté par le zéphir à hauteur convenable, Mr Jolibois (car hélas la passion aveugle) s'efforce de rompre ces criminels liens. Mais il manque de point d'appui.
Après quoi le petit Zéphir s'amuse à faire tourbillonner le tout.
8.

The burgher, having imprudently let go his umbrella, is fortunate enough to fall on the shoulders of Mrs. Jolibois.

Seeing which (for passion blinds alas) Mr. Jolibois is persuaded that his wife is carrying off her lover. He immediately strips himself of his clothing to seek death in the waves, but he finds that it is not so easy a matter.

Carried off by the Zephyr to the right height, Mr. Jolibois (for passion blinds, alas) attempts to break the criminal bonds. But he is lacking in any point of support.

After which the little Zephyr playfully makes everything swirl around.

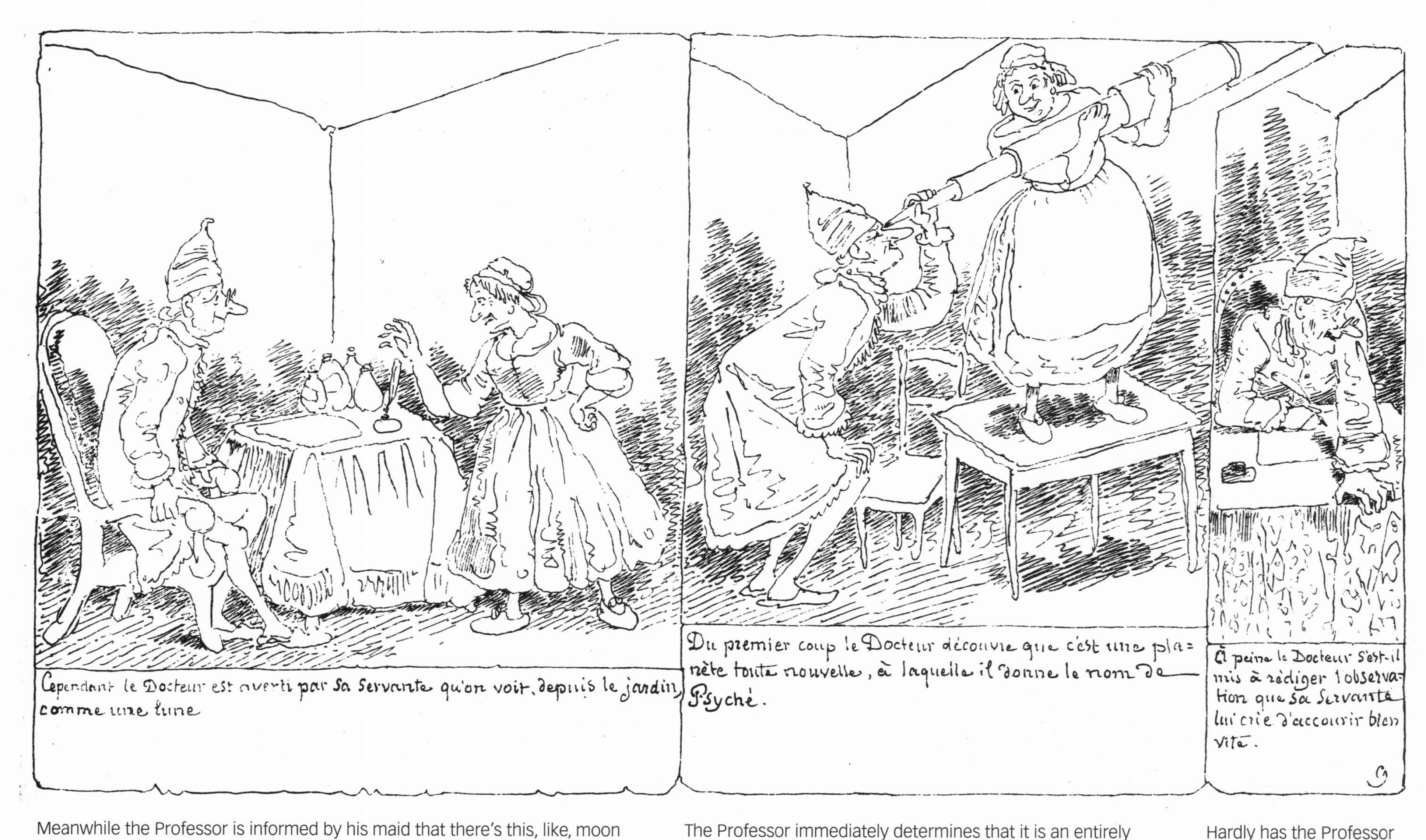
Cependant le Docteur est averti par sa Servante qu'on voit, depuis le jardin, comme une lune
Du premier coup le Docteur découvre que c'est une pla= nète toute nouvelle, à laquelle il donne le nom de Psyché.
À peine le Docteur s'est-il mis à rédiger l'observation que sa Servante lui crie d'accourir bien vite.

Meanwhile the Professor is informed by his maid that there's this, like, moon to be seen from the garden.

The Professor immediately determines that it is an entirely new planet, to which he gives the name Psyche.

Hardly has the Professor begun to write up his observation, than his maid shouts to him to hurry over quickly.

C'est le soulier de madᵉ Jolibois et le parapluie du bourgeois qui viennent de tomber du haut des airs.... Le Docteur s'écrie : Habitée !! habitée !!!! (la planète)
Assailli tout à coup par une trop grande quantité d'inductions et d'hypothèses, Le Docteur défaille dans les bras de sa Servante.
A peine revenu à lui, le Docteur reprend la plume pour décrire précipitamment les habitans de sa planète, leurs mœurs probables, leurs usages possibles, et leur civilisation virtuelle etc. etc. etc. etc. etc. etc. etc.....
10.

It is Mrs. Jolibois's shoe and the burgher's umbrella which have just fallen from the sky above. . . . The Professor cries Inhabited! ! Inhabited! ! ! ! (the planet).

Suddenly overcome by an excessive intake of inductions and hypotheses, the Professor faints into the arms of his maid.

As soon as he recovers consciousness, the Professor takes up his pen again to begin his hasty description of the inhabitants of his planet, their probable customs, their possible habits, and their potential civilization etc. etc. etc. etc. etc. etc etc. . . . .

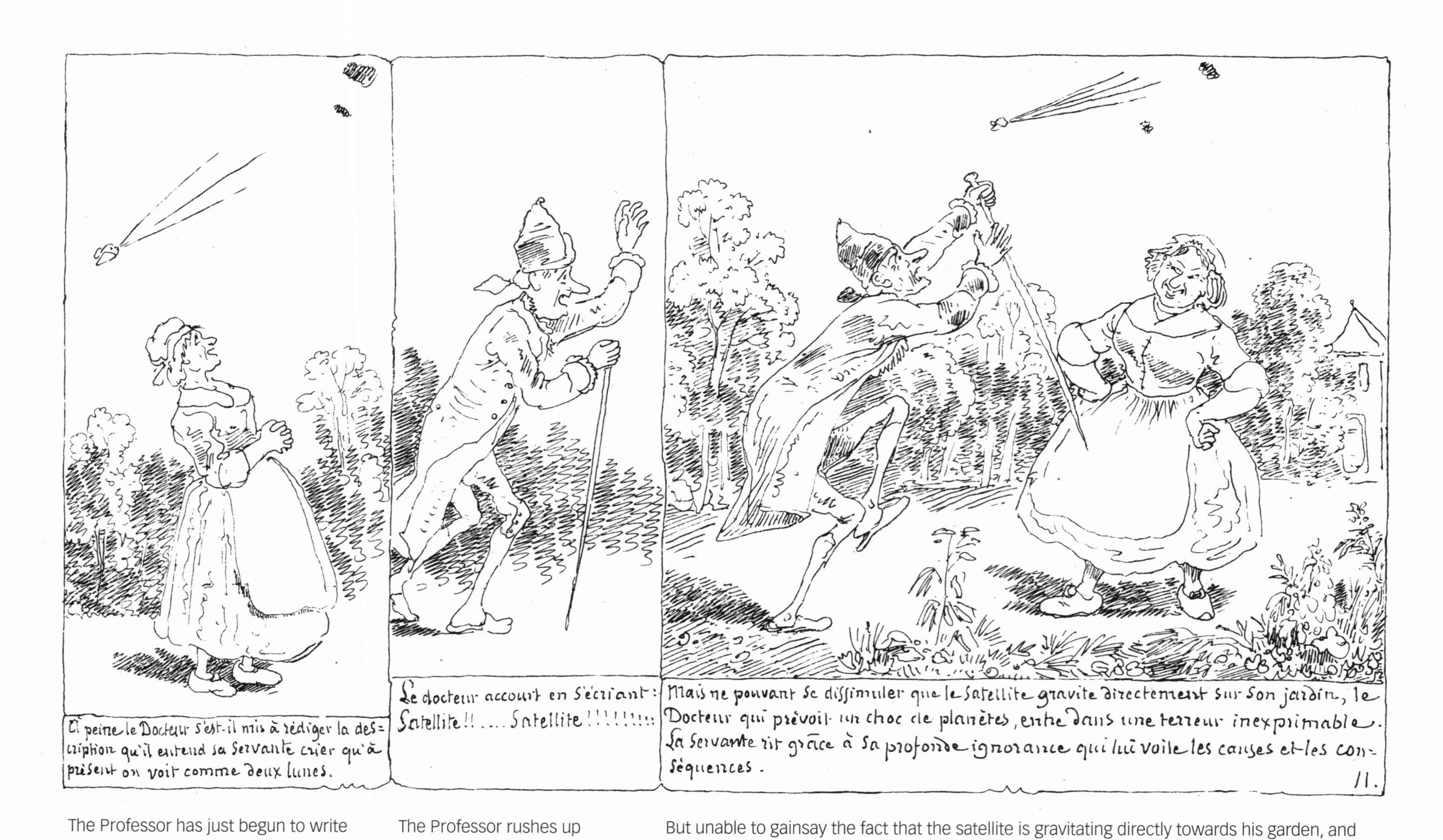
À peine le Docteur s'est-il mis à rédiger la des=
cription qu'il entend sa Servante crier qu'à
présent on voit comme deux lunes.
Le docteur accourt en s'écriant :
Satellite !! .... Satellite !!!!!!!!
Mais ne pouvant se dissimuler que le satellite gravite directement sur son jardin, le
Docteur qui prévoit un choc de planètes, entre dans une terreur inexprimable.
La Servante rit grâce à sa profonde ignorance qui lui voile les causes et les con-
séquences.
11.

The Professor has just begun to write up his description, when he hears his maid shouting that she can now see, like, these two moons.

The Professor rushes up exclaiming: Satellite! ! . . . . Satellite! ! ! ! ! ! ! !

But unable to gainsay the fact that the satellite is gravitating directly towards his garden, and foreseeing a collision of the planets, the Professor enters into an inexpressible terror. The maid laughs, owing to her profound ignorance which conceals causes and effects from her.

Le Docteur sent déjà une chaleur insolite, et une extrême raré=
faction de l'air. La Servante ne sent rien grâce à sa pro=
fonde ignorance qui lui voile les effets.
Le Docteur entend aussi un bruit sourd de rotation ellipsoïde et parabolique. La
Servante n'entend rien, grâce à sa profonde ignorance qui lui voile les
rotations.
12

The Professor already senses an unusual heat, and an extreme rarefaction of the atmosphere. His maid senses nothing owing to her profound ignorance, which conceals effects from her.

The Professor also hears a dull sound of ellipsoid and parabolic rotation. His maid hears nothing, owing to her profound ignorance which conceals rotations from her.

Le Docteur Subodore aussi des exhalaisons sulfureuses. La Servante ne subodore rien, grâce à sa profonde ignorance qui lui bouche le nez.
Eclairé par la science, le Docteur, prévoyant la fin du monde, va faire son testament, se met au lit, et attend le choc d'un moment à l'autre.
La Servante qui ne prévoit rien grâce à sa profonde ignorance s'en va cueillir des salades pour le dîner.
13

The Professor scents sulfurous exhalations. The maid scents nothing, owing to her profound ignorance which stops her nose.

In his scientific enlightenment, and foreseeing the end of the world, the Professor makes his will, takes to his bed, and expects the collision at any moment.

The maid, who foresees nothing owing to her profound ignorance, goes off to pick lettuce for dinner.

Cependant Mr Jolibois, sa chemise s'étant entortillée, est détaché du tourbillon, et vient tomber dans les salades.
À peine le Docteur s'est mis à attendre le choc, qu'il entend sa servante crier : Tiens! Quel oiseau!
Pendant que le Docteur s'habille pour accourir, la servante retourne du pied Mr Jolibois qui lui paraît un homme comme un autre.
Profonde admiration du Docteur qui découvre du premier coup que c'est un habitant de sa planète.
14.

Meanwhile Mr. Jolibois, twisted up in his shirt, is detached from the whirlwind, and falls into the lettuce patch.

The Professor is just composing himself to await the collision, when he hears the maid shout: Wow! What a bird!

While the Professor dresses before rushing to the scene, the maid turns Mr. Jolibois over with her foot. He appears to her to be a man like any other.

Profound astonishment of the Professor as he instantly recognizes that it is an inhabitant from his planet.

La première chose que fait le Docteur, c'est de mettre son habitant
sous clé dans la grande volière.

The first thing the Professor does is to put his inhabitant under lock and key in the big birdcage.

Cependant le Bourgeois ayant lâ=
ché Madame Jolibois se détache
du tourbillon et s'en vient tom=
ber sur une meule de foin.

Meanwhile, having released Mrs. Jolibois, the Burgher detaches himself from the whirlwind, and lands in a haystack.

Le chien ayant voulu suivre
son maître, s'en vient tomber
sur le tèlègraphe.

Trying to follow his master, the dog lands on a telegraph pole.

Cependant le Docteur
se hâte d'achever son
grand mémoire sur
un vent souterrain tout
nouveau et de l'adresser
à l'Académie Royale
afin de pouvoir s'occu=
per sans distraction
de son habitant.

15.

Meanwhile the Professor hastily finishes off his great scientific report on an entirely new subterranean wind, and addresses it to the Royal Society, so as to free himself for undisturbed study of his inhabitant.

Après avoir terminé et expédié son mémoire, le Docteur voulant commencer par les caractères internes se dispose à pratiquer l'incision cruciale sur son habitant.
À peine Mr Jolibois a-t-il senti la pointe du scalpel que, revenu de son étourdissement, d'une seule crispation cruciale, il met le Docteur hors de combat. (car hélas, la passion aveugle!)
Le Docteur rédige aussitôt: ..... léthargiques... impétueux aussi..... ils ruent avec une adresse remarquable.
16.

Having finished and sent off his report, and deciding to begin with the internal characteristics, the Professor prepares to make the cross incision on his inhabitant.

As soon as Mr. Jolibois feels the point of the scalpel, he recovers from his daze, and with a single cross convulsion, puts the Professor out of action. (for passion blinds, alas!)

The Professor immediately writes: . . . . lethargic . . . also impetuous . . . . . they kick with remarkable dexterity.

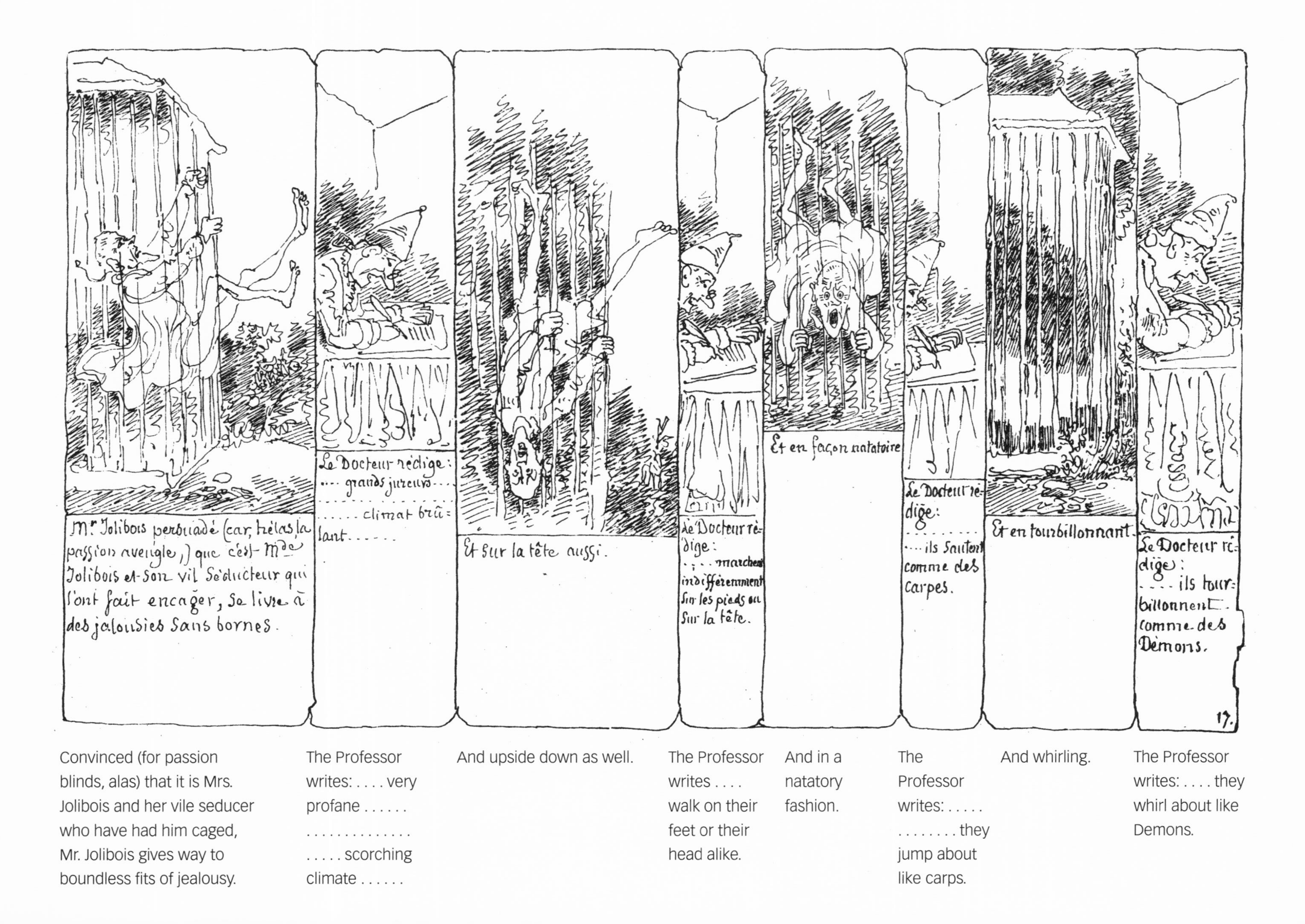

Mr. Jolibois persuadé (car, hélas, la passion aveugle,) que c'est Mde Jolibois et son vil Séducteur qui l'ont fait encager, se livre à des jalousies sans bornes.
Le Docteur rédige: .... grands jureurs .... climat brûlant......
Et sur la tête aussi.
Le Docteur rédige: ..... marchent indifféremment sur les pieds ou sur la tête.
Et en façon natatoire
Le Docteur rédige: .... ils sautent comme des carpes.
Et en tourbillonnant.
Le Docteur rédige: .... ils tourbillonnent comme des Démons.
17.

Convinced (for passion blinds, alas) that it is Mrs. Jolibois and her vile seducer who have had him caged, Mr. Jolibois gives way to boundless fits of jealousy.

The Professor writes: . . . . very profane . . . . scorching climate . . . . . .

And upside down as well.

The Professor writes . . . . walk on their feet or their head alike.

And in a natatory fashion.

The Professor writes: . . . . they jump about like carps.

And whirling.

The Professor writes: . . . . they whirl about like Demons.

En ayant assez des bourgeois et des bourgeoises, le petit Zéphir rebrousse pour chercher le dessin, ensorte que Madame Jolibois commence à redescendre.
Ce que voyant, Mr Jolibois, (car, hélas, la passion aveugle) il ramasse le scalpel laissé dans la volière, et il s'en sert pour couper un des barreaux.
Et sans attendre que son épouse ait pris terre, il l'accueille (car, hélas, la passion aveugle,) à coups de barreau de cage.
18.

Tiring of burghers and their wives, the little Zephyr returns to look for the drawing, so that Mrs. Jolibois begins to descend again.

Seeing which (for passion blinds, alas), Mr. Jolibois picks up the scalpel left in the birdcage, and uses it to cut one of the bars.

And without waiting for his wife to land, he greets her (for passion blinds, alas) with blows from the cage bar.

Madame Jolibois ayant crié : Au Secours!! .... le Docteur quitte la rédaction pour l'observation. Il examine l'effet produit par la vue d'une dame de notre globe sur un habitant de Psyché ; et il note dans son esprit les plus petites circonstances.
Le Docteur rédige.
19.
La Science étant satisfaite, le Docteur juge bon d'aller délivrer Mad^e. Jolibois; mais Mr Jolibois juge mauvais qu'on se mêle de ses affaires, (car, hélas, la passion aveugle) et il tourne sa fureur contre le Docteur. Mad^e. Jolibois profite du quart d'heure pour s'enfuir.

Mrs. Jolibois cries: Help! ! . . . . and the Professor leaves writing for observation. He studies the effect produced on an inhabitant of Psyche by the sight of a lady of our globe; and he makes a mental note of the minutest circumstances.

The Professor writes.

With science satisfied, the Professor sees fit to go to the rescue of Mrs. Jolibois; but Mr. Jolibois sees him unfit to meddle in his affairs (for passion blinds, alas), and turns his fury against the Professor. Madame Jolibois takes advantage of this moment to flee.

Le Docteur poursuivi jusque dans son cabinet est secouru par sa Servante qui trouve moyen d'y enfermer Monsieur Jolibois.
Après quoi le Docteur rédige la chose le moins péniblement qu'il peut :
. . . . ils assènent des horions formidables
Madame Jolibois qui se croit poursuivie se cache dans la meule où est tombé le bourgeois. Mr. Jolibois qui assiste à ce spectacle, de la fenêtre du cabinet, se persuade (car, hélas, la passion aveugle) que c'est un rendez-vous.
20.

Pursued into his study, the Professor is saved by his maid, who manages to lock Mr. Jolibois up in it.

After which the Professor writes the matter up as painlessly as possible: . . . . they inflict terrific beatings.

Believing that she is being pursued, Mrs. Jolibois hides in the haystack where the burgher fell. Observing the spectacle from the study window, Mr. Jolibois (for passion blinds, alas) convinces himself that it is a rendezvous.

Cependant le petit Zéphir rencontrant le nouveau dessin de Mr. Pencil s'amuse à le faire voltiger

Mr. Pencil ne voulant pas céder son dessin, se trouve avoir affaire au petit Zéphir.

Mr. Pencil essaie de se retenir au chapeau d'un particulier.

21.

Meanwhile the little Zephyr finds Mr. Pencil's new drawing and playfully makes it flutter about.

Unwilling to give up his drawing, Mr. Pencil finds himself having to deal with the little Zephyr.

Mr. Pencil tries to hold on to an individual's hat.

M^r. Pencil ayant eu du dessous est enlevé à une hauteur prodigieuse.
Heureusement que, laissé par le Zéphir, il vient tomber sur la meule.
Voyant cela, (car hélas la passion aveugle) M^r. Jolibois croit que c'est encore un sé=ducteur, et il prend mal de jalousie ren=trée.
Le Docteur se hâte de profiter de cette léthargie pour lier son Psychiote, et le suspendre dans son cabinet d'a=nimaux.
22.

Having lost out, Mr. Pencil is carried to a prodigious height.

Fortunately, dropped by the Zephyr, he lands on the haystack.

Seeing this (for passion blinds, alas), Mr. Jolibois thinks that it is another seducer, and becomes ill with suppressed jealousy.

The Professor hastens to profit from this lethargy to tie his Psychiot up, and hang him in his animal collection.

Revenu à lui, Mr. Jolibois, (car, Hélas, la passion aveugle) se persuade que les deux vils séducteurs, de concert avec son épouse, l'ont livré aux bêtes, et ses cheveux se dressent sur sa tête.

L'Académie Royale écoute la lecture du Mémoire sur un Vent Souterrain tout nouveau, et nomme une commission de trois membres pour analyser le contenu des phioles. 23.

Regaining consciousness, Mr. Jolibois (for passion blinds, alas) convinces himself that the two vile seducers, in complicity with his wife, have thrown him to the beasts, and his hair stands on end.

The Royal Society hears a reading of the report on the entirely new subterranean wind, and appoints a commission of three members to analyze the contents of the phials.

La commission procède à l'analyse du contenu.
Le gaz s'étant dégagé, il s'en suit des soupçons atroces.
Et des explications très vives.
24.

The commission proceeds to the analysis of the contents.

As the gas is released, atrocious suspicions are aroused.

And very lively discussions.

Les phioles s'étant cassées au milieu du désordre, les trois Savans tom=
bent asphyxiés.

Cependant le chien du
bourgeois en cherchant
à se tirer d'affaire
fait légèrement basculer
le télégraphe.

Aussitôt toutes les lignes télégraphiques basculent lé=
gèrement

25

When the phials break amidst all the disorder, the three scientists collapse asphyxiated.

Meanwhile the burgher's dog tries to get down and causes the telegraph to tip slightly.

Immediately all the telegraph lines tip slightly.

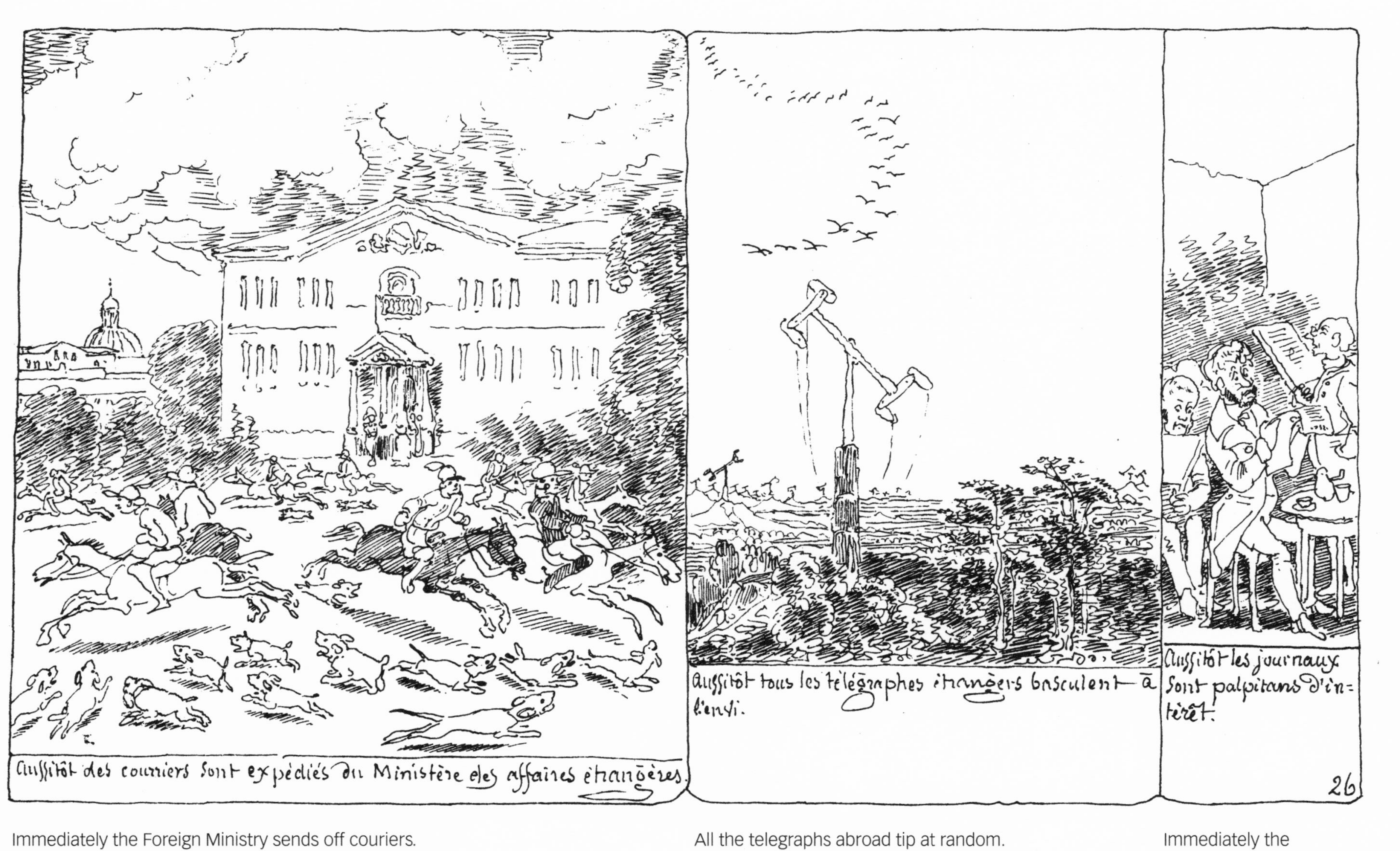
Aussitôt des courriers sont expédiés du Ministère des affaires étrangères.
Aussitôt tous les télégraphes étrangers basculent à l'envi.
Aussitôt les journaux sont palpitans d'intérêt.
26

Immediately the Foreign Ministry sends off couriers.

All the telegraphs abroad tip at random.

Immediately the newspapers become of palpitating interest.

Les politiques prévoient une rupture funeste entre les cinq puissances.

The politicians foresee a fatal rupture between the five powers.

Le trois pour cent est lourd.

The three percents are sluggish.

Les sucres fléchissent.

Sugars weaken.

Les cafés languissent

Coffees languish.

Les ateliers se ferment et il se forme des attroupements d'ouvriers.

27.

Workshops close, and workers gather into mobs.

Le ministre annonce à la Chambre que trois cent mille hommes menacent la frontière.

The Minister announces to the Chamber that three hundred thousand men are threatening the frontier.

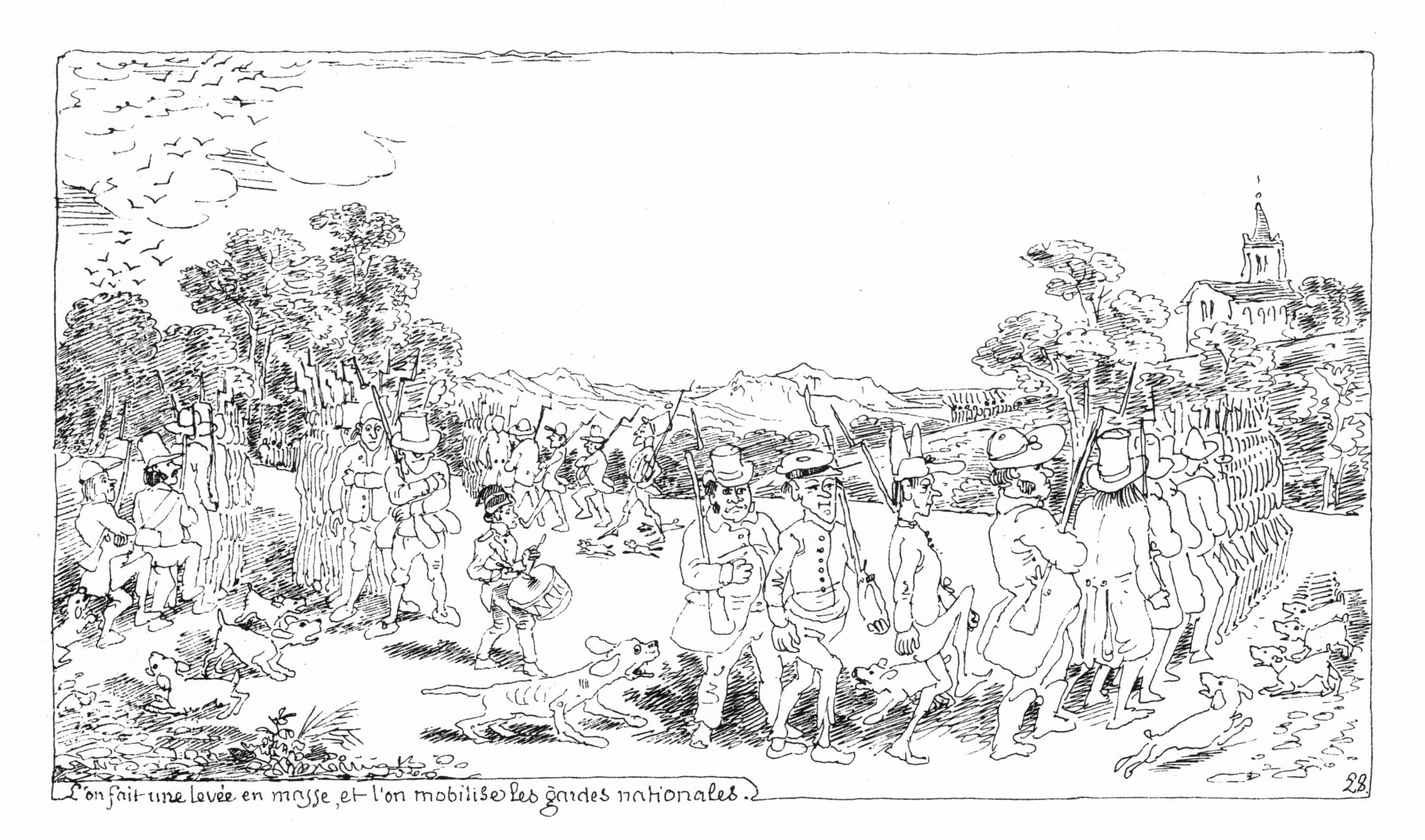
L'on fait une levée en masse, et l'on mobilise les gardes nationales.
28.

There is a mass levy of troops, and the national guard is mobilized.

Et on les forme aux grandes manoeuvres.

There are drills, and grand maneuvers.

Et l'on fait la remonte des chevaux.
29.

Horses are sent for cavalry remounting.

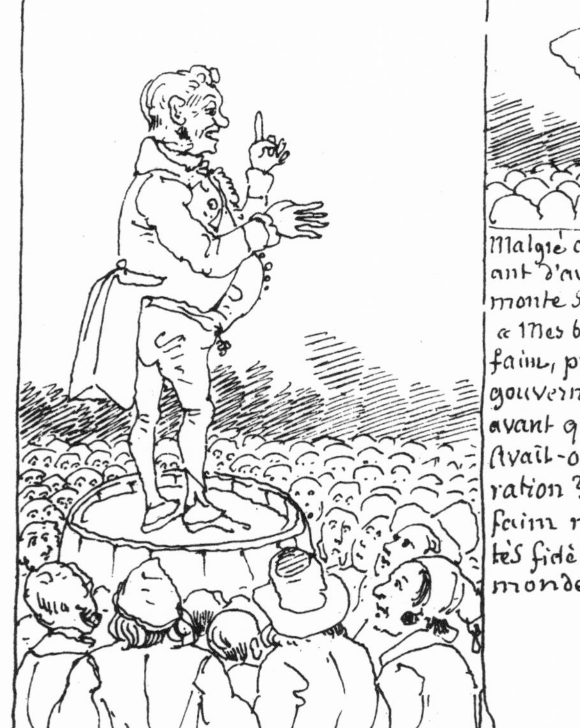
Cependant les Ouvriers continuant à demander du pain par attroupemens, Mr Mondor monte sur un tonneau:
« Mes bons amis, tout tient à la rente. En ce moment la rente monte; ne bougez pas et alors elle montera plus haut encore, et alors les capitalistes voudront faire valoir leurs fonds, et alors vous aurez du pain!
Malgré cela les ouvriers continuant d'avoir faim, Mr de Pibrac monte sur le tonneau:
« Mes bons amis, si vous avez faim, prenez-vous-en à votre gouvernement. Avait-on faim avant quatre vingt neuf? Non. Avait-on faim sous la restauration? Non. Avons-nous faim nous qui sommes restés fidèles? Pas le moins du monde!
Malgré cela les Ouvriers continuant d'avoir faim Mr Grelot monte sur le tonneau:
« Mes bons, mes excellens amis, je pleure sur vous. Mais pour guérir vos maux, il faudrait l'occupation de la Belgique, l'épuration des Préfets, la chûte du trône et la guerre générale!!..
Malgré cela, les Ouvriers continuant d'avoir faim Mr Truffet monte sur le tonneau:
« Braves gens, retirez vous tranquillement, car les attroupemens peuvent nous conduire à l'anarchie, qui nous conduirait au despotisme militaire, qui nous conduirait à une troisième restauration!..
Malgré cela les Ouvriers continuant d'avoir faim Mr Raffle, St Simonien, monte sur le tonneau:
« Mes fils et mes filles! Tout est amour. La transmission par héritage est le dernier anneau de la chaîne des privilèges.
Mes pères et mes mères! Beaux-Arts, Sciences, industrie! À chacun selon sa capacité, à chaque capacité selon ses oeuvres. Le passé est fini. L'avenir commence. Encore mille ans, et tout ira bien!
30.

Meanwhile the mobs of workers continue to make demands for bread, and Mr. Mondor gets up on a barrel: "My good friends, it all depends on revenues. At the moment, revenues are rising; stay put, and they will rise further still, and then the capitalists will want to sell their stocks, and then you will have bread!"

In spite of that the Workers still continue to go hungry, and Mr. Pibrac gets up on the barrel: "My good friends, if you are hungry, blame your government. Was there hunger before eighty-nine? No. Was there hunger under the Restoration? No. Are we hungry, we who remained faithful? Not in the least!"

In spite of that, the Workers continue to go hungry, and Mr. Grelot gets up on the barrel: "My good, my excellent friends, I weep upon you. But in order to cure your woes, we would have to occupy Belgium, clean out the Prefecture, overthrow the throne, and have a general war! ! . ."

In spite of that, the Workers continue to go hungry, and Mr. Truffet gets up on the barrel: "Good people, go quietly home, for demonstrations like this may lead to anarchy, which would lead to a military despotism, which would lead to a third restoration! . ."

In spite of that, the Workers continue to go hungry, Mr. Raffle, Saint-Simonian, gets up on the barrel: "My sons and daughters! All is love. Inheritance laws are the last link in the chain of privilege.

My fathers and mothers! Fine Arts, Science, Industry. To each according to his capacity, to each according to his work. The past is over. The future begins. Another thousand years, and all will be well!

La garde nationale dissipe l'attroupement par la persuasion.
Cependant le Docteur ayant achevé son mémoire, emballe son Psychiote et son mémoire, qu'il adresse à l'Académie Royale.
Ce qui est cause que Mr. Jolibois (car hélas la passion aveugle) voyage franc de port sur l'impériale de la malleposte
31.

The national guard uses persuasion to disperse the mob.

Meanwhile, having finished his report, the Professor packs up his Psychiot and his report, which he addresses to the Royal Society.

Which causes Mr. Jolibois (for passion blinds, alas) to travel carriage-free on the roof of the mail coach.

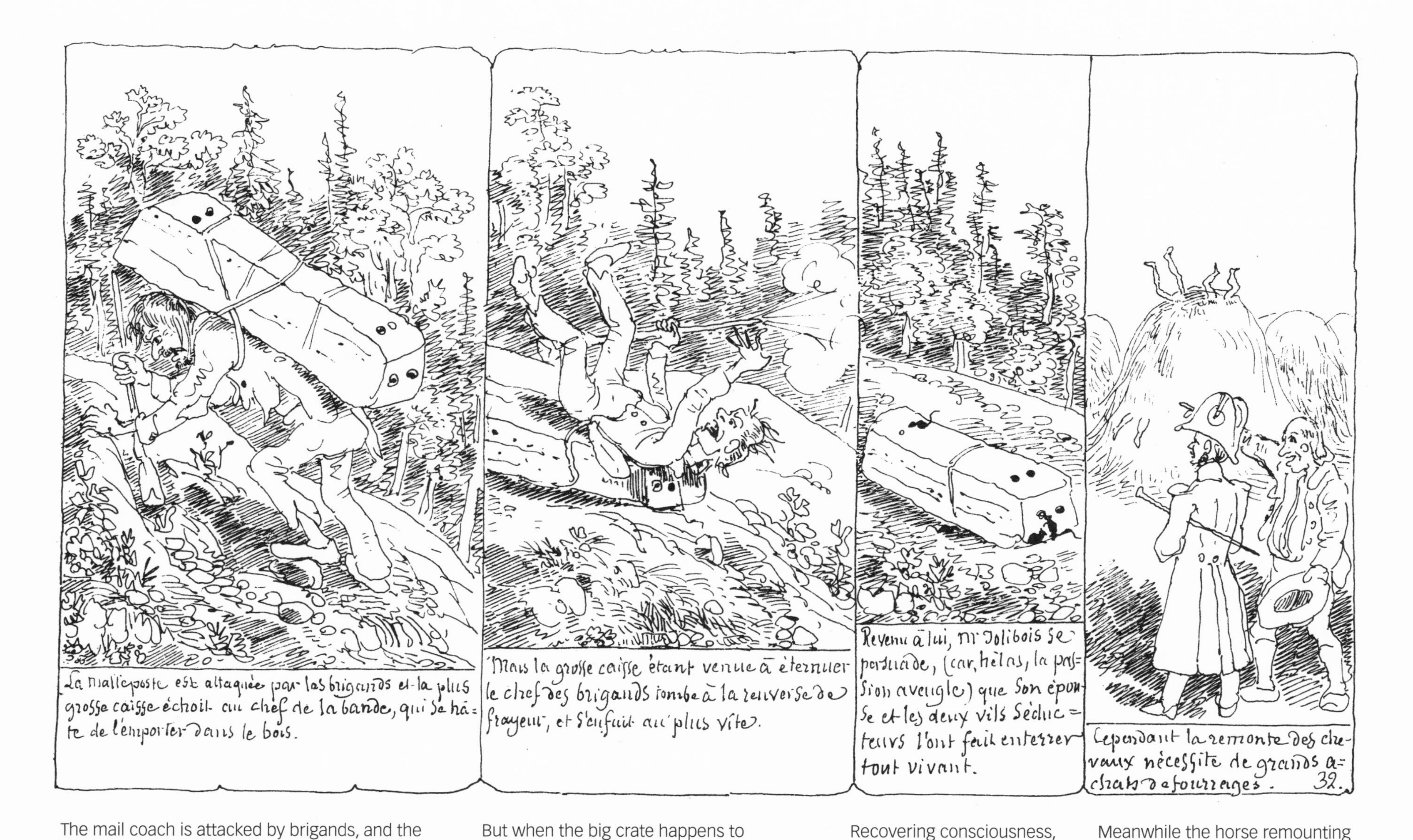
La malleposte est attaquée par les brigands et la plus grosse caisse échoit au chef de la bande, qui se hâte de l'emporter dans le bois.
Mais la grosse caisse étant venue à éternuer le chef des brigands tombe à la renverse de frayeur, et s'enfuit au plus vite.
Revenu à lui, Mr Jolibois se persuade, (car, hélas, la passion aveugle) que son épouse et les deux vils séducteurs l'ont fait enterrer tout vivant.
Cependant la remonte des chevaux nécessite de grands achats de fourrages.
32.

The mail coach is attacked by brigands, and the biggest crate falls to the chief of the band, who hastily carries it off into the wood.

But when the big crate happens to sneeze, the brigand chief falls over backwards with fright, and flees as fast as he can.

Recovering consciousness, Mr. Jolibois is convinced (for passion blinds, alas) that his wife and the two vile seducers have had him buried alive.

Meanwhile the horse remounting necessitates great purchases of forage.

Les fourrages ayant été achetés sont livrés au vingtième-léger.

Once bought, the forage is delivered to the Twentieth Light (cavalry).

qui les livre à ses chevaux.

33.

Who deliver it to their horses.

Après qu'ils se sont familiarisés avec la situation, Mde Jolibois et ses deux cavaliers se servent des chevaux pour fuir, pendant que le Vingtième-léger joue aux quilles.
34.

As soon as they have acquainted themselves with the situation, Mrs. Jolibois and her two escorts use the horses for their getaway, while the Twentieth Light play skittles.

S'étant aperçus de quelque chose, le Vingtième Léger se met à la poursuite des voleurs.

En poursuivant les voleurs le Vingtième Léger gâte beaucoup de blés.

35.

Noticing that something is up, the Twentieth Light set off in pursuit of the thieves.

In pursuit of the thieves, the Twentieth Light do great damage to the corn.

Pour plus de vitesse, le Vingtième Léger s'aide des chariots et des montures des paysans
36.

To increase their speed, the Twentieth Light help themselves to the carts and mounts of the peasants.

Le Vingtième Léger ouvre les écluses pour inonder les lieux bas à cause des voleurs.

Le Vingtième Léger brûle un bois pour incendier les lieux hauts, à cause des voleurs.

37.

après quoi, le Vingtième Léger ayant chaud se fait rafraîchir par le Maire

The Twentieth Light open the sluices so as to flood the low-lying land, because of the thieves.

The Twentieth Light set a wood on fire so as to burn off the high-lying land, because of the thieves.

After which, being hot, the Twentieth Light partake of refreshments at the Mayor's.

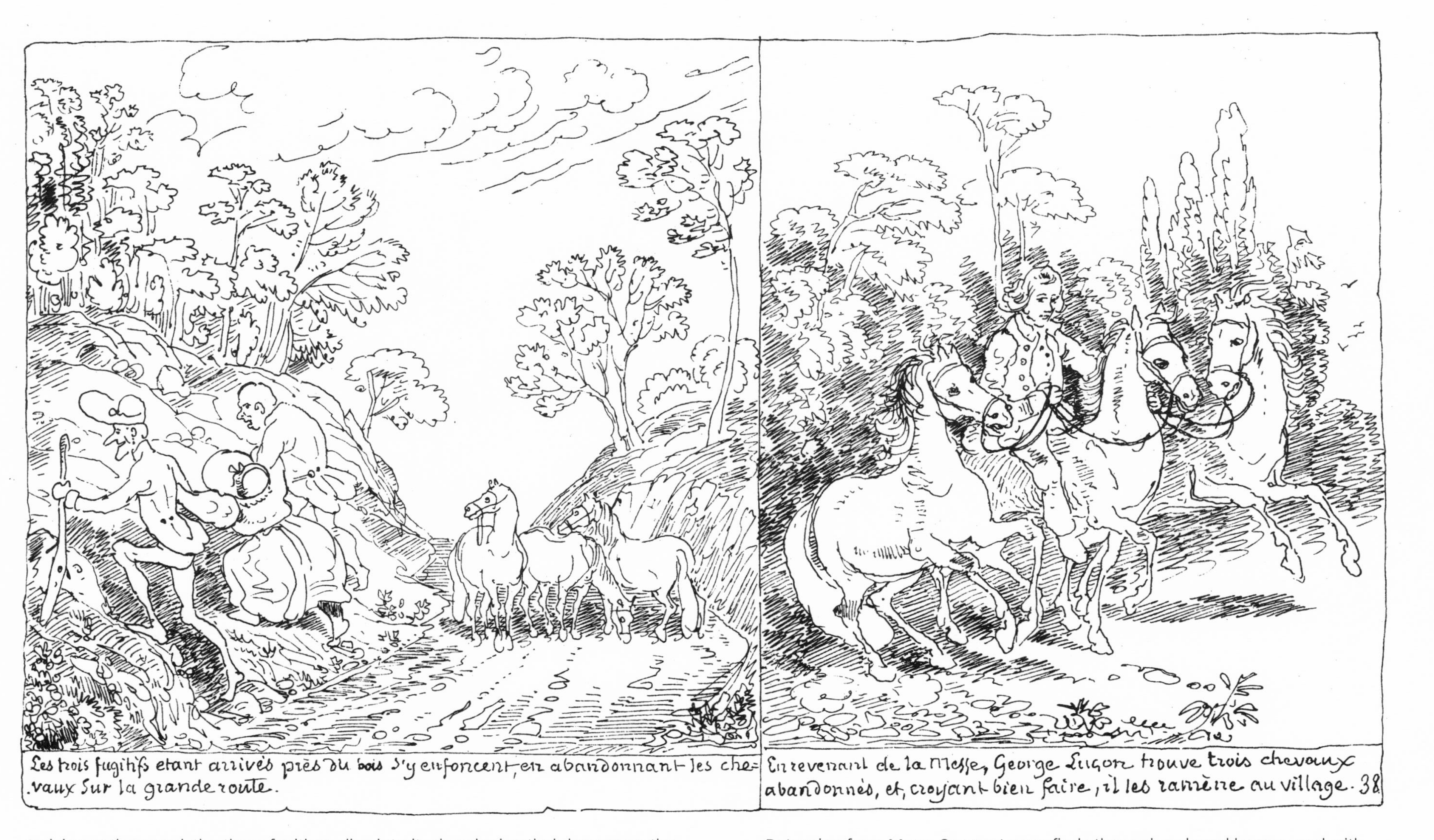
Les trois fugitifs etant arrivés près du bois s'y enfoncent, en abandonnant les che-
vaux sur la grande route.
En revenant de la Messe, George Luçon trouve trois chevaux
abandonnés, et, croyant bien faire, il les ramène au village. 38

Arriving at the wood, the three fugitives dive into it, abandoning their horses on the highway.

Returning from Mass, George Luçon finds three abandoned horses, and with the best intentions, brings them back to the village.

Comme il passe devant le jardin du Maire, George Luçon se voit arrêté par le Vingtième Léger et traîné devant le Conseil de guerre.

Ouïs les témoins, et le flagrant délit constaté, George Luçon est condamné à être fusillé 39.

Passing by the Mayor's garden, George Luçon finds himself arrested by the Twentieth Light, and hauled before a Court-martial.

The witnesses heard, and the heinous crime proven, George Luçon is condemned to be shot.

Le vingtième Léger ayant bu un coup de trop chez le Maire, manque Geor=
ge Luçon et pique le Capitaine Ricard qui a commandé le feu.
George Luçon n'attend pour ressusciter que de voir le Vingtième Léger un peu plus loin.
40.

Having drunk a glass too much at the Mayor's, the Twentieth Light miss George Luçon, and hit Captain Ricard who gave the firing order.

To come to life again, George Luçon waits only to see the Twentieth Light a bit further off in the distance.

Après que le Vingtième Léger s'est éloigné, George Luçon revêt les habits du Capitaine Ricard, l'habille des siens, et gagne les champs. Ce qui est cause que le Capitaine Ricard est enterré sans les honneurs militaires.

41.

Once the Twentieth Light have disappeared, George Luçon puts on Captain Ricard's clothes, dresses the captain in his own, and takes to the fields. Which causes Captain Ricard to be buried without military honors.

Cependant Mr. Jolibois (car, hélas, la passion aveugle) est inquiété par les rats qui ont agrandi les trous de la caisse.

Meanwhile Mr. Jolibois is bothered (for passion blinds, alas) by the rats which have enlarged the holes in his crate.

Cependant les trois fugitifs qui sont harassés de fatigue, ont le malheur de s'asseoir sur une fourmilière.

Meanwhile, overcome with fatigue, the three fugitives are unfortunate enough to sit down on an anthill.

Ce qui triple leurs démangeaisons.
Heureusement qu'ayant trouvé la caisse ils vont s'y asseoir à l'abri des fourmis.
42.

Which triples their itching.

Finding the crate, they are fortunately able to sit down free of the ants.

A peine Mr. Jolibois a-t-il reconnu la voix de son épouse, (car hélas la passion aveugle) que, poussant une apostrophe immense et désordonnée, il cherche à se ressaisir de l'infidèle.

43.

Croyant entendre le Vingtième Léger, George Luçon tire sur la gauche.

As soon as Mr. Jolibois recognizes the voice of his wife (for passion blinds, alas), emitting an immense, disordered reprobation against her, he tries to grab hold of the unfaithful one.

Thinking he hears the Twentieth Light, George Luçon veers to the left.

Revenus de leur frayeur, Mr Pencil et le Bourgeois cherchent à délivrer Madame Jolibois.
44.
Entendant un bruit de caisson, George Luçon tire sur la droite.
Les pans de la veste de Mr Pencil ayant cédé, le Bourgeois roule jusqu'à la grande route où il prend place dans la diligence.

Recovering from their fright, Mr. Pencil and the Burgher try to rescue Mrs. Jolibois.

Hearing the sound of the crate, George Luçon veers to the right.

When Mr. Pencil's coattails give way, the Burgher rolls backwards onto the highway, where he takes a seat in the coach.

Entendant rouler, George Luçon tire sur la gauche.

Hearing the sound of carriage wheels, George Luçon veers to the left.

Mr. Pencil ayant eu une idée, délivre Mde Jolibois au moyen d'une paire de ciseaux.

Mr. Pencil has an idea, and rescues Mrs. Jolibois with the aid of a pair of scissors.

Mr. Jolibois, (car hélas la passion aveugle) essaie de poursuivre l'infidèle.

Mr. Jolibois (for passion blinds, alas) attempts to pursue the unfaithful one.

George Luçon croyant voir l'ombre du cercueil du Capitaine Ricard, fuit épouvanté.

45.

George Luçon thinks he sees the shadow of the coffin of Captain Ricard, and flees in horror.

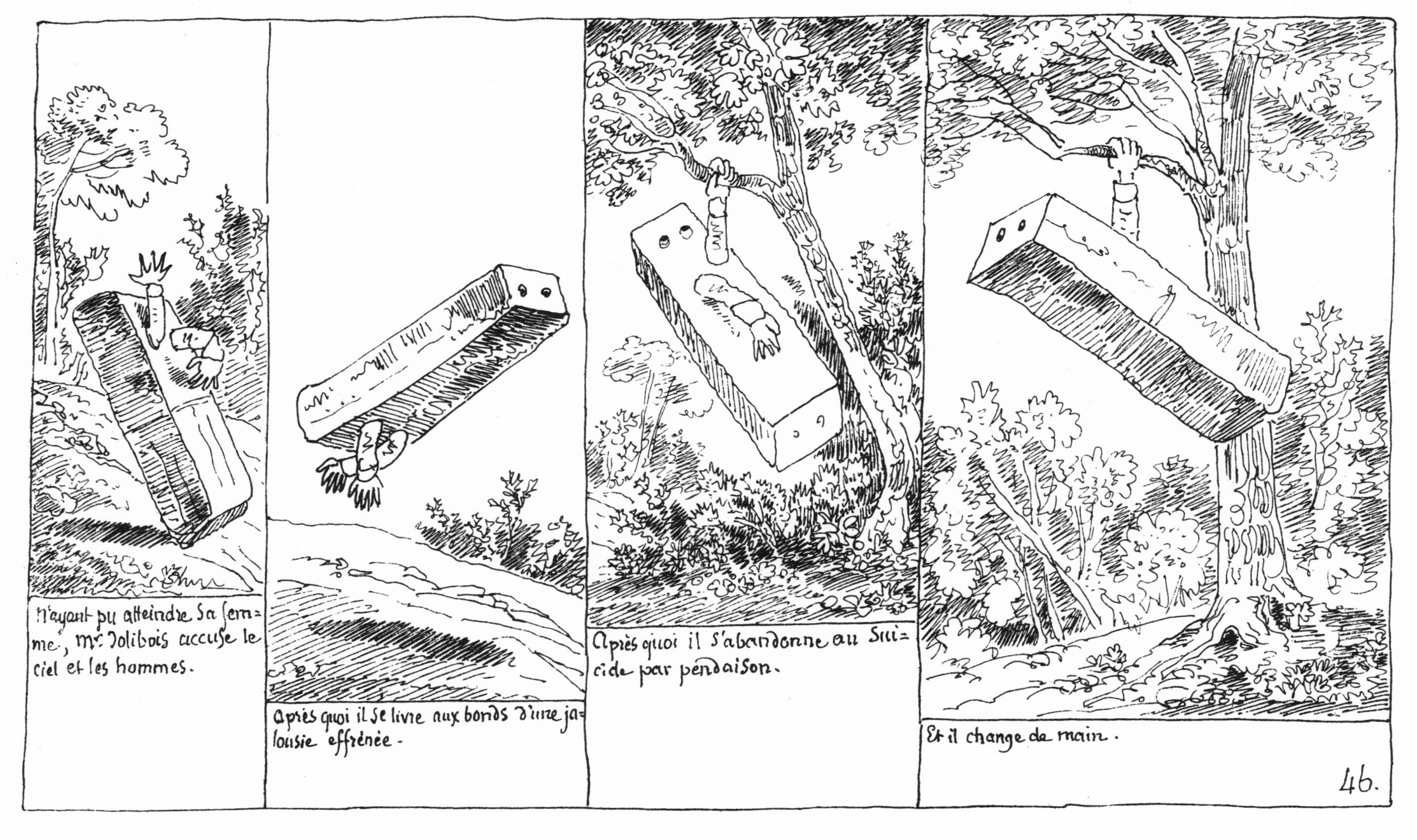
N'ayant pu atteindre sa femme, Mr. Jolibois accuse le ciel et les hommes.
Après quoi il se livre aux bonds d'une jalousie effrénée.
Après quoi il s'abandonne au suicide par pendaison.
Et il change de main.
46.

Unable to reach his wife, Mr. Jolibois accuses heaven and man.

After which he gives himself up to the springs of frenetic jealousy.

After which he gives way to suicide by hanging.

And changes hands.

Après quoi, il essaie des charmes d'une mélancolie contemplative.

After which, he tries the charms of contemplative melancholy.

Cependant George Luçon ayant trop tiré sur la gauche, tombe au milieu du vingtième léger
qui est à la recherche du Capitaine Ricard.
47.

Meanwhile, having veered too far to the left, George Luçon runs into the Twentieth Light looking for Captain Ricard.

Se voyant reconnu à l'habit pour le Capitaine Ricard, George Luçon commande la manoeuvre au bord du lac Batracien et crie : À droite, alignement ! ! . . .
Puis : Pas accéléré, en avant, ... Marche ! ! . . . . et tout le Vingtième Léger tombe dans l'eau.
48.

Seeing that he is taken, by his costume, for Captain Ricard, George Luçon drills them at the edge of the Batracian lake, and cries: By the right, dress! ! . .

Then: At the double, forward, ... March! ! . . . . and the entire Twentieth Light fall into the water.

Cependant la diligence passant au pied du Télégraphe, le bourgeois croit reconnaître son chien perché sur l'instrument et il prie le conducteur de faire arrêter.
Après quoi, le bourgeois étant monté sur l'impériale, il a le bonheur d'attraper le chien par la patte.
Malheureusement le chien se met à hurler, et les chevaux s'emportent.
49.

Meanwhile, the coach passing by the foot of the telegraph, the Burgher thinks he recognizes his dog perched on top of the apparatus, and begs the driver to stop.

After which, the burgher climbs on top of the coach, and manages to seize the dog by the paw.

Unfortunately, the dog begins to howl, and the horses bolt.

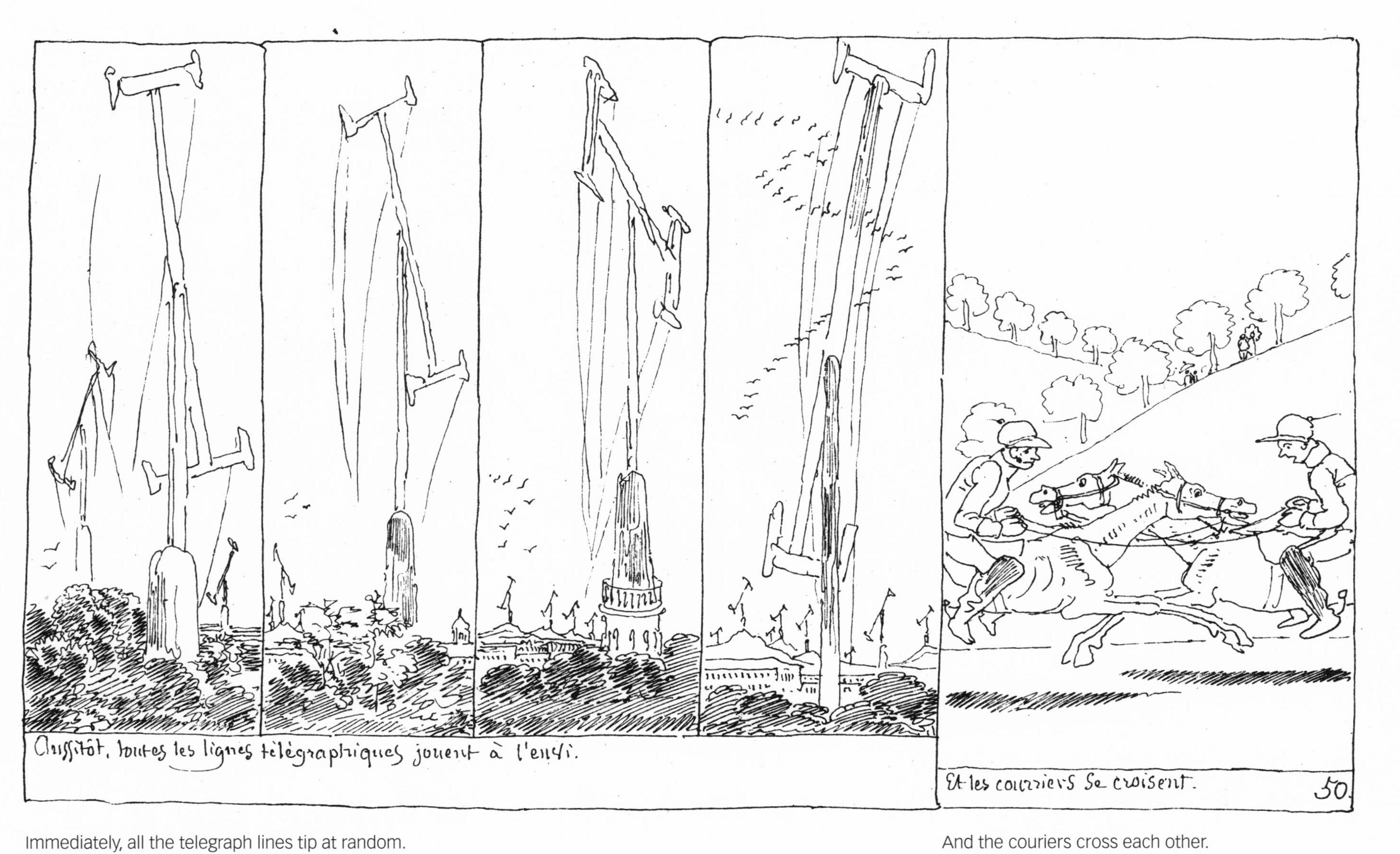
Aussitôt, toutes les lignes télégraphiques jouent à l'envi.
Et les courriers se croisent.
50

Immediately, all the telegraph lines tip at random.

And the couriers cross each other.

Et le Ministre de la guerre imprime une immense activité à ses bureaux
51.

And the War Minister exacts immense activity from his offices.

Et les journaux redeviennent palpitans d'intérêt.
Et l'on chante la Marseillaise.
Et l'on chante Henri Quatre.
52.

And the newspapers become once again of palpitating interest.

And the [revolutionary] *Marseillaise* is sung.

And *God Save the King* is sung.

Ce qui amène des discordances,

des gendarmes,

et des plaies et bosses.

53.

Which leads to differences of opinion,

police,

and cuts and bruises.

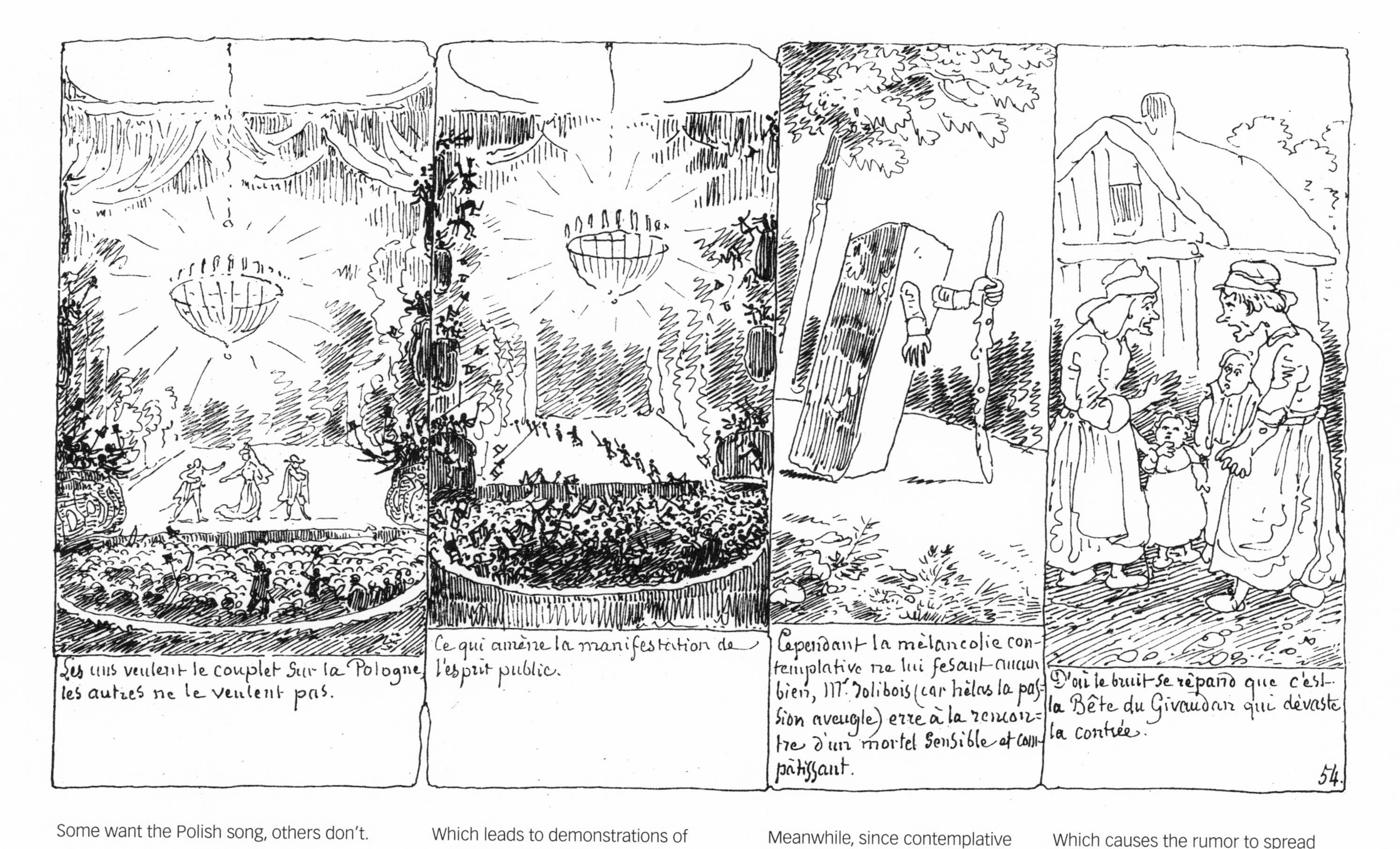
Les uns veulent le couplet sur la Pologne les autres ne le veulent pas.
Ce qui amène la manifestation de l'esprit public.
Cependant la mélancolie contemplative ne lui fesant aucun bien, Mr. Jolibois (car hélas la passion aveugle) erre à la rencontre d'un mortel sensible et compatissant.
D'où le bruit se répand que c'est la Bête du Givaudan qui dévaste la contrée.
54.

Some want the Polish song, others don't.

Which leads to demonstrations of public opinion.

Meanwhile, since contemplative melancholy does him no good at all, Mr. Jolibois (for passion blinds, alas), wanders about looking for some sensitive and compassionate mortal.

Which causes the rumor to spread that it is the Beast of Gévaudan devastating the country.

Le Maire se met à la tête d'une battue, et l'on aperçoit la bête qui grimpe sur un noyer de cinq ans.

Voyant tant de mortels sensibles, et un maire compâtissant (car hélas la passion aveugle) la Bête accourt à grands pas, et toute la battue s'enfuit à grands pas aussi. 55.

The Mayor places himself at the head of a scouting party, who see the beast climbing up a five-year-old walnut tree.

Seeing so many sensitive mortals, and a compassionate mayor (for passion blinds, alas), the Beast rushes forward, and the whole scouting party rushes backwards.

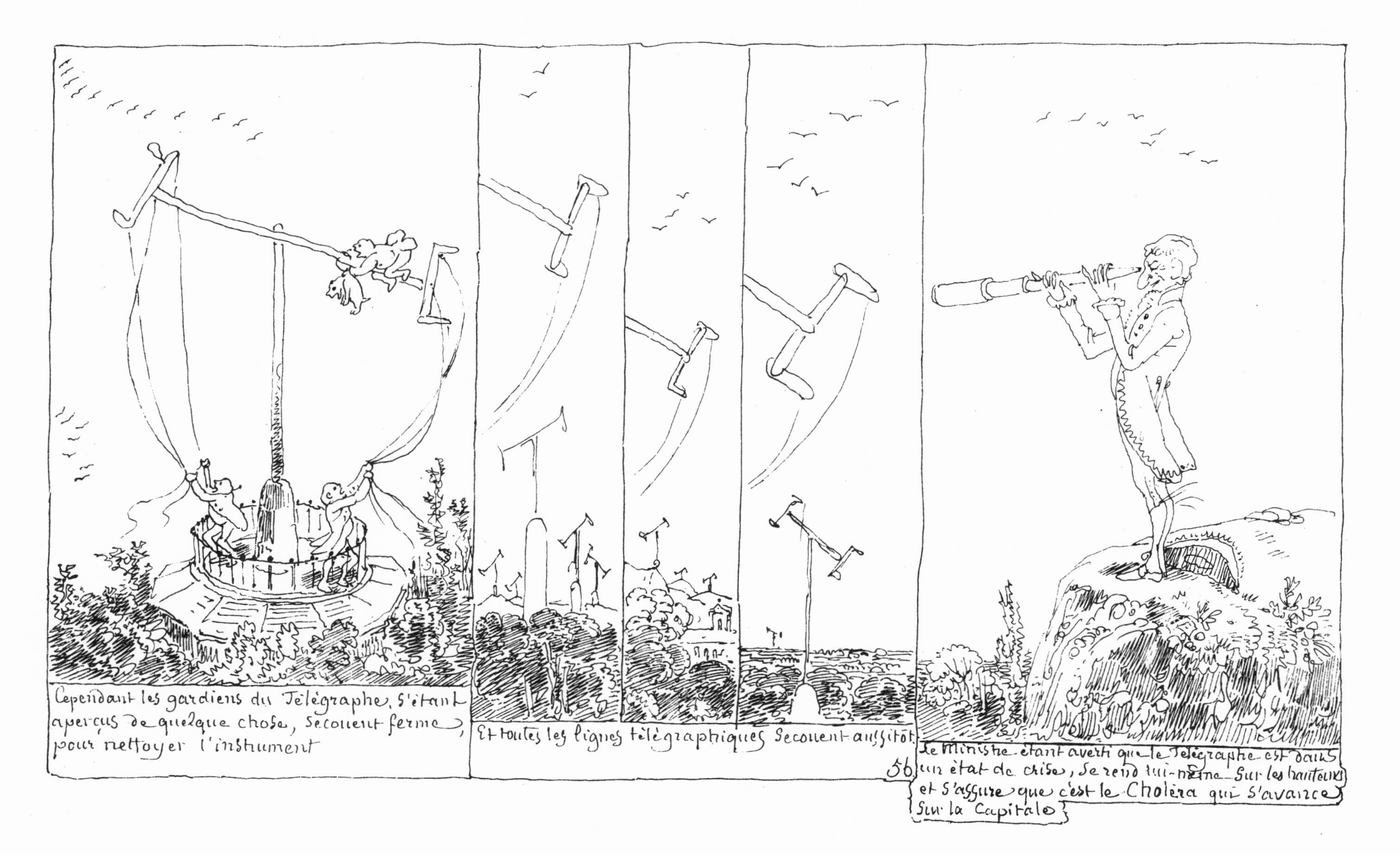
Cependant les gardiens du Télégraphe, s'étant aperçus de quelque chose, secouent ferme, pour nettoyer l'instrument
Et toutes les lignes télégraphiques secouent aussitôt.
56
Le Ministre étant averti que le Télégraphe est dans un état de crise, se rend lui-même sur les hauteurs et s'assure que c'est le Choléra qui s'avance sur la Capitale

Meanwhile the Telegraph attendants, noticing that something is up, shake the apparatus thoroughly in order to clear it.

And all the telegraph lines immediately shake likewise.

Informed that the telegraph is in a state of crisis, the Minister personally betakes himself to the hilltops, and ascertains that it is the cholera itself advancing on the capital.

Aussitôt Mr. Mondor joue à la baisse.

Mr. Mondor immediately speculates on a falling market.

Mr de Pibrac accuse l'usurpation.

Mr. de Pibrac makes charges of usurpation.

Mr. Grelot interpelle chaleureusement le Ministère.

Mr. Grelot warmly challenges the Minister.

Mr. Truffet se purge.

57.

Mr. Truffet takes a purgative.

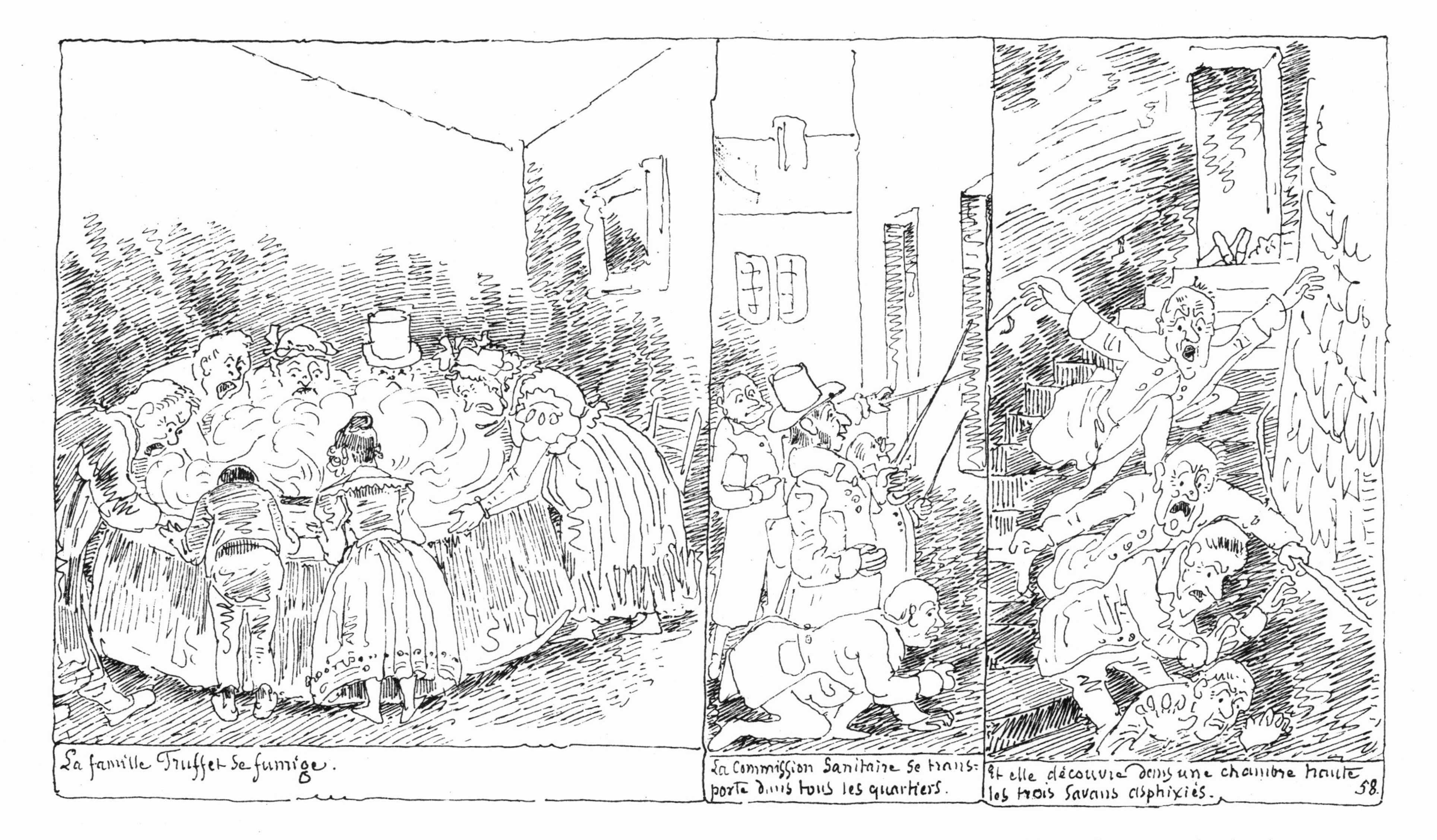
La famille Truffet se fumige.
La Commission Sanitaire se transporte dans tous les quartiers.
Et elle découvre dans une chambre haute les trois savans asphixiés.
58.

The Truffet family fumigate themselves.

The sanitary commission makes the rounds of the whole town.

They discover in an upper chamber three asphyxiated experts.

La Médecine ayant analysé les trois Savans déclare
qu'effectivement ils sont morts du Choléra.
EAUX MINERALE
PHARMACIE DE PURGON
Les Pharmaciens s'en frottent les mains.
Et les employés aux pompes funèbres prévoyant une belle
saison d'affaires, boivent à crédit.
59.

After examining the three experts, the medical profession declares that they did indeed die of cholera.

The Pharmacists rub their hands in anticipation.

And people in the funeral business, foreseeing a good season, drink on credit.

Cependant le Docteur ne recevant point de nouvelles ni de son mémoire, ni de son Psychiote, tombe dans un grand abattement.
A la fin, sur le conseil de sa servante, il se détermine à en aller chercher lui-même.
60.
En poursuivant la battue, Mr. Jolibois (car hélas la passion aveugle) arrive sur la grande route juste au moment où le Docteur y cheminait paisiblement.

Meanwhile, hearing no news either of his report or his Psychiot, the Professor falls into a great depression.

Finally, on his servant's advice, he decides to go look for them himself.

Pursuing the scouting party, Mr. Jolibois (for passion blinds, alas) reaches the highway just at the moment the Professor is passing peacefully by.

Le Docteur ayant reconnu son Psychiote en personne, descend précipitamment de cheval pour le prendre et le mettre en croupe
Mr. Jolibois ayant reconnu son Docteur (car hélas la passion aveugle) rebrousse précipitamment pour lui échapper.
Et se voyant poursuivi, il résiste.
61.

Recognizing his Psychiot in person, the Professor hurriedly gets off his horse in order to put him up behind.

Having recognized his Professor (for passion blinds, alas), Mr. Jolibois turns suddenly back in order to escape him.

And seeing that he is pursued, he resists.

Et voyant que la Servante s'en mêle, il détale.
La lutte s'engage.
Et la victoire se déclare.
62.

And seeing that the maid is joining in the fray, he scurries off.

Battle is engaged

And victory declared.

Après quoi le Docteur prend en croupe son Psychiote et continue son voyage.
LAZARET DES HOMMES
Arrivé à la frontière, le Docteur est mis en quarantaine et on lui prend ses effets pour les fumiger.
LAZARET DES Femmes
La Servante traite fort mal l'Inspecteur Sanitaire qui lui ordonnait de purger sa quarantaine, et elle lui réplique: Purge-toi toi-même, vieux démon!
63

After which the Professor puts his Psychiot up behind, and continues his journey.

Reaching the frontier, the Professor is put into quarantine and his effects are taken to be fumigated.

The maid mauls the sanitary Inspector who orders her to purge her quarantine, and she replies: Go purge yourself, you old demon!

Cependant Mr Pencil et Mde Jolibois arrivant au même lieu, la même invitation leur est faite. Mr Pencil répond qu'il s'est purgé en route; et Mde Jolibois qu'elle ne se purge jamais. Ce qui fait rire l'Officier sanitaire, homme de beaucoup d'esprit.
Les effets du Docteur sont fumigés. Mr Jolibois (car hélas la passion aveugle) y voit la continuation du complot tramé par sa femme et les deux vils séducteurs, et il suffoque de jalousie.
Les ais de la caisse ayant cédé, les deux valets de Santé n'ont que le temps de crier: au Choléra! … au Choléra!!
64.

Meanwhile Mr. Pencil and Mrs. Jolibois reach the same point (on the frontier), and receive the same invitation. Mr. Pencil replies that he has purged himself along the way and Mrs. Jolibois replies that she never purges herself. Which makes the sanitary officer, a man of great wit, laugh.

The Professor's effects are fumigated. Mr. Jolibois (for passion blinds, alas) sees a thickening of the plot hatched by his wife and the two vile seducers, and he suffocates with jealousy.

The planks of the crate give way, and the two sanitary assistants have only the time to shout: the Cholera! . . . the Cholera! ! !

à la vue du Choléra en personne les Officiers de
Santé prennent le mors aux dents.

At the sight of the Cholera in person, the health officials take the bit between their teeth.

Et les infirmiers aussi.

And the male nurses too.

Et les infirmières
pareillement.

And the female nurses similarly.

Heureusement la Servante s'aperçoit
que c'est le Psychiote de son maître
qui s'est échappé, et elle l'a bientôt
repris.
65.
aeiou

Fortunately the maid realizes that it is her master's Psychiot who has escaped, and she quickly seizes him.

Accourue au bruit Mme Jolibois reconnait que c'est son époux qui est enlevé par une femme.
Et à son tour (car hélas la passion a=veugle) elle ôte son chapeau pour s'abandonner aux amertumes de sa situation d'épouse.
Et aux larmes de sa position de mère.
Et aux rages de sa nature de femme,
66.

Running up at the noise, Mrs. Jolibois recognizes that it is her husband being abducted by a woman.

And in turn (for passion blinds, alas), she removes her hat in order to give herself up to the bitterness of her situation as wife.

And to the tears of her position as mother.

And to the rage of her nature as woman.

Après-quoi, dans un entretien intime, elle charge Mr. Pencil de lui rendre son époux et le bonheur inclusivement.
Cependant le Psychiote replacé dans un cabinet vitré, brise les vitres, et se montre de plus en plus indomptable et effréné.
67

After which, in an intimate conversation, she engages Mr. Pencil to bring back to her both husband and happiness.

Meanwhile, placed back in the glass cabinet, the Psychiot breaks the windows and proves more and more unmanageable and frantic.

Le Docteur commence à être fatigué de son Psychiote, et la Servante est d'avis qu'il faut s'en défaire.
Sur ces entrefaites Mr. Pencil introduit Mde Jolibois, et il expose qu'elle vient réclamer un époux
Le Docteur approuve fort, et la Servante ajoute qu'on le trouvera dans le cabinet vitré.
68.

The Professor begins to tire of his Psychiot, and the maid's advice is to get rid of him.

At this juncture Mr. Pencil introduces Mrs. Jolibois, and explains that she has come to reclaim a husband. The Professor approves strongly, and the maid adds that he can be found in the glass cabinet.

Première entrevue

First Interview.

Après quoi Mr Pencil prend la parole, et émet, à distance, des propos adoucissans.

69.

After which Mr. Pencil takes the floor, and makes, at a distance, some soothing remarks.

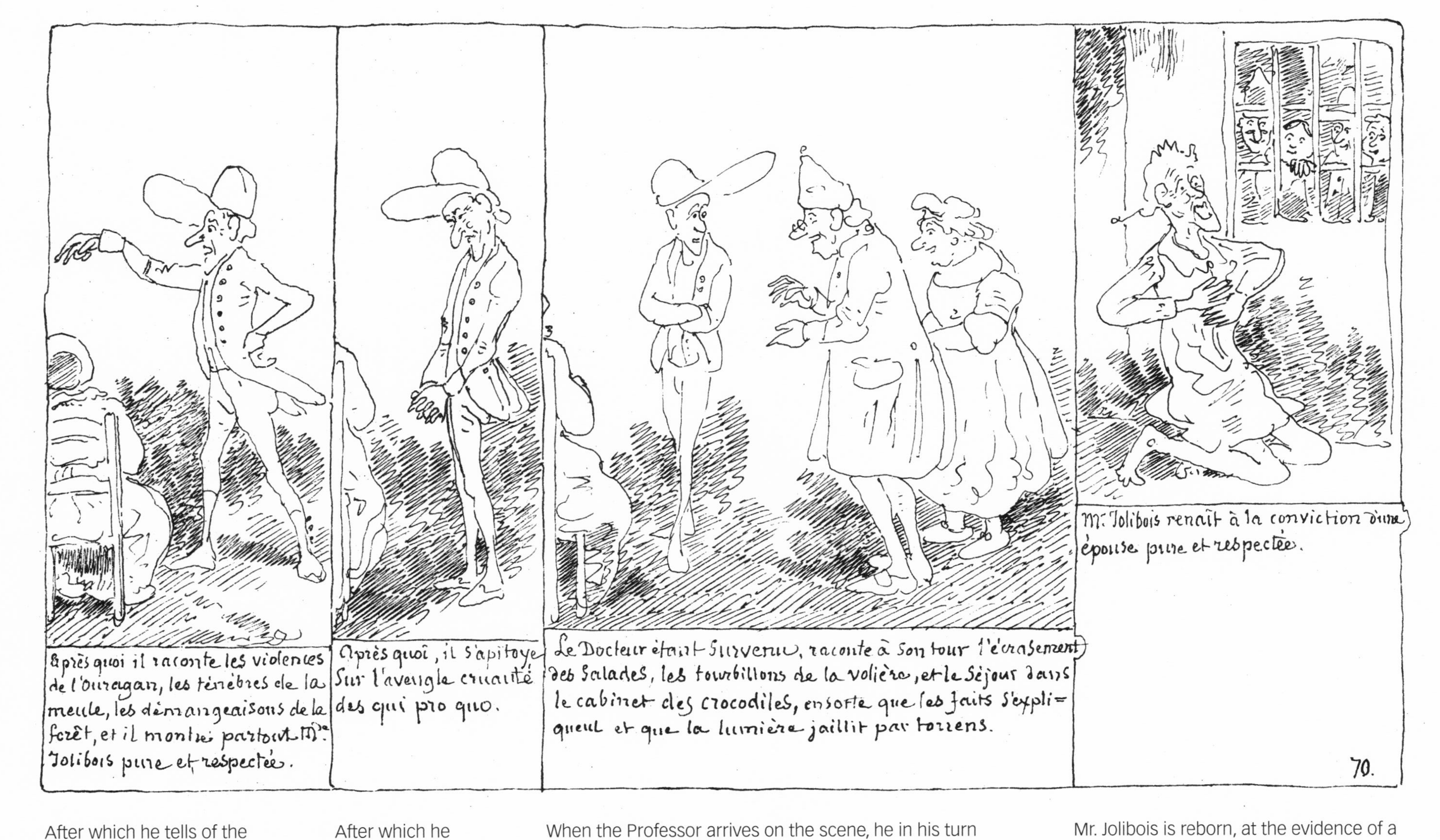
Après quoi il raconte les violences de l'ouragan, les ténèbres de la meule, les démangeaisons de la forêt, et il montre partout Mme Jolibois pure et respectée.
Après quoi, il s'apitoye sur l'aveugle cruauté des qui pro quo.
Le Docteur étant survenu, raconte à son tour l'écrasement des Salades, les tourbillons de la volière, et le séjour dans le cabinet des crocodiles, ensorte que les faits s'expliquent et que la lumière jaillit par torrens.
Mr. Jolibois renaît à la conviction d'une épouse pure et respectée.
70.

After which he tells of the violence of the Hurricane, the darkness of the haystack, the itching of the forest, and he shows how through it all, Mrs. Jolibois remained pure and respected.

After which he bewails the blind cruelty of this comedy of errors.

When the Professor arrives on the scene, he in his turn tells of the crushing of the lettuce, the whirlwinds of the birdcage, the sojourn in the crocodile cabinet, with the result that facts are cleared up, and enlightenment pours forth in torrents.

Mr. Jolibois is reborn, at the evidence of a pure and respected wife.

Etant tout à fait rené, Mr Jolibois (car hélas la passion ne l'aveugle plus) demande qu'on ouvre le cabinet vitré, et il se jette dans les bras de son épouse pure et respectée Mr Pencil embrasse la servante, et le Docteur s'embrasse lui-même.)
71.
Une voiture ayant été louée en commun, l'on reprend ensemble la route du pays, et l'on recueille en passant le bourgeois et son chien qui étaient restés sur le Télégraphe.)

Entirely reborn, Mr. Jolibois (for passion no longer blinds him, alas) asks that the glass cabinet be opened, and throws himself into the arms of his pure and respected wife. Mr. Pencil embraces the maid, and the Professor embraces himself.

Having rented a coach in common, they resume the road home, and pick up in passing the Burgher and his dog, who had remained stuck on the Telegraph.

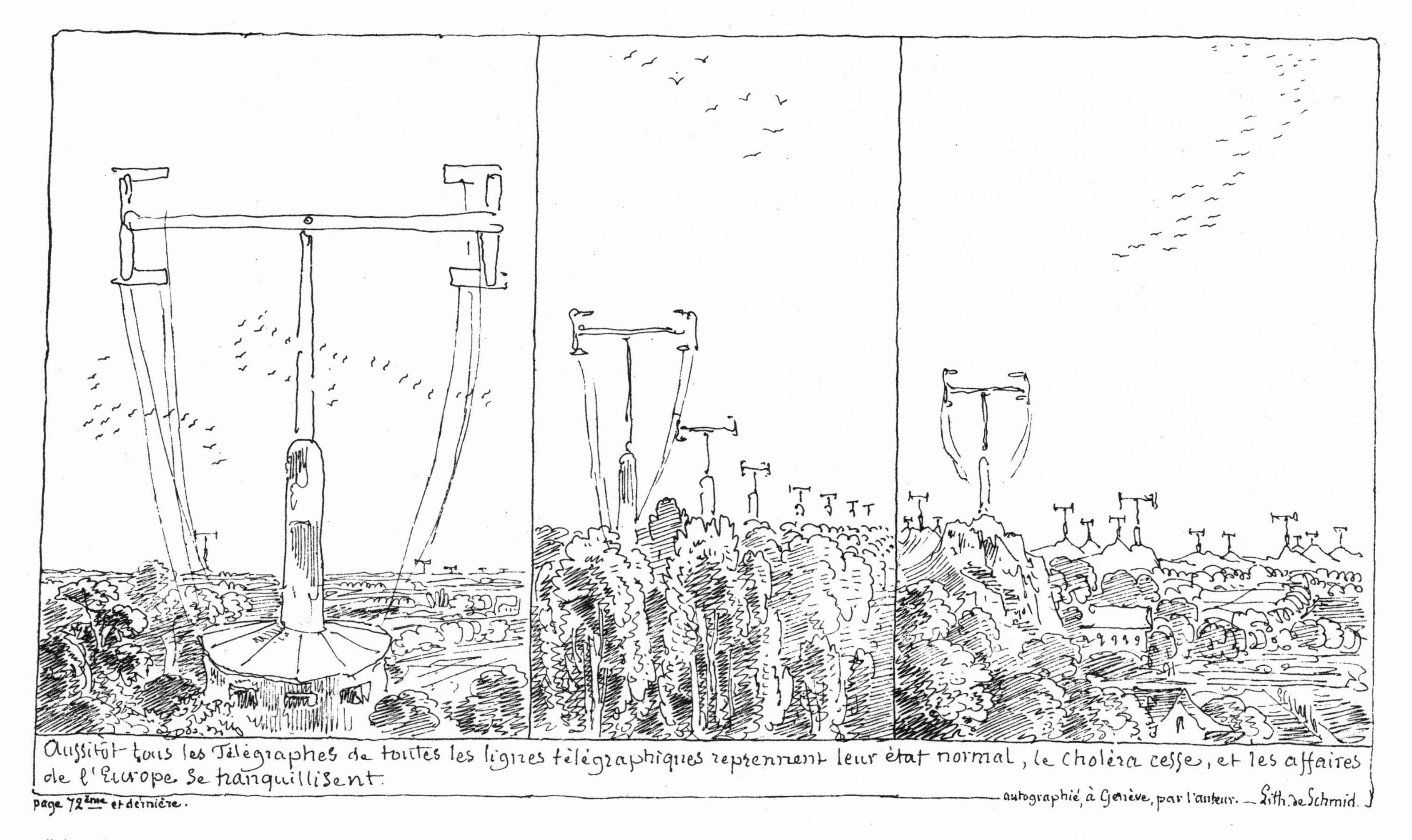
Aussitôt tous les Télégraphes de toutes les lignes télégraphiques reprennent leur état normal, le Choléra cesse, et les affaires de l'Europe se tranquillisent.
page 72ème et dernière.
autographié, à Genève, par l'auteur. — Lith. de Schmid.

All the Telegraphs of all the telegraphic lines resume their normal state, the cholera stops, and the European situation resumes its wonted calm.

Le Docteur Festus
PARIS
Librairie d'Abm. Cherbuliez et Cie. rue
de Tournon. 17.

In this notebook are represented to the life the Travels and Adventures of Dr. Festus, together with the misfortunes of the Mayor, the maneuvers of the Armed Force, and the facts concerning Milord and his wife.

Go little book and choose your world, for at crazy things, those who do not laugh, yawn; and those who do not yield, resist; and those who reason, are mistaken, and those who would keep a straight face, can please themselves.

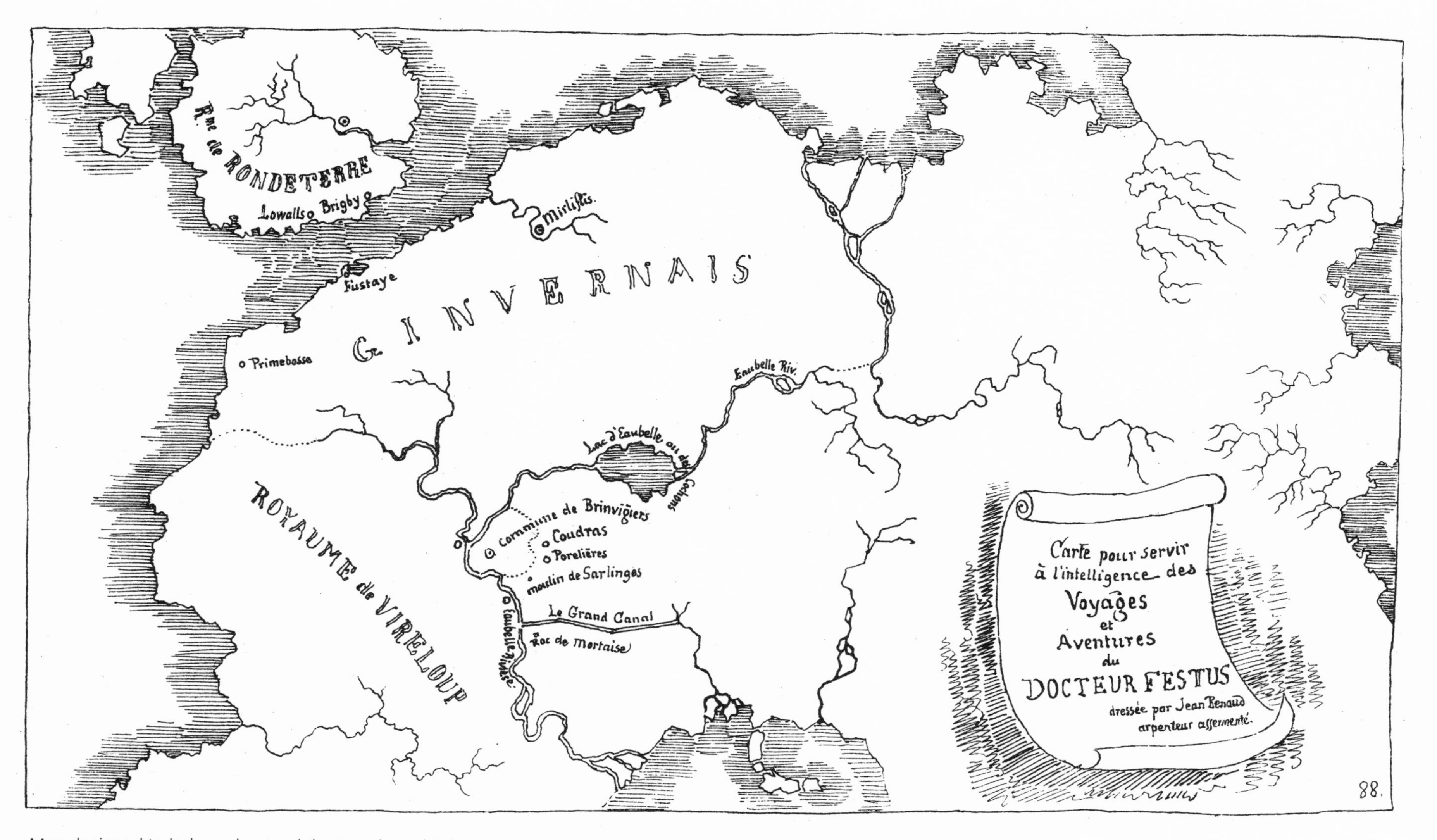

Map designed to help understand the Travels and Adventures of Dr. Festus, drawn up by Jean Renaud, sworn surveyor.

Étant entré un soir dans son écurie, le Docteur Festus y trouve un fort joli petit mulet.

Ayant attendu quatre ans, pour laisser grandir le mulet, le Docteur Festus part pour son grand voyage d'instruction.

2

Entering his stable one evening, Dr. Festus finds a very pretty little mule.

Having waited for four years to let the mule grow up, Dr. Festus leaves for his great educational tour.

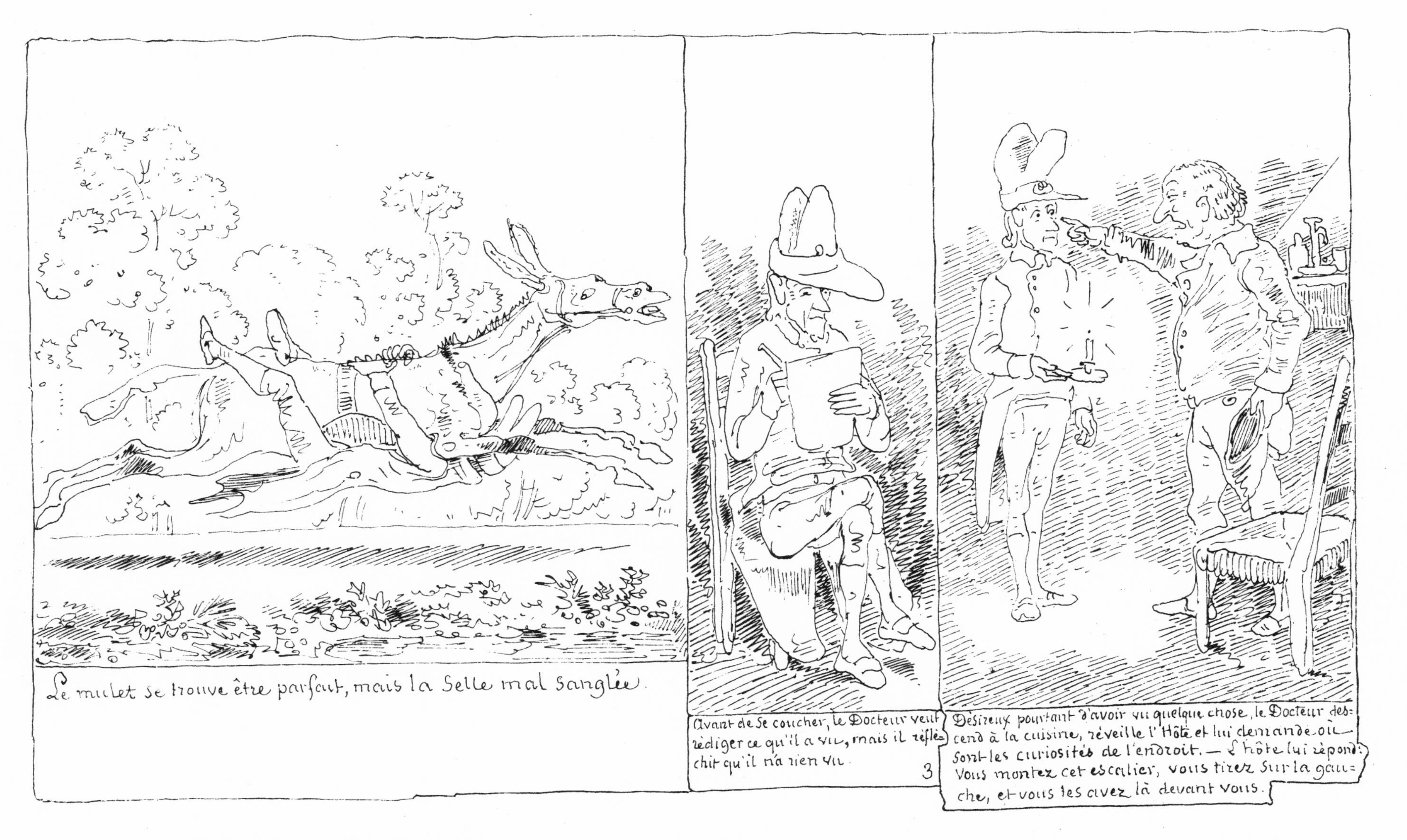
Le mulet se trouve être parfait, mais la Selle mal sanglée.
Avant de se coucher, le Docteur veut rédiger ce qu'il a vu, mais il réfléchit qu'il n'a rien vu.
3
Désireux pourtant d'avoir vu quelque chose, le Docteur descend à la cuisine, réveille l'Hôte et lui demande où sont les curiosités de l'endroit. — L'hôte lui répond: Vous montez cet escalier, vous tirez sur la gauche, et vous les avez là devant vous.

The mule turns out to be perfect, but the saddle is badly secured.

Before going to bed, Dr. Festus tries to write up what he has seen, but he reflects that he has seen nothing.

Wanting however to have seen something, Dr. Festus goes down to the kitchen, wakes up his Host, and asks him where to find the local places of interest.—The host replies: You go up this stairway, take the left, and there they are in front of you.

Il n'y a que la canaill
Qui mette son nom sur
les muraille

Malheureusement le courant d'air éteint la lumière au moment où le Docteur allait jouir du Spectacle

Renonçant pour ce jour là à toute curiosité, le Docteur gagne son lit. Mais il se trompe de chambre, et se couche dans la grande malle de Milady.

4

Unfortunately a draft puts out the light at the moment when Dr. Festus was about to enjoy the spectacle. [Graffiti on wall of privy:] Only the riff-raff feel the call / To write their names upon the wall.

Renouncing for the time being all places of interest, Dr. Festus gets into his bed. But he mistakes the room, and settles into Milady's great trunk.

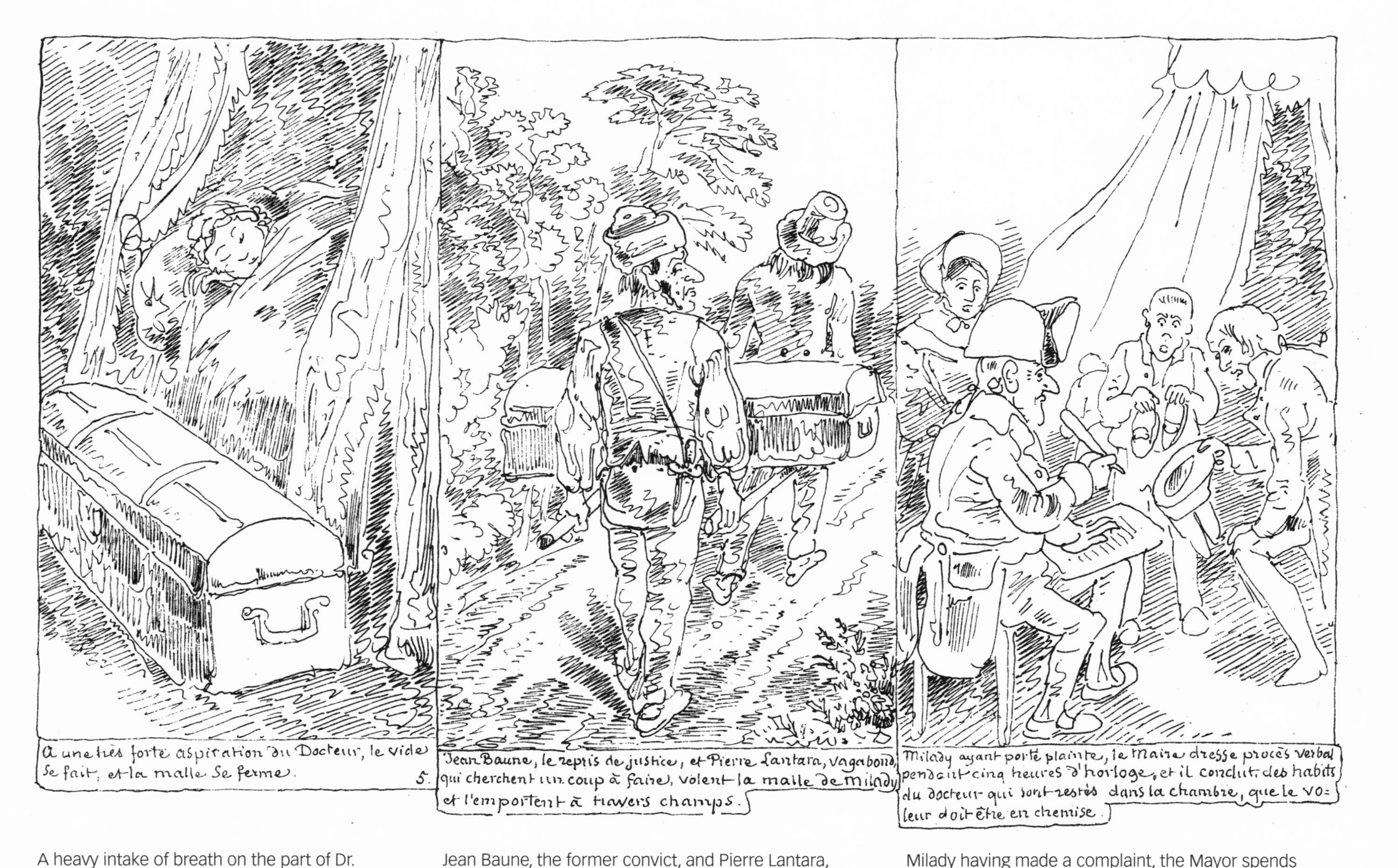
A une très forte aspiration du Docteur, le vide se fait, et la malle se ferme.
5.
Jean Baune, le repris de justice, et Pierre Lantara, vagabond, qui cherchent un coup à faire, volent la malle de Milady et l'emportent à travers champs.
Milady ayant porté plainte, le Maire dresse procès verbal pendant cinq heures d'horloge, et il conclut, des habits du docteur qui sont restés dans la chambre, que le voleur doit être en chemise.

A heavy intake of breath on the part of Dr. Festus creates a vacuum and the trunk closes.

Jean Baune, the former convict, and Pierre Lantara, the tramp, looking for a trick to play, steal Milady's trunk and carry it off through the fields.

Milady having made a complaint, the Mayor spends five hours drawing up a report, and concludes from Dr. Festus's clothes that he left in the room, that the thief must be in shirt sleeves.

Après quoi, le civil achevé, il réunit la force armée, composée de George Blême, dit *La Mèche*, et de Joseph Rouget, dit *l'Amorce*, et il se met à la poursuite du voleur.

Cependant Milord qui venait pour rejoindre son épouse, est dévalisé par Jean Baune et Pierre Lantara qui chargent la malle sur son cheval, et le laissent en chemise dans le bois.

6

After which, civil procedures accomplished, he gathers the armed force, composed of George Blême, called *The Wick*, and Joseph Rouget, called *The Bait*, and he sets off in pursuit of the thief.

Meanwhile Milord, who was coming to join his wife, is robbed by Jean Baune and Pierre Lantara who load the trunk on his horse, and leave him in shirt sleeves in the wood.

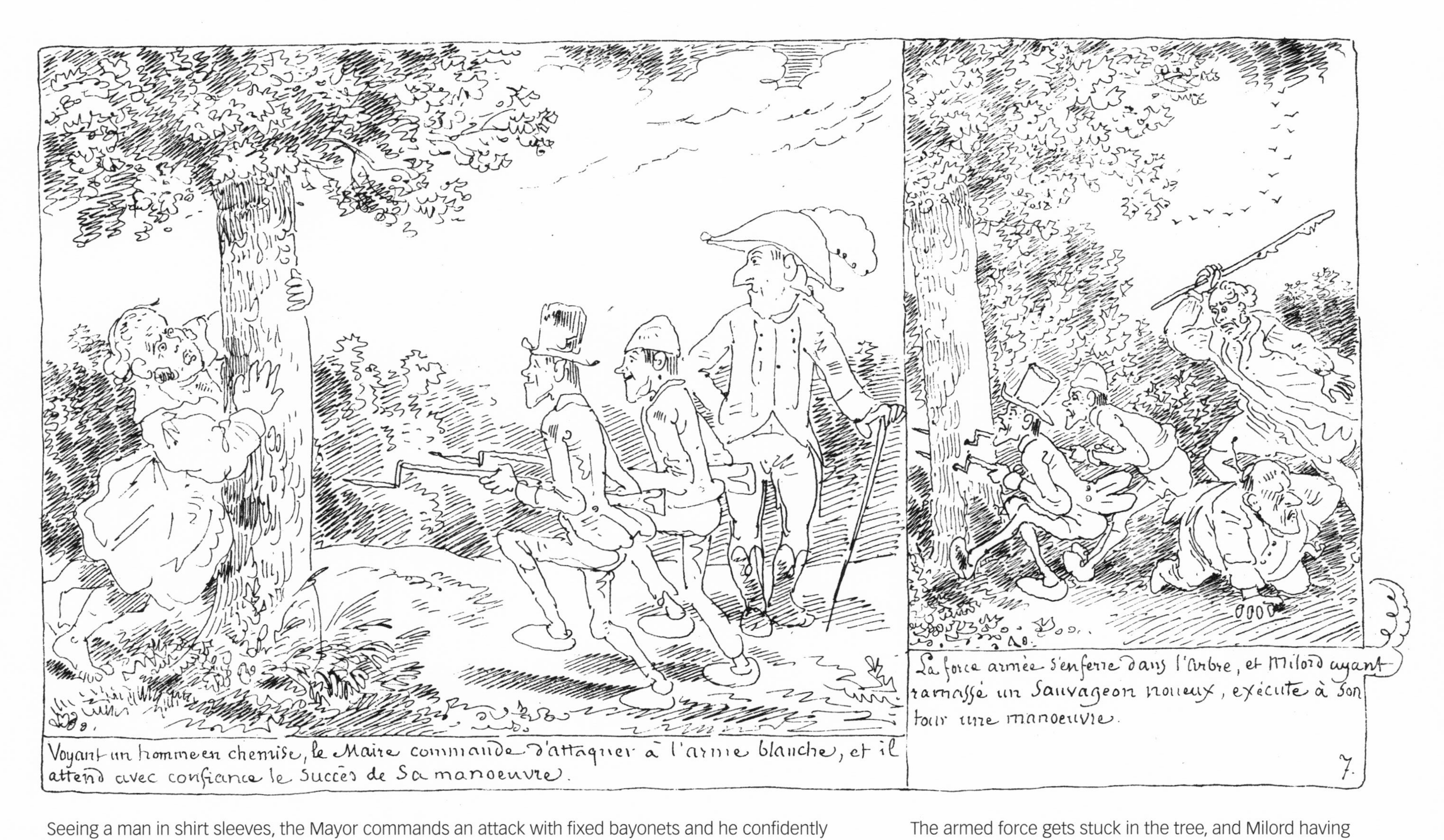
Voyant un homme en chemise, le Maire commande d'attaquer à l'arme blanche, et il attend avec confiance le succès de sa manoeuvre.
La force armée s'enferre dans l'arbre, et Milord ayant ramassé un Sauvageon noueux, exécute à son tour une manoeuvre.
7.

Seeing a man in shirt sleeves, the Mayor commands an attack with fixed bayonets and he confidently awaits the success of his maneuver.

The armed force gets stuck in the tree, and Milord having picked up a knotty stick, executes a maneuver likewise.

Pendant ce temps le Docteur Festus continue son grand voyage d'instruction.

Meanwhile Dr. Festus continues his educational tour.

Milord s'étant vêtu des habits du Maire reprend sa route. La force armée suit l'habit.

8.

Milord having donned the Mayor's clothes, goes on his way. The armed force follows the uniform.

Cependant Milady ne voyant pas arriver Milord, monte le mulet laissé par le Docteur Festus, et part pour aller à sa rencontre. Elle est bien surprise de trouver sur son chemin le Maire en chemise.
9.
Le Maire pressé par ses devoirs administratifs et n'osant reparaître en chemise dans sa commune, se décide, contrairement à toutes ses habitudes de légalité, à abattre Milady d'un coup de sauvageon, et à s'emparer de ses habits.
9

Meanwhile Milady failing to see Milord arrive, mounts the mule left by Dr. Festus, and sets off to meet him. She is very surprised to find en route the Mayor in shirt sleeves.

The Mayor, under pressure from his administrative duties and not daring to reappear in his commune in his shirt sleeves, decides, contrary to all his habitual legality, to knock down Milady with his stick, and seize her clothes.

Cependant Jean Baune et Pierre Lantara, arrivés dans un endroit écarté, ouvrent la malle et ils tombent à la renverse d'épouvante, en voyant qu'ils ont volé un homme

De son côté le Docteur trouvant à ces gens mauvaise mine, leur passe sur le corps et vient se cacher dans les foins de George Luçon.

10.

Meanwhile Jean Baune and Pierre Lantara, arriving in a remote spot, open the trunk and fall over backwards with horror seeing that they have stolen a man.

For his part Dr. Festus finding these men to be shady looking, passes over their bodies and hides in the haystacks of George Luçon.

Arrivé sur les bords de la rivière d'Eaubelle, Milord se dépouille de ses habits, et s'y baigne avec délices. La force armée voyant Milord d'un côté, l'habit de l'autre, sent bien (il y a un instinct dans les masses) que son véritable chef est au saule et s'alignant à dix pas, elle garde une exacte discipline.
Un souffle de vent ayant soulevé la manche droite, la force armée fait demi-tour à gauche, pas accéléré.
11.

Reaching the banks of the Eaubelle river, Milord strips off his clothes and takes a delightful dip there. The armed force seeing Milord on one side and the uniform on the other, recognizes (there is an instinct among the masses) that its true chief is on the willow and taking up position six feet away, maintains a perfect discipline.

A gust of wind having raised the right sleeve, the armed force executes a half-turn to the left, at the double.

Sur un nouveau mouvement, la force armée fait halte, et présente armes! avec une étonnante précision.

Le vent ayant beaucoup fraîchi, la force armée fait la charge en douze temps, reprend l'arme au bras, croise la baïonnette et s'avance au pas de charge.

12.

At a new movement [of the sleeve] the armed force comes to a halt, and executes a present arms! with astonishing precision.

With a sudden freshening of the wind, the armed force charges in double time, cradles arms, crosses bayonets, and advances at the charge.

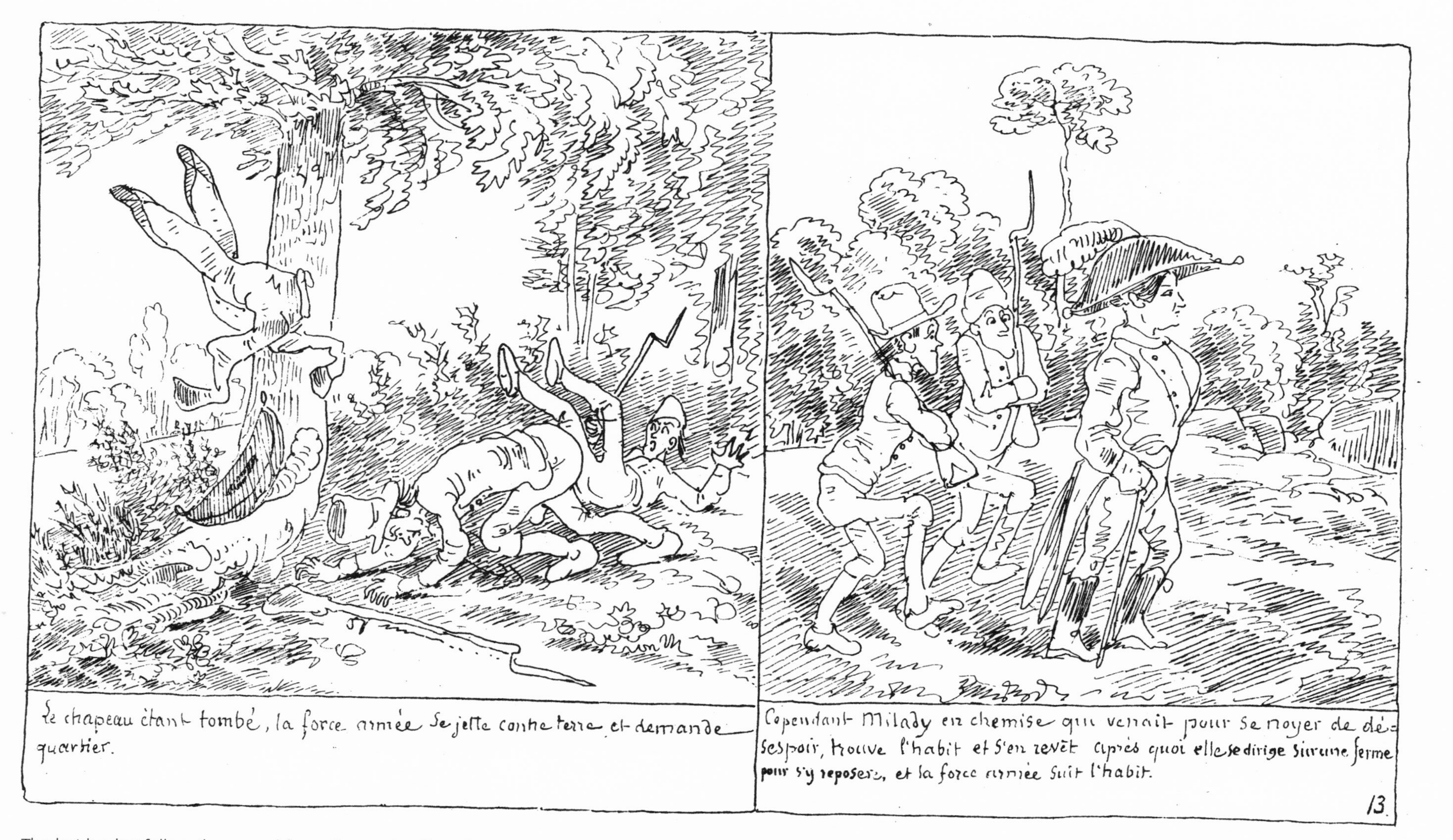
Le chapeau étant tombé, la force armée se jette contre terre et demande quartier.
Cependant Milady en chemise qui venait pour se noyer de désespoir, trouve l'habit et s'en revêt après quoi elle se dirige sur une ferme pour s'y reposer, et la force armée suit l'habit.
13.

The hat having fallen, the armed force throws itself on the ground and demands quarter.

Meanwhile Milady who came to drown herself in despair, finds the uniform and dons it, after which she sets off for a farm in order to rest, and the armed force follows the uniform.

Cependant George Luçon, dit *le Trèfle*, fait ses foins, et le Docteur est hissé sur le char.

D'où il est hissé dans la fenière.

14.

Meanwhile George Luçon, called *The Clover*, takes in his hay and Dr. Festus is hoisted upon the cart.

From where he is hoisted into the hay barn.

Ou il voit Milady qui s'y repose, et la force armée qui attend des ordres.
15.
Après y avoir réfléchi, le Docteur Festus croit pouvoir s'emparer d'un habit d'homme sans faire tort à un Sexe aimable et digne de protection ensorte qu'il s'en revêt et reprend son voyage d'instruction, jusque-là si heureusement commencé.

Where he sees Milady resting, and the armed force awaiting orders.

Upon reflection, Dr. Festus thinks it permissible to seize male clothing without prejudice to the gentle sex otherwise worthy of protection, so that he dons it and resumes his educational tour, so happily begun thus far.

Cependant Milord, après s'être baigné avec délices, regagne la rive, où il ne trouve plus ses habits, et se met aussitôt à la poursuite du voleur.

Les ayant trouvés sur le dos du Docteur, il s'apprête à les reprendre et à lui faire un mauvais parti, mais la force armée défend l'habit à l'arme blanche

16.

Meanwhile Milord, having finished his delightful dip, regains the river bank, where he finds his clothes missing, and immediately sets off in pursuit of the thief.

Having found them on Dr. Festus, he is about to recover them and knock him about, but the armed force defends the uniform with fixed bayonets.

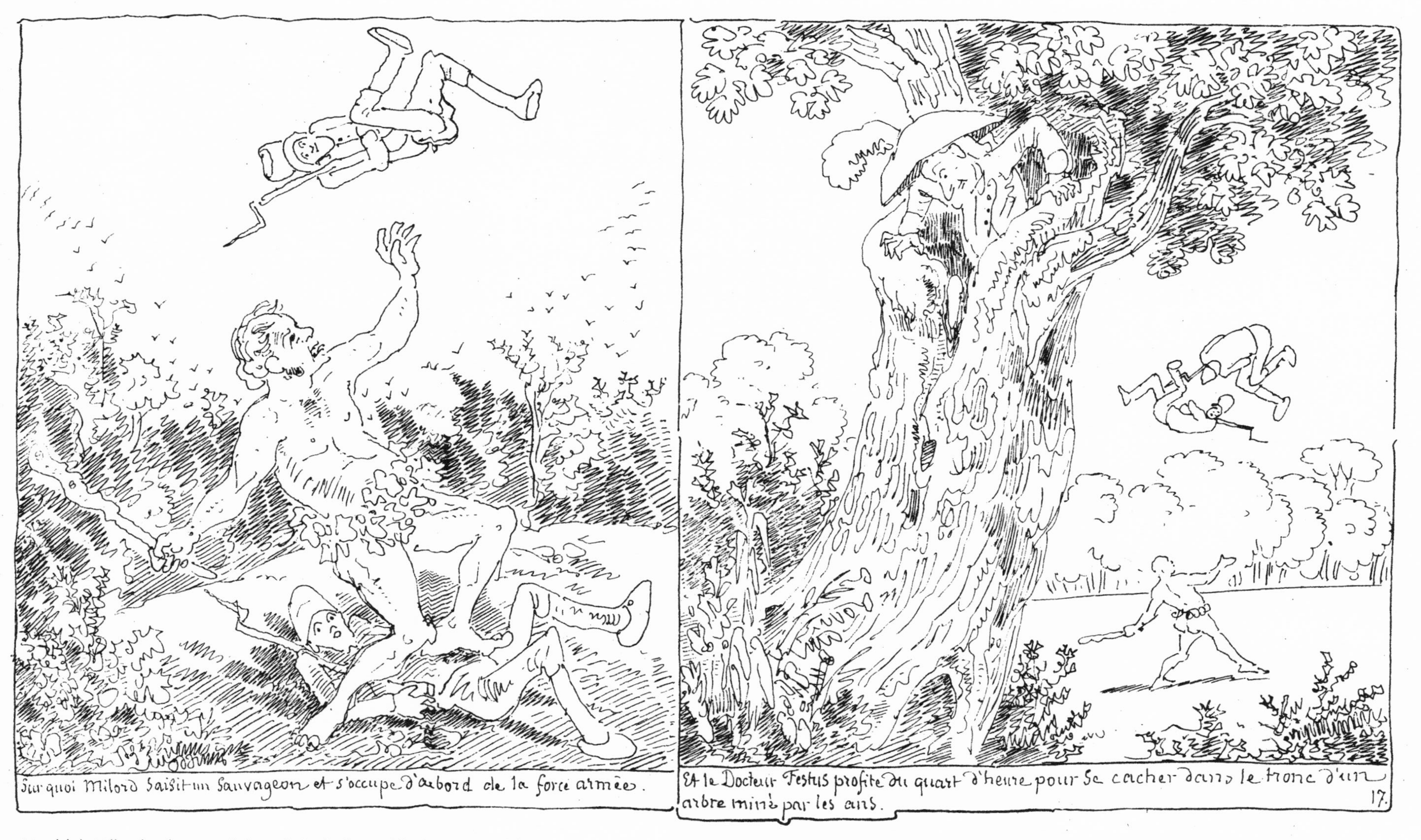
Sur quoi Milord saisit un sauvageon et s'occupe d'abord de la force armée.
Et le Docteur Festus profite du quart d'heure pour se cacher dans le tronc d'un arbre miné par les ans.
17.

At which Milord seizes a stick and deals first with the armed force.

And Dr. Festus seizes the moment to hide in the trunk of a tree hollowed out by the passage of time.

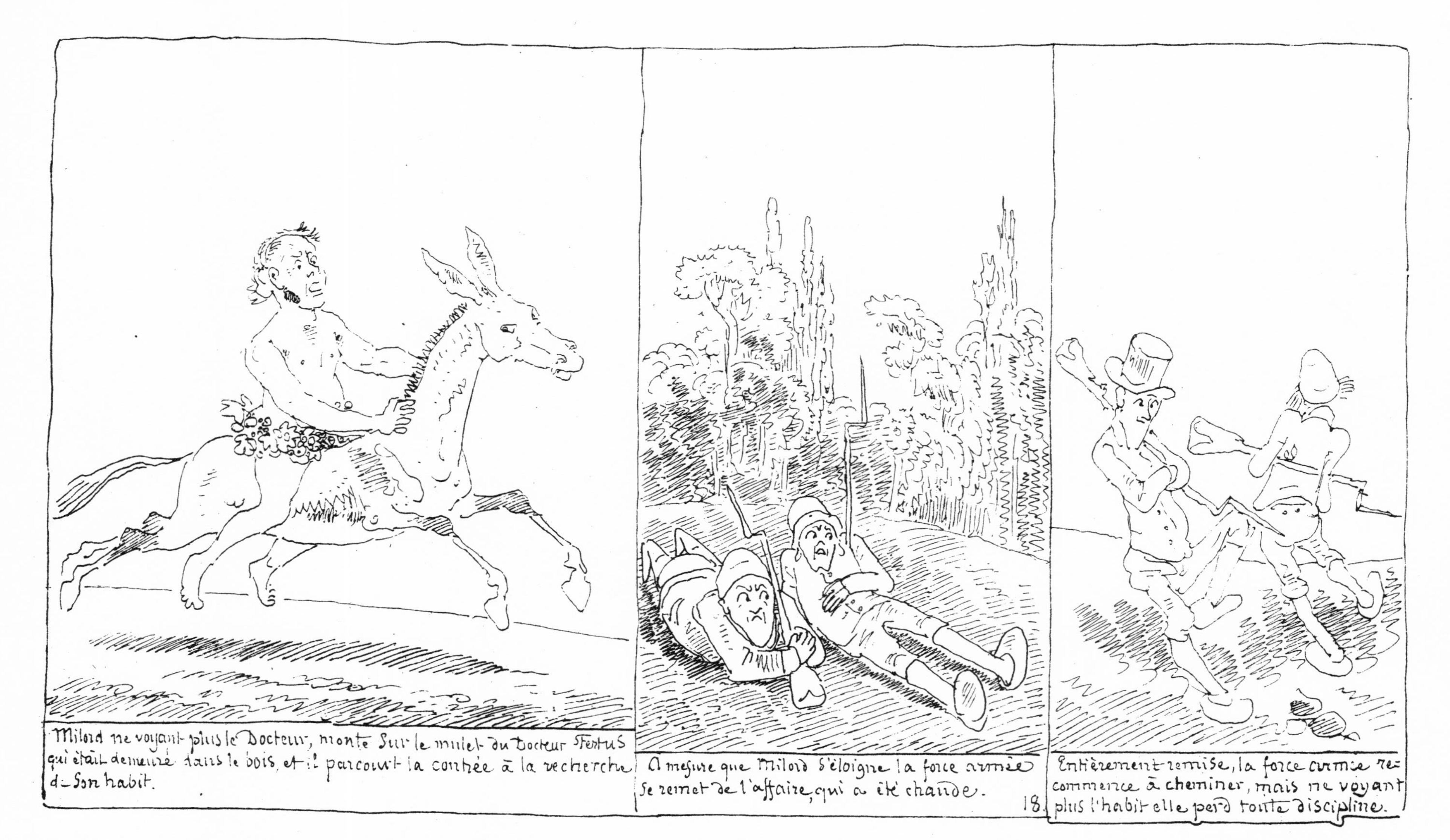
Milord ne voyant plus le Docteur, monte sur le mulet du Docteur Festus qui était demeuré dans le bois, et il parcourt la contrée à la recherche de son habit.
A mesure que Milord s'éloigne la force armée se remet de l'affaire, qui a été chaude.
18.
Entièrement remise, la force armée recommence à cheminer, mais ne voyant plus l'habit elle perd toute discipline.

Milord no longer seeing Dr. Festus, mounts Dr. Festus's mule left in the wood, and ranges over the countryside looking for his clothes.

With the disappearance of Milord the armed force recovers from the affair, which was a warm one.

Entirely recovered, the armed force takes off again, but with no uniform in sight loses all discipline.

Et les paysans lui lancent des carottes parce qu'elle couche les seigles.
Le Maire qui voit cela d'une hauteur voisine, en est profondément mortifié.
Et étant venu se poster en face des délinquans: Gredins! ... leur dit-il ... Mais la force armée ne voyant pas l'habit, lui passe sur le ventre.
19.

And the peasants throw carrots at them, because they flatten the rye.

The Mayor who sees this from a neighboring height, is profoundly mortified.

And confronting the delinquents face-to-face: Wretches! . . . he tells them . . . But the armed force not seeing the uniform, marches over his belly.

Le maire affligé et meurtri tâche de ga=
gner une ferme.

The Mayor, distressed and bruised, tries to reach a farmhouse.

Et il se présente à celle de George Luçon qui lui ouvre la fenière où
il s'endort profondément.

And he shows up at that of George Luçon who opens up his hay barn, where he falls fast asleep.

20.

Milady qui vient de se réveiller, croit ne pas faire
tort au maire en lui reprenant ses habits.

Milady, who has just woken up, thinks it is no prejudice to the Mayor if she takes back his clothes.

C'est ce jour là que le Maire fait son grand rêve normal. Il se voit d'abord ravi dans une commune-modèle, où il est assis sur vingt six volumes d'archives, constatant l'acquisition par ladite de trois fontaines coulantes, de vingt pieds de haie vive, et deux chemins vicinaux; le tout par prescription ou saisie, tant sur le propriétaire que sur les hoirs.
Il voit ensuite un procès-verbal de huit pieds de haut qui danse la matelote avec la Déesse Thémis, pendant que cette Déesse lui a confié, à lui Maire, sa balance.
21.

That is the day the Mayor has his great habitual dream. First he sees himself transported to a model commune, where he is seated on twenty-six volumes of archives, confirming the acquisition by that commune of three running fountains, twenty feet of live hedge, and two local roads; the whole by prescription or seizure, on the owner as on the heirs.

He then sees an eight-foot-long report, which dances the matelote [hornpipe] with the Goddess Thémis, while that Goddess has entrusted to him, the Mayor, her scales.

Il voit ensuite trois cents huissiers en robe courte, qui chantent les cinq codes sur l'air de Marlborough, avec une plume de paon sur l'oreille gauche, et un exploit en façon de jabot.

Il voit ensuite trois mille cinq cent quatre textes de loi encore inconnus qui cuisent dans une marmite de parchemin, dont soixante deux clercs lèchent les parois, pour attraper la bouillie descendante

22.

He then sees three hundred bailiffs in short tunics, singing the five codes to the tune of Marlborough, with a peacock feather behind their left ear, and a writ as a shirt frill.

He then sees three thousand five hundred and four hitherto unknown legal texts boiling in a parchment pot, the walls of which are licked by sixty-two clerks to catch the overflowing pulp.

Mais au milieu de la fête, il voit une force armée qui fume la pipe auprès d'un magasin à poudre, en pouffant la fumée dans les yeux d'un respectable caporal à chevrons.
Alors ne pouvant se maîtriser, le Maire s'élance sur les délinquans pour les arrêter lorsqu'il est arrêté lui-même comme suspect d'être le voleur en chemise que cherche la police.
23

But in the middle of the festivities, he sees an armed force smoking a pipe near the powder magazine, and puffing the smoke into the eyes of a respectable, veteran corporal.

Then, unable to control himself, the Mayor pounces upon the delinquents to arrest them, when he is himself arrested on suspicion of being the thief in shirt sleeves the police are looking for.

Conduit en prison, le Maire y rêve à son rêve.

Cependant André Luçon, Scieur de long, voulant travailler de son métier pour le Sieur Taillandier qui refait sa toiture et planche son fenil, vient trouver son frère George Luçon, et fait pache avec lui pour des pieds de chêne qui sont dans son bois.

André Luçon, levé dès l'aube, vient au bois et fait abattre un pied de chêne. 24.

Taken to prison, the Mayor dreams there of his dream.

Meanwhile André Luçon, sawyer, wishing to ply his trade on behalf of Master Taillandier who is fixing his roof and putting a new floor on his hayloft, comes to fetch his brother George Luçon, and contracts with him with respect to some lengths of oak in his wood.

André Luçon, rising at dawn, comes to the wood and has an oak tree cut down.

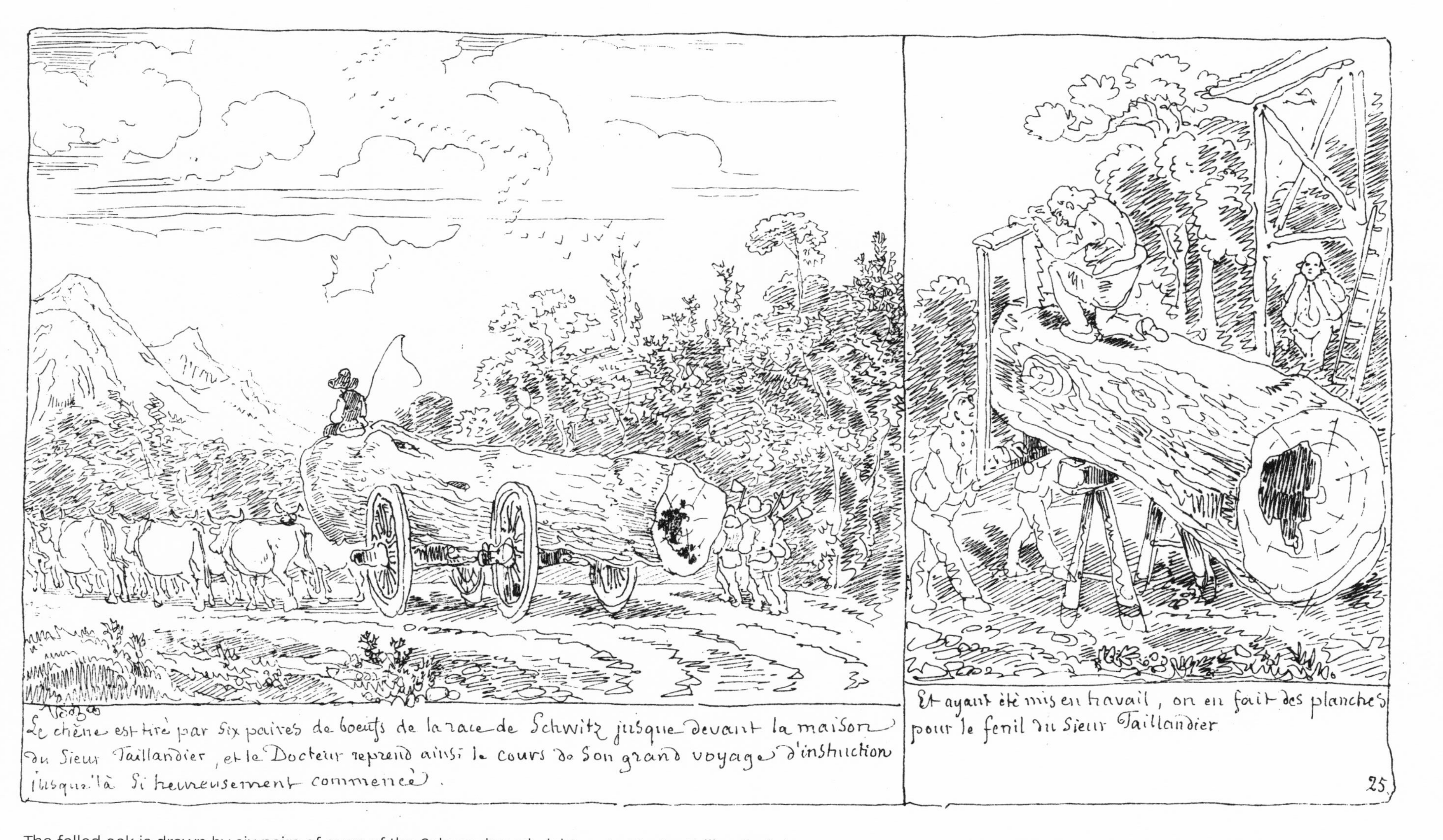
Le chêne est tiré par six paires de boeufs de la race de Schwitz jusque devant la maison du Sieur Taillandier, et le Docteur reprend ainsi le cours de son grand voyage d'instruction jusqu'à là si heureusement commencé.
Et ayant été mis en travail, on en fait des planches pour le fenil du Sieur Taillandier
25

The felled oak is drawn by six pairs of oxen of the Schwyz breed, right up to Master Taillandier's house, and Dr. Festus thus resumes his great educational tour so happily started thus far.

Set up for working, the tree is cut into planks for Master Taillandier's hayloft.

Au trente deuxième coup la Scie mord l'orteil du Docteur qui pousse un énorme cri en vingt deux langues. A ce cri, le Sieur Taillandier tombe dans un baquet de chaux maigre, et les Scieurs de long s'en vont porter la nouvelle d'un arbre parlant dans les hameaux de Porelières et de Coudraz.

Le Docteur Festus trouve prudent de sortir de l'arbre, mais il trouve suspecte la figure du Sieur Taillandier qui est blanchi de chaux maigre

26.

At the thirty-second cut the saw bites into the toe of Dr. Festus who utters a tremendous scream in twenty-two languages. At this scream, Master Taillandier falls into a bucket of quiet lime, and the sawyers run off to broadcast the news of a talking tree in the hamlets of Porelières and Coudraz.

Dr. Festus deems it prudent to crawl out of the tree, but he finds the figure of Master Taillandier suspect, covered as he is in quiet lime.

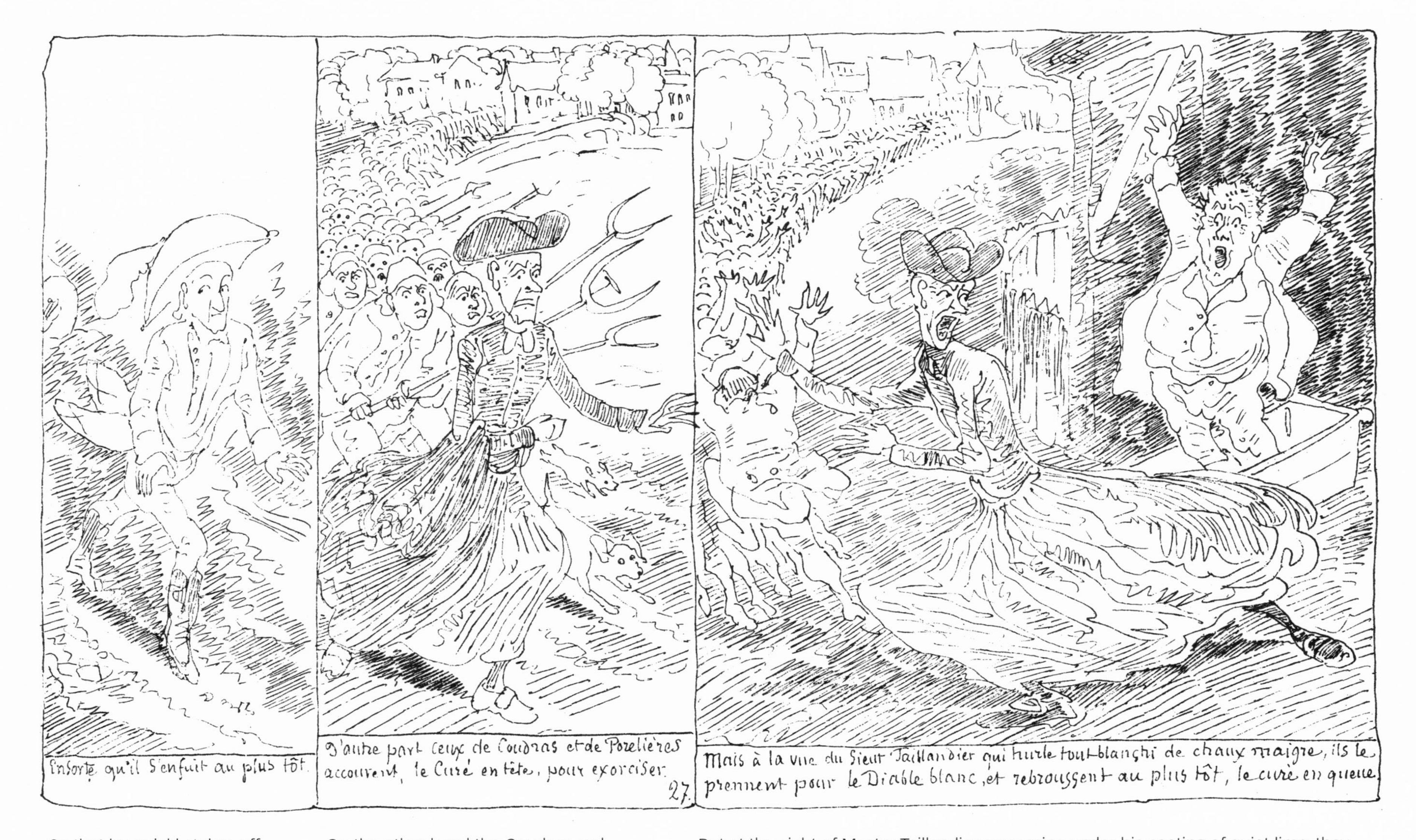
Ensorte qu'il s'enfuit au plus tôt.
D'autre part ceux de Coudras et de Porelières accourent, le Curé en tête, pour exorciser.
27.
Mais à la vue du Sieur Taillandier qui hurle tout blanchi de chaux maigre, ils le prennent pour le Diable blanc, et rebroussent au plus tôt, le curé en queue.

So that he quickly takes off.

On the other hand the Coudras and Porelières folk run up, headed by their Priest, in order to perform an exorcism.

But at the sight of Master Taillandier screaming under his coating of quiet lime, they take him for the White Devil, and turn back as fast as they can, the priest in the rear.

À l'ouïe de tant de monde, le Docteur entre de plein saut dans le grenier à blé de Samuel Porret, où il se déguise en sac de blé pour n'être pas reconnu.

Le lendemain, Samuel Porret charge le sac sur son âne, et prend le chemin du moulin. De cette façon le Docteur Festus continue son voyage d'instruction jusque là si heureusement commencé.

28.

L'âne, qui a ses idées à lui, ne voulant pas passer le ruisseau, Samuel Porret frappe ferme, au grand détriment du Docteur.

Hearing the rush of so many people, Dr. Festus leaps into the corn barn of Samuel Porret, where he disguises himself as a sack of corn to avoid recognition.

The next day, Samuel Porret loads the sack on his ass, and takes the road to the mill. In this way Dr. Festus continues his educational tour so happily begun thus far.

The ass, which has his own ideas, refuses to cross the stream, and Samuel Porret gives it a good beating, to the great detriment of Dr. Festus.

Le Docteur ayant poussé un immense cri en vingt deux langues, Samuel Porret s'enfuit à tire de jambes, et l'ane s'en va paisiblement au moulin, paissant aux herbes, et philosophant au Soleil.
Voyant arriver l'âne, Claude Thiolier, dit Benaîton, décharge le sac en disant à Gamaliel de tout préparer pour moudre le lendemain
29.

Dr. Festus having uttered an immense scream in twenty-two languages, Samuel Porret takes off as fast as his legs will carry him, and the ass goes off peaceably to the mill, cropping the grass and philosophizing in the sun.

Seeing the ass arrive, Claude Thiolier, called *Big Booby*, unloads the sack telling Gamaliel to prepare it all for milling the next day.

Entendant ce propos, le Docteur Festus veut prendre la fuite, et Claude Thiolier, dit Benaîton, croit que le diable l'emporte.

Hearing this conversation, Dr. Festus tries to flee, and Claude Thiolier, called *Big Booby*, thinks that the devil is carrying him off.

Le sac tombe, Claude Thiolier s'en va quérir du secours, et Gamaliel se cache derrière un van, où il dit des Ave.
30.

The sack falls, Claude Thiolier runs off to get help, and Gamaliel hides behind a winnowing basket, where he recites Aves.

La meunière revenant d'en champs avec ses huit cochons d'Islande trouve le sac par terre et le traîne dans le moulin.
Mais le sac s'étant fortuitement dénoué, le Docteur Festus met le nez à l'air et admire la beauté du paysage, tandis que la meunière tombe sur le nez et se casse trois dents, dont deux incisives et une oeillère.
31.

The Miller's Wife, returning from the fields with her eight Irish pigs, finds the sack lying on the ground ands drags it into the mill.

But the sack having come fortuitously undone, Dr. Festus sticks his nose out and admires the beauty of the landscape, while the Miller's Wife falls on her nose and breaks three teeth, including two incisors and one eye-tooth.

Entendant le village qui arrive, Claude Thiolier en tête, le Docteur Festus enjambe la Meunière et saute dans le moulin sans être aperçu.

La Meunière disant n'avoir rien vu, les paysans cognent de leur fourche Claude et Gamaliel comme poltrons et couards, prenant sacs pour démons, et grains de blé pour charbons d'enfer.

32.

Hearing the village come upon him, Claude Thiolier at the head, Dr. Festus steps over the Miller's Wife and into the mill, unnoticed.

The Miller's Wife saying she has seen nothing, the peasants pin Claude and Gamaliel against the wall with their forks, calling them funks and cowards who take sacks for demons and grains of corn for the coals of hell.

Quand le village s'est éloigné, Claude Thiolier bat sa femme pour avoir dit qu'elle n'a rien vu.
La meunière bat le garçon pour avoir dit qu'il a vu quelque chose.
Le garçon bat l'âne pour avoir causé tout ce mal. Après quoi la paix revient dans le moulin 33.

When the village has withdrawn, Claude Thiolier beats his wife for having said she saw nothing.

The Miller's Wife beats the boy for having said he saw something.

The boy beats the ass for having caused all this trouble. After which peace returns to the mill.

Cependant le Docteur Festus, qui s'est caché dans le comble du moulin, soulève qques tuiles et met le nez à l'air

La force armée qui se trouve sous le vent de l'habit, manifeste quelques symptômes de discipline.

Faute d'échelle, le Docteur Festus se décide à descendre le long de l'aile, qui commence à tourner

La force armée qui voit l'habit reprend toute sa discipline et double le pas.

34.

Meanwhile Dr. Festus, who has hidden in the roof of the mill, raises some tiles and pokes his nose out.

The armed force moving into the lee of the uniform, manifests some symptoms of discipline.

For lack of a ladder, Dr. Festus decides to descend along the mill arm, which begins to turn.

The armed force sees the uniform and resumes its wonted discipline and doubles its pace.

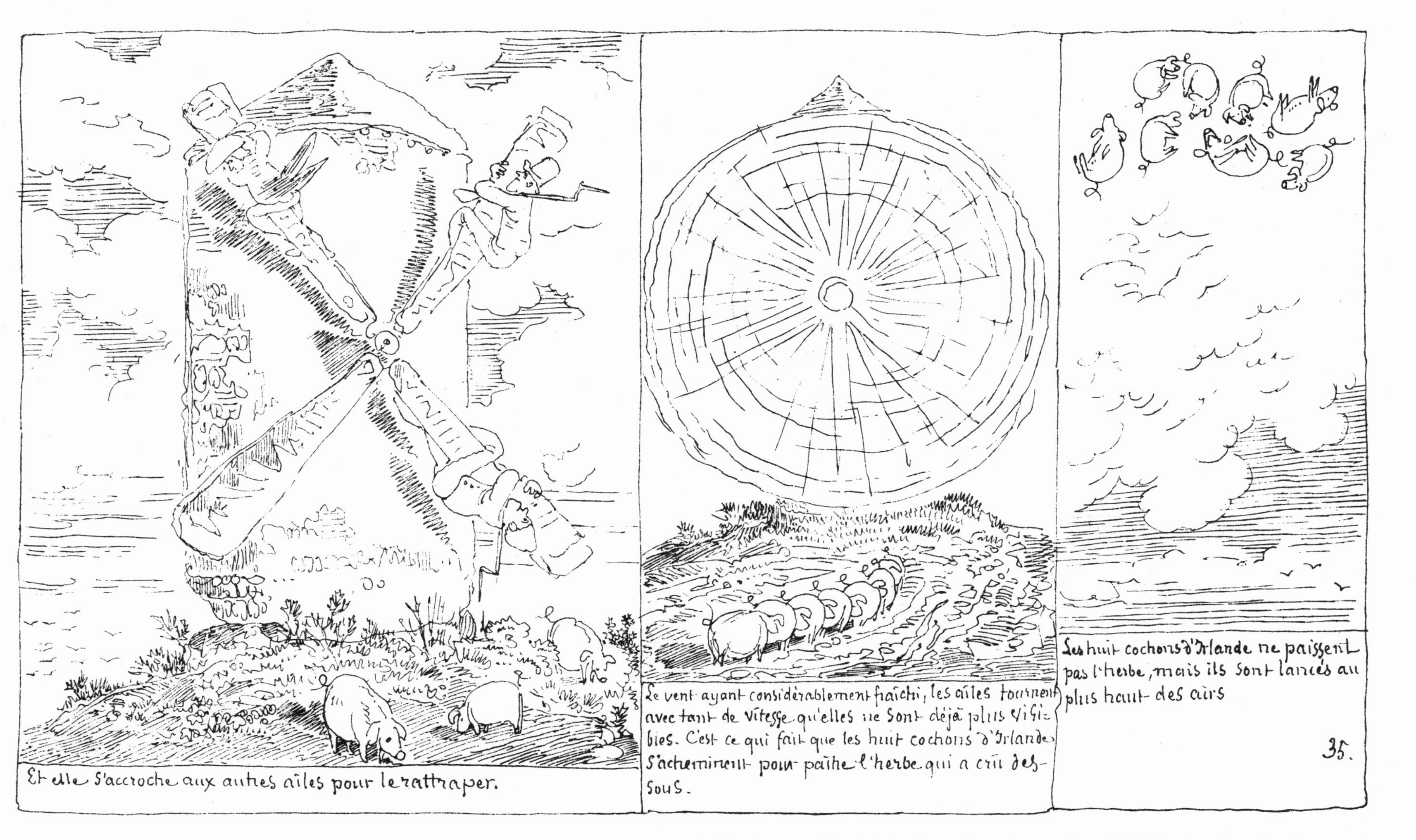
Et elle s'accroche aux autres ailes pour le rattraper.
Le vent ayant considérablement fraîchi, les ailes tournent avec tant de vitesse qu'elles ne sont déjà plus visibles. C'est ce qui fait que les huit cochons d'Irlande s'acheminent pour paître l'herbe qui a crû dessous.
Les huit cochons d'Irlande ne paissent pas l'herbe, mais ils sont lancés au plus haut des airs
35.

And hangs on to the other arms to catch up with him.

The wind having considerably freshened, the arms turn with such speed that they are already no longer visible. Which causes the eight Irish pigs to proceed to the grass that has grown beneath.

The eight Irish pigs do not get to graze, but are thrown high up into the air.

Et au bout de trois semaines ils tombent dans le lac d'Eaubelle, au nombre de vingt huit, car les femelles ont mis bas durant la traversée.

And after three weeks they fall into Lake Eaubelle, twenty-eight in number, for the females have brought forth young in flight.

L'ouragan étant devenu irrésistible, le Docteur Festus est lancé par la tangente à une élévation où aucun Docteur n'est parvenu ni avant ni après lui. La force armée suit l'habit.

The hurricane having become irresistible, Dr. Festus is thrown by the tangent to a height which no scientist has ever reached, before or after him. The armed force follows the uniform.

Cependant privée de son Maire et de la force armée la Commune enfreint les réglemens, brûle les bois communaux, et met l'Hôtel de Ville en cabaret. 36.

Meanwhile, deprived of their Mayor and the armed force, the Commune breaks the rules, burns the communal woods, and turns the town hall into a tavern.

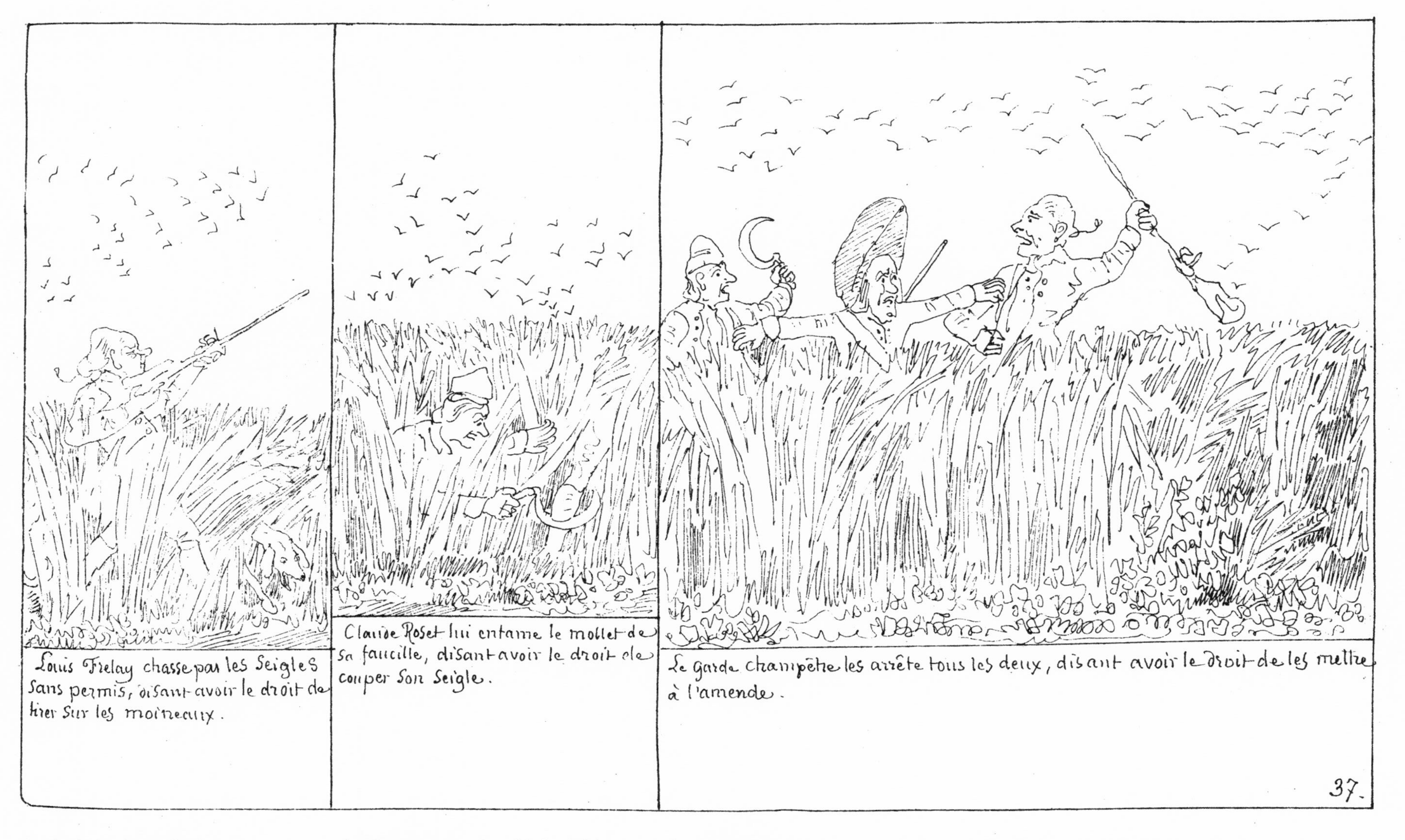
Louis Frelay chasse par les Seigles Sans permis, disant avoir le droit de tirer Sur les moineaux.
Claude Roset lui entame le mollet de sa faucille, disant avoir le droit de couper Son Seigle.
Le Garde champêtre les arrête tous les deux, disant avoir le droit de les mettre à l'amende.
37.

Louis Frelay hunts in the rye without a permit, saying he has the right to shoot at sparrows.

Claude Roset cuts into his leg with his sickle, saying he has the right to cut his rye.

The rural guard arrests both of them, saying he has the right to levy a fine on them.

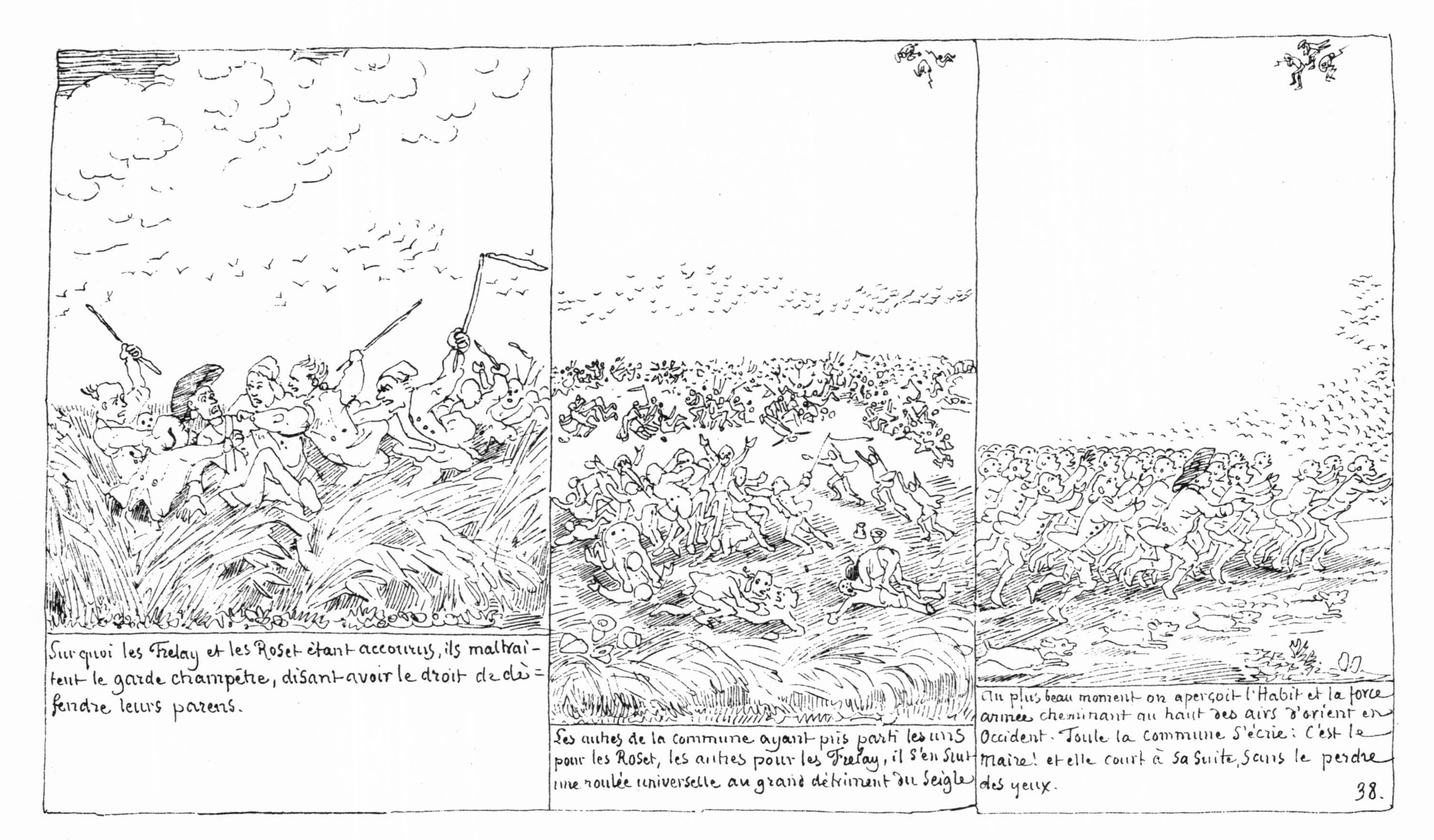
Sur quoi les Frelay et les Roset étant accourus, ils maltraitent le garde champêtre, disant avoir le droit de défendre leurs parens.
Les autres de la commune ayant pris parti les uns pour les Roset, les autres pour les Frelay, il s'en suit une roulée universelle au grand détriment du seigle.
Au plus beau moment on aperçoit l'Habit et la force armée cheminant au haut des airs d'orient en Occident. Toute la commune s'écrie: C'est le Maire! et elle court à sa suite, sans le perdre des yeux.
38.

At which the Frelays and the Rosets rush up and maltreat the rural guard, saying they have the right to defend their relatives.

Other members of the Commune having taken sides, some for the Rosets and the others for Frelays, there ensues a general free-for-all, to the great detriment of the rye.

At the height of it all the Uniform and the armed force are seen careering high up in the sky from East to West. The whole commune cries out: It's the Mayor! and they run after him, without losing him from sight.

Cependant le Maire, pressé par ses besoins administratifs, quitte pour un instant ses habitudes de légalité, casse sa cruche sur la tête du geolier, lui prend ses clés, et s'échappe de la prison.
Et comme il regagne sa commune il croit la voir qui accourt pour se jeter dans ses bras.
« Chers Administrés! leur dit-il ..... Mais la Commune qui regarde en l'air lui marche sur le ventre et passe outre
39.

However the Mayor, pressed by his administrative duties, abandons for the moment his habits of legality, breaks a jug over the head of the jailer, takes his keys and escapes from prison.

And as he returns to his Commune, he thinks he sees them running to throw themselves into his arms.

"Dear Citizens of the Commune!" he tells them ..... But the Commune looking up into the sky walks over his belly and passes on.

Et, arrivée au bord du grand Canal, elle y tombe faute de voir son chemin et s'arrêter à temps.

C'est depuis ce tems que l'autorité a fait mettre dans cet endroit une forte barrière qui s'y voit encore dans les basses eaux. 40.

And reaching the bank of the Grand Canal they fall in, having lost their way and failed to stop in time.

It is from this moment that the authorities had a strong barrier put up in this place, which is still to be seen in low water.

Cependant Milady, après avoir recouvré ses habits, prend le parti de retourner à l'hôtellerie pour y attendre Milord. Mais à sa grande stupeur, elle ne retrouve plus dans la Commune une âme vivante, excepté l'âne de Julien le borgne, qui lèche la boîte à sel.
Repartie en toute hâte pour l'Angleterre, Milady est arrêtée, faute de papiers, à la frontière de Vireloup, et l'on saisit sur elle un carnet contenant dix pages de chiffres suspects qui sont les notes de sa blanchisseuse. Elle est en conséquence écrouée à la prison royale de Vireloup, sous le N°. 36.
Cependant le maire s'étant relevé à grand'peine, fait d'amères reflexions sur le sort des grands ici-bas, et aigri par la conduite de ses administrés, il se décide à s'exiler.
41.

Meanwhile Milady, having recovered her clothes, decides to return to the hostelry to wait for Milord. But to her great astonishment, she finds in the Commune not a living soul, except the ass of One-eyed Julien, licking the salt box.

Setting off again in a hurry for England, Milady is arrested for lack of papers at the Vireloup frontier, and a notebook is found on her containing ten pages of suspicious figures, which represent her laundress's accounts. She is therefore consigned to the royal prison of Vireloup, under No. 36.

Meanwhile, sitting up with great difficulty, the Mayor reflects bitterly on the fate of the great here below, and soured by the conduct of the population in his charge, decides to go into excile.

UANE ROYALE

Tout en s'exilant, le Maire arrive à la frontière de Vireloup, où il est fouillé sévèrement, et on lui demande s'il n'a rien à déclarer.

Le Maire n'ayant point de papiers, est arrêté comme suspect, et écroué sous le No. 36 où il est mal accueilli par Milady qui le reconnaît fort bien. 42.

On his way into exile, the Mayor arrives at the frontier of Vireloup, where he is thoroughly searched, and asked if he has nothing to declare.

The Mayor having no papers is arrested as a suspect and consigned to prison under the No. 36, where he is ill received by Milady who recognizes him very well.

Cependant Milord las de parcourir la contrée en cherchant inutilement ses habits prend le parti de rejoindre Milady à l'Hôtellerie. Mais à sa grande stupeur il ne trouve pas une âme vivante dans toute la Commune, si ce n'est l'âne de Julien le borgne, qui lèche la boîte à sel.
OUANE ROYALE
Reparti en toute hâte pour l'Angleterre, Milord arrive à la frontière de Vireloup, où il est fouillé sévèrement, et on lui demande s'il n'a rien à déclarer.
Milord n'ayant point de papiers est arrêté comme suspect et écroué sous le No 36 où il boxe le Maire et l'accule sur la cruche parce qu'il le reconnaît fort bien.
43

Meanwhile Milord, tired of running around the country on a useless search for his clothes, decides to join Milady at the hostelry. But to his great astonishment, he finds not a living soul in the entire Commune, except for one-eyed Julien's ass, licking the salt box.

Leaving in a hurry for England, Milord arrives at the Vireloup frontier, where he is thoroughly searched, and asked if he is has nothing to declare.

Milord having no papers is arrested as a suspect and jailed under No. 36, where he boxes the Mayor and drives him back onto the water jug because he recognizes him very well.

Cependant la Commission chargée d'examiner les pièces saisies étudie les chiffres de la blanchisseuse, trouve la clé de cette correspondance secrète, et découvre une vaste conspiration ramifiée.

Meanwhile the commission charged with examining the seized documents, studies the laundry lists, finds the key to this secret correspondence, and discovers a vast ramified conspiracy.

Informé des dangers qu'a couru le Trône, le Roi de Vireloup prend mal, et la Reine aussi. Après quoi il ordonne par un Edit que la chose publique n'ait à souffrir aucun détriment dans sa personne.

44

Informed of the dangers that the Throne has run, the King of Vireloup falls ill, and the Queen also. After which he issues an edict that the state should not suffer any harm in his person.

Milord, Milady et le Maire, condamnés à être pendus, sont acheminés nuitamment sur la Capitale
Mais par un admirable enchaînement de circonstances, la force armée que le poids des armes a fait graviter plus rapidement que le Docteur, vient se ficher dans la poitrine des deux gendarmes, et les bat complètement. Les prisonniers se hâtent de fuir.
45.

Milord, Milady, and the Mayor, condemned to be hanged, are taken nocturnally to the capital.

But by an admirable chain of circumstances, the armed force whose weight of arms has caused them to gravitate more rapidly than Dr. Festus, on landing stick their bayonets into the two policemen, in a crushing victory. The prisoners hastily take to their heels.

La force armee se dèfiche et s'en va pleine de gloire, mais sans discipline, malheureusement.
Cependant le Docteur Festus étant reste en l'air, l'Astronome Guignard qui habite en Rondeterre (c'est un grand royaume insulaire, au nord du Ginvernais) découvre par delà le Capricorne un nouveau corps céleste qui ne lui paraît qu'à trois mille milliards de lieues de la Terre.
46.
Aussitôt l'Astronome Guignard convoque la Société Royale pour lui communiquer sa découverte et dans un discours de trois heures de long, il prouve jusqu'à l'évidence que le nouvel astre est une comète opaque.

The armed force unsticks itself and goes off in a blaze of glory, but without discipline, unfortunately.

Meanwhile Dr. Festus having remained up in the air, the Astronomer Guignard who lives in Rondeterre (this is a great island kingdom, to the north of Ginvernais) discovers beyond the Capricorn a new asteroid that appears to him only three thousand billion leagues from Earth.

Immediately Astronomer Guignard convokes the Royal Society to communicate his discovery and in a three-hour speech, he proves conclusively that the new asteroid is an opaque comet.

Pendant que l'Astronome Guignard fait sa dé-
monstration, le Docteur Festus vient tomber
droit dans le Télescope.
Ce qui fait que l'Astronome Guignard retour=
ne à l'observation, découvre que son corps
Céleste n'est plus qu'à six millions de lieues
de la Terre. Et il tombe malade d'effroi.
47.
Pendant que l'Astronome Guignard garde le lit d'effroi, l'Astronome Lunard
dans un mémoire parfaitement écrit, prouve jusqu'à l'évidence que, bien
au contraire, le corps en question est un aerolithe ferrugineux et lu-
naire. Ensorte que Guignard a du dessous.

While Astronomer Guignard is making his demonstration, Dr. Festus falls right into the Telescope.

Which causes Astronomer Guignard to return to his observations, and discover that his celestial body is only six million leagues from the Earth. And he falls ill with fright.

While Astronomer Guignard takes to his bed in fright, Astronomer Lunard in a perfectly written report proves conclusively that on the contrary the body in question is a ferruginous, lunar aerolith. So that Guignard loses out.

Dans une improvisation chaleureuse, l'Astronome Nébulard prouve jusqu'à l'évidence, que, bien au contraire, le corps en question est la nébuleuse qui a déjà été vue par Sosigène, sous Jules César. En sorte que Guignard et Lunard ont du dessous.

Mais, à peine rétabli, Guignard étant venu annoncer avec douleur que l'astre n'est plus qu'à six millions de lieues de la terre, tous les savans prennent mal au ventre, et s'en vont faire leur testament. En sorte que Guignard a réellement du dessus.

48.

In an ardent improvisation, Astronomer Nébulard proves conclusively that, very much to the contrary, the body in question is the nebula that was already seen by Sosigenes under Julius Caesar. So that Guignard and Lunard lose out.

But barely recovered, Guignard having come to make the painful announcement that the asteroid is only six million leagues from earth, all the scientists get the stomach ache, and go off to make their will. So that Guignard really wins.

Cependant, de l'autre côté du détroit, les Savans de Mirliflis, qui est la Capitale du Ginvernais, ayant reçu communication de la découverte de l'astronome Guignard, cherchent dans tout le Zodiaque l'astre nouveau qui n'y est déjà plus.
49.

However, on the other side of the straits, the scientists of Mirliflis, which is the capital of Ginvernais, having been informed of Astronomer Guignard's discovery, search the whole of the Zodiac for the new asteroid which is already gone.

L'Institut est convoqué pour une réponse à faire, et l'Astronome Parrallax propose de répondre 1° que le Ginvernais a précédé toutes les nations dans les inventions et découvertes. 2° que le Ginvernais n'a rien à envier à ses voisins. 3° que, tout au contraire, il n'y a jamais eu moins d'astres au Zodiaque que dans ce moment. — Il est vivement applaudi par les Savans qui ont chacun un emplâtre sur l'oeil droit pour avoir trop regardé le Zodiaque.

La Société Royale pense que l'Institut s'est fourvoyé, faute de bons instrumens et elle lui expédie le grand Telescope de Guignard, escorté des trois Commissaires Guignard, Lunard et Nébulard. En sorte que le Docteur Festus continue son voyage d'instruction jusque là si heureusement commencé. 50.

The Institute is convoked to respond to this, and Astronomer Parrallax proposes accordingly that 1st. Ginvernais preceded all other countries in the matter of inventions and discoveries. 2nd. That Ginvernais has nothing to envy in its neighbors. 3rd. That, very much to the contrary, there have never been so few asteroids in the Zodiac than at this moment. He gets lively applause from the scientists who all have a plaster over their right eye for having stared too long at the Zodiac.

The Royal Society considers that the Institute has gone astray, for lack of good instruments, and sends it Guignard's great Telescope, escorted by the three Commissioners Guignard, Lunard, and Nébulard. So that Dr. Festus continues his educational tour, so happily begun thus far.

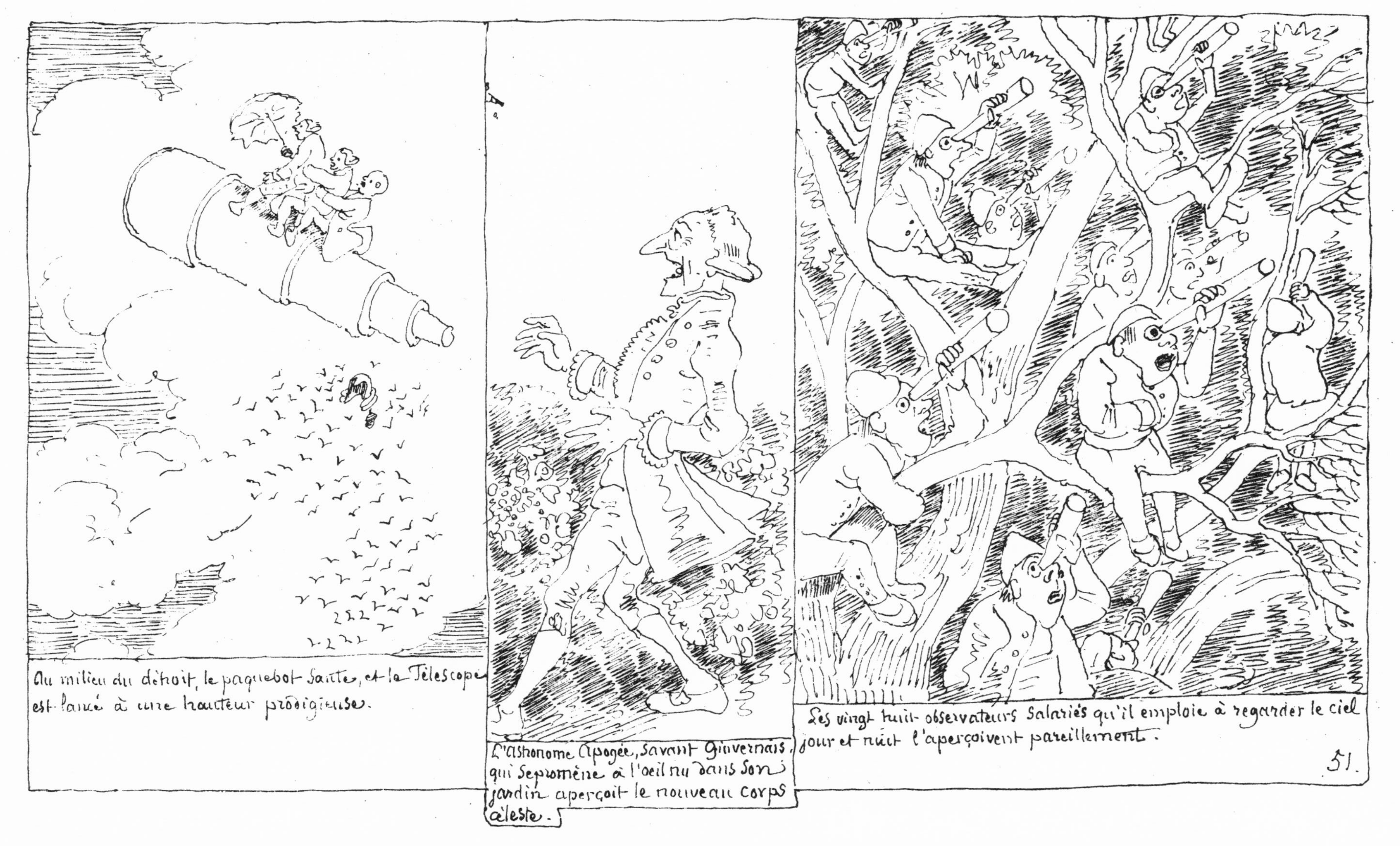
Au milieu du détroit, le paquebot saute, et le Télescope est lancé à une hauteur prodigieuse.
L'astronome Apogée, savant Ginvernais, qui se promène à l'oeil nu dans son jardin aperçoit le nouveau corps céleste.
Les vingt huit observateurs salariés qu'il emploie à regarder le ciel jour et nuit l'aperçoivent pareillement.
51.

In the middle of the channel, the steam packet explodes, throwing the Telescope to a prodigious height.

Astronomer Apogée, a scientist from Ginvernais, who is walking in his garden, perceives with his naked eye the new celestial body.

The twenty-eight salaried observers whom he employs to watch the sky day and night, perceive it likewise.

Ayant aussitôt fait seller sa jument, l'Astronome Apogée galope à Mirliflis, sans perdre son astre de vue.

L'Institut convoqué immédiatement, s'assemble en toute hâte.

52.

Having immediately saddled his mare, Astronomer Guignard gallops to Mirliflis, without losing his asteroid from sight.

The Institute, immediately convoked, assembles in all haste.

« Une planète immense !... opaque !... fortement habi=
tée ! ..... Un Satellite !!!!! ...
Tout l'Institut, par un mouvement spontané se lève en
criant : Un Satellite ...... Vive le Roi !!!!!! .....
53.
Arrêté, séance tenante : Que la priorité de
la découverte appartient au Ginvernais,
soit à cause du Satellite qui en fait tout
le prix ; soit, éventuellement, parce que
Guignard est le fils d'un père qui descend
d'un aïeul dont le grand père maternel a
épousé la nièce d'une particulière de Mir=
liflis.

"An immense planet! . . . opaque! . . . densely inhabited! . . . . . A Satellite! ! ! ! . . ."

The whole Institute, in a spontaneous outburst, rises up shouting: A Satellite . . . . Long Live the King! ! ! ! ! ! . . . . . .

Passed, in session: that priority in the discovery goes to Ginvernais, either because of the satellite which is the whole point of it; or, eventually, because Guignard is the son of a father who descends from an ancestor whose maternal grandfather married the niece of a Mirliflis citizen.

Cependant Milord et Milady se rendent sur le paquebot qui doit les ramener en Angleterre.

Meanwhile Milord and Milady proceed to the steamer which will take them to back to England.

Cependant le Maire dégouté de l'exil par ses dernières aventures, reprend à pied le chemin de sa commune.

54.

Meanwhile the Mayor, disgusted with exile by his latest adventures, resumes on foot the road to his commune.

Le Télescope projetant une ombre qui accompagne le Maire, celui ci en prend de l'ombrage et se retire dans le bois pour lui laisser prendre les devans

The telescope projecting a shadow that accompanies the Mayor, the latter takes umbrage and retires to a wood in order to let it pass ahead of him.

Après quoi, pour égayer le voyage, le Maire achète à crédit du papier tim=
bré, et s'asseyant sous les ombrages, il interroge des témoins possibles, et
il rédige des procès-verbaux fictifs.
Mais Sentant l'inanité de Ses considérans, le
Maire n'y goûte aucun charme, ensorte que
Son existence Se décolorant il lui vient à l'esprit des projets Sinistres.
Ayant emprunté le Sabre d'un Caporal à
chevrons, le Maire ouvre Sa chemise et
lève Sur Son Sein l'arme fatale.
55.

After which, in order to brighten his journey, the Mayor buys stamped paper on credit, and seating himself in the shade, interrogates possible witnesses, and draws up fictive reports.

But sensible of the inanity of his proceedings, the Mayor finds no charm in them, so that his existence loses its luster and sinister plans come to mind.

Having borrowed a veteran corporal's sabre, the Mayor opens his shirt and raises against his breast the fatal weapon.

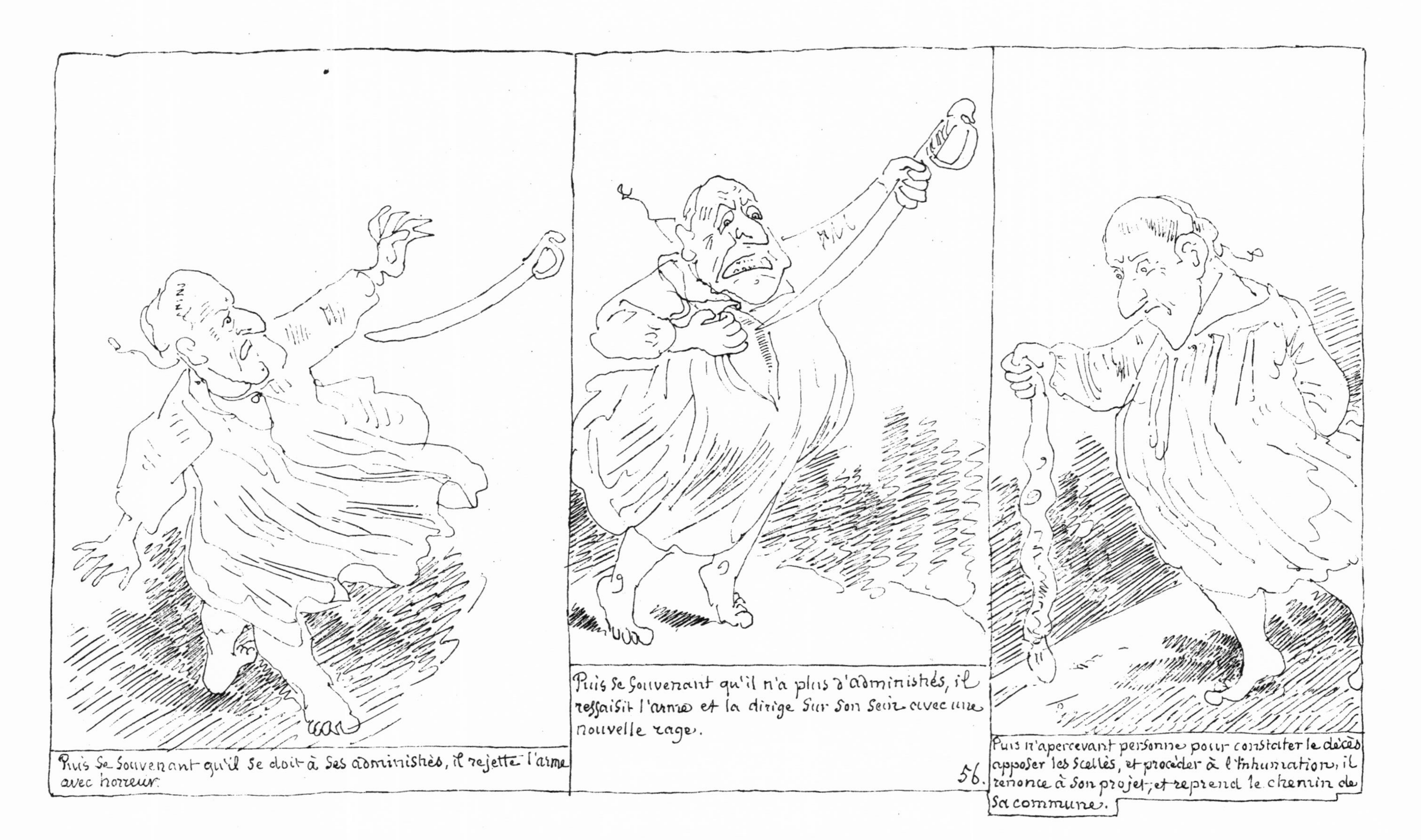
Puis se souvenant qu'il se doit à ses administrés, il rejette l'arme avec horreur.
Puis se souvenant qu'il n'a plus d'administrés, il ressaisit l'arme et la dirige sur son sein avec une nouvelle rage.
56.
Puis n'apercevant personne pour constater le décès apposer les scellés, et procéder à l'inhumation, il renonce à son projet, et reprend le chemin de sa commune.

Then remembering what he owes to the citizens under his administration, he throws away the weapon with horror.

Then remembering that he has no such citizens any more, he seizes the weapon again and places it against his breast with renewed rage.

Then realizing that there is no one to record his death, append the seals, and proceed to burial, he renounces his plan, and resumes the road to his commune.

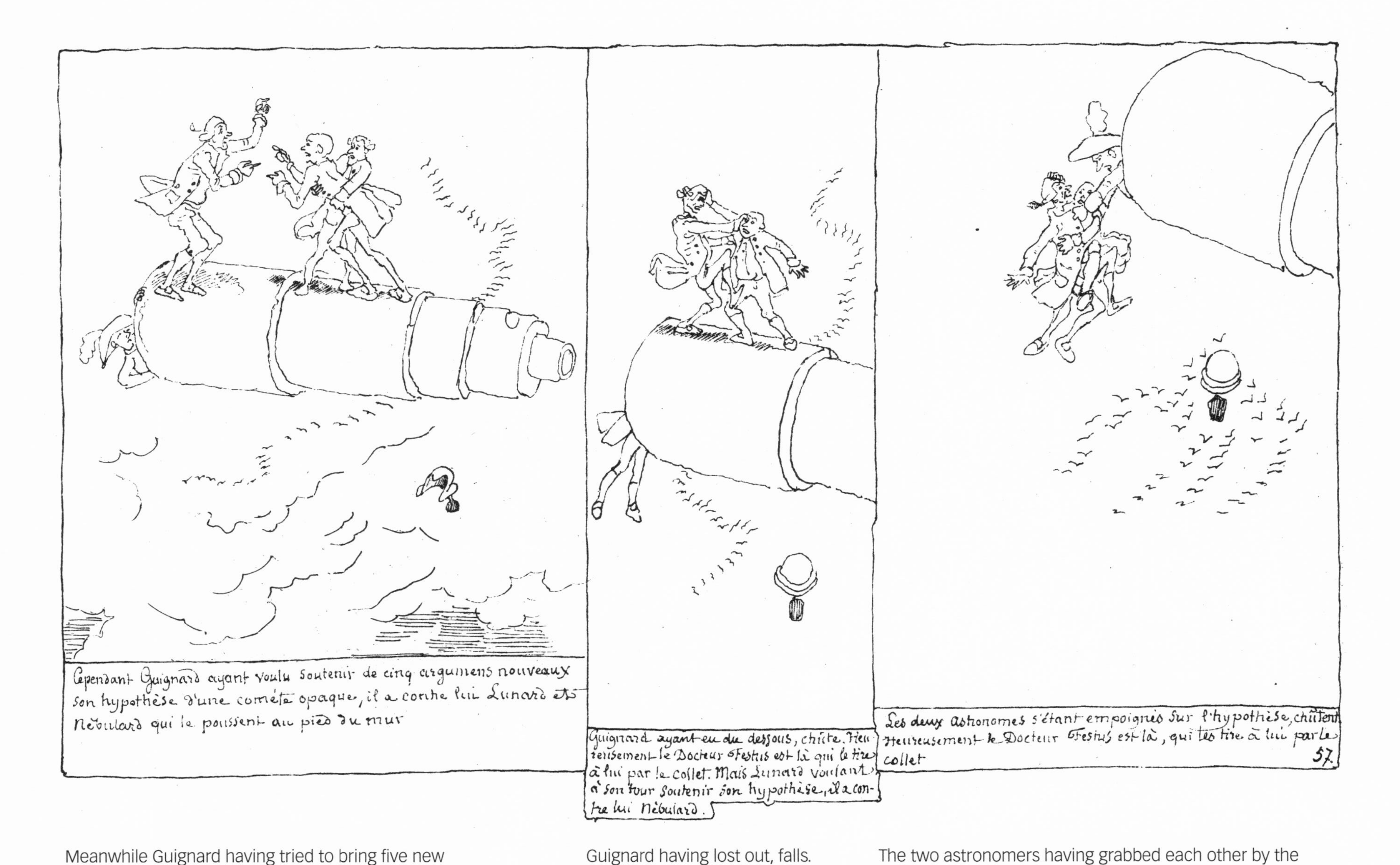
Cependant Guignard ayant voulu soutenir de cinq argumens nouveaux son hypothèse d'une comèta opaque, il a contre lui Lunard et Nébulard qui le poussent au pied du mur
Guignard ayant eu du dessous, chûte. Heureusement le Docteur Festus est là qui le tire à lui par le collet. Mais Lunard voulant à son tour soutenir son hypothèse, il a contre lui Nébulard.
Les deux astronomes s'étant empoignés sur l'hypothèse, chûtent. Heureusement le Docteur Festus est là, qui les tire à lui par le collet
57.

Meanwhile Guignard having tried to bring five new arguments in support of his hypothesis about an opaque comet, finds himself opposed by Lunard and Nébulard who drive him into a corner.

Guignard having lost out, falls. Fortunately Dr. Festus is there to pull him up by the collar. But Lunard trying in turn to support his hypothesis, finds he has Nébulard against him.

The two astronomers having grabbed each other by the hypothesis, fall. Fortunately Dr. Festus is there, to pull them up by the collar.

La discussion continue à l'intérieur si vivement que le Docteur Festus croit devoir y demeurer étranger.
Cependant Milord et Milady passent le détroit. Le Capitaine ayant regardé en l'air voit une trombe solide qui arrive dans la direction du paquebot et il ordonne de forcer la marche.
La trombe approchant, le Capitaine perd la tête, ferme les écoutilles, et fait jeter dans le feu cinquante trois boisseaux de charbon à la fois.
58.

The discussion continues inside, in so lively a manner that Dr. Festus finds it better to stay out of it.

Meanwhile Milord and Milady pass over the channel. The Captain having looked up, sees a solid whirlwind advancing in the direction of the steamer and gives the order full speed ahead.

As the whirlwind approaches, the Captain loses his head, closes the hatches, and has fifty-three bushels of coal thrown onto the fire all at once.

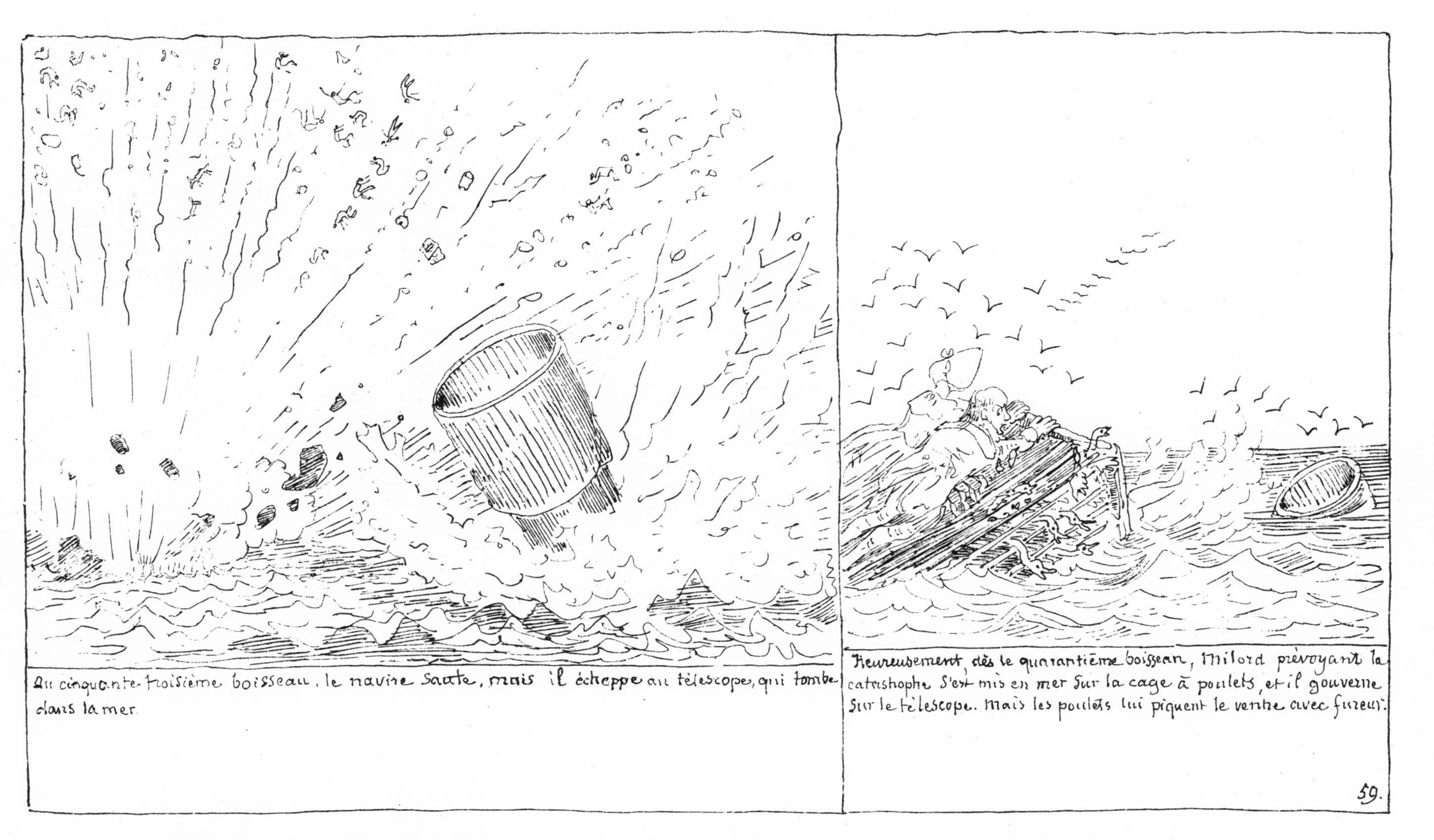
Au cinquante-troisième boisseau, le navire saute, mais il échappe au télescope, qui tombe dans la mer.
Heureusement, dès le quarantième boisseau, Milord prévoyant la catastrophe s'est mis en mer sur la cage à poulets, et il gouverne sur le télescope. Mais les poulets lui piquent le ventre avec fureur.
59.

At the fifty-third bushel, the ship explodes, but it escapes the telescope, which falls into the sea.

Fortunately, at the fortieth bushel, Milord foreseeing the catastrophe, throws himself into the sea on the chicken cage, and he steers to the telescope. But the chickens peck at his belly furiously.

Milord est astonishé beaucoup en écoutant sortir du télescope un grand cliquetis d'hypothèses.

Cependant Monsieur et Madame Apogée, après une nuit délicieu-
se sont réveillés par un bruit de vingt-huit mâchoires qui cra-
quent de consternation.

60.

Milord is most astonished to hear a great clicking of hypotheses issuing from the telescope.

However Mr. and Mrs. Apogée, after a delicious night, are awakened by the sound of twenty-eight jaws cracking in consternation.

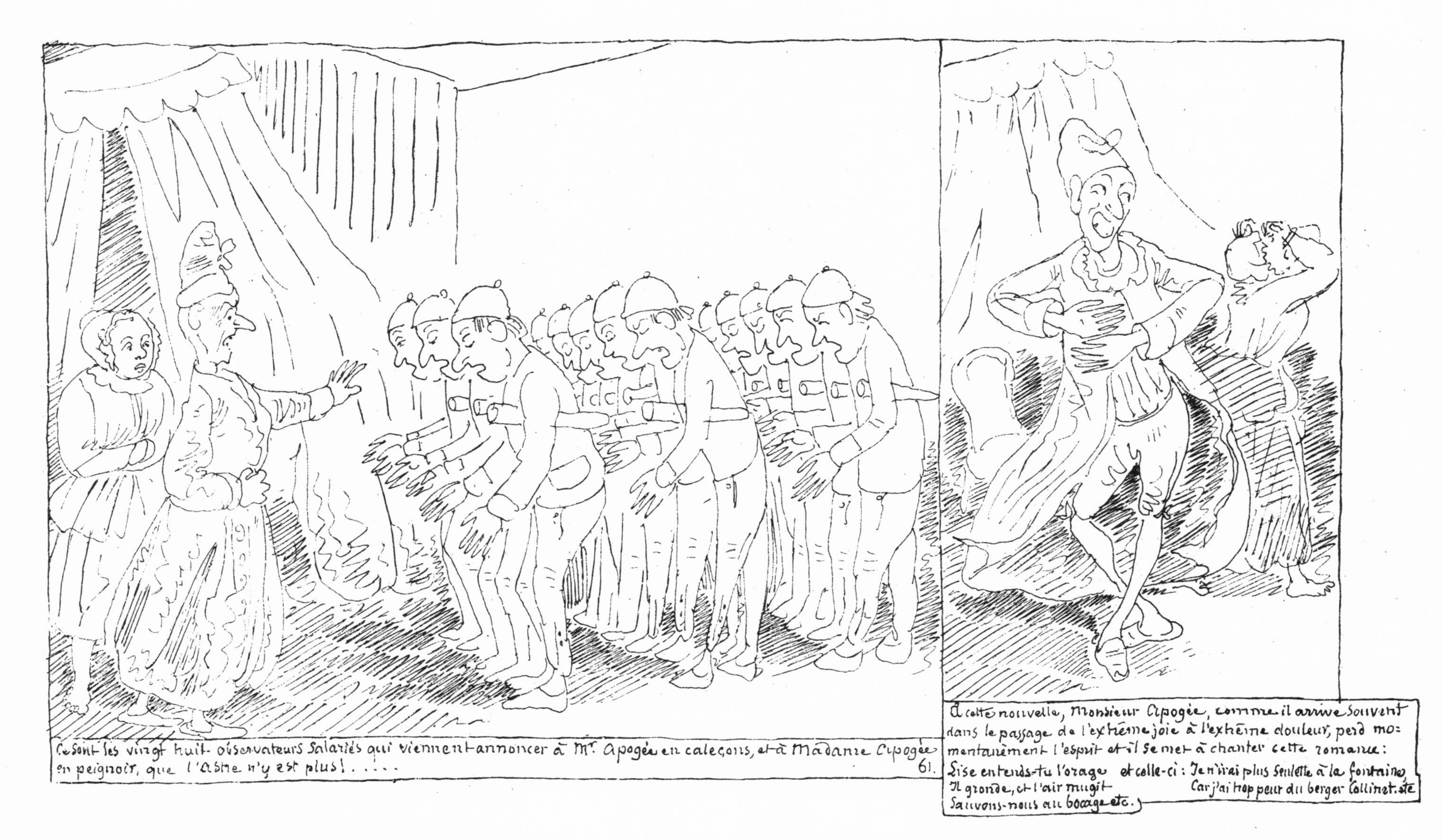
Ce sont les vingt huit observateurs salariés qui viennent annoncer à Mr. Apogée en caleçons, et à Madame Apogée en peignoir, que l'astre n'y est plus! . . . . .
61.
A cette nouvelle, Monsieur Apogée, comme il arrive souvent dans le passage de l'extrême joie à l'extrême douleur, perd momentanément l'esprit et il se met à chanter cette romance:
Lise entends-tu l'orage
Il gronde, et l'air mugit
Sauvons-nous au bocage etc.
et celle-ci: Je n'irai plus seulette à la fontaine,
Car j'ai trop peur du berger Collinet. etc

It is the twenty-eight salaried observers who come to announce to Mr. Apogée in his undershorts, and to Mrs. Apogée in her dressing gown, that the asteroid is gone!

At this news, Mr. Apogée, as happens often in the transition from extreme joy to extreme grief, temporarily loses his mind, and begins to sing this ballad:
Lise, do you hear the storm / It roars, and the air howls / Let us escape to the grove etc.
and this one:
I shall no longer go all on my own to the fountain, / For I am too afraid of the shepherd Collinet. etc.

Puis il force Madame Apogée à danser le menuet.

À la cinquième révérence, il plante là sa femme, saute dans le jardin, et escalade le grand pommier dont il cueille les pommes avec une activité vraiment fébrile

62.

Then he forces Mrs. Apogée to dance the minuet.

At the fifth reverence, he forsakes his wife, leaps into the garden, and climbs up the big apple tree where he gathers apples in a truly feverish manner.

Madame Apogée ordonne aux vingt-huit observateurs salariés de poser la grande échelle et d'aller ôter leur maître de dessus le pommier.
Quand Mr Apogée les voit tous sur les échelons, il poussa l'échelle du pied, et les vingt-huit observateurs salariés tombent, le dos dans le gazon, et l'échelle sur le ventre.
63

Mrs. Apogée orders the twenty-eight salaried observers to place the big ladder and to go and remove their master from the midst of the tree.

When Mr. Apogée sees them all perched on the rungs, he kicks off the ladder, and the twenty-eight salaried observers fall with their backs onto the grass and the ladder on their bellies.

Alors Monsieur Apogée leur lance ses pommes sur le nez, et les vingt-huit prennent la fuite en criant: Sauve qui peut! . .

64.

À cette vue Monsieur Apogée rit avec une telle véhémence, qu'entrant en faiblesse il tombe du pommier sur le terreau, où il reste empreint comme un bronze dans du plâtre frais. C'est là que Madame Apogée en peignoir retrouve son époux en caleçons.

Then Mr. Apogée throws apples in their face, and the twenty-eight take flight shouting: Each man for himself! . .

At the sight of which Mr. Apogée laughs so violently that, in his weakness, he falls from the apple tree into the compost heap, where he remains impressed like a bronze in fresh plaster. There it is that Mrs. Apogée in her dressing gown finds her husband in his undershorts.

La chûte et la fraîcheur du terreau ayant produit une révolution dans le sang, Mr. Apogée revient à la raison, mais pour être en proie à une tristesse amère et profonde.
On essaie, mais sans succès, de frictionner Mr. Apogée avec des étuis de lunettes en peau de chagrin.
65.

The fall and the chill of the compost having induced a revolution in his blood, Mr. Apogée recovers his reason, but only to become prey to a bitter and profound sadness.

Attempts are made, but without success, to rub Mr. Apogée down with telescope cases in grain-leather.

Madame Apogée tâche d'agir sur le moral en disant: Con-
sole-toi, Salomon, il en viendra d'autres. . . .
En se couchant, Mr. Apogée sent
que c'est là . . .
En se levant, Mr. Apogée congédie définitivement
ses vingt huit observateurs salariés qui venaient
prendre ses ordres pour la journée
66.

Mrs. Apogée tries to raise his morale by saying: take comfort, Salomon, there will be others. . . .

Going to bed, Mr. Apogée feels that it is there . . .

On rising, Mr. Apogée gives their definitive discharge to his twenty-eight salaried observers who came to take his orders for the day.

Après quoi, Mr Apogée dépérit malgré les Secours de l'Art et les conso=
lations de l'amitié.
Et il meurt le dix août, à quatre heures, d'un astre rentré.
67.

After which Mr. Apogée wastes away despite the succor of Art and the consolations of friendship.

And he dies August tenth, at four o'clock, of a repressed star.

Cependant le télescope poussé par une brise du Nord Ouest, rebrousse vers le Ginvernais, où il échoue sur la côte. Milady prend terre et aussi Milord qui croit reconnaître sur le dos du Docteur l'habit qu'il a tant cherché.

Voyant Milord qui se dispose à boxer, le Docteur Festus prend la fuite et se cache pendant deux jours dans un plant de pois-gourmands.

68.

Après quoi Milord et Milady marchent le long de la côte, jusqu'au port de Fustaye, où ils s'embarquent de nouveau pour l'Angleterre.

Meanwhile the telescope, pushed by a Nor'westerly wind, turns back to Ginvernais, where it runs aground on the coast. Milady steps onto land and Milord also, who thinks he recognizes on the back of Dr. Festus the clothes he was so much looking for.

Seeing Milord preparing for fisticuffs, Dr. Festus takes flight and hides for two days in a patch of snow peas.

After which Milord and Milady walk along the coast, as far as the port of Fustaye, where they embark again for England.

Cependant les trois Commissaires sortent du télescope sans cesser de sophistiquer contradictoirement au sujet de leurs trois hypothèses respectives.
Ils sont rattrapés par la marée montante qui les ramène dans le détroit. Heureu=sement la discussion, en produisant des mouvemens natatoires les maintient à la surface.
69.

Meanwhile the three commissioners leave the telescope, without ceasing their contradictory quibbling over their three respective hypotheses.

They are caught up in the rising tide that draws them back into the channel. Fortunately the discussion, involving them in natatory movements, keeps them on the surface.

Cinq jours après, ils sont pris au filet par des pêcheurs de Rondeterre.

Les pêcheurs passent deux jours à les détortiller des mailles, et ils trouvent leurs poches pleines de harengs.

70.

Five days later they are taken in a net by the fishermen of Rondeterre.

The fishermen spend two days disentangling them from the meshes, and find their pockets full of herrings.

Abandonnés sur la rive, les trois Commissaires s'avancent dans l'intérieur, sans cesser de sophistiquer contradictoirement, ce qui effraie les troupeaux
à Lowalls, ils troublent le service divin.
71.

Abandoned on the shore, the three commissioners advance into the interior, without ceasing their contradictory quibbling, which frightens the beasts of the field.

At Lowalls, they disturb the divine service.

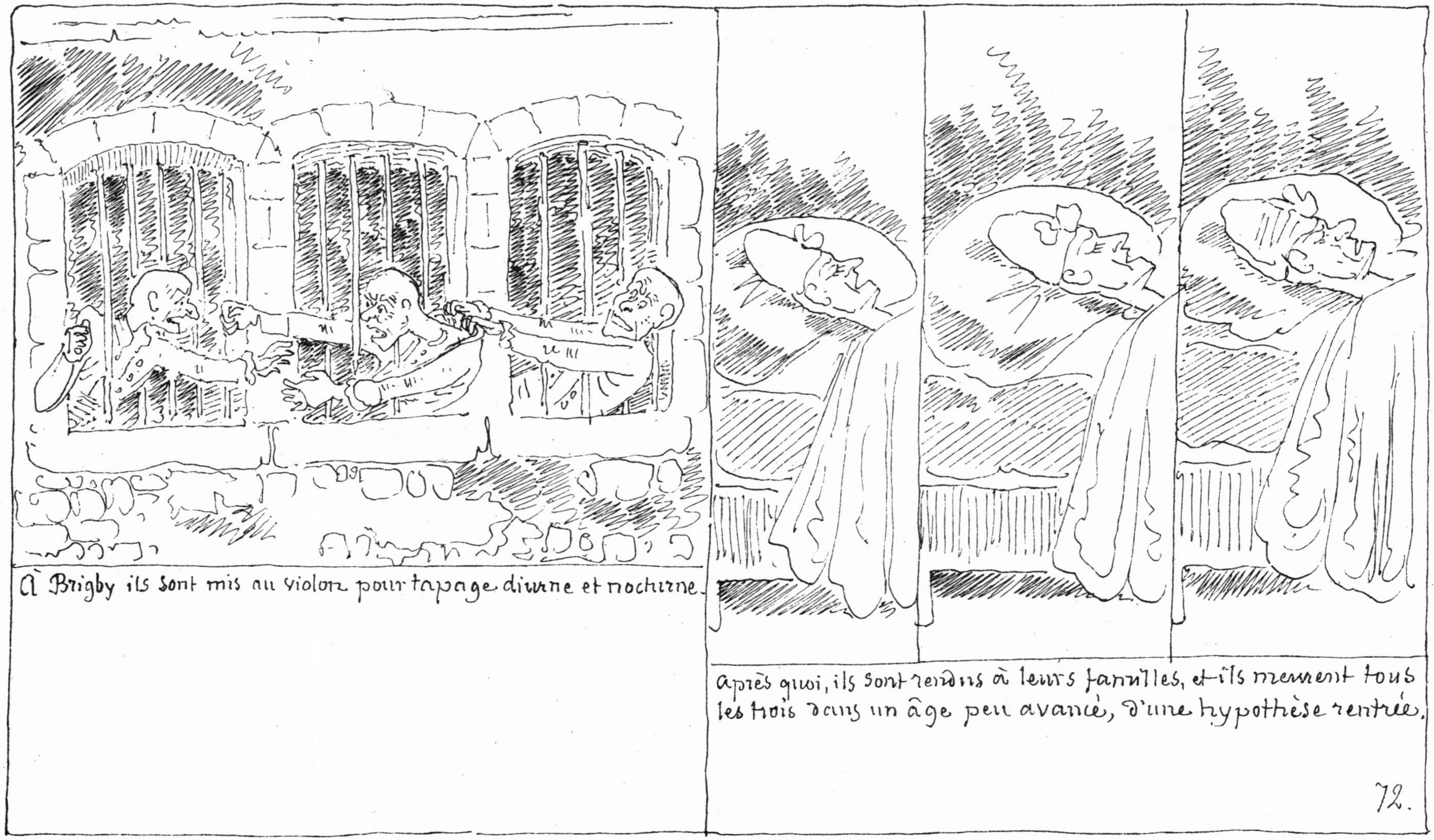

À Brigby ils sont mis au violon pour tapage diurne et nocturne.

Après quoi, ils sont rendus à leurs familles, et ils meurent tous les trois dans un âge peu avancé, d'une hypothèse rentrée.

72.

At Brigby they are put in the lock-up, for disturbing the peace by day and night.

After which they are returned to their families, and all three die prematurely, of a repressed hypothesis.

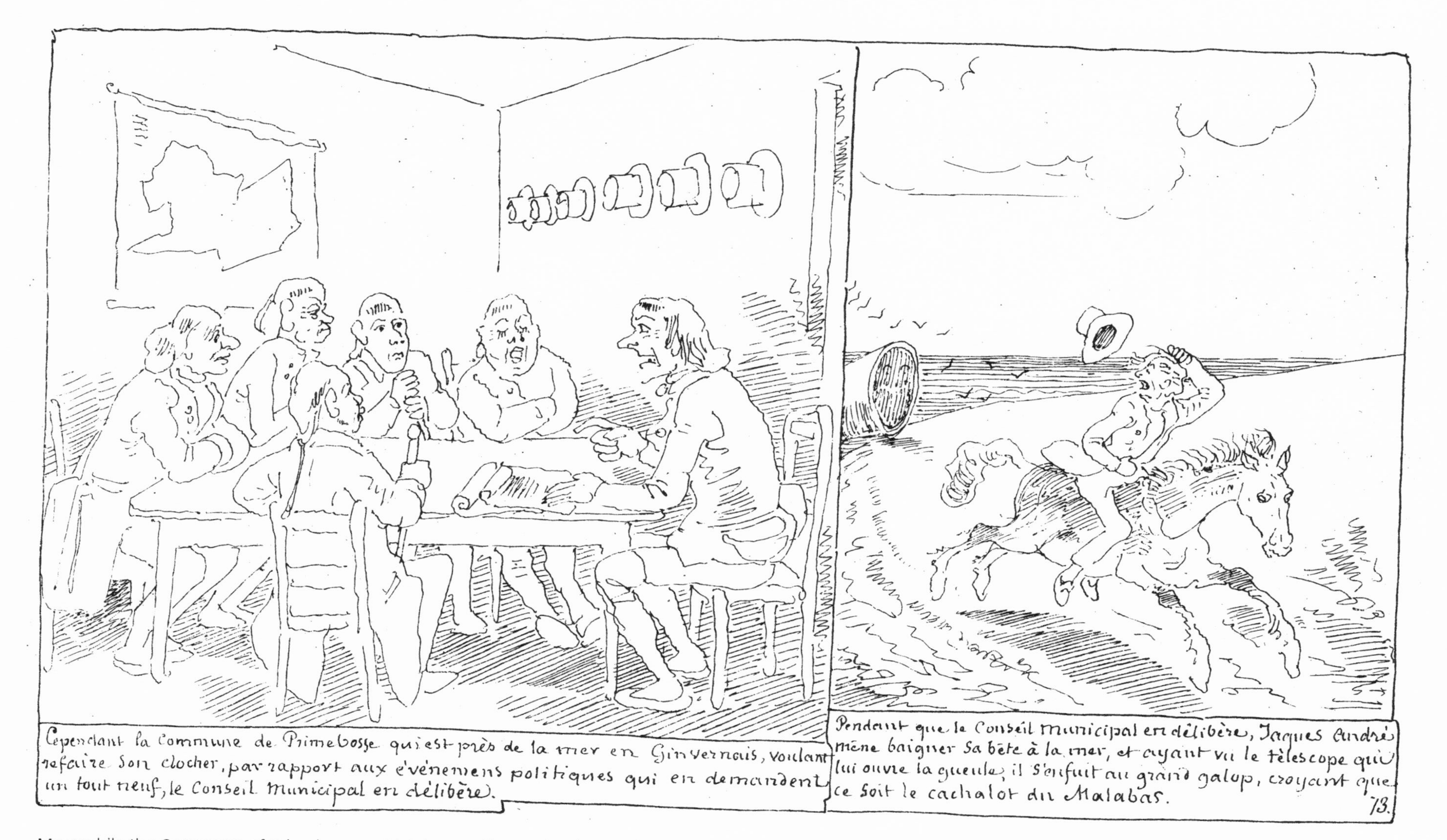
Cependant la Commune de Primebosse qui est près de la mer en Ginvernais, voulant refaire son clocher, par rapport aux événemens politiques qui en demandent un tout neuf, le Conseil Municipal en délibère.
Pendant que le Conseil Municipal en délibère, Jaques André mène baigner sa bête à la mer, et ayant vu le télescope qui lui ouvre la gueule, il s'enfuit au grand galop, croyant que ce soit le cachalot du Malabar.
73.

Meanwhile the Commune of Primebosse, which is near the sea in Ginvernais, desiring to redo their bell tower, with respect to political events which demand a new one, the Municipal Council deliberates on the matter.

While the Municipal Council is deliberating, Jaques André takes his animal to water by the sea, and having seen the telescope with its gaping maw, he flees at a full gallop, thinking that it is the cachalot of Malabar.

On bat la générale dans la Commune et ils viennent en armes au rivage, où, voyant de loin la bête, ils lui tirent dessus durant neuf heures d'horloge, attendant qu'elle ferme la gueule pour s'en approcher sans risque.
74.
Comme ils n'avancent rien, quatre déterminés s'en vont à deux lieues de là pour s'embarquer sans être vus du monstre, puis faisant un grand contour pour venir l'examiner par derrière, ils s'écrient : Miracle ! Miracle ! c'est un clocher ! ! . . . . . . Alors la Commune approche sans crainte, le Curé en tête, qui prend possession au nom de l'Église.

The alarm is sounded in the Commune and they come armed to the shore where, seeing the beast from afar, they fire on it for nine hours of the clock, waiting for it to close its maw in order to approach it safely.

Since this gets them nowhere, four determined men set off to embark two leagues away in order to avoid being seen by the monster, then making a big detour to allow them to examine it from behind, they exclaim: Miracle! Miracle! It's a bell tower! ! . . . . . . Then the Commune feels safe in drawing near, the Curé at the head, who takes possession in the name of the Church.

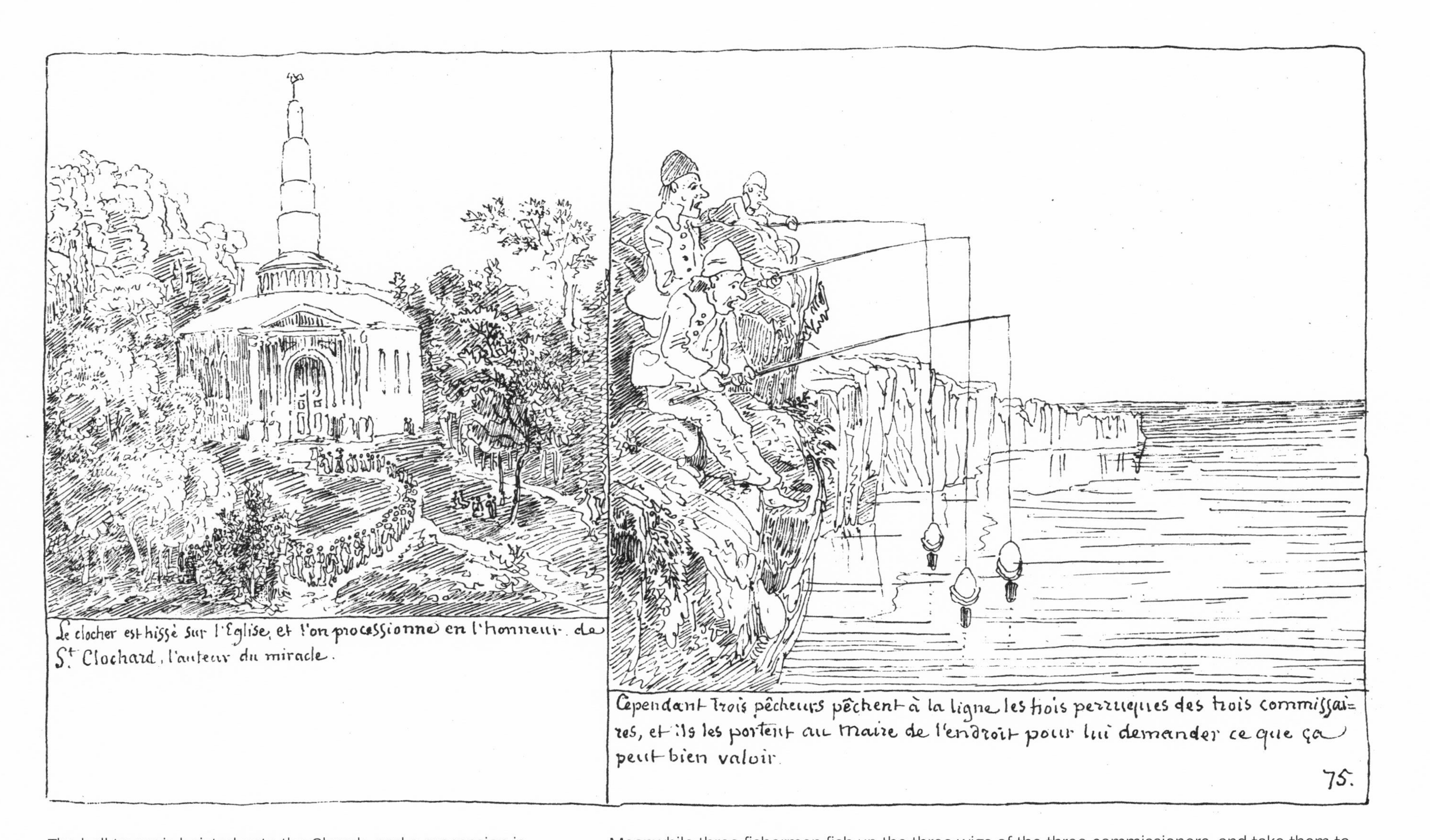
Le clocher est hissé sur l'Eglise, et l'on processionne en l'honneur de
S.t Clochard, l'auteur du miracle.
Cependant trois pêcheurs pêchent à la ligne les trois perruques des trois commissai=
res, et ils les portent au maire de l'endroit pour lui demander ce que ça
peut bien valoir.
75.

The bell tower is hoisted onto the Church, and a procession is held in honor of St. Clochard, author of the miracle.

Meanwhile three fishermen fish up the three wigs of the three commissioners, and take them to the local Mayor to ask what those things might be worth.

Le Maire leur dit que c'est des bêtes d'eau Salée, et qu'il y a quelque chose à gagner, mais il ne leur en offre rien, en sorte qu'ils vont à Prévot l'Ecrivain public.
PREVOT
ECRIVIN PUBLIC
Prévot, l'Ecrivain public, leur dit que c'est des fausses couches de Baleine, et que ça ne vaut rien à manger, par rap=port à ce que ça n'a pas eu son excroissance, et qu'on ne mange le veau qu'après huit mois. Ensorte que, moyennant trois sous, il leur écrit une lettre pour Favras le Botaniste, qui demeure à huit lieues de là.
Favras, le Botaniste, leur dit que c'est une pulpe filamenteuse qui a recouvert une noix du Micisispi, et il leur en donne deux écus patagons.
76.

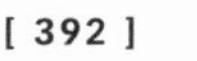

The Mayor tells them that they are salt-water creatures and that there is something to be got for them; but he offers them nothing, so that they go to Prévot the Public Letter-writer.

Prévot the Public Letter-writer tells them that they are aborted bits of Whale fetus, and that they are no good to eat, since they have not had their excrescence, and that one eats veal only after eight months. So that, for a fee of three sous, he writes a letter for Favras the Botanist, who lives eight leagues away.

Favras the Botanist tells them it is a filamentary pulp covering a Micisispi nut, and gives two Patagonian écus for them.

Favras le botaniste, part pour Mirliflis, et va droit à Mr. Dubalay, conservateur en chef des Musées Royaux, qui trouve que c'est trois magnifiques crustacés non encore classés, et qui les achète pour douze écus patagons la pièce.
Mr. Dubalay, moyennant mille écus la pièce, en enrichit le Musée, où ils font l'admiration des Étrangers de marque.
Cependant le Maire à mesure qu'il approche de sa Commune, à mesure aussi se sent plus de drôlerie et de félicité
77.

Favras the Botanist leaves for Mirliflis, and goes straight to Mr. Dubalay, head keeper of the Royal Museums, who finds that they are three magnificent hitherto unclassified crustaceans, and who buys them for twelve patagonian écus each.

Mr. Dubalay, at the price of a thousand écus the piece, enriches the Museum with them, where they are objects of admiration by distinguished Foreigners.

Meanwhile the Mayor, the closer he approaches to his Commune, the more affable and happy he feels.

Mais n'y retrouvant âme vivante, excepté l'ane de Julien le borgne qui lèche la boîte à sel, le Maire ploye sous le faix, perd toute dignité, et parcourt toutes les phases de la démoralisation.

But finding not a living soul there, except One-eyed Julien's ass licking the salt box, the Mayor collapses under the burden, loses all dignity, and runs the gamut of demoralization.

D'abord le Maire s'étourdit dans les plaisirs, et il se donne à lui même un grand bal dans la Salle de l'Hôtel de Ville, ayant pris les rafraîchissemens dans la boutique de Frelay, l'Oncle, qui vent de l'anisette et du pain d'épices. Les fêtes durèrent huit jours.

78

At first the Mayor drowns himself in pleasures, and gives himself a big ball in the banqueting chamber of the Town Hall, having lifted the refreshments from the shop of Frelay, the Uncle, who sells aniseed and gingerbread. The festivities lasted a week.

Ensuite le Maire se livre à la boisson, s'étant établi chez Roset, au grand Pressoir, où il met tous les tonneaux en perce, et boit aussi du bouché.

Then the Mayor surrenders to drink, having established himself at the Roset's, at the big Wine Press, where he broaches all the casks, and drinks the bottles too.

Ensuite le maire se livre à l'extrême dévotion, se faisant hermite dans le fond d'une bosse défoncée, et se fustigeant d'un trousseau de clés trois fois le jour.
Ensuite le Maire se livre aux raffinemens d'une mollesse efféminée, se mettant des papillottes dès l'aurore, et allant s'étendre du matin au soir sous l'ombre énervante des platanes.
79.

Then the Mayor surrenders to extreme piety, becoming a hermit in a broken barrel, and beating himself three times a day with a bunch of keys.

Then the Mayor surrenders to the refinements of an effeminate weakness, putting on hair curlers at dawn, and resting from morning until evening in the enervating shade of the plane trees.

Ensuite le Maire se livre à l'amour des richesses, et il prévarique dans l'exercice de ses fonctions; s'adjugeant à tout bout de champ les immeubles de ses administrés par prescription ou défaut.

80.

Ensuite le Maire s'ennuyant de sa richesse recourt aux émotions fortes. Il met le feu aux quatre coins du village, après avoir jeté la pompe à feu dans un puits; après quoi il sonne lui-même le tocsin pendant cinq jours consécutifs.

Afterwards the Mayor gives way to the love of riches, and he prevaricates in the exercise of his function; awarding himself left, right, and center the real estate of the citizens by prescription or default.

Then the Mayor becoming bored with riches, has recourse to strong emotions. He sets fires all over the village, after having thrown the fire pump into a well, after which he sounds the tocsin himself for five days on end.

Au bruit de la cloche, le Maire revient à la raison; d'où il est sur le point de perdre l'esprit, tant il se repent d'avoir profané son caractère.
S'étant choisi une cave en façon de catacombe, il s'y ensevelit durant quinze jours dans une douleur muette et profonde.
Après quoi voulant se procurer des administrés pour reconstituer sa commune, il prend une bêche et se dirige vers la grande route.
Arrivé sur la grande route, le Maire y creuse tout au milieu, une fosse de sept pieds de profondeur, sur cinq de large
81.

At the sound of the bell, the Mayor recovers his reason; at which point he is about to lose his mind, so much does he repent of having profaned his character.

Having chosen a cellar by way of catacomb, he hides himself away in it for a fortnight in profound and silent pain.

After which, with the intent of procuring for himself citizens to reconstitute his commune, he takes a spade and directs his steps towards the highway.

Arriving at the highway, the Mayor digs in the middle a pit seven feet deep and five feet wide.

Après quoi, ayant placé sur la fosse un treillis d'osier recouvert de terre, le Maire s'embusque, pour voir venir et être tout prêt.

After which, having placed over the pit a willow trellis covered in earth, the Mayor lies in ambush, to watch for any passer-by, and to be all prepared.

Cependant, au bout de deux jours, le Docteur Festus quitte le plant de pois-gourmands et se remet en route.

Meanwhile, after two days, Dr. Festus leaves the patch of snow peas and sets off again.

La force armée qui se trouve dans le voisinage sent l'habit et double le pas.

82.

The armed force lurking in the area smells the uniform and doubles its pace.

Croyant s'apercevoir qu'il est poursuivi par deux hommes armés, le Docteur prend la fuite, et la force armée suit l'habit.
Tous les trois tombent dans la fosse du maire de qui la joie est grande.
Avant toute chose le maire exige qu'on lui rende l'habit, dont il se revêt incontinent avec une inexprimable félicité.
83.

Thinking that he sees himself pursued by two armed men, Dr. Festus takes flight, and the armed force follows the uniform.

All three fall into the pit dug by the Mayor, whose joy knows no bounds.

Before anything else, the Mayor demands that he be given back his uniform, which he puts on immediately with inexpressible satisfaction.

Incontinent aussi, le Docteur saisit l'habit par les pans, entraîne le Maire dans la fosse, grimpe le long de son dos et s'échappe au plus vite.

No less immediately Dr. Festus seizes the uniform by the coattails, drags the Mayor into the pit, climbs along his back, and quickly escapes.

Le Maire, pour se dédommager de ses longues privations commande la manoeuvre, durant douze heures d'horloge, dans la fosse même.

84.

The Mayor, to compensate for his long privations, orders maneuvers for twelve hours of the clock, inside the pit itself.

Après quoi, réfléchissant qu'il ne dispose plus d'un seul administré, le Maire se voue à la carrière militaire, et il part en marquant le pas.

After which, reflecting that he no longer disposes of a single citizen, the Mayor dedicates himself to a military career, and he sets off marking time.

Le Maire continue pendant trois années à parcourir le pays à la tête de ses forces, couchant à la belle étoile, et marchant le chef nu, comme Trajan, car il a perdu son chapeau.
85
Et il serait mort dans un âge très avancé sans sa grande manoeuvre normale, dans laquelle, après neuf heures de marches et contremarches, il commanda tout à coup le pas de course au bord du grand canal, de façon qu'ils y tombèrent tous les trois.

The Mayor continues for three years to rove the countryside at the head of his forces, sleeping in the open, and marching bareheaded, like Trajan, for he has lost his hat.

And he would have died at an advanced age but for his great standard maneuver, in which, after nine hours of marches and counter-marches, he suddenly gave the order "at the run" at the edge of the grand canal, so that all three of them fell in.

Et ils ont été enterrés sous le Saule des Pierrettes, en face du roc de Mortaise, rière l'écluse du grand canal.

Cependant le Docteur retrouve sur la lisière du bois son mulet, qui, se sentant son maître sur le dos, reprend au galop le chemin de l'écurie.

86.

And they were buried under the Pierrettes Willow, opposite the Mortaise rock, [be]hind the grand canal lock.

Meanwhile Dr. Festus finds at the edge of the wood his mule which, feeling his master on his back, picks up the road to the stable at the gallop.

En approchant de l'écurie, le Mulet fait une telle pétarade de joie que le Docteur lancé en l'air retombe sur un poirier où il demeure accroché et évanoui.
Le Fermier du Docteur et son fils Jean étant venus pour cueillir les poires, décrochent leur maître et le transportent dans son lit.
Le Docteur revenu à lui le lendemain matin, s'imagine qu'il n'a pas quitté le logis, et, tout en contemplant l'aurore, il songe au beau rêve qu'il a fait.
87.
Fin des Voyages et Aventures du Docteur Festus

Approaching the stable, the Mule gives such a backfire of joy that Dr. Festus is thrown into the air and falls into a pear tree where he remains suspended and unconscious.

Dr. Festus's tenant farmer and his son Jean having come to pick the pears, unhook their master and carry him into his bed.

Dr. Festus, recovering consciousness the next day, imagines that he has not quit his home, and even as he contemplates the Dawn, he muses over the lovely dream he has had.

End of the Travels and Adventures of Dr. Festus.

1845
Histoire d'Albert.
par Simon de Nantua

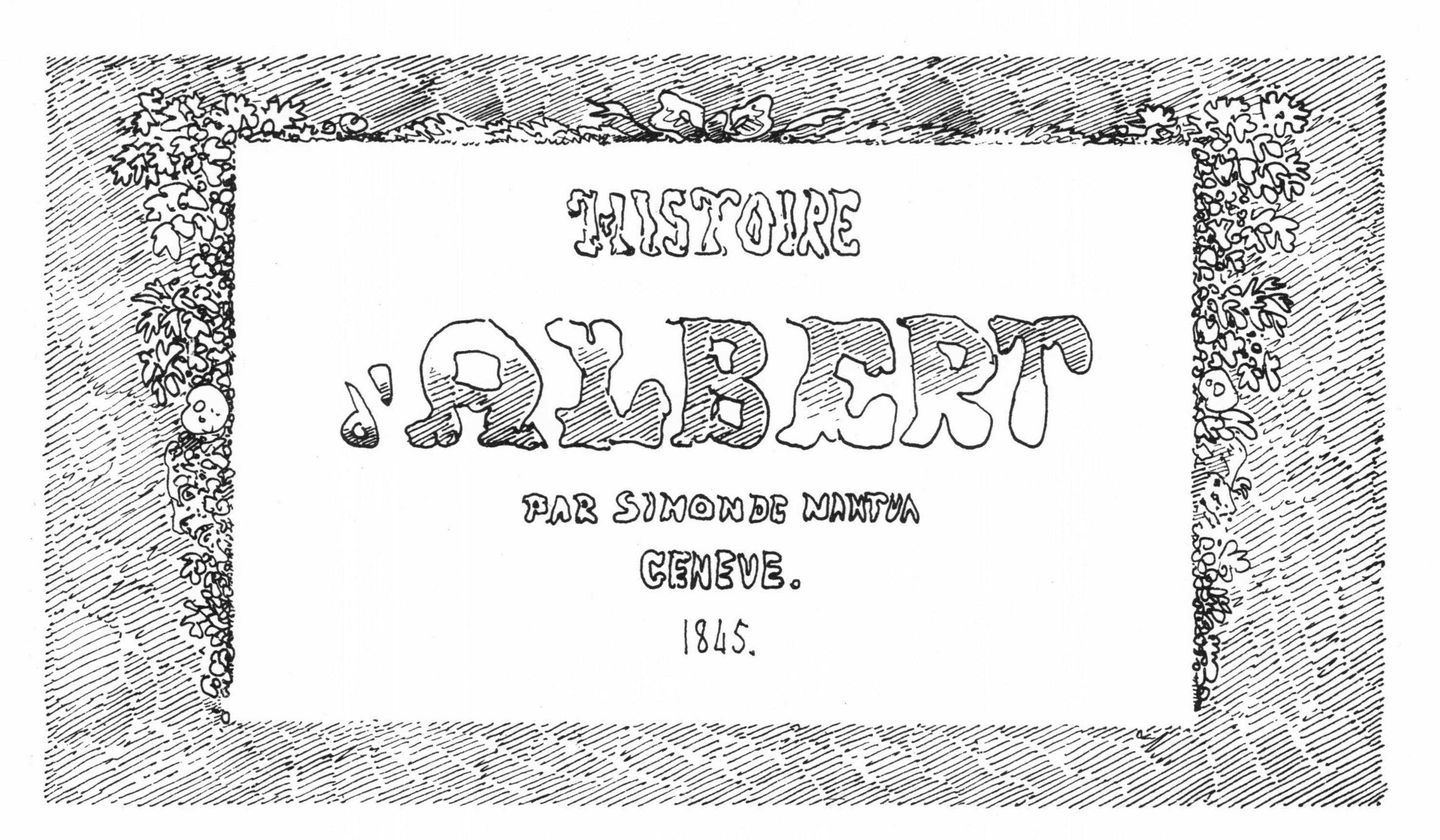
HISTOIRE
d'ALBERT
PAR SIMON DE NANTUA
GENEVE.
1845.

Préface.
Ci-contre, et rien qu'à tourner les pages, l'on verra figurée au naturel toute l'histoire d'Albert, et comme quoi, n'étant bon à rien, il finit par trouver sa vocation.
Va, petit livre, et choisis ton monde; car, aux choses folles, qui ne rit pas, baille; qui ne se livre pas, résiste; qui raisonne se méprend; et qui veut rester grave, en est maître.
Fol. 1
Vers l'âge de douze ans, Albert est mis au collège, où il continue d'occuper le dernier banc.
Ce qui est cause que son père le morigène.

Preface. Hereafter, and merely by turning the pages, you will find represented the whole history of Albert from the life, and how, being good for nothing, he ended by finding his vocation.

Go little book and choose your world, for at crazy things, those who do not laugh, yawn; and those who do not yield, resist; and those who reason, are mistaken, and those who would keep a straight face, can please themselves.

At about the age of twelve years, Albert is put in secondary school, where he always occupies the bottom bench.

Which causes his father to scold him.

2.

et que sa mère le reconforte.

And his mother to comfort him.

Comme le concours approche,
Albert s'y prépare.

Since exams are getting near,
Albert prepares himself.

et son père veille à ce qu'il ne s'endorme pas.

And his father makes sure that he does not fall asleep.

3.
Par malheur, le jour du concours, Albert s'oublie devant une ménagerie.
Ce qui est cause que son père le morigène,
et que sa mère le reconforte.
Le collège terminé, on délibère sur la carrière d'Albert qui insiste pour poursuivre celle des études, parceque, au collège, ce qui l'ennuyait, c'étaient les élémens.

Unfortunately, the day of the exams, Albert dallies in front of a menagerie.

Which causes his father to scold him.

And his mother to comfort him.

When school is finished, a debate is held on the future of Albert who insists on pursuing his studies, because, in school, it was the elements that bored him.

4.

On cède au vœu d'Albert qui est habillé en étudiant. Pour l'encourager son père lui fait présent d'une badine, et sa mère d'un pantalon à sous-pieds.

Albert's wishes prevail, and he is dressed as a student. His father gives him a walking cane to encourage him, and his mother trousers with foot-straps.

En attendant l'ouverture des cours Albert déclame du Hugo

While waiting for the beginning of classes, Albert declaims Victor Hugo.

Ce qui frappe Albert dans son Hugo, ce sont les préfaces, à cause des doctrines.

What strikes Albert in his Hugo, is the prefaces, because of the ideology.

à partir de ce jour, Albert comprend pourquoi les élémens l'ont tant ennuyé; c'est qu'il lui fallait des doctrines.

From this moment, Albert understands why the elements bored him so; it's because he needed ideology.

Les cours académiques s'ouvrent enfin, et Albert écoute avec avidité.

The academic lectures begin at last, and Albert listens avidly.

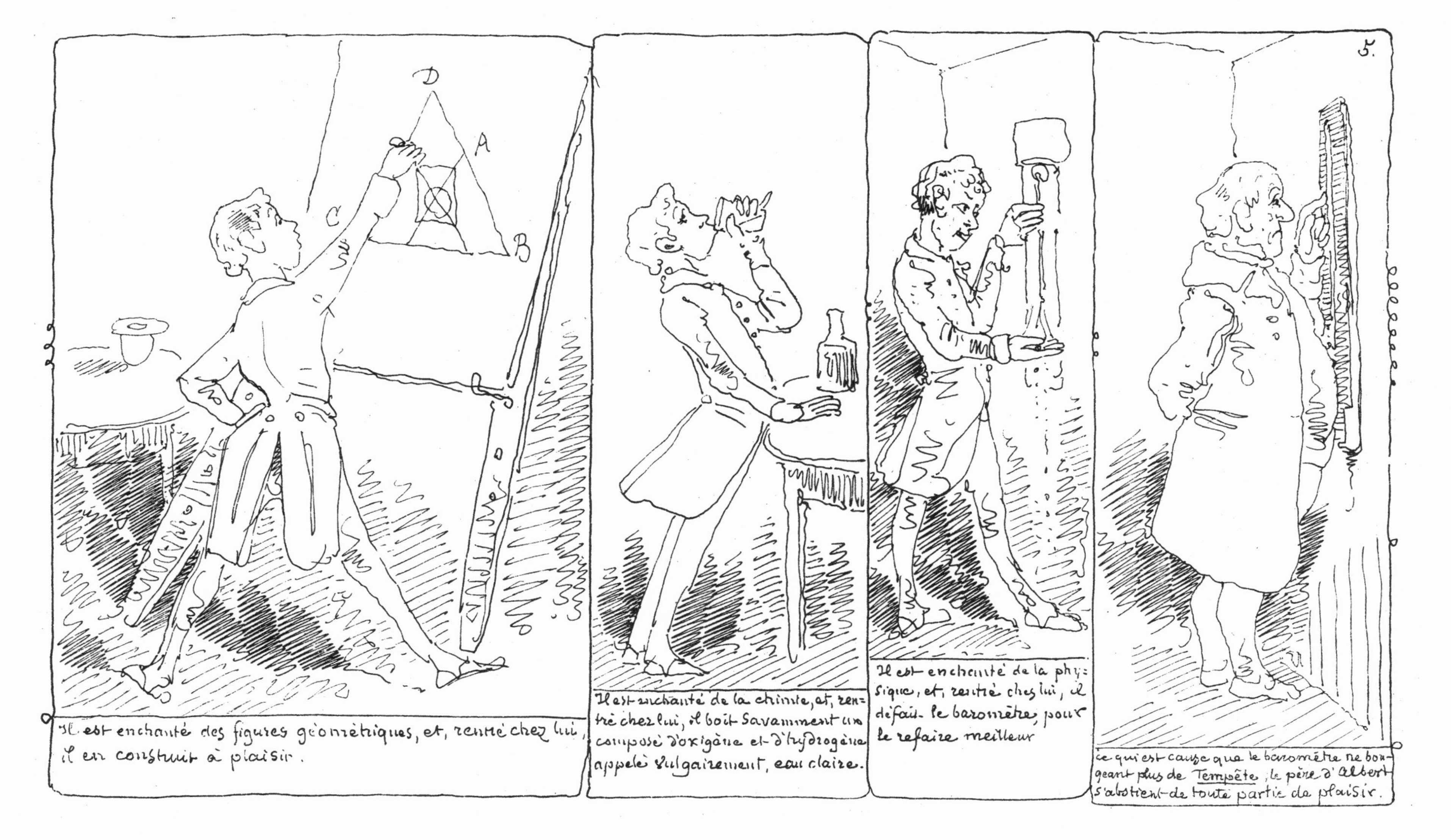
5.
D
A
C
B
Il est enchanté des figures géométriques, et, rentré chez lui, il en construit à plaisir.
Il est enchanté de la chimie, et, rentré chez lui, il boit savamment un composé d'oxigène et d'hydrogène appelé vulgairement, eau claire.
Il est enchanté de la physique, et, rentré chez lui, il défait le baromètre, pour le refaire meilleur
ce qui est cause que le baromètre ne bougeant plus de Tempête, le père d'Albert s'abstient de toute partie de plaisir.

He is enchanted by geometric diagrams, and back home, constructs them to his heart's content.

He is enchanted by chemistry, and back home, he cleverly drinks a concoction of oxygen and hydrogen commonly called water.

He is enchanted by physics, and, back home, he takes apart the barometer, to make it work better.

Which causes the barometer to get stuck at *Storm*, so that Albert's father gives up on any pleasure trips.

6.
alors Albert lui explique que ce qui fait que le Baromètre est bas, c'est l'extrême pesanteur de l'air.
Albert explique aussi à la Servante que ce qui produit l'ébullition, c'est l'extrême chaleur du feu.
Albert explique aussi à sa mère que ce qu'elle admire là, ce sont des cé-pales
et que ce qu'elle a sous les yeux, c'est un arc soustendu.

So Albert explains to him that what causes the Barometer to go down is the increased weight of the air.

Albert explains also to the Maid that what causes boiling is the increased heat of the fire.

Albert explains also to his mother that what she is admiring there are cepales.

And what she sees in front of her is a subtended arc.

7.
Cependant, à mesure que les constructions géométriques vont se compliquant davantage, Albert en est insensiblement moins épris.
Ce qui fait que son père est insensiblement moins content de lui.
et que sa mère le reconforte.
A mesure aussi que la chimie s'éloigne de l'eau claire, Albert y met moins d'intérêt.

Meanwhile, as the geometric constructions get more and more complicated, Albert becomes gradually less enthusiastic about them.

Which causes his father to become gradually less happy with him.

And his mother to comfort him.

And the more chemistry goes beyond water, the more Albert loses interest in it.

8.

Ce que sa mère comprend jusqu'à un certain point.

Which his mother understands up to a certain point.

Mais pas du tout son père.

But his father not at all.

à mesure aussi que les autres Sci= ences tournent davantage aux notions positives, Albert s'en occupe avec moins d'ardeur.

The more the other sciences turn towards positive concepts, the less keen Albert becomes on them.

Ce que sa mère s'explique un peu par des suites de petite vérole.

Which his mother explains as the consequence of smallpox.

mais son père pas du tout.
Albert fait de sérieuses réflexions.
Cependant on lui permet de faire son droit, parce que, au fond, ce qui l'ennuyait en philosophie, c'étaient les notions positives.
Ce qui enchante surtout Albert, ce sont les origines du droit naturel, parce qu'elles se perdent dans la nuit des temps.
9.
Mais à mesure que l'on s'éloigne de la nuit des temps, Albert se désenchante du droit naturel.

But his father not at all.

Albert does some deep thinking.

He is however allowed to study law because, basically, what bored him in philosophy was the positive notions.

What delights Albert above all is the origins of natural law, because they are lost in the mists of time.

But the further off the mists of time, the less delighted Albert becomes with natural law.

10.
Malgré le droit naturel, Albert est arrêté comme n'ayant pas de permis de chasse.
Et à cause du droit naturel son père lui administre une correction quelque part.
Forcé de retourner aux Cours Albert y porte son Hugo et il s'y repaît de Djinns, de néant, de mort, d'océans et de doctrines.
Mais le droit n'en va pas mieux, en sorte que Albert s'essaie à peindre en vers le vide intime de son âme...
La tombe qui ouvre à sa jeunesse décolorée une gueule séduisante.

Despite natural law, Albert is arrested for not having a hunting license.

And natural law permits his father to administer a correction on some part of him.

Forced to return to the lectures, Albert brings his Victor Hugo and indulges in Djinns, voids, death, oceans, and ideology.

But the law is none the better for this, so that Albert tries painting in verse the inner void of his soul . . .

The tomb that opens a seductive maw to his washed-out youth.

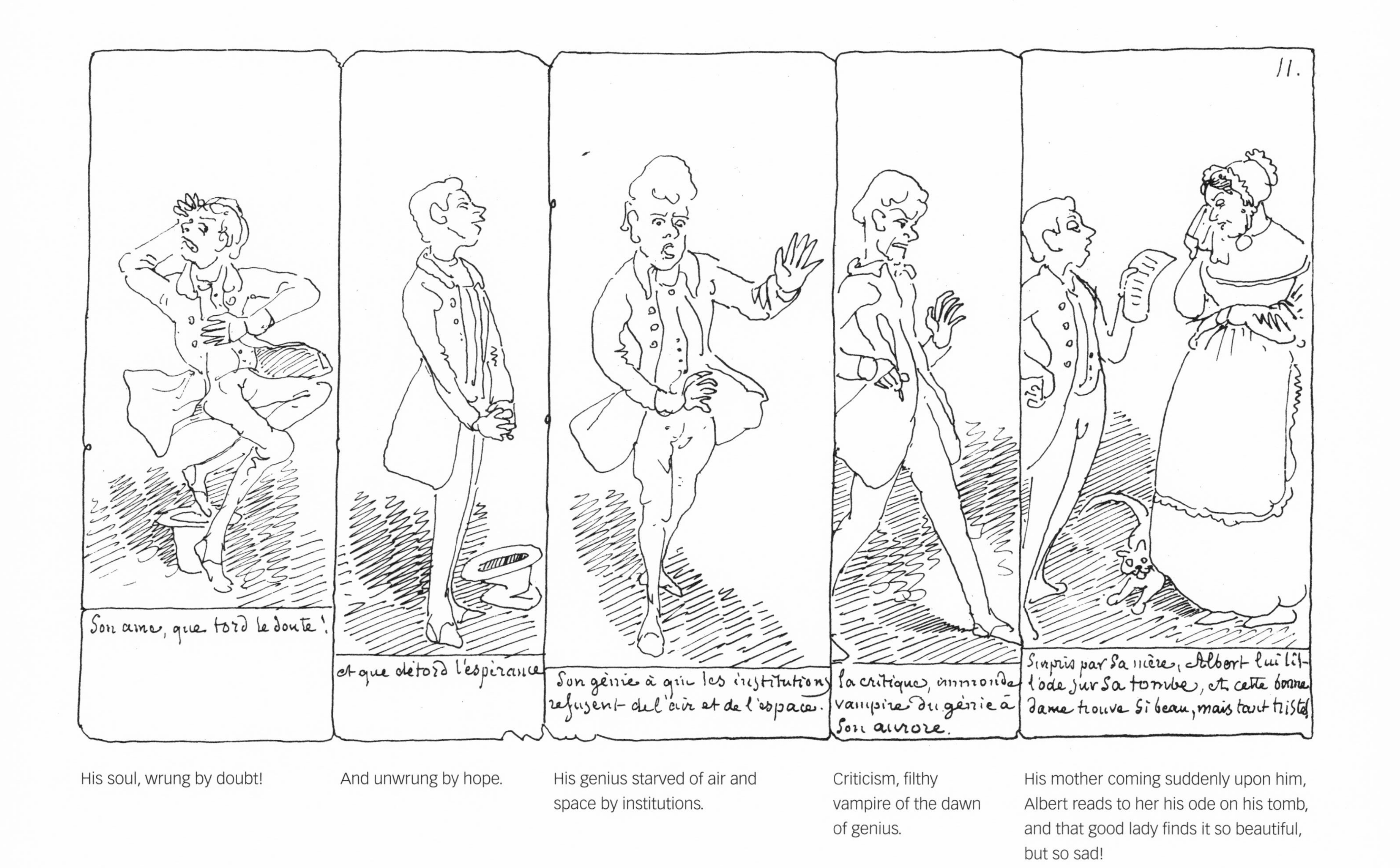
11.
Son ame, que tord le doute!
et que détord l'espérance
Son génie à qui les institutions refusent de l'air et de l'espace.
la critique, immonde vampire du génie à son aurore.
Surpris par sa mère, Albert lui lit l'ode sur sa tombe, et cette bonne dame trouve si beau, mais tant triste!

His soul, wrung by doubt!

And unwrung by hope.

His genius starved of air and space by institutions.

Criticism, filthy vampire of the dawn of genius.

His mother coming suddenly upon him, Albert reads to her his ode on his tomb, and that good lady finds it so beautiful, but so sad!

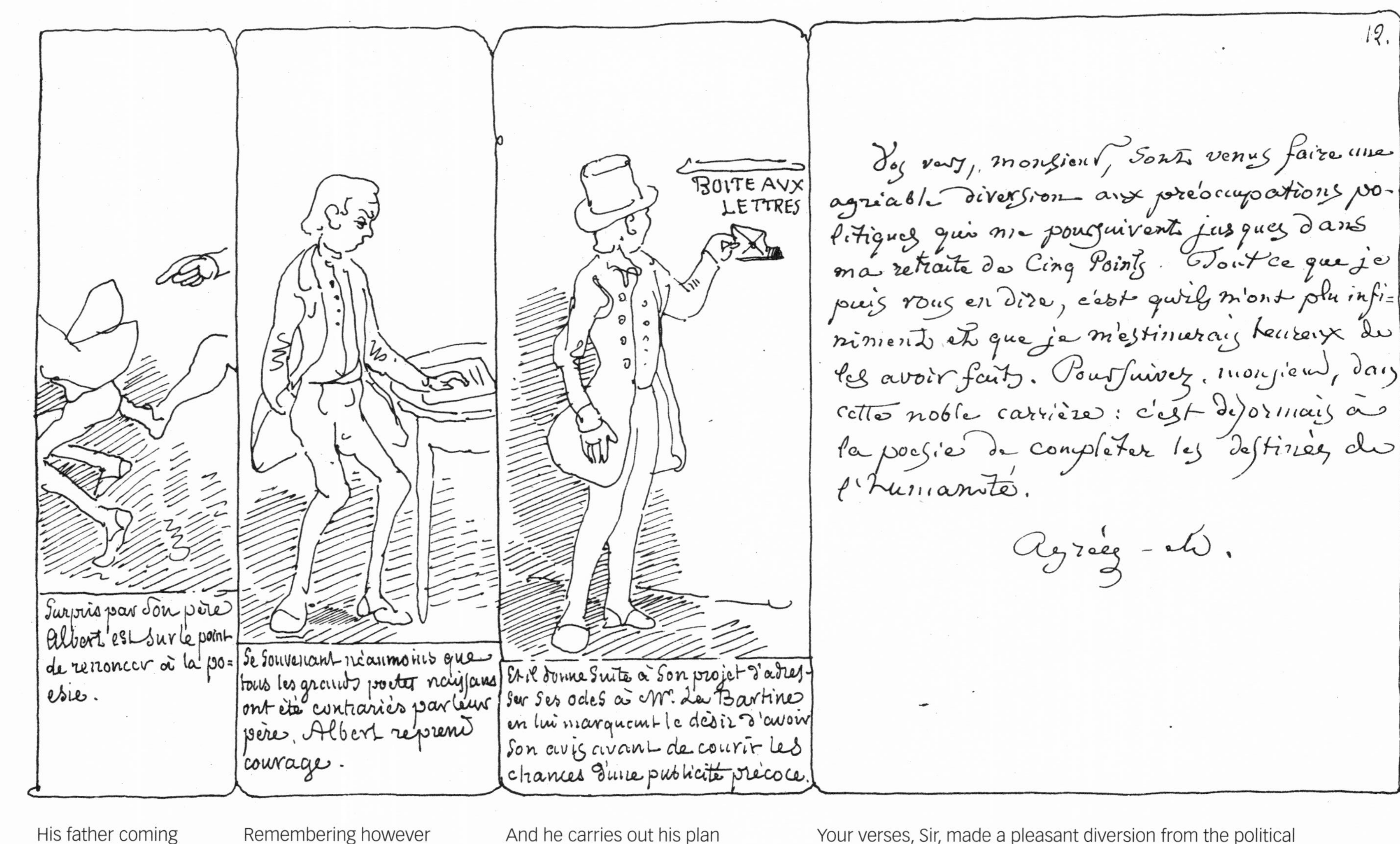
Surpris par son père
Albert est sur le point
de renoncer à la po=
ésie.
Se souvenant néanmoins que
tous les grands poetes naissans
ont été contrariés par leur
père, Albert reprend
courage.
BOITE AUX
LETTRES
Et il donne suite à son projet d'adresser ses odes à Mr. La Bartine
en lui marquant le désir d'avoir
son avis avant de courir les
chances d'une publicité précoce.
12.
Vos vers, monsieur, sont venus faire une
agréable diversion aux préoccupations politiques qui me poursuivent jusques dans
ma retraite de Cinq Points. Tout ce que je
puis vous en dire, c'est qu'ils m'ont plu infi=
niment et que je m'estimerais heureux de
les avoir faits. Poursuivez, monsieur, dans
cette noble carrière : c'est désormais à
la poésie de compléter les destinées de
l'humanité.
Agréez - etc.

His father coming suddenly upon him, Albert is on the point of giving up poetry.

Remembering however that all great budding poets were thwarted by their fathers, Albert summons up his courage.

And he carries out his plan of sending his odes to Mr. La Bartine with a request for advice before running the risk of going public prematurely.

Your verses, Sir, made a pleasant diversion from the political preoccupations which pursue me even to my retreat of Cinq Points. All I can tell you is that I liked them enormously and that I would be happy to have written them myself. Pursue, Sir, this noble career: it is from now on for poetry to make the destinies of humanity complete.

Sincerely—etc.

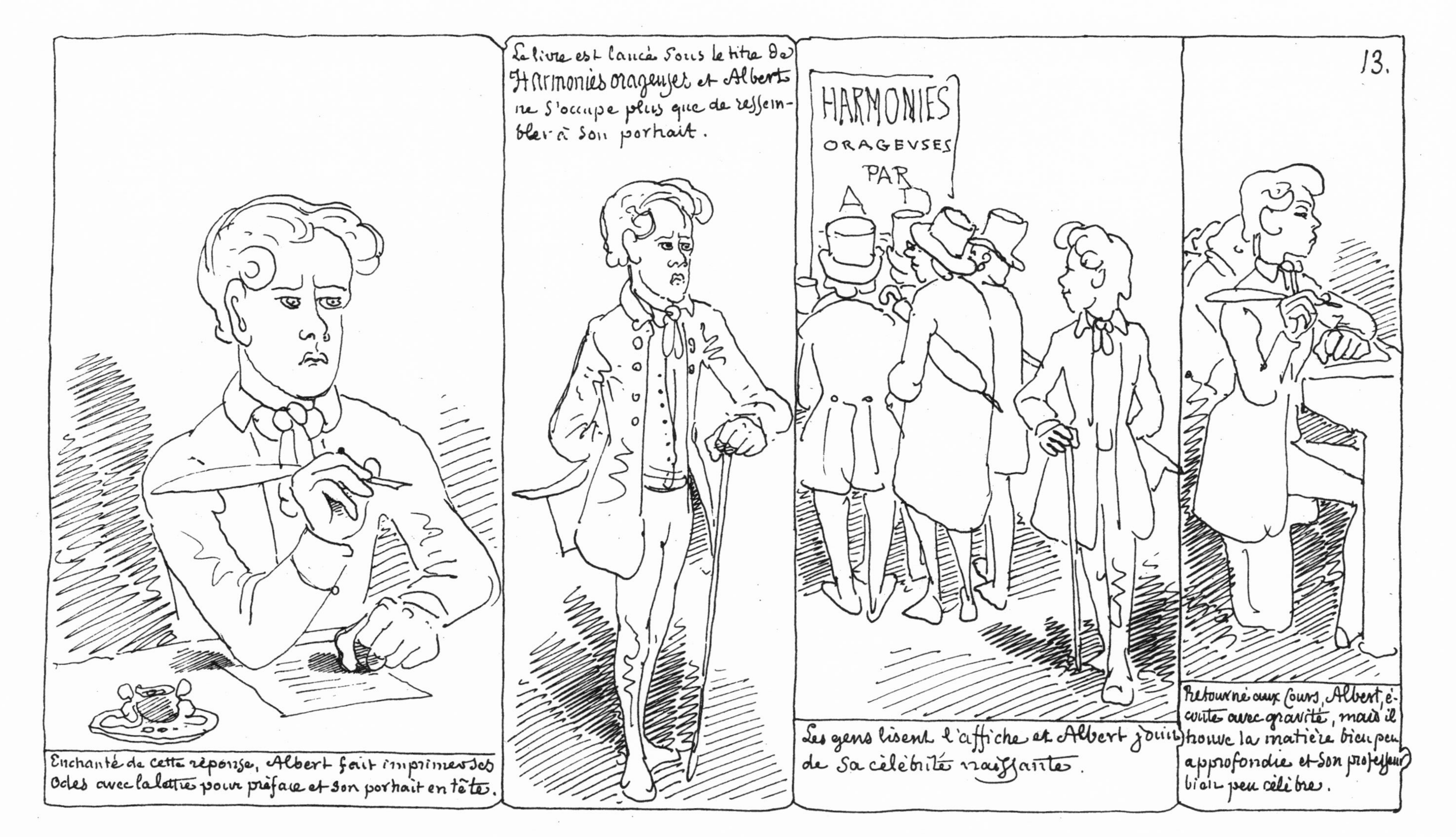
13.
Enchanté de cette réponse, Albert fait imprimer ses Odes avec la lettre pour préface et son portrait en tête.
Le livre est lancé sous le titre de Harmonies orageuses et Albert ne s'occupe plus que de ressembler à son portrait.
HARMONIES
ORAGEVSES
PAR
Les gens lisent l'affiche et Albert jouit de sa célébrité naissante.
Retourné aux cours, Albert écoute avec gravité, mais il trouve la matière bien peu approfondie et son professeur bien peu célèbre.

Delighted with this response, Albert has his verses printed with the letter as a preface and his portrait as frontispiece.

The book is launched under the title *Stormy Harmonies*, and Albert dedicates himself entirely to looking like his portrait.

People read the poster and Albert enjoys his budding fame.

Back at the lectures, Albert listens gravely, but finds the material far too shallow and his professor not at all famous enough.

14.

fcs 600.

Cependant le livre ne se vendant pas, l'imprimeur a l'idée d'adresser sa note au père.

Ah! tu aimes les harmonies orageuses!! ! . . . .

Se trouvant décidément trop contrarié dans sa vocation, Albert renonce pour tout de bon à la poésie.

Et étant retourné aux cours, il s'y tient debout les premiers jours.

When the book does not sell, it occurs to the printer to send a bill to the father.

Ah! So you like stormy harmonies! ! ! . . . .

Finding himself decidedly thwarted in his vocation, Albert gives up on poetry for good.

And back at the lectures, he remains standing at first.

TAMINET.
Mais le droit civil ne laisse pas que de l'attirer bien peu.
à l'Estaminet, Albert se lie avec le Carbonaro Mangini qui lui explique le plan central du grand comité secrets.
Albert assiste riens que pour voir à une Séance du Comité local.
15.
Après quoi, renonçant à ressembler à son portrait, Albert ne s'occupe plus que de se laisser croître une moustache et un collier.

But civil law continues to hold few attractions for him.

At the pub, Albert falls in with the Carbonaro Mangini who explains to him the central plan of the great secret committee.

Albert is present at a meeting of the local committee, just to see.

After which, giving up on any resemblance to his portrait, Albert dedicates himself entirely to growing a moustache and a chinstrap beard.

16.

a mesure que son collier croît, Albert recouvre insensiblement toute sa dignité de l'homme, et il ne voit plus dans les fonctionnaires civils que les horribles exploitateurs du peuple;

dans les fonctionnaires de l'ordre militaire, que les abjects suppôts de la tyrannie organisée;

dans les Curés, que les abrutisseurs du peuple et la valetaille du trône.

As his beard grows Albert gradually recovers all his manly dignity, and he sees in all civil servants nothing but horrible exploiters of the people;

in military officials, only the abject tools of organized tyranny;

in Priests, only the stultifiers of the people and the lackeys of the throne.

17.
Dans les Sacristains et dans les Suisses d'Eglise, que des créatures dégradées, honte à la fois et vermine d'un état social absurde.
Qu'un Sang im-pur.... Abreuve nos Sillons.... Abreuve nos Sillons!!

In sacristans and church guards, only degraded creatures, at once the disgrace and the vermin of an absurd social entity.

May a foul Blood . . . . Drench our Furrows . . . . Drench our Furrows! !

18.

Dans la séance suivante du comité local, Albert jure haine aux Rois, reconstitution de la Pologne, affranchissement de l'Italie, émancipation du Nord, et, généralement parlant tout ce qui fera des cinq parties du monde une seule famille gouvernée par la liberté, unie par l'Egalité, heureuse par la vertu!

Albert s'ouvre à sa mère au sujet de son initiation et il lui révèle les projets du comité local sur les cinq parties du monde. Cette bonne dame trouve tant beau, mais si difficile!

Albert ne s'ouvre pas à son père parce que celui-ci trouve que le droit ne va déjà pas très bien.

Albert trouve sa dignité de l'homme un peu compromise, et il hésite à s'occuper davantage de l'avenir des cinq parties du monde.

In the next meeting of the local committee, Albert swears hatred to Kings, the reconstitution of Poland, the liberation of Italy, emancipation of the North, and generally speaking everything that will make a single family of the five parts of the world governed by liberty, unified by Equality, and happy in its virtue!

Albert reveals to his mother the matter of his initiation and the plans of the local committee for the five parts of the world. That good lady finds it all so fine, but so difficult!

Albert does not reveal anything to his father because the latter finds that the law is already not doing very well.

Albert finds his manly dignity somewhat compromised, and hesitates to dedicate himself further to the future of the five parts of the world.

19.
aussi étant retourné aux cours, il mord ferme au droit constitutionnel.
Mais quand le Professeur en est venu à l'absurdité d'une royauté possible et d'un représentatif applicable, il tousse d'indignation et il quitte brusquement la salle.
Cependant, au dehors, de l'agitation se manifeste, et le Comité local se constitue en permanence.
Des masses s'ébranlent dans une petite rue.
Albert court s'avinner en toute hâte, et il rejoint les masses au moment où elles vont surprendre le poste.

So back at his lectures, he gets his teeth solidly into constitutional law.

But when the Professor comes to the absurdity of the idea of a monarchy with associated parliament, he coughs indignantly and abruptly quits the room.

Outside meanwhile there are disturbances and the local Committee remains permanently in session.

Mobs break forth in a back street.

Albert hurriedly gets himself tipsy and rejoins the mobs at the moment when they are about to attack the police station.

20.

GOUVERNEMENT PROVISOIRE

Pendant qu'on surprend le poste, le Comité local fait afficher dans une petite rue le gouvernement provisoire.

While the police station is under attack, the local Committee announces the formation of a provisional government in posters put up in a back street.

Le poste ayant riposté vivement, les masses se retranchent dans une petite maison d'une petite rue.

When the police station gives a warm riposte, the mobs take refuge in a little house of a back street.

L'avenir des cinq parties du monde est manqué, et des arrestations s'opèrent.

The future of the five parts of the world is aborted, and arrests are made.

Pendant que les arrestations s'opèrent, Albert s'efforce plus que jamais de ressembler à son portrait.

While arrests are being made, Albert tries more than ever to look like his portrait.

Toutefois, averti que les papiers du comité local sont tombés au pouvoir de la Police, Albert déménage.

Alerted however that the local committee's papers have fallen into the hands of the Police, Albert decamps.

21.
N'ayant tout à l'heure plus le sou, Albert entre comme aide
chez un chirurgien dentiste.
Mais s'ennuyant bientôt de l'état de chirurgien dentiste, Albert
entre comme aide, chez un extirpeur de cors et durillons.

Being soon penniless, Albert takes a job as assistant to a dental surgeon.

But soon getting tired of dental surgery, Albert gets a job as an assistant to an extirpator of corns and calluses.

22
Au bout d'un mois, Albert quitte son maître et il extirpe pour son compte.
Par malheur, tous ses sujets étant venus à mourir du tétanos, Albert déménage.
Entré chez un négociant propriétaire à Bordeaux, Albert y tâte furtivement les vins, pour s'instruire.
Ayant fait de rapides progrès, Albert devient commis voyageur en vins, et il assassine d'étage en étage.

After a month of this, Albert leaves his boss and extirpates independently.

Unfortunately all his patients die of tetanus, so Albert decamps.

Getting a job with a vintner owning a business in Bordeaux, Albert furtively test-tastes the wine, just to get the hang of it.

Advancing rapidly, Albert becomes a commercial traveler in wines, pestering people from one floor to the next.

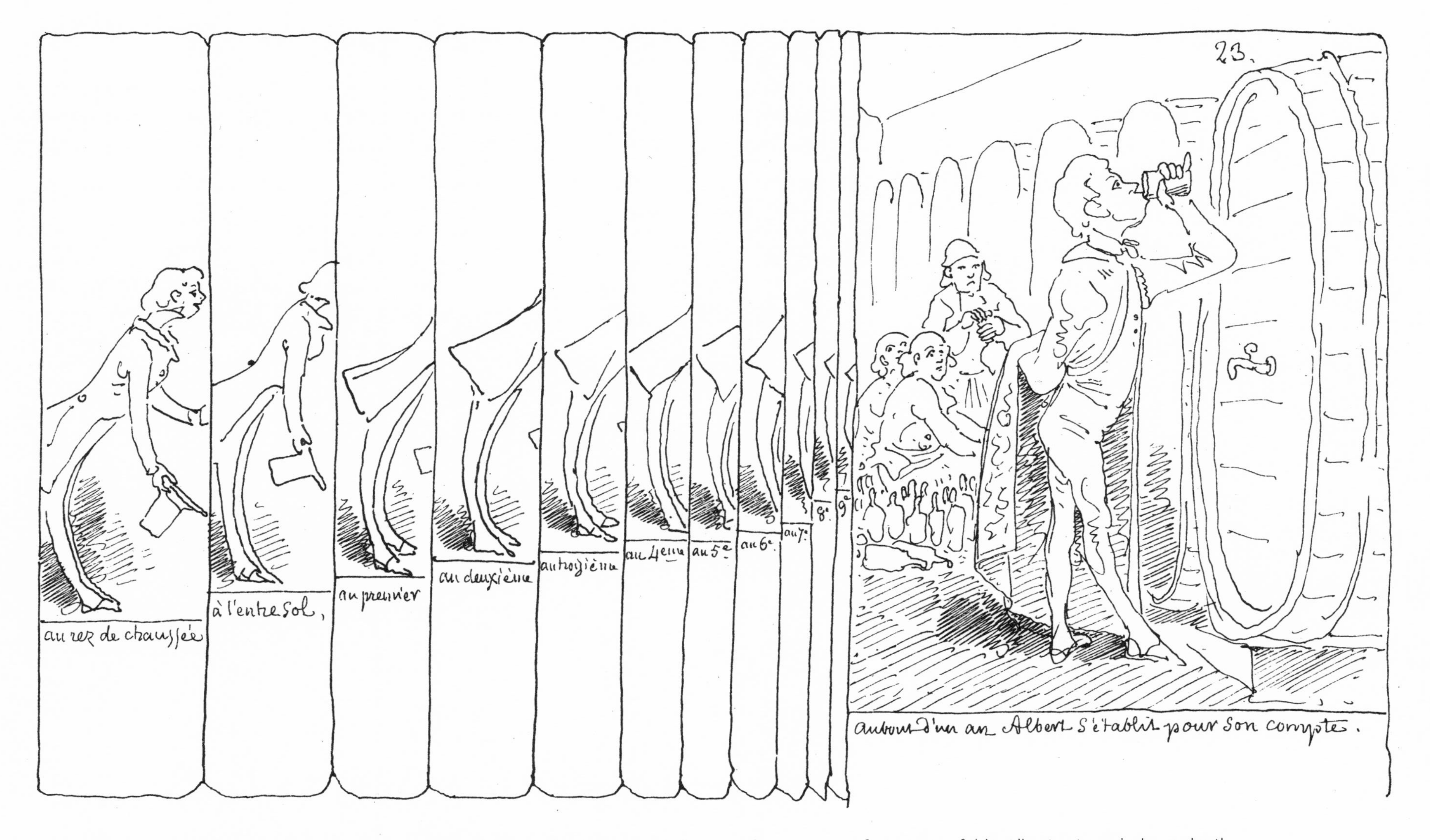

On the ground floor —mezzanine, —first floor —second floor —third floor —4th floor —5th —6th —7th —8th —9th

After a year of this, Albert sets up independently.

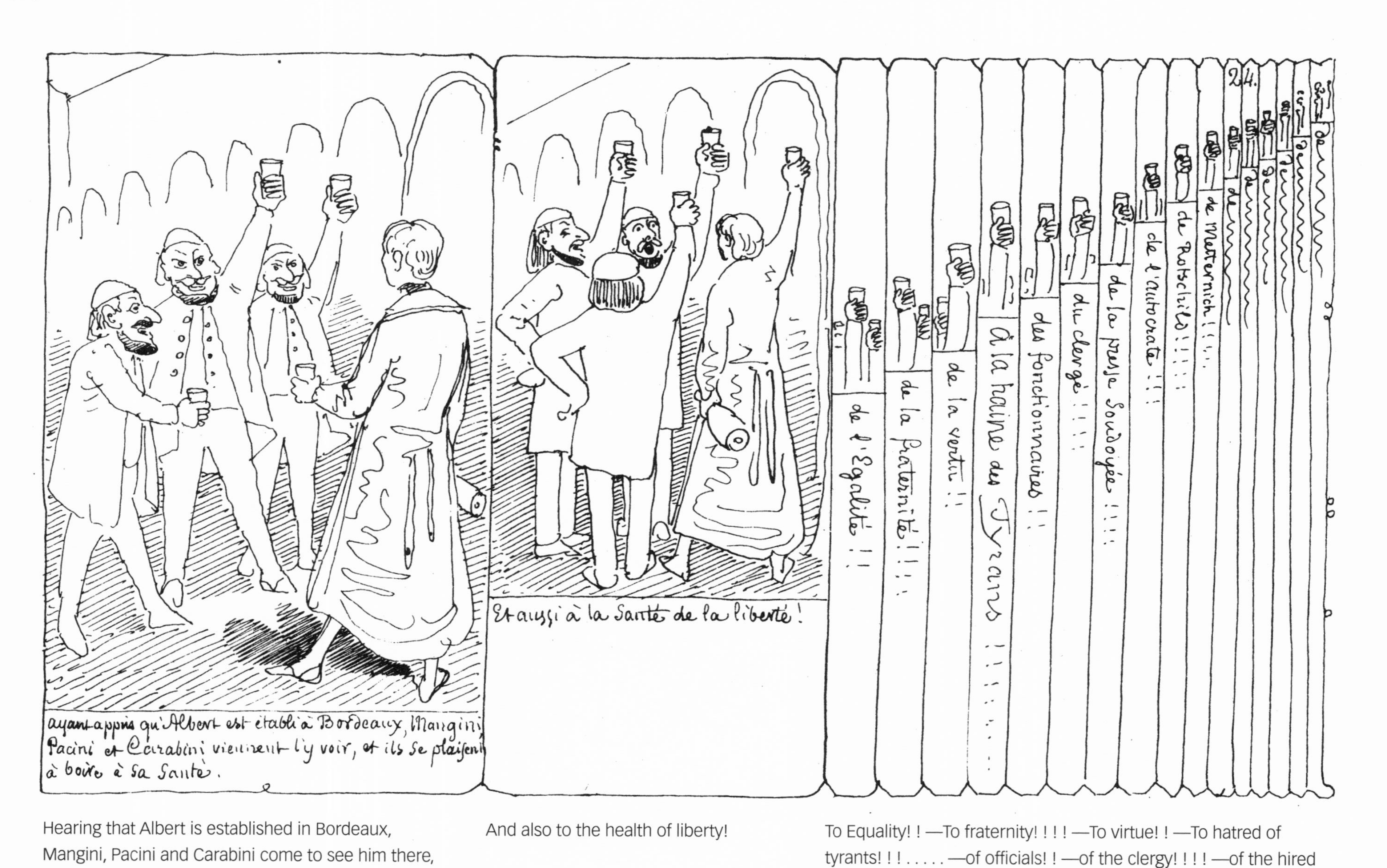
ayant appris qu'Albert est établi à Bordeaux, Mangini Pacini et Carabini viennent l'y voir, et ils se plaisent à boire à sa santé.
Et aussi à la santé de la liberté!
24.
de l'Egalité !!
de la fraternité !!!..
de la vertu !!
à la haine des Tyrans !!!.....
des fonctionnaires !!
du clergé !!!!
de la presse soudoyée !!!!
de l'autocrate !!!
de Rotschild !!!!!
de Metternich !!...
de
de
de
de
de

Hearing that Albert is established in Bordeaux, Mangini, Pacini and Carabini come to see him there, and have the pleasure of drinking to his health.

And also to the health of liberty!

To Equality! ! —To fraternity! ! ! ! —To virtue! ! —To hatred of tyrants! ! ! . . . . . —of officials! ! —of the clergy! ! ! ! —of the hired press! ! ! ! —of the Rothschilds! ! ! ! ! —of Metternich! ! ! . . —of . . . —of . . . —of . . . —of . . . —of . . . —of . . .

25.
Par malheur, la faillite est déclarée, et Jaques déménage.
Entré chez un Editeur libraire, Albert est chargé du placement de la grande édition de la Metaphysique pittoresque, texte et gravures, en sorte qu'il recommence à assassiner d'étage en étage.
au rez de chaussée
au premier
au 2eme
au 3eme
au 4eme

Unfortunately bankruptcy is declared, and Jaques decamps.

Getting a job with a bookseller-publisher, Albert is charged with selling the big edition of METAPHYSICS IN PICTURES, text and engravings, which means that he resumes his pestering of people from floor to floor.

on the ground floor —first floor —2nd —3rd —4th.

Au troisième de la maison voisine, Albert insiste pour être introduit, et il fait antichambre pendant qu'on va prévenir Monsieur.

On the third floor of the house next door, Albert insists on being let in, and he sits in a waiting room while the gentleman of the house is informed.

Monsieur dont l'épouse est sur le point d'accoucher déplore qu'on lui fasse des visites dans un moment pareil.

The gentleman whose wife is on the point of giving birth, finds it deplorable that he should be bothered with visits at such a moment.

Au premier mot de métaphysique pittoresque, Monsieur entre en grande fureur.

At the first mention of metaphysics in pictures, the gentleman gets really furious.

Albert ayant reçu plusieurs contusions se dégoûte de l'état, et il déménage.

Thoroughly bruised, Albert becomes disgusted with the job, and decamps.

27.
TABAC
Entré chez un épicier, Albert y trouve toute l'édition de ses harmonies Orageuses mise en cornets.
Et tant de poésie lui inspirant le dégout du poivre et de la canelle, il méprise son état et forme des rêves de gloire.
ayant traité son patron d'homme vulgaire, Albert est dans le cas de déménager.
En route, Albert achète pour trois francs cinquante centimes, le secret de la méthode d'Aubusson par laquelle on enseigne l'histoire universelle en quatre leçons.

Getting a job with a grocer, Albert finds the whole printing of his *Harmonious Storms* used for paper screws.

And with so much poetry inspiring him with a disgust for pepper and cinnamon, he despises his job and begins to dream of glory.

After calling his boss a common man, Albert finds himself decamping.

On the way, Albert buys for three francs fifty centimes the secret of the Aubusson method of teaching universal history in four lessons.

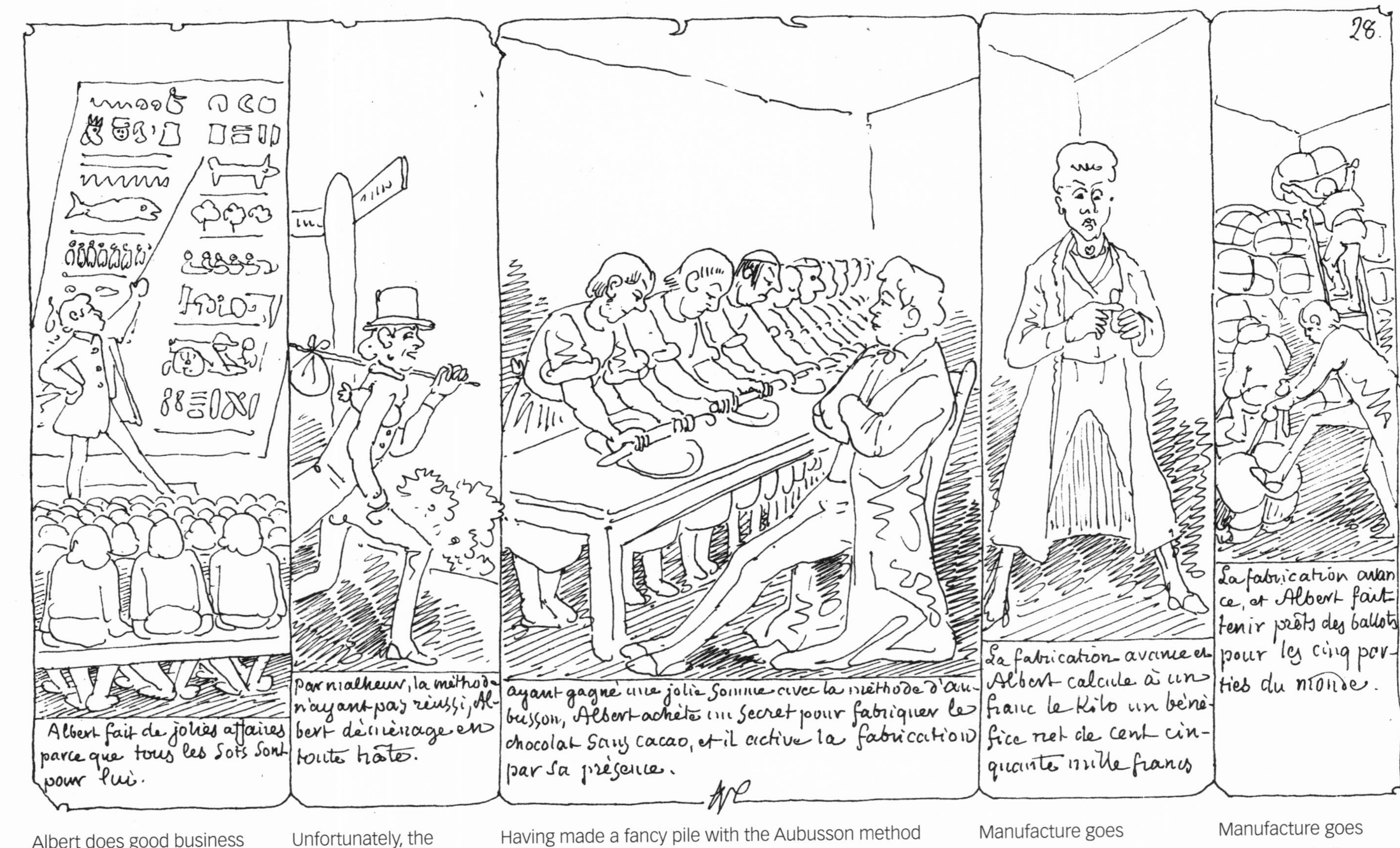
28.
Albert fait de jolies affaires parce que tous les sots sont pour lui.
Par malheur, la méthode n'ayant pas réussi, Albert déménage en toute hâte.
ayant gagné une jolie somme avec la méthode d'Aubusson, Albert achète un secret pour fabriquer le chocolat sans cacao, et il active la fabrication par sa présence.
La fabrication avance et Albert calcule à un franc le kilo un bénéfice net de cent cinquante mille francs
La fabrication avance, et Albert fait tenir prêts des ballots pour les cinq parties du monde.

Albert does good business because all the idiots are for him.

Unfortunately, the method doesn't work, and Albert decamps in a hurry.

Having made a fancy pile with the Aubusson method Albert buys a secret for the manufacture of cocoa-less chocolate, and he expedites production by his presence.

Manufacture goes forward and Albert calculates at one franc per kilo a net profit of a hundred and fifty thousand francs.

Manufacture goes forward and Albert has the bales readied for the five parts of the world.

29.
Par malheur le chocolat se trouve avoir le goût de Guano, et la consistance de la craie de Briançon.
La faillite est déclarée et Albert déménage.
Dégoûté du commerce, Albert entre comme instituteur chez le Comte Baldaquin.
mais le Comte lui explique qu'il veut pour ses enfants point du tout de physique de droit naturel ni de doctrines, et, au contraire, beaucoup d'orthographe et d'arithmétique.

Unfortunately the chocolate turns out to have the taste of Guano, and the consistency of Briançon chalk.

Bankruptcy is declared and Albert decamps.

Disgusted with business, Albert takes a job as a tutor with Count Baldaquin.

But the Count explains that what he wants for his children is not physics at all, nor natural law, nor ideology, but, on the contrary, a lot of spelling and arithmetic.

30.
Dès le lendemain, Albert met les enfans à l'arithmétique, mais cela ne va plus du tout, parce qu'alors il se trouve que les petits Baldaquin l'ont déjà poussée plus loin que lui.
Au bout d'un mois le Comte remercie Albert de ses soins.
En chemin, Albert rencontre Simon de Nantua qui l'interroge, apprend son histoire et lui dit: Un seul des métiers que vous avez essayés pouvait vous faire vivre honorablement, mais il fallait l'apprendre et s'y tenir. Venez avec moi, je vous placerai, et si vous faites bon commencement, vous ferez bonne fin.
Albert est placé par Simon de Nantua chez un fabricant de bougies, et il fait un bon commencement.
Au bout de six mois Albert passe des mèches à la tremperie.

The next day, Albert sets the children to learning arithmetic, but that doesn't work at all, because it turns out that the little Baldaquins are already well ahead of him.

After a month the count discharges Albert for his efforts.

On the way, Albert meets Simon of Nantua who questions him, learns his history and tells him: Any one of the trades you have tried could have provided you with an honorable living, but you would have had to learn it thoroughly and keep at it. Come with me, I will find you a job, and if you start well you will end well.

Simon of Nantua gets Albert a job with a candlemaker, and he starts well.

After six months Albert passes from wicks to dipping.

31.
au bout de six autres mois, Albert passe de la tremperie à aider la bourgeoise pour la vente.
au bout de six autres mois, le bourgeois étant mort, Albert se trouve être à la tête de l'établissement et tout en se promenant dans le comptoir, il médite de donner une grande extension à la fabrication
Il y a même des moments où il calcule un bénéfice net de cinquante mille francs.
Albert tout à la fois active la fabrication, achète un secret pour tirer de la cire des os de chevaux et prépare des ballots pour les cinq parties du monde
au bout de trois mois, la faillite est déclarée et Albert déménage.

After another six months Albert passes from dipping to helping the owner's wife in sales.

After another six months, the owner dies and Albert takes over as head of the business, and pacing behind the counter, he thinks up a way towards a massive increase of production.

There are even moments when he calculates a net profit of fifty thousand francs.

Albert all at once expedites production, buys a secret for extracting wax from horse bones, and makes ready bales for the five parts of the world.

After three months, bankruptcy is declared, and Albert decamps.

Albert se fait agent d'affaires

L'état irait encore n'était la comptabilité où Albert n'entend rien.

32.

N'en pouvant plus de comptabilité manquée, Albert plante là son bureau et déménage.

Albert becomes a business agent.

The job would be alright, but for accountancy of which Albert understands nothing.

Sick of his failed accountancy, Albert forsakes his bureau and decamps.

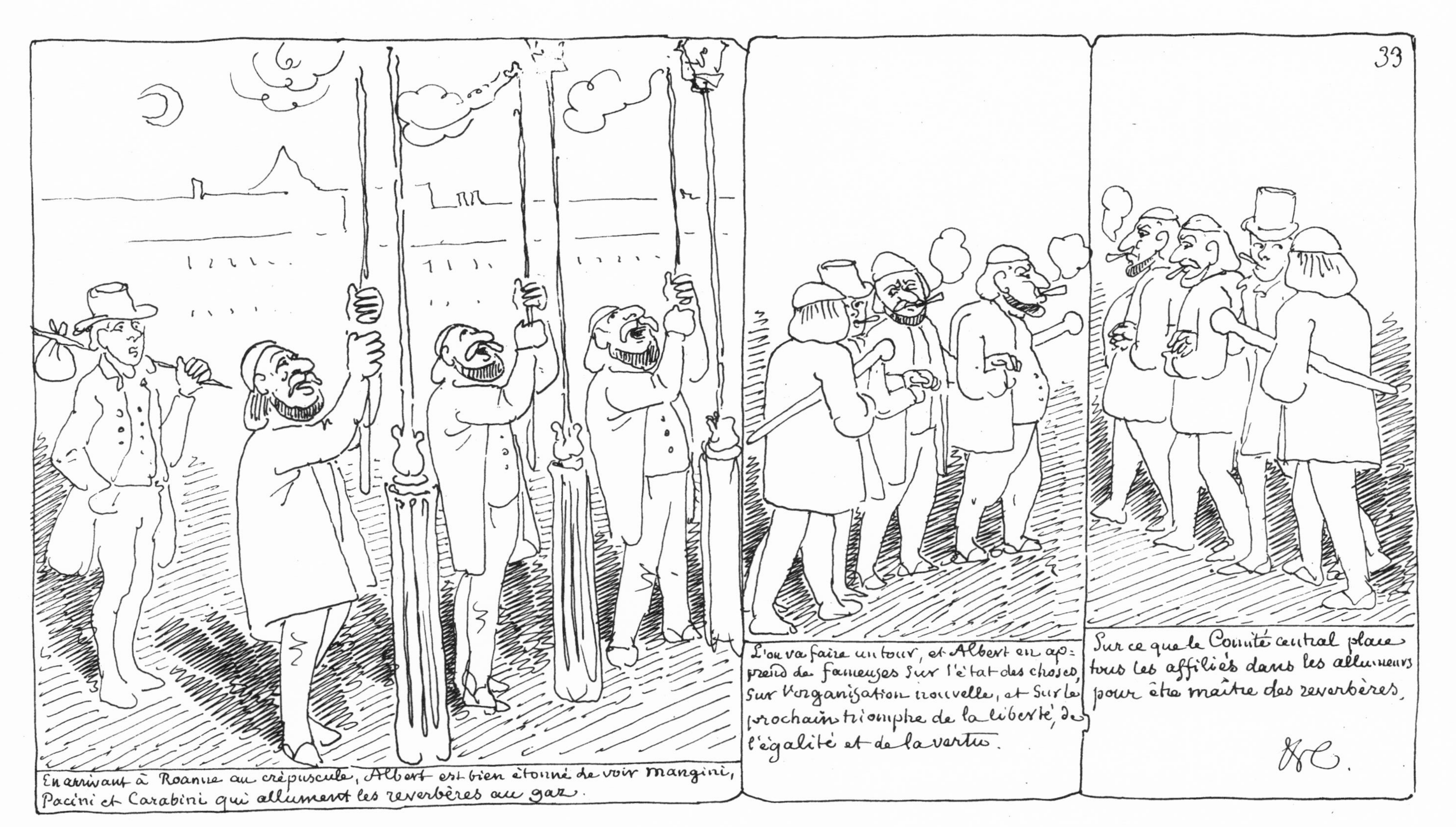
33
En arrivant à Roanne au crépuscule, Albert est bien étonné de voir Mangini, Pacini et Carabini qui allument les reverbères au gaz.
L'on va faire un tour, et Albert en apprend de fameuses sur l'état des choses, sur l'organisation nouvelle, et sur le prochain triomphe de la liberté, de l'égalité et de la vertu.
Sur ce que le Comité central place tous les affiliés dans les allumeurs pour être maître des reverbères.
HC.

Reaching Roanne at dusk, Albert is very surprised to see Mangini, Pacini, and Carabini lighting gas lamps.

They go for a walk, and Albert is told some wild stuff about the state of things, about the new organization, and about the imminent triumph of liberty, equality, and virtue.

About the Central Committee getting all the members into lamp-lighting, so as to take control of the street lamps.

Sur ce que le mouvement n'éclatera que quand l'éclairage au gaz aura été établi dans toutes les préfectures et les Sous-préfectures.
Sur ce qu'il doit lui-même s'inscrire dès ce soir pour la première place vacante d'allumeur.
Présenté au Comité local, Albert expose qu'il a vu partout le travailleur obligé de déménager devant l'obstacle d'institutions bâtardes, de lois absurdes et de capitalistes égoïstes; que lui-même est une victime ambulante de l'ordre Social et que partout l'air et l'espace ont manqué à sa vertu.
Pendant quatre mois, Albert allume les reverbères au gaz à Roanne.
34.
Mais la Police ayant surpris les allumeurs réunis en corps délibérant, Albert et ses trois amis parviennent à déménager.
Et en passant le Cerdon, ils s'y nourrissent de fruits Sauvages.

About the movement breaking out only when gas lighting is established in all prefectures and sub-prefectures.

About his having to apply that very evening for the first vacancy in lamp-lighting.

Presented to the local Committee Albert tells them how he has seen the worker obliged to migrate in the face of bastard institutions, absurd laws, and selfish capitalists; that he himself is an itinerant victim of the social order and that everywhere virtue has been deprived of space to breathe and live.

Albert spends four months in Roanne lighting gas lamps.

But the police catch the lamplighters in the midst of a meeting, while Albert and his three friends manage to decamp.

And passing through the Cerdon, they live on wild fruit.

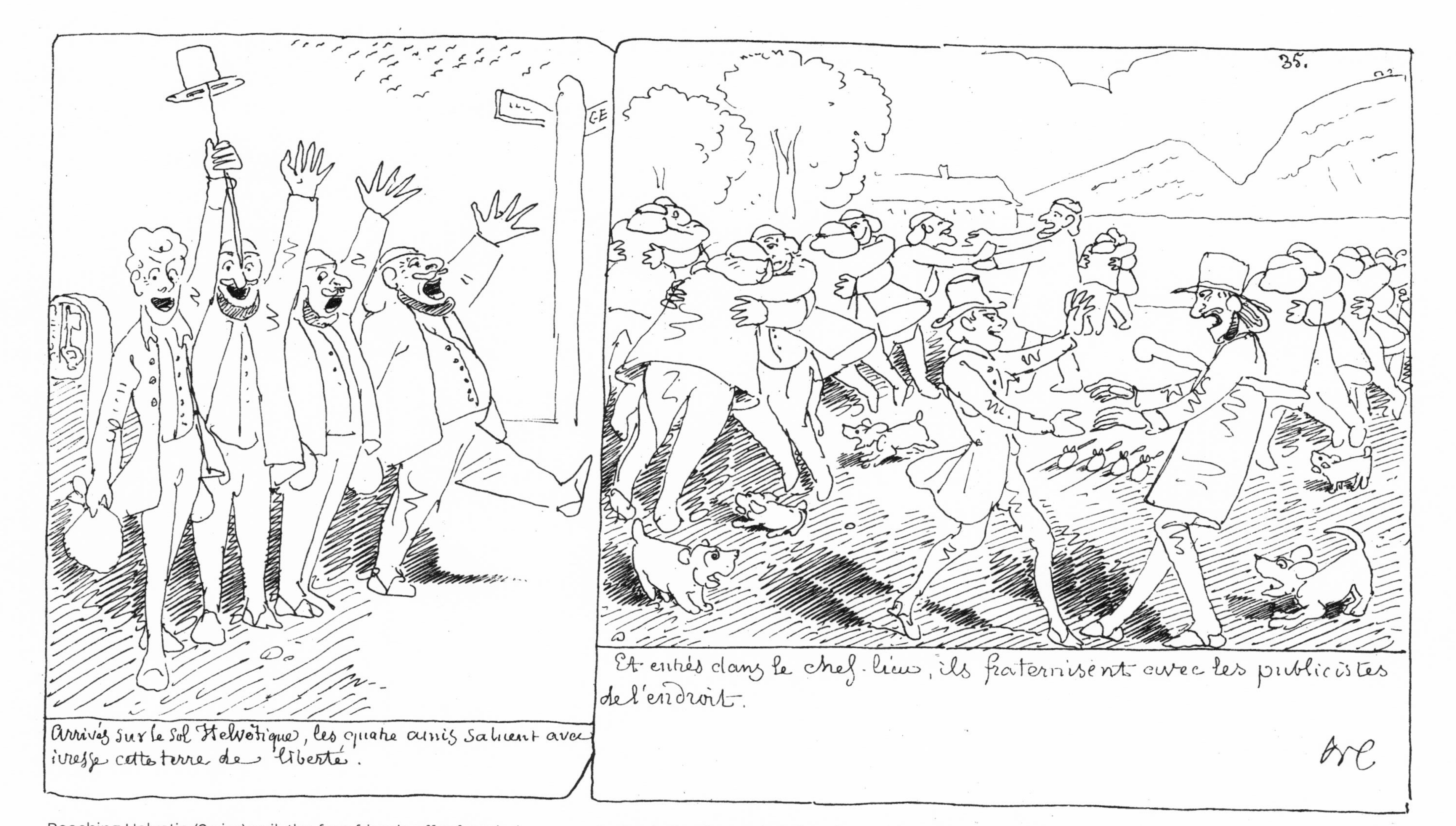
Arrivés sur le sol Helvétique, les quatre amis saluent avec ivresse cette terre de liberté.
35.
Et entrés dans le chef-lieu, ils fraternisent avec les publicistes de l'endroit.

Reaching Helvetic (Swiss) soil, the four friends offer frenzied salutations to this land of liberty.

And entering the capital, they fraternize with the local journalists.

36.
L'on va faire un tour, et les quatre amis ont bientôt appris des publicistes de l'endroit que le Canton gémit sous le joug sans nom d'une aristocratie échevelée.
Que le gouvernement y est la proie d'hommes personnellement doux et habiles, mais politiquement astucieux et incorrigibles.
Que le peuple y est heureux et libre, mais ne se comprenant pas et n'étant pas compris.
Qu'en conséquence le moment est venu d'apprendre au peuple à se comprendre et à être compris.
Secondé par ses amis politiques et par des publicistes de l'endroit, Albert fonde un journal.

Walking around together, the four friends soon learn from the local journalists that the Canton is groaning under the nameless yoke of a disorderly aristocracy.

That the government is under the sway of men who are personally mild and able, but politically cunning and incorrigible.

That the people there are happy and free, but misunderstand themselves and are misunderstood.

That therefore the moment has come for the people to understand themselves and to be understood.

With the help of political friends and the local journalists, Albert founds a newspaper.

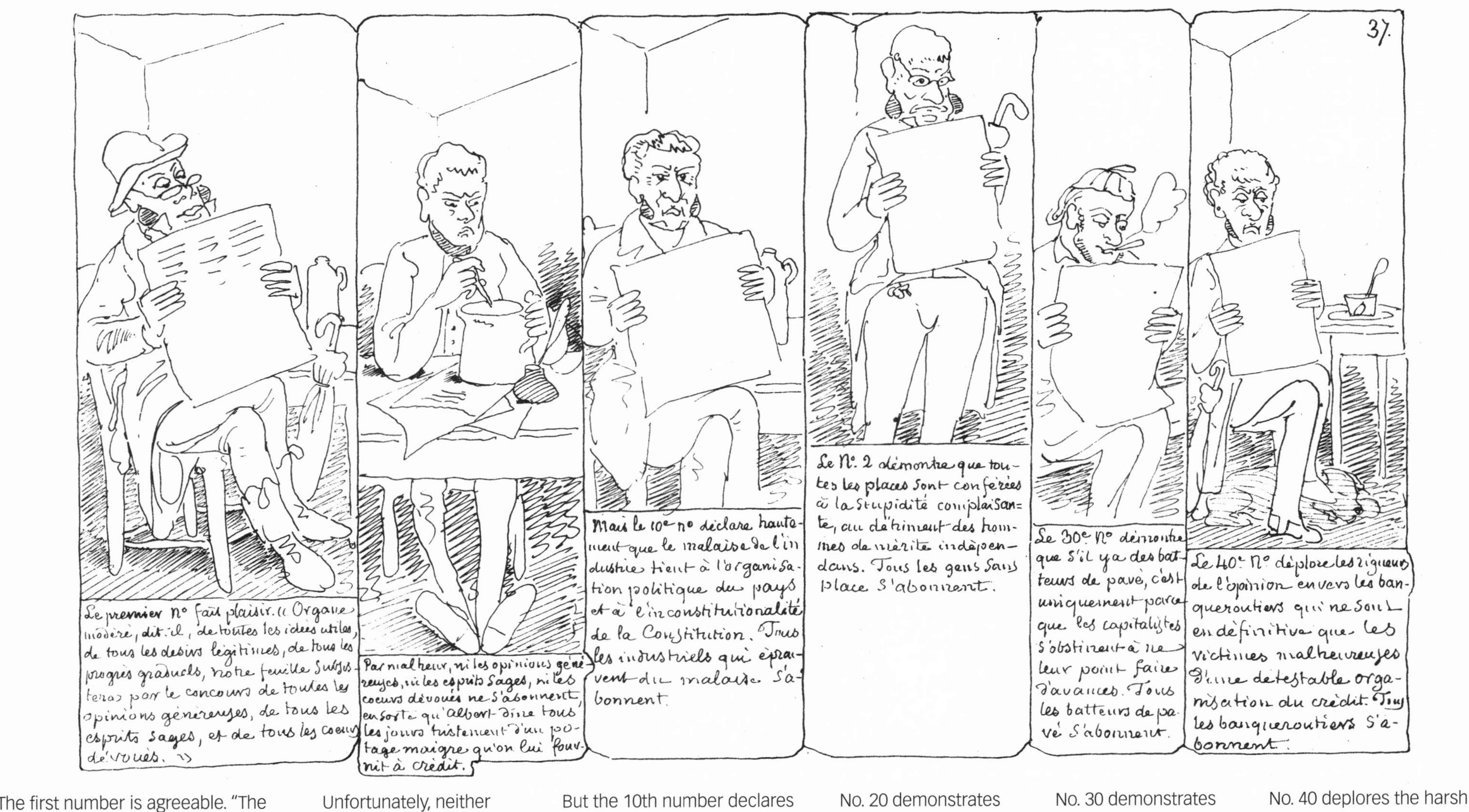
37.
Le premier n° fait plaisir. « Organe modéré, dit-il, de toutes les idées utiles, de tous les desirs légitimes, de tous les progrès graduels, notre feuille subsistera par le concours de toutes les opinions généreuses, de tous les esprits sages, et de tous les coeurs dévoués. »
Par malheur, ni les opinions généreuses, ni les esprits sages, ni les coeurs dévoués ne s'abonnent, en sorte qu'Albert dîne tous les jours tristement d'un potage maigre qu'on lui fournit à crédit.
Mais le 10e n° déclare hautement que le malaise de l'industrie tient à l'organisation politique du pays et à l'inconstitutionalité de la Constitution. Tous les industriels qui éprouvent du malaise s'abonnent.
Le N°. 2 démontre que toutes les places sont conférées à la stupidité complaisante, au détriment des hommes de mérite indépendans. Tous les gens sans place s'abonnent.
Le 30e N° démontre que s'il y a des batteurs de pavé, c'est uniquement parce que les capitalistes s'obstinent à ne leur point faire d'avances. Tous les batteurs de pavé s'abonnent.
Le 40e N° déplore les rigueurs de l'opinion envers les banqueroutiers qui ne sont en définitive que les victimes malheureuses d'une detestable organisation du crédit. Tous les banqueroutiers s'abonnent.

The first number is agreeable. "The moderate organ," it proclaims, "of all useful ideas, of all legitimate desires, and all gradual progress, our paper will depend on the support of all liberal opinions, of all wise minds, and all generous hearts."

Unfortunately, neither the liberal opinions, nor the wise minds, nor the generous hearts subscribe, so that Albert makes a gloomy daily dinner of thin soup furnished on credit.

But the 10th number declares loudly that the malaise in industry is caused by the political organization in place, and the unconstitutionality of the Constitution. All the industrialists suffering from the malaise subscribe.

No. 20 demonstrates that all the jobs are being given to time-serving stupidity, to the disadvantage of the competent and independent. All the unemployed subscribe.

No. 30 demonstrates that if there are idle men, it is wholly because the capitalists obstinately refuse to give them a chance. All the idle men subscribe.

No. 40 deplores the harsh criticism of the bankrupts who are after all only the unfortunate victims of a detestable organization of credit. All the bankrupts subscribe.

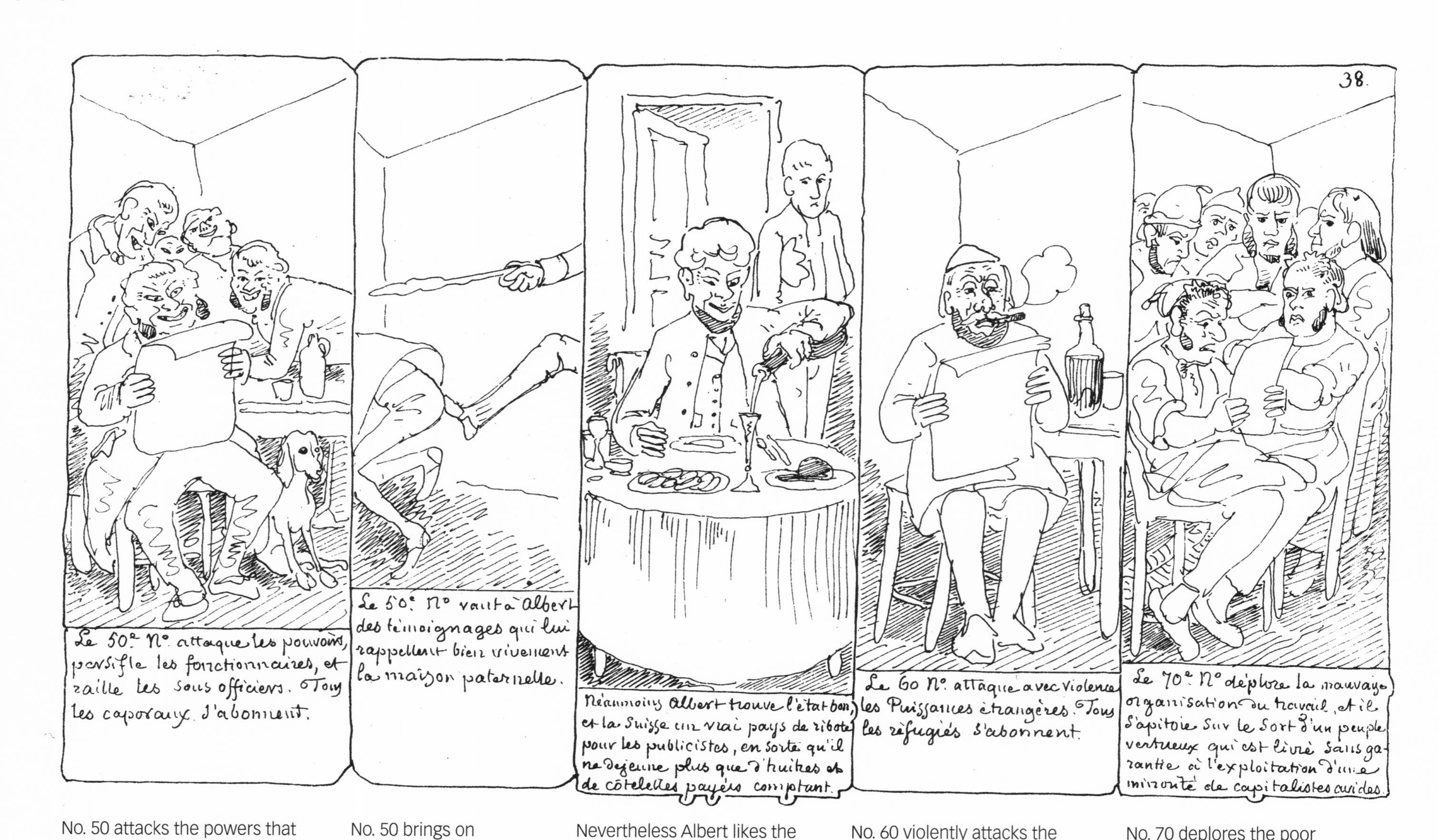
38.
Le 50e No. attaque les pouvoirs, persifle les fonctionnaires, et raille les sous officiers. Tous les caporaux s'abonnent.
Le 50e No vaut à Albert des témoignages qui lui rappellent bien vivement la maison paternelle.
Néanmoins Albert trouve l'état bon, et la Suisse un vrai pays de ribote pour les publicistes, en sorte qu'il ne déjeune plus que d'huîtres et de côtelettes payées comptant.
Le 60 No. attaque avec violence les Puissances étrangères. Tous les réfugiés s'abonnent.
Le 70e No déplore la mauvaise organisation du travail, et il s'apitoie sur le sort d'un peuple vertueux qui est livré sans garantie à l'exploitation d'une minorité de capitalistes avides.

No. 50 attacks the powers that be, makes fun of the officials, and mocks the under-officers. All the corporals subscribe.

No. 50 brings on testimony that reminds Albert keenly of the paternal home.

Nevertheless Albert likes the work, and finds Switzerland a good place for journalists to binge in, so that he dines only on oysters and cutlets paid for in cash.

No. 60 violently attacks the foreign Powers. All the refugees subscribe.

No. 70 deplores the poor organization of work, and sheds tears over the lot of a virtuous, helpless people subject to the exploitation of a minority of greedy capitalists.

39.
Qu'un-Sang-im-pur
A— breuve nos Sillons!
A— breuve nos Sillons!
Le N.° 80.e conjure le pouvoir d'accorder au peuple ses justes demandes.
Le N.° 90.e conjure le peuple de s'apaiser, puis que le pouvoir ne saurait lui refuser plus long-temps ses justes demandes.
Cependant le peuple commençant à se comprendre et à être compris, il s'ensuit que les citoyens se tirent les uns contre les autres, que la Constitution est culbutée, que la ville est en deuil, que les affaires sont ruinées......

May a foul Blood Du-rench our furrows! Du-rench our furrows! Du-rench our furrows!

No. 80 entreats the government to give in to the people's just demands.

No. 90 entreats the people to calm down, since the government cannot refuse their just demands any longer.

Meanwhile, with the people beginning to understand themselves and to be understood, the result is that the citizens fire on each other, that the Constitution is overthrown, that the town is in mourning, that business is ruined . . . . . .

40 et dernière.

Autographié chez Schmidt à Genève 1845.

Mais Albert a trouvé une existence.

Fin de l'Histoire d'Albert. — par R.T.

But Albert has found a life.

End of the Story of Albert. — by R.T.

Histoire de
Monsieur
Cryptogame
1845

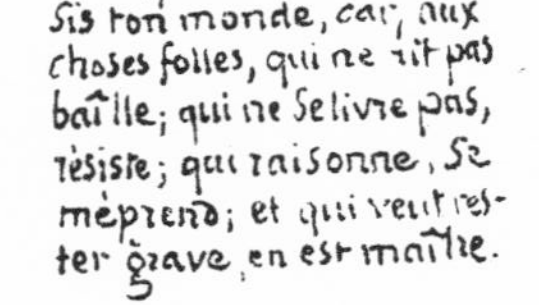

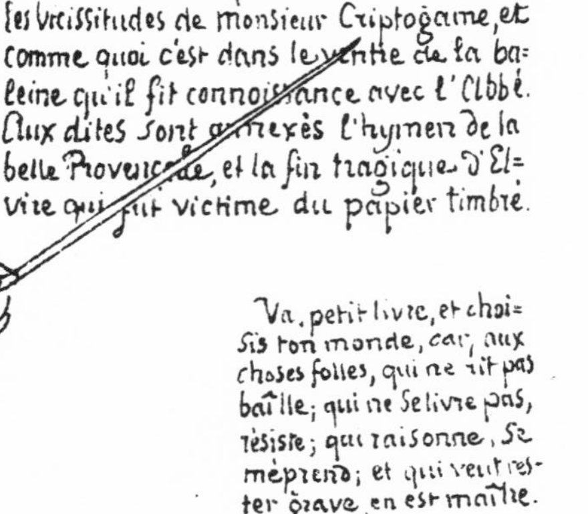
Ci-derrière sont représentées au naturel
les vicissitudes de monsieur Criptogame, et
comme quoi c'est dans le ventre de la baleine qu'il fit connoissance avec l'Abbé.
Aux dites sont annexés l'hymen de la
belle Provençale, et la fin tragique d'Elvire qui fut victime du papier timbré.
Va, petit livre, et choi-
sis ton monde, car, aux
choses folles, qui ne rit pas
baîlle; qui ne se livre pas,
résiste; qui raisonne, se
méprend; et qui veut res-
ter grave, en est maître.
autographié par l'auteur
Lithog. de Schmidt à Genève

Hereafter are represented from the life the vicissitudes of Mr. Criptogame, and how it was in the belly of the whale that he made the acquaintance with the Abbé. To which are appended the nuptials of the Beauty from Provence, and the tragic end of Elvire who was a victim of stamped document paper.

Go little book and choose your world, for at crazy things, those who do not laugh, yawn; and those who do not yield, resist; and those who reason, are mistaken, and those who would keep a straight face, can please themselves.

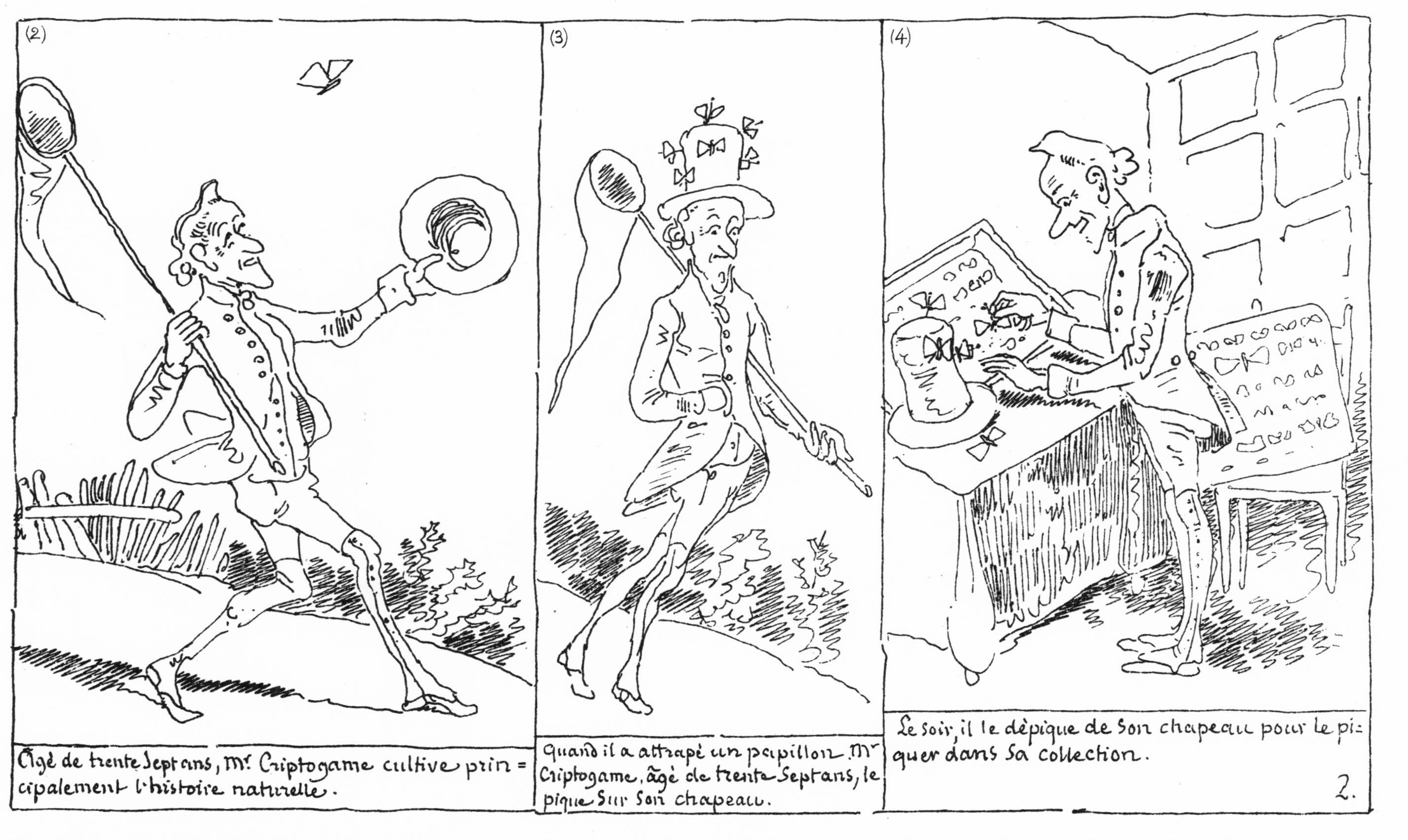
(2)
Âgé de trente Sept ans, Mr. Criptogame cultive prin=
cipalement l'histoire naturelle.
(3)
Quand il a attrapé un papillon Mr
Criptogame, âgé de trente Sept ans, le
pique sur son chapeau.
(4)
Le soir, il le dépique de son chapeau pour le pi=
quer dans sa collection.
2.

Thirty-seven years old, Mr. Criptogame cultivates principally natural history.

When he catches a butterfly, Mr. Criptogame, thirty-seven years old, pins it to his hat.

In the evening he unpins it from his hat and re-pins it into his collection.

(5)
Après quoi il va se coucher satisfait, et rêve une contrée où l'on trouve les papillons tout piqués.
(6)
Pendant que Mr. Criptogame rêve papillons, Elvire, âgée de trente-huit ans, rêve les délices d'une prochaine union avec le choisi de son coeur.
(7)
Mais l'Aurore lui est fade parce qu'elle ramène la réalité qui est si inférieure aux rêves.
(8)
Au fait, Mr. Criptogame est plus naturaliste que passionné.
3.

After which he goes satisfied to bed, and dreams of a land full of ready-pinned butterflies.

While Mr. Criptogame dreams of butterflies, Elvire, thirty-eight years old, dreams of the delights of an imminent union with the chosen of her heart.

But the dawn holds no charms for her, because it brings on a reality that is so inferior to her dreams.

In fact, Mr. Criptogame is more of a naturalist than a lover.

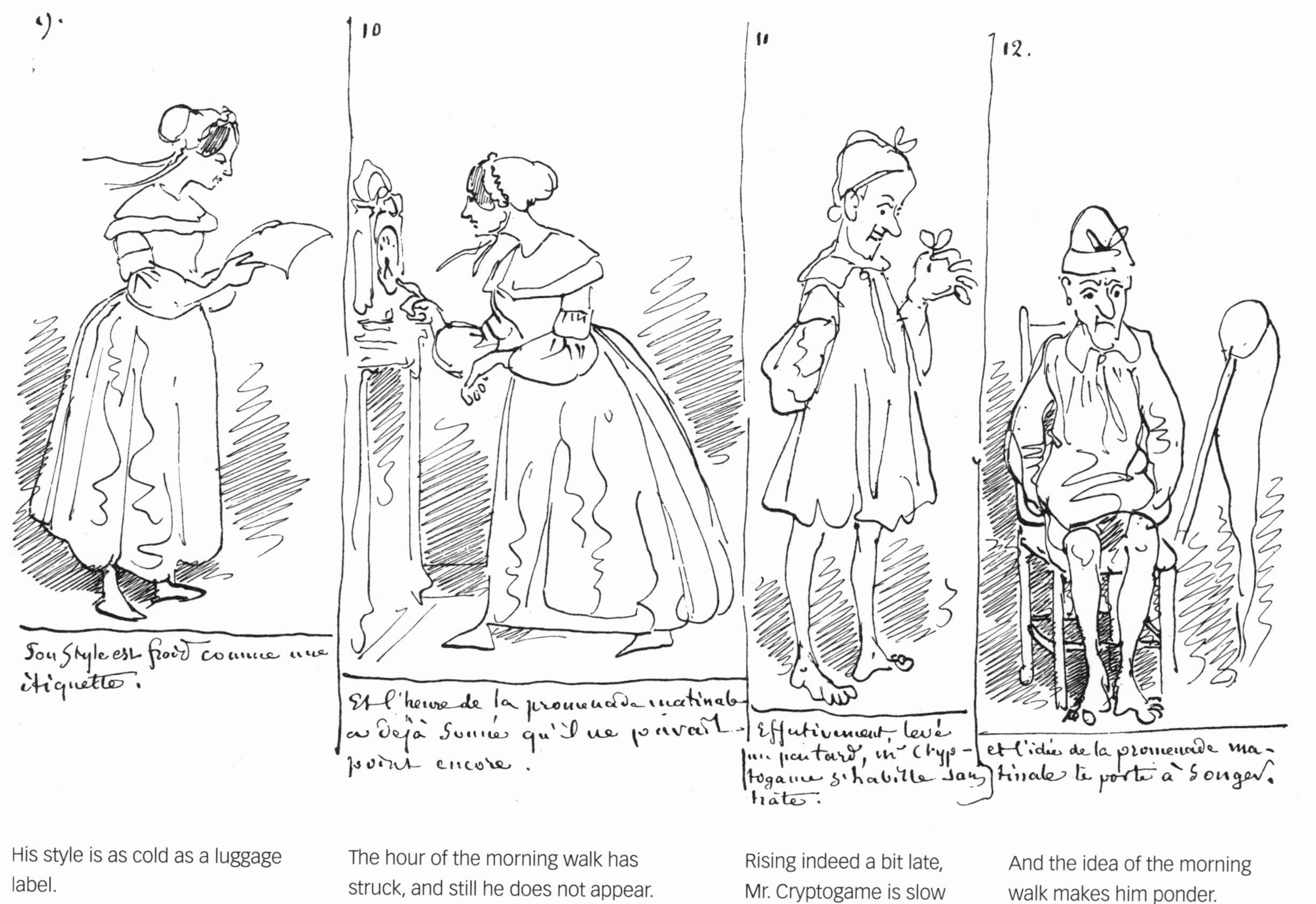
9.
Son Style est froid comme une étiquette.
10
Et l'heure de la promenade matinale a déjà sonné qu'il ne paraît point encore.
11
Effectivement, levé un peu tard, M. Cryptogame s'habille sans hâte.
12.
Et l'idée de la promenade matinale le porte à songer.

His style is as cold as a luggage label.

The hour of the morning walk has struck, and still he does not appear.

Rising indeed a bit late, Mr. Cryptogame is slow in dressing.

And the idea of the morning walk makes him ponder.

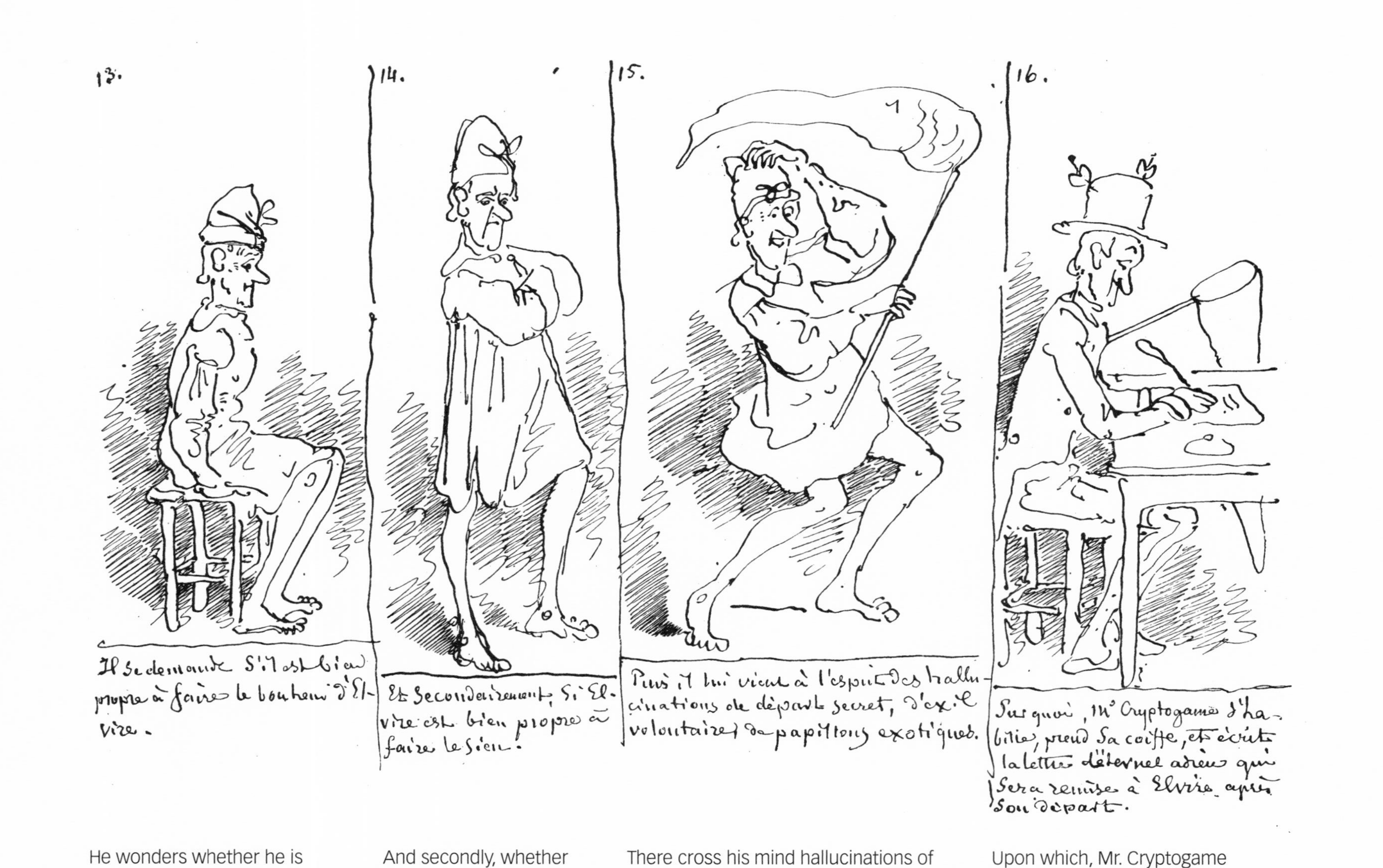
13.
Il se demande s'il est bien propre à faire le bonheur d'Elvire.
14.
Et secondairement, si Elvire est bien propre à faire le sien.
15.
Puis il lui vient à l'esprit des hallucinations de départ secret, d'exil volontaire, de papillons exotiques.
16.
Sur quoi, Mr Cryptogame s'habille, prend sa coiffe, et écrit la lettre d'éternel adieu qui sera remise à Elvire après son départ.

He wonders whether he is the right man to make Elvire happy.

And secondly, whether Elvire is the right person to make him happy.

There cross his mind hallucinations of secret departure, of voluntary exile, of exotic butterflies.

Upon which, Mr. Cryptogame dresses, takes his headgear, and writes the letter of everlasting farewell to be given to Elvire after his departure.

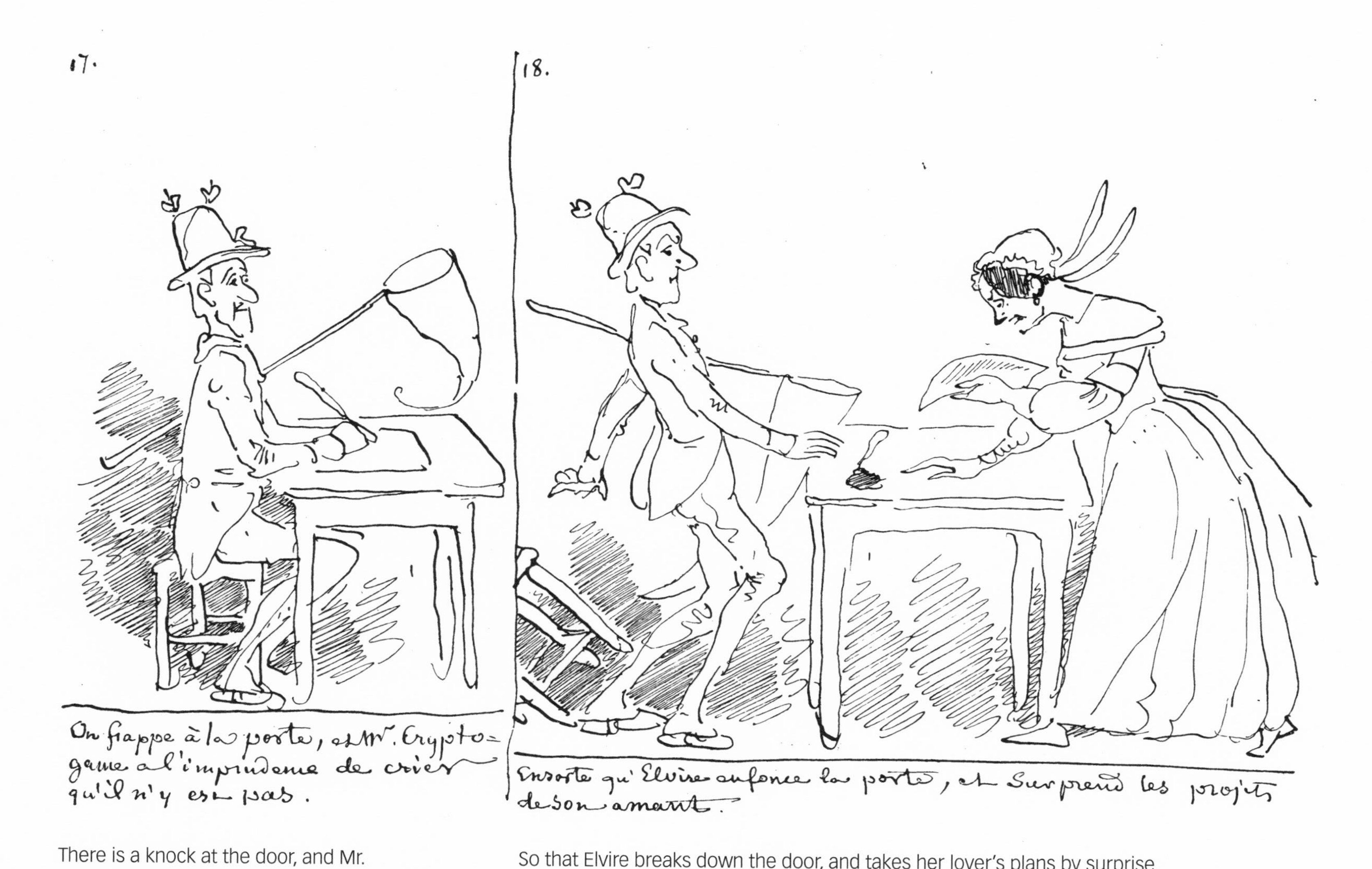
17.
On frappe à la porte, et Mr. Cryptogame a l'imprudence de crier qu'il n'y est pas.
18.
En sorte qu'Elvire enfonce la porte, et surprend les projets de son amant.

There is a knock at the door, and Mr. Cryptogame is rash enough to cry that he is not at home.

So that Elvire breaks down the door, and takes her lover's plans by surprise.

19.

Les premiers moments d'explication sont bien pénibles pour Mr. Cryptogame.

The initial moments of explanation are very painful for Mr. Cryptogame.

20.

Mais mis au pied du mur, il déclare renoncer à ses projets.

But backed against the wall, he declares he will renounce his projects.

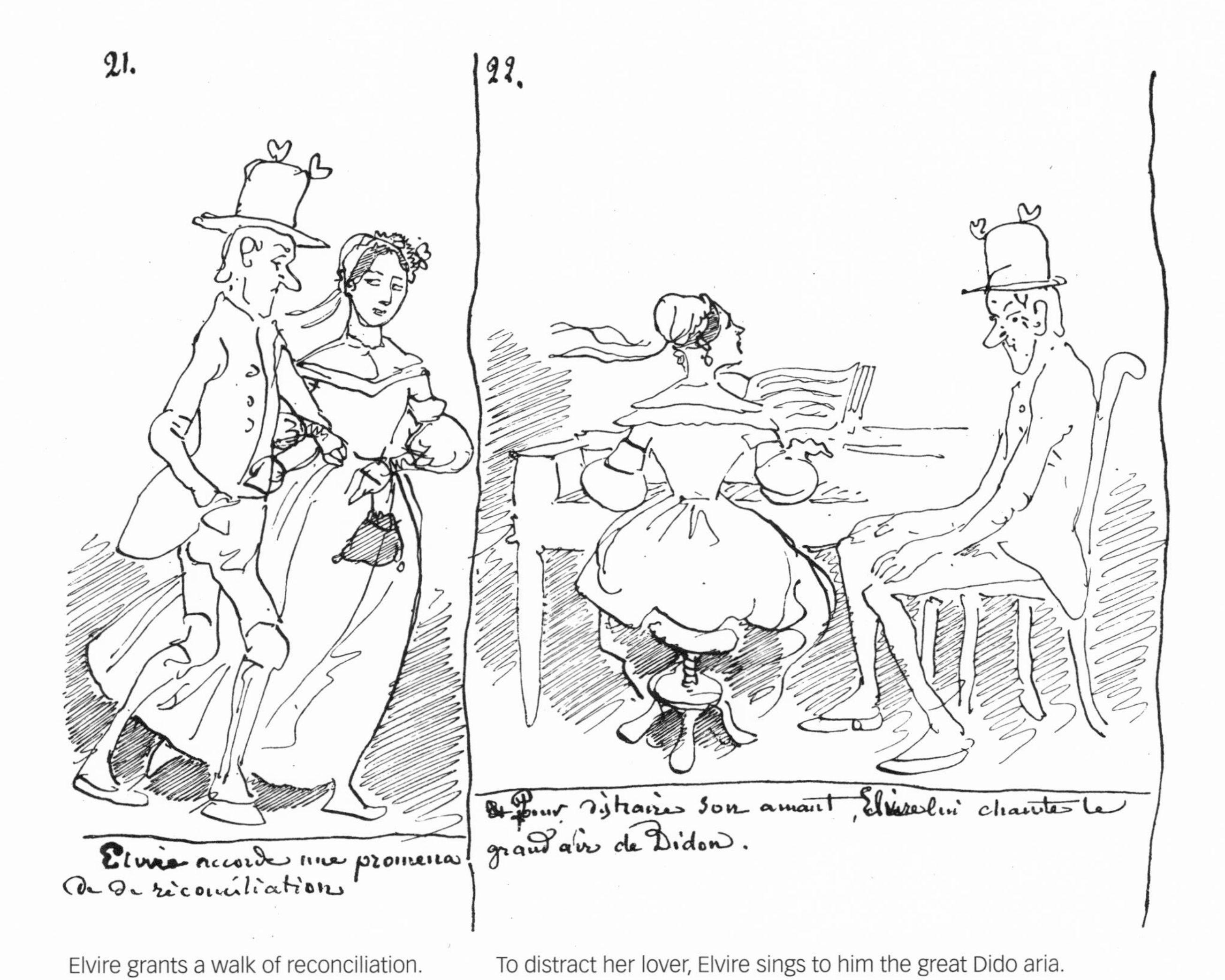
21.
Elvire accorde une promenade de réconciliation
22.
Pour distraire son amant, Elvire lui chante le grand air de Didon.

Elvire grants a walk of reconciliation.

To distract her lover, Elvire sings to him the great Dido aria.

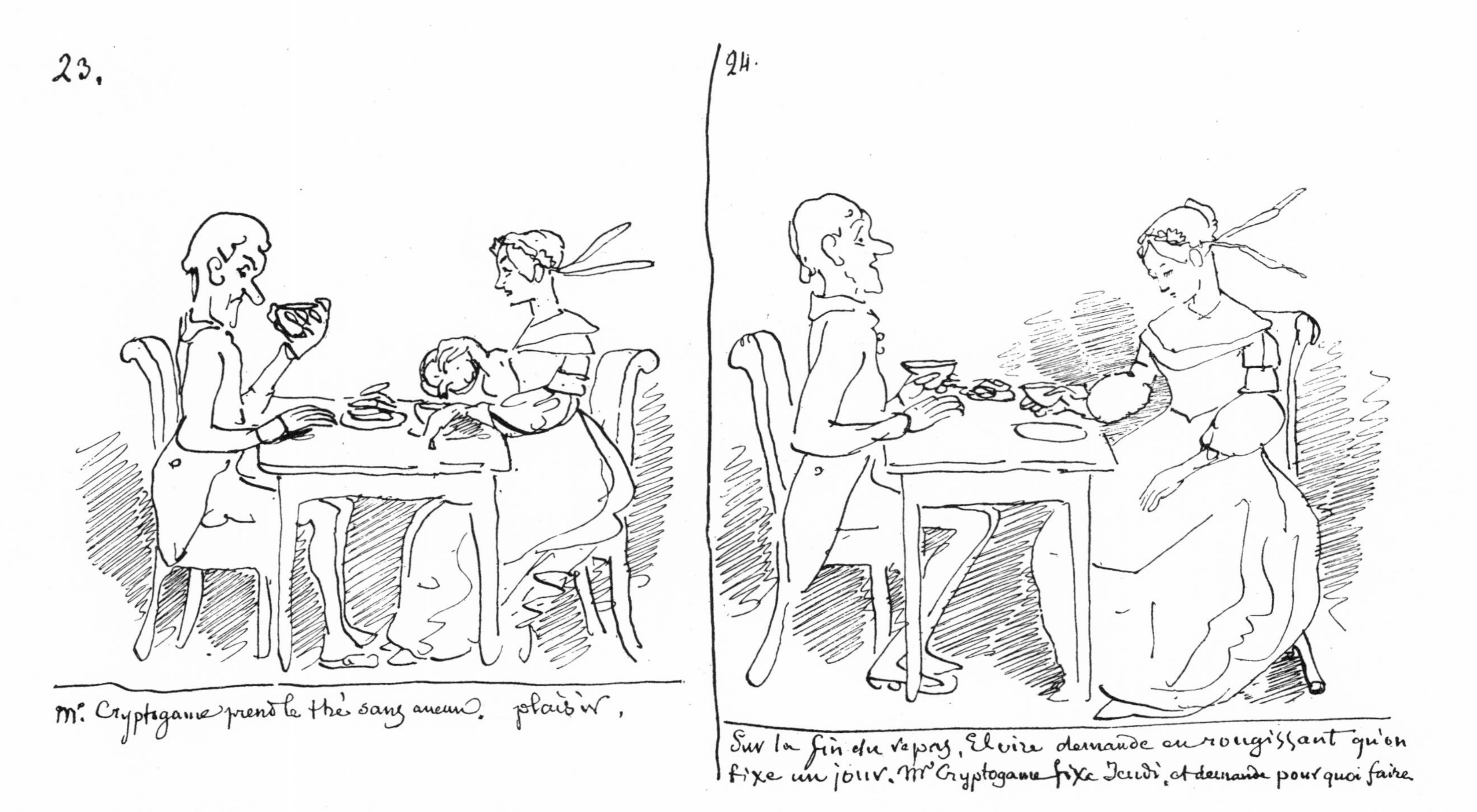
23.
Mr. Cryptogame prend le thé sans aucun plaisir.
24.
Sur la fin du repas, Elvire demande en rougissant qu'on fixe un jour. Mr Cryptogame fixe Jeudi, et demande pourquoi faire

Mr. Cryptogame takes tea with no pleasure at all.

At the end of the meal, the blushing Elvire aks him to fix a day. Mr. Cryptogame fixes Thursday, and asks to do what.

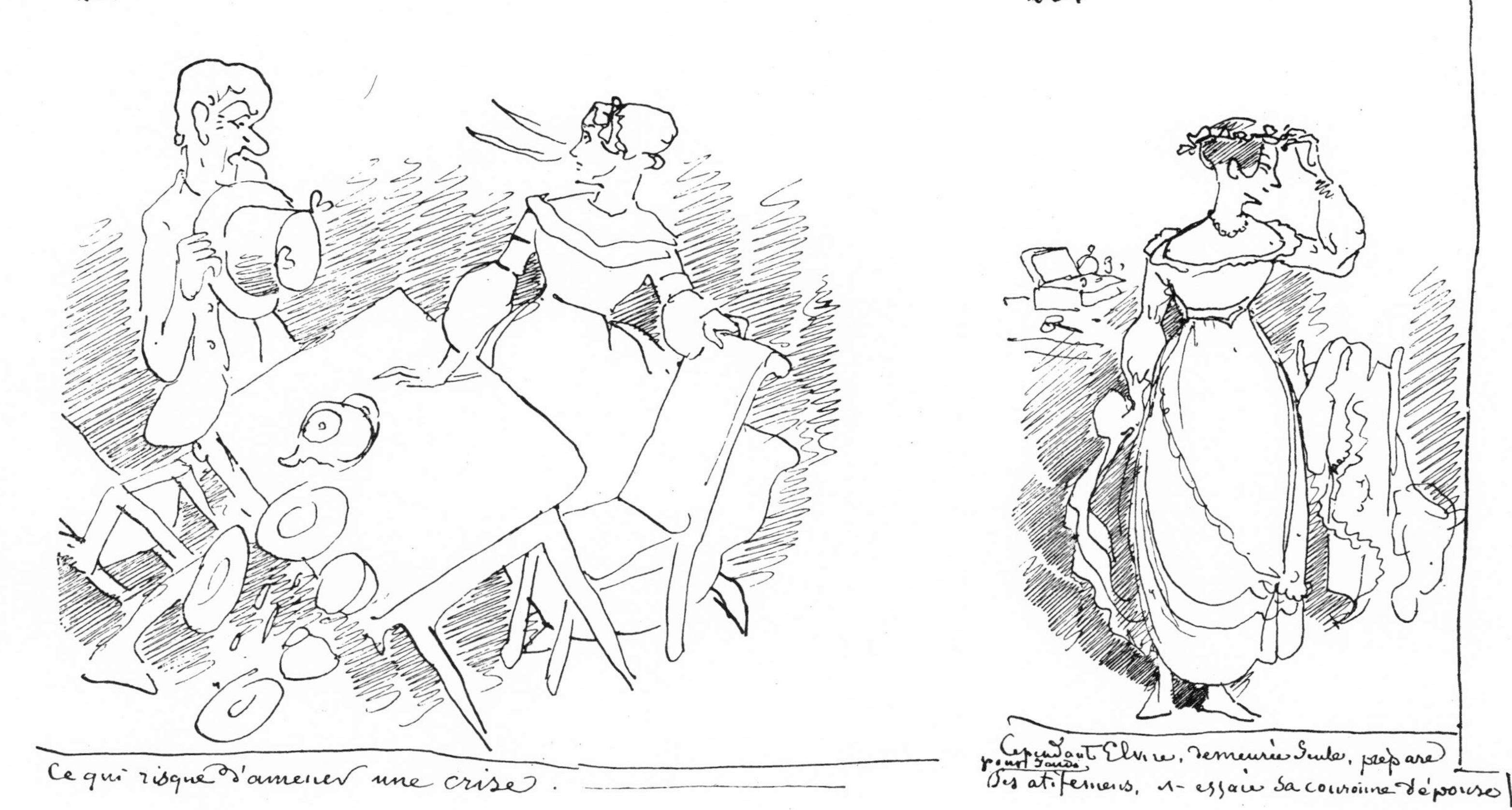
25.
Ce qui risque d'amener une crise.
26.
Cependant Elvire, demeurée seule, prépare
ses atifemens, et essaie sa couronne d'épouse

Which threatens to provoke a fit.

Left alone, however, Elvire prepares her outfit for Thursday, and tries on her bridal wreath.

(27)

De son côté, demeuré seul, Mr. Cryptogame s'accoutre, ferme sa porte à clé, et part nuitamment pour Marseille.

(28)

À peine hors des murs, Mr. Cryptogame éprouve un affranchissement inexprimable.

(29)

À Nantua, il fait trois fois le tour du lac à la poursuite d'un Manteau Royal.

(30.)

À Avignon, il manque une phalène et attrape un chat-huant.

9.

For his part, left on his own, Mr. Cryptogame gets dressed, locks his door, and leaves nocturnally for Marseille.

Hardly outside the walls, Mr. Cryptogame experiences an inexpressible liberation.

At Nantua, he runs around the lake three times in pursuit of a *Monarch*.

At Avignon, he misses a moth and catches an owl.

(31.)
A Arles, il manque un Apollon et n'attrape pas un Sphinx
(32.)
Mais à Marseille il attrape une dame, et ne manque pas un factionaire.
10.

At Arles he misses a Swallowtail and fails to catch a Painted Lady.

But at Marseille, he catches a real lady and does not miss a sentry.

(33.)

Dès le lendemain, Mr Cryptogame dit adieu aux rivages de l'Europe, et s'embarque pour le Nouveau Monde.

(34.)

Arrivé sur le vaisseau, il s'approche avec bonté d'une dame au désespoir.

(35.)

C'est Elvire! . . . Mr Cryptogame trouve que sa situation change du tout au tout, et il regrette presque l'ancien monde.

11.

The next day, Mr. Cryptogame says goodbye to the shores of Europe, and embarks for the New World.

Stepping on board, he sympathetically approaches a lady in the throes of despair.

It is Elvire! . . . Mr. Cryptogame finds the situation altogether changed, and almost regrets the Old World.

(36)
Néanmoins, pour conjurer la crise, il proteste de l'ardeur de son amour, et de l'ingénuité de ses intentions.
(37.)
En sorte qu'Elvire lui fait écrire le tout sur du papier timbré dont elle s'est pourvue
(38.)
Elvire satisfaite redevient intéressante et tendre.
12.

Nonetheless, to stem the crisis, he protests the ardor of his love and the sincerity of his intentions.

In consequence, Elvire makes him write it all down on stamped document paper which she carries with her.

Satisfied, Elvire becomes interesting and tender again.

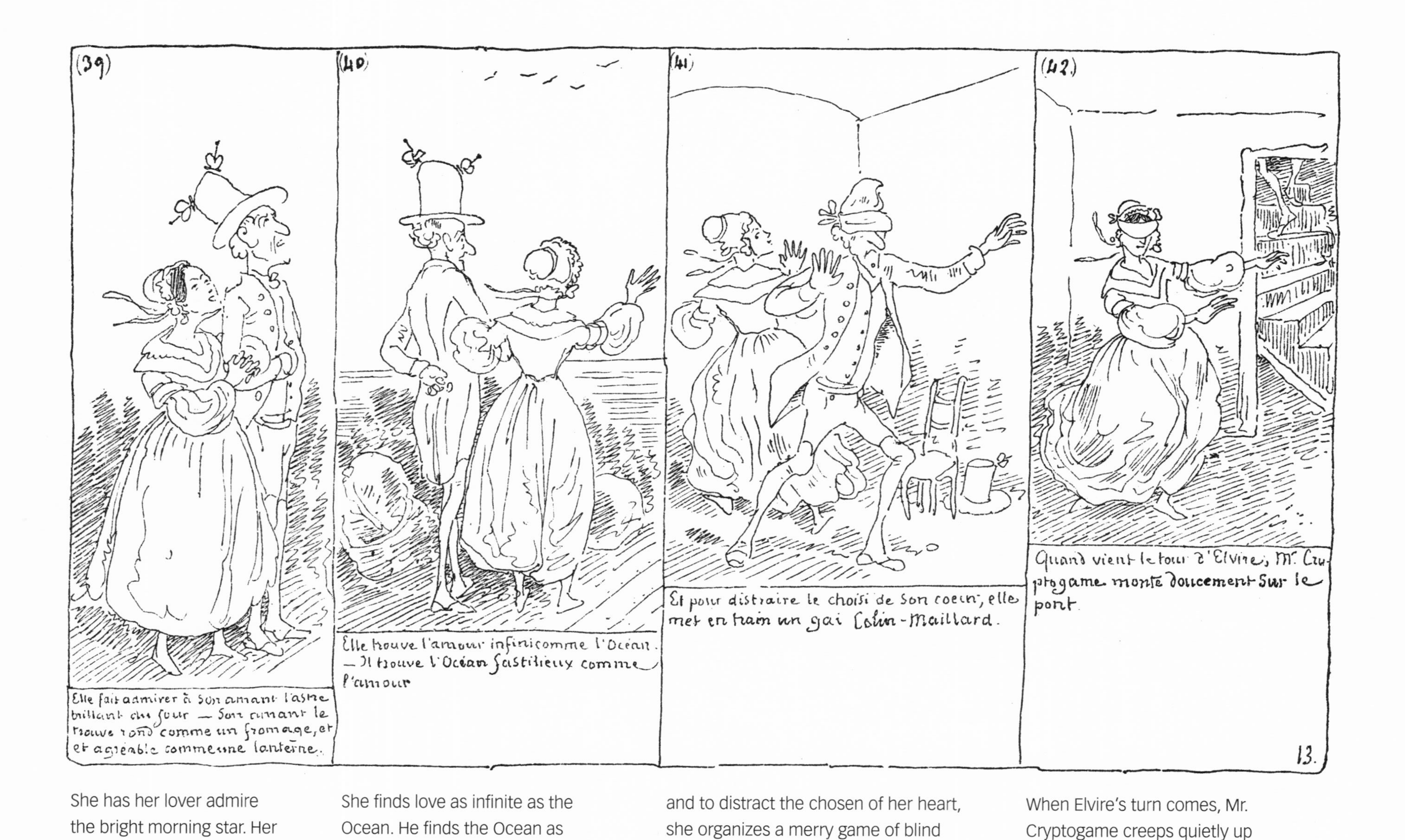
(39)
Elle fait admirer à son amant l'astre brillant du jour — Son amant le trouve rond comme un fromage, et et agréable comme une lanterne.
(40)
Elle trouve l'amour infini comme l'Océan. — Il trouve l'Océan fastidieux comme l'amour
(41)
Et pour distraire le choisi de son coeur, elle met en train un gai Colin-Maillard.
(42)
Quand vient le tour d'Elvire, Mr. Cryptogame monte doucement sur le pont
13.

She has her lover admire the bright morning star. Her lover finds it as round as a cheese, and as amusing as a lantern.

She finds love as infinite as the Ocean. He finds the Ocean as tedious as love.

and to distract the chosen of her heart, she organizes a merry game of blind man's buff.

When Elvire's turn comes, Mr. Cryptogame creeps quietly up on deck.

(43.)
où il se met à sonder la profondeur de sa situation.
(44.)
Et il se refuse à répondre aux agaceries d'une superbe Amphitrite.
(45.)
Tant son avenir est brisé!
(46.)
Cependant après avoir cherché pendant deux heures, Elvire abaisse le bandeau; et s'apercevant qu'elle est seule, elle s'élance sur le pont.
14

Where he proceeds to ponder the depths of his situation.

And he refuses to respond to the provocations of a superb Wood Nymph.

So blighted is his future!

Meanwhile after having searched for two hours, Elvire lowers her blindfold, and seeing that she is alone, darts up on deck.

(47.)

De son côté, Mr Cryptogame s'apercevant qu'il n'est plus seul saute à la mer.

(48.)

Elvire saute après le choisi de son coeur.

(49)

Le Capitaine saute pour sauver Elvire.

15.

For his part, Mr. Cryptogame seeing that he is no longer alone, jumps into the sea.

Elvire jumps after the chosen of her heart.

The Captain jumps to save Elvire.

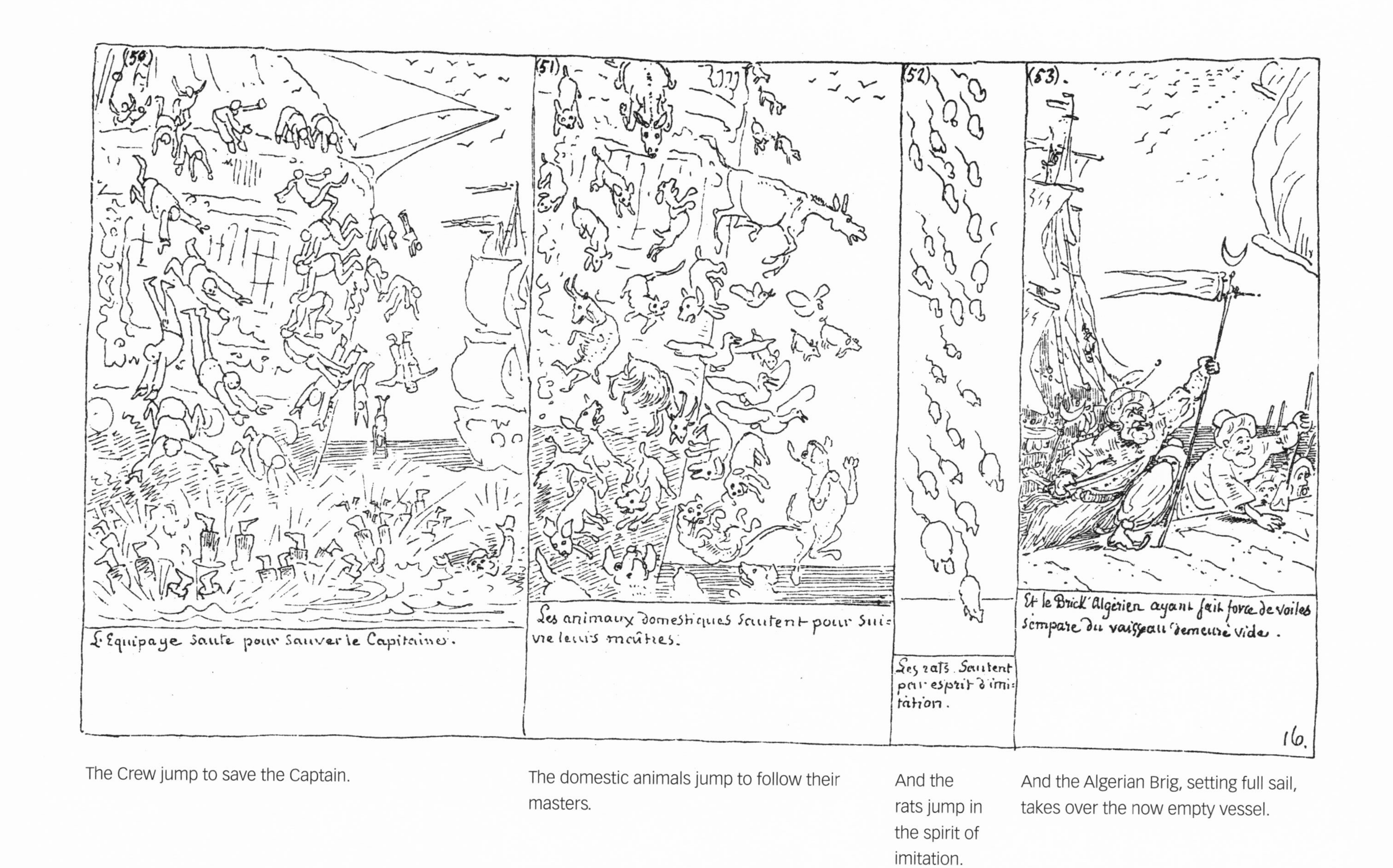
(50)
L'Equipage saute pour sauver le Capitaine.
(51)
Les animaux domestiques sautent pour suivre leurs maîtres.
(52)
Les rats sautent par esprit d'imitation.
(53).
Et le Brick Algérien ayant fait force de voiles s'empare du vaisseau demeuré vide.
16.

The Crew jump to save the Captain.

The domestic animals jump to follow their masters.

And the rats jump in the spirit of imitation.

And the Algerian Brig, setting full sail, takes over the now empty vessel.

(54.)

Ses maures, une fois maîtres du vaisseau, se hâtent de repêcher l'équipage, pour en tirer rançon.

Having made themselves masters of the ship, the Moors hasten to fish up the crew, with a view to getting a ransom out of them.

(55.)

Voyant qu'on repêche Elvire, Mr Cryptogame tâche de n'être pas repêché.

Seeing that Elvire is being fished up, Mr. Cryptogame tries not to be fished up.

(56)

Mais il boit deux tonnes d'onde amère avant d'atteindre à un îlot qui est en vue.

But he drinks two tons of bitter saltwater before landing on an islet he espies.

(57)
Par malheur, l'îlot, qui est très chatouilleux, éprouva d'énormes tressaillements.
(58)
Puis il replonge.

Unfortunately the islet, which is very ticklish, undergoes tremendous shuddering.

Then dives down again.

59.

Puis d'une bouchée il avale Mr. Cryptogame.

Then in a single gulp, swallows Mr. Cryptogame.

60.

Parvenu heureusement dans la baleine, Mr. Cryptogame y lutte contre le courant digestif.

Arriving safely inside the whale, Mr. Cryptogame struggles against the digestive current.

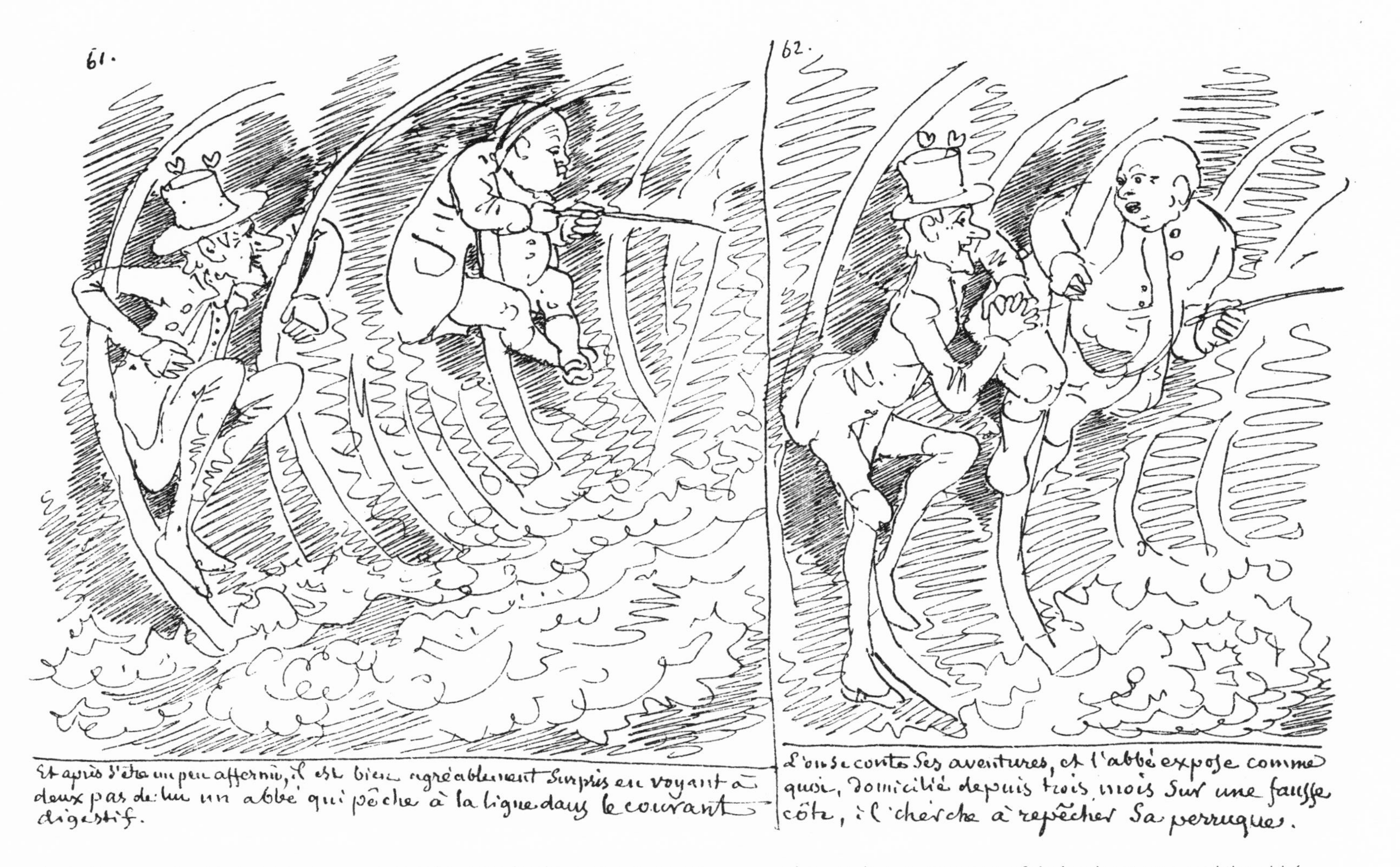
61.
Et après s'être un peu affermi, il est bien agréablement surpris en voyant à deux pas de lui un abbé qui pêche à la ligne dans le courant digestif.
62.
L'on se conte ses aventures, et l'abbé expose comme quoi, domicilié depuis trois mois sur une fausse côte, il cherche à repêcher sa perruque.

And after securing his hold, he is very agreeably surprised to see, two paces away, an abbé who is fishing with rod and line in the digestive current.

They exchange accounts of their adventures, and the abbé explains how, residing for three months on a false rib, he has been trying to fish up his wig.

63

Entre les repas de la baleine, les deux amis descendent sur les îlots digestifs, où ils jouent au palet, avec des coquilles d'huîtres.

64.

Mais quand viennent les repas de la baleine, les deux amis remontent bien vite dans leurs domiciles res= pectifs.

Between the whale's meals, the two friends descend to the digestive islets, where they play quoits with oyster shells.

But when the whale's meals arrive, the two friends quickly climb back to their respective perches.

65.
Cependant le courant digestif amène un beau matin deux missionnaires, un ménétrier, et une Provençale d'une beauté extraordinaire.
66.
Grâce à cette recrue, le séjour de la Baleine devient presque agréable, car pendant que les deux missionnaires entreprennent la conversion de l'abbé, d'une part Mr. Criptogame s'éprend de la belle Provençale, tandis que d'autre part le Ménétrier joue du violon.

The digestive current however brings one fine morning two missionaries, a minstrel, and a woman from Provence of extraordinary beauty.

Thanks to these new recruits, the sojourn in the whale becomes almost agreeable, for while the two missionaries undertake the conversion of the Abbé, Mr. Criptogame falls in love with the Beauty of Provence, while the Minstrel plays his fiddle.

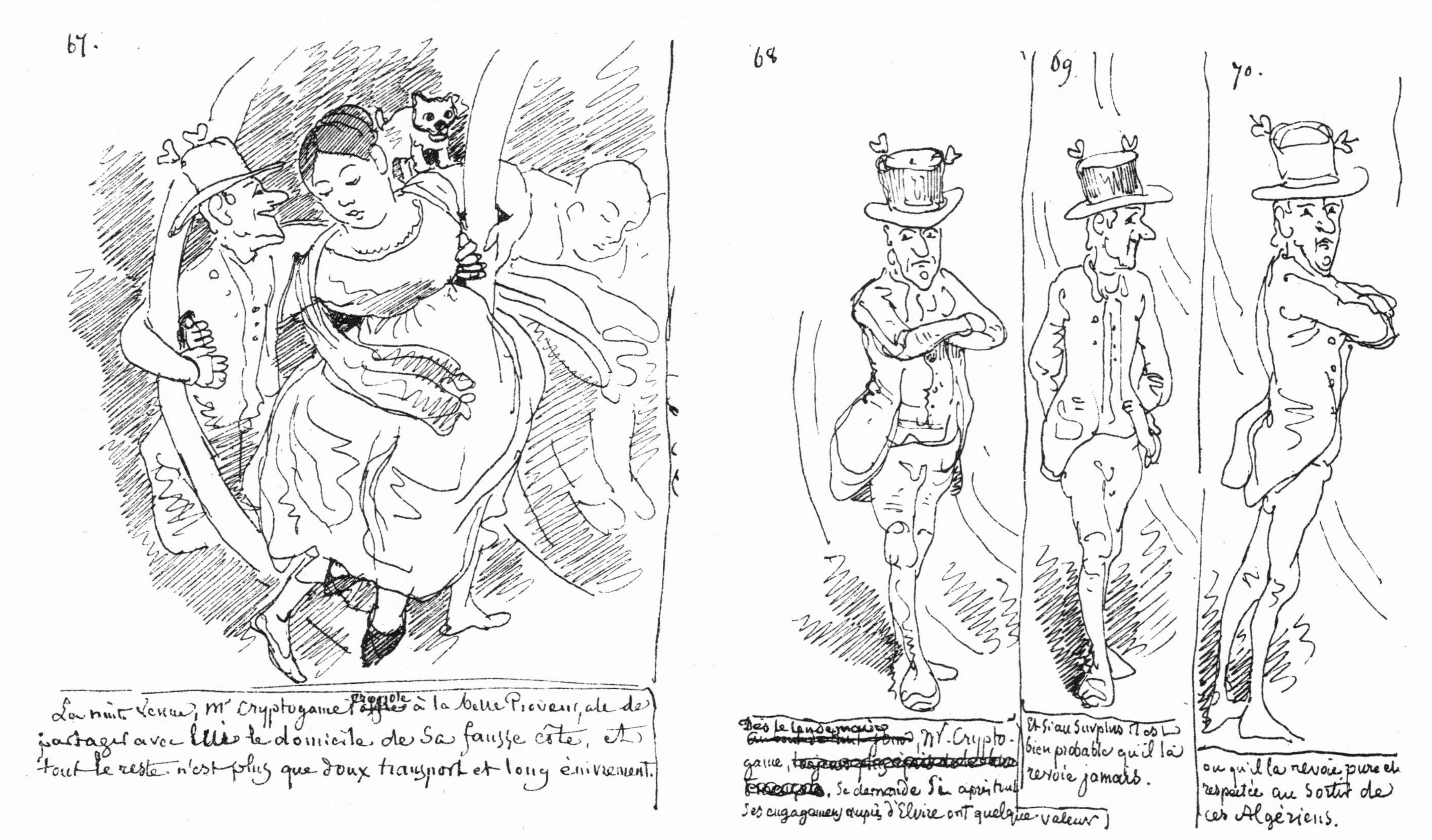
67.
La nuit venue, Mr Cryptogame propose à la belle Provençale de partager avec elle le domicile de sa fausse côte, et tout le reste n'est plus que doux transport et long enivrement.
68
Mr. Cryptogame, se demande si après tout ses engagements auprès d'Elvire ont quelque valeur
69.
Et si au surplus il est bien probable qu'il la revoie jamais.
70.
ou qu'il la revoie pure et respectée au sortir de ces Algériens.

At nightfall, Mr. Cryptogame proposes to the Beauty from Provence to share with him his perch on the false rib, and all the rest is nothing but sweet rapture and prolonged delirium.

The next day Mr. Cryptogame wonders whether after all his commitments to Elvire are truly valid.

And whether moreover there is much chance that he will ever see her again.

Or whether he will see her again pure and respected once she has left the hands of those Algerians.

71
Ayant pris son parti, Mr Cryptogame vient prier l'un des deux Missionnaires de vouloir bien l'unir à la choisie de son coeur.
72.
Dès ce jour même, à midi moins un quart, Mr. Cryptogame est uni à la choisie de son coeur en présence de tout le public de la Baleine.

Having made up his mind, Mr. Cryptogame approaches one of the missionaries and asks him to be so kind as to unite him to the chosen of his heart.

That very day, at a quarter to midday, Mr. Cryptogame is united to the chosen of his heart in the presence of the whole population of the Whale.

73.
Et aussitôt la cérémonie terminée, monsieur Cryptogame engage le Ménétrier et donne un grand bal de noces à sa belle provençale.

And as soon as the ceremony is over, Mr. Cryptogame engages the minstrel and gives a great wedding ball for his Beauty from Provence.

74.
Par malheur le bal de noces donne un vaste mal de coeur à la Baleine en telle sorte que le courant digestif commence à remonter.

By misfortune the wedding ball makes the Whale tremendously sick, so that the digestive current starts to flow back up.

75

Et que la Baleine rejette les deux tiers de ses alimens

And the Whale throws up two thirds of its food.

76

Heureusement les deux Missionnaires, le ménétrier et la belle Provençale sont recueillis par un canot que le Vesuvio, Brik napolitain envoie à leur secours.

Happily the two Missionaries, the Minstrel, and the Beauty from Provence are picked up by a rowing boat that the Vesuvius, a Neapolitan brig, sends to help them.

77
Monsieur Cryptogame demeuré seul avec l'abbé ne se console pas de n'avoir pas été compris dans l'indigestion de la Baleine, c'est pourquoi l'abbé lui propose une partie de palets.
78.
Pendant que les deux amis jouent au palet, la Baleine donne un coup de reins qui les fait trébucher.

Mr. Cryptogame, left alone with the abbé, is inconsolable at not having been included in the indigestion of the Whale; which is why the abbé proposes a game of quoits.

While the two friends are playing quoits, the Whale gives a shake which knocks them over.

79.

C'est du sang qui dégoutte du plafond,
L'abbé n'y comprend rien.

80.

Cependant, au dehors, les baleiniers tirent, tirent.

It is blood dripping from the ceiling. The abbé is nonplussed.

Meanwhile, outside, the whalers are shooting, shooting.

81.
Et la baleine ayant été amenée, ils sont bien étonnés d'en voir sortir deux particuliers très bien mis.

And bringing the whale on shore, they are astonished to see two very well dressed individuals issuing from it.

82.
L'abbé a la satisfaction de retrouver sa perruque dans l'intestin grêle de la baleine, tandis que Mr Cryp-togame y retrouve le papier timbré sur lequel Elvire lui a fait signer un double de ses sentimens.

The abbé has the satisfaction of finding his wig again in the small intestine of the whale, while Mr. Cryptogame finds the copy of the stamped document which Elvire made him sign, attesting to his intentions.

83.
Cependant l'île étant polaire, Mr Cryptogame et l'abbé qui sont légèrement vêtus passent de mauvais moments.

Meanwhile since the island is polar, Mr. Cryptogame and the abbé who are lightly dressed have a hard time.

84.
Mr. Cryptogame gèle sur place. L'abbé gèle au moment où il prenait de l'exercice.

Mr. Cryptogame freezes on the spot. The abbé freezes at the moment when he was taking some exercise.

85.
Les baleiniers ayant terminé leur pêche, embarquent Mr Cryptogame
et l'abbé tout gelés pour retourner en Norwège. —
86.
Mr. Cryptogame et l'abbé sont suspendus tels quels au mat de misaine.

After finishing their expedition, the whalers embark Mr. Cryptogame and the abbé all frozen, before returning to Norway.

Mr. Cryptogame and the abbé are suspended as they are from the foremast.

87.
Cependant la tempête ayant poussé dans ces parages le brik algérien, les Baleiniers s'emparent de tout ce qu'ils y trouvent de précieux y compris l'équipage gelé qu'ils comptent vendre en Espagne aux entrepreneurs d'autodafés.

A storm having meanwhile blown the Algerian brig into the same waters, the whalers seize all they can find of value, including the frozen crew whom they plan on selling in Spain to contractors for auto-da-fés.

88.
Parmi les gelés, les Baleiniers sont surpris de trouver une femme qu'ils jugent devoir être une chrétienne.

Among the frozen parties the Whalers are surprised to find a woman they take to be Christian.

89.
Tous les Maures sont transportés à fond de cale.
90.
Le capitaine seul et Elvire sont mis à part, et suspendus au mât de misaine.
91.
Mais à quelques jours de là un matelot ayant eu l'imprudence d'allumer sa pipe au pied du mât, la barbe du capitaine prend feu en sorte qu'Elvire et Mr Cryptogame dégèlent chacun de l'œil droit.
92.
Le dégel continue, Elvire saute à terre, mais Mr Cryptogame estime qu'il lui est avantageux de paraître toujours gelé. —

All the Moors are carried into the hold.

Only the Captain and Elvire are set apart, and hung on the foremast.

But a few days afterwards when a sailor is careless enough to light his pipe at the foot of the mast, the Captain's beard catches fire so that Elvire and Mr. Cryptogame thaw out a bit, each in the right eye.

The thaw continues, Elvire jumps down, but Mr. Cryptogame deems it to his advantage to appear still frozen.

93.
Elvire décroche son amant, mais Mr. Cryptogame, en tant que gelé, lui tombe dessus.

Elvire unhooks her lover, but Mr. Cryptogame, still of frozen mien, falls on top of her.

94
Désespoir d'Elvire qui tourne et retourne le choisi son coeur. Sans pouvoir le dégeler.

Despair of Elvire who turns and turns again the chosen of her heart, without being able to thaw him out.

95.
Elvire essaie des boissons chaudes. mais Mr. Cryptogame, en tant que gelé, n'en tient compte.

Elvire tries hot toddies. But Mr. Cryptogame, of frozen mien, takes no notice.

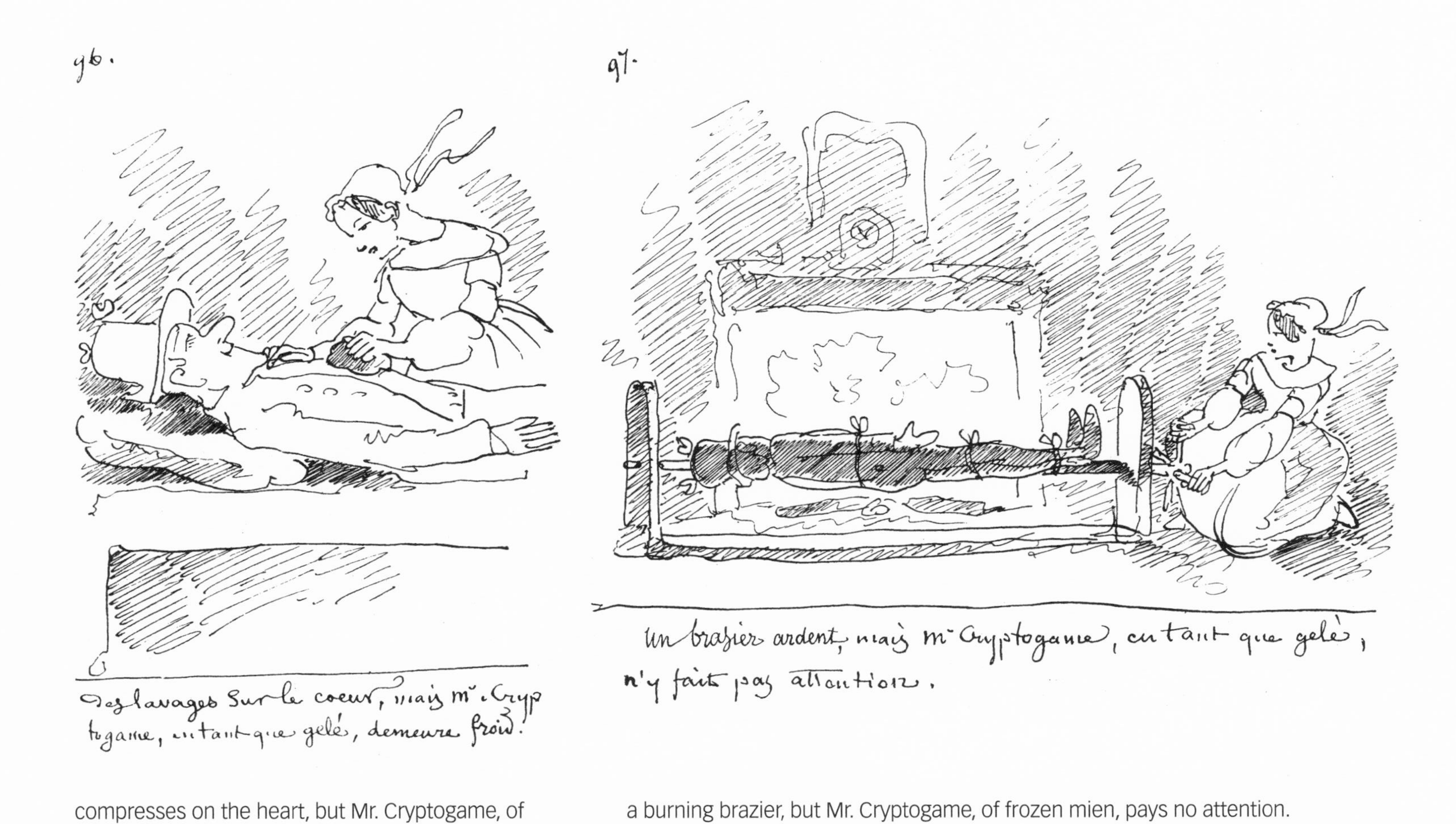
96.
Des lavages sur le coeur, mais Mr Cryp
togame, en tant que gelé, demeure froid.
97.
Un brazier ardent, mais Mr Cryptogame, en tant que gelé,
n'y fait pas attention.

compresses on the heart, but Mr. Cryptogame, of frozen mien, remains cold.

a burning brazier, but Mr. Cryptogame, of frozen mien, pays no attention.

98.

Cependant vers le 54e. de latitude la chaleur commence à pénétrer à fond de cale, et les Algériens dégèlent un peu.

Meanwhile towards the 54th latitude the warmth begins to penetrate down to the hold, and the Algerians thaw out a little.

99.

Une fois dégelés, les Algériens tirent le yatagan, montent sur le pont, et massacrent tout l'équipage de Baleiniers.

Once thawed out, the Algerians draw their yatagans, climb up on deck, and massacre the whole crew of Whalers.

100.

Accourue au bruit, Elvire devient la proie d'un vieux Turc qui s'occupe aussitôt de la mettre à part pour son Sérail.

Running up at the noise, Elvire becomes the prey of an old Turk who immediately sets about reserving her for his seraglio.

101
Mais Elvire se dégage, et saisissant le vieux Turc par la barbe, elle le fait pirouetter de plus en plus rapidement.
102.
Et le vieux Turc s'en va tomber dans la mer, à deux milles sud est nord est.

But Elvire escapes and seizing the old Turk by the beard, she swings him around faster and faster.

And the old Turk goes flying into the sea, at two thousand miles southeast northeast.

103.

Pendant ce temps, Mr Cryptogame demeuré seul, entend distinctement cuire son flanc gauche, en sorte qu'il crie à tue tête qu'il est depuis longtemps entièrement dégelé.

During all of this, Mr. Cryptogame left on his own, distinctly feels his left side burning, so that he shouts at the top of his voice that he has been completely thawed out long since.

104.

Elvire accourue, sauve d'un même coup elle même et le choisi de son coeur, en affirmant aux musulmans que Mr Cryptogame n'est autre chose qu'un chrétien qu'elle faisait griller. —

Elvire runs up, and saves both herself and the chosen of her heart at one go, by telling the Muslims that Mr. Cryptogame is only a Christian dog she was roasting on a spit.

105.
Ensorte que le chrétien est débroché, à condition qu'il prendra le turban
106.
L'abbé dégèle le dernier, mais il a bien de la peine à se déficeler.

So that the Christian is unspitted, on condition that he take the turban.

The abbé is the last to thaw out, but he has some trouble disentangling himself.

107.

Une fois déficelé, en voyant des Turcs au lieu de baleiniers, l'abbé n'y comprend rien.

Once disentangled, seeing Turks instead of whalers, the abbé is nonplussed.

108.

Et en voyant un de ces Turcs qui ressemble comme deux gouttes d'eau à son ami Cryptogame, l'abbé tombe net à la renverse.

And seeing one of these Turks who resembles his friend Cryptogame like two peas in a pod, the abbé falls sheer over backwards.

109.
Bientôt tout s'explique, et pour plus de sûreté, l'Abbé lui-même prend le turban.
110.
Cependant Elvire, pour plus de sûreté aussi, exige du choix de son cœur, qu'il lui signe par devant témoin, une promesse d'amour ardent, suivie de mariage immédiat au prochain débarquement.
111.
Mr. Cryptogame qui s'est déjà marié une fois dans la Baleine tremble d'aller devenir bigame.

Soon all is explained, and for extra safety, the Abbé himself takes the turban.

Meanwhile Elvire, for extra safety too, demands that the chosen of her heart sign in front of a witness a promise of ardent love, followed by immediate marriage at the next disembarkation.

Mr. Cryptogame who has already married once in the Whale, trembles at the prospect of becoming bigamous.

But what he finds reassuring is that his dear lady from Provence must be dead by now, and that Turkish law is indulgent in that respect, anyway.

So the meal of reconciliation is charming, and the abbé who finds Elvire to his taste is as amiable as he is courteous.

114
De son côté, Elvire pour inquiéter Mr. Cryptogame et allumer sa jalousie, favorise l'abbé de quelques préférences,
115
Suite des préférences.

For her part, in order to provoke Mr. Cryptogame and kindle his jealousy, Elvire shows the abbé certain favors,

The favors continued.

116.

Suite des préférences.

The favors continued.

117.

Voyant cela, Mr. Cryptogame prend l'abbé à part, et il lui conseille de demander pour son propre compte la main d'Elvire.

Seeing which, Mr. Cryptogame takes the abbé aside, and advises him to ask for the hand of Elvire for himself.

118.
L'abbé appuyé de Mr Cryptogame demande la main d'Elvire qui n'en croit pas ses yeux.
119.
et une épouvantable crise commence. L'abbé n'y comprend rien

The abbé, seconded by Mr. Cryptogame, asks for the hand of Elvire, who cannot believe her eyes.

And a dreadful fit breaks out. The abbé is nonplussed.

120.
Elvire épuisée de rage s'évanouit mais les deux amis n'osent pas se relever encore.
121
Au bout d'une demi heure pourtant, ils se hasardent tout doucement.....

Exhausted with rage, Elvire faints but the two friends do not dare to get up yet.

Half an hour later, however, they furtively creep . . . . .

122
Et Convaincus que pour cette fois Elvire est bien décédée, Mr Cryptogame et l'abbé emportent le corps pour le jeter à la mer.
123
mais Elvire ayant éternué, Mr Cryptogame lâche prise et s'enfuit.

And convinced that this time Elvire really is dead, Mr. Cryptogame and the abbé pick up the body to throw it into the sea.

But Elvire sneezes, Mr. Cryptogame lets go and flees.

124

Le coup fait qu'Elvire revient à elle, et l'abbé serre ferme, crainte d'être poursuivi.

This revives Elvire, and the Abbé holds fast, for fear of being pursued.

125

Elvire tape, étrangle, égratigne, et l'abbé n'y comprend rien.

Elvire thumps, strangles, scratches, leaving the Abbé nonplussed.

126

Elvire se dégage enfin, et l'abbé a du dessous.

Elvire at last frees herself, and the Abbé has the worst of it.

127-

Cependant, Mr Cryptogame fait neuf fois le tour du pont sans trouver d'issue.

Meanwhile Mr. Cryptogame runs nine times around the deck without finding a way out.

128

Accourue sur le pont, Elvire se met à la poursuite de Mr. Cryptogame.

Dashing onto the deck, Elvire sets off in pursuit of Mr. Cryptogame.

129.
Voyant cela, l'abbé fuit et poursuit tout ensemble, sans y comprendre rien.
130.
Voyant cela, les Maures aussi.
131.
Voyant cela, les animaux domestiques aussi.

seeing which, the Abbé flees and pursues all at once, still nonplussed.

seeing which, the Moors too.

seeing which, the domestic animals too.

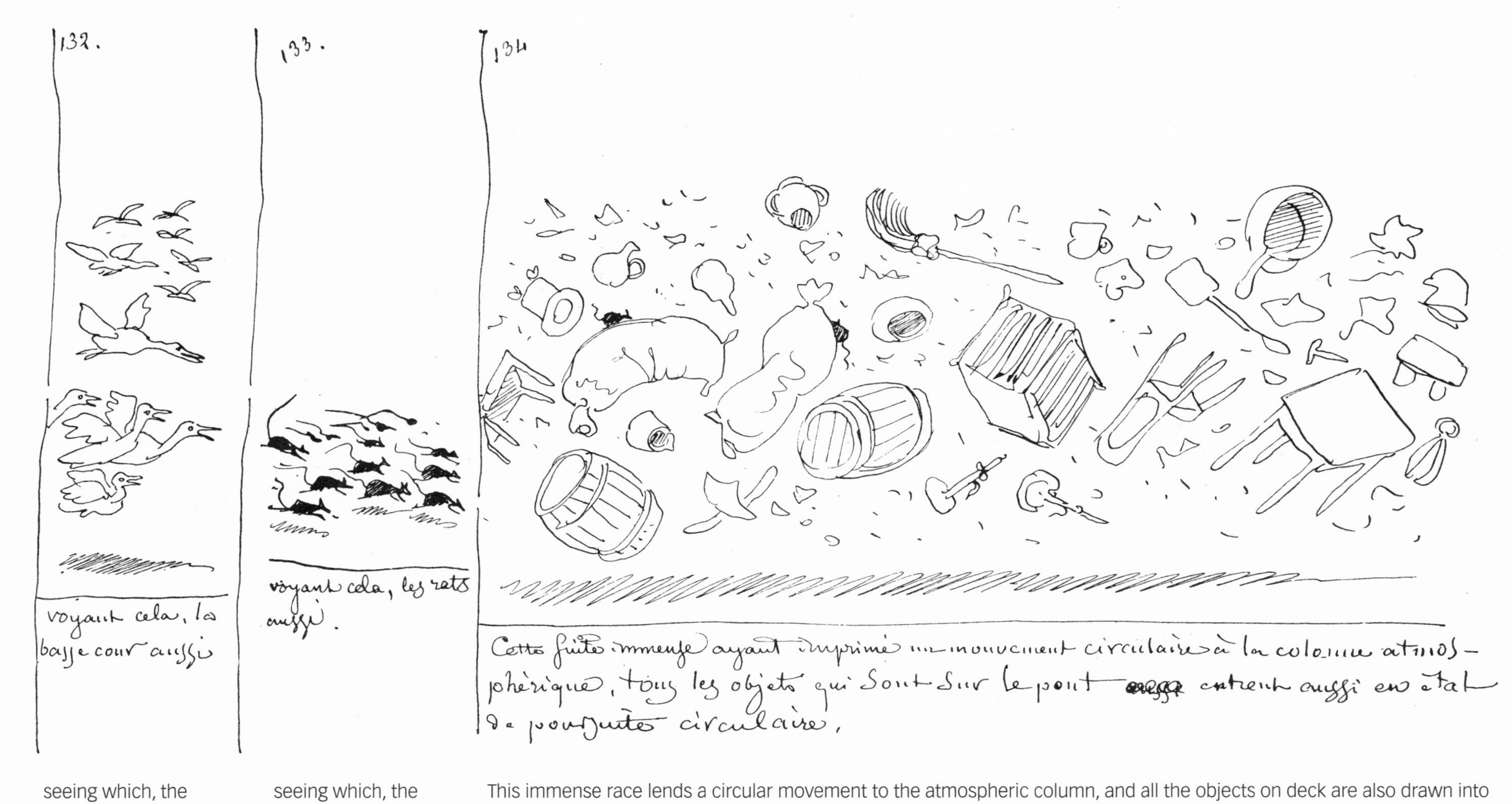
132.
voyant cela, la basse cour aussi
133.
voyant cela, les rats aussi.
134
Cette fuite immense ayant imprimé un mouvement circulaire à la colonne atmosphérique, tous les objets qui sont sur le pont entrent aussi en état de poursuite circulaire.

seeing which, the farm birds too.

seeing which, the rats too.

This immense race lends a circular movement to the atmospheric column, and all the objects on deck are also drawn into a state of circular pursuit.

135.

Et au bout de peu de temps, le vaisseau lui-même, se met à pirouetter huit tours par seconde.

And very soon the ship itself begins to spin at a rate of eight revolutions per second.

Meanwhile the dey of Algiers, smoking his pipe on the seashore, perceives something like a whirlwind.

137.

N'y comprenant rien, le dey d'Alger assemble ses Savans, et il leur ordonne d'expliquer le phénomène

Nonplussed, the dey of Algiers gathers together his scientists and orders them to come up with an explanation of the phenomenon.

138

Les Savans procèdent aussitôt à leurs observations.

The scientists proceed at once to their investigations.

139.

Dans un mémoire en bon arabe, qui a huit coudées de long, les Savans déclarent à l'unanimité que le phénomène en question est un météore aqueux de toute première classe et présageant à Sa Majesté des félicités sans nombre, des jours sans fin, et la mort de tous ses ennemis. Le dey leur fait remettre à chacun deux mille sequins.

In a report in good Arabic, eight ells long, the scientists declare unanimously that the phenomenon in question is an aqueous meteor of the first water, presaging joys innumerable and life everlasting to his Majesty, and death to all his enemies. The dey rewards each of them with two thousand sequins.

140.
En attendant le vaisseau vient échouer dans la rade d'Alger et hommes et biens sont sauvés, mais l'équipage a horriblement mal au coeur.

Meanwhile the ship runs aground in the Algiers roadsteads, and men and goods are saved, but the crew is horribly sick.

141
Le Dey, dans sa justice, fait pendre tous
ses savans pour n'avoir pas dit les
choses telles qu'elles sont, dans
sa clémence, il fait grâce de la vie
aux femmes et aux enfans.

The Dey, in his justice, has all the scientists hanged for having failed to tell things the way they are, but in his mercy he spares the life of the wives and children.

142.
Les officiers du Dey, sur l'avis qu'il y avait trois chrétiens à
bord, viennent pour en prendre possession, et ils commencent par
destiner Elvire au sérail de leur maître.

Officers of the Dey, hearing that there are three Christians on board, come to take possession of them, and they begin by reserving Elvire for the master's seraglio.

143.

Mr. Cryptogame s'étant donné pour naturaliste, il est acheté par Aboul Hassan, qui se propose de lui faire planter ses salades.

Professing himself a naturalist, Mr. Cryptogame is bought by Aboul Hassan, who proposes to have him plant his lettuce.

144.

L'abbé s'étant donné pour homme de lettres Moustacha l'achète pour en faire le précepteur de ses enfants et la première leçon va très bien.

Professing himself a man of letters, the Abbé is bought by Moustacha to act as tutor to his children, and the first lesson goes very well.

145
mais dès la seconde leçon, les petits Moustachas proposent à leur précepteur de jouer à tiens toi bien et l'instruction en souffre un peu
146.
Dès la troisième leçon les petits Moustacha ne voulant plus que jouer à tiens toi bien, l'abbé s'y refuse, et l'instruction n'en va pas mieux

but at the second lesson, the young Moustachas propose a game of piggy-back with some prejudice to the teaching.

At the third lesson the young Moustachas wanting only to play piggy-back, the abbé refuses, and the teaching is not improved thereby.

147.

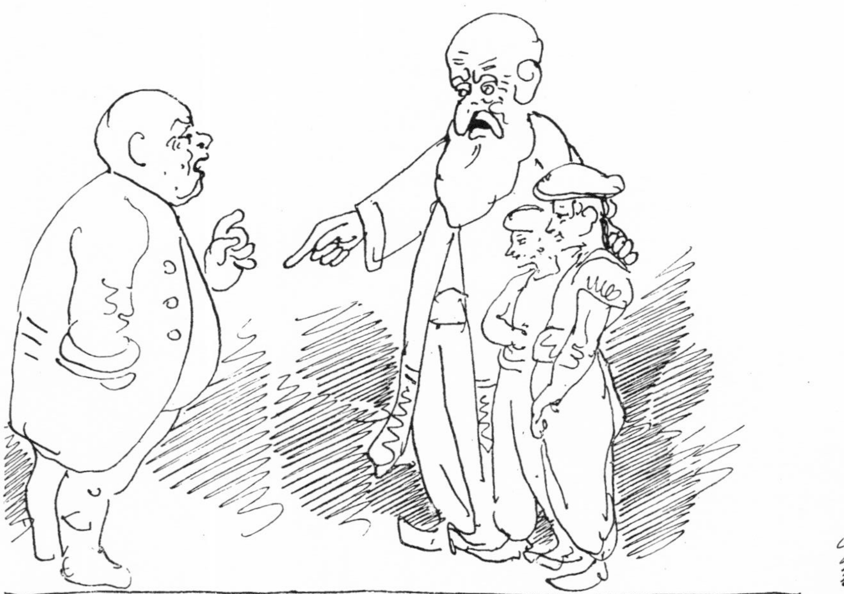

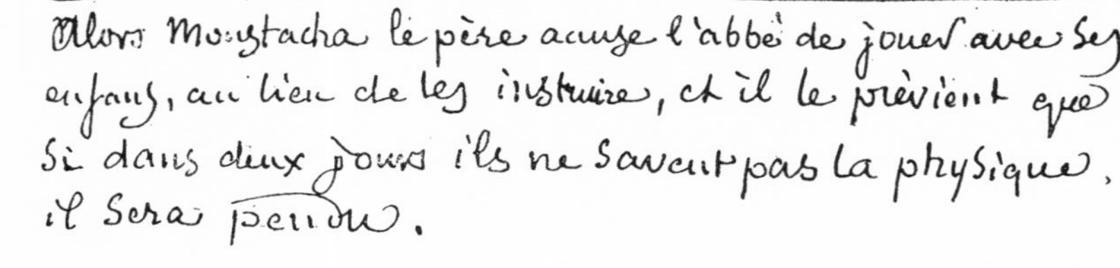
Alors Moustacha le père accuse l'abbé de jouer avec ses
enfans, au lieu de les instruire, et il le prévient que
si dans deux jours ils ne savent pas la physique,
il sera pendu.

Then Moustacha the elder accuses the abbé of playing games with his children instead of educating them, and warns him that if they do not know physics within two days, he will be hanged.

148

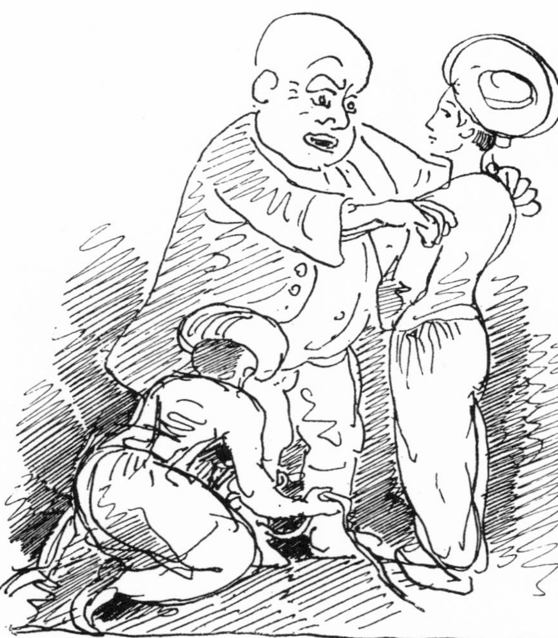

L'abbé ayant horriblement peur d'être pendu,
imagine une méthode prompte et sure, c'est
de n'occuper qu'un enfant à la fois, pendant
que l'autre repose son attention fatiguée

Horribly afraid of being hanged, the abbé thinks up a quick and sure method, that is to keep one child at a time busy, while the other takes a good rest.

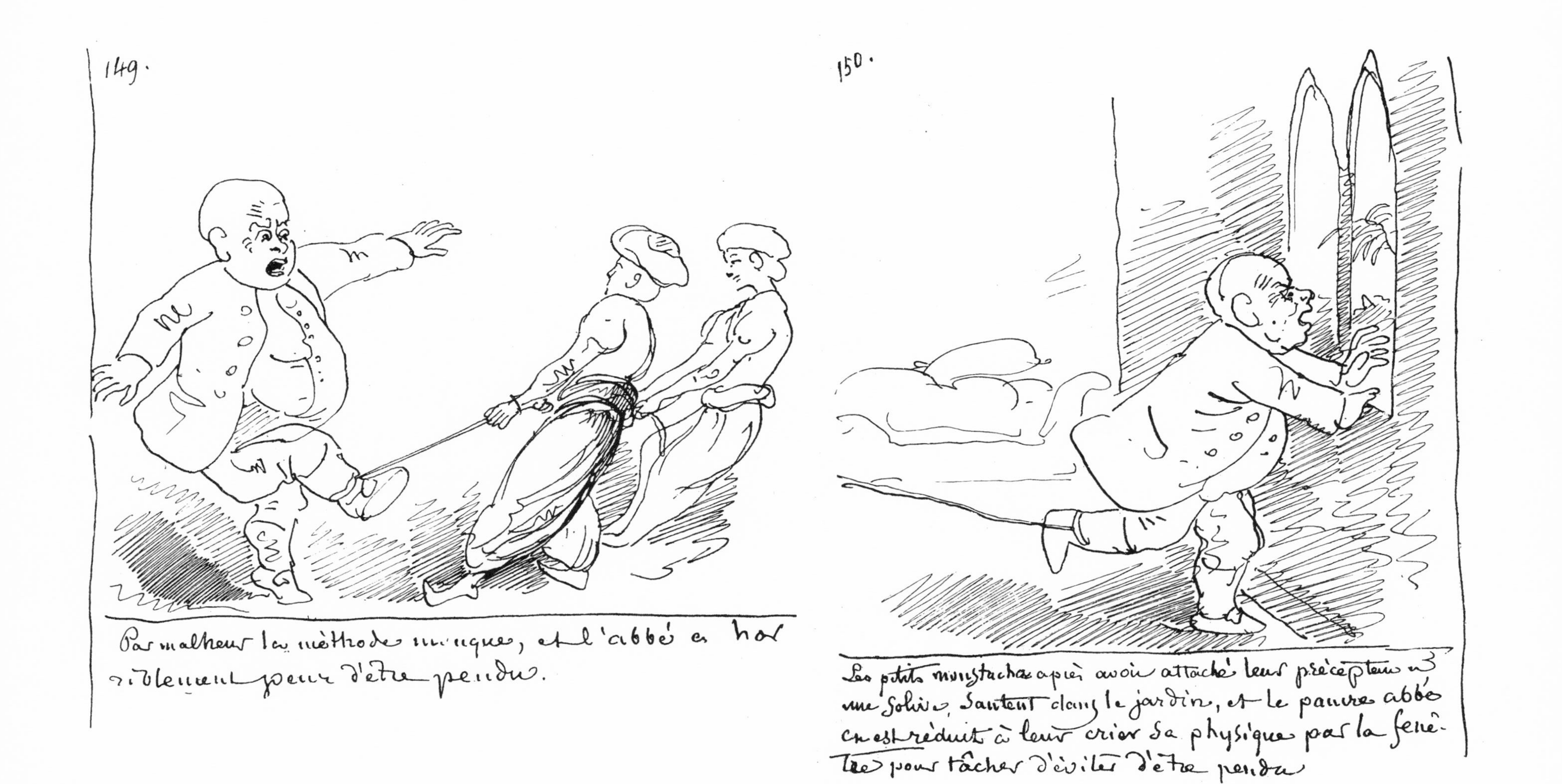
149.
Par malheur la méthode manque, et l'abbé a hor
riblement peur d'être pendu.
150.
Les petits Moustachas après avoir attaché leur précepteur à
une solive, sautent dans le jardin, et le pauvre abbé
en est réduit à leur crier sa physique par la fenêtre pour tâcher d'éviter d'être pendu

Unfortunately the method fails, and the abbé is horribly afraid of being hanged.

Having tied their tutor to a beam, the young Moustachas jump into the garden, and the poor abbé is reduced to shouting his physics at them through the window, in his attempt to avoid being hanged.

151.
ayant horriblement peur d'être pendu, l'abbé tire, tire, dans l'espoir de casser la corde pour s'échapper ensuite
152.
La corde tient bon, mais la poutre casse, le plafond vient en bas, et Moustacha aussi. L'abbé qui a doublement peur d'être pendu fuit à tire d'aile.

Horribly afraid of being hanged, the Abbé pulls and pulls, in the hope of escaping by breaking the rope.

The rope holds, but the beam breaks, bringing down the ceiling, and Moustacha with it. The abbé, doubly afraid of being hanged, flees pell mell.

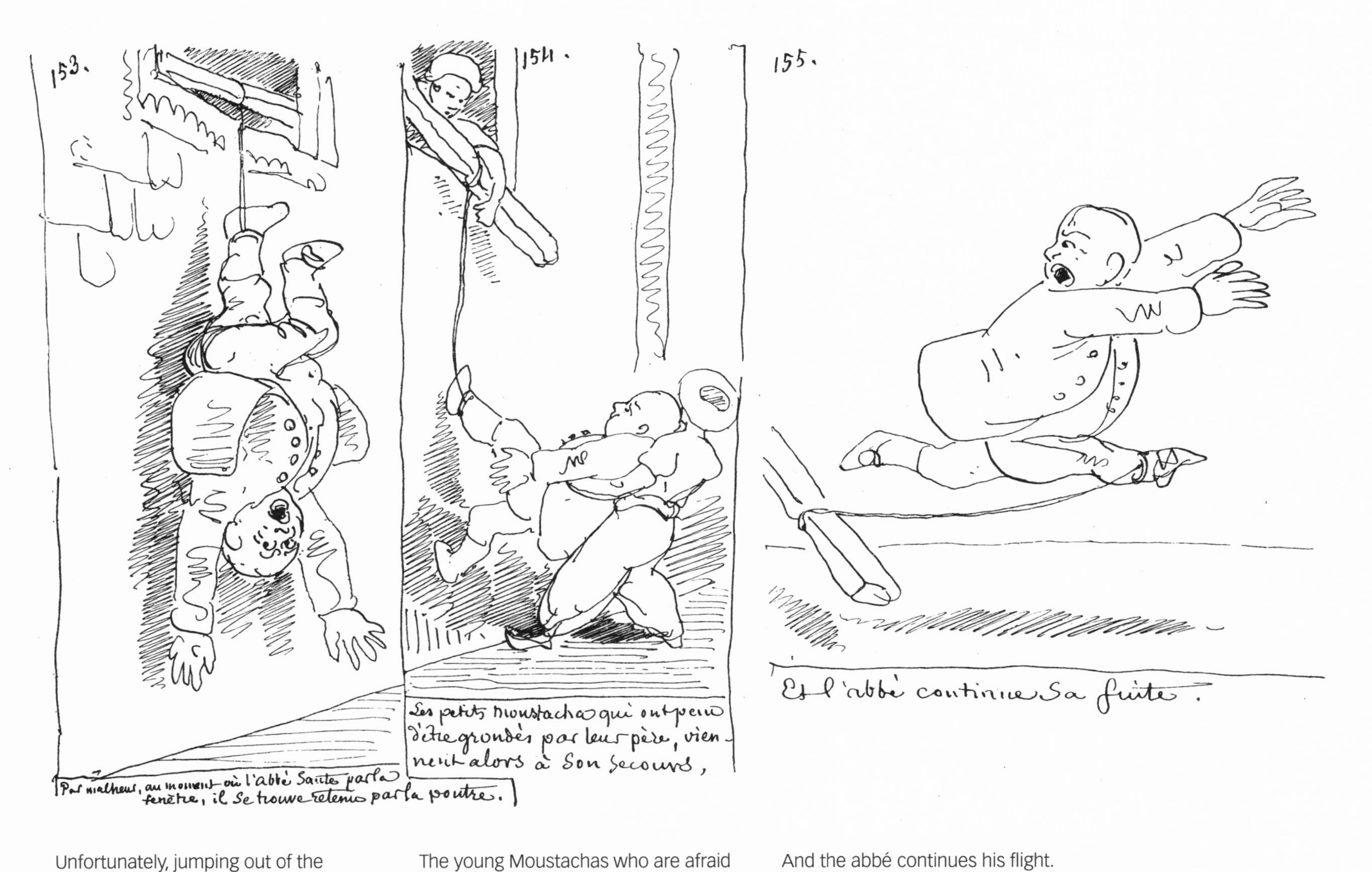
153.
Par malheur, au moment où l'abbé Saute par la fenêtre, il se trouve retenu par la poutre.
154.
Les petits Moustachas qui ont peur d'être grondés par leur père, viennent alors à son secours,
155.
Et l'abbé continue sa fuite.

Unfortunately, jumping out of the window the Abbé finds himself blocked by the beam.

The young Moustachas who are afraid of being scolded by their father, come to his rescue.

And the abbé continues his flight.

156.
Pendant ce temps, Mr. Cryptogame plante des Saz
Pades sous la surveillance de Tapesalé, le porte
bâton d'aboul Hassan.

Meanwhile Mr. Cryptogame plants lettuce under the supervision of Tapesalé, Aboul Hassan's slavedriver.

157.
Pendant ce temps aussi, Elvire tourne la tête au Dey qui accède à toutes ses fantaisies.
158.
Puis, le moment venu, comme Judith, Elvire égorge son Holofernes.

At the same time, Elvire turns the head of the dey, who falls in with all her caprices.

Then, at the right moment, like Judith, Elvire slays her Holofernes.

159.
après quoi elle rengaine et s'enfuit.

After which she sheathes the dagger, and flees.

160.
Cependant Mr Cryptogame ayant aperçu comme une forme d'Elvire qui viendrait à lui, plante là ses Salades, et monte sur un grand arbre.

Meanwhile Mr. Cryptogame, perceiving as it were the shape of Elvire coming towards him, leaves his lettuce there and then, and climbs up a tall tree.

161.
Effectivement c'est Elvire qui apprend à Mr Cryptogame qu'elle est rendue à sa tendresse, et qu'il faut fuir en toute hâte.
162.
à cette proposition, Mr Cryptogame essaie de se cacher dans l'intérieur de l'arbre pour suggérer à Elvire l'idée de fuir en toute hâte sans lui.

It is indeed Elvire, who tells Mr. Cryptogame that she is returned to his tender love, and that they must flee in all haste.

At this proposal, Mr. Cryptogame tries to hide inside the tree, to give Elvire the idea of fleeing in all haste without him.

163.
Mais ce procédé n'aboutit qu'à provoquer une crise si violente que Mr. Cryptogame doit se retirer bien vite à l'extrémité de la branche suprême.
164.
Cependant l'Abbé fuyant toujours, dans la crainte d'être pendu, le frottement finit par enflammer la poutre.

But this proceeding serves only to provoke so violent a fit that Mr. Cryptogame has to withdraw to the tip of the topmost branch.

Meanwhile with the Abbé still in full flight in fear of being hanged, friction on the beam eventually sets it on fire.

165
Et le feu se communique aux herbes, et les lions sortent
de leurs repaires.
166
Et tous les habitans des campagnes
fuient vers Alger
emportant leurs
effets les plus pré-
cieux.
167.
à Alger on ne s'aperçoit de
rien encore parce qu'on
s'y occupe de l'élection
d'un nouveau Dey.

And the desert grass catches fire, and the lions come forth from their lairs.

And the all the inhabitants of the countryside flee towards Algiers, carrying their most precious possessions.

This passes unnoticed in Algiers, where people are busy electing a new dey.

Meanwhile Mr. Cryptogame sees from the tip of the topmost branch an immense fire advancing towards him, preceded by a vanguard of lions, so that he shouts to Elvire that he is going to be returned to her tender love, and that they must indeed flee in all haste.

Mr. Cryptogame and Elvire are joined by the abbé who is still horribly afraid of being hanged.

170
Le vent soufflant de terre, les flammes poursuivent jusqu'à la mer toute la population d'Alger et du territoire;
mais Elvire, Mr. Cryptogame et l'abbé trouvent un refuge sur le reste de poutre, et celui-ci a l'avantage
de narguer Moustacha le père qui lui demande les larmes aux yeux une place sur son bord.

With the wind blowing off the land, the flames pursue the population of Algiers and its territory into the sea; but Elvire, Mr. Cryptogame, and the abbé take refuge on the remains of the beam, and the latter has the pleasure of turning the tables on Moustacha the Elder who begs with tears in his eyes for a place on board.

171.
Le Vent de terre pousse au large, et un vaisseau s'étant montré à l'Est Nord Est, Sud Sud-ouest, l'on s'empresse de faire force signaux.

The wind from the land pushes them into the open sea, and a vessel showing up at East-Nor'-East, South-Sou'-West they hurriedly raise all distress signals.

172.
Les Signaux sont aperçus du Vaisseau, qui se trouve être le Vesuvio, Brick napolitain, et aussitôt un canot est envoyé

The signals are seen by the vessel, which turns out to be the Neapolitan brig Vesuvius, which instantly sends out a jolly-boat.

173.
A peine arrivée à bord, Elvire qui a pris un refroidissement se met au lit, et elle exige tendrement que le choisi de son cœur ne s'éloigne pas d'auprès d'elle.
174.
Et elle lui peint sous les plus délicieuses couleurs leur débarquement prochain, suivi de mariage immédiat.

Once on board, Elvire who has taken a chill, goes to bed, and demands tenderly that the chosen of her heart should stay close to her side.

And she paints in the most glowing colors their imminent disembarkation, followed by immediate marriage.

175.

Et elle lui fait un affreux tableau de sa position s'il venait à la perdre,

And she draws a frightful picture of his position if he should lose her.

176.

Et elle lui propose de boire en commun ses potions, afin d'être malades ensemble.

And she proposes they drink the medicines together, so as to be ill together.

177.

après quoi, épuisée de fatigue, elle s'endort.

After which, exhausted by the effort, she falls asleep.

178.
à peine remonté sur le pont, Mr Cryptogame y retrouve son épouse, la belle provençale qui lui saute au cou, et le ménétrier qui lui joue la bienvenue,

Hardly has he stepped on deck, but Mr. Cryptogame finds his wife there, the Beauty from Provence who throws herself upon his neck, and the minstrel who plays a tune of welcome.

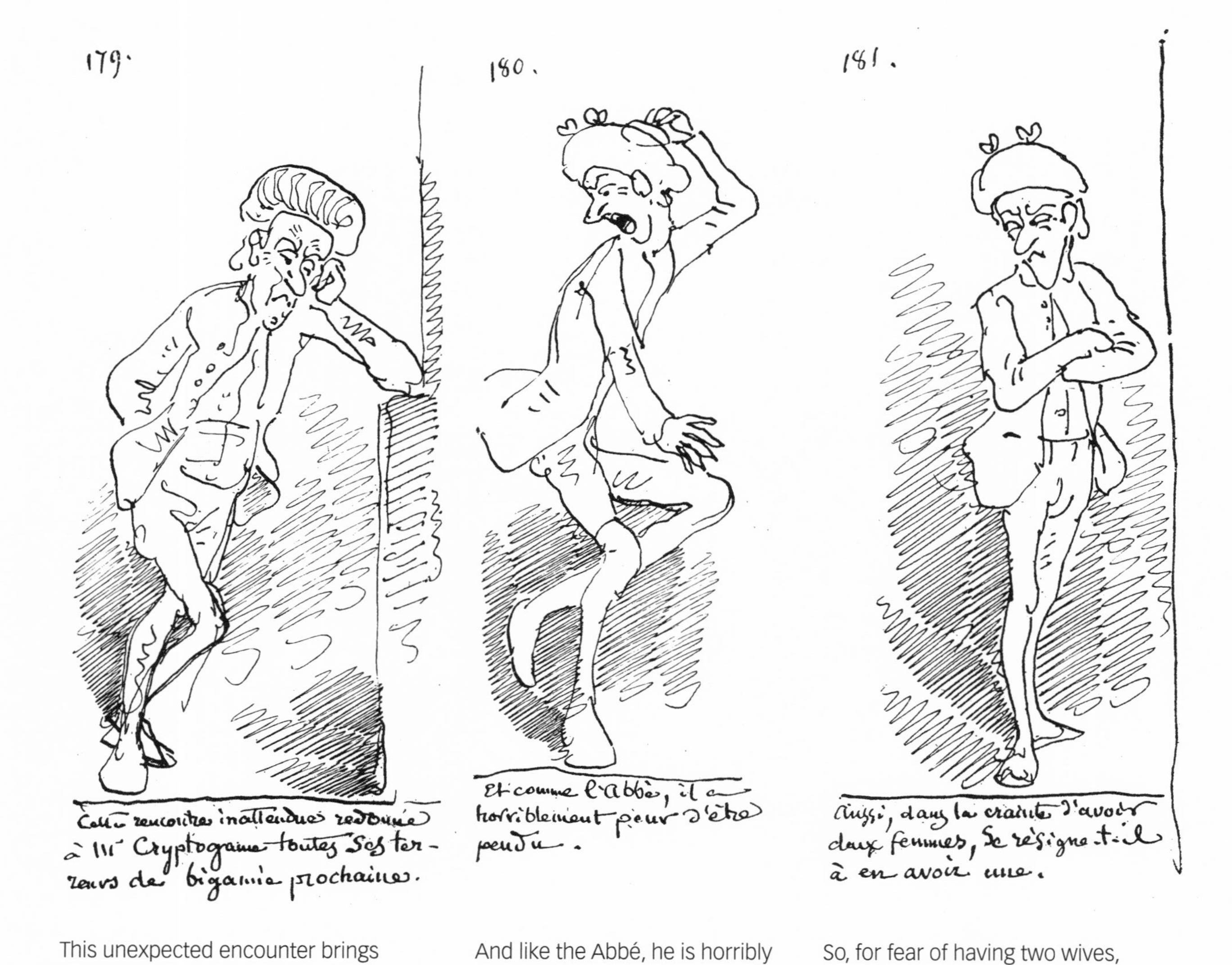
179.
Cette rencontre inattendue redonne à Mr Cryptogame toutes ses terreurs de bigamie prochaine.
180.
Et comme l'Abbé, il a horriblement peur d'être pendu.
181.
Aussi, dans la crainte d'avoir deux femmes, se résigne-t-il à en avoir une.

This unexpected encounter brings back to Mr. Cryptogame all his dread of imminent bigamy.

And like the Abbé, he is horribly afraid of being hanged.

So, for fear of having two wives, he resigns himself to having one.

182
Et il obtient du Capitaine la faveur d'être débarqué cette nuit même sur la côte d'Italie qui est toute prochaine.
183.
Cependant Elvire se réveille à l'aube, et ne voyant plus à son chevet le choisi de son cœur, elle en conçoit des soupçons convulsifs.

And he obtains from the Captain the favor of being disembarked that same night on the coast of Italy which is close by.

Meanwhile Elvire wakes up at Daybreak, and no longer seeing the chosen of her heart by her bedside, she entertains convulsive suspicions.

184.

Et d'un seul bond elle atteint au sommet du grand mât.

In a single bound she reaches the top of the main mast.

185.

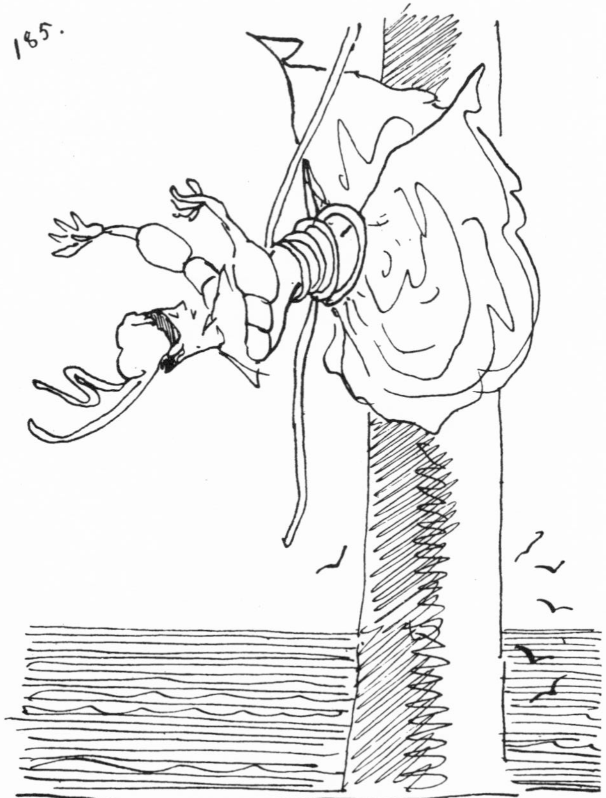

à la vue des deux amans fugitifs Elvire se laisse choir. Heureusement que, ficelée dans un agrès où elle s'entortille, elle n'éclate pas de jalousie.

At the sight of the two fugitive lovers Elvire lets go. Fortunately entangled fast in the rigging, she does not explode with jealousy.

186.
Pendant ce temps, les deux amans ont touché la terre, M. Cryptogame
affranchi qu'il se voit de la bigamie d'Elvire, donne essor à sa joie.

Meanwhile, the two lovers have landed, and Mr. Cryptogame seeing himself freed from bigamy with Elvire, gives vent to his joy.

187.
après quoi, de plus en plus épris de sa chère Provençale, Mr. Cryptogame hante amoureusement les bosquets de la côte
188.
Et les anfractuosités des promontoires.

After which, deeper and deeper in love with his dear Provençale, Mr. Cryptogame amorously haunts the coastal groves.

And the rugged winding cliffs.

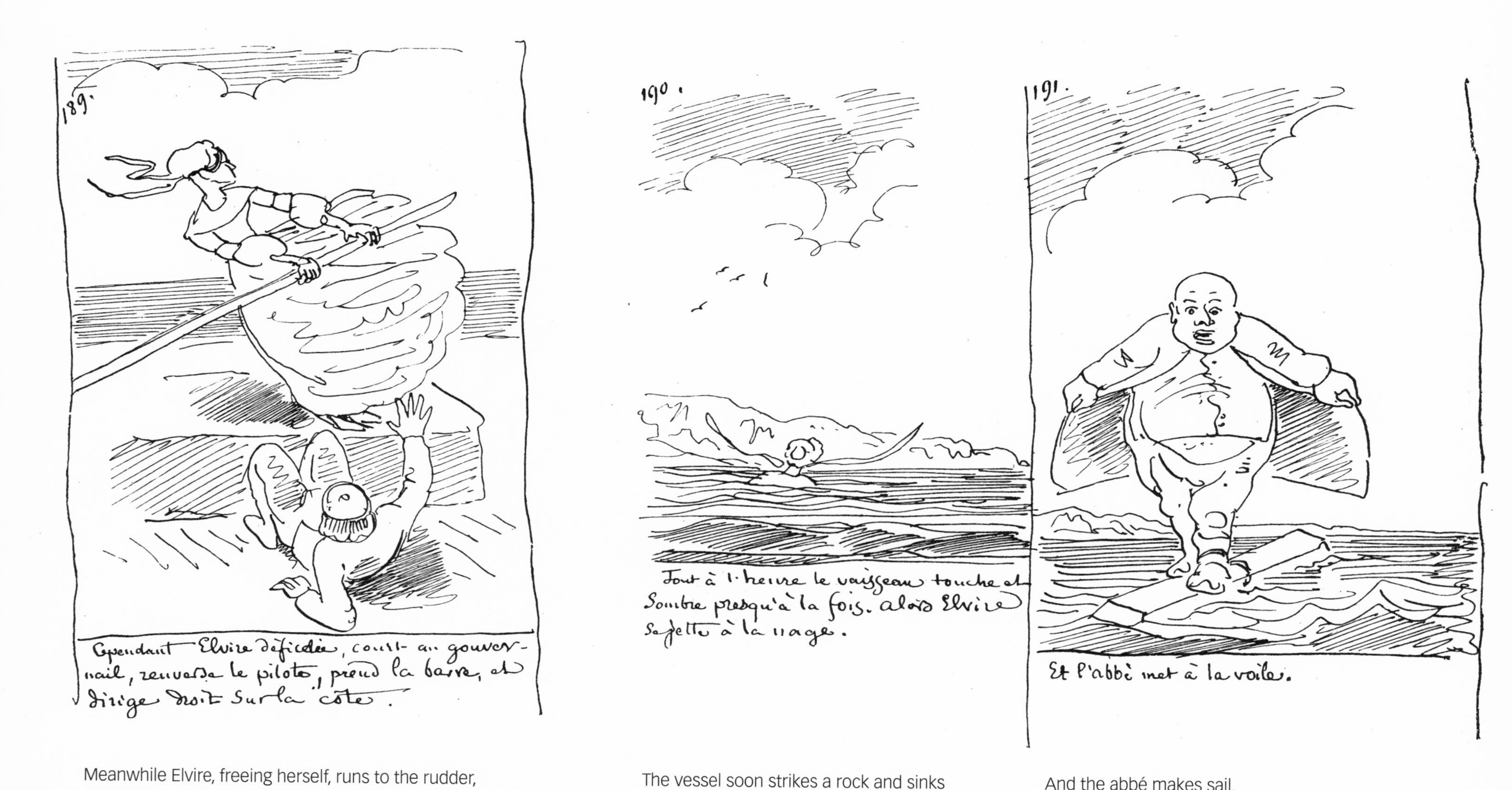
189.
Cependant Elvire défcelée, court au gouvernail, renverse le piloto, prend la barre, et dirige droit sur la côte.
190.
Tout à l'heure le vaisseau touche et sombre presqu'à la fois. alors Elvire se jette à la nage.
191.
Et l'abbé met à la voile.

Meanwhile Elvire, freeing herself, runs to the rudder, knocks down the pilot, takes the helm and heads straight for the coast.

The vessel soon strikes a rock and sinks almost at once. Then Elvire throws herself in and swims.

And the abbé makes sail.

192.

En percevant Elvire qui arrive droit sur l'anfractuosité Mr. Cryptogame reprend ses terreurs de bigamie et déménage en toute hâte.

Seeing Elvire reaching his crag, Mr. Cryptogame is visited again with the terrors of bigamy and moves off in all haste.

193.

et l'abbé, débarqué le premier, déménage pareillement.

and the Abbé, the first to land, moves off likewise.

194.
Se voyant serré de près, Mr Cryptogame fait volte
face, il dispose le ménétrier et l'abbé en front de
bataille, la provençale sur les ailes, puis
prenant son grand courage, il crie à Elvire qu'il
est marié!!!!
195.
Fin malheureuse d'Elvire qui à l'ouïe de ces
seules paroles, éclate de jalousie et de rage.

Seeing himself hard pressed, Mr. Cryptogame wheels around, disposes his forces in battle array, with the minstrel and the abbé in the vanguard and the Provençale on the wings, and then, summoning up all his courage, he shouts to Elvire that he is married! ! ! !

Unfortunate end of Elvire who on hearing these dread words, explodes with jealousy and rage.

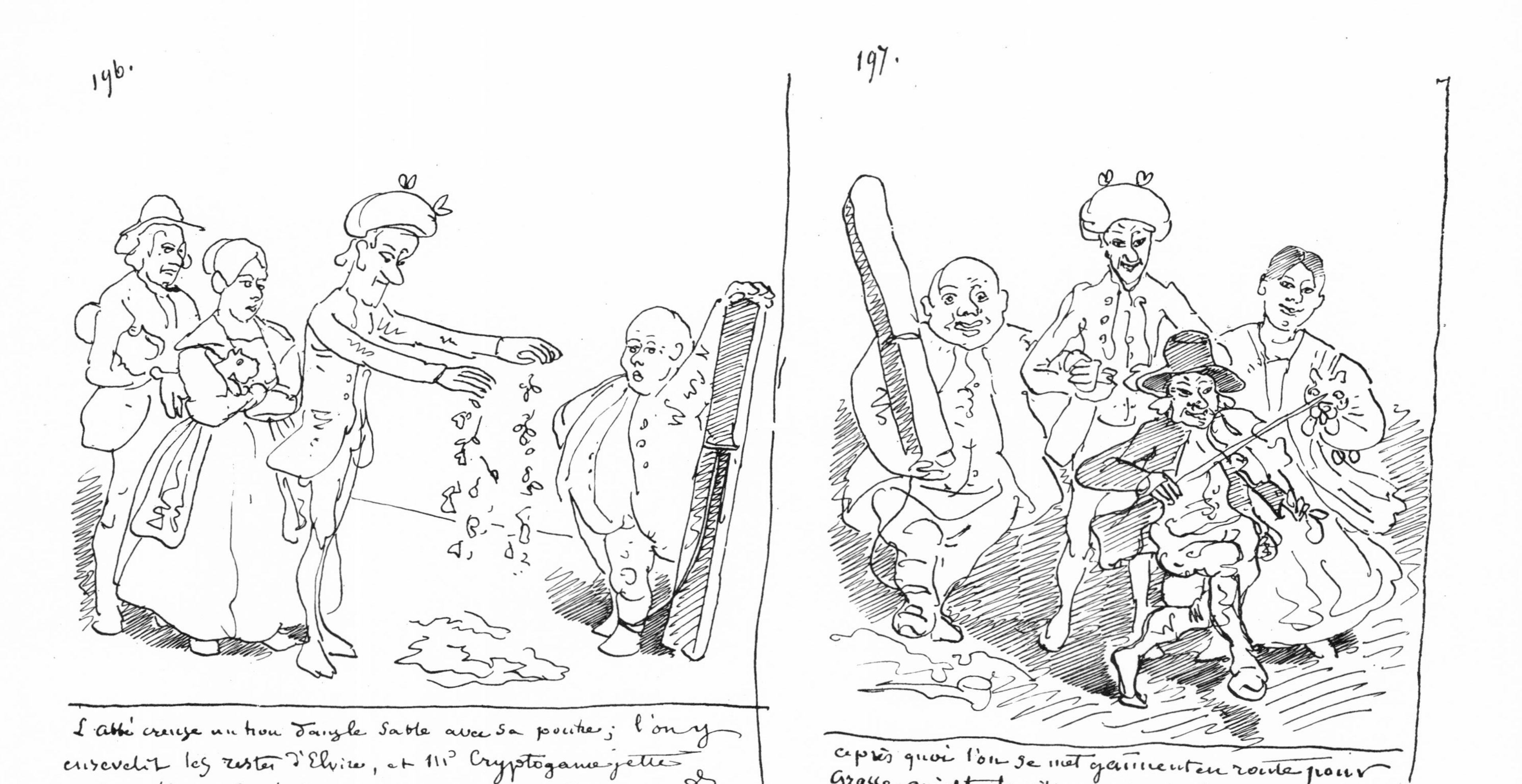
196.
L'abbé creuse un trou dans le sable avec sa poutre; l'on y ensevelit les restes d'Elvire, et Mr Cryptogame jette quelques fleurs sur la tombe de cette amante bien digne d'un meilleur sort.
197.
après quoi l'on se met gaiement en route pour Grasse qui est la ville natale de la belle provençale.

The Abbé digs a hole in the sand with his beam; the remains of Elvire are buried there. And Mr. Cryptogame strews flowers on the tomb of this lover so worthy of a better lot.

After which all set off gaily for Grasse, which is the hometown of the Beauty from Provence.

198.
En route, la belle provençale profite d'une halte pour faire à
Mr Cryptogame l'aveu qu'elle a huit enfans d'un premier lit.
199.
En effet, arrivé à Grasse, Mr Cryptogame
y est chaudement accueilli par une petite
famille tout éclose.

En route, the Beauty from Provence takes the occasion of a rest to make the confession to Mr. Cryptogame, that she has eight children from a first marriage.

Reaching Grasse, Mr. Cryptogame is indeed warmly welcomed by a blooming little family.

200.

Le ménétrier se fixe à Grasse, l'abbé est nommé précepteur des enfans, et Mr Cryptogame coule des jours suffisamment heureux, au sein d'un grand tapage domestique.

The minstrel stays in Grasse, the Abbé is appointed tutor to the children, and Mr. Cryptogame passes his days moderately happy, amid a great domestic racket.

201.
Fin de l'histoire de Mr. Cryptogame

The End of the Story of Mr. Cryptogame.

HISTOIRE DE M. TRICTRAC

Mr. Trictrac est dévoré de l'amour de la Science.
Vagues désirs de célébrité.
Commencement de projets.

Mr. Trictrac is devoured by love of science.

Vague aspirations to celebrity.

Plans hatched.

4.
Nouvelles idées !!!!
5
Mr. Trictrac communique à sa famille son projet de découvrir les sources du Nil.

New ideas! ! ! !

Mr. Trictrac tells his family about his plan to discover the sources of the Nile.

6
Les parens de Mr. Trictrac s'opposant à
son projet ne veulent pas le laisser partir.
Mr. Trictrac ayant pris le parti de dissimuler, salue ses parens, comme allant se
coucher. Les parens lui font encore des remon-
trances amicales.

Mr. Trictrac's parents are opposed to his plan and do not want him to leave.

Deciding to engage in a deception, Mr. Trictrac bids his parents good night, as if going to bed. His parents still offer some gentle remonstrances.

8

Le père ferme à clé la porte de Mr. Trictrac. pour plus de sûreté.

The father locks Mr. Trictrac's door just to make sure.

9

au moment où Mr. Trictrac allait partir pour les Sources du Nil par la cheminée, un Voleur en descend.

At the moment when Mr. Trictrac was about to depart for the sources of the Nile by the chimney, a thief comes down it.

10.

Mr. Trictrac voyant que le Voleur a peur, prend courage, et l'intimide.

Mr. Trictrac seeing that the thief is afraid, takes courage, and intimidates him.

11
12
13.
Mr Trictrac après avoir pris du voleur des informations pour savoir où conduit la cheminée, l'engage à se mettre dans son lit à sa place, et s'évade pour les sources du nil
Cependant la police, ayant eu vent qu'un voleur est sur le toit, cerne la maison de Mr. Trictrac.
Arrivé sur le toit, Mr Trictrac délibère de quel côté il doit descendre pour aller aux sources du Nil.

Mr. Trictrac has the thief tell him where the chimney leads, then gets him to lie down in his bed in his place, and escapes for the sources of the Nile.

Meanwhile the police getting wind of a thief on the roof, surround Mr. Trictrac's house.

Reaching the roof, Mr. Trictrac considers in what direction he should descend, to make for the sources of the Nile.

14
La police ayant aperçu Mr. Trictrac, le prend pour son voleur et escalade à dessein de l'envelopper habilement par derrière.
15.
La police ayant sommé Mr Trictrac de se rendre — Il répond avec esprit qu'il se rendra aux Sources du Nil.
16.
Profond embarras de la Police. Mr. Trictrac pour s'en débarrasser, pousse l'échelle contre l'autre côté de la rue.

The police espying Mr. Trictrac take him for their thief and climb up in order to surround him cleverly from behind.

The police having summoned Mr. Trictrac to give himself up—He responds wittily that he will rather give himself up to a search for the Nile.

Great trouble for the Police. Mr. Trictrac in order to get rid of them, pushes the ladder against the other side of the street.

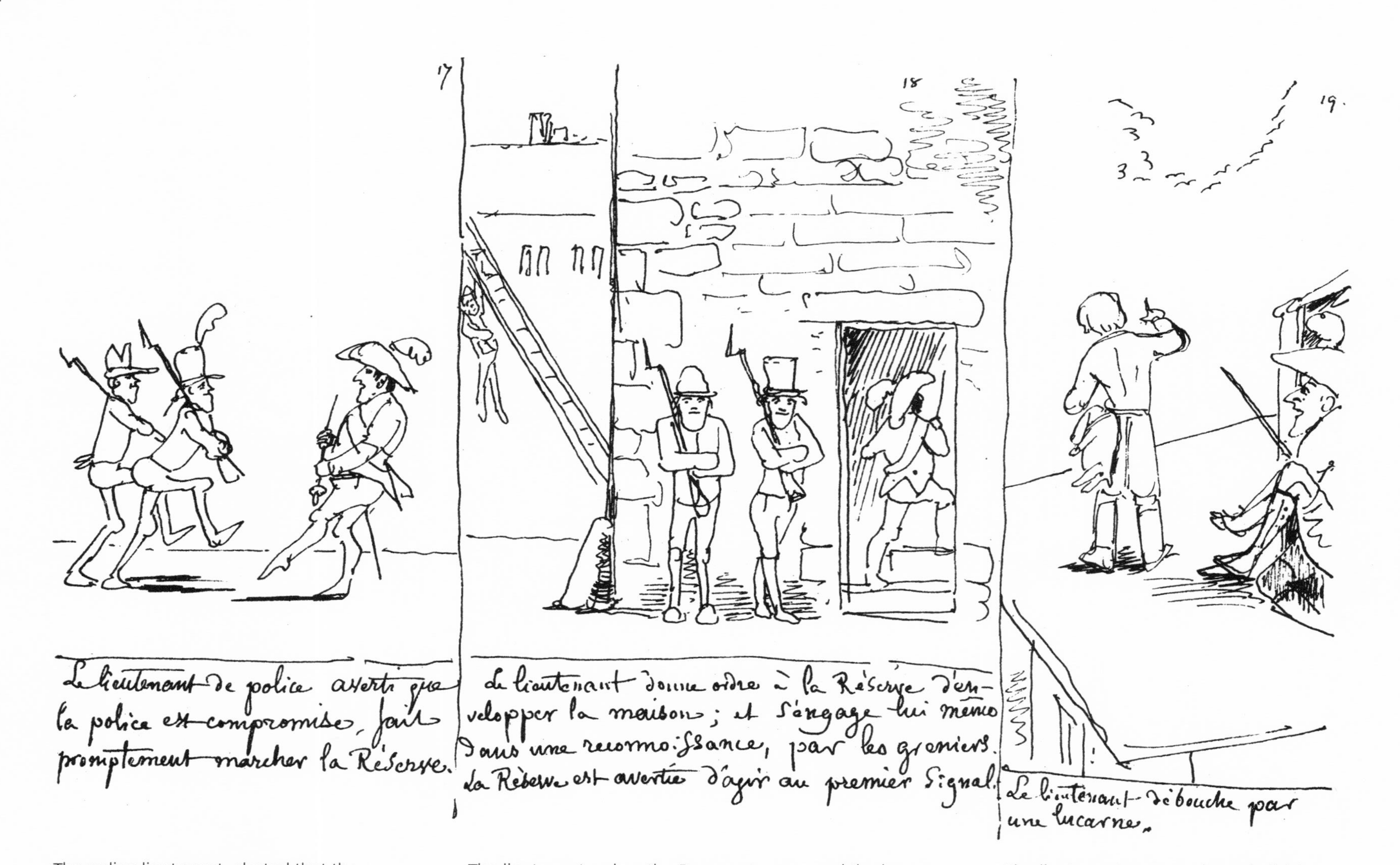
17
Le lieutenant de police averti que la police est compromise, fait promptement marcher la Réserve.
18
Le lieutenant donne ordre à la Réserve d'envelopper la maison; et s'engage lui même dans une reconnaissance, par les greniers. La Réserve est avertie d'agir au premier signal.
19.
Le lieutenant débouche par une lucarne.

The police lieutenant, alerted that the police are in jeopardy, promptly calls up the Reserve.

The lieutenant orders the Reserve to surround the house; and himself engages in a reconnaissance, by the attics. The Reserve is alerted to act at the first signal.

The lieutenant emerges by a skylight.

20

Cependant le père demande à travers la porte si son fils est toujours dans les mêmes sentiments. Le voleur répond que oui, d'après ses instructions.

Meanwhile the father asks through the door whether his son is still of the same humor. The thief replies yes, according to his instructions.

21

Le père trouve son fils horriblement changé.

The father finds his son horribly changed.

22.

Le médecin venu se fait décrire les symptômes, depuis l'origine.

The doctor sent for, has the symptoms described to him, from the beginning.

23

Les Symptomes connus le Médecin explique au père toute la maladie de son fils, comme quoi c'est un cas très commun; provenant de surabondance dans le chyle, mêlé d'échauffement des glandes lombaires, et comme quoi malgré la gravité du cas, il le tirera de là sans aucun doute, à moins d'accidens.

The symptoms established, the Doctor explains to the father all of his son's illness, how it is a very common case resulting from a superabundance in the chyle, in conjunction with a heating of the lumbar glands; and how despite the gravity of the case, he is bound to bring him out of it, barring accidents.

24.

Le docteur ayant prescrit les évacuans, l'Apothicaire est mandé.

The doctor having prescribed purges, the Apothecary is sent for.

25.

Le voleur voyant approcher le danger, s'empare de l'arme. L'apothicaire désarmé a du dessous.

The thief seeing danger approach, seizes the weapon. The apothecary, disarmed, gets the worst of it.

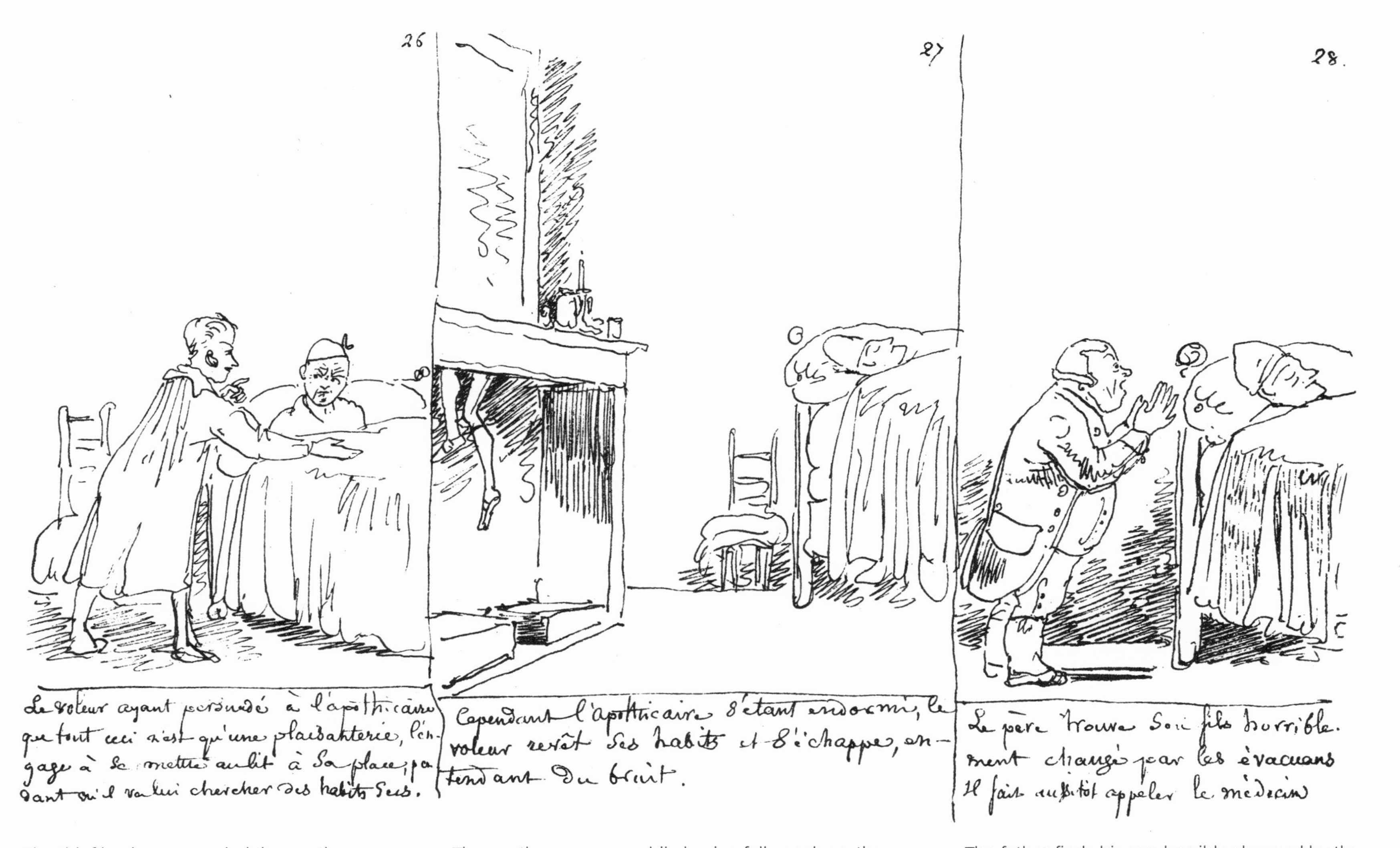
26
27
28.
Le voleur ayant persuadé à l'apothicaire que tout ceci n'est qu'une plaisanterie, l'engage à se mettre au lit à sa place, pendant qu'il va lui chercher des habits secs.
Cependant l'apothicaire s'étant endormi, le voleur revêt ses habits et s'échappe, entendant du bruit.
Le père trouve son fils horriblement changé par les évacuans Il fait aussitôt appeler le médecin

The thief having persuaded the apothecary that it was all only a joke, has him get into the bed in his place, while he goes to fetch some dry clothes.

The apothecary meanwhile having fallen asleep, the thief puts on his clothes and hearing a noise, escapes.

The father finds his son horribly changed by the purges. He calls instantly for the doctor.

29
Le médecin venu, explique au père que c'est le cours de sa maladie; que l'effet de l'évacuation est d'agir sur les fibres qui constituent l'état normal de la physionomie; qu'il avait prévu cet effet, et qu'en conséquence il est très content de l'état du malade. Le cas est grave, très grave sans doute, mais il le tirera de là sans aucun doute, à moins d'accidens imprévus. Il ordonne des boissons chaudes.
30
Cependant le Lieutenant de Police ayant voulu arrêter son voleur, une lutte s'engage entre lui et Mr. Trictrac, au moment où le voleur débouche.
31
Le voleur ayant reconnu le lieutenant de police, s'empresse de bien vite redescendre.

On arriving, the doctor explains to the father that this is the normal course of the sickness; that the effect of the purges is to act on the fibers that constitute the normal state of the physiognomy; that he had foreseen this result, and that as a consequence he is very satisfied with the state of the patient. The case is serious, very serious without doubt, but he will certainly pull him through, barring unforeseen accidents. He orders hot toddies.

Meanwhile the Police Lieutenant having tried to arrest the thief, a struggle is engaged between him and Mr. Trictrac, at the moment when the thief emerges.

The thief having recognized the lieutenant of police, very hurriedly descends again.

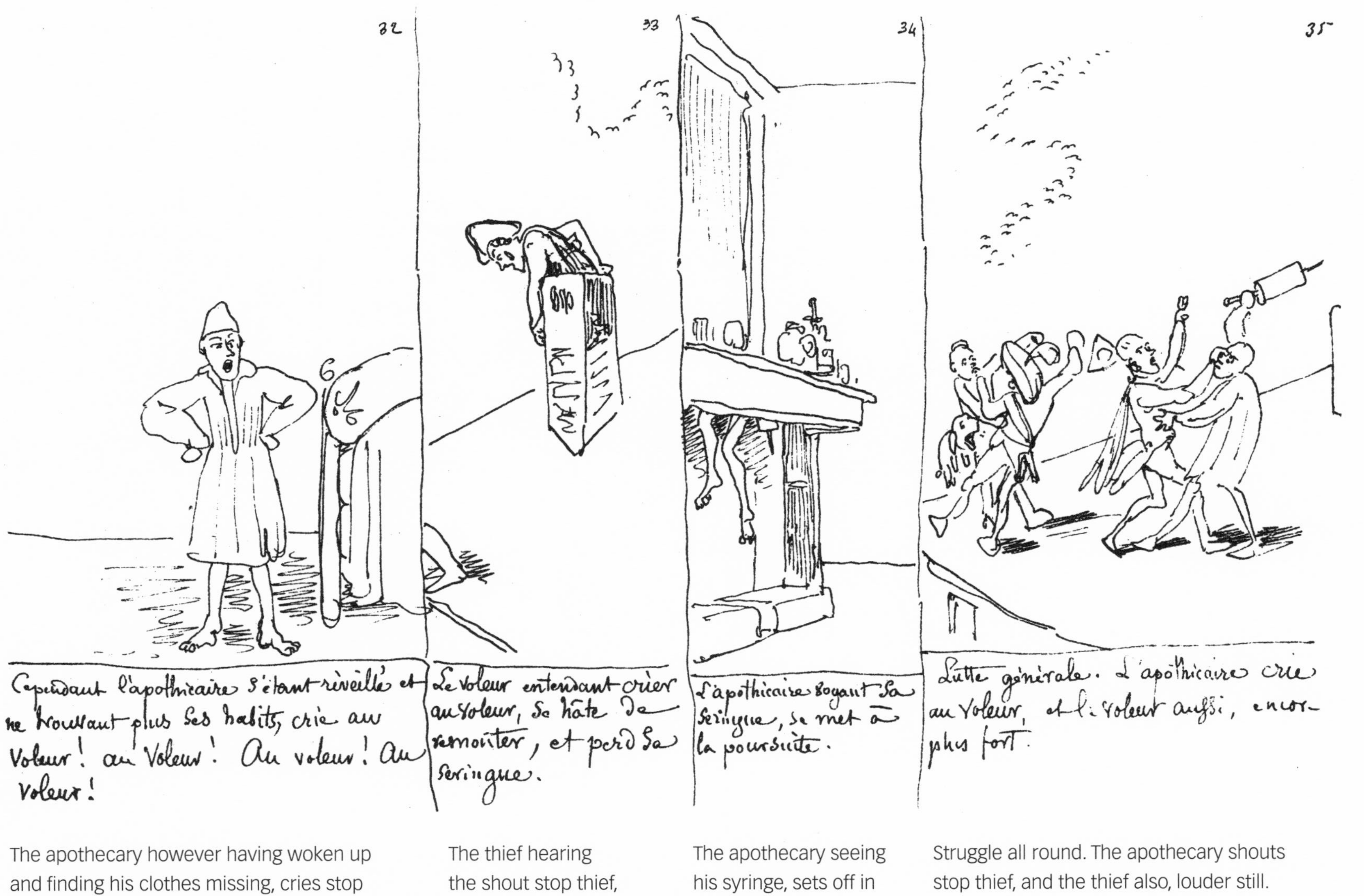
32
Cependant l'apothicaire s'étant réveillé et ne trouvant plus ses habits, crie au voleur! au Voleur! Au voleur! Au voleur!
33
Le voleur entendant crier au voleur, se hâte de remonter, et perd sa seringue.
34
L'apothicaire voyant sa seringue, se met à la poursuite.
35
Lutte générale. L'apothicaire crie au voleur, et le voleur aussi, encore plus fort.

The apothecary however having woken up and finding his clothes missing, cries stop thief! Stop thief! Stop thief! Stop thief!

The thief hearing the shout stop thief, hurriedly climbs up again, and loses his syringe.

The apothecary seeing his syringe, sets off in pursuit.

Struggle all round. The apothecary shouts stop thief, and the thief also, louder still.

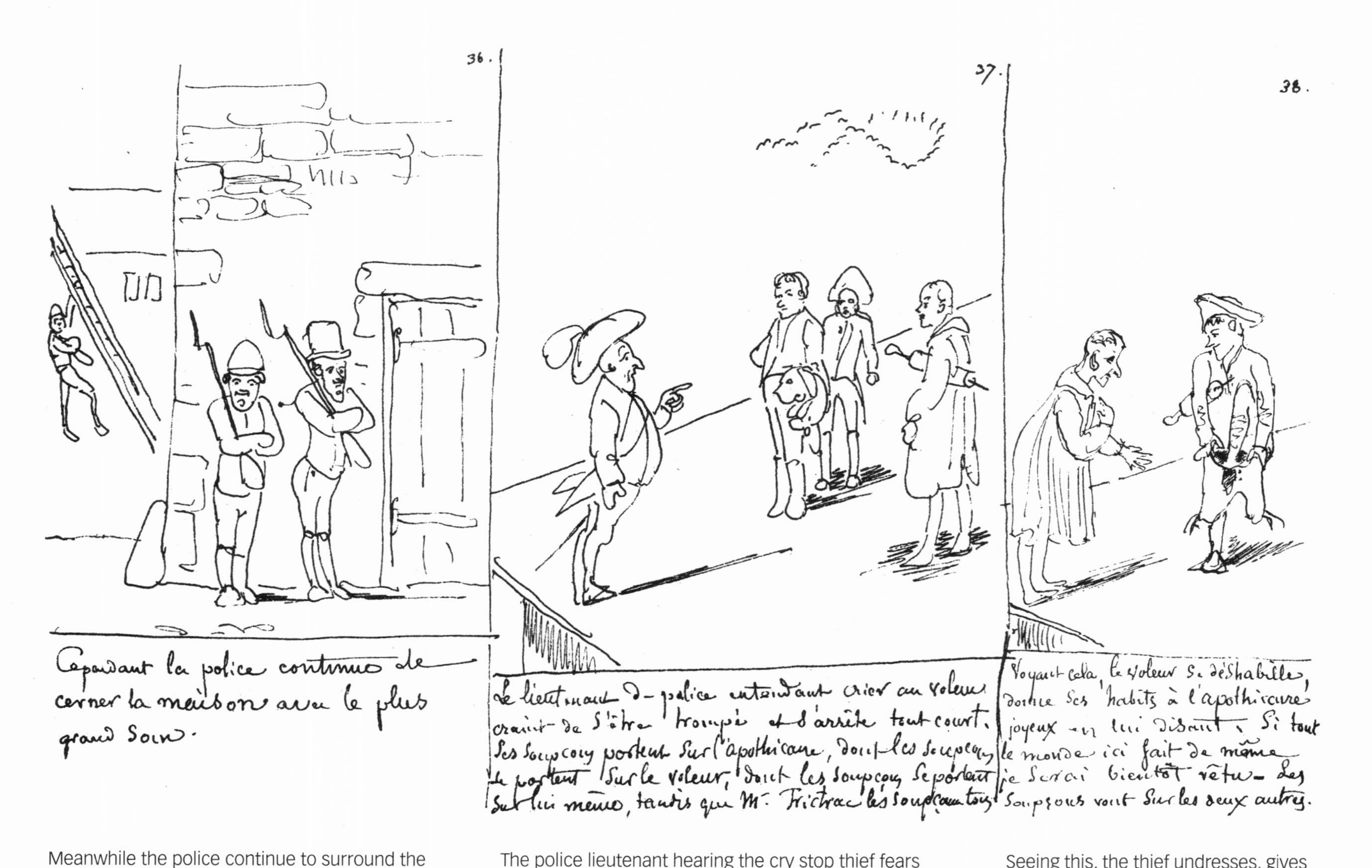
36.
Cependant la police continue de cerner la maison avec le plus grand soin.
37.
Le lieutenant de police entendant crier au voleur craint de s'être trompé et s'arrête tout court. Ses soupçons portent sur l'apothicaire, dont les soupçons se portent sur le voleur, dont les soupçons se portent sur lui même, tandis que Mr. Trictrac les soupçonne tous.
38.
Voyant cela, le voleur se déshabille, donne ses habits à l'apothicaire joyeux en lui disant: Si tout le monde ici fait de même je serai bientôt vêtu. Les soupçons vont sur les deux autres.

Meanwhile the police continue to surround the house most punctiliously.

The police lieutenant hearing the cry stop thief fears he is mistaken and stops abruptly. Suspicions fall on the apothecary, whose suspicions fall on the thief, whose suspicions fall on himself, while Mr. Trictrac suspects them all.

Seeing this, the thief undresses, gives his clothes to the delighted Apothecary, saying to him: If everyone here does likewise, I shall soon be clothed. Suspicions fall on the two others.

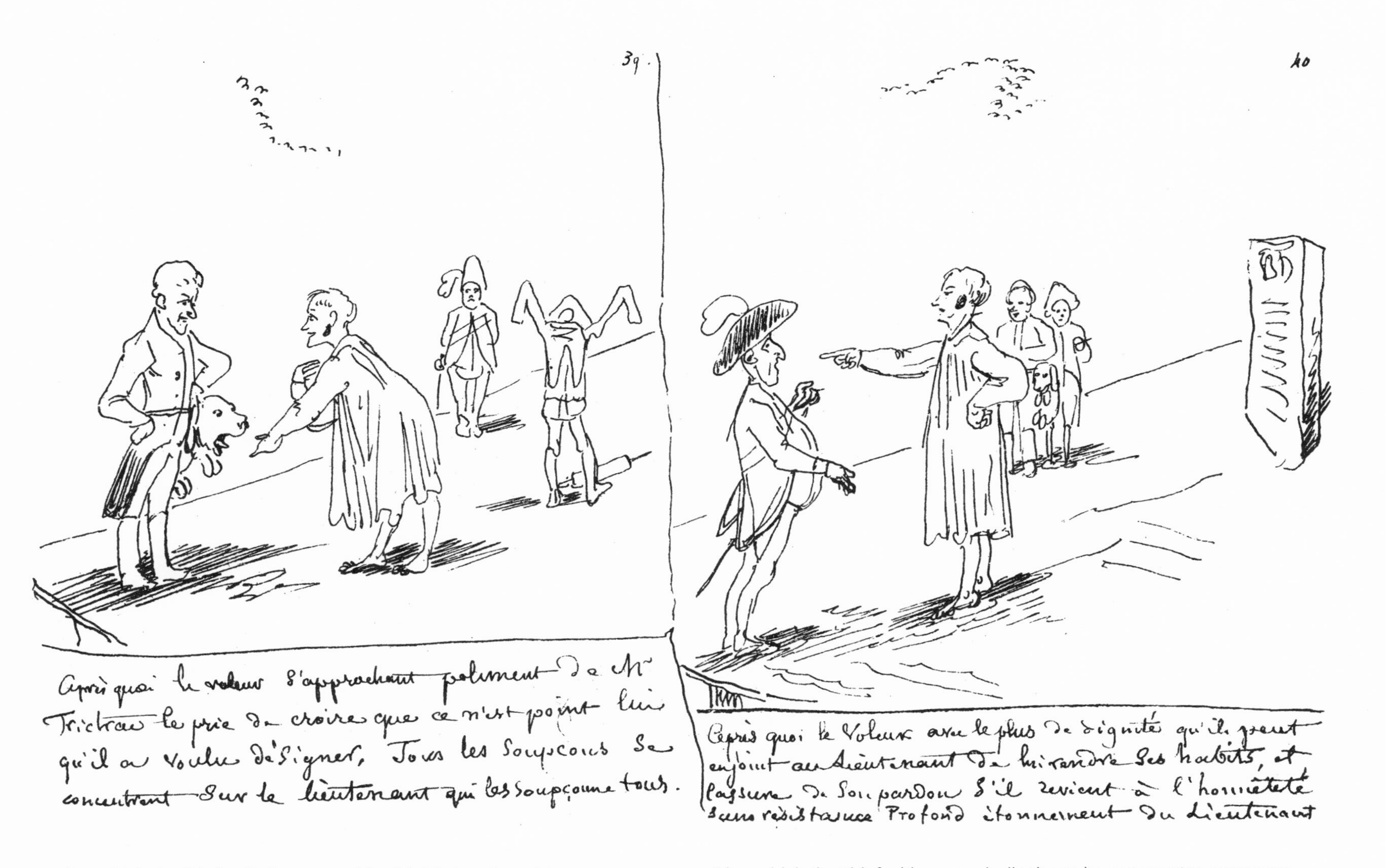
39.
Après quoi le voleur s'approchant poliment de Mr Trictrac le prie de croire que ce n'est point lui qu'il a voulu désigner, Tous les soupçons se concentrent sur le lieutenant qui les soupçonne tous.
40
Après quoi le Voleur avec le plus de dignité qu'il peut enjoint au Lieutenant de lui rendre ses habits, et l'assure de son pardon s'il revient à l'honnêteté sans résistance Profond étonnement du Lieutenant

After which the thief politely approaching Mr. Trictrac, begs him to believe that he was not thinking of him. All suspicions are now concentrated on the lieutenant who suspects them all.

After which the Thief with as much dignity as he can muster, summons the Lieutenant to give him back his clothes, and assures him of his pardon if he returns unresisting to an honest life. Profound astonishment of the Lieutenant.

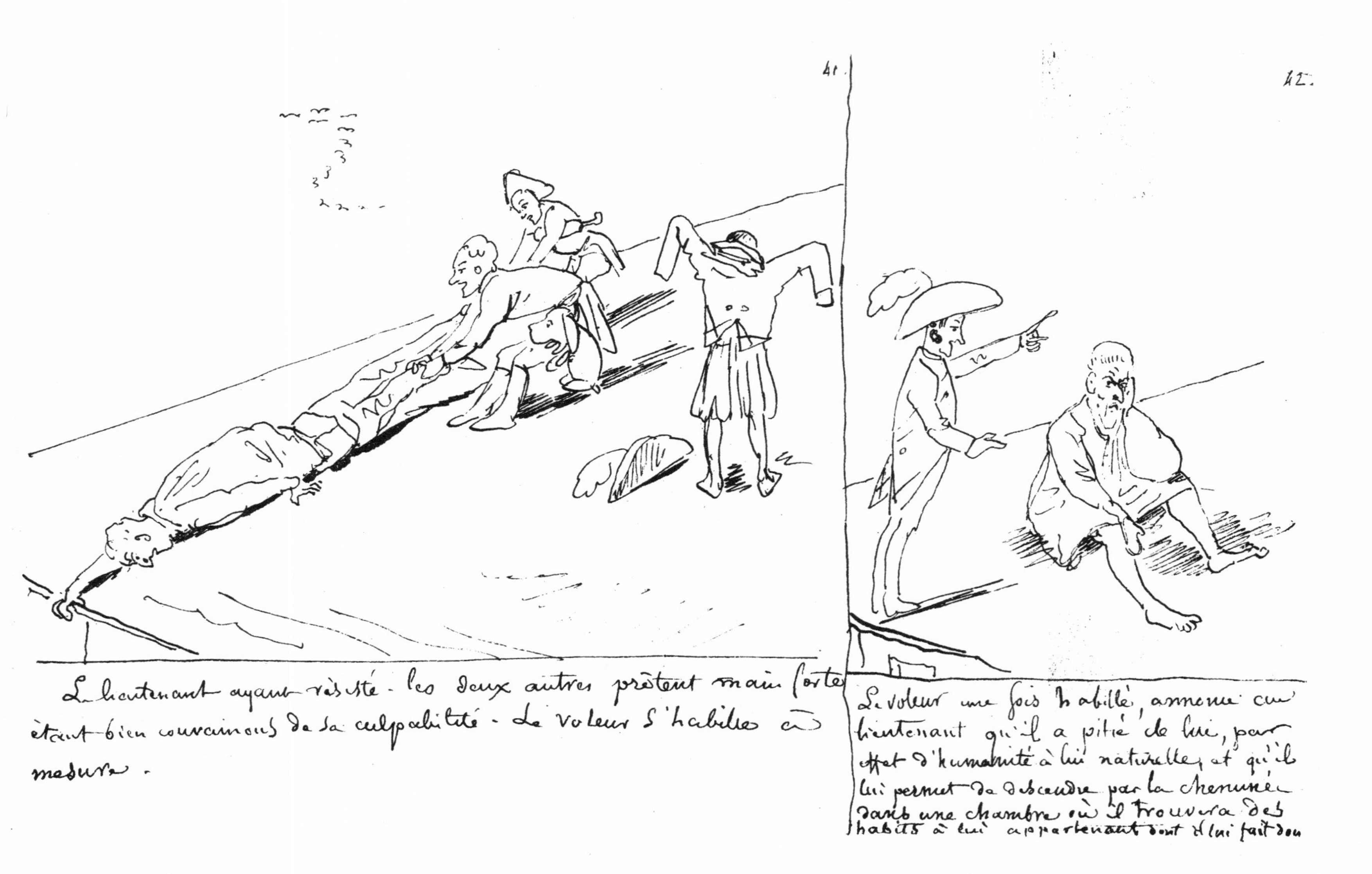
41.
Le lieutenant ayant résisté - les deux autres prêtent main forte
étant bien convaincus de sa culpabilité - Le voleur s'habille en
mesure.
42.
Le voleur une fois habillé, annonce au
lieutenant qu'il a pitié de lui, par
effet d'humanité à lui naturelle, et qu'il
lui permet de descendre par la cheminée
dans une chambre où il trouvera des
habits à lui appartenant dont il lui fait don

The lieutenant resists and the two others lend a hand, being convinced of his guilt. The thief dresses accordingly.

The thief, once dressed, tells the lieutenant that he is sorry for him, by reason of a humanity natural to him, and that he will allow him to descend by the chimney into a room where he will find clothes belonging to himself, which he can take as a gift.

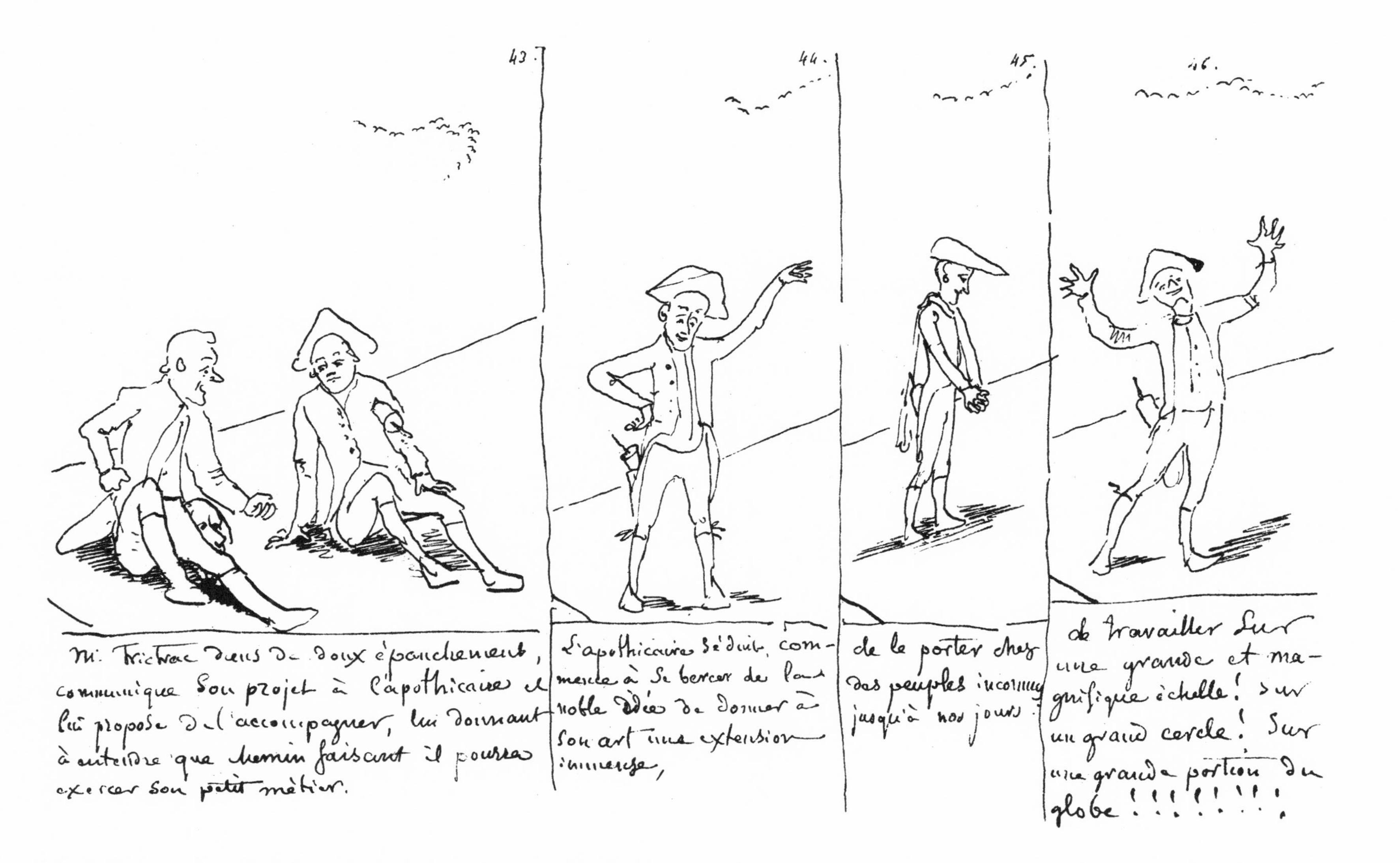

43.
Mr. Trictrac dans de doux épanchements, communique son projet à l'apothicaire et lui propose de l'accompagner, lui donnant à entendre que chemin faisant il pourra exercer son petit métier.
44.
L'apothicaire séduit, commence à se bercer de la noble idée de donner à son art une extension immense,
45.
de le porter chez des peuples inconnus jusqu'à nos jours.
46.
de travailler sur une grande et magnifique échelle! sur un grand cercle! Sur une grande portion du globe!!!!!!!!

Mr. Trictrac calmly venting his heart tells the apothecary of his plan and proposes that he accompany him, giving him to understand that along the way he would be able to exercise his modest trade.

The apothecary is won over, and begins to cherish the noble idea of massively extending his art,

of bringing it to hitherto unknown peoples,

of working on a grand and magnificent scale! With a huge range! Over a large part of the globe! ! ! ! ! ! !

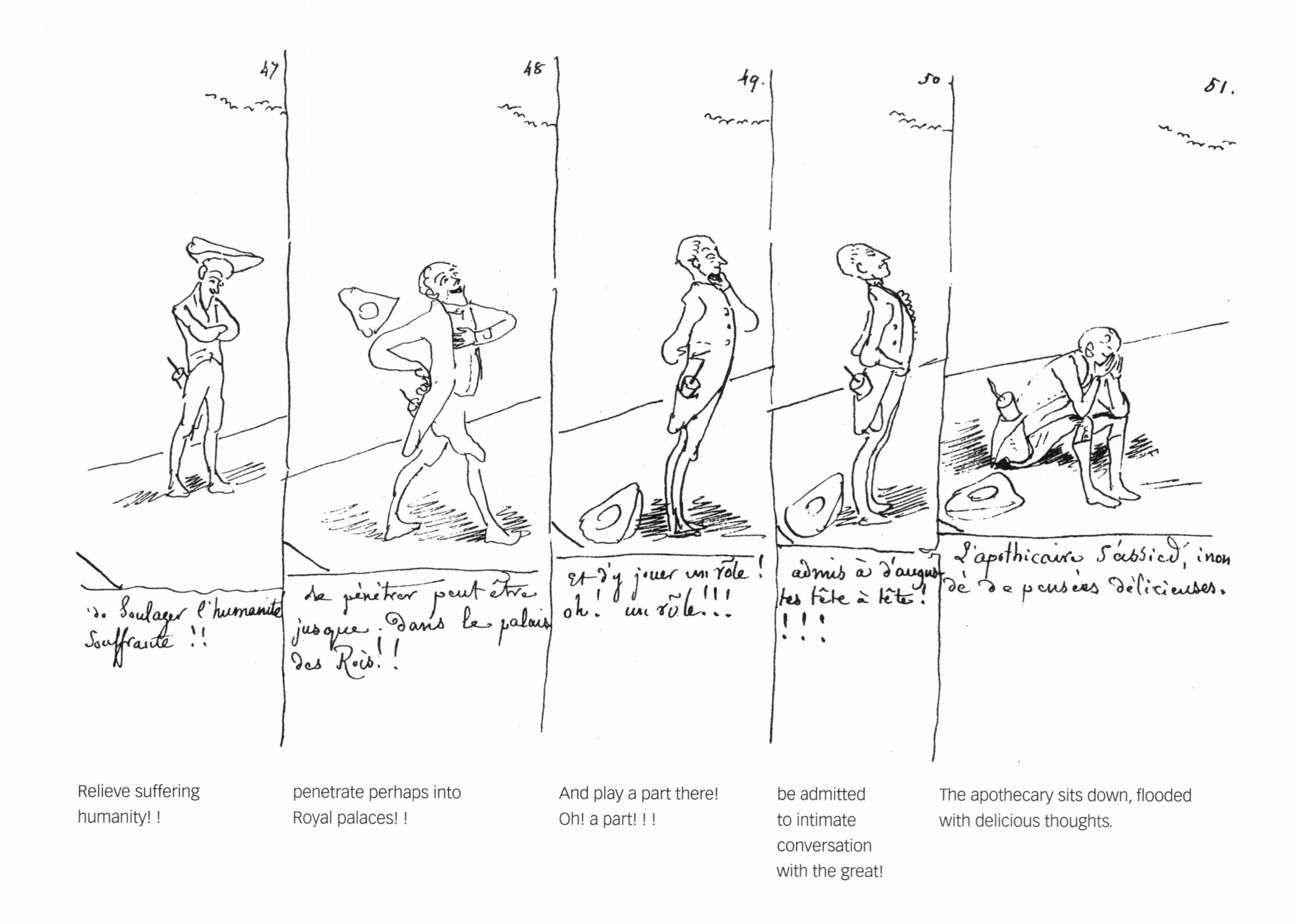
47
.. Soulager l'humanité Souffrante !!
48
de pénétrer peut être jusque dans le palais des Rois!!
49.
et d'y jouer un rôle! oh! un rôle!!!
50
admis à d'augustes tête à tête! !!!
51.
L'apothicaire s'assied, inondé de pensées délicieuses.

Relieve suffering humanity! !

penetrate perhaps into Royal palaces! !

And play a part there! Oh! a part! ! !

be admitted to intimate conversation with the great!

The apothecary sits down, flooded with delicious thoughts.

52.
Cependant le lieutenant qui a pris froid, trouvant un bon lit encore chaud, y entre.
53.
Le père trouve son fils horriblement défiguré par les boissons
chaudes. il fait aussitôt
chercher le médecin.
54.
Le médecin venu
examine l'état du
malade.

Meanwhile the Lieutenant who has taken cold, finding a good bed, still warm, gets into it.

The father finds his son horribly disfigured by the hot drinks. He sends immediately for the doctor.

The doctor arrives and examines the patient's condition.

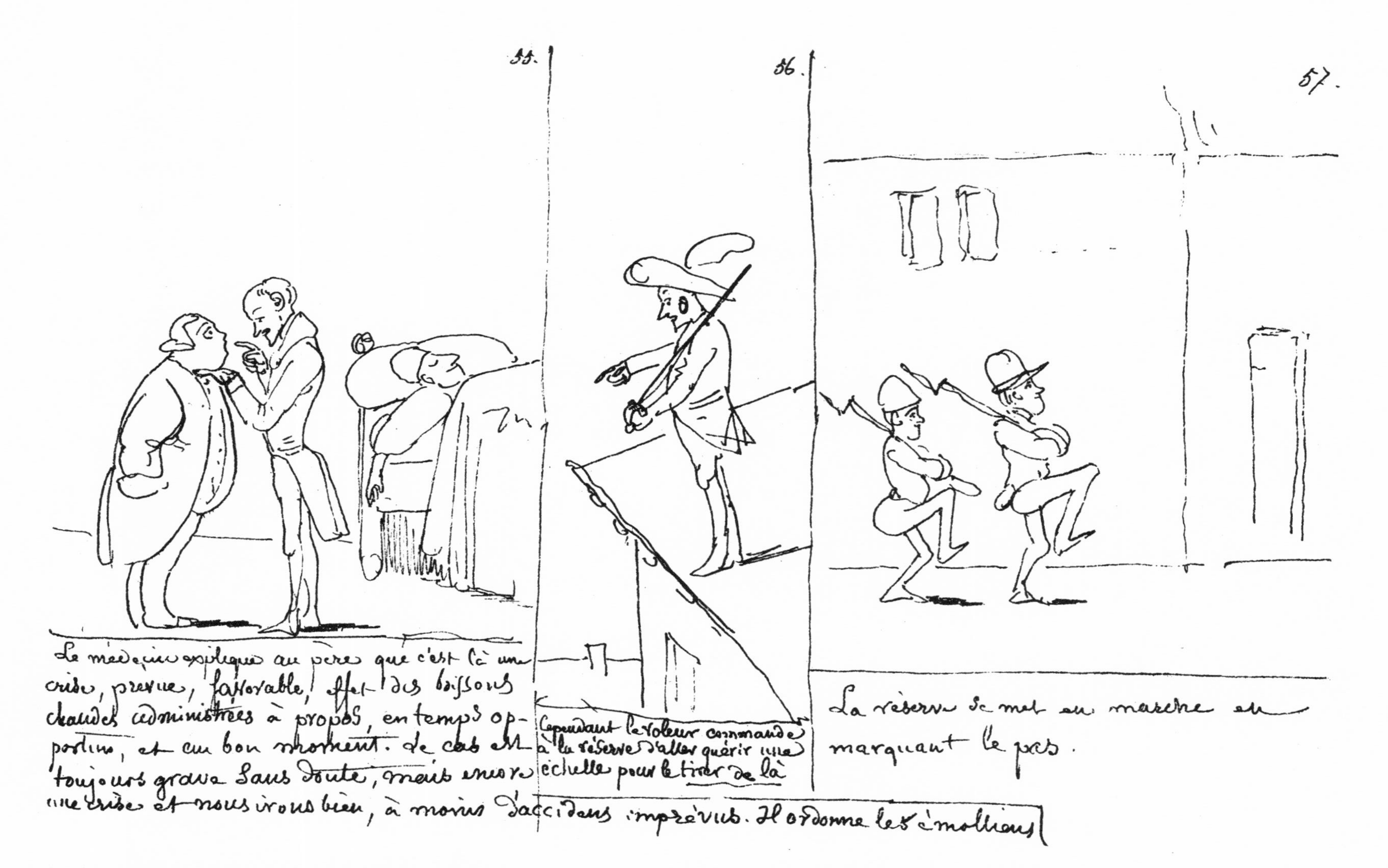
55.
Le médecin explique au père que c'est là une crise, prévue, favorable, effet des boissons chaudes administrées à propos, en temps opportun, et au bon moment. Le cas est toujours grave sans doute, mais encore une crise et nous irons bien, à moins d'accidens imprévus. Il ordonne les émolliens
56.
Cependant le voleur commande à la réserve d'aller quérir une échelle pour le tirer de là
57.
La réserve se met en marche en marquant le pas.

The doctor explains to the father that this is a crisis he had foreseen, and favorable, the effect of the hot drinks correctly administered, in good time, and at the right moment. The case is still serious without a doubt, but another such crisis and all will be well, barring unforeseen accidents. He prescribes emollients.

Meanwhile the thief orders the reserve to go look for a ladder to get him off the roof.

The reserve sets off, marching in step.

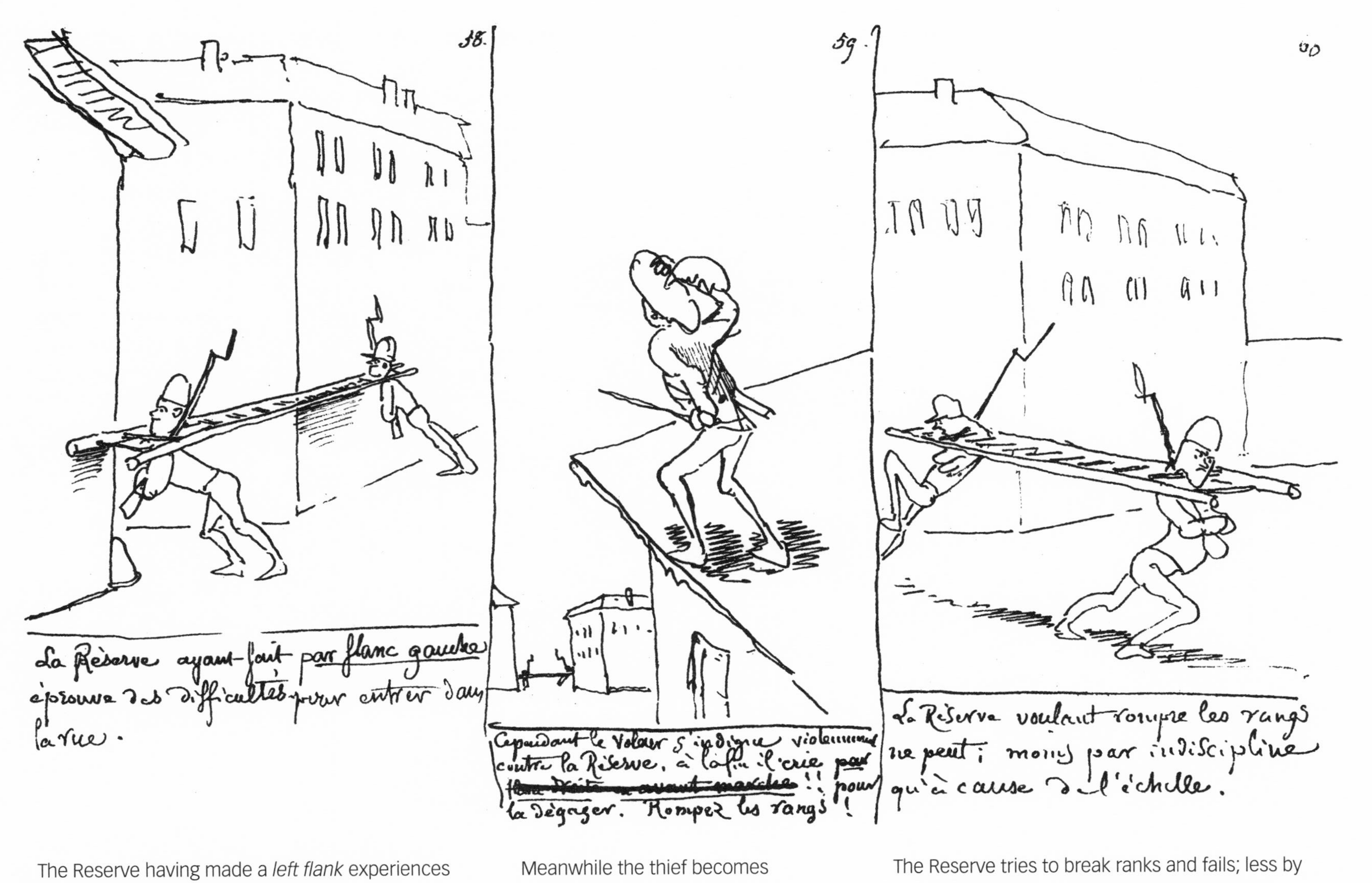
58.
La Réserve ayant fait par flanc gauche
éprouve des difficultés pour entrer dans
la rue.
59.
Cependant le Voleur s'indigne violemment
contre la Réserve, à la fin il crie par
!! pour
la dégager. Rompez les rangs !
60
La Réserve voulant rompre les rangs
ne peut ; moins par indiscipline
qu'à cause de l'échelle.

The Reserve having made a *left flank* experiences some difficulty in entering the street.

Meanwhile the thief becomes violently angry at the Reserve, finally shouting in order to extricate them: Break ranks!

The Reserve tries to break ranks and fails; less by lack of discipline, than because of the ladder.

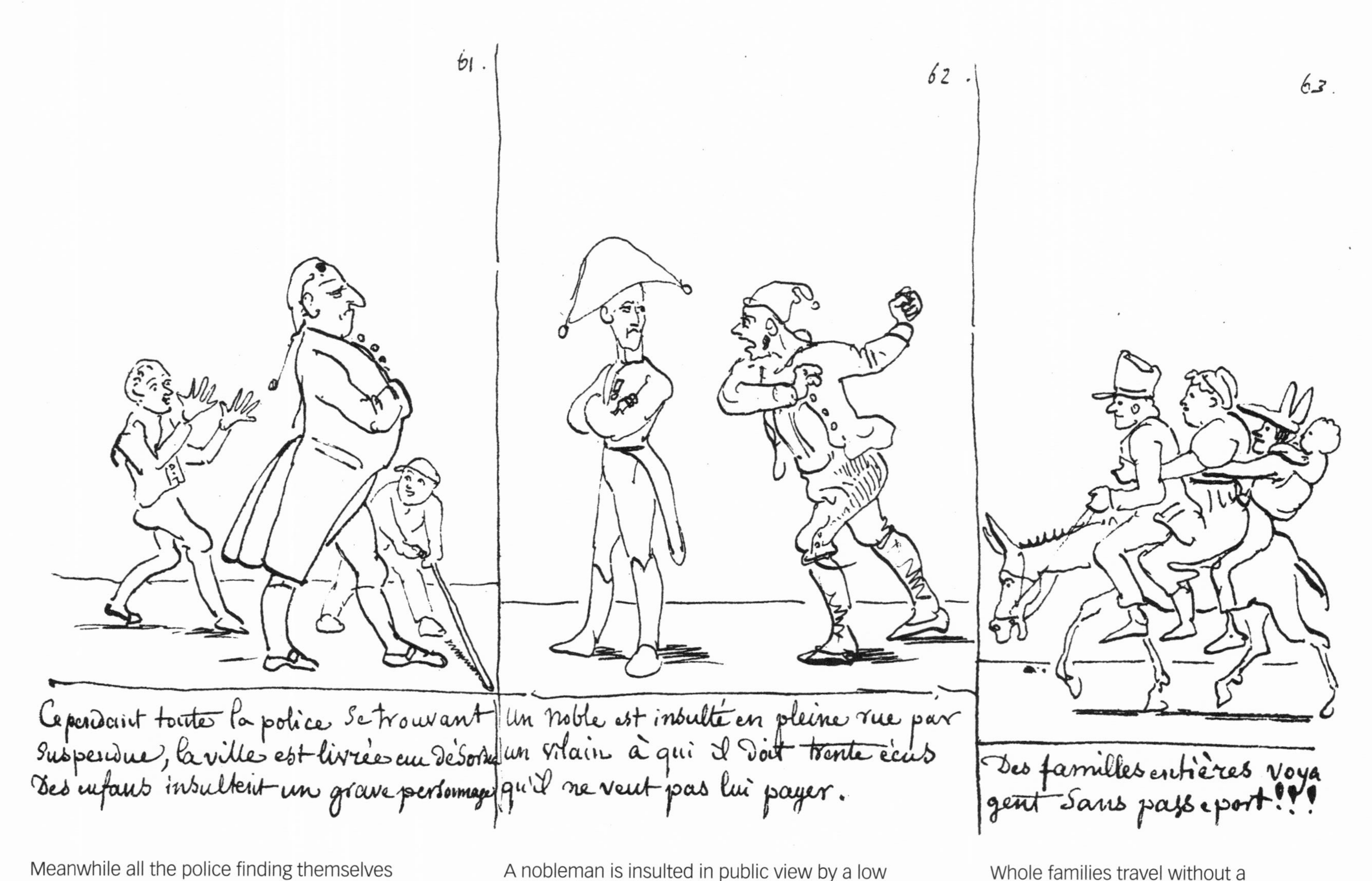
61.
Cependant toute la police se trouvant suspendue, la ville est livrée au désordre
Des enfans insultent un grave personnage
62.
Un noble est insulté en pleine rue par un vilain à qui il doit trente écus qu'il ne veut pas lui payer.
63.
Des familles entières voyagent sans passeport!!!

Meanwhile all the police finding themselves suspended, the town is given over to disorder. Children insult a distinguished personage.

A nobleman is insulted in public view by a low fellow to whom he owes thirty écus which he won't pay.

Whole families travel without a passport! ! !

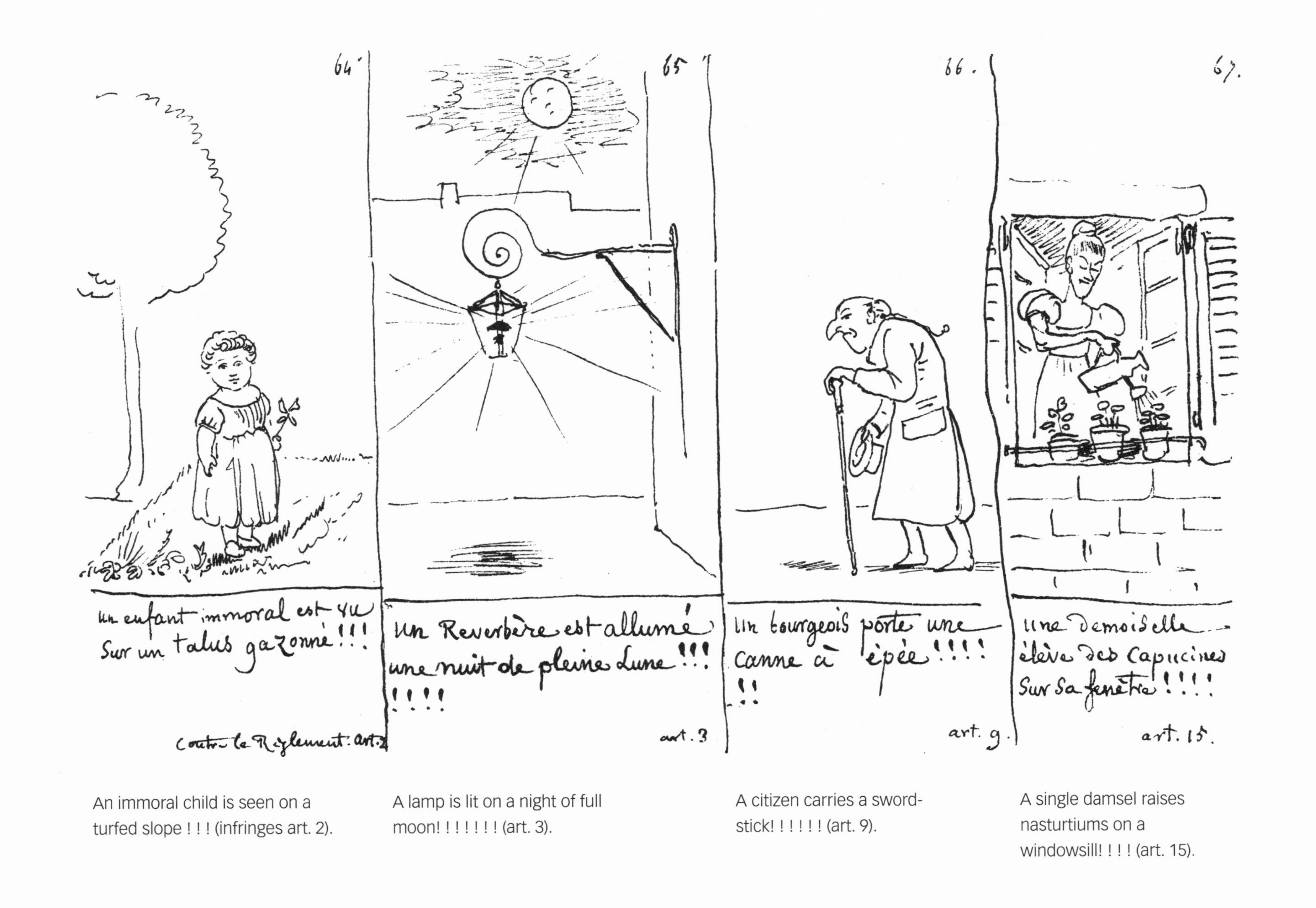
64.
un enfant immoral est vu
Sur un talus gazonné !!!
Contre le Reglement: art. 2
65
Un Reverbère est allumé
une nuit de pleine Lune !!!
!!!!
art. 3
66.
Un bourgeois porte une
canne à épée !!!!
!!
art. 9.
67.
une demoiselle
élève des Capucines
Sur sa fenêtre !!!!
art. 15.

An immoral child is seen on a turfed slope ! ! ! (infringes art. 2).

A lamp is lit on a night of full moon! ! ! ! ! ! ! (art. 3).

A citizen carries a sword-stick! ! ! ! ! ! (art. 9).

A single damsel raises nasturtiums on a windowsill! ! ! ! (art. 15).

68
Une Sérénade a lieu à Minuit et 20 minutes.
!!!!
art. 20.
69.
Un incendie ayant éclaté, le désordre est à son
comble. De simples citoyens, sans insignes, vont
eux mêmes chercher les pompes, établir la chaîne, et
éteignent l'incendie, avant même que le corps
des Sapeurs pompiers soit rassemblé, avant
que leur capitaine soit arrivé de sa campagne
où on l'a été quérir; avant que le sous capitaine qui attend un habit d'uniforme tout neuf,
ait pu le recevoir et venir donner ses ordres. Une
femme sonne le tocsin au lieu d'attendre que le Marguillier
ait achevé de se raser. Les citoyens font la chaîne avec des Seilles au lieu d'aller chercher des seaux à l'autre bout de la ville.

A serenade is played at 20 minutes past midnight! ! ! ! (art. 20).

A fire breaks out, and the chaos reaches a climax. Ordinary, unqualified townspeople go to fetch the pumps themselves, set up a chain, and put out the fire before the fire brigade can muster, before the captain arrives from his country house where he is sent for; before the deputy captain, delayed by waiting for the delivery of a brand new uniform, could meet him and give his orders. A woman sounds the alarm without waiting for the Churchwarden to finish shaving. The townspeople make a chain with wooden pails instead of fetching large buckets from the other end of the town. The disorder is terrible.

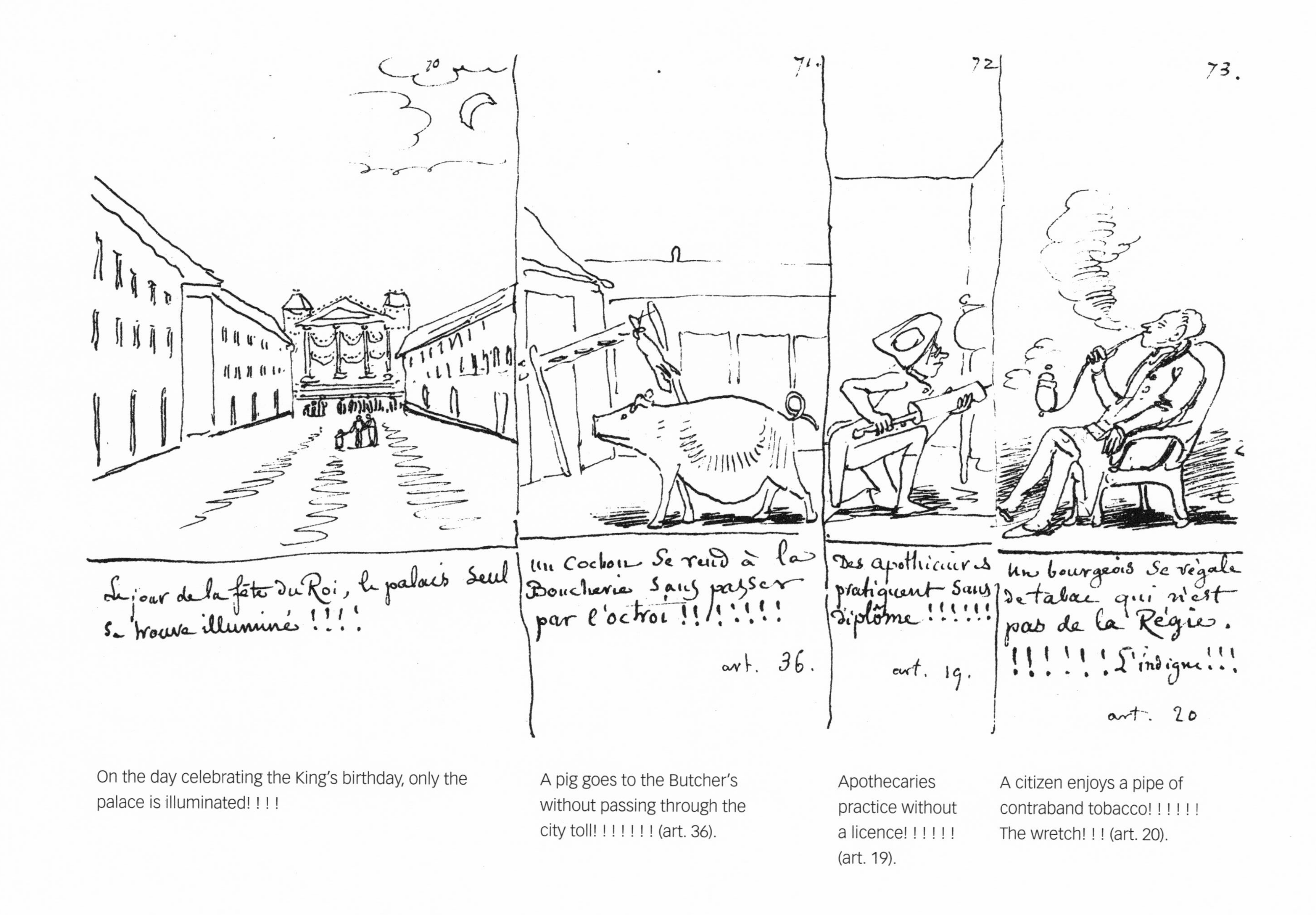
70
Le jour de la fête du Roi, le palais seul se trouva illuminé !!!!
71.
Un Cochon se rend à la Boucherie sans passer par l'octroi !!!!!!!
art. 36.
72
Des apothicaires pratiquent sans diplôme !!!!!!
art. 19.
73.
Un bourgeois se régale de tabac qui n'est pas de la Régie.
!!!!!! L'indigne!!!
art. 20

On the day celebrating the King's birthday, only the palace is illuminated! ! ! !

A pig goes to the Butcher's without passing through the city toll! ! ! ! ! ! ! (art. 36).

Apothecaries practice without a licence! ! ! ! ! ! (art. 19).

A citizen enjoys a pipe of contraband tobacco! ! ! ! ! ! The wretch! ! ! (art. 20).

Tout ce qu'il y a de bons citoyens, s'afflige, et regrette le bon temps.

All the good old boys grieve, and regret the good old times.

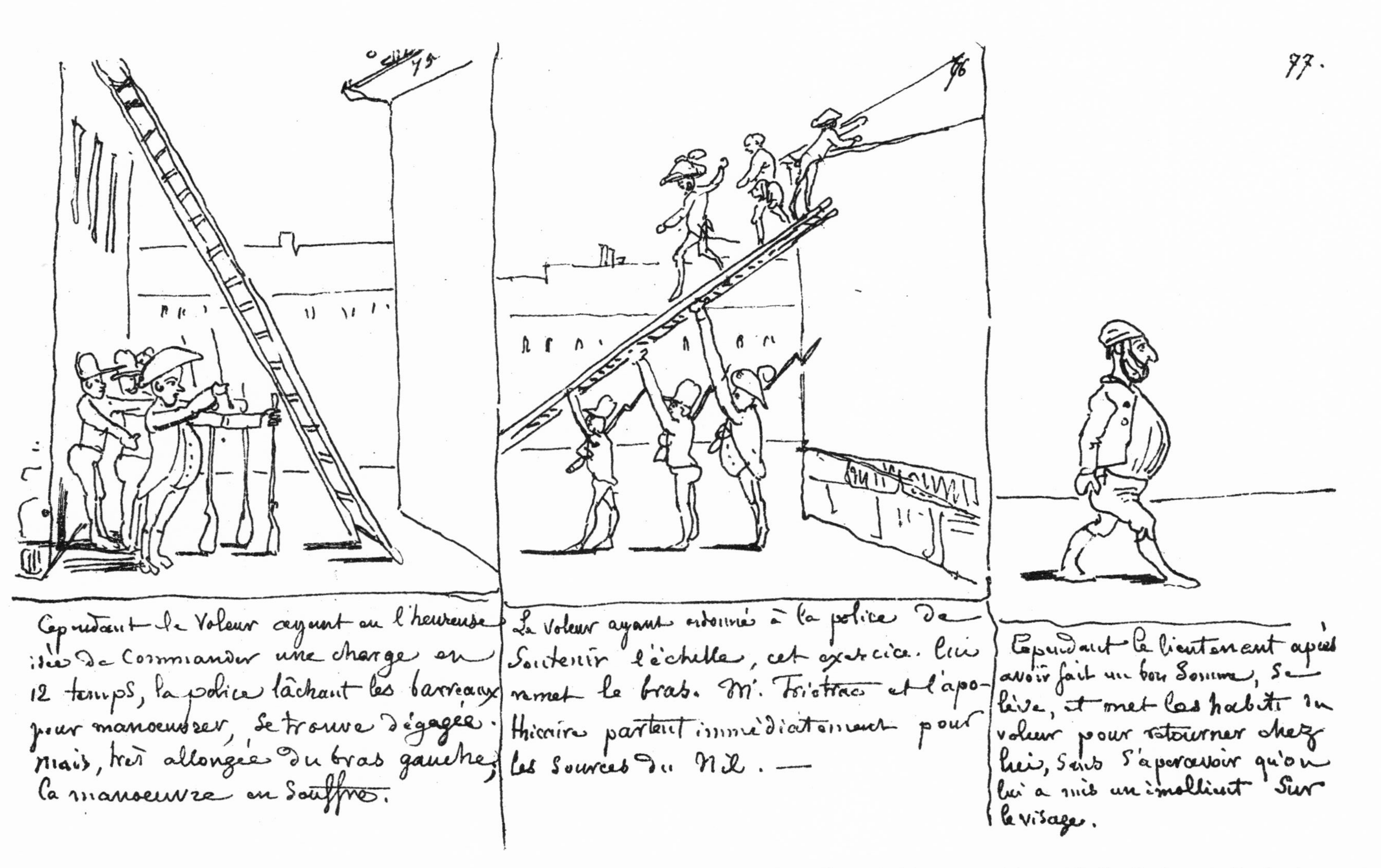
75
76
77.
Cependant le Voleur ayant eu l'heureuse idée de commander une charge en 12 temps, la police lâchant les barreaux pour manoeuvrer, se trouve dégagée. mais, très allongée du bras gauche, la manoeuvre en souffre.
Le voleur ayant ordonné à la police de soutenir l'échelle, cet exercice lui remet le bras. Mr. Trictrac et l'apothicaire partent immédiatement pour les sources du Nil. —
Cependant le lieutenant après avoir fait un bon somme, se lève, et met les habits du voleur pour retourner chez lui, sans s'apercevoir qu'on lui a mis un émollient sur le visage.

Meanwhile the thief having had the happy idea of ordering a charge in double time, the police extricate themselves by letting go the rungs of the ladder in order to execute their maneuver. But, with their left arm much lengthened, the maneuver suffers.

When the thief gives orders to the police to hold up the ladder, they find their arm restored to its proper length. Mr. Trictrac and the apothecary leave immediately for the sources of the Nile.

Meanwhile the lieutenant after having had a good nap, rises and puts on the thief's clothes in order to return home, without noticing that an emollient has been put on his face.

78.
79.
Le lieutenant et le voleur s'étant reconnus, s'arrêtent
mutuellement au même instant, et se livrent mutuellement à la police qui reste immobile,
sollicitée à égale force, d'un côté par la
voix du lieutenant; de l'autre, par son habit
Mais le voleur ayant tiré de sa poche son propre signalement
prouve bien aisément qu'il se rapporte à l'habit du lieutenant.
Sauf l'émollient, qui est une ruse dit-il pour cacher la figure.
Le lieutenant est conduit en prison le 7. courant.

The lieutenant and the thief having recognized each other, mutually arrest each other simultaneously, and mutually deliver each other to the police who stand pat, attracted by equal forces, on one side the lieutenant's voice, on the other, his uniform.

But the thief having pulled from his pocket his own description, easily proves that it relates to a lieutenant in uniform, but for the emollient, which is a trick, he says, to conceal his face. The lieutenant is taken to prison on the 7th of the current month.

80

Cependant le père ne trouvant plus son fils entre dans une angoisse inexprimable. Il fait aussitôt chercher le médecin.

Meanwhile the father no longer finding his son, undergoes inexpressible anguish. He immediately sends for the doctor.

81

Le médecin venu, examine l'état du lit

The doctor comes, and examines the state of the bed.

82

Les Symptômes reconnus, le médecin explique au père que son fils a le délire, que l'on devait s'y attendre, l'émollient ayant agi sur le cerveau au moyen des parotides et de la région palatine; qu'il a donc eu tort de laisser la porte ouverte, très tort; que s'il agit ainsi on ne peut répondre de rien, qu'avant tout, il doit retrouver son fils x

x que s'il continue ainsi, il ne s'en mêlera plus.

Recognizing the symptoms, the Doctor explains to the father that his son has become delirious, which was to be expected, the emollient having acted on the brain via the parotid glands and the palatine region. That he was therefore wrong to leave the door unlocked, very wrong; and if he behaves like this, he cannot take responsibility for anything, and if he goes on like this, he washes his hands of the case, and that above all he must find his son.

88.

Le père après avoir fait des excuses au médecin, dépêche des gens à la recherche de son fils, leur disant qu'ils le reconnoîtront à l'émollient. qu'ils amènent toute personne ayant un émollient ou cataplasme.

The father excuses himself to the doctor, sends off people in search of his son, telling them they will recognize him by his emollient, and that they should bring him any person wearing an emollient or cataplasm.

89.

Cependant la Réserve, en tourbillonnant, cause d'affreux désordres le 16. courant.

The Reserve however, whirling around, causes terrible disruption on the 16th inst.

90.

Voyant cela le voleur ordonne une charge sur la Réserve, à l'arme blanche.

Seeing this the thief orders a charge on the Reserve, with fixed bayonets.

91.

La réserve qui a entendu le commandement fait aussi une charge, à l'arme blanche comme par instinct.

The Reserve who have heard the order also make a charge, with fixed bayonets, as if by instinct.

92.

Toute la police s'embroche, ayant mal visé. D'affreux désordres renaissent. La majeure partie de la population reçoit des contusions et avaries.

The whole police force, aiming badly, get stuck. There are terrible disorders anew. Most of the population suffers bruises and injuries.

94.
BUREAU
distributoire
N°. 3.
Cependant l'autorité vient au secours de la population en établissant des chaudières d'émolliens
économiques, dans chaque quartier. Ils sont déli-
vrés sur une carte attestant la moralité.
M. le Baron C.D.... profite de l'occasion pour établir sur
des bonnes données, une table comparative de la
moralité des différens quartiers, en comptant les
têtes à émolliens depuis sa fenêtre.

The civic authorities meanwhile come to the help of the population by establishing in each district cauldrons for cheap emollients. They are issued on production of a certificate of good conduct.

The Baron C.D . . . . takes the opportunity to establish on reliable data a comparative table of the morality of different districts, counting the heads with emollients from his window.

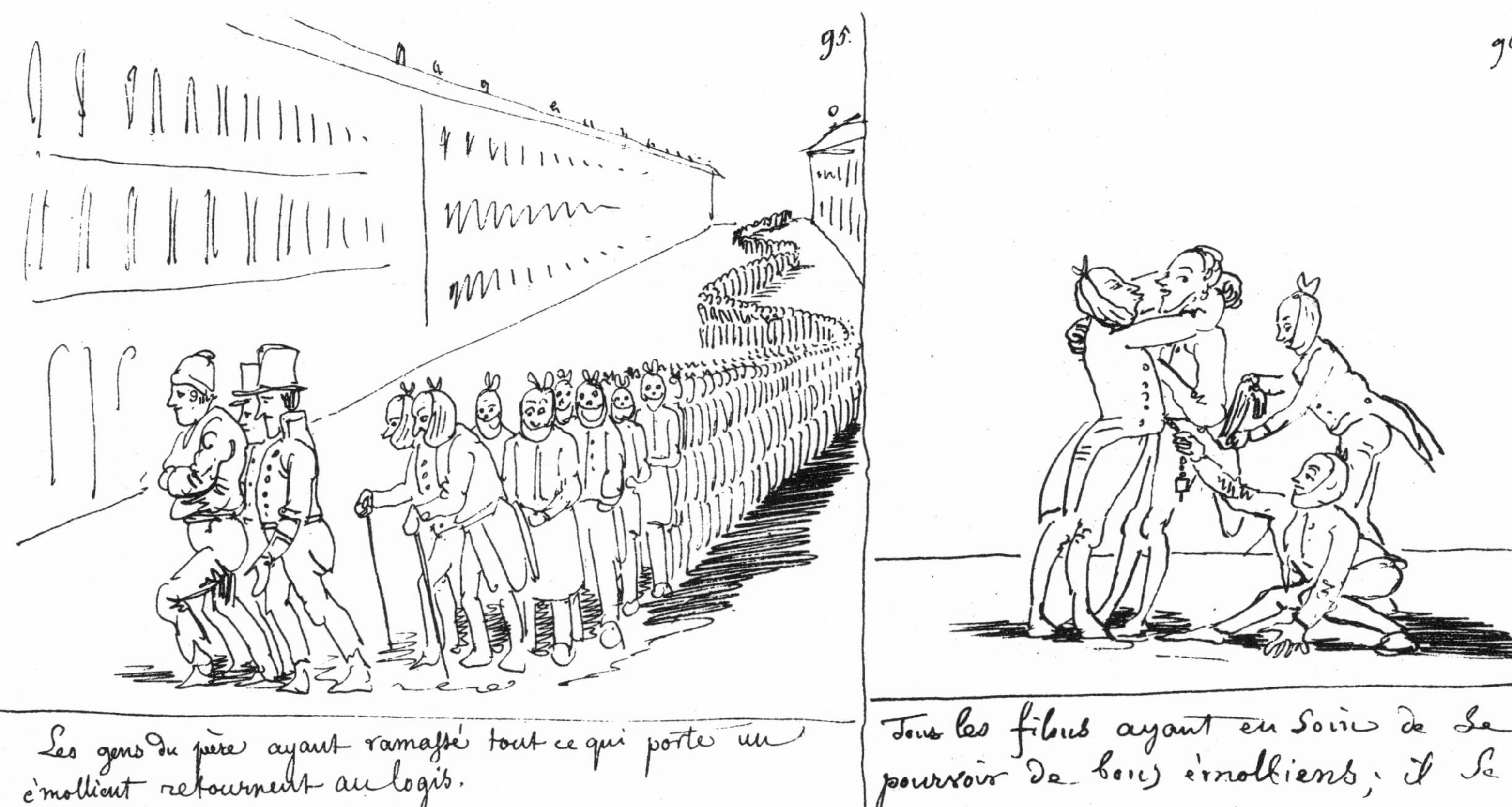
95.
Les gens du père ayant ramassé tout ce qui porte un émollient, retournent au logis.
96.
Tous les filous ayant eu soin de se pourvoir de bons émolliens; il se passe de grands désordres; mais le chiffre des gens de bien en est accru.

The father's agents after gathering together all those wearing an emollient, return to his house.

All the pickpockets having taken the precaution of procuring good emollients, great disorder results; but the number of respectable people is augmented thereby.

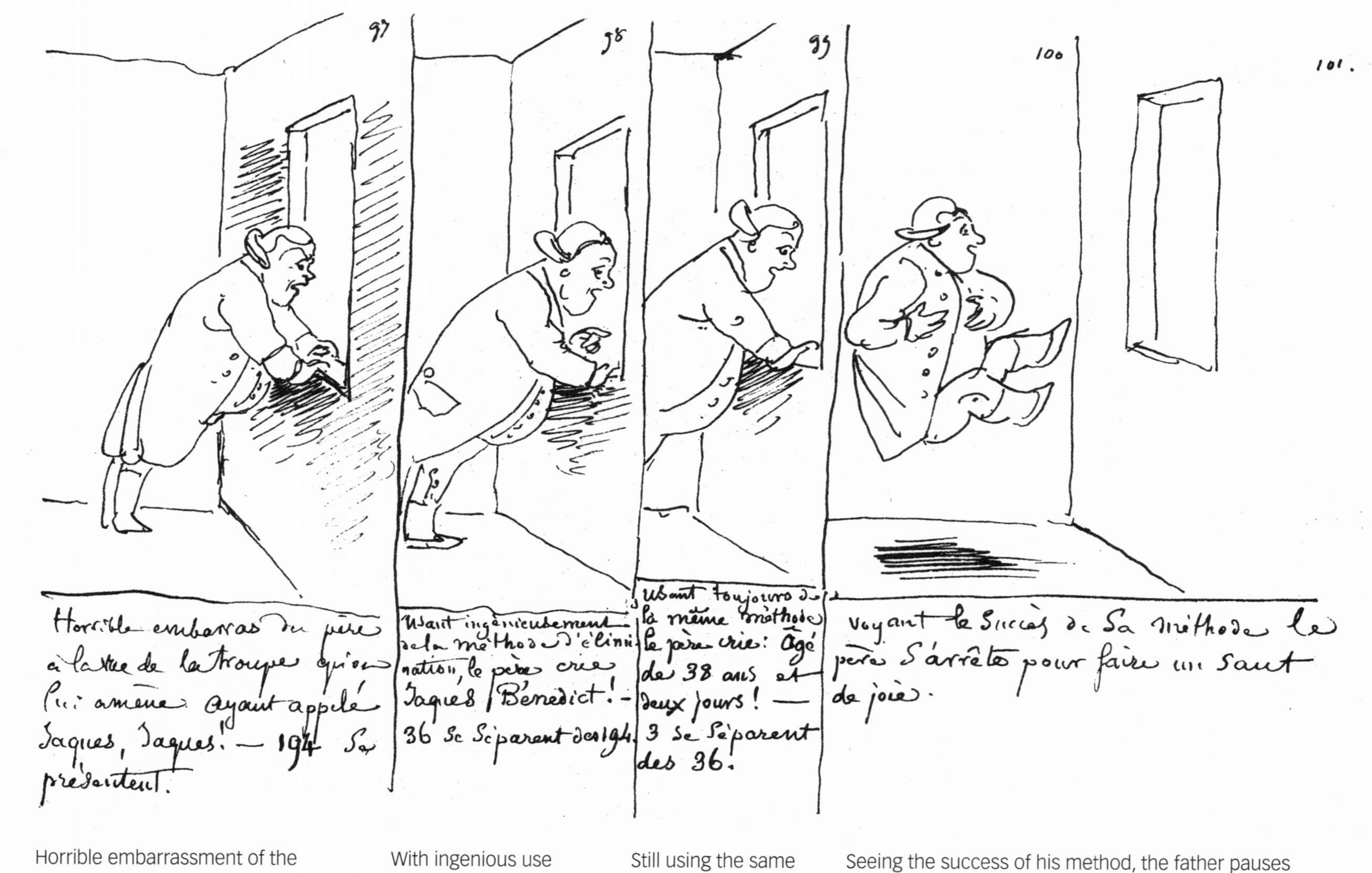
97
98
99
100
101.
Horrible embarras du père à la vue de la troupe qu'on lui amène. Ayant appelé Jaques, Jaques! — 194 se présentent.
Usant ingénieusement de la méthode d'élimination, le père crie Jaques Bénédict! — 36 se séparent des 194.
Usant toujours de la même méthode le père crie: Agé de 38 ans et deux jours! — 3 se séparent des 36.
Voyant le succès de sa méthode le père s'arrête pour faire un saut de joie.

Horrible embarrassment of the father at the sight of the crowd being brought to him. After he calls out Jaques, Jaques!—194 present themselves.

With ingenious use of the process of elimination, the father cries Jaques Bénedict!—36 detach themselves from the 194.

Still using the same process, the father cries: Aged 38 years and two days!—3 detach themselves from the 36.

Seeing the success of his method, the father pauses to jump for joy.

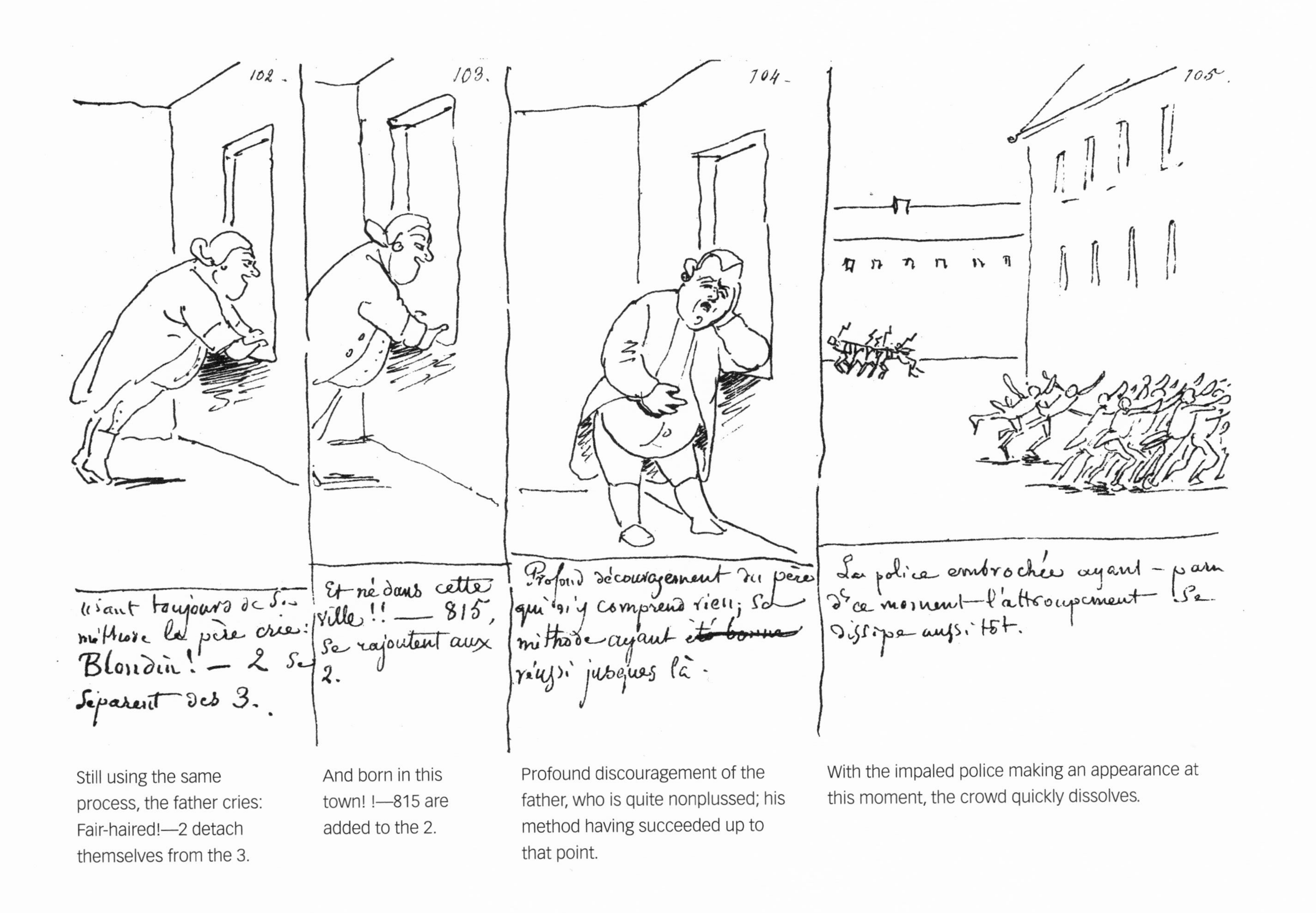
102.
Usant toujours de sa méthode le père crie: Blondin! — 2 se séparent des 3.
103.
Et né dans cette ville!! — 815, se rajoutent aux 2.
104.
Profond découragement du père qui n'y comprend rien; sa méthode ayant ~~été bonne~~ réussi jusques là.
105.
La police embrochée ayant paru dès ce moment l'attroupement se dissipe aussitôt.

Still using the same process, the father cries: Fair-haired!—2 detach themselves from the 3.

And born in this town! !—815 are added to the 2.

Profound discouragement of the father, who is quite nonplussed; his method having succeeded up to that point.

With the impaled police making an appearance at this moment, the crowd quickly dissolves.

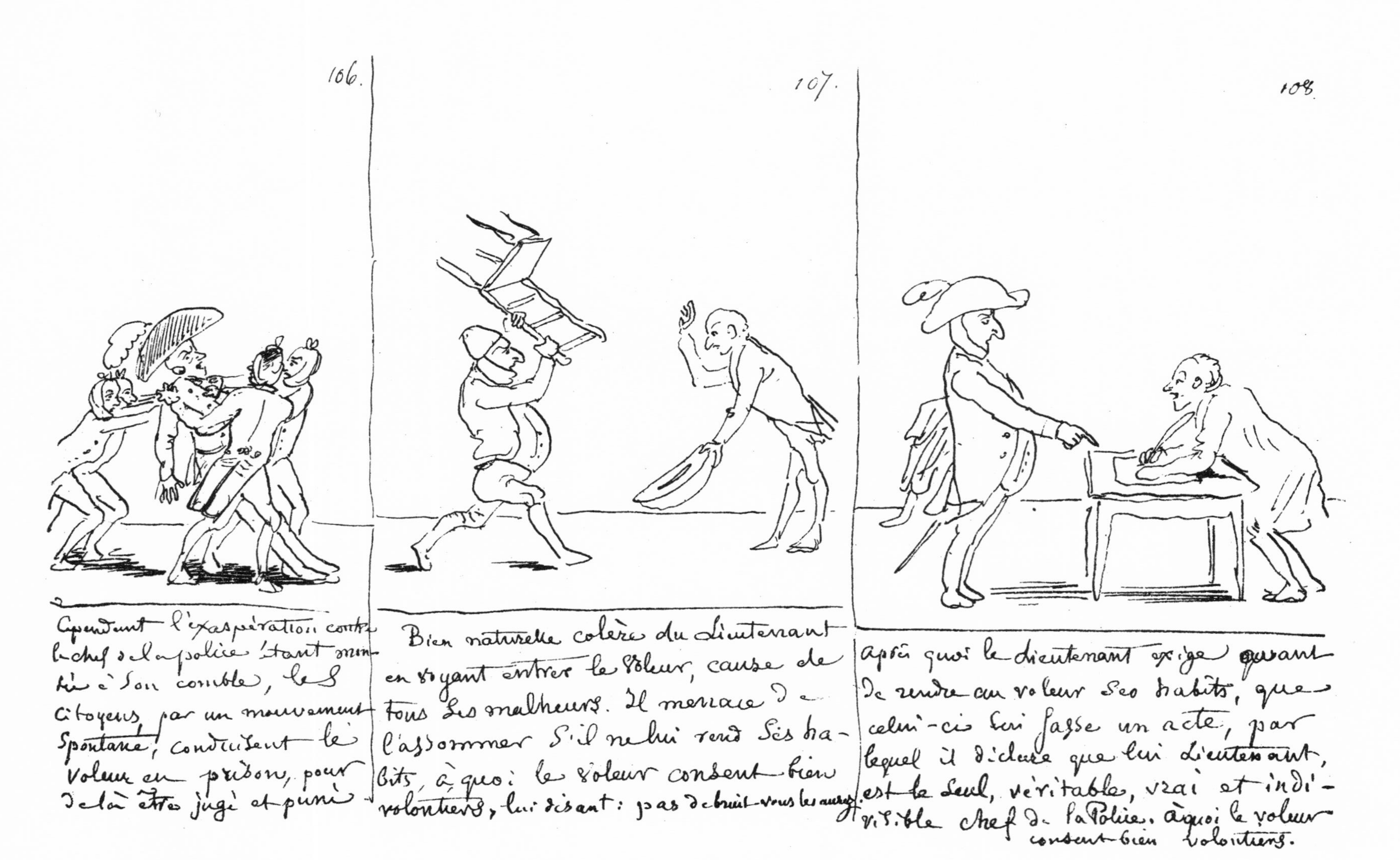
106.
Cependant l'exaspération contre
le chef de la police étant mon-
tée à son comble, les
citoyens, par un mouvement
spontané, conduisent le
voleur en prison, pour
de là être jugé et puni.
107.
Bien naturelle colère du Lieutenant
en voyant entrer le voleur, cause de
tous ses malheurs. Il menace de
l'assommer s'il ne lui rend ses habits, à quoi le voleur consent bien
volontiers, lui disant: pas de bruit vous les aurez.
108.
Après quoi le Lieutenant exige avant
de rendre au voleur ses habits, que
celui-ci lui fasse un acte, par
lequel il déclare que lui Lieutenant,
est le seul, véritable, vrai et indivisible chef de la Police. À quoi le voleur
consent bien volontiers.

Meanwhile the exasperation against the chief of police reaching its climax, the citizens spontaneously take the thief off to prison, to be tried and punished.

Very natural anger of the Lieutenant at the entrance of the Thief, the cause of all his misfortunes. He threatens to knock him down if he doesn't give him back his clothes. To which the thief willingly agrees, telling him: not so loud, you'll get them.

After which the lieutenant demands that, before returning his clothes to the thief, the latter shall sign a document by which he declares that he, the lieutenant, is the only, authentic, true and indivisible chief of police. To which the thief very willingly agrees.

109
110.
Cependant le Concierge étant venu chercher le Chef de la Police, et faisant qques difficultés sur sa figure, le lieutenant lui dit : Bête ; regardez. en montrant son acte et ses habits.
En conséquence, le Lieutenant est conduit devant la Cour Suprême, où lui sont lus ses crimes, consistant à avoir corrompu la police, lui ôtant sa discipline et la poussant à attenter aux jours des citoyens. Profonde surprise du Lieutenant. Les bras lui en tombent et son chapeau aussi.

Meanwhile the warder having come to fetch the Chief of Police, and made some difficulties about his face, the lieutenant tells him: Fool; take a look, and shows him his document and his uniform.

As a result, the lieutenant is taken before the Supreme Court, where his crimes are read out to him, consisting in having corrupted the police, let them run riot, and having them threaten the lives of the citizens. Profound surprise of the Lieutenant. He is floored, and his hat too.

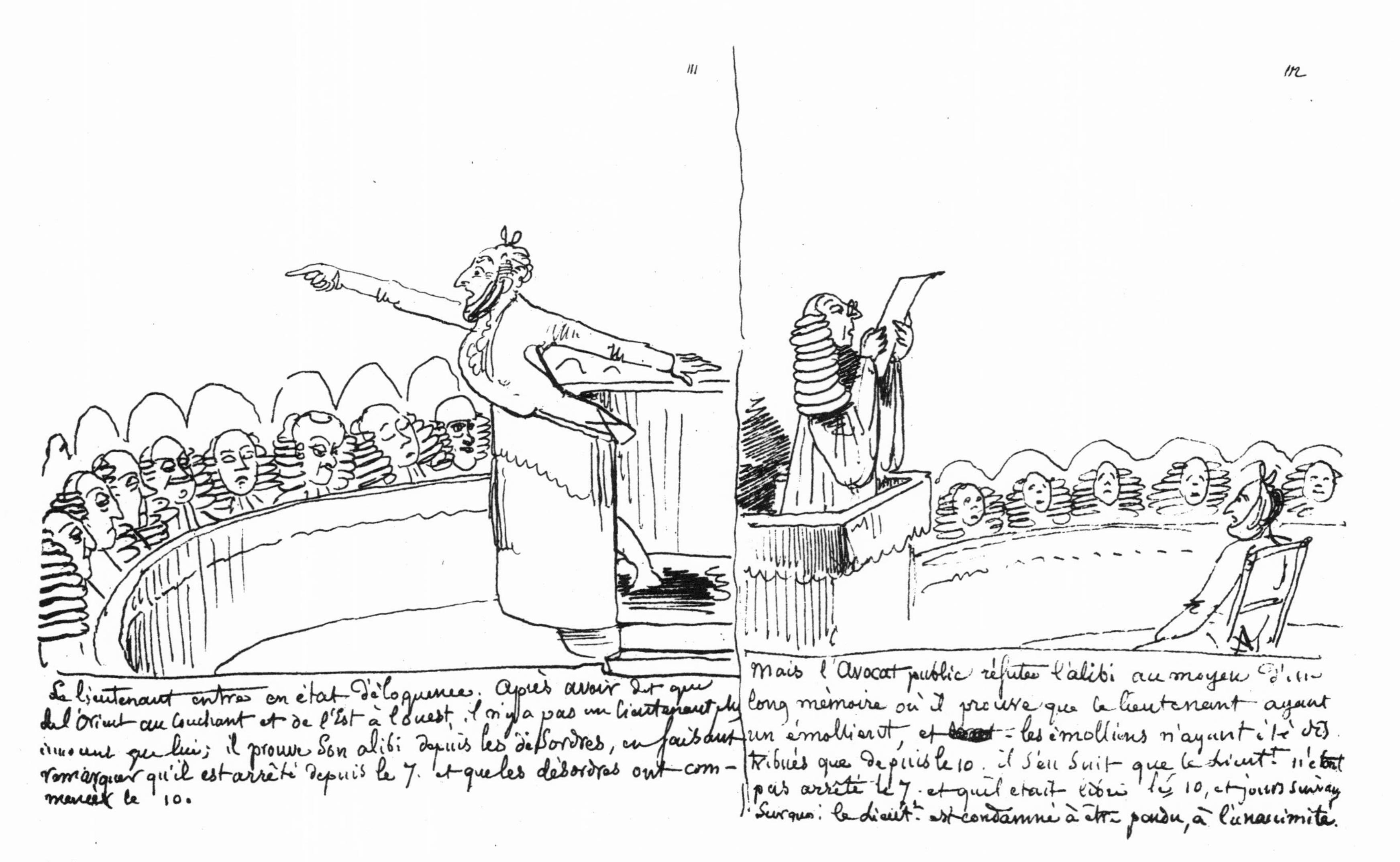
111
112
Le lieutenant entre en état d'éloquence. Après avoir dit que de l'Orient au Couchant et de l'Est à l'Ouest, il n'y a pas un lieutenant plus innocent que lui; il prouve son alibi depuis les désordres, en faisant remarquer qu'il est arrêté depuis le 7. et que les désordres ont commencé le 10.
Mais l'Avocat public réfute l'alibi au moyen d'un long mémoire où il prouve que le lieutenant ayant un émollient, et les émollients n'ayant été distribués que depuis le 10. il s'en suit que le lieut. n'était pas arrêté le 7. et qu'il était libre le 10, et jours suivants. Sur quoi: le lieut. est condamné à être pendu, à l'unanimité.

The lieutenant takes an eloquent turn. Having said that from Orient to Occident and from East to West, there is no lieutenant more innocent than he, he proves his alibi since the disorders by noting that he was arrested on the 7th and the disorders did not begin until the 10th.

But the Public Prosecutor refutes the alibi by means of a long report where he proves that the lieutenant having an emollient, and emollients having been distributed only since the 10th, it follows that the lieutenant cannot have been arrested on the 7th, and that he was free on the 10th and following days. Upon which the lieutenant is condemned to be hanged, unanimously.

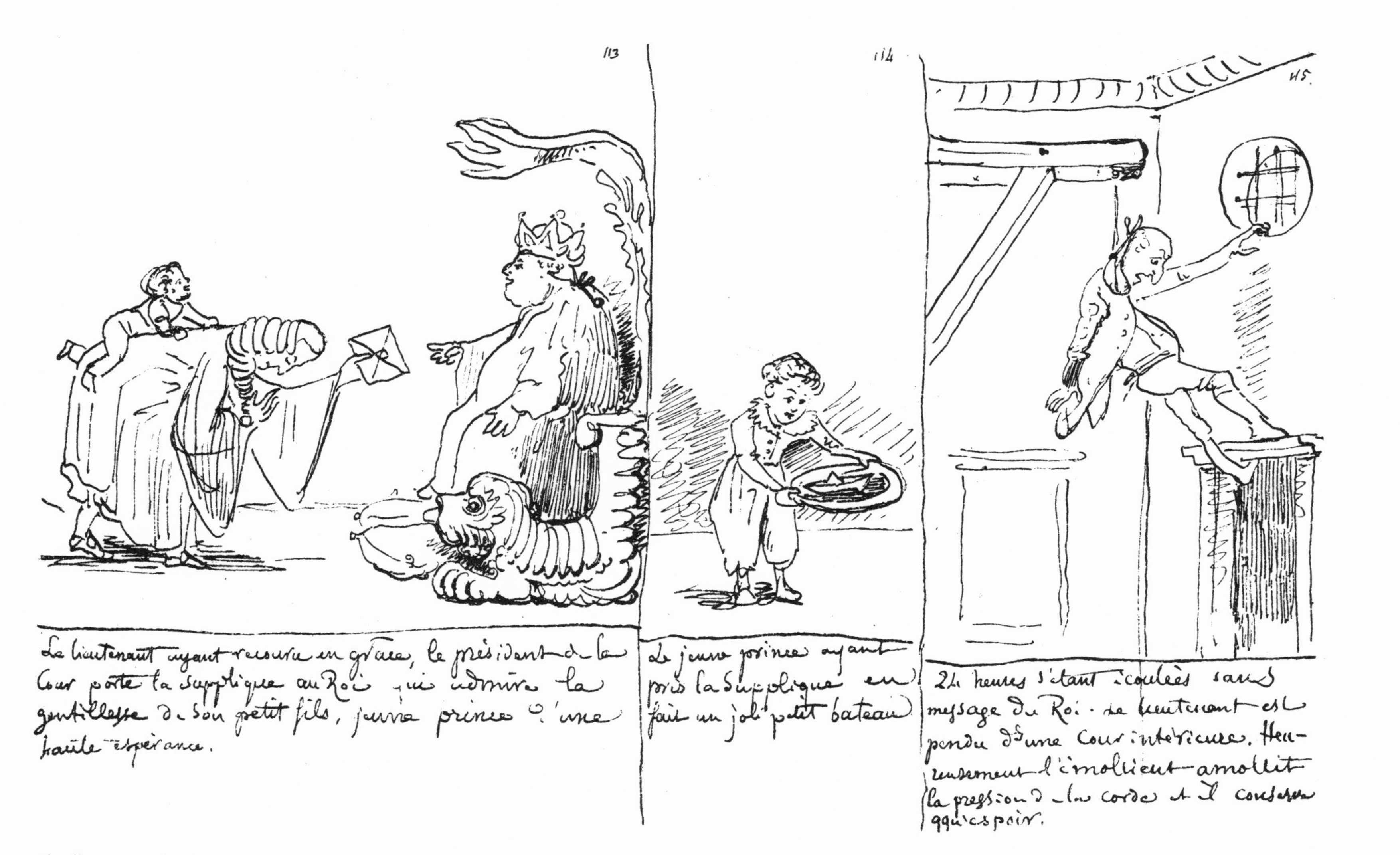
113
Le lieutenant ayant recours en grâce, le président de la Cour porte la supplique au Roi qui admire la gentillesse de son petit fils, jeune prince d'une haute espérance.
114
Le jeune prince ayant pris la supplique en fait un joli petit bateau
115
24 heures s'étant écoulées sans message du Roi, le lieutenant est pendu dans une Cour intérieure. Heureusement l'émollient amollit la pression de la corde et il conserve quelqu'espoir.

The lieutenant having recourse to a petition of mercy, the president of the Court carries the petition to the King who is admiring the cuteness of his little son, a young prince of great promise.

The young prince having taken the petition makes a pretty little boat out of it.

24 hours have gone by with no message from the King. The lieutenant is hanged in an interior courtyard. Fortunately the emollient lessens the pressure of the rope and he does not lose all hope.

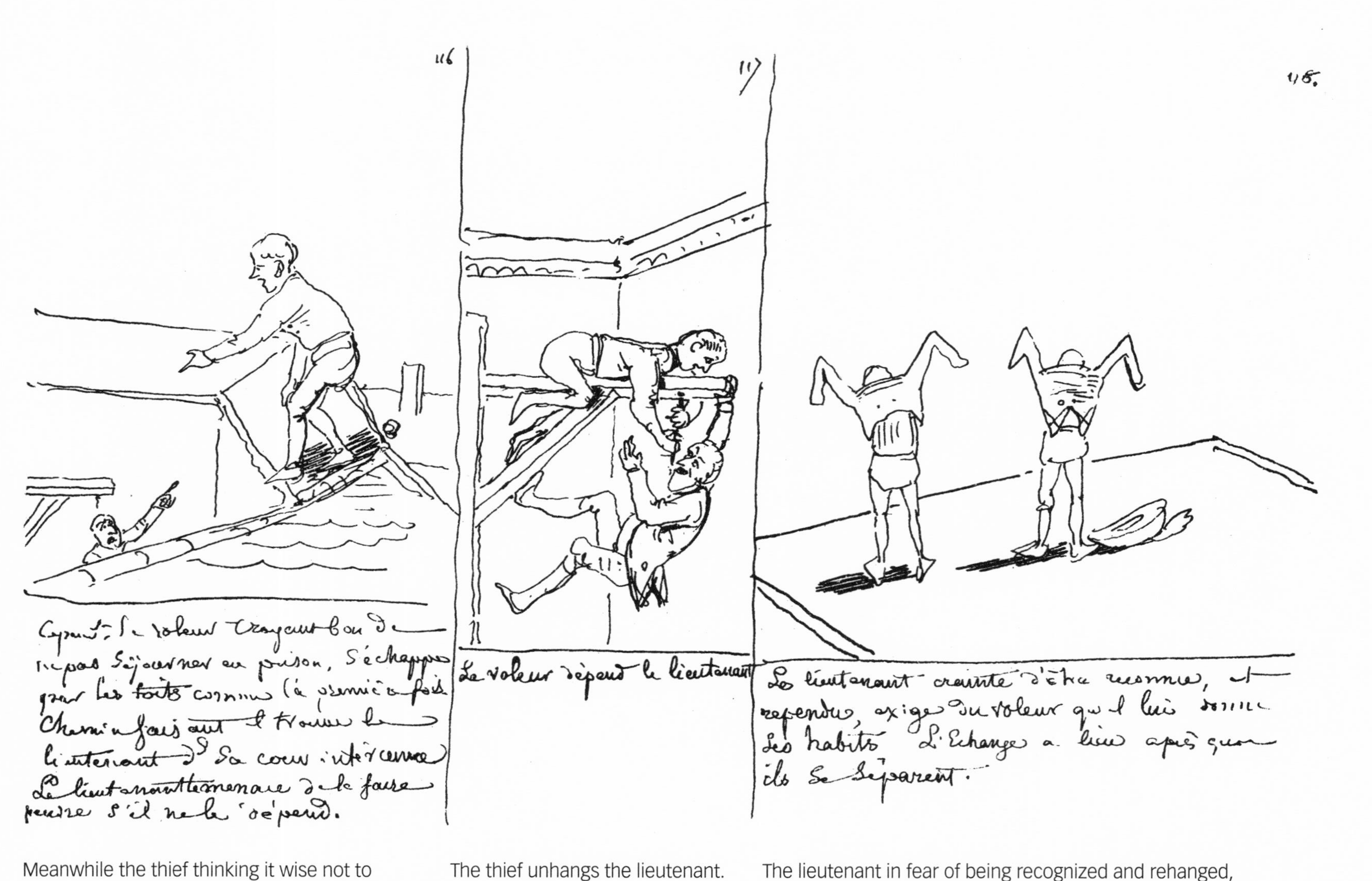
116
117
Le voleur dépend le lieutenant
118.

Meanwhile the thief thinking it wise not to stay in prison, escapes by the roofs like the first time. On the way he finds the lieutenant in his interior courtyard. The lieutenant threatens to have him hanged if he doesn't unhang him.

The thief unhangs the lieutenant.

The lieutenant in fear of being recognized and rehanged, demands that the thief give him his clothes. The Exchange takes place after which they go their own ways.

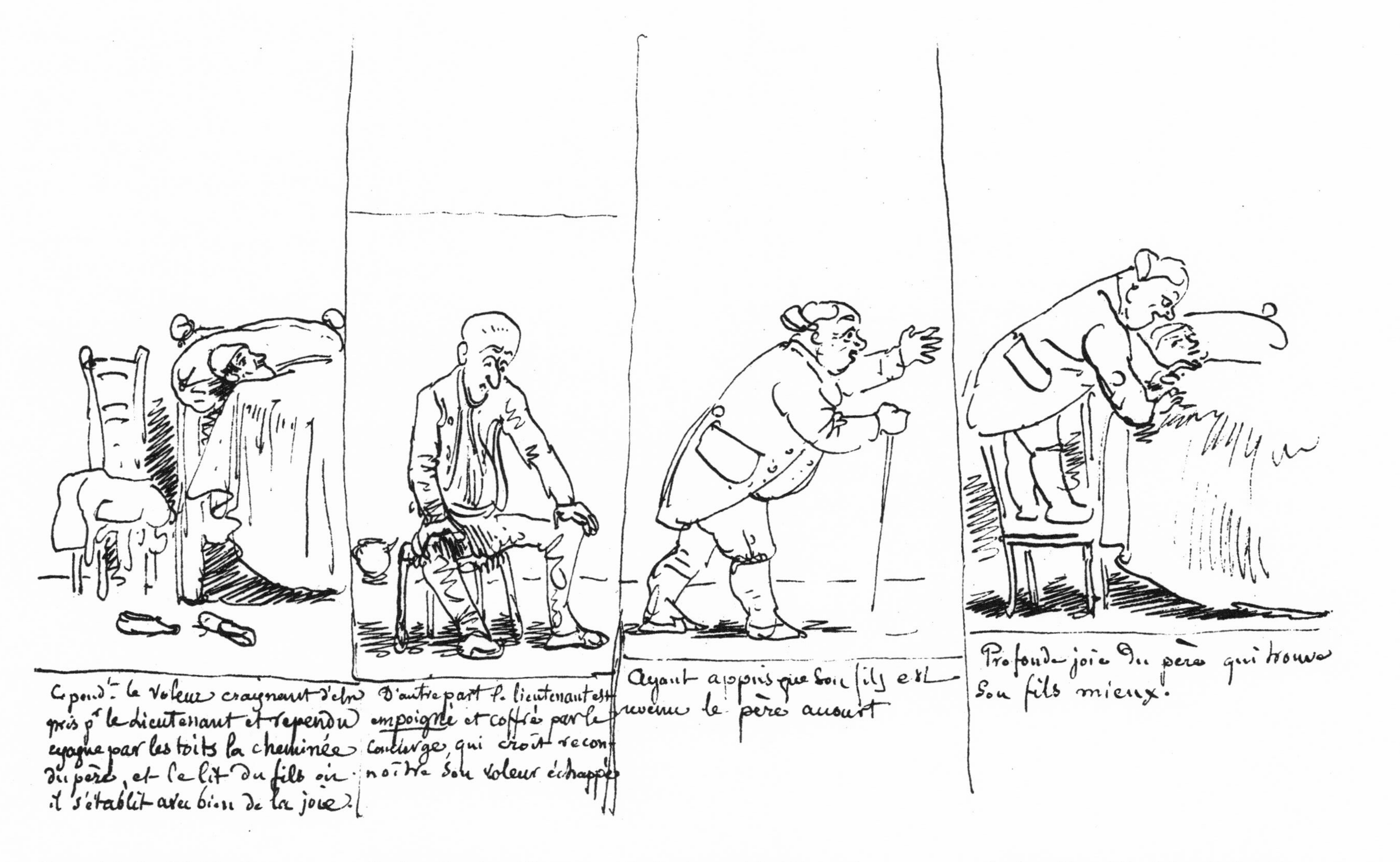
Cependt. le voleur craignant d'être pris pr le lieutenant et rependu gagne par les toits la cheminée du père, et le lit du fils où il s'établit avec bien de la joie.
D'autre part le lieutenant est empoigné et coffré par le concierge, qui croit reconnaître son voleur échappé
Ayant appris que son fils est revenu le père accourt
Profonde joie du père qui trouve son fils mieux!

Meanwhile the thief fearing to be taken for the lieutenant and rehanged, reaches via the rooftops the elder Trictrac's chimney, and the son's bed which he is very glad to occupy.

On the other hand the lieutenant is *seized* and jailed by the warder, who thinks he recognizes his escaped thief.

Having learned that his son has returned, the father runs up.

Profound joy of the father finding his son better.

The doctor comes and learning that the son is better, explains to the father that it is the expected effect of his last prescription, the emollient having as a result of the delirium necessarily evaporated the rachitic fluids accumulated under the scalp. He prescribes broths, poultry, and Spanish wine to fortify the stomach, horseback riding to refresh the internal organs and in general very careful treatment of all kinds.

The father delights in the revived appetite of his son, for whom he has a new suit made.

The thief refreshes his internal organs.

Appendix A

MANUSCRIPT SEGMENTS OMITTED FROM PUBLISHED VERSIONS

STORY OF MR. JABOT

Although the design was actually lithographed and printed, the page was cut from the published version. RT joked about this in his correspondence.

10.
Mr Jabot ayant eu un malheur, un léger nuage compromet ses succès.
Mr Jabot conduit la galope avec le plus heureux succès.

Mr. Jabot having suffered a misfortune; a slight cloud compromises his success.

Mr. Jabot leads the gallopade with great success.

MR. CRÉPIN (Cut from between pages 67 and 68)

Les puces ne trouvant plus à dévorer passent chez Madame Pétuble qui voyage avec Craniose sur l'impériale de la diligence
Madame Pétuble est obligée de quitter la voiture et de se réfugier dans l'endroit le plus obscur du bois.
Et de se livrer à une fuite désordonnée qui fait lever les lièvres, et épouvante les oiseaux de l'air

Finding nothing more to devour, the fleas pass to Mrs. Pétuble who is traveling with Craniose on the top of the diligence.

Mrs. Pétuble is obliged to leave the coach and take refuge in the darkest spot of the wood.

And to abandon herself to a disorderly flight which raises the hares, and terrifies the birds of the air.

MR. CRÉPIN (Cut from between pages 70 and 71)

Cependant Bonichon qui est en patrouille poursuit madame Pétuble qu'il prend pour un homme déguisé en balle de coton.
Mr Pétuble, qui cherche son épouse, étant survenu Bonichon bat en retraite, ne voulant pas se risquer contre deux balles de coton.
Mr Pétuble baigne sa femme dans le grand canal, et toutes les puces y périssent

Meanwhile Bonichon who is on patrol pursues Mrs. Pétuble, whom he takes for a man disguised as a bale of cotton.

When Mr. Pétuble arrives, looking for his wife, Bonichon beats a retreat, having no desire to risk himself against two bales of cotton.

Mr. Pétuble dips his wife in the Grand Canal, and all the fleas perish there.

DR. FESTUS

(follows from page 36)

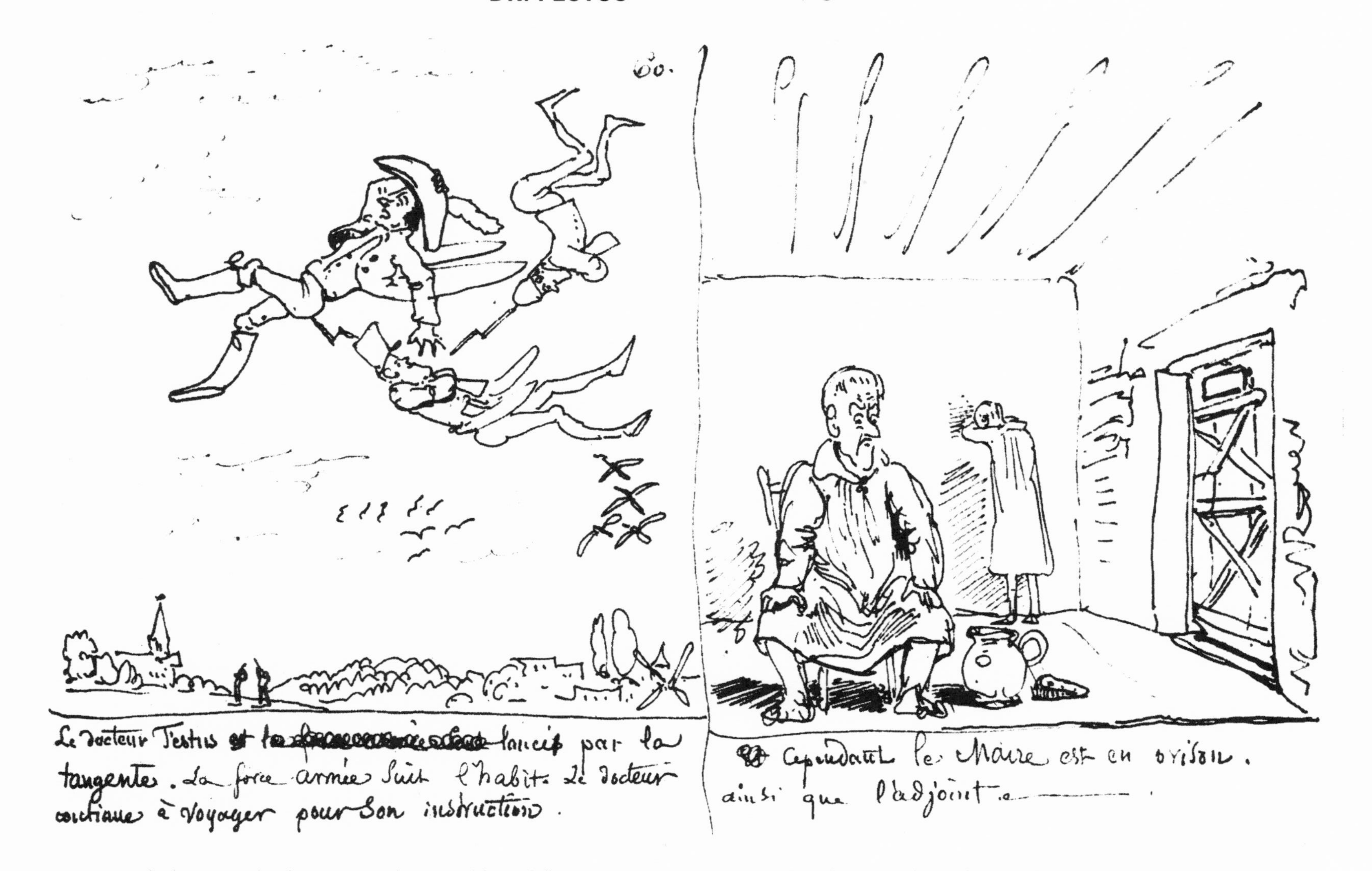
Le docteur Festus lancé par la tangente. La force armée suit l'habit. Le docteur continue à voyager pour son instruction.
Cependant le Maire est en prison, ainsi que l'adjoint.

Dr. Festus is thrown up by the tangent. The armed force follows the uniform. Dr. Festus continues his educational tour.

Meanwhile the mayor is in jail, as is his deputy.

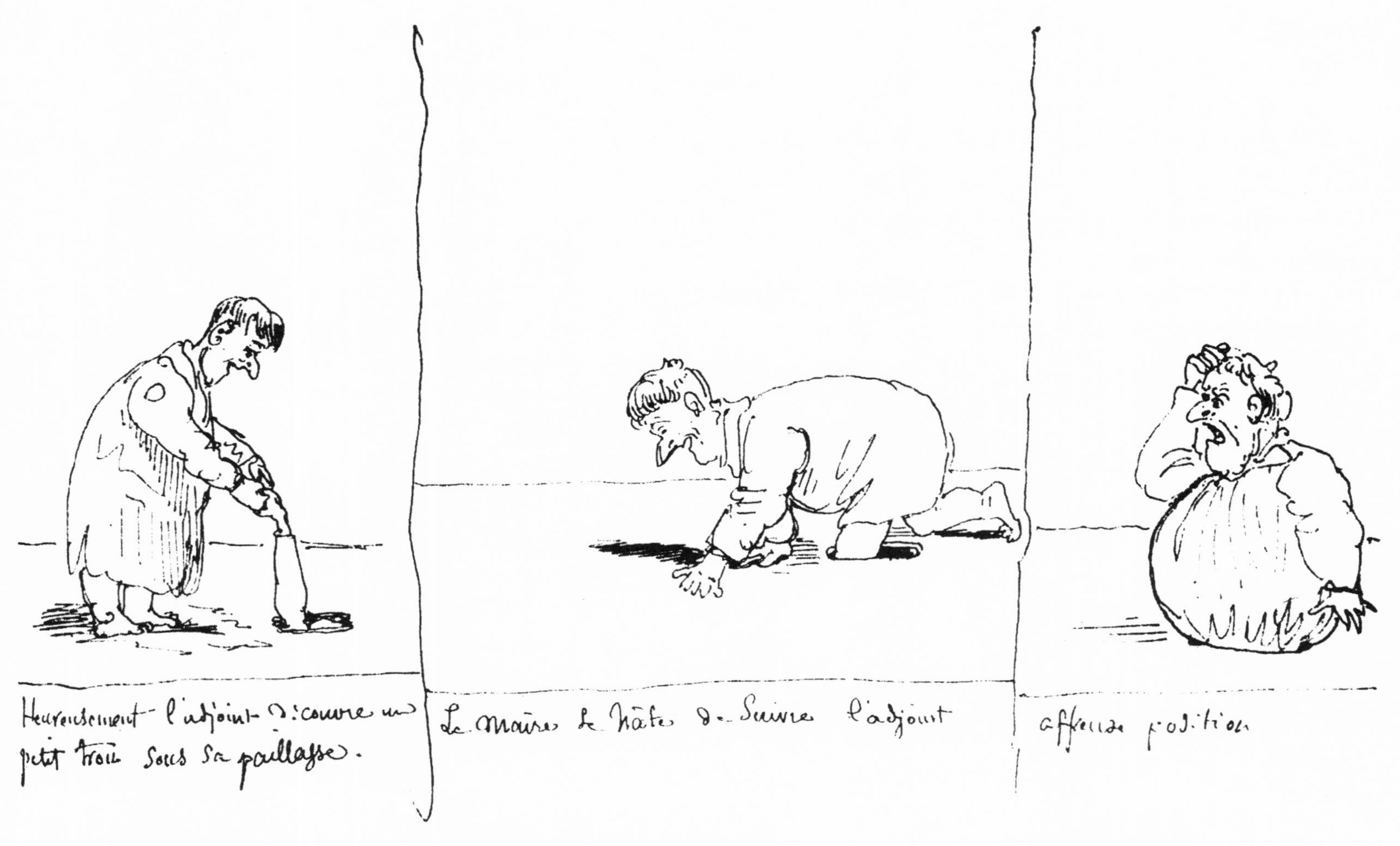
Heureusement l'adjoint découvre un petit trou sous sa paillasse.
Le Maire se hâte de suivre l'adjoint
affreuse position

Fortunately his deputy discovers a little hole under his straw mattress.

The Mayor hurriedly follows the deputy.

Terrible position.

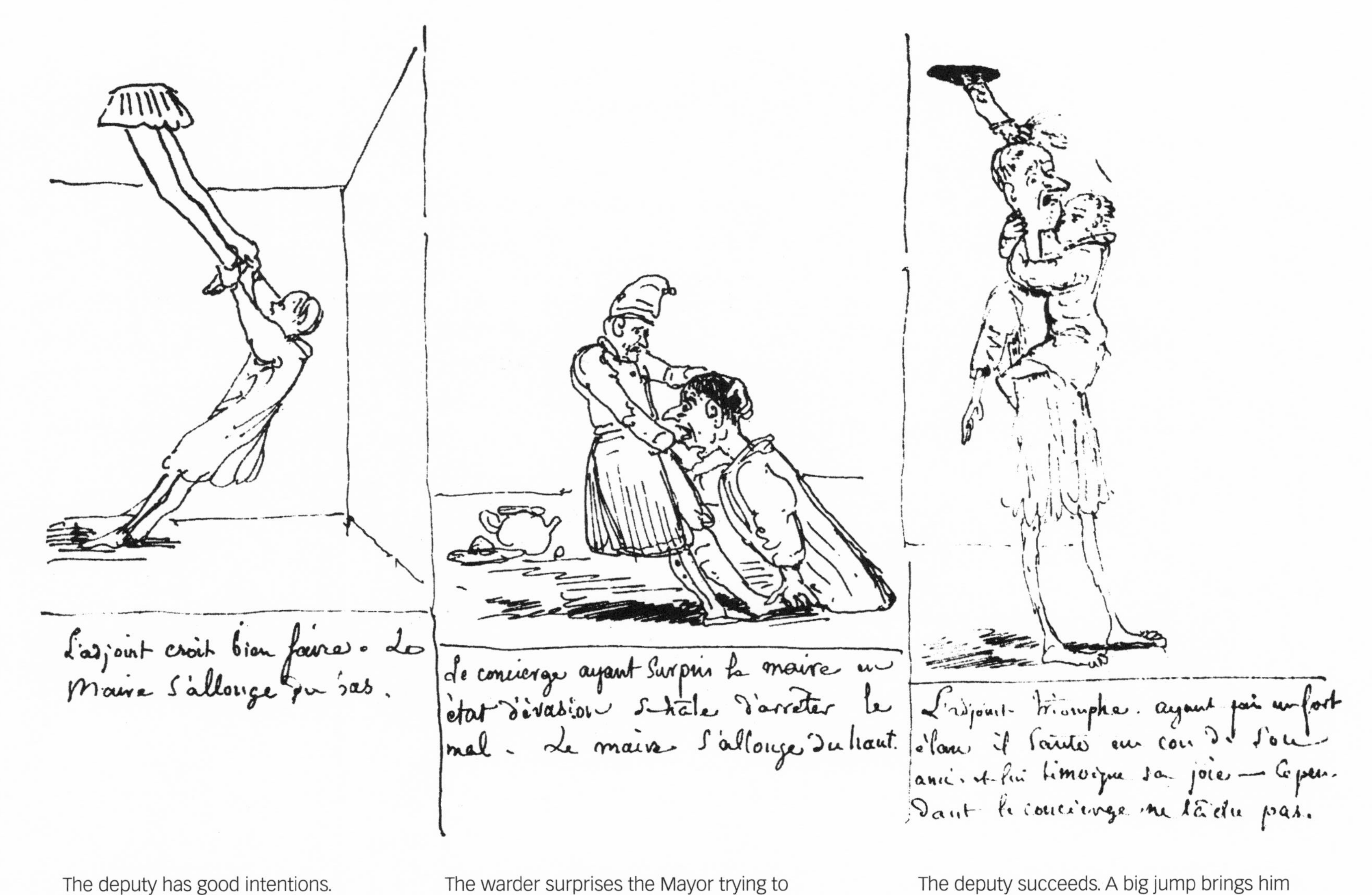
L'adjoint croit bien faire. Le
Maire s'allonge par bas.
Le concierge ayant surpris le maire en
état d'évasion se hâte d'arrêter le
mal. Le maire s'allonge du haut.
L'adjoint triomphe. ayant pris un fort
élan il saute au cou de son
ami et lui témoigne sa joie — Cependant le concierge ne lâche pas.

The deputy has good intentions.
The Mayor is stretched from below.

The warder surprises the Mayor trying to escape, and quickly sets about stopping him. The mayor is stretched from above.

The deputy succeeds. A big jump brings him to his friend's neck, and he demonstrates his delight. Meanwhile the warder does not let go.

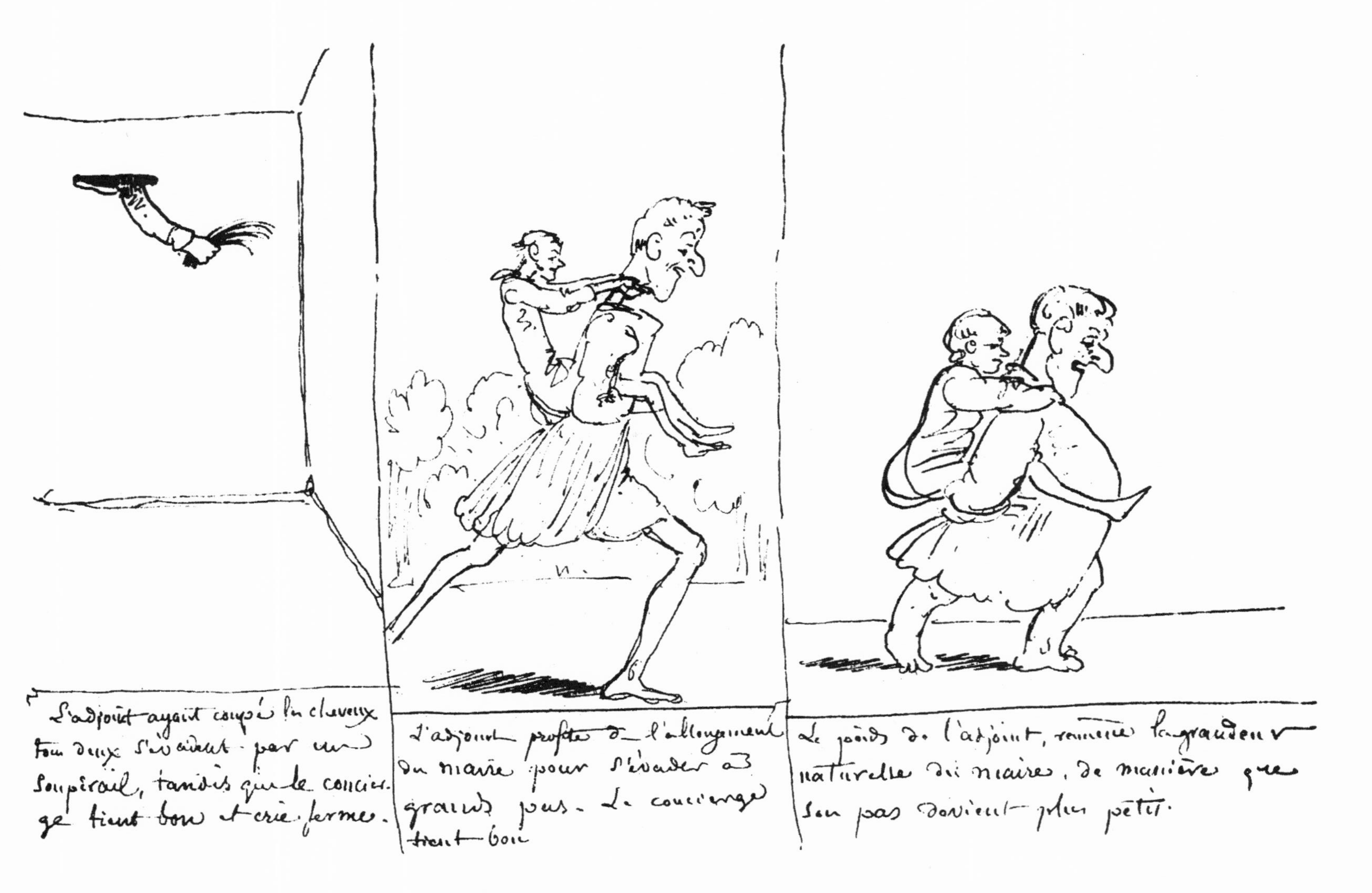
L'adjoint ayant coupé les cheveux
tous deux s'évadent par un
soupirail, tandis que le concierge tient bon et crie ferme.
L'adjoint profite de l'allongement
du maire pour s'évader à
grands pas. Le concierge
tient bon
Le poids de l'adjoint ramène la grandeur
naturelle du maire, de manière que
son pas devient plus petit.

The deputy having cut the Mayor's hair off, both escape by a vent, while the warder holds on and shouts out loud.

The deputy uses the lengthening of the Mayor to take great steps to escape. The warder holds on.

The deputy's weight brings the Mayor down to his normal size, so that his steps become smaller.

au lion d'or.
Milord arrivé à l'hotellerie où il compte retrouver Milady, ne trouve personne toute la Commune étant à la recherche du maire

Milord arriving at the hostelry, where he expects to find Milady again, finds no one, the whole Commune having gone to search for the Mayor.

STORY OF MR. CRYPTOGAME

1830 manuscript, scenes 168–225 (end of ms)

Mr. Criptogame sees for the first time a beautiful woman from Provence whom he had never seen before.

Mr. C. feels that it is for life.

And yet his commitments to Elvire! ! . . .

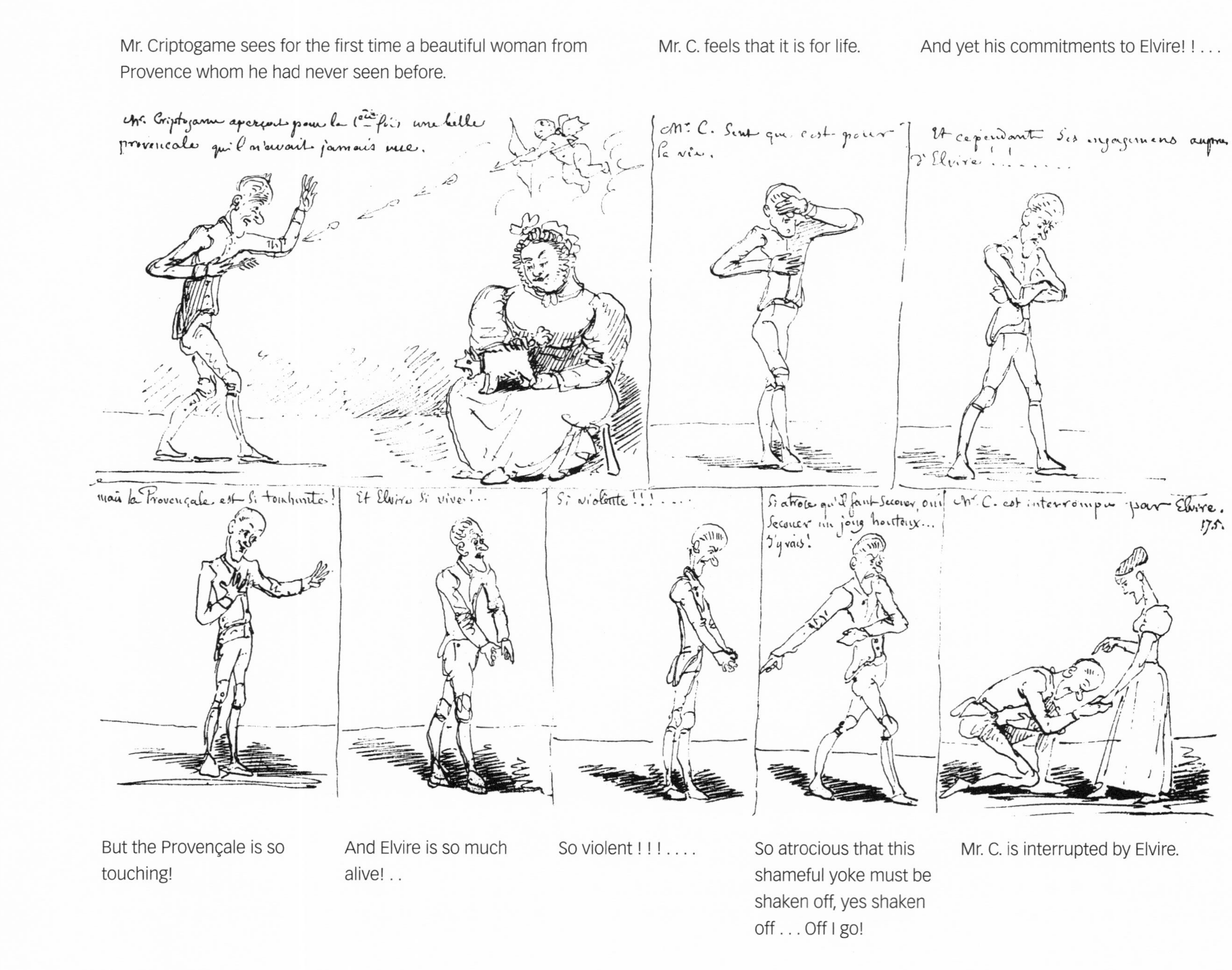
Mr. Criptogame aperçoit pour la 1ère fois une belle provençale qu'il n'avait jamais vue.
Mr. C. sent que c'est pour la vie.
Et cependant ses engagemens auprès d'Elvire ! ! . . . . . .
mais la Provençale est si touchante !
Et Elvire si vive ! . .
Si violente ! ! ! . . . .
Si atroce qu'il faut secouer, oui secouer un joug honteux... j'y vais !
Mr. C. est interrompu par Elvire.
175.

But the Provençale is so touching!

And Elvire is so much alive! . .

So violent ! ! ! . . . .

So atrocious that this shameful yoke must be shaken off, yes shaken off . . . Off I go!

Mr. C. is interrupted by Elvire.

Declaration, while Elvire is at supper. The Provençale takes it all badly and screams like a banshee.

Elvire cries out from below: What is going on! Hearing this Mr. C. hurriedly comes back to her, and assures her that the noise was caused by poultry being bled on the deck.

The abbé running up at the noise, finds himself upbraided and is nonplussed.

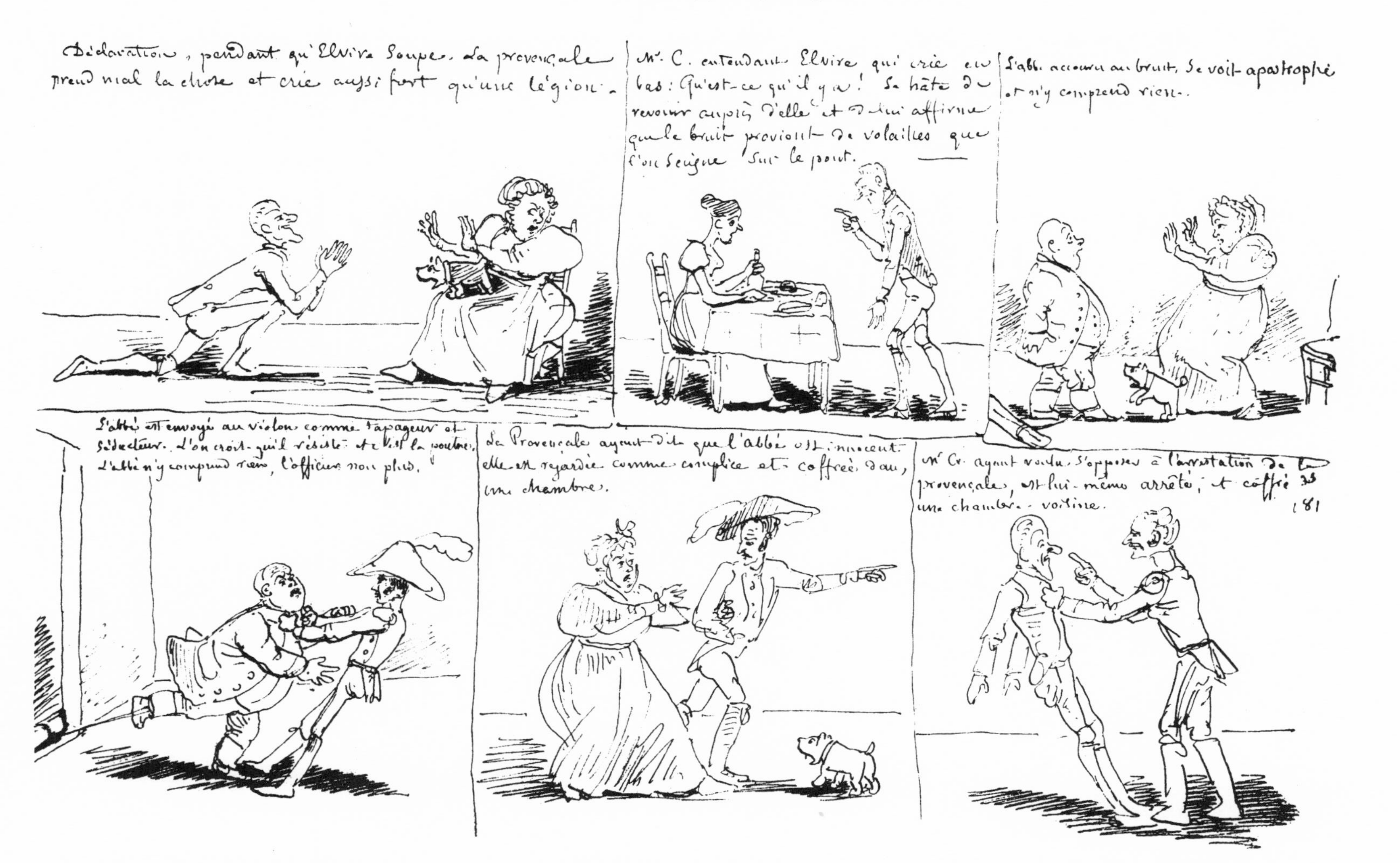
Déclaration, pendant qu'Elvire soupe. La provençale prend mal la chose et crie aussi fort qu'une légion.
Mr. C. entendant Elvire qui crie en bas: Qu'est-ce qu'il y a! Se hâte de revenir auprès d'elle et de lui affirme que le bruit provient de volailles que l'on seigne sur le pont.
L'abbé accourant au bruit, se voit apostrophé et n'y comprend rien.
L'abbé est envoyé au violon comme tapageur et séducteur. L'on croit qu'il résiste et c'est la poutre, L'abbé n'y comprend rien, l'officier non plus.
La Provençale ayant dit que l'abbé est innocent. elle est regardée comme complice et coffrée dans une chambre.
Mr Cr. ayant voulu s'opposer à l'arrestation de la provençale, est lui-même arrêté, et coffré dans une chambre voisine.
181

The abbé is sent to jail as a rowdy and seducer. He is thought to be resisting arrest when it is only the beam.
The abbé is nonplussed, so is the officer.

The Provençale having told them that the abbé is innocent, is regarded as an accomplice and shut up in a room.

Mr. Cr. having tried to prevent the arrest of the Provençale, is himself arrested, and shut up in a neighboring room.

After claiming Mr. C. as her property Elvire is also shut up elsewhere as an accomplice.

The abbé in jail thinks he can hear Mr. Criptogame singing.

Mr. C. on hearing the Provençale cough in the neighboring room, gives vent to love songs.

The arrow strikes the target.

Each having made holes in the wall on the side where their affections lie, simultaneously push through them.

Mr. C. averts the storm by protesting to Elvire that he was merely on his way to join her.

The abbé held back by the beam screams like 3 banshees, the beautiful Provençale like two, and the dog like one.

Elvire determined to discover the cause of this racket, is held back by Mr. C., on the pretext that she will be exposing her precious life.

The abbé is obliged, in order to free himself, to return by the same hole. The noise ceases and the Provençale is left alone.

When Mr. C. tries to make a hole in order to escape while Elvire is asleep, the water gushes violently out and knocks him down.

Great distress.

The water penetrates by the hole in the beautiful Provençale's room.

Seeing the water flow, the abbé gets into a swimming position on the floor, in order to be all ready.

Fortunately a fat dolphin trying to enter gets stuck in the hole.

The beautiful Provençale is saved by her balloon sleeves.

The abbé having forgotten about the beam is held back by it, head downwards. Fortunately he is able to cut through the floor with a knife.

When the water subsides the abbé has no idea how to get off the top of his head.

When the water runs under the wall into the abbé's room, the beautiful Provençale finds herself back on her feet.

The same [water running] into the neighboring room. They are very cold.

Down in the hold, which is flooded, the leak is sought everywhere. The accused are freed for fear of drowning.

Colds and catarrh: the doctor prescribes hot Drinks. The anxious Elvire has demanded that Mr. C. be tied by his foot to a string, the other end of which she holds in her hand.

Mr. C. decides to decide to write.

The abbé takes charge of the message. He receives a flattering response.

Transports of joy at the return of the abbé. The latter is almost suffocated.

The anxious Elvire pulls on the string, the abbé is nonplussed, and screams like ten banshees in a bass voice.

The Provençale runs up at the noise. The anxious Elvire pulls even harder.

Elvire has her nurse pull the string and goes to see for herself the cause of the resistance. Meanwhile the woman pulls in everybody.

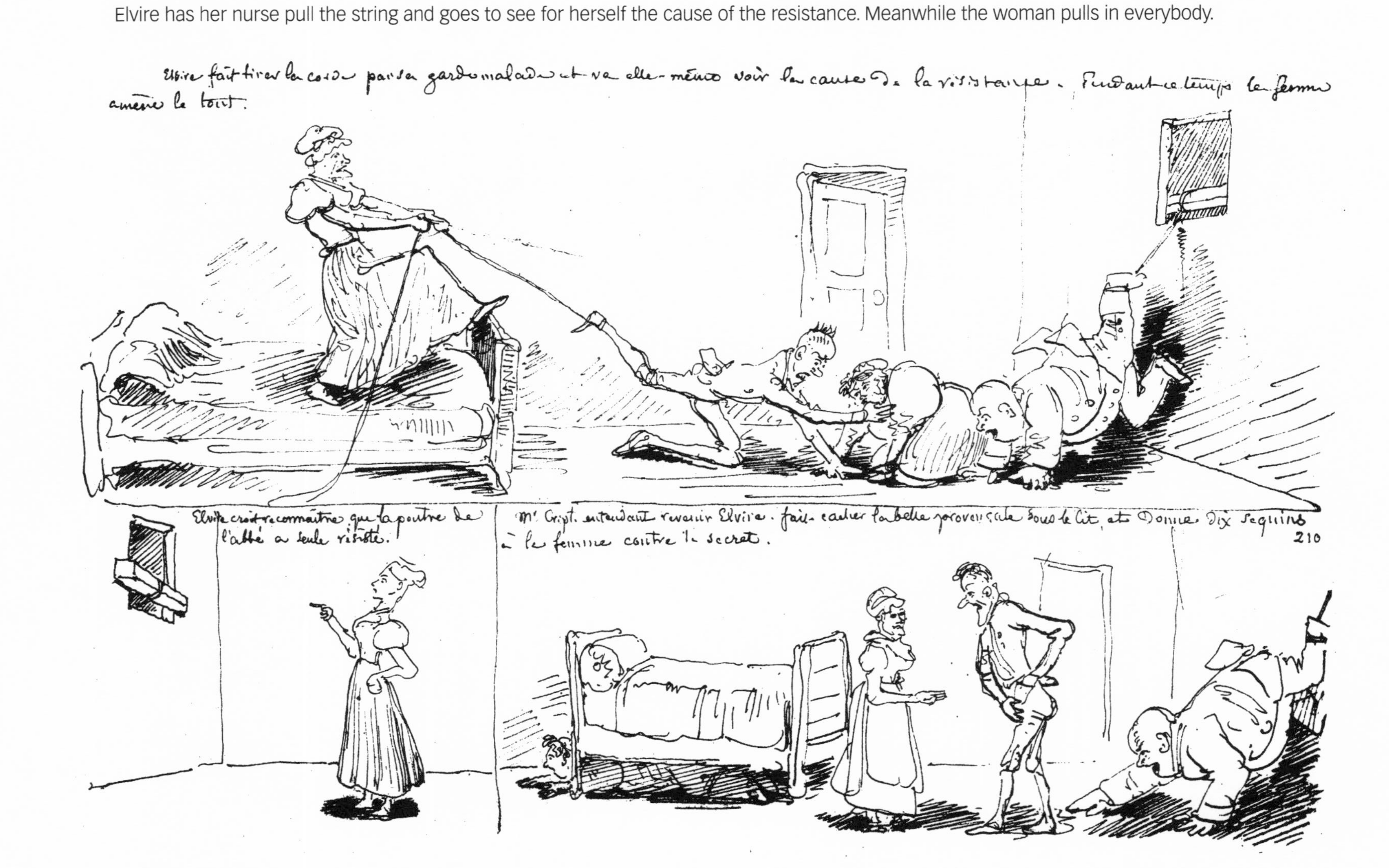
Elvire fait tirer la corde par sa garde-malade et va elle-même voir la cause de la résistance. Pendant ce temps la femme amène le tout.
Elvire croit reconnaître que la poutre de l'abbé a seule résisté.
Mr Cript. entendant revenir Elvire. fait cacher la belle provençale sous le lit, et donne dix sequins à la femme contre le secret.
210

Elvire seems to recognize that the abbé's beam alone has held out.

Mr. Cript. hearing Elvire return gets the beautiful Provençale to hide under the bed, and gives six sequins to the woman to keep the secret.

Protestations d'amour et de soumission. après quoi on dégage l'abbé.
La Belle Provençale ayant toussé, Mr Cript. s'efforce de faire croire que c'est l'abbé. On lui fait prendre des boissons chaudes.
L'abbé transpire ferme; pendant que Mr Criptog. a engagé Elvire à faire une promenade sur le pont.
La Belle Provençale prie l'abbé de lui donner un coup de main.
En achevant de le dégager, la Belle Provençale fait chavirer le lit sur l'abbé et s'enfuit. — 215.
Surprise d'Elvire au retour. Mr Cript. s'efforce de lui persuader que l'abbé s'est mis ainsi pour mieux transpirer, en raison de son rhume.

Protestations of love and submission, after which the abbé is freed.

When the Beautiful Provençale coughs, Mr. Cript. tries to have them believe that it is the abbé. He is made to take hot drinks. The Abbé is nonplussed.

The abbé sweats profusely, while Mr. Criptog. engages Elvire to take a turn on the deck.

The Beautiful Provençale asks the Abbé to lend a hand.

At the moment of freeing him, the Beautiful Provençale tips over the bed on top of the abbé and makes off. Surprise of Elvire when she returns. Mr. Cript. tries to persuade her that the abbé has taken this position in order to facilitate sweating, because of his cold.

Naples heaves in sight, and full speed is made to get there. But the dolphin messes with the rudder, and the ship passes by the harbor without being able to enter.

The captain convinced that he is dealing with a strong current, immediately draws up a fine report on this discovery and dispatches it to Paris. He is received unanimously into the Institute.

Delicious moments while the abbé stands guard.

L'on arrive à la vue de Naples. et l'on fait force de voile p^r y aborder. Mais le dauphin contrariant le gouvernail, le vaisseau passe devant le port sans y pouvoir entrer
Le capitaine bien certain que c'est un fort courant rédige sur le champ un beau mémoire sur cette découverte et l'envoie à Paris. Il est reçu à l'Institut à l'unanimité.
Moments délicieux - pendant que l'abbé fait la garde.
Duo divin – deux coeurs qui s'idolâtrent. Roulades amoureuses. bémols passionnés. – dièzes ardents – L'abbé fait la garde.
Ris et jeux célestes. L'abbé fait la garde.
220

Divine duet of two hearts which worship each other. Amorous roulades. Soft flats of passion. Ardent sharps. The abbé stands guard.

Laughter and heavenly games. The abbé stands guard.

Intoxicating dance. The abbé stands guard.

Sweet repose and charms of glowing exhaustion. The abbé stands guard.

There is a noise. The abbé stands at the ready.

The noise increases and the voice of Elvire is heard. Mr. Cript. and the Abbé fall ill. After giving help, the Beautiful Provençale makes off.

Elvire meets the beautiful Provençale leaving the room and falls downright ill with suspicion.

Appendix B

FRAGMENTS OF PICTURE STORIES, STARTED AND ABANDONED

Mr. Anatole asks the way of old Patu, who replies: straight ahead of you.

Mr. Anatole demande la route au père Patu qui lui répond : droit devant vous.
Et sur une pente roide, le père Patu pense que c'est pour aller plus vite.
et dans un champ d'orties, le père Patu pense que c'est un original.

This direction having led Mr. Anatole into a swamp, old Patu supposes that's his fancy.

And on a steep cliff, old Patu thinks he is trying a short cut.

And in a nettle field, old Patu thinks this is a queer 'un.

MR. BOISSEC

Elise dort dans un Bois-
Mr Boissec dort aussi dans un bois
Mr Boissec s'étant réveillé aperçoit Elise et chante aussitot: Dormez donc mes chères amours.

Elise sleeps in a Wood.

Mr. Boissec sleeps also in a wood.

Mr. Boissec, awakening, sees Elise and immediately sings: Sleep away, my dear love.

Mr. Boissec sent que le vide de son coeur est enfin rempli.

Mr. Boissec feels that the void of his heart is at last filled.

Mr. Boissec cherche à réveiller Elise par le parfum des fleurs.

Mr. Boissec tries to awaken Elise with the scent of flowers.

M. Boissec sentant que ça ne suffit pas, essaie le secouement du pied.
M. Bois-Sec se livre à un immense vacarme pour parvenir à son but.
M. Bois-Sec ayant crié pendt. trois heures, perd la voix.

Mr. Boissec realizing that this is not enough, tries giving her foot a shake.

Mr. Bois-Sec gives vent to an immense racket to achieve his ends.

Mr. Bois-Sec having shouted for three hours on end, loses his voice.

Mr. Boissec voyant passer un Meunier veut l'appeler pour lui emprunter son âne, il ne peut retrouver le moindre filet de voix !
Mr. Bois-Sec s'étant retourné, aperçoit avec délices qu'Elise est réveillée, et dans le quart d'un clin-d'oeil il est à ses pieds. Elise n'y comprend rien.

Mr. Boissec seeing a miller pass by, tries to call him in order to borrow his ass, but cannot raise the slightest whisper of a voice.

Mr. Bois-Sec turning back sees with delight that Elise has woken up, and in a quarter of a wink is at her feet. Elise is nonplussed.

Mr Boissec fait d'immenses et indicibles efforts pour s'expliquer, mais la voix manquant tout à fait, il ne fait qu'effray l'intéressant Elise qui le somme de s'éloigner
Mr Boissec continuant ses efforts est sur le point d'éclater, d'où Elise appelle du Secours.
Cependant Elise ayant crié au Secours pendant trois heures perd aussi la voix.

Mr. Boissec makes immense and unspeakable efforts to explain himself, but his voice fails him altogether; all he does is scare the interesting Elise who summons him to depart.

Mr. Boissec persists in his efforts, and is on the point of exploding, when Elise calls for help.

But Elise after calling for help for three hours on end, also loses her voice.

MR. CALICOT

Mr. Calicot attend le chalant.

Mr. Calicot awaits customers.

Mr. Calicot aune pour la pratique.

Mr. Calicot takes measures for practice.

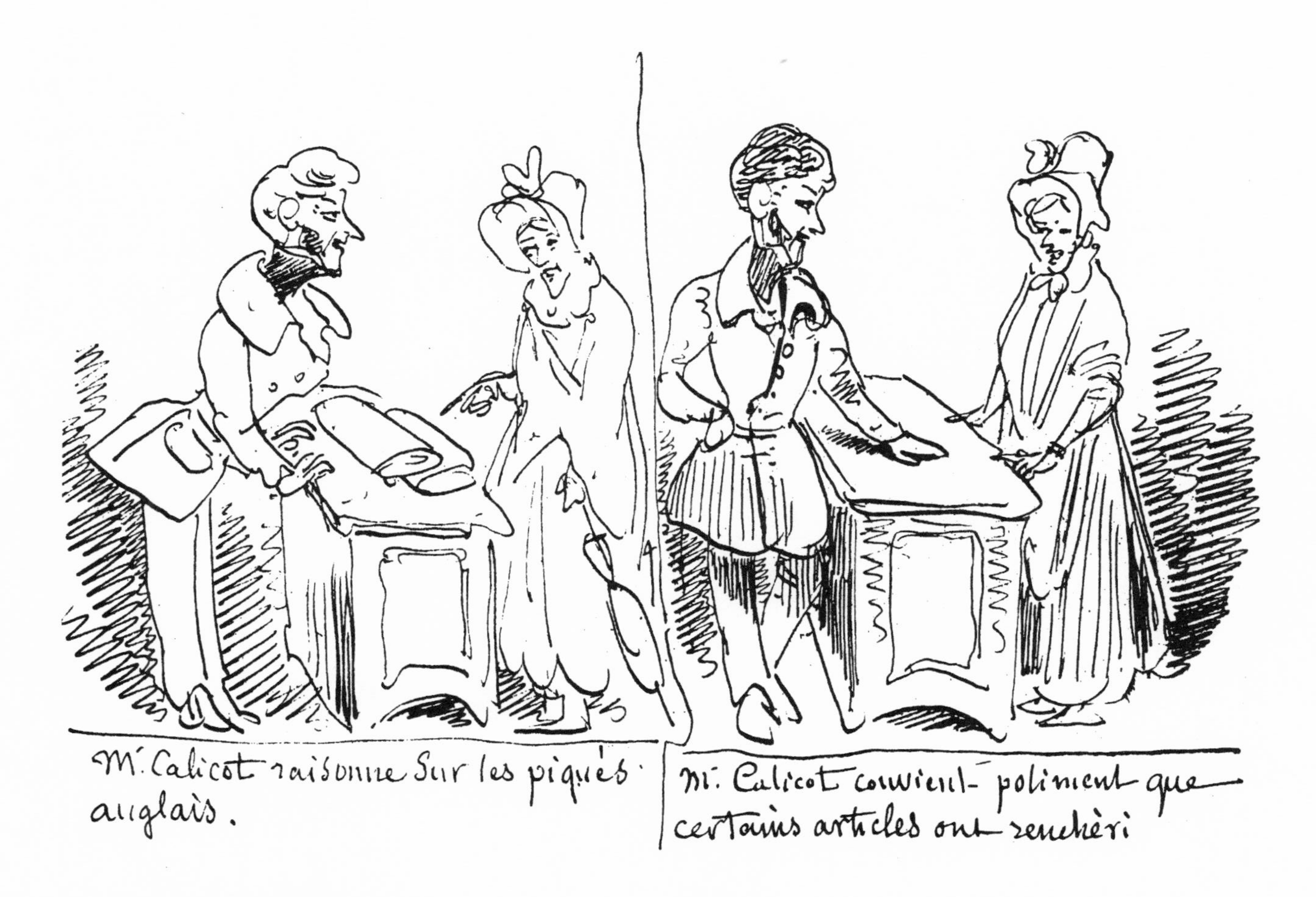
M. Calicot raisonne sur les piqués anglais.
Mr. Calicot convient poliment que certains articles ont renchéri

Mr. Calicot discourses on English quilts.

Mr. Calicot politely concedes that certain articles have gone up in price.

Mr. Calicot n'a pas de monnoie..
Mr. Calicot a de la monnoie

Mr. Calicot has no change.

Mr. Calicot does have change.

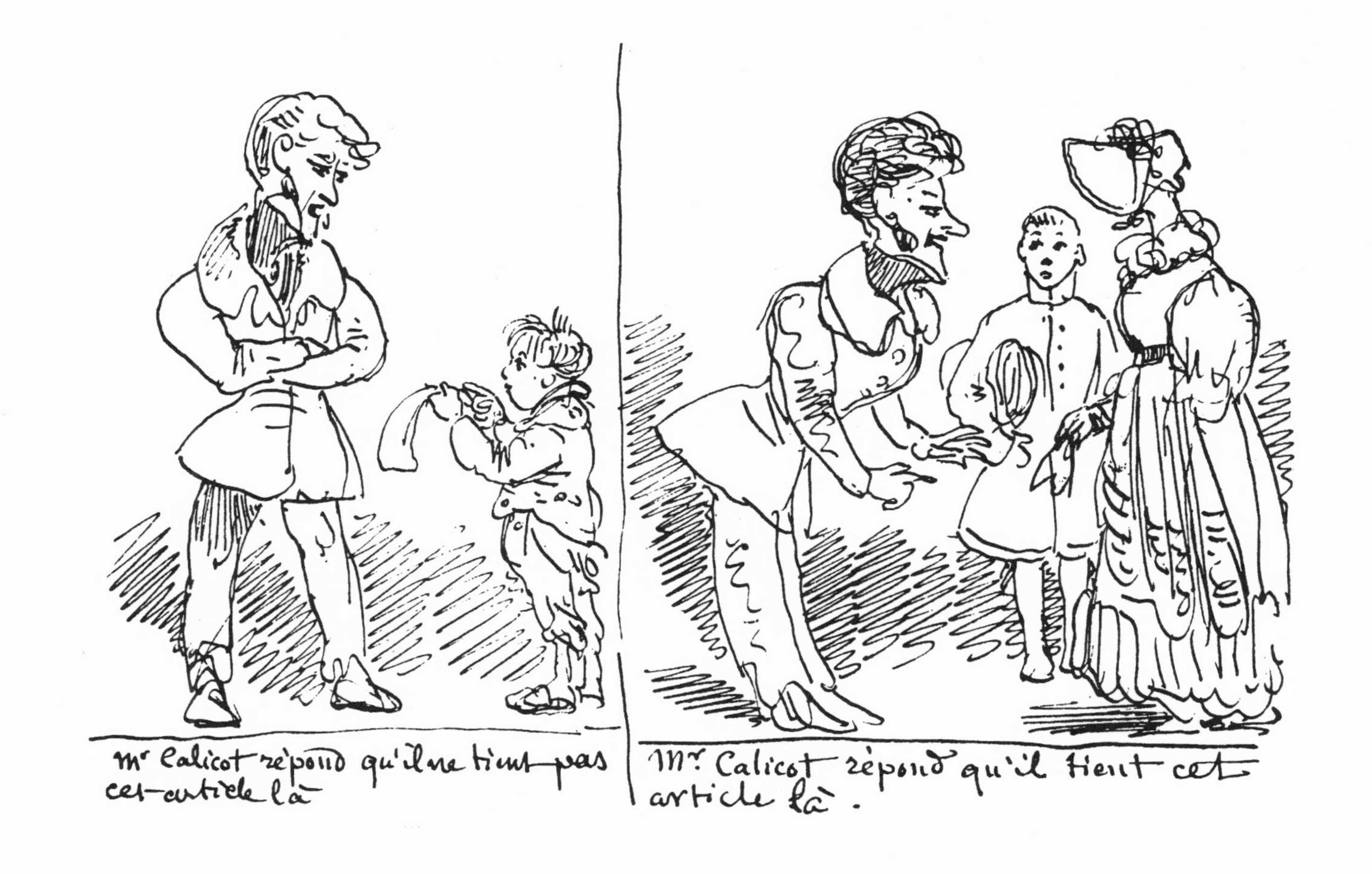
Mr Calicot répond qu'il ne tient pas cet article là
Mr. Calicot répond qu'il tient cet article là.

Mr. Calicot replies that he does not carry that particular article.

Mr. Calicot replies that he does carry that particular article.

Mr Calicot improuve fortement le ministère, et dit qu'ils sont toujours les mêmes !!
Et que c'est pire que sous l'ancien régime.
Et qu'on n'en veut plus !

Mr. Calicot strongly disapproves of the ministry, and says that they are always the same! !

And that it is worse than under the Ancien régime.

And that this can't go on!

MR. BRUTUS CALICOT

Mr. Brutus Calicot on leaving an open air civic banquet gets the chills and takes to his bed.

Mr. Brutus Calicot is carried off in the prime of life leaving his young wife pregnant.

The political friends of Mr. Brutus Calicot subscribe to place a marble slab on his tomb. ["Here lies Brutus Calicot. He was pure. He fought tyranny and died for fraternity, Equality and liberty"]

The widow Calicot gets on with her life, despite the death of her husband . . . After three days the widow Calicot re-opens up her shop, and sells half a pound of pepper to Mr. Tiberius Graccus Robinet.

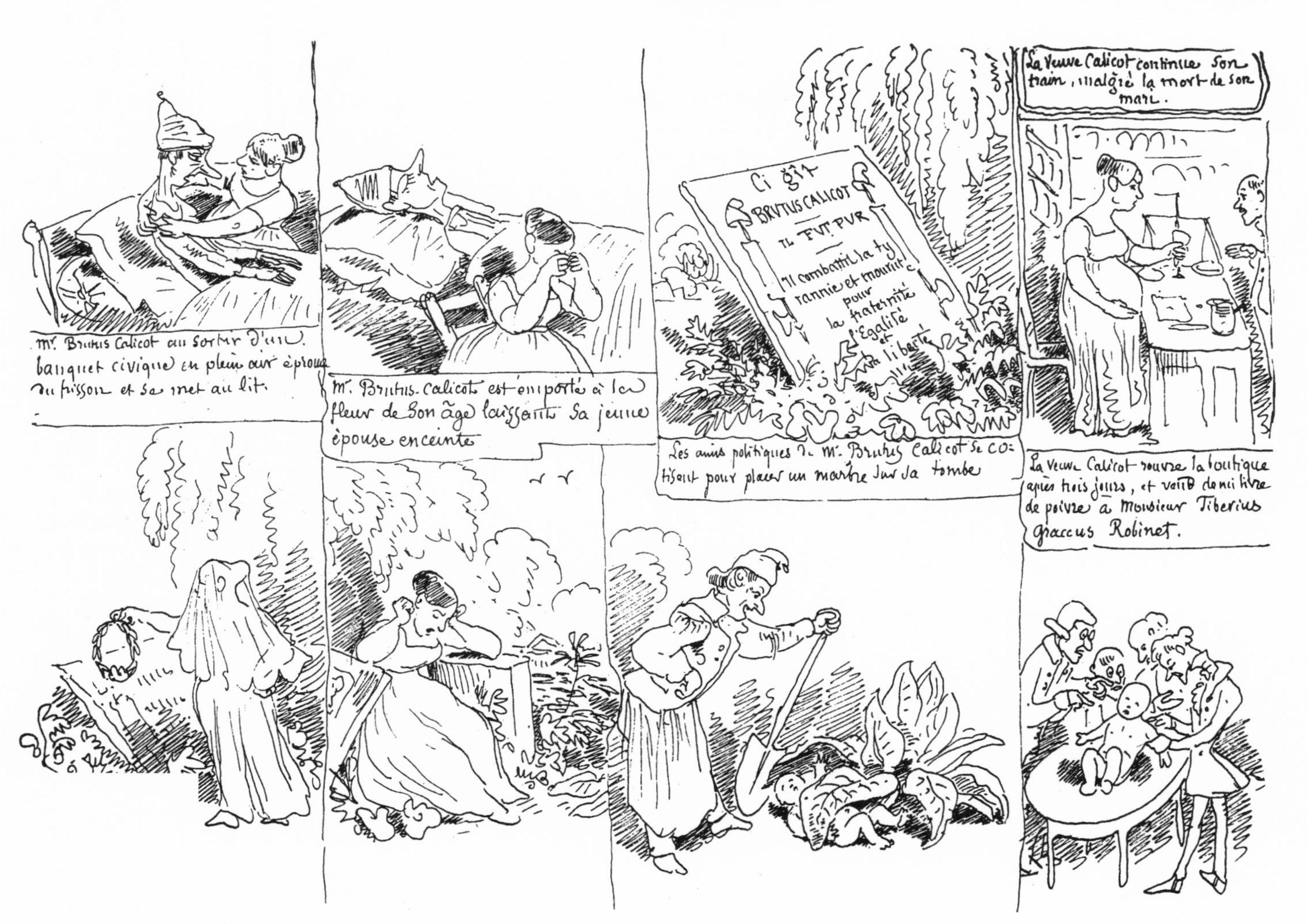
Mr. Brutus Calicot au sortir d'un banquet civique en plein air éprouve un frisson et se met au lit.
Mr. Brutus Calicot est emporté à la fleur de son âge laissant sa jeune épouse enceinte
Ci gît
BRUTUS CALICOT
IL FVT PVR
Il combattit la tyrannie et mourut pour la fraternité l'Egalité et la liberté
Les amis politiques de Mr. Brutus Calicot se cotisent pour placer un marbre sur sa tombe
La Veuve Calicot continue son train, malgré la mort de son mari.
La Veuve Calicot rouvre la boutique après trois jours, et vend demi livre de poivre à Monsieur Tiberius Graccus Robinet.

MR. FLUET

au bout de 15 ans d'absence Mr
fluet retrouve son épouse bien portante
et ses 15 filles prospères.

After 15 years of absence Mr. Fluet finds his wife in good health and his 15 daughters prosperous.

C'est je vous jure
la passion la plus pure...

I swear, mine in the purest passion . . .

Mr. Fluet will receive daily from 7 to 9 requests for marriage.

Miss Fluet the seventh is intoxicated with sentimental romances.

Hearing this, Mr. Verpale falls down in sheer ecstasy on the staircase.

The Fluet girls who have all received the same education from the same governess, run up with hot drinks.

5-footed horse, or painful ride of Mr. X.xx, whose steed has gone deaf.

Sad state of Mr. Verpale after having drunk the 15 hot drinks. But he reflects.

Mr. X.xx's ride continued.

Mr. Fluet receives proposals from 7 to 9.

Waiting room from 7 to 9.

Miss Fluet the 7th gives a horrible reception to her father's choice of husband.

The same ride continued.

The fact is that Miss Fluet, who has a lively imagination, wants a hero for a husband.

A horrible quarrel breaks out among grave men.

Mr. Verpale appears under the windows of Miss Fluet the 7th, having decided to make his passion known. But he can only sing in a gargling voice, having hot drinks right up to and including the larynx.

Hearing this, Miss Fluet thinks she recognizes a tender cooing. She abandons herself to passionate impulses.

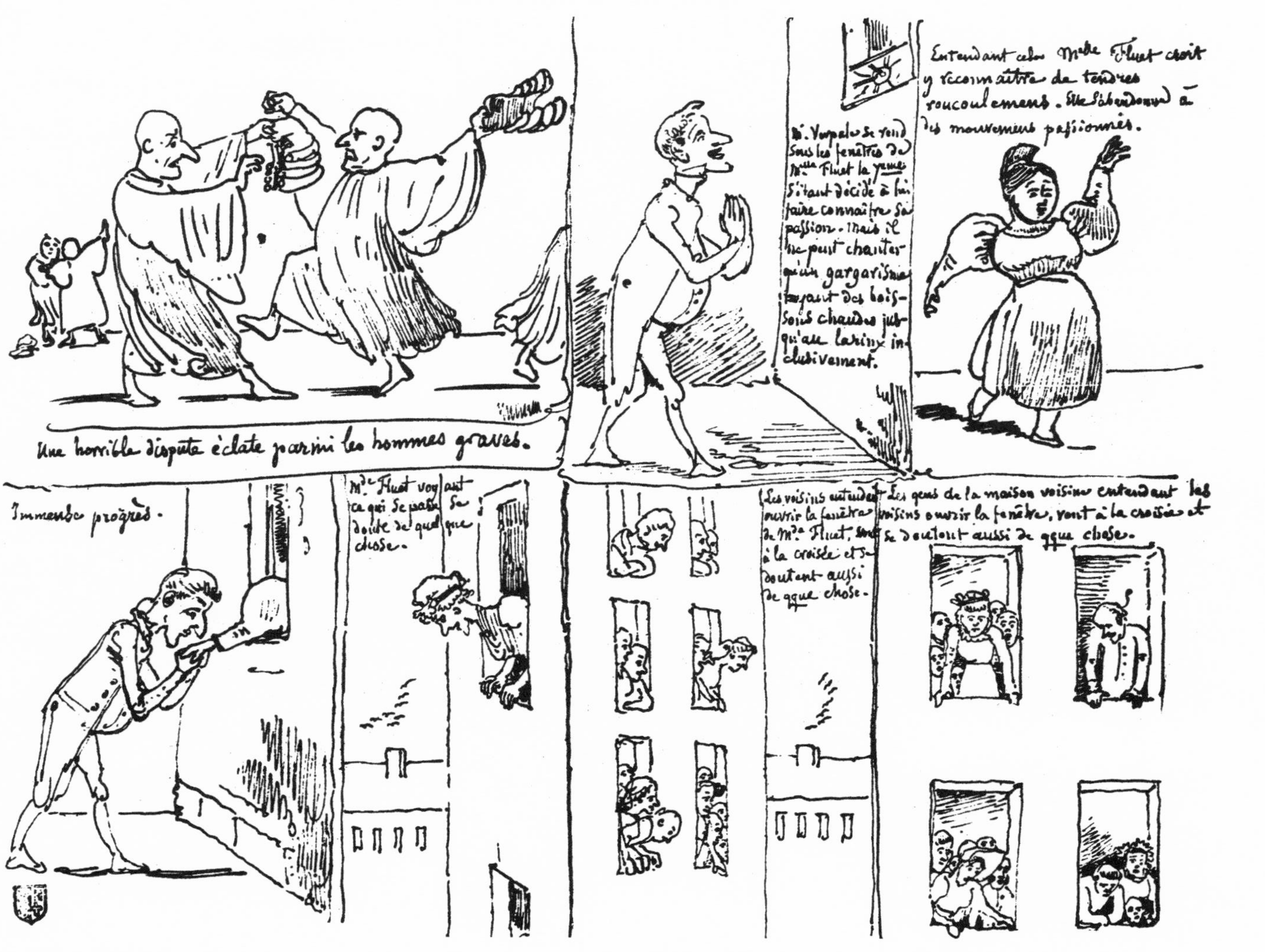
Une horrible dispute éclate parmi les hommes graves.
Mr. Verpale se rend sous les fenêtres de Mlle Fluet la jeune s'étant décidé à lui faire connaître sa passion. Mais il ne peut chanter qu'un gargarisme ayant des boissons chaudes jusqu'au larinx inclusivement.
Entendant cela Mlle Fluet croit y reconnaître de tendres roucoulements. Elle s'abandonne à des mouvements passionnés.
Immense progrès.
Mme Fluet voyant ce qui se passe se doute de quelque chose.
Les voisins entendant ouvrir la fenêtre de Mme Fluet, vont à la croisée et se doutent aussi de qque chose.
Les gens de la maison voisine entendant les voisins ouvrir la fenêtre, vont à la croisée et se doutent aussi de qque chose.

Immense progress.

Mrs. Fluet seeing what is going on, suspects something.

The neighbors hearing Mrs. Fluet open her window, go to their windows and also suspect something.

The people in the house next door hearing the neighbors opening the window, go to their window and suspect something.

Madame Fluet vient instruire son mari de ce qui se passe. Les bras lui en tombent. Et sa chaise aussi.
nouveaux progrès.

Mrs. Fluet comes to inform her husband of what is happening. He is floored. And his chair also.

More progress.

MR. VERTPRÉ

Mr. Vertpré, after the ship sinks, fights the fury of the waves.

When the waves subside, Mr. Vertpré recovers his hat.

Mr. Vertpré, le vaisseau ayant sombré, lutte contre la fureur des flots.
Les flots s'étant calmés, Mr. Vertpré, rattrape son chapeau.
Le soleil ayant lui, Mr Vertpré se rajuste et sent avec plaisir les boucles de sa chevelure se reformer.
Mr. Vertpré offre galamment le bout de sa badine à Melle d'Espagnac.

When the sun shines forth, Mr. Vertpré straightens himself out and takes pleasure in the sensation of his hair recovering its curl.

Mr. Vertpré gallantly offers the point of his cane to Miss d'Espagnac.

A Shark threatening to compromise the health of Miss d'Espagnac, Mr. Vertpré scolds the insolent creature with his cane.

Miss d'Espagnac having freed herself, the Shark trying to grab her leg again, catches the mast. Mr. Vertpré considers the success of his gallant devotion.

Mr. Vertpré uses his cane to shove the mast further down the Shark's throat.

un Requin pouvant compromettre la santé de Melle d'Es-
pagnac, Mr Vertpré, tance de sa badine l'insolent animal
Melle d'Espagnac, s'étant dégagée, le Requin, voulant ressaisir
sa jambe, attrappe le mât. Mr Vertpré considère le succès de son galant dévouement.
Mr Vertpré pousse de sa badine pour enferrer
le Requin toujours davantage
après quoi Mr Vertpré essuie sa badine, s'é-
tonnant que Melle d'Espagnac tarde tant
à remercier son libérateur.
s'entendant traiter de lâche et de pol-
tron, Mr Vertpré trouve le mot fort,
pour ne pas dire absurde.
Le requin ayant fait des mouvemens convulsifs Mr Vertpré supplie Melle d'Espagnac de s'appuyer sur
sa badine.

After which Mr. Vertpré wipes his cane, surprised that Miss d'Espagnac is so slow in thanking her liberator.

Hearing himself called a coward and a poltroon, Mr. Vertpré finds it a bit much, not to say absurd.

The shark having made some convulsive movements, Mr. Vertpré begs Miss d'Espagnac to use his cane for support.

Mr. Vertpré decides to row with his cane to reach Miss d'Espagnac, and offer her gallant hospitality on board his mast.

Failing altogether, Mr. V.pré has the idea of throwing his dog into the sea in the hope that he will fly to the aid of Miss d'Espagnac.

Since the dog tries to get back on board, Mr. V. pushes him sharply away, with his cane.

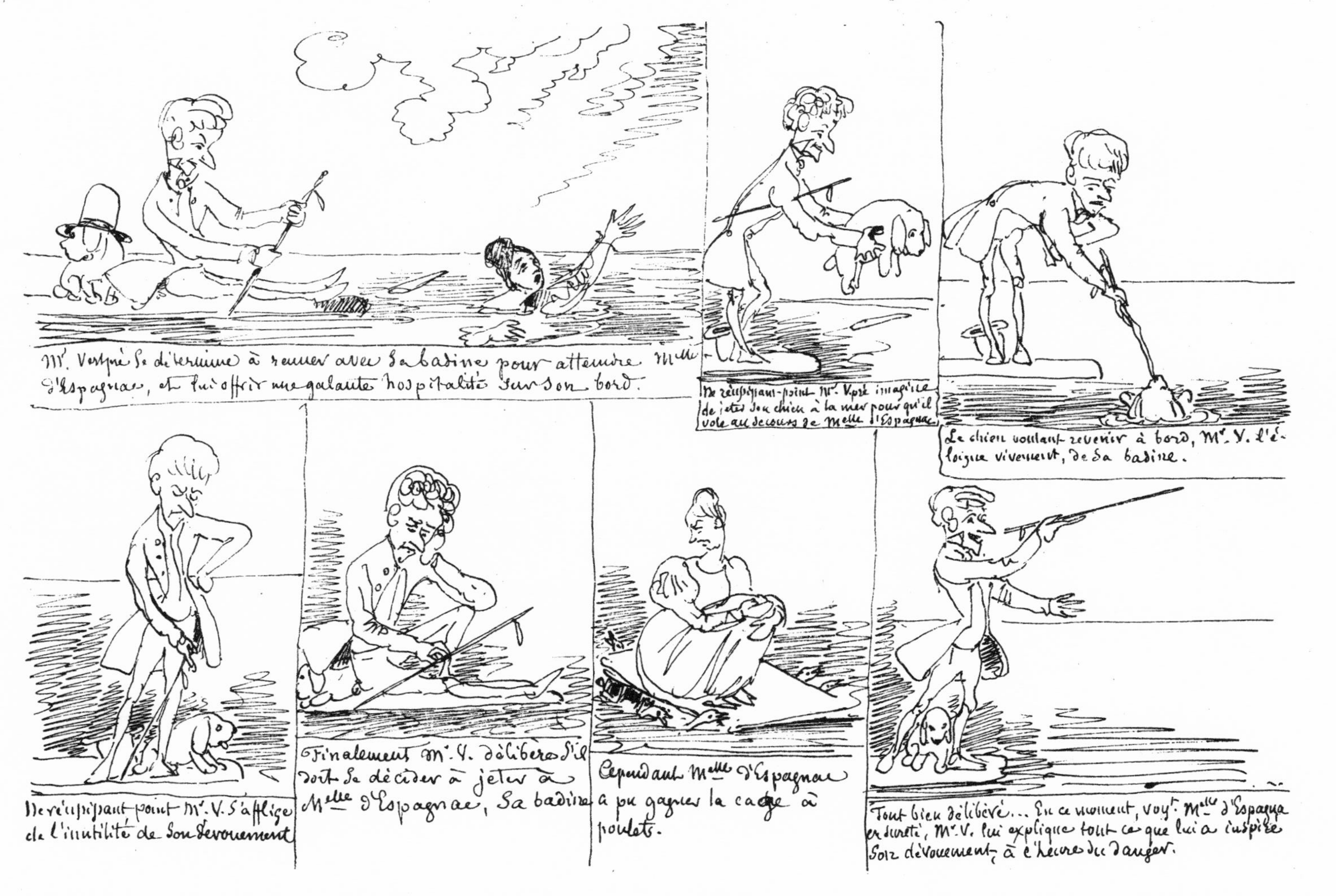

Mr. Vertpré se détermine à ramer avec sa badine pour atteindre Melle d'Espagnac, et lui offrir une galante hospitalité sur son bord.
Ne réussissant point Mr. Vpré imagine de jeter son chien à la mer pour qu'il vole au secours de Melle d'Espagnac.
Le chien voulant revenir à bord, Mr. V. l'éloigne vivement, de sa badine.
Ne réussissant point Mr. V. s'afflige de l'inutilité de son dévouement
Finalement Mr. V. délibère s'il doit se décider à jeter à Melle d'Espagnac, sa badine
Cependant Melle d'Espagnac a pu gagner la cage à poulets.
Tout bien délibéré... En ce moment, voyt. Melle d'Espagnac en sûreté, Mr. V. lui explique tout ce que lui a inspiré son dévouement, à l'heure du danger.

Failing again, Mr. V. grieves at the uselessness of his devotion.

Finally Mr. V. deliberates whether he should decide to throw his cane at Miss d'Espagnac.

Meanwhile Miss d'Espagnac was able to reach the chicken cage.

All things considered . . . At this moment seeing that Miss d'Espagnac is safe, Mr. V. explains to her everything that has inspired his devotion, in the moment of danger.

Miss d'Espagnac gives him the finger.

Mlle D'Espagnac lui fait les cornes.

Mr. Vertpré gets angry.

Mr. Vertpré s'emporte.

The westerly wind comes up.

Le vent d'ouest se lève

Ever stronger.

Toujours plus fort.

Toujours plus fort

Ever stronger.

Toujours plus fort.

Ever stronger.

Toujours plus fort.

Ever stronger.

Et Mr V. touche heureusement à la côte.

And Mr. V. fortunately lands on the coast.

Mr. Vertpré juge que la côte est fort peu habitée.

Mr. Vertpré esteems the coast to be very uninhabited.

Appendix C

MR. BERLU AND LORD TURNEPS (FRAGMENT): TEXT-ONLY SCENARIOS

STORY OF CLAUDIUS BERLU

(baptised in Brumaire)

—Aged 32 years, Mr. Berlu has a stomach ache.
—Returning home he calls for his mother, Mrs. Berlu, the mother?
—The doctor comes, examines the symptoms.
—after which he reflects on the case.
—then he prescribes 10 pills of antimony which Mr. Berlu goes to fetch.
[inserted] A thief introduces himself at the Cavagné (?) couple's (take up from above)
—Meanwhile the police chase a thief, who escapes by the rooftops.
—The thief enters by the chimney
—Mr. Berlu has a dreadful fright at the first sight of the feet. He flees.
—The thief slips into the bed.
—The police who have seen the thief enter by the chimney, surround the house.
—and they arrest Berlu junior, who is jailed in cell no. 4 where he is dressed in
[A Puseyite takes the opportunity to convert Berlu junior with respect to his crimes—struck]
—Meanwhile Mr. Berlu does not recognize his son so changed, who is made to take the 10 pills all at once while the doctor is sent for.
—The doctor examines the symptoms (identical)—[tiny drawing of taking pulse]
—He reflects on the case and declares that the whole trouble comes from the fact of taking 10 pills at once instead of successively which has produced etc etc. .....
—And he prescribes a poultice of one metre / 20 centimeters which Mrs. Berlu goes to fetch.
[P. 2]
—? Meanwhile [Puseyite prison chaplain attempts to convert Berlu junior—struck] Berlu junior's fits of colic having redoubled, the chaplain who enters at this moment deduces apparent remorse for previous crimes committed.
—? And being Puseyite he undertakes immediately a conversion to his sect. All, he says, may be forgiven if you become a Puseyite.
—? Berlu junior becomes a Puseyite, but without his stomach ache getting any better, so that he regrets the antimony.
—Meanwhile Mrs. Berlu goes to fetch the poultice (she is made to wait—pharmacist's mistake)??
—The thief being horribly afraid of that meter-long poultice takes advantage of being left alone and hides in the courtyard in order to escape at nightfall.
—With the result that when Uncle Berlu returns from his travels, he is quite astonished to find the door open and no one in the house. (take up from above? Trunk?) and not finding his bed made he takes his nephew's where he goes fast asleep. NB have the thief worn out, then astonishment at his being so much fatter, and from there use of meter-long absorbant.
—The poultice goes into action and Uncle Berlu begins to experience the stinging.
—Until awakening, he is baffled by this cuirasse and utters frightful screams, while the doctor is [P. 3] hastily called.
—The doctor (identical formula) examines the symptoms,
—And having reflected on the case he declares that the trouble has a dartrous cause which, having been brought out by the antimony administered at too high a dosage, has turned into a spasmodic fever. Not significant however.
—And he prescribes three cataplasms, two .... four fumigations and one anti-spasmodic potion which will make all these symptoms disappear very promptly.
—Meanwhile, the symptoms get worse.
—While Mrs. Berlu is absent Uncle Berlu tries in vain to remove the poultice. . . . .the incident . . . campagne [several words illegible]
—Then he goes up to the fourth floor where they try to help him, but the skin comes away [with the poultice]

—And Uncle Berlu goes into spasms and contortions which horrify the neighbors who go to fetch the police.
[Ten lines crossed out]
[p. 4]
—and running off, he cries for help.
—And he hits someone who tries to relieve him.
—And he plunges into the public fountain.
—And followed by the street kids, he takes it out on them.
—Two good citizens immediately go to alert the police.
—And he collides with a sugar-barrel.
—And the barrel beginning to roll, Uncle Berlu knocks over a patrol running to arrest him.
—And the barrel slows down only on the big quayside.
—From where it rolls into the port. Yesterday all in disorder and riotous, and the people become sovereign in Geneva, the government is changed.
—Meanwhile the thief seeing the arrival of the police summoned by the neighbors, imagines they are after him, and returning quickly to Mrs. Berlu's, he slips again into the bed.
—The police search the house, and finding nothing to arrest, return to make their report and take further orders.
—Immediately afterwards Mrs. Berlu returning home prepares the 3 cataplasms, then she fumigates, and then administers the anti-spasmodic draught.
—The draught begins to have the opposite effect and the thief visibly goes into spasms: Mrs. Berlu runs for the doctor.
—The spasms continued.
—And when the neighbors run up, he throws poultices at them.
[p.5]
—after which, having drunk some water from his fumigations, he feels relieved.
—And falls fast asleep.
—So the doctor is very much happier with his appearance.
—Examines the symptoms.
—Finds that the poultice has been neutralized and that the draught has restored the etc.
—He finds also that the cataplasms have
—He assures himself likewise that the fumigations have
—And he finds that the physiognomy is gradually returning to its natural state.
—And he predicts complete recovery within a few days.
—Except that, one must
—So that the good lady Berlu is beside herself with joy and she overwhelms the patient with caresses.
—goes to fetch a remedy
—Meanwhile on the 6th the Berlu junior affair is brought up, and he is acquitted for lack of proof.
—Hardly has Berlu junior been acquitted, than he returns home where finding no one, he gets into the bed and falls fast asleep.
—Meanwhile the poultice comes off Uncle Berlu, who is fished up alive but furious.
[p.6]
—and put in jug for violent behavior.
—and taken to a sanitarium because his explanations are so incoherent and the tale about a gigantic poultice being put on him while he was asleep, so senseless.
—Nonetheless the poultice floats along the quayside, where a Jew eyes it avidly.
—The Jew who sells leather pants fishes up the poultice so as to use it to patch his merchandise.
—Meanwhile Mrs. Berlu cannot get over the effect of the remedies and the accuracy of the predictions.
—Unfortunately her son speaks of a prison where he has been locked up for six weeks and of a law court which has acquitted him, so that she is nonplussed.

—Unfortunately again her son tells her that he has had no stomach ache for six weeks, so that he sees no reason to take any remedies.
—Fortunately the doctor comes and examines the symptoms.
—And has the matter repeated to him.
—And declares that this business of the prison and acquittal is the perfectly natural result of the feverish dreams and severe delirium which have prevailed constantly during the course of his illness.
[p.7]
We call that, he says, a mucous typhoidal.
—The recovery of Berlu junior makes a big noise in the area and Mr. P. gets a lot of business. (burial) [i.e. shown in drawing]
—And in the moments left to him by his practice he composes an article on the mucuous typhoidal, its treatment, and statistics of cases.
—And he recommends antimony and poultices.
—He attributes to this treatment a fair degree of success, saving on average five patients in nineteen.
—Meanwhile every Monday the madhouse doctor examines Uncle Berlu and since his talk about the poultice is still incoherent he is kept as an incurable.
—And he is treated now with very sudden douches of cold water
—now with inside.
—But the moment anyone tries to treat him with a poultice, he becomes uncontrollable.
—Finally realizing that his release depends upon it, he resigns himself to denying the poultice business.
[p.8]
—And he is released as cured.
—And he figures in medical statistics of the year . . . as having been cured by . . . . .
—And returning to his sister's he discovers that, on the contrary, a poultice has cured his nephew.
—Meanwhile the Jew having patched some pants with bits of the poultice, a number of accidents ensue.
—And the doctor has all the more work to do.
—And he notes in his article that the disease is endemic . . . here, the worst.
—And the burials proliferate.
—And the thief passes by
—And the doctor too.
—And the story ends there. 92 [pictures/captions]

Lord Turneps

—arrives in Geneva a great satisfaction because the people here take tea
—and who have a very much estimable government
—and the 3rd day takes chamomile tea he has brought with him in order to drive out his humors.
—From his hotel window Lord Turneps watches a large troop marching with a flag and he rings to ask what it is.
—The waiter tells Lord Turneps that it is simply some radicals [crossed out: being led to their popular meeting because they] who are persuaded that they are the people of Geneva so that they are taken to a barn to talk about politics, administration, and government.
—Lord Turneps finds the idea very foolish [this word in English] and decides to go and watch.
—And the 4th day, he leaves for Chamonix

Notes and References

Notes to Individual Comic Strips

Page numbers refer to book pages of this edition.

STORY OF MR. JABOT

p. 3 "Jabot": as a noun, shirt-frill; "jaboter" = to jabber.

p. 5 "Go little book . . . ": This is a spiced version of a traditional literary farewell, found in Chaucer, Spenser, and Southey, among others.

p. 7 "Belgian affairs": In 1830 Belgium broke away from the kingdom of the Netherlands to which it had been joined since 1815. Some copies of the Parisian plagiary (see below), finding this reference too controversial, change it to "affairs in the East."

p. 11 The *Journal des Débats* was an official French newspaper. "L'autocrate": presumably King Charles X, dethroned in the July 1830 revolution.

p. 26 "entrechat": a difficult crisscrossing of the legs in the air, normally associated with classical, professional dance, not a social quadrille as here. Jabot is, of course, showing off. "Posomby" is an English name (for Ponsonby).

p. 28 Pun on "galope" and "galopin," which means "scamp." Forgive my version.

p. 29 "Tory": British conservative party.

p. 55 Partitives: the "de" in French connotes nobility.

Jabot is a satire on the social upstart, a type in which nineteenth-century life and literature abounds. He is the typical upwardly striving petty bourgeois, probably from a family in trade. (His cousin, whom he rejects, is a haberdasher). This type, as a readily understood butt of literary satire, made a relatively safe debut for Töpffer in the picture story and was much appreciated by Goethe. Politically conservative, Jabot is probably moneyed, which would make him attractive to a presumably destitute, widowed aristocrat. His tasseled knee-breeches, at a time when gentlemen generally wore trousers, define him as old-fashioned but his wasp-waist and padded chest is that of the corseted dandy of the period. Note that he is the only figure caricatured.

There is an element of self-persiflage here, for Töpffer characterized himself as a Jabot strutting around with a copy in his pocket of Goethe's *Kunst und Alterthum* praising his work. Several years before, about the time he started his school (1824), Töpffer wrote a verse satire on the social climber called *Les Pots*, set very much in the Genevan milieu (never published, for fear of repercussions; excerpts in Blondel and Mirabaud, pp. 34–36). His farces, also unpublished, notably *Les Grimpions* (*The Upstarts*, 1829), are full of the type.

The first part of *Jabot* is a relatively conventional, farcical account of his adventures at a ball, always the test of social presence; the second part offers an escalating chain of truly Töpfferian absurdity. The subsequent albums will fuse the two humorous modes, old and new.

MANUSCRIPT ALBUMS

MAH, ms suppl. 1198, no. 57 (1910—171 53A). Paper size 10.5 x 17 cm. 154 scenes on 112 numbered pages. Starts with two pages of doodled figures and profiles. Manuscript title page virtually the same as published, but where the latter starts "go little book . . . " RT puts his habitual warning, "You are requested not to dirty or crumple the pages." Followed by "started 29 January and finished 5 February 1831," and three illegible words (the first ending "–phié," the last "plume" or "plusr" ("plusieurs").

This is the shortest of Töpffer's picture stories, written in the smallest album, one row of mostly two to three scenes per page, the scenes numbered (probably later) at the top right hand corner of each page, 2–154, the captions often squeezed in awkwardly, clearly written after the drawings. The leaving blank of the ninth and thirteenth pages of the story with only the injunction "Turn the pages without dirtying or crumpling them, please" indicates that the first eighteen drawings were done in one session, and the next three in another, and handed over each time to the curious. On the endpaper are thirteen lines of notes filling most of the page, apparently made when the author proceeded to lithography, crossing out the scenes as he redid them.

Album in collection of Marianne Gouraty, New York, since 1980. It is my belief that this newly discovered manuscript is in RT's hand and done in preparation for the lithographed edition of 1833, to which it is very similar, with significant small changes (mostly to correct small errors and to make small improvements), with just one page considerably changed for the general distribution of 1835, not used then, but inserted in later editions (Kessmann and Garnier). I hope to put my arguments in a future *Bulletin de la Société d' Etudes Topffériennes*.

LITHOGRAPHIC EDITION

Geneva, 1833. The only one of Töpffer's albums to be printed on just one side of the paper. A very small distribution was made among friends that year, but further dissemination was delayed, despite Goethe's imprimatur of 1832, on the advice of his friends, and not released to general distribution (of 800 copies printed) until 1835, after he was tenured as professor at the Academy. There are almost exactly the same number of drawings (153 to 154 of manuscript) and few changes of any substance. Over half the manuscript page layouts (1833 ed., pp. 24–52) are preserved.

The only significant difference vis-à-vis the manuscript album (apart perhaps for the change of the name of the écarté-playing baron from Derlighighectigt to Baron de la Canardière) is the reduction in farting. RT replaced a broad scene (manuscript scene #29; see Appendix A, p. 584) of dancers holding their noses and looking askance at the culprit, to the caption "Mr. Jabot having suffered a misfortune; a slight cloud compromises his success," with two narrow scenes of Jabot trying to make agreeable conversation with his partner. Later he cut scene #58 of servants opening the windows, as a result of the "unpleasant interruption" at which "everyone demands air! Air! Quickly, air —Mr. Jabot promises himself to change his diet the next day." But RT kept the "private" fart emitted by Jabot on getting into bed (1833 ed., p. 29). The English plagiary changed even this from "a little noise emitted from behind" to "a noise as of thieves," and prudish to the hilt, translated "culotte" (underpants) as "inexpressibles" (1833 ed., p. 45).

The surviving "private" fart may have caused problems among the "bégueules" (prudes) in notoriously prudish England, where (according to a letter of 8 July 1836) he was encouraging a correspondent in England to facilitate the entrée there of his "dear child." The author wrote a friend that he actually printed the original scene of the fart at the dance and then removed it, "but I keep for you a copy of this abominable variant" (repr. our p. 582).

The correspondence reveals details of a delay and a quarrel with the printer, who spoiled pages, and indications of an intention to print more copies in 1834. The author was however determined not to allow copies to circulate or go on sale prematurely (probably before mid-October 1835), that is before his nomination to the academy professorship was confirmed. By January 1839 stocks of the album were running out, and he was planning a second edition, which never materialized. Nor did the idea of doing a woodcut version, mooted later (letter of 10 May 1845 to Dubochet).

REVIEW-ADVERTISEMENTS

Eighteen months after it went on sale, Töpffer placed a semi-laudatory, semi-deprecatory review-advertisement for *Jabot*, stressing its peculiar "mixed" character, in *La Bibliothèque Universelle de Genève*, the magazine he helped edit, for June 1837 (pp. 334–37; extract in Blondel and Mirabaud, p. 376). There was another announcement in the same magazine April 1839 (pp. 342–43).

PLAGIARIES

Le Charivari, 27 February 1839. The idea of a continuation after this one page of reproductions of the first drawings was evidently substituted by that of complete lithographic reproduction of the album, by the same publisher: *Histoire de Mr. Jabot*, Paris, chez Aubert, Place de la Bourse (or Galerie Véro-Dodat). In April 1839 (*La Bibliothèque Universelle de Genève*, pp. 342–43) Töpffer complained about the piracy which he found "gloomy," and the drawings, "sadly faithful and scrupulously ponderous." He also notes that the piracy truncated his story and transposed the drawings, rendering it unintelligible in those places. According to Cailler (*Caricatures*, vol. 11, p. 60) seventeen drawings were omitted, but in later printings replaced, giving the full complement. I have not seen this truncated edition. The complete one has fifty-two pages in the same pagination as the original. Aubert's draftsman has updated the women's costume, Paris style, and reversed all the designs, except in scenes on pages 10, 16, 17, 19, 25, and 32, in order to preserve right-handedness in dancing and dueling; the first two scenes of page 7 are printed in reverse order. RT's failure of continuity, the lack of a necklace on Mlle. du Bocage on pages 9 and 11, is corrected. On page 41 the reversal loses Töpffer's frame line functioning as a wall with a door through which Marquise spies on Jabot. The captions are calligraphed, as in normal lithography.

The Comical Adventures of Beau Ogleby, London, Tilt and Bogue [1842]. Copied (traced) from, and in same reversed direction as, the Aubert edition. The new title page with figures from the story surrounding the title, and possibly the whole copy, is by Robert Cruikshank, whose more famous brother George co-financed it.

As usual with the plagiaries, RT's broken and wavering contours and frame lines are straightened out and made continuous. The amusing refrain "Mr. Jabot thinks it proper" is omitted. Worse is the normalization of the inanity of Ogleby's conversation about the loss of his life and worst of all that of the inanity of his love-letters, and many jokes, one of which involves a deliberate change in the drawing: the Marquise ("Miss Pruder") closing only one eye to sleep (this however via Aubert, 42). There is altogether a great loss in the verbal parodic flavor, especially of pseudo-aristocratic elegance (Alphonse *du* Jabot" becomes simply "Timothy Jabot"), and a banalization of verbal subtleties. A whole level of social satire, in which the Marquise never rises above the denomination "Miss Pruder" and "Suzanne Pruder," is dissipated.

OPERA

See Roger Vuataz, *Monsieur Jabot*, 1958. Opéra bouffe en un acte. Livret de George Hofmann, d'après un album de Rodolphe Töpffer et Musique de Roger Vuataz Op. 100-1857. (BPU, Ib 3659). Omits dogs and duels.

MR. CRÉPIN

p. 59 "Crépin" (Crispin): many verbal associations, none obviously relevant to the role.

p. 60 "Craniose:" from crâne, skull. "Bonichon": "boniche" is slang for maidservant, skivvy. "Fadet": "fade" means dull, ill or drunk; "fadaise" means nonsense. "Pécrin": anagram of Crépin.

p. 61 "travels": Manuscript has "exile," a political touch removed.

p. 79 "*Adventures of Telemachus*" (1699): a very moralistic novel and ever-popular schoolroom classic by Fénélon, and a youthful favorite of RT. "Jacotot": Joseph Jacotot invented a method of universal instruction, to the slogan "All is in All," promoting rote learning and the transference of principles, ideas, and facts from one domain to an entirely different one.

p. 81 "Ecole Polytechnique": elite science school founded 1794 in Paris, still in existence under this name.

p. 83 "sorites": argument where propositions have predicates forming the subject of the next, and the conclusion unites the subject of the first with the predicate of the last.

p. 105 "Chiffon": chiffonnier, ragpicker. "Gagneprin": gagne-pain, bread-winner.

p. 115 "balances": Oddly, this word ("équilibre") replaces "combat" (struggles against) crossed out in the manuscript, but "combat" appears in the printed version. For once, I have kept the manuscript thought.

p. 117 "duck-egg, quacks": for "ventilateur" and "fumistes," a pun on the idea of a smoking ventilator, "fumiste" also meaning a humbug or cheat, like the phrenologist himself.

p. 127 "[Passing by] Berg[en]-op-Zoom": a town in Holland. I have supplied the words in brackets, missing in most editions old and new, from the 1860 edition.

p. 129 "Gribouille": fool, scribbler.

p. 130 "Danaides": in classical mythology, the fifty (or more) daughters of Danaus, destined to marry the sons of Aegyptus. The theme, popular in opera, presumably required much crowding on the stage. RT saw in Paris *Les Petites Danaides ou les 99 victimes* (1819).

p. 133 "Parpaillozzi": "parpaillot," pejorative for Calvinist (plus "Pestalozzi," see below).

p. 134 "Bonnefoi": good faith.
p. 137 Dog smuggler: as in reality.
p. 141 "Péclot": "Péclotier" is a Genevan pejorative for clockmaker. "killer of eighty-nine": The reference is the popular civil disturbance of January 1789 in Geneva, where a few people were killed over increase in the price of bread.

This is, with *Albert*, the most serious of Töpffer's comic picture stories, and text-heavy at times. The irrelevant comic episode with the Pécrin poultice may be seen as an attempt to mitigate this seriousness, while another brief irrelevant episode in the manuscript, that of the Pétuble fleas (see Appendix A, pp. 585–86), was cut, perhaps for its vulgarity. (The superior's fart in the manuscript, from which the Crépin boys are trained to divert attention by looking out of the window, becomes a sneeze of Mr. Crépin into his soup, p. 93). Beginning with the farcical antics of the Crépin boys, which may be read as little more than the natural exuberance and the mischievousness of the very young exacerbated by neglect and indulgence, the story quickly takes on vulnerable satiric targets: first on various fraudulent educational methods, including social etiquette as a militaristic and mechanical exercise; and finally on the fashionable pseudo-science and popular entertainment known as phrenology, or craniology, that is, the reading of an individual's character from the bumps on or shape of the skull, which entered new, European-wide spasms of popularity in the 1830s.

As an educator himself, and one averse to new-fangled theory at a time when Geneva, like most countries, was itself debating all kinds of educational reform, Töpffer takes issue with leading new educational systems and pedagogues of the period. The name Parpaillozzi (actually, scarcely satirized here) evokes Pestalozzi, perhaps the single most famous Swiss whose name has endured in history, and Farcet (farce means joke) is clearly Fröbel, whose name is still attached to a kind of school that emphasizes play in early years. The highly authoritarian pedagogue and agronomist Emmanuel von Fellenberg of Berne, under attack already in the caricatures of RT's father, was not amused; other humorless pedagogues were also offended.

Having himself risen above the dim prospect of becoming a private tutor and recognizing that this type, associated with rich and aristocratic families, was historically doomed in a more democratic age, and with his own private school thriving, Töpffer has no compunction about introducing Mr. Bonnefoi (Mr. Goodfaith) as an alter ego, one who spurns systems and applies common sense in a small private school—one can count just thirty-six heads on p. 134, exactly the median size of the Pension Töpffer.

The interpolation at the end of an episode featuring the murder of the customs officer, and phrenological theory justifying the exoneration of the murderer, may be read as reflecting the author's concern that determinist social theories were vitiating ideas of free will and personal moral responsibility. The episode also tries to discredit arguments in favor of abolition of the death penalty, which was hardly carried out in Geneva anyway, but much in France. The application of phrenological theory to criminology lay in the future, with Cesare Lombroso. With the "Great Palpator" Töpffer intuits the totalitarian tendency of much science and education, then as now.

MANUSCRIPT

MAH, 1910—176, 53. F. At 22.5 x 30 cm, the largest of the manuscript albums, with 177 drawings for the story, a total noted at the very end, on thirty-seven pages, with author's initials and the date 1837. The drawings are arranged in two rows on each page, larger than usual and thus close in scale to the printed version. The front endpaper has some very brief content notes, starting in pencil and then in ink. The first page, preceding a page with four pairs of drawings showing a peasant with a flail threatening, attacking, and triumphing over a bourgeois type, and following the usual preface as printed, contains the following, the longest of such admonitions, in slightly different handwriting, evidently added later:

> Said story belongs to Mr. R.T., who strongly advises the persons to whom he has the pleasure of lending it, to turn the pages by the edge. You can see just as well, and the book stays clean and in good condition.
>
> But there are, says La Bruyère, "people who are both interested and negligent, and imagine that a thing has been made to be used only once, that once that they are using it. Lend these people a drawing made on a clean, white page, and they will return it to you in no time crumpled and dirty, so that although they admire the work, and thank you for the pleasure, internally you send them packing."
>
> ch. IV, line 17.

The attribution to the classic French seventeenth-century moralist is certainly fanciful, and the corrections in the original show he was not copying the passage out, but it may be observed that (by coincidence?) the fourth chapter in La Bruyère's version of Theophrastus from his famous *Caractères* concerns vulgar, thoughtless behavior.

The compositions and captions are in almost all cases identical or very close to the printed version. Two groups of three scenes each, originally placed between pages 67 and 68, and between 70 and 71, introducing a new, irrelevant character called Madame Pétuble ("pétufle" = Genevan for a sausage skin), who catches fleas from Craniose, are omitted (see Appendix A, pp. 585–86). The amusing bathos of "[the bump of] paternitivity" as associated with "those who gave buns to their children" yields to a more conventional "knowledge . . . man of learning" (1837 ed., p. 53).

PUBLISHED EDITION

Mr. Crépin, autographié chez Frutiger, à Genève, 1837, signed only at end, R.T. Printed in 500 copies. 171 drawings.

ATTEMPTED SEQUEL

According to a letter to his wife, Kity, of 11 July 1843, written from Lavey where he was taking a cure, RT amused fellow patients with a series of drawings showing "Crépin at Lavey." There were at least five: "The Source," "At the Bath," "In Bed," "Taking Coffee," and "Playing Whist." He gave away other drawings which were much appreciated, including "Monsieur Crépin Tormented by Flies."

PLAGIARY

Mr. Crépin, chez Aubert, galerie Véro-Dodat, Paris 1839. The copyist, who must have traced the drawings and is very accurate in preserving facial expressions, is evidently, from the shading, left-handed. He adds a touch of official illiteracy, with DOUAN ROYALE for Töpffer's correct "douane" (1837 ed., p. 28). Some linguistic refrains, so characteristic of Töpffer, are removed as redundant. The impinging captions on pages 52 and 78 of the 1837 edition are "corrected." The crude shop sign of the tinker on page 67, the rough hand-lettering of which RT has realistically imitated, quite wrongly imitates three different typographic fonts. On the final page, Töpffer's caption, happily waving in concert with the proposal of a toast, is straightened.

TRANSLATION

Eppie Wiese translated, edited, and provided an introduction to *Enter: The Comics: Rodolphe Töpffer's Essay on Physiognomy and The True Story of Monsieur Crépin*, Lincoln: University of Nebraska Press, 1965. The rather free translation is of the manuscript version, on a much reduced reproduction of the drawings, which are unfortunately sometimes cropped in order to make room for the English captions. I have often taken advantage of Wiese's wording in my translation, and some of her references in these notes.

MR. VIEUX BOIS

p. 164 Scene and caption were added in the 1839 edition. The French caption "ayant feint de feindre, afin de mieux dissimuler" has achieved a certain proverbial status, having been cited recently in both Parisian and Genevan national assemblies. It is used by RT in a letter of 1830 (Droin, vol. 2, p. 386). "Mr. Vieux Bois sur un arbre perché," with its poetic inversion, recalls Fable 2 in Book 1 of La Fontaine, "Maître Corbeau sur un arbre perché . . . "

pp. 211–14 "Thyrsis": a shepherd in Virgil.

The fanatical pursuit of a Beloved Object, a Rival, the duel, unjust incarceration and hair-raising escape, abductions, persecution by superstitious, murderous monks, repeated suicide attempts, highway robbery, resuscitation from the dead, a ghost, the pastoral interlude, excesses of emotional self-indulgence, plus the sheer implausibility and bizarre coincidences of the narrative twists—all this parodies clichés of romantic fiction and the Gothic novel in particular. The namelessness and morose supineness of the Beloved Object, comic in itself (how on earth could such a supine creature inspire such heroic passion?) seems to mock the very concept of irrational romantic love and the helplessness of heroines. Töpffer's hostility to monks as idle and dirty is well attested in his *Voyages en Zigzag*.

MANUSCRIPT

MAH, recently acquired, BA 2002—51D, 17 x 28.5 cm. On a slip of paper pasted into the album, "croquis par, et à R. Töpffer—1827." The earliest of Töpffer's drafts. Dark brown ink, with faint pencil numbering of the scenes on many pages. The album opens on the upper part of the page with two unrelated drawings of a traveler encountering the ghosts of his ancestors, before passing directly, via the title "Histoire de Mr. Vieux Bois" to the first three drawings for the story, as if in doing so the author had at first no idea he would develop it at length. The scenes are arranged in two rows per page, with the captions generally written rather tight above, indicating he wrote them after the drawings were done.

The 1827 manuscript has 156 drawings on thirty pages; the 1837 edition (and the Aubert plagiary) has 198 drawings on eighty-eight pages, and the 1839 edition has 221 drawings on ninety-two pages.

LITHOGRAPHIC EDITIONS

Les Amours de Mr. Vieux Bois first edition, Geneva: Frutiger, 1837. According to a letter to Monvert of 18 February (BPU Te 1293), the printing was almost ready, but according to a letter to the same correspondent of 18 May, held up ("au crochet") because of a missing page. Meanwhile, RT was anxious for advance orders. On 28 June his friend and translator Heinrich Zschokke was writing to tell him that "M. Vieuxbois [sic] surrounded by his funny fellows ["bamboccioli"], made us faint with laughter," followed by a long eulogy. By May 1838 (Gautier, no. 33, p. 85), "the pile is almost gone," and the same in a letter of 23 January 1839 (Gautier, no. 95, p. 223).

There was an alternative title page/preface with Vieux Bois seated on rock, gazing at the Beloved Object, while a monk creeps up from the other side and is barked at by a little dog (see Kunzle, 2007, p. 125).

Second edition, 1939. RT engaged in a second edition after he saw that the first had been plagiarized by Aubert in Paris, and his stock of the first edition was exhausted (letter to Monvert, 23 June 1839). He is justified in his claim that "Cette édition présente des changements et des augmentations considérables" (Cailler, *Caricatures*, 4, notes [unattributed]).

We compare primarily the 1837 and 1839 editions, with note of a few differences from the 1827 manuscript. Landscape and background effects are heightened consistently through the three versions. In the 1839 preface page, a crowd of spectator figures is added pressing spookily on the banner-holder, isolated in 1837.

Among the significant improvements and additions: the gamut of burgeoning suspicion (1839 ed., pp. 6–7) much extended in 1839 from 1837, replacing an episode of Vieux Bois trying to drown himself 1827; in 1839 he also added a full-width "splash" page detailing chaos caused to civilians as well as military (p. 10, entirely missing in 1827); also the beam yanking Vieux Bois backwards (p. 12), which renders better the sudden impact repeated in the next scene where the frame line now goes into sudden squiggles. Here, as elsewhere, RT benefits from greater width of scene, consistently 1:1.9, where in 1837, 1:1.6.

The duel on page 18 (1839 ed.) has the sword pass under the Rival's arm, followed by a scene of the Rival resuscitating, absent in 1837, where both swords merely cross through Rival's hat hovering in the air between them. On page 20 we now see only the top of Vieux Bois's face peering over the jail door, where before he was visible to the waist through the bars: less is more, and more pathetic. The landscape on page 22 is more distant and wilder, and omits the brigands' guns poking from bushes of 1837, and brigands' bodies visible in 1827. Vieux Bois shows greater despair in the cave (p. 23). Vieux Bois sitting in his monastic jail (p. 24) loses the companionship of his dog, replaced by a water jug. A comic moment is added, of a traveler (a brigand who robbed him earlier and acquired his clothes) romantically accosting and dining him as an available female (p. 25). An allegorical bouquet is delivered to a very morose Beloved Object (p. 30), and there are increased bunches of excited monks at the recapture of Vieux Bois and Beloved Object (p. 31). The courtroom, and Vieux Bois's subsequent emotional peroration is much extended from 1837 which is in turn much extended from 1827, in rivalry perhaps with Daumier, the design of whose now-famous *Ventre Législatif* (1834, see Kunzle, 2007, p. 69) underlies the (increased) sweeping view of bored and somnolent judges (p. 41).

There is a major increase (from five to seven pages) in the dunking of the Rival in the river, intercut with the pastoral pleasures of Vieux Bois. On page 74

Vieux Bois, instead of simply leading his mule by the reins, has his arm affectionately on the Beloved Object's lap, fondles her hand, and looks up in adoration at her ever-morose face. In the mêlée between Vieux Bois and the monks (p. 77), the hero's mule kicks a monk high into air. More monks, more excitement.

Fashion note: skirts are a couple of ankle-revealing inches shorter in 1839 than 1837, on all four ladies visible at Vieux Bois's wedding (p. 92).

NOTES

Notes for a continuation (prequel? merger?), overtaken by *Cryptogame*? MS Suppl. 1256 env. 5, pp. 1–2.

"[p. 1] Story of Mr. Vieux Bois and the Beloved Object. Join this Story to the best of Criptogame . . . This remarkable man was born under the sign. . . .

[p. 2] At the age of forty-five years Mr. Vieux Bois has been strolling in public for two and a half hours and in his own company, and begins to feel a bit fatigued in the legs.

[added later in a different handwriting]

Sudden passions much more common formerly than nowadays. Specifically I know of no lover who suffered more setbacks and who triumphed over the obstacles arising from his ardor with a more praiseworthy presence of mind and courage.

Two quite distinct parts may be observed in the life of Mr. Vieux Bois, well known at the time. One where he flees a woman who adores him excessively, and the other where he pursues a woman who adores him with a moderation most rare in a lover, if one can suppose her impassioned."

PLAGIARIES

French plagiary of 1837 edition. Same title and same text of preface page, retaining (remarkably) initials RT, Chez Aubert Galerie Véro Dodat, 1839, pages numbered 1–84. Töpffer's "U" in the title is rendered virtually as an "I" so that "Vieix Bois" appears in major library catalogues. The plagiary is mentioned in a letter to RT from Mlle. d'Angeville of 11 April 1839. RT himself characterized it as "pitoyablement véridique, la chose moins la chose" (pitiably truthful, the thing without the thing), and thought (hoped) that his own album at 15 francs (usually 10) would be found cheaper than the Paris version at 6 francs.

This is a plain, literal copy, in the same direction and the same medium (transfer lithograph) with a correspondence too close not to point to careful tracing, scene by scene, with frames ruled straight and captions calligraphed. There is a careless transposition of scenes on page 49 (1839 ed., p. 52).

English plagiary of 1837 edition. *The Adventures of Mr. Obadiah Oldbuck, wherein are duly set forth the crosses, chagrins, calamities, checks, chills and circumgirations by which his courtship was attended. Showing also, the issue of his suit and his espousal to his ladye-love*, London: Tilt and Bogue. Hoone's gypsography, 1842. Pages numbered 1–80. The title page, an original composition with various figures taken from the story, and the title held as a banner by an official-looking person, is by Robert or George Cruikshank.

The English captions are typographic, as in a woodcut version, but the compositions are in the same direction. The retention here of the Aubert transposition of scenes on page 49 (1839 ed., p. 52) proves what would otherwise be hard to determine, that this copy was made from Aubert's. It is however much more free (not traced) and shows stylistic variations, especially in the treatment of background, testifying to the collaboration of several hands. The Tilt and Bogue craftsmen tended to fill in the facial ellipses of RT respected by Aubert's version.

Some of the often free translations of the captions exhibit a certain ingenuity of their own, e.g., "Mr. Oldbuck turns over a new leaf" for "Mr. Vieux Bois changes his shirt"; and "he returns to life dying of hunger" (p. 6).

The English plagiary was reviewed in *The Gentleman's Magazine* for January 1842 (p. 73), as copied from a work by a "French artist," referring presumably to the Töpffer original, not the Aubert, since he says, "Such merit as they [the absurdities] had, however, in the original Vieux-Bois, has we think pretty well evaporated in the transcription; besides which, the adventures are chiefly peculiar to continental habits, and do not suit the English name. It would have been better to have called it, the New Munchausen."

U.S. plagiary. *The Adventures of Mr. Obadiah Oldbuck*, with the subtitle as above. Published by Wilson & Company in New York, 14 September 1842, as a supplement to *Brother Jonathan* (Extra, no. IX), and advertised as printed from the "English plates of the original," and (the whole thing) "got up on an entirely original plan" (see *New York Times*, 3 September 1904, p. 598, under "Queries"). The captions are however reset. Another version of the subtitle runs "Wherein are set forth the Curious, Comical, Despairing, Disastrous, Extraordinary, extravagant, funny, farsical [sic], lively, Lackadaisical, Pathetical and Perplexing INCIDENTS by which his courtship was attended. Showing also the issue of his suit and his espousal to his ladye-Love." A new printing from Wilson appeared in 1849.

The same English source was used by Dick and Fitzgerald, also of New York, also in 1849, in an edition reissued 185–? and 186–?, with a variant subtitle starting "Wherein are set forth his unconquerable passion . . ."

Dutch plagiary. *De wonderbaarlijke lotgevallen van Jubal Jubelslee* . . . , with Dutch rhymes by Gerrit Komrij, Amsterdam 1975, based on the original 1839 edition.

PLAY

Alfred Jarry, *L'Objet Aimé*. Pastorale en un acte (Arcanes, Paris 1953, note de Roger Shattuck). This avatar of the theater of the absurd (preceded by Jarry's better known *Ubu Roi* in 1896) was composed in 1903 and published in 1908, under the title *L'Objet Aimé, le premier suicide de Mr. Vieuxbois* [sic], *d'après Töpffer*. It indulges in word-play and nonsense in the spirit of Töpffer. Elsewhere Jarry also used *Dr. Festus* (as Faustroll).

A SERIES OF DRAWINGS ON CARDS

BPU Suzannet 112, where designated "premier essai" and accepted as such by Cailler (*Caricatures*, vol. 11, p. 66, 28B). 156 pen drawings mounted on as many cards copying (tracing?) exactly the 156 drawings of the 1827 manuscript. Each drawing is numbered (in the manuscript album numbers appear intermittently). The captions are copied below the drawings, while in the manuscript album they were written above each scene. Frame lines are given intermittently, then consistently from #74. The writing appears to be Töpffer's, although rather less legible and more hasty, as if written only for himself, and for a further transcription. The following drawings, and no others, appear reversed: #39, #43, #46, #54.

Numerous small changes and errors (of haste), and corrections to the captions which another copyist would not make, are evidence for these drawings being by Töpffer's own hand. The only compositional change is prompted by a shortening of the panel (#133).

ANIMATED FILM

Mr. Vieux Bois et l'objet aimé, by the Frenchmen Lortac and Cavé, 1921, said to be 700 metres, 35,000 drawings, and 45 minutes long, technically more paper cut-out than animation proper. Shown locally through 1930s, as pre-main feature and separated into three segments. RT was hailed in 1920 by Jean Choux as precursor of the cinema (*Bulletin de la Société d' Etudes Topffériennes*, no. 34, October 2004, pp. 2–3, with bibliography).

MR. PENCIL

p. 242 I have throughout used "the Professor" to designate a man of learning (but not necessarily one attached to a university), as the best equivalent for the (unnamed) "le Docteur," since "the doctor" in English suggests a medical man. The "mad professor" has of course a resplendent future ahead of him in the comic strip.

p. 268 "The Five Powers": Britain, France, Prussia, Austria and Russia, who dominated European affairs.

p. 269 "National Guard": volunteer police recruited from the middle classes in France, especially Paris.

p. 271 Some equivalents: "Goldsax" for "Mondor" (also mondain = worldly); "Pibroch" or "bagpipe" for "Pibrac"; "Bell" for "Grelot"; "Truffler" for "Truffet" (also truffe = idiot); "Cleansweep" for "Raffle." "Occupy Belgium": In 1815 Belgium was joined by the allies after the fall of Napoleon to Holland as the kingdom of the Netherlands; in 1830 it broke away with international support. "Saint Simonian": follower of social philosopher Henri de Saint Simon (1760–1825), founder of French socialism. "To each according to his capacity." was a slogan associated with him.

p. 293 "God Save the King": for the "Henri Quatre," a French song in favor of the legitimist Bourbon line, thus anti-Orleanist King Louis-Philippe as well as anti-republican.

p. 295 "Polish song": song supporting the liberation of Poland from Russia. "Beast of Gévaudan": In the years 1764–1766 wolves (or a wolf, and/or possibly an escaped hyena) ravaged the Gévaudan in southern France, killing an estimated one hundred or more people, mostly women and children, causing widespread terror, and giving rise to an enduring legend. Töpffer who liked to mock Catholic superstition may be here thinking also of the local bishop at the time, who characterized the beast as one sent by God as a punishment for sin. The Beast has a considerable literature, representation today in all media, and a website. Best historical documentation: Guy Crouzet in several editions, the latest called *La Grande Peur du Gévaudan* (2003).

p. 297 "Cholera" (see below).

In this (with *Albert*) most overtly political of Töpffer's stories (first version sketched March–July 1831), the motivating political force is that social and political stability can easily be thrown into chaos and slip willy nilly into a possible European war. Töpffer was sharing the general disillusion with the French Revolution of July 1830 and its aftermath, and reacting to the dangers, absurdities, and injustices of the new government which were richly represented in caricatures (by Daumier and others) in the relatively uncensored years 1830–1835. RT must have known these. In the manuscript he added a note (in 1840) to specify the date 1831 of the "political business," which does not appear in the printed version, as superfluous and derogating from the idea of a historically generalized madness. There were mild echoing disturbances in Switzerland, especially nearby Neuchatel and Lausanne 1830–1831, with which, together with the more serious ones in France, Töpffer claimed to be thoroughly fed up ("indijectionné" is the word he invents). *Pencil* balances and intertwines the idea of political chaos with that of personal flights of artistic fancy, against which politics and perhaps even "reality" itself intrudes, while the album also embraces and conjures the caprices of fate as a kind of superior reality.

Monsieur Pencil represents Töpffer himself, the author-artist whose capricious imagination (symbolized by a little zephyr playing with a sketch) gives the first shake to the kaleidoscope of adventure. Although Pencil intervenes "authorially" at the end to straighten out the tangle, he is in fact the progenitor, rather than recorder, much less editor, of a self-propelled fantasy that imbibes sketch paper and human bodies alike, willfully suspending gravity and disbelief before finally letting all down to earth again. The return to the real and wider social world was decided only in the final version, which ends on the telegraph poles, agents of social commotion become emblems of social peace. This peace was a celebration of the relative peace enjoyed by Geneva, before the civil commotions starting the following year.

The episode of worker distress (p. 271) reflects RT's short-lived "democratic" sympathy or at least respect for the travails of the French, if not Genevan, working class (there were great upheavals in Lyons 1831 and 1834), retained from his liberal period up to around 1830. His satire on a destructive and stupid military is traditional to caricature and grows out of his Genevan-republican suspicion of neighboring absolutist states. The sympathy for the simple decent peasant (George Luçon = Clare) is quite exceptional at the time in caricature, possibly very Swiss. The telegraph malfunction precipitating a war crisis stands as a metaphor of RT's resistance to scientific progress in general, and his sense that a highly strung political system was apt to overreact to false alarms. The cholera scare, which had only just started in 1831 when RT was sketching *Pencil*, did not actually hit Paris, where the epidemic was terrible, until May 1832, and it never reached Geneva. Cholera was widely associated with the political disease of socialism and revolution. Geneva would be shaken by serious political passions the year after *Pencil* came out, and undergo a real political revolution a few months after RT's premature death in 1846.

MANUSCRIPT

MAH 1910—173, No. 53C and 53C.2, occupying most of two albums (carnets) of forty-three leaves each. 14 x 24 cm. The first page contains doodles of faces and figures.

The albums themselves were ready drawn, if not finished, and available to his schoolboys and presumably friends and family in the summer of 1831, to judge by the preface complaint which is dated 31 August. The first sentence of this reads as printed. The second starts with the phrase "Le tout mêlé aux affaires du temps présent" ("All mixed with the affairs of our times") which is changed to "drôleries du temps présent" ("fun of our present times"), as a decoy from the author's latent seriousness of intent. Instead of continuing with the usual envoi ("go little book . . . ") Töpffer writes:

> Which history, certified truthful, contains good teachings, within the reach of those who are jovial by nature and love to laugh without worrying too much what about; which is a more certain sign of contentment in this world than any I know.
>
> And this book will be lent initially most willingly to all persons who request it, on the sole condition to return it as clean and spotless and free of all dirt and crumpling as they received it.
>
> There is indeed nothing so foolish, in my opinion, as borrowing in order to set about stupidly marking and soiling these pages that the author scribbled carefully and cleanly. Some however make a practice of it, imagining that they have been given a nice white margin to wipe or wrap their thumbs on: which people I instantly invite to lend me some linen, a shirt, a cotton cap, that my laundress can restore, but not a book which, once dirtied, cannot be undirtied.
>
> I wrote these things the thirty-first day of August, the year of grace eighteen thirty-one.

RT left the manuscript unfinished on the flight of the sanitary officers and the hospital patients from the Cholera Morbus in person (i.e. Mr. Jolibois, escaped from his crate [1840 ed., p. 65]); the Professor recognizing his Psychiot; Madame Jolibois and her husband; and Pencil sketching the whole scene, all from a window; the police arriving; and finally the distressed Jolibois seated, perhaps in jail. This figure the author (subsequently?) surrounded with notes for a quick ending. Spread over several pages at the end of the second album are various sets of such notes for a conclusion, which evidently caused the author some perplexity, and their chronology is not certain. At one point he considered the (unfortunate) idea of having Mr. Pencil take up the maid's plan to sell the recaptured Mr. Jolibois, who had become uncontrollable in his cage, offering two écus including cage for him. On a page with notes for scenes he finally used, he appended reminders to bring back Luçon (and, on another page, the heirs of Captain Ricard), and have the little Zephyr give Pencil back his drawing after having carried it around the world.

The manuscripts show that RT decided when he came to revise the whole, to keep more or less intact all the ideas represented in the first thirty-nine drawings, spread over ten pages, for on the blank page opposite the eleventh he began to make notes for changes (both albums are drawn on the right hand pages only). He kept making such notes after every two, and then three and again two pages, discontinuing the notes only where large cuts were made and the drawings marked "remove" or "skip." At the end of the first sketchbook, and the 157th drawing, there appear notes on the right hand page and in different handwritings suggesting they were written at different times, for a continuation which would introduce an (English) Milord buying the artist's drawing and the Zephyr arranging a reunion of characters in a haystack beyond (?) what appears in scene #70. RT also thought of cutting out Mr. Pencil at the start, leaving just the playing of the Zephyr. This he fortunately did not do. In the second album, he continued the practice of making notes, on the opposite page, after every two or three pages. After some blank pages in the first carnet, before the preface, there is a sheet of scribbles of faces and figures, including one of Mr. Pencil sketching.

At the end of the second carnet, among more notes for a conclusion, there are two pages with large drawings of a whale, and a tree. All the pages of the story carry at the top right corner the number of the scene, accurately totalized, presumably done in 1840 as a guide to the revision.

LITHOGRAPHIC EDITION

Librairie Abraham Cherbuliez, Paris, lithography Schmid, Geneva 1840.

The new drawings, totaling 219 (including title pages) were just finished on 8 May 1840, and (with *Festus*) fully printed by 4 July, ready for shipment to Paris. A date for the printing may be derived from a page of cost calculations at the beginning of the second manuscript album, stating that on 17 June he paid to the lithographer Schmid in Geneva 1,000 francs for 800 printed copies, presumably of *Pencil*.

Major reductions from the manuscript: In the scenes of parliamentary debate and in the long captions attached, a total of twenty-four are reduced to six (scenes #93, and #99–#117 are cut). The crazy scientific theories of the windbag windologists (#76–#80) are reduced. Scenes of scientists accusing each other of farting were mitigated (#84–#85 cut). Scene #48 with a series of absurd conclusions about the Psychiot's external appearance is cut. In total, discounting a few fusions of scenes, Töpffer cut about fifty-five scenes from the manuscript, and added about thirty-five scenes.

Reduction in geographic, personal, and political specifics: RT cut location names for the operations of the telegraph—"Prussia to Berlin," "Austria to Vienna," "Russia to St Petersburgh,"—as well as references to France as the country where the story basically takes place (in manuscript scene #131 "la belle France" is to be defended by 300,000 men). He cut the use of political "Left," "Right," and "Center," current in French debate, and the allusion to "Rotchild" (sic), a figure with high-value banknotes bulging out of his pockets and debating within himself the relative profitability war and peace (#116). Scene #148 of soldiers burning a whole village was cut—as too drastic? On the other hand, Töpffer added (1840 ed., p. 27a) the specificity of the dread thought that "the politicians foresee the fatal rupture of the five powers."

Increase in graphic effects: The wonderfully cinematic intercut, syncopated sequence of the Professor writing and his specimen raging in the cage (scenes #53–#57, 1840 ed., pp. 16–17) is much extended from four to thirteen scenes. The sublime interlude of Jolibois in his crate pursuing his wife, despairing, and trying to hang himself by the arms is added (five scenes, 1840 ed., pp. 46–47), as is the same crated Jolibois climbing a tree and scaring the villagers (four scenes, 1840 ed., pp. 54–55), and later trying to escape and battling the servant from his crate (six scenes, 1840 ed., pp. 61–62).

Minor changes of significance: In scene #12 RT self-censors the "vulgarity" of showing the whole latrine with the Professor holding his fan over it. It was marked "changer" and replaced by a view of the Professor opening the door slightly to the latrine (1840 ed., p. 5). Latrine seat is cut in scene #17. Scenes #18–#19 of connoisseur rejecting as worthless Pencil's drawing, which is wrapped in a sausage and sent to M. Jolibois, are cut (marked "ôter"). In scene #45 the crude pun on "plonger" is cut. "Institut Royal" changed to "Académie Royale" throughout. The only significant change in the captions, which are sometimes simply reduced, is to the scene where the soldiers fall into a lake, to which RT considered adding "and were much drowned (or else never heard of again)"—in the final version (1840 ed., p. 48) the drawing says enough.

DR. FESTUS

Throughout I have reverted to Dr. Festus's name when he is referred to simply as "le Docteur," since "the Doctor" in English connotes a medical man.

p. 327 Eaubelle river refers to the Rhone which flows into the lake of Geneva.

p. 338 "tune of Marlborough": famous French folk-song "Malbruck s'en va' t'en guerre . . ." referring to the British duke and general who defeated Louis XIV.

p. 340 "Master Taillandier": "Sieur" is the title given to a well-propertied peasant.

p. 342 "Quiet lime": literally "thin chalk."

p. 343 "Coudras," where p. 342 has "Coudraz": example of Töpffer's haste; Coudraz is the more likely Lake-of-Genevan ending.

p. 346 "Aves": Hail Marys, Catholic prayers.

p. 357 "Vireloup": see below; name of actual village on French border with customs post.

p. 360 Illness of the King of Vireloup: This scene was cut from the 1846 Collected Edition of Kessler, no doubt for fear of offending the King of France.

p. 362 The manuscript here (scene #94) has HERSCHEL INVENIT inscribed on the telescope, after the famous astronomers, Sir John and his son. The latter was a frequent correspondent to RT's magazine, the *Bibliothèque Universelle.* It was safer not to associate him with this nonsense. "Guignard": from "guigner" ("to envy") and/or "guigne" ("ill-luck").

p. 363 "Lunard": from "lune" ("moon"; plus "lunatic"?)

p. 364 "Nébulard": from "nebulaire."

p. 365 "Mirliflis" would be Paris, and "Givernais," France, with a touch of Geneva; "straits": presumably the English Channel, since Guignard delivers his speech to the Royal Society in Rondeterre (Angleterre, England).

p. 366 In order to keep the movement from left to right, Töpffer has to show the audience from the (orator's) right, and the left eye covered.

p. 368 The scientists' wigs are symbolic of their old-fashioned, retrograde character.

p. 370 A rare pun: on "shadow" ("ombre") and "umbrage" ("ombrage").

p. 375 As his *Voyages* attest RT was always nervous about travel on water, particularly by the new steamers on Swiss lakes.

p. 376 "Astonishé": sic, Frenchified English

p. 391 "St Clochard": pun on "cloche," meaning bell, and "clochard," meaning tramp.

p. 392 "Micisispi": RT misspells "Mississippi."

I have summarized the reception of the manuscript by Goethe and some of the many and major differences between manuscript and published version in Kunzle, 2007, as well as the particular appeal to the German poet of the satire on scientific pretension. The leading scientific controversy of the day, pitting two famous naturalists against each other, was between Geoffroy de Saint-Hilaire and Georges Cuvier. Geneva was an important center for astronomical research and used astronomical observations to aid in its time-keeping, so essential to this city of watchmakers. There is no reason to suppose RT was satirizing particular Genevan astronomers or natural scientists, among whom he counted some close friends; rather, he was aiming Europe-wide at their reputation for vanity, greed, competitiveness, and gullibility, in an age of industrial enterprise that attracted charlatans as well as scientific talent.

The satire on bureaucratic fanaticism became a staple of nineteenth-century culture. The mockery of the stupidly repressive monarchical government of Vireloup (a name composed of "virulent" and "loup" meaning wolf with a touch of vireux = noxious), with its paranoid frontier control, is that of a republican, Protestant Geneva feeling itself beset by the neighboring Catholic French and Savoyard monarchies, a source also of his mockery of Catholic superstition.

MANUSCRIPT

MAH 53B 1910—172. 13.5 x 21.5 cm. Drawn in 149 scenes, arranged in one row, between one and three scenes per page, on sixty-five pages. The 1840 edition is much expanded to 213 scenes on eighty-seven pages. The manuscript album starts, after pencil notes for the story on the inside cover pages, with the usual warning about turning the pages carefully and cleanly, followed by one page of doodles, and then a page with the title, dated 14 July 1829, followed below by more warning about handling dated 9 September 1829. These are presumably the dates within which RT executed the manuscript. There are two pages of notes in pencil at the end.

The title runs: "Here follow the travels and adventures of Dr. Festus. Combyned (sic: archaic) with the misfortunes and calamities of the Mayor and the facts concerning Milord Dobleyou and his wife. All in etching, and certified true."

LITHOGRAPHIC EDITION

Librairie Abraham Cherbuliez, 1840. The major cut, a hilarious bit of cartoon farce, is reproduced here (Appendix A, pp. 587–91). There are many additions and extensions of incidents, notably those of the armed force obeying the disembodied uniform of the Mayor (1840 ed., pp. 11–13), the Mayor's bureaucratic dream (pp. 21–22), piglets born midair to the airborne sows (pp. 35–36), Festus and Taillandier taken for devils (pp. 26–27), more Mayoral suicide attempts, much increased civic chaos caused by his absence (pp. 36–40), and interpretation of the washed-up wigs (pp. 75–77). The madness of astronomer Apogee becomes a major insertion of fifteen scenes (pp. 61–67). Suicide was a primary romantic theme, as was madness. The mechanical folly of the armed force and the degeneration into social chaos recall *Pencil*.

PROSE VERSION

Voyages et Aventures du Dr. Festus. Töpffer chose to publish, just after the comic album, a Rabelaisian prose version of the story of *Festus*, which he probably wrote experimentally to test the differences between two media, around the same time as he drew the sketches. Never reprinted in the nineteenth century, it seems to have failed. In Kunzle, 2007 (pp. 81–82), I have summarized the differences with the picture story, which are mainly a matter of specification and intensification, especially in the satire on the monarchical repression in the kingdom of Vireloup under the "Barbons" (i.e., the France of Charles X), the parody of philosophical and syllogistical mania of the ever and explicitly dreaming and not-knowing-he-is-dreaming Festus, plus a few scatological details considered improper for the album. It is assumed he was dissuaded from earlier publication of this prose version, as he was from publication of the album of sketches, by his friends. There was, indeed, a harsh review of it when published (*Journal de Genève*, no. 111, 17 Sept. 1840)

THE STORY OF ALBERT

p. 406 *Simon de Nantua ou le Marchand Forain*, by Laurent Jussieu (4th ed. Geneva 1825, 1st ed. 1818, innumerable reprintings in the nineteenth century) is a didactic children's book about a philanthropic, good-(conservative)-advice peddling peddler.

p. 416 "Victor Hugo": leader of the Romantic school, of which Töpffer disapproved. "Djinns": refers to his collection, *Les Orientales* (1829).

p. 481 "La Bartine": obviously Alphonse de Lamartine, prominent romantic poet, statesman, and, as a democrat, suspect to Töpffer. His *Harmonies Politiques et Religieuses* was published in 1829. "Cinq Points": Lamartine acquired the chateau of Saint-Point on his marriage in 1820.

p. 421 "Mangini": Giuseppe Mazzini, leader of the Carbonari conspirators, friend of Fazy, later the unifier of Italy, but suspect to Genevan conservatives for having tried to stir up revolution in Italy from within their borders. The name puns on "manger" ("to eat").

p. 423 "foul blood . . . ": from *La Marseillaise*, the anthem of the French Revolution.

p. 424 Poland had been occupied by Russia.

p. 425 "monarchy": Presumably Töpffer means a constitutional monarchy, English style, which the radical Albert opposes.

p. 430 "Rotschild" (Rothschild): already famous (or notorious) international banking house. "Metternich": Austrian chancellor, and architect of Restoration Europe.

p. 431 "Jaques": original name of Albert in the manuscript, introduced here by error.

p. 440 "Cerdon": Cerdagne valley

By far the most serious, most overtly political, and least funny of Töpffer's picture stories, as well as (for those reasons) the least popular, *Albert* was conceived, drawn, and written under the impact of the growing revolutionary ferment in Geneva, and the first revolution starting November 1841, which the author combated tirelessly with a twice-weekly journal, *Courrier de Genève*. This he co-founded and for it he wrote about 105 articles, between January 1842 and March 1843. His enemy, after whom Albert is (mis)modeled, was James Fazy (in the manuscript the hero was called "Jaques," French for "James"), poet in his youth, a passionate and single-minded, but brilliant and responsible revolutionary who took power in a relatively bloodless coup just after Töpffer's death, and led Geneva to a stable, more democratic and prosperous future. Albert is the typical feckless youth, victim not of faulty educational methods as in *Crépin*, but a faulty personal temperament, exacerbated by contradictory parenting. His dabbling in various professions follows a picaresque literary tradition, but in a oblique, mocking way, fairly represents the predicament of the worker rendered shiftless and migratory by industrial change and profiteering.

Thus towards the end of his life, and in failing health, the author became a journalist to fight what he saw as the evils of journalism and democratic radicalism, the jargon of which is accurately, if simplistically, rendered in *Albert*. Töpffer satirizes conspiracy, which did so much during the Restoration to keep democratic, as well as nationalist, ideas alive, and shiftlessness, a quality hardly a characteristic of Fazy or Mazzini, but which conservatives tended to see in the great mass of under- and unemployed. The simultaneous attack on fraudulent business practices, typified here in the petty entrepreneur but in reality also the style of big business enterprise, may be influenced by the famous *Robert Macaire* series of Daumier and Philipon, and the contemporary novel. In Geneva, which lacked a true industrial proletariat, it was the skilled artisans in the watchmaking industries who, led by Fazy, made the revolution. This was fomented by a remarkably free press whose very freedom Töpffer both deplored and exploited. Although directly born of Genevan politics, *L'Histoire d'Albert* is a scurrilous indictment of democratic struggle everywhere.

MANUSCRIPT

MAH 1910—174, No. 53D. 16 x 22.5 cm. In blue ink, unlike the other albums which are in brown. The preface, text as printed, is dated 7. 9 (=November) 1844. The second page has drawings of a younger boy and generic notes for the story, including "false theories in newspapers on education," indicating that RT originally (also) thought of starting with a younger Albert, with more emphasis on his education.

The narrative that follows is carried by pieces of paper cut out and pasted in, with many paste-overs, substitutions, deletions, and changes in the captions, as if the author had lost confidence in his capacity to easily improvise a final product. Töpffer kept 173 scenes, which he duly numbered, run in a single row over sixty-four pages.

Starting as Jaques, at the eleventh drawing the hero's name is changed to John, then back again to Jaques, in which form it continues to the end. This attempt to dilute the identification with Töpffer's target, James Fazy, can have fooled few; RT also crossed out in the manuscript (scene #151; 1845 ed., p. 36), "qu'en Suisse aussi, et en particulier à Genève" in favor of "que le Canton." According to Corleis (p. 259), Lyon was changed to Roanne because Fazy had worked in Lyon in his father's business.

The physical farce is largely limited to a remarkable, much repeated, pars pro toto refrain of Albert being kicked by his father. Other prophetic graphic tricks include the much-admired accelerando of six narrow frames of Albert pestering from floor to floor, which will be almost doubled (1845 ed., p. 23), and a similar tactic with the toasts which will be more than doubled, from six to sixteen (1845 ed., p. 24). A caption for a deleted drawing (between manuscript scenes #159 and #160), where No. 40 attacked the (moral) "rigorisme" of a pleasure-hating government, and recommended "rapports plus fréquents et plus faciles qu'autrefois entre le citoyen et la citoyenne" (more frequent and easier relations than heretofore between the male and female citizen), a reference to demands for free love particularly anathema in Geneva, was *very* thoroughly crossed out.

At the other end of the album (in reverse to *Albert*) Töpffer started (previously?) another picture story, four scenes about a Mr. Anatole (see Appendix B, p. 604), continuing with a series of ten pages of miscellaneous humorous doodles.

LITHOGRAPHIC EDITION

Being printed by 18 December 1844 (letter to Dubochet of that date). Advertised in *Le Fédéral* (Geneva) for 7, 15, 17, and 21 January 1845, and in *L'Illustration*, 19 April 1845. RT sent a copy to Pictet de Rochemont in January 1845. The work influenced *The Deeds and Opinions of Herr Piepmeyer* by Detmold and Schrödter (for which, see Kunzle, 1990, p. 227).

STORY OF MR. CRYPTOGAME

p. 447 "Cryptogame": Greek for "secretly married."

p. 449 The first version has Cryptogame as botanist; the butterfly is an ancient symbol of dream, beauty, self-transformation, and transience. The title page and pages 451 and 452 revert to the first manuscript spelling "Criptogame"—simply because Töpffer was referring back to it rather than the 1844 manuscript?

p. 450 "Elvire": The name recalls that of a famous abandoned lover, in Mozart's *Don Giovanni*.

p. 455 "Dido aria": a dire and prophetic choice, since Dido (in Purcell's opera *Dido and Aeneas*, for instance) complains of being abandoned by her lover, Aeneas, and will commit suicide.

p. 482 "auto-da-fés": executions performed by the Spanish Inquisition. The English plagiary substitutes the currently controversial sales to slave-traders.

p. 486 "54th latitude" (north): This would be the temperate climate level of Danzig or Hamburg.

p. 509 "piggy-back": I derive this from the drawing rather than the French "behave yourself" ("tiens-toi-bien"). The English plagiary has "jump my little nag-tail."

p. 514 "Tapesalé": "Hit-hard."

p. 519 "electing a new dey": The satire is less on Algerian than Genevan politics, undergoing sometimes violent revolutionary ferment.

This was the last of Töpffer's picture stories to be revised for publication, undergoing many changes between its conception in 1830 and its appearance in *L'Illustration* in 1845. Like *Vieux Bois* it burlesques the idea of romantic love. This time instead of showing a single-minded male passion in the face of all kinds of obstacles, it features the more unusual theme of a single-minded, indeed heroic female passion overcoming but finally defeated by the obstacles. The most physically adventurous of Töpffer's stories, it stands as the first in a long distinguished line of exotic adventure comics.

The earliest manuscript responds to the initial French invasion of Algeria in 1830, and the course of publication of the first, much revised printed version coincides, with amazing precision, with the massive publicity at the French victory over their tenacious opponent, Abd-el-Kadr, in 1845. The whole intervening period was one of orientalism in all the arts (for instance, Delacroix's *Femmes d'Alger*). RT might have seen *L'Italiana in Algeri* performed in Geneva in 1813, where the Bey of Algiers has a wife called Elvire (Corleis p. 252). The episode in the belly of the whale is of course biblical-mythic and reminiscent of the *Adventures of Baron Munchausen*.

The story is relatively straight and coherent, lacking in the customary digressions and interwoven subplots, and spiced with well-placed silly gags. With its accumulation of incidents in chain reaction, developed here as nowhere else, it was already admired by Goethe and was well-thumbed, too well-thumbed, as the author had cause to complain, by others, so that it is puzzling why the author kept it back from print for so long.

MANUSCRIPTS

MAH 1910—177 53g. [1830]. 17 x 26 cm. 225 scenes in two rows, on eighty-six pages. The "final" version has 201 drawings on eighty-nine pages.

The first page warns, "And please avoid crumpling, dirtying, or pulling the pages about, being careful to turn only by the edge." There are also some warm-up scribbles, including animals, "Cryptogame à l'âge de 35 ans," followed by sketches for names that do not appear later: Mr. Triptolème à l'âge de 45 ans. Mr. Diakos [with fiery face and hair!] à l'âge de 32 ans. On the next, facing page, there are more injunctions for clean handling, with the date 20 July 1830, and the phrase "the above entreaty renewed for 10 years."

Opposite page 4 are twenty-six lines of pencil notes, several crossed out as they were dealt with, which have a continuous look, as if the author conceived in advance the first part of the story (the first ten pages, or thirty-two drawings), at least. There are many more notes, in pencil and ink, at intervals on later pages (16, 18, 22, 24, 26, 28, 36, 52). The drawings end on page 86, on the encounter of Elvire with the belle Provençale, which is followed by many blank pages, then seven pages of complete-looking notes for a continuation and conclusion. There are three pages of notes at the end for the beginning of the story; RT evidently planned at least five scenes of a docile Cryptogame accompanying Elvire to different places.

Reproduced by Maschietto, Club des Libraires de France, 1967.

MAH 1910—178 53H [1844]. 18 x 16 cm, 201 drawings, each numbered, on seventy-eight pages. Dedication to his daughter Adèle Töpffer. Drawings all remade, and the story much changed. This must be the manuscript sent to Dubochet for translation to woodcut. It was described as done in a letter to Calame of 19 November, and in Dubochet's hands by 27 November. The sketches are cut out and glued onto the page, except for scenes #27–#53. On pages 11–16 the lithographic version is cut out and glued in. I have restored the manuscript version in our reproduction at this point (see Preface).

SERIAL PUBLICATION

L'Illustration, Journal Universel, 1845. Run complete in eleven installments from 25 January to 19 April: vol. 4, pp. 332–33 (18 scenes), pp. 348–49 (20 scenes), (one week gap), pp. 380–81 (24 scenes), pp. 396–97 (20 scenes); vol. 5, pp. 12–13 (21 scenes), pp. 28–29 (20 scenes), pp. 44–45 (17 scenes), (one week gap), pp. 76–77 (17 scenes), pp. 92–93 (16 scenes), pp. 108–9 (16 scenes), pp. 124–25 (13 scenes). Summary and title: "*Histoire de Mr. Cryptogame*, par l'auteur de M. Vieux-Bois, de M. Jabot, de M. Crépin, du Dr. Festus." A fake anonymity is thus maintained.

After deciding not to submit a prose work to *L'Illustration*, the first illustrated news magazine in France, published by his second cousin Jacques-Julien Dubochet and very successful, Töpffer offered *Cryptogame*, duly revised. The complicated story of this revision and the translation onto wood by Cham, the author's Parisian admirer and imitator, after receiving a barrage of polite, sometimes contradictory instructions from Geneva, and the censorious changes made by the magazine is told at some length in Kunzle, "Histoire de Monsieur Cryptogame (1845) : une bande dessinée de Rodolphe Töpffer pour le grand public" (*Genava*, 32 [1984] : pp. 139–69) and in summary in Kunzle, 1990. For the general character of the magazine, see Kunzle, "L'Illustration, Journal Universel," *Nouvelles de Estampe* no. 43 (Jan.–Feb. 1979) : pp. 8–19. Suffice it to point out here that the Parisian journal, wary of offending the religious sensibilities of its considerable public (which reached Algeria), felt the need to change the abbé into a doctor, and the missionaries into a mayor with his deputy.

The copy drawn by Cham onto and cut into the block by a team of engravers headed by Best and Leloir, is, culpably, in reverse, which vitiates the essential forward movement of the narrative. It is, however, considering the difference of medium and public, in my view a creditable performance, despite the aspersions usually cast upon it (where Cham is usually wrongly called the engraver).

ALBUM EDITION

Histoire de M. Cryptogame, J. J. Dubochet, Paris, 1846.

Dubochet sold copies of the *Illustration* blocks to England long before he got out his own album edition. RT expressed great annoyance at the delay (letter to Dubochet of 22 June 1845), which was blamed on the need to recut certain blocks. It was described by Dubochet as "in press, appetizing, cheap" (letter to RT of 30 July), but RT did not receive a copy until 25/27 April 1846 (letter to Dubochet of that date).

Dubochet added a floral title page showing four principal characters (but not Elvire) in the corners, and hiding behind a rock bearing the publisher's name, some little turbaned dark children who, one might reasonably and scandalously suppose, represent offspring sired by the hero in North Africa.

The most visible improvements are in the printing of the captions, very defective in *L'Illustration*, now cleaned up and slightly smaller, and in the punctuation and word breaks. The latter worsen towards the end, suggesting sudden haste in already very tardy production. Seven scenes are recut: a block of five on album page 3, with the face of Mr. C. made more subtle and the addition of deep shadows. On page 17 the confusion of minstrel and company in the belly of the whale is sorted out. On page 44 the scene of the Docteur (Abbé) running to the window is ruined by too much hatching, which blends him into his own shadow. One cannot believe Cham did this.

There were a large number of subsequent Paris editions, notably in 1849: *Autour de la Table. Histoire de M. Cryptogame*, 201 Dessins par R. Töpffer [here named for the first time]; 5th ed. [sic], Paulin and Lechevalier, and used by the magazine as a premium to subscribers, very cheap at F.1.50; 5th ed. [sic], Imp. J. Claye, 1861; 6th ed., Imp. Blot, 1873.

PLAGIARIES

The Veritable History of Mr. BACHELOR BUTTERFLY, showing how it was diversified by many changes: for after being married in the belly of a whale he narrowly escaped bigamy, and became the step-father of eight hopeful children. London: D. Bogue, 1845, sixty-six pages.

Printed from copies of the *Illustration* blocks supplied by Dubochet, with a free and not unimaginative translation of the captions. The Abbé remains a doctor, but Töpffer's (Protestant) missionaries are now Irish priests from Maynooth; the Provençale is a "beauty from Cork." Omits references to a "seraglio" where Elvire (as "Dorothy") is immured, but not her two homicides.

The Strange Adventures of Bachelor Butterfly, setting forth how his passion for natural history wholly eradicated the tender passion implanted in his breast, and induced him to discard the chosen of his heart—also, detailing his dire misfortunes and hair-breadth escapes both by sea and by land, and his singular marriage to a "beauty from Cork," who proves to be an extremely interesting widow with eight small children—then, his domestic bliss. New York: Wilson & Co., 1849. Copy as above.

J. Jullien, Geneva, 1896. This reproduces the 1844 drawings for the first eight (plus title and preface) pages, instead of the lithographic version of this portion appearing in all subsequent editions, which use the whole lithographic segment available down to page 26. I have, as explained in the preface, substituted the original drawings at scenes #9–#26, which I consider better than the lithographs, done when the author was very ill. Was scene #25 radically changed, from Elvire chasing Mr. C. instead of kicking over the tea table, because RT feared it was too reminiscent of the second scene in Hogarth's *Harlot's Progress*? A pity. Some proof sheets for the lithographs are in BPU Suzannet, 125.

FOREIGN VARIANT EDITIONS
(all use copies of the original Dubochet blocks)

Fahrten und Abenteuer des Herrn Steckelbein. Eine wunderbare und ergötzliche Historie. Nach Zeichnungen von Rudolf Töpffer in lustigen Reimen von Julius Kell. Lepizig, Brockhaus & Avenarius, 1847. 153 drawings on seventy-five pages. 2nd ed. (or printing?), 1858; 3rd ed., 1865 (seventy-nine pages); 4th ed., 1879; 5th ed., 1900 (sixty-seven pages), etc. This edition used for subsequent Danish (*Stankelben*), Norwegian, and Swedish (*Spindelben*, 1847) editions.

Fiancée Elvire is changed into the "horrid sister Ursula" (böse Schwester Ursula), trying to cure Mr. Cryptogame of his passion for butterflies. This and the Dutch edition (below) are designed for younger children, whom it was evidently considered inappropriate to expose to a woman trying desperately to force a man into marriage with her. A sister trying to force a brother to stay with her was presumably acceptable. This switch involves the patent absurdity of a spinster sister going berserk when a brother tries to fix up her marriage with a perfectly respectable, if stupid, figure of neutral social identity, for Töpffer's abbé is always called "der Dicke" (the fat guy). The missionaries become a farmer (Bauer) and his servant, and the beauty from Provence is his daughter Barbara. Elvire in bed or any kind of undress, the harem, and her killing of Turks are omitted. We pass over other oddities.

Reizen en Avonturen van Mijnheer Prikkebeen. Een wonderbaarlijke en kluchtige historie, naar teekeningen (getekend) door Rodolphe Töpffer en voor de neerlandse jeugd berijmd door J. J. Goeverneur. First published in 1858, there have been innumerable editions, down to today, making it one of the leading and most lasting Dutch children's classics. Many children know the effortless, jingly verses by heart. Gouverneur follows much of Kell's text and most of his changes, and corrects some of his errors. The 201 original designs are reduced to 150.

The verses of this edition have been turned into the Groningen dialect (. . . *Meneer Prikkebain* . . . , 1964), which ends with Prikkebain fleeing the pestering of his new family to rejoin his butterflies; the Friesian language; Afrikaans; French (. . . *M. Maigrichon* . . . , transl. René Burdet, Lausanne, n.d.), and Esperanto (. . . *Sinjoro Lonkrurolo* . . . , Hilversum, 1927).

A Portuguese version (*Sr Cryptogamo*, 1850) is mentioned by Castelli (2003, p. 11, no. 5), but the Portuguese "Cryptogame imitation" at no. 4 there is in fact a copy after Stop's Töpfferish "M. Verdreau" in *L'Illustration* (January–February 1850). No. 6 reproduces from a "colored edition" of the English *Bachelor Butterfly* unknown to me.

"Togten en Avonturen van den Heer Spillebeen" (in the Dutch *Humoristisch Album* 1866) reproduces the first third of *Cryptogame*. The verse refers to Hamlet, Socialism, and Mozart.

There are three curious Dutch spinoffs:

De Zoon van Prikkebeen. Tekst en Tekeningen van Jac. A. Hazelaar, Kruseman, The Hague, 1951, a kind of continuation, ending with Prikkebeen's son in the U.S. and China, before returning home.

Töpffer, mijn Zoon. Roman over de vader van Prikkebeen, by Paul de Vaan (pseud. J. P. Naeff), The Hague 1984. This ingenious work, told in the words of Rodolphe's octogenarian father, part embroidered biography of RT, imagines him not drawing in the presence of his pupils, but to a larger public of friends, a sensational performer everywhere in demand. He plays as it were on an organ, or as a Paganini, improvising from the public reactions on huge sheets of paper placed on an easel, a kind of graphic orator and conjuror. The elder Töpffer dislikes the story as is, deemed by him a roman a clé where he is caricatured as the hero, and plans to turn it (as it were) into the Gouverneur edition, for children.

De Neef van Prikkenbeen (Prikkenbeen's cousin or nephew), by Oom Abraham, with drawings by Doan Hoeksema, Naarden-Bussum 1950, is another continuation, taking Mr. Cryptogame to Africa, where he marries and has lots of black children.

There are also Dutch editions with new rhymes closer to Töpffer's captions.

MR. TRICTRAC

p. 539	"Trictrac": "backgammon".
p. 541	"the sources of the Nile": an eternal nineteenth-century quest, in which the Swiss John Ludwig Burckhardt engaged in 1812, under the auspices of the British African Association.
p. 561–63	The ordinances referred to are all represented in contemporary police regulations for the city of Geneva (Archives d'Etat, Geneva, ADL I no. 32, fo. 12 (printed): *Règlement de Police pour la ville de Geneve*, 1809, sec. 2, arts. ix and xv; sec. 4, art. xxv; sec. 6, art. xxxv; and sec. 9, art. lxv).
p. 562	"Fire": an autobiographical reminiscence, recorded also in the novel *L'Héritage* (1834).
p. 568	Scenes misnumbered to omit 84–88, apparently because RT misread his "83" for "88," continuing with 89.
p. 577	"petit fils": "petit-fils" would be "grandson," perhaps intended here since the king looks quite old; Töpffer was not too careful about punctuation.

Although unfinished, *Trictrac* must rank as one of Töpffer's best efforts, with a particularly concentrated system of switched identities such as one associates with theatrical farce of a later age. The ladder business, surely new to caricature, looks forward to Laurel and Hardy, and identities become more entangled than the police in the ladder. Switches of clothes and identities seem almost to be the raison d'être of the story, coming so pell mell that they tend to sweep aside the other satirical flourishes: against medical vanity and obscurantism (note that the doctor is not caricatured, his absurdity lies entirely in the speech reported in the captions), against petty civic bureaucracy, the corruption and stupidity of the law, the criminal frivolity and negligence of the highest (here, royal) authority, and, above all, the destructive idiocy of the police. Insofar as the story, spinning out of control, turns out to be less about the titular hero than about the thief, a polite and ingenious thief who has no trouble passing himself off as a police officer—he seems to have prior military experience, knowing the commands—we may see here a classic topos of equation or complicity of crime with law, of criminal with police, worthy of a political radical which the author certainly never was in reality. Balzac's Vautrin in *Le Père Goriot* (1834) was based on Vidocq, a real-life former criminal who became police chief in Paris and hired mostly ex-cons like himself.

MANUSCRIPT

MAH 1996—14 x 22.5 cm. With no title page, the album opens with two pages of doodled faces, figures, and animals, followed by five pages of the story of *M. Boissec* (see Appendix B, pp. 605–9), three more pages of doodled figures and faces, and then forty-one pages of the present story. The album has been dated by Philippe Kaenel (1988) to around 1830, the era of several other first drafts of picture stories, and a *Voyage* of 1829, which has a preface decorated with three stupid policemen. In a letter dated 20 March 1831, *Trictrac* is implicitly described as done, while a *Docteur Saitout*, possibly a medical satire, now lost, such as occurs episodically here, is described as in process ("sur le métier"). In 1840, in the well-known autobiographical letter to Sainte-Beuve, *Trictrac*, the story of a thief, is ironically described as "for the moment, stolen" ("pour le moment, volé"). Whether it remained stolen, and for that reason Töpffer could not return to it and publish it, we do not know. The numbering of the scenes almost to the end suggests serious thought of completion and printing. There are few signs of use at the page edges.

The manuscript was found in the library of M. Panchaud de Bottens, the syndic of Vich (canton Vaud), and first published by Paul Chaponnière in 250 copies with the *Journal de Genève* in 1937. It then passed into the collection of Pierre-Yves Gabus of Bevaix (NE), from whom it was acquired by the MAH in 1996.

A good modern facsimile, in a 20 percent enlargement, with commentary, was published by Philippe Kaenel in 1988 (*Mr. Trictrac et autres Dessins, Fac-similé d'un album de dessins originaux de Rodolphe Töpffer*. Lausanne: Favre).

MR. ANATOLE FRAGMENT

This is a parody of what Töpffer describes happening when he and his boys took shortcuts in their excursions in the Alps.

MANUSCRIPT: MAH 1910—174 (8). Four drawings on one sheet.

MR. BOISSEC FRAGMENT

p. 603 "Boissec": "drink-dry."

MANUSCRIPT: MAH 1996—4. These thirteen scenes on five pages precede Mr. *Trictrac* in the same album.

MR. CALICOT FRAGMENT

p. 608 "Calicot": "draper's assistant" as well as "calico."

p. 612 "Ancien régime": French (and Genevan) régime before the Revolution of 1789.

MANUSCRIPT: MAH 1910 512-516. Eleven scenes on five sheets.

MR. BRUTUS CALICOT FRAGMENT

p. 613 All the names suggest (Roman) republicanism, "Brutus" that of a revolutionary capable of tyrannicide. Brutus's tomb slab is carved with the French revolutionary slogan, and the revolutionary cap of liberty on top of fasces.

MANUSCRIPT: BPU Suz. 170a.

MR. FLUET FRAGMENT

p. 615 "Verpale": "pale green."
p. 615–16 Are the three scenes with Mr. X.xx and his horse, which do not seem to belong thematically, the beginning of a subplot?
p. 618 The last two phrases of the last caption but one occur in very similar form in *Trictrac* (p. 577, scene #110), suggesting a similar date.

MANUSCRIPT: MAH 1910—545-549 (Legs Töpffer 1910, Alb. 51) Carton T Q 54
22 (not including landscape) scenes on six pieces of paper.

MR. VERTPRÉ FRAGMENT

MANUSCRIPT: MAH 1910—175, 16.5 x 24.5 cm.

Twenty-six drawings on five pages, preceded by gutters of two pages excised, presumably the start of the story. The rest of the album is blank.

HISTOIRE DE CLAUDIUS BERLU (SCENARIO)

p. 624 "Berlu": "Berlue" is a medical term for false vision (metamorphopsia). "Puseyite": The reference to "Puseyism," named after the catholicizing Anglican controversialist Edward Pusey, who was not known in France or Switzerland, must be a cover for the Methodists, feared for their proselytizing among Genevan Calvinists.
p. 624 "Brumaire": November/December in French revolutionary calendar.

This must be the "crazy medical story, all thought out but not drawn and there is for the moment no way I can put the least character on paper. We'll see later" (letter to Dubochet 25/26 May 1845). Writing from his useless cure at Vichy, RT was very ill and unable to draw, which evidently cost more effort than writing.

Mr. Berlue bears marked similarities to themes in *Trictrac*, sketched by 1831 (the switches of identity in bed, a thief descending a chimney, the medical satire, the play with a poultice), but it reminds one also of the recently published *Histoire d'Albert* (1845) and the disturbances of the 1840s with its reference to the sovereignty of the people and change in government (ninth caption on manuscript, p. 4). These were made more explicit in the first, shorter set of notes for the scenario (not printed here), which locates the story specifically in Switzerland, where the government is "pure demo[cracy]," the "militia is disarmed," there is a draft for a provisional constitution, and the name "Carabini" appears. The earlier draft bears the title "Histoire de Claudius Berlu, baptized in Brumaire," a month of the French revolutionary calendar. A date close to that of *Albert*, a few notes for which appear at the head of the first pages of the longer draft, as noted, is therefore likely.

Was the story a kind of replacement for *Trictrac*, maybe still lost, and then became superceded by *Albert*?

MANUSCRIPT: BPU MS Suppl. 1256b, eight pages. The first three pages with the list of entries numbered 1–20 ("end") obviously constitute the first sketch for the following scenario, here omitted. The page (numbered 1) starts with four lines of notes for the *Histoire d'Albert*, crossed out, and some more, on a slant, for *Berlu*. A couple of significant passages which the author struck appear here in brackets; the many others I have omitted. Many words in the original are abbreviated. The underlining and question marks are in the original.

LORD TURNEPS

MANUSCRIPT: MS Suppl. 1256/115 env. 2, p. 73 (date c. 1942). The French imitates, in part, the bastard attempts at French of the English tourist.

Sources

BIOGRAPHY

The only two complete biographies, which also include criticism, are Pierre-Maxime (L'Abbé) Relave, *La Vie et les Oeuvres de Töpffer*, Paris, 1886; and Auguste Blondel and Paul Mirabaud, *Rodolphe Töpffer: L'écrivain, l'artiste, et l'homme*, Paris, 1886.

MONOGRAPHS AND MODERN CRITICAL ANTHOLOGIES

Gisela Corleis, "Die Bildergeschichten des Genfer Zeichners Rodolphe Töpffer," typescript dissertation,

Munich 1973, printed Munich 1979. Comprehensive with excellent allusions to local and European history.

Thierry Groensteen and Benoît Peeters, *Töpffer, Inventeur de la Bande Dessinée*, Paris: Hermann, 1996.

Daniel Maggetti, editor, *Töpffer*, Skira: Geneva, 1996. Nine essays by different authors on various aspects of the oeuvre, including three on the prose *Voyages*, one on the theater, and one on the art criticism.

Danielle Buyssens et al., editors, *Propos Topffériens: Actes du colloque international de Genève, Juin 1996*, Geneva: Société des Études Töpffériennes and Georg, 1998. Eleven essays on various aspects of the Töpffer production.

Useful synthetic chapters can also be found in David Kunzle, *The History of the Comic Strip, volume 2, The Nineteenth Century*, Berkeley: University of California, 1990, pp. 28–71; and Philippe Kaenel, *Le Métier d'Illustrateur (1830–1880): Rodolphe Töpffer, J. J. Grandville, Gustave Doré*, second edition, Paris 1996.

Kunzle, *Father of the Comic Strip: Rodolphe Töpffer*, University Press of Mississippi, 2007.

CORRESPONDENCE

Léopold Gautier, *Un bouquet de Lettres de Rodolphe Töpffer*, Lausanne: Payot, 1974.

Jacques Droin editor, *Correspondance complète de Rodolphe Töpffer*, Geneva: Droz, 2002. Two volumes have appeared of a projected five.

RECENT COLLECTED EDITIONS

Oeuvres Complètes de Rodolphe Töpffer, edited by Pierre and Henri Cailler and Henri Darel, Geneva: Skira, 1943–1952). Volumes IV–IX of "Caricatures" reproduce the picture stories. Rare.

Rodolphe Töpffer, with preface by François Caradec, Paris: Horay, 1975. Basic modern edition of seven published picture stories (omits *Trictrac*).

A three-volume edition with six stories edited by Thierry Groensteen was published by Paris: Seuil, 1996. Volume 1: *Monsieur Jabot, Monsieur Vieux Bois: deux histoires d'amour;* Volume 2: *Monsieur Crépin, Monsieur Pencil: deux égarements de la science;* Volume 3: *Le Docteur Festus, Histoire de Monsieur Cryptogame: deux odyssées*.

Innumerable republications of individual picture stories have appeared in French and German.

Manuscripts of *Vieux Bois*, *Festus*, *Jabot*, *Crépin*, and *Albert* (described above in the notes to individual comic strips) were published in original formats as a boxed set, edited and with an introduction by Manuela Maschietto, translated into Italian and with a preface by

COLLECTION
DES
HISTOIRES EN ESTAMPES
DE
R. TOEPFFER.
1er Volume
Mr. Jabot.
GENÈVE
1846.
Librairie allemande de J. Kessmann,
Rue du Rhône 171.

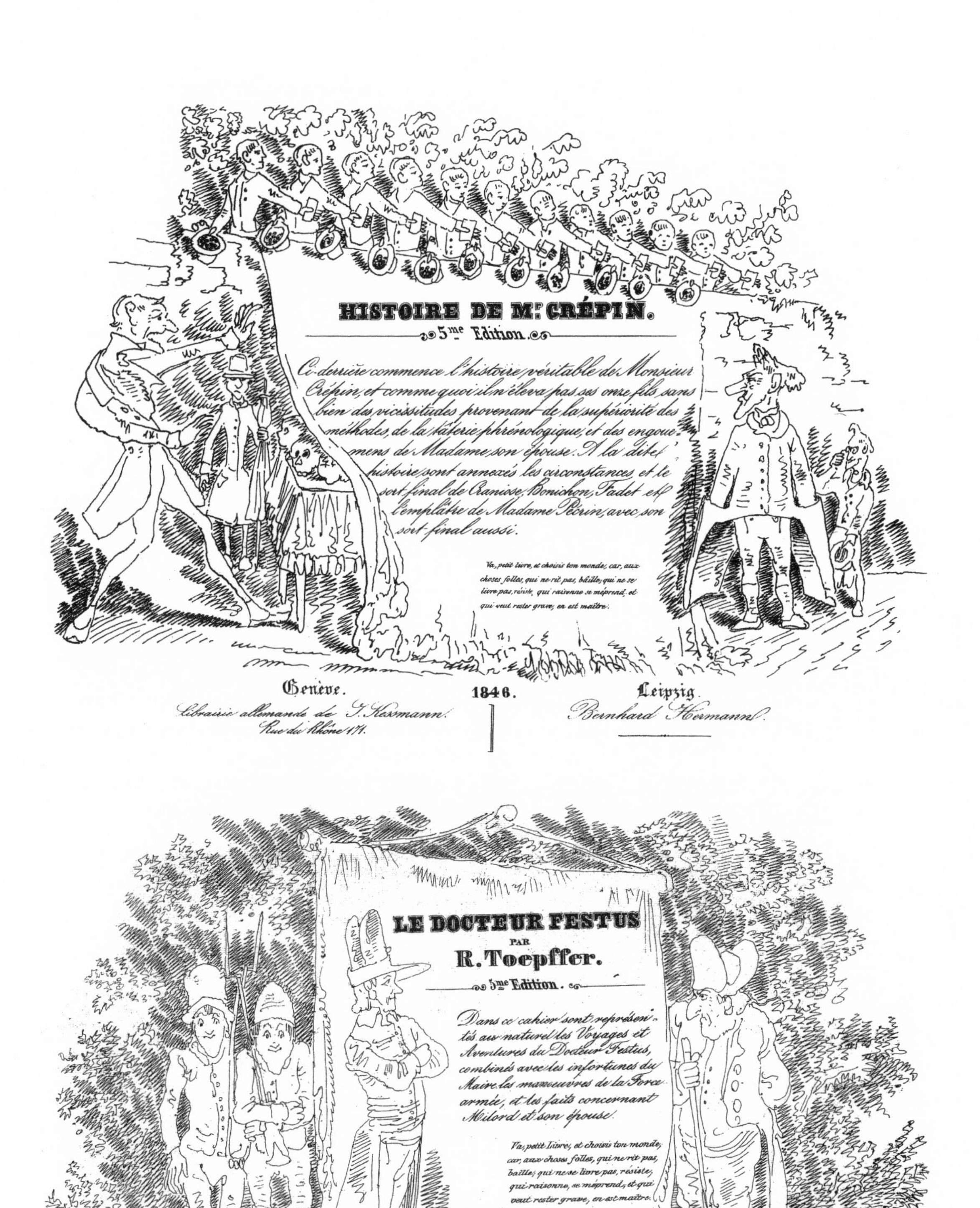
HISTOIRE DE Mr. CRÉPIN.
5me Edition.
Ci-derrière commence l'histoire véritable de Monsieur Crépin, et comme quoi il n'éleva pas ses onze fils sans bien des vicissitudes provenant de la supériorité des méthodes, de la tâterie phrénologique, et des engouemens de Madame son épouse. A la dite histoire sont annexés les circonstances et le sort final de Craniose, Bonichon, Fadet et l'emplâtre de Madame Pécrin, avec son sort final aussi.
Va, petit livre, et choisis ton monde; car, aux choses folles, qui ne rit pas, bâille; qui ne se livre pas, résiste; qui raisonne se méprend; et qui veut rester grave, en est maître.
Genève.
1846.
Leipzig.
Librairie allemande de J. Kessmann.
Rue du Rhône 171.
Bernhard Hermann.
LE DOCTEUR FESTUS
PAR
R. Toepffer.
5me Edition.
Dans ce cahier sont représentés au naturel les Voyages et Aventures du Docteur Festus, combinés avec les infortunes du Maire, les manœuvres de la Force armée, et les faits concernant Milord et son épouse.
Va, petit Livre, et choisis ton monde; car, aux choses folles, qui ne rit pas, baille; qui ne se livre pas, résiste; qui raisonne, se méprend; et qui veut rester grave, en est maître.
Genève.
1846.
Leipzig.
Librairie allemande de J. Kessmann
Rue du Rhône 171.
Bernhard Hermann.

Mr. Pencil
PAR
R. Toepffer.
GENÈVE
1846.
Librairie allemande de J. Kessmann,
Rue du Rhône 171.

HISTOIRE D'ALBERT
PAR
R. Toepffer.
GENÈVE
1846.
Librairie allemande de J. Kessmann, Rue du Rhône 171.

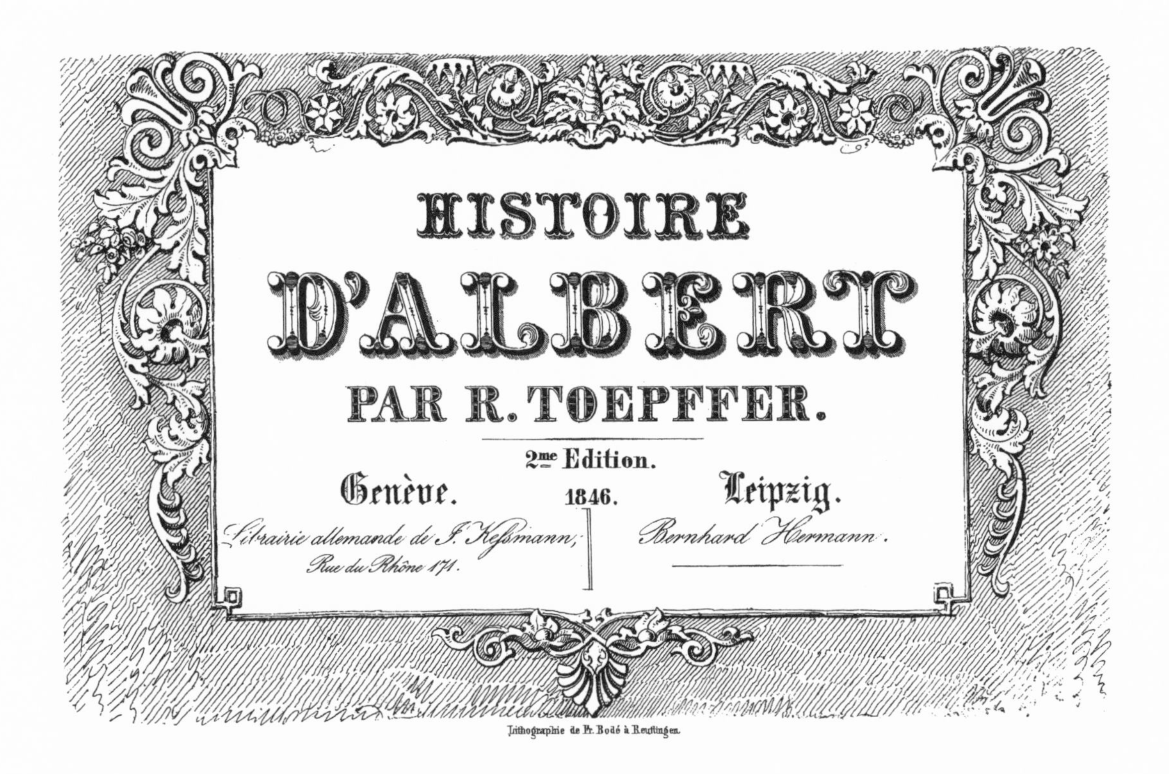

Luciano Erba, Milan: Garzanti, 1973. Very rare. Maschietto also edited Rodolphe Töpffer, *Trois Histoires en Images*, Club des Libraires de France, 1962, with facsimiles of *Vieux Bois*, *Festus*, and *Cryptogame* manuscripts.

NINETEENTH-CENTURY COLLECTED EDITIONS

Collection des Histoires en Estampes de R. Toepffer, Genève, 1846, Librairie allemande de J. Kessmann, rue du Rhône 171. Kessmann's main branch was in Leipzig.

This edition is very rare. I have used and described here the copy in the BPU, Geneva (Ia 1309), which puts into one binding the six volumes, each with its own dust cover and new title page, after the running overall title showing M. Pencil admiring a portrait of Crépin, with other characters distributed in trees and landscape. The volumes, varying slightly in size, were evidently sold separately. All volumes are printed on both sides of the page. The price for each volume is given as 6 French francs, and 1.15 Russian Sgr. The author sold the rights to Kessmann by 14 October 1845, and lived to see the first two volumes, *Jabot* and *Crépin*, out by March 1846, and to express pleasure at being unable to tell the difference from his own lithographic versions. His intention to include a lithographed version of *Cryptogame* was frustrated by his last illness and death.

Jabot is marked, oddly, "5e éd." (it was, conceivably, the 3rd: preceded by that dated 1833 and that dated 1835), and "autographié chez Schmid à Genève, 1845," which suggests the publisher wanted the public to think that Töpffer himself redid the whole book. The initials R.T. are however removed throughout this edition. *Crépin* was printed by Gruaz of Geneva, *Vieux Bois* by C. Mäcken Sohn, Reutlingen (this installment contains the Friedrich Vischer essay translated in Kunzle, 2007, *Festus* and *Albert* are marked "lithographie de Fr. Bodé à Reutlingen." For *Pencil* no lithographer is given.

Fr. Bodé, reasonably assumed to have copied (traced) the whole edition, is presumably the Fritz Bode mentioned in the Thieme-Becker lexicon (and no more) as the brother of Louis Bode (1812–1859) who ran the L. Bode lithographic shop in Stuttgart (document from 1858).

About ten drawings for *Festus*, possibly connected either with this or the 1860 edition, some on very fine tracing paper, are in the collection of Mr. Fontanel in Geneva.

The captions in the Kessmann edition are written in small calligraphic script in both the German translation and the French original, which is of course a great loss. With often slightly broader scenes, adjusted perhaps in order to fit in the German translation (in *Jabot*, the scenes are consistently 10 percent wider), Bodé has generally had to add to the background settings (and even fragments of squabbling children in *Crépin* 9a). The airier effect may be termed an improvement. The frames are regularized, but still not ruled-looking. A few ambiguities in the writing of the text (e.g., what looks like "dèbolé" is corrected to "désolé" in *Jabot* 50b), and a few graphic imperfections—the bed-curtain in *Vieux Bois* 3a, evidently started and then aborted by RT, here window-like scribbles, and in the Garnier edition, better, turned into paintings on the wall as in previous and succeeding views of the same room—are corrected or improved. In *Jabot* 22c, the angle of Milady's head is changed, to express shock rather than sympathy, the position of Jabot's legs is clarified, and the sharp tip of Jabot's nose is blunted to conform with its shape throughout. Oddly, RT's misspelling "vent" for "vend" (*Festus* 78b) is kept in both Kessmann and Garnier.

Both Kessmann and Garnier keep the Gourary *Jabot* manuscript major variant version with the date 1835 on page 27.

There is one substantial act of censorship: In *Festus* (44b), as noted, the scene of the king of Vireloup (i.e., France or Savoy) fainting at the news of a supposed conspiracy was cut, which necessitated considerably extending the preceding drawings.

Garnier edition, published 1860 by Garnier frères.

These volumes, published at Fr. 7.50 as separate, bound volumes with gold-tooled designs on the cover, and in roan and marbled boards, printed on thick paper on one side only, must have recommended themselves as a cheap but substantial and handsome gift. All the designs, including captions, were carefully traced by Rodolphe's son François (1830–1876, listed as a "commis négociant" in the contract), imitating his father's handwriting with astonishing fidelity, in frames slightly broader and deeper, with the necessary occasional small addition of background (as in Kessmann), leaving more room for the captions, and no objective need for caption-induced excrescences in the bottom frame lines. The caprices of the frame lines are otherwise faithfully observed.

François makes a number of very small corrections to the text: missing and too-hastily formed accents (especially RT's habit of sloping the acutes to look like graves), the occasional misspellings such as "soupçons croisants" (8a)—but not "occuppent" (*Crépin* 76b, corrected in Kessmann). FT keeps the awkward word breaks (e.g., "l'É-glise in *Festus* 74b). While generally faithful to the slightest nuance of expression, the son ventures some minute graphic improvements: The face of the suicidal Vieux Bois peering through his shirt (32c); the awkward circular cheekbone on Crépin (48b) and the same on Vieux Bois (32d), modified to a semicircle; and the important hole in the roof made by Vieux Bois jumping for joy (53b), scarcely visible in RT, now duly emphasized. Garnier omits the map in *Festus*.

Nef edition: *Rudolphe Töpffer-Album. Töpffer's Komische Bilder-Romane. Lustige Geschichten und Karikaturen d. berühmten Verfassers der Genfer Novellen*. Published in twenty installments Stuttgart: Nef, 1887 (and Esslingen, 1899, according to Thieme-Becker, *Künstlerlexikon*, but I have not seen or otherwise heard of this edition). Lamentably removes the Töpffer frames.